Total Solution for the **GED**® Test

Laurie Callihan, Ph.D.

Stacey Kiggins, M.S.

Lisa Gail Mullins, M.A.

Stephen Reiss, M.B.A.

Research & Education Association

Visit our website: www.rea.com

Research & Education Association

61 Ethel Road West
Piscataway, New Jersey 08854
Email: info@rea.com

REA's Total Solution for the GED® Test, 2nd Edition

Printed in the United States of America

Library of Congress Control Number 2016954066

ISBN-13: 978-0-7386-1217-1
ISBN-10: 0-7386-1217-0

Foreword

Congratulations! In purchasing this REA Book + Online prep, you have taken the first step toward earning your GED® credential. Completing your high school education will open doors to many career and educational opportunities. A recent report from the U.S. Office of Vocational and Adult Education described the GED® test as "the only high school equivalency exam strongly aligned with the new adult education voluntary college and career readiness standards. These standards will help prepare more adult learners for the college courses needed to qualify for most jobs."

A Tough Test

The GED® test is not easy. I know this because I have more than 20 years' experience as a teacher and administrator helping adults to prepare for the test. This REA prep will serve as a beacon as you work toward achieving your goal. REA's authors are experienced educators and know the expectations of the GED® test. This test prep is strictly aligned to the information, subjects, and types of questions that you will see on the GED® test. Still, no matter how good the study guide is, the burden of being successful is on *you*.

Making the Commitment

There is no standard timeframe that works for everyone looking to complete the GED® test. Some will take a few weeks, some a few months and, yes, some a year or more. It depends on you, your ability, and how committed you are to this goal. If you do not have a minimum of 4 hours a week that you can devote to studying, I suggest you wait until your schedule is less busy before you prepare for the test. The time that you commit to studying should be constant (the same time and day and/or night every week). Develop a regular study routine and make sure you will not have any interruptions.

Developing a Strategy

Many people take the GED® test one module (or section) at a time. Which module you take first is entirely up to you. However, since all sections of the GED® test require good reading skills, you may want to start with the Reasoning Through Language Arts section of this book. Pay extra attention to lessons addressing reading skills such as how to ferret out the main idea, supporting details, inference, the writer's point of view, sequencing, drawing conclusions, and summarizing. You will be asked to apply these skills not only in the Language Arts section of the test, but also in the Social Studies, Science, and in some parts of the Mathematical Reasoning test. The best way to become better at anything is to practice. The same is true if you want to become a better reader. Make it a habit to read something substantive every day.

After completing the Language Arts section, I suggest you study the Math section. If you do not have a good foundation in basic math, such as knowing your addition, subtraction, multiplication, and division facts, you will need to strengthen those areas before you start studying for the test. Once again, set aside a special time to practice these skills.

Once you have studied the Language Arts and Math content, you will be ready to move on to the Social Studies and Science sections. Because you will have strengthened your reading ability by completing the Language Arts section, I think you will find that the Social Studies and Science sections will be less difficult.

Previewing the Array of Question Types

Throughout this test prep you will be shown excellent examples of the types of questions asked on the GED® test: multiple-choice questions, short-answer items, several different types of technology-enhanced items, drop-down items embedded in passages, and one 45-minute extended-response item. Take every opportunity to practice answering these questions as you study. Also, be sure to practice writing a 45-minute response.

In helping students prepare for the GED® test, I have found that those who truly commit themselves to reaching their goals ultimately succeed. Getting your high school equivalency diploma cannot be accomplished overnight, and no single timeline works for everyone. But if you continue to put forth the effort, you will pass the GED® test.

I wish you the best of luck.

Rubianna M. Porter, Ed.D.
Former Director of Education
Re-Start–The Center for Adult Education
Chattanooga, Tennessee

Contents

Introduction   1

REASONING THROUGH LANGUAGE ARTS 17

Chapter 4: Analyzing the Structure of Texts — 65

Chapter 5: Author's Purpose — 75

Chapter 6: Evaluating the Argument and Claims — 85

Chapter 7: Analyzing Similar Themes or Topics — 103

Chapter 8: Applying Rules of Standard English: Grammar and Usage 117

Chapter 9: Applying Rules of Standard English: Capitalization and Punctuation 145

Chapter 10: Written English in Context: Extended Response 157

Chapter 1: Operations with Real Numbers   175

Chapter 2: Fractions, Percents, and Decimals   193

Chapter 3: Algebraic Expressions and Equations   213

Chapter 4: Ratios and Proportions   257

Chapter 5: Linear Equations and the Coordinate Plane   271

Chapter 6: Measurement and Geometric Figures   311

Chapter 7: Area, Surface Area, and Volume 339

Chapter 8: Statistics and Data Analysis 365

Chapter 9: Real-World Applications of Mathematical Models 391

Chapter 1: Life Science   411

Chapter 2: Physical Science   469

Chapter 3: Earth and Space Science   495

Chapter 4: Science Practices   525

SOCIAL STUDIES   545

Chapter 1: Civics and Government   549

Chapter 2: United States History — 575

Chapter 3: Economics — 621

Chapter 4: Geography and the World   649

Practice Tests   671

Practice Test Battery 1   673

Practice Test Battery 2   833

Appendix $\qquad$ **1003**

Index $\qquad$ **1011**

About Our Authors

Reasoning Through Language Arts: Stacey Kiggins, M.S.

Stacey Kiggins is the English Department Chair at Thomas A. Edison High School in Fairfax County, Virginia, where she teaches International Baccalaureate Language and Literature, and Speech and Debate. She received her B.A. in English Education from the University of North Carolina at Greensboro, and her M.S. in Initiatives in Educational Transformation from George Mason University. Ms. Kiggins was the 2010 Virginia Association of Communication Arts and Sciences Speech Teacher of the Year and the 2011 National Communication Association's National Speech Teacher of the Year. Ms. Kiggins is an IB English HL Examiner, and serves as the president of the Northern Virginia Chapter of the National Forensics League.

Mathematical Reasoning: Stephen A. Reiss, M.B.A.

Stephen A. Reiss is the founder and owner of the Math Magician, which has provided math tutoring for a wide array of tests including the GED® test since 1988. Mr. Reiss also operates Reiss SAT Seminars, test preparation centers in San Diego, California. In addition to teaching more than 300 SAT seminars over a 30-year period, Mr. Reiss has authored, co-authored, or edited more than 40 test preps. He earned his B.A. from Clark University and his M.B.A. from Arizona State University. Mr. Reiss is also a member of Mensa, the world's largest and oldest high IQ society.

Science: Laurie A. Callihan, Ph.D.

Dr. Laurie Callihan is a veteran science author, public speaker, educator, editor, mentor, and researcher. She has served in many capacities in both the private and public sectors. From 2012 to 2013, she was a Research Implementation and Curriculum Specialist at NYU Steinhardt Department of Teaching and Learning, where she managed the Promoting Science Among English Language Learners (P-SELL) Scale-Up project, funded by a $3.5 million National Science Foundation grant. The study, aimed at improving science achievement of all students with a focus on English language learners, involved 66 schools across three Florida school districts. As a curriculum consultant for CPALMS, the official source for Florida state K–12 education standards and course information, she reviewed and produced science curricula and supplements geared to achieve adherence to the Next Generation Sunshine State Standards for Science. In a career spanning 30 years, she has taught science to all age groups. Dr. Callihan received her B.S. in Biology from San Diego Christian College and earned her Ph.D. in Science Education from Florida State University. She is also the author of numerous books, including REA test preps for CLEP Biology and CLEP Natural Sciences, and has been featured at national and international speakers' forums.

Social Studies: Lisa Gail Mullins, M.A.

Lisa Gail Mullins worked for 16 years, through 2016, as an adult education teacher in Tennessee's Hawkins-Hancock County Adult Education Program, where she prepared students to succeed on the GED® test. Ms. Mullins also taught English as a Second Language and adult basic education and literacy. She has logged a great many professional development hours with the Tennessee Adult Education Program. Ms. Mullins is a member of the Tennessee Association of Adult and Community and the Commission of Adult Basic Education. She also has served on the the Association of Adult Literacy Professional Developers, the Adult Education National Credential Advisory Panel, and the Tennessee Adult Education ESOL Transition Task Force as well as the Smoky Mountains Area Workforce Board. In addition, Ms. Mullins is an adjunct professor at Walters State Community College, where she teaches American History. She earned her B.S. and M.A. at East Tennessee State University.

About REA

Founded in 1959, Research & Education Association (REA) is dedicated to publishing the finest and most effective educational materials—including study guides and test preps—for students of all ages. Today, REA's wide-ranging catalog is a leading resource for students, teachers, and other professionals. Visit *www.rea.com* to see a complete listing of all our titles.

Acknowledgments

Technical Editors:

Julie Clark (Reasoning Through Language Arts)

Janice Hildreth (Mathematical Reasoning)

Pepper Stackhouse (Science)

Lynn Elizabeth Marlowe (Social Studies)

Tyson Smith (Economics)

Copyeditors: S4 Carlisle, Karen Lamoreux (RLA content)

Proofreader: Ellen Gong

Correlations: CSA, Inc.

Typesetter: Kathy Caratozzolo

Indexer: Terry Casey

REA Test Prep Team

Publisher: Pam Weston

VP, Editorial: Larry B. Kling

VP, Technology: John Paul Cording

Managing Editor: Diane Goldschmidt

Copywriter: Kelli Wilkins

Cover Design: Jennifer Calhoun

We would like to thank GED Testing Service® and ProCert Labs for conducting a detailed formal review of this publication. GED Testing Service® has certified that this publication is fully aligned with the GED® test.

Introduction

Welcome to REA's *Total Solution for the GED® Test,* your key to mastering the GED® test. Choosing REA as your study partner puts you on a path to join the millions of people who have benefited from the educational and career advantages offered by earning one of America's most recognized credentials.

Since its launch in1942, more than 20 million adults have earned their GED® high school credential. You may have heard of some of them—actors Nicholas Cage, Michael J. Fox, Christina Applegate, Hilary Swank, and Kelly McGillis, the late rock musician David Bowie, former professional boxer Oscar De La Hoya, the late ABC News correspondent Peter Jennings, Olympic gold medalist Mary Lou Retton, former Delaware Governor Ruth Ann Minner, rap artists 50 Cent and Eminem, and comedian Chris Rock.

The GED® test has changed with the times. The test is no longer meant to be viewed as an end in itself but rather as a springboard for adults looking to move on to college, learn a trade, or land a better-paying job. There's no doubt about it: The GED® credential is a major door-opener. In fact, nearly all U.S. colleges and and U.S. employers accept the GED® credential in place of a high school diploma.

About This Book + Online Prep

This REA Book + Online Prep was developed to give you all you need to know to perform well on the GED® test. Built from the ground up to ensure that our content thoroughly reflects today's GED® Assessment Targets, it spans all four test subjects: Reasoning Through Language Arts, Mathematical Reasoning, Science, and Social Studies. Prepared under the supervision of GED Testing Service®, this book is guaranteed to cover 100% of the test objectives—fully and accurately.

This book, along with the valuable tools at the online REA Study Center, provides you with everything you need to master the GED® test content. Our GED® test prep package includes:

- Detailed coverage of how the new GED® test works

- 4 online diagnostic tests (1 for each test section)

- Targeted review for all test sections

- 2 full-length practice tests

We know your time is valuable and you want an efficient study experience. At the online REA Study Center, you'll get feedback right from the start on what you know and what you don't. Armed with this information, you can focus your study time on the topics where you need the most help.

Here's what you'll find at the online REA Study Center:

4 Diagnostic Exams (1 for each test subject) — Our online diagnostic exams will identify your knowledge gaps in each of the test sections. The diagnostic exams are scored automatically and pinpoint the topics where you need the most review. Detailed answer explanations for each question show you why the correct answer is right, and explain why the other answer choices are incorrect.

To access this content, visit *http://studycenter.rea.com.*

GED® Item Types

The GED® test is entirely computer-based. Because the test is given on computer, test administrators have added interactive questions, or as they're known in testing circles, item types. Learning how these seven item types function is central to understanding the GED® test as a whole:

- Drag-and-drop

- Hot spot

- Fill-in-the-blank

- Drop-down

- Multiple-choice

- Short answer

- Extended response

It's also important to know that, according to the best information available from test officials, approximately half of the questions on the test will still be in classic multiple-choice format and will have four answers, lettered (A) through (D), from which you will need to choose the best answer.

Not sure what a drag-and-drop question looks like? No worries. We've included samples of all the GED® question types to familiarize you with what you can expect to see on test day.

Drag-and-Drop:

Drag-and-drop questions allow you to answer questions by moving objects around on the screen. You "drag" the object or icon where you want it and "drop" it into place.

GED Layouts - Candidate Name	Question **2** of **13**

✍ Comment   ⚑ Flag for Review

Read the following paragraph from a student's essay about Susan B. Anthony's speech.

Although Susan B. Anthony was an integral part of the women's right to vote movement, she was not the sole player in the cause. There were many other women who participated in the movement, but because of their more radical approaches to suffrage, they were largely ignored by history. Consequently, the only way students can find out more information about these integral women is often to research outside of traditional textbooks. History for the classroom is written, after all, not only by the victor, but with the idea of promoting proper behavior for those who would again attempt such radical changes.

Drag and drop all of the transitional or signal words or phrases in this paragraph.

A. Although

B. Integral

C. But

D. Suffrage

E. Consequently

F. After all

Answer

In this instance, you would drag and drop answers (A), (C), (E), and (F). All transitional words, save perhaps "after all", should be relatively clear to you, and the only way you can identify them is to memorize them or recognize when an author is indicating a shift in thought.

◀ Previous | Next ▶

Hot Spot Item:

To answer this type of question, you will have to move your computer cursor to a specific "hot spot" on a graphic. In the example below, the test-taker is asked to complete a dot plot.

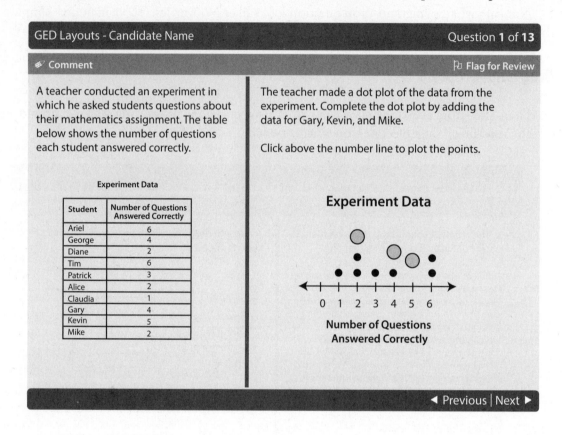

Fill-in-the-blank

This type of question asks you to fill in a single blank space (or in some cases, a few blank spaces). You'll use the keyboard to type in your answers.

✎ Comment   ⚑ Flag for Review

Type your answer in the box.

4. Lori needs an 85% average in her math class to move on to the next class. On her first three exams, she earned scores of 81%, 78% and 97%. What must Lori score on her fourth and final test to earn an 85% grade for the class? Place your answer in the box below.

Answer:

The average of Lori's test scores is calculated by finding the sum of the four scores and then dividing by four.

Let x = Lori's fourth test score

$$\frac{81 + 78 + 97 + x}{4} = 85$$

$$\frac{256 + x}{4} = 85$$

$$(4)\left(\frac{256 + x}{4} = 85\right)(4)$$

$$256 + x = 340$$

$$x = 84$$

◄ Previous │ Next ►

Drop-down Item:

Choose your answer from a drop-down menu embedded in the text.

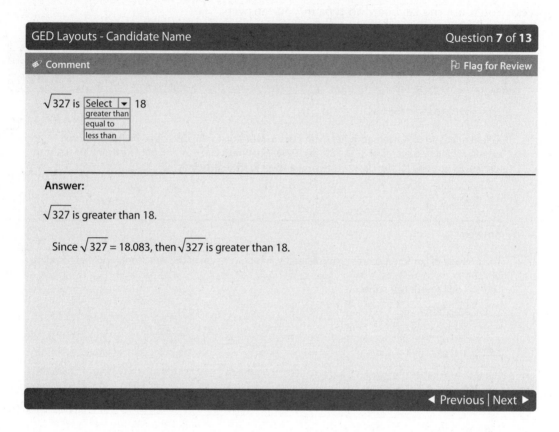

Short-Answer & Extended-Response Boxes:

You will see this screen when you write short-answer items (for the Science section) or for the longer extended-response items in the Reasoning Through Language Arts test.

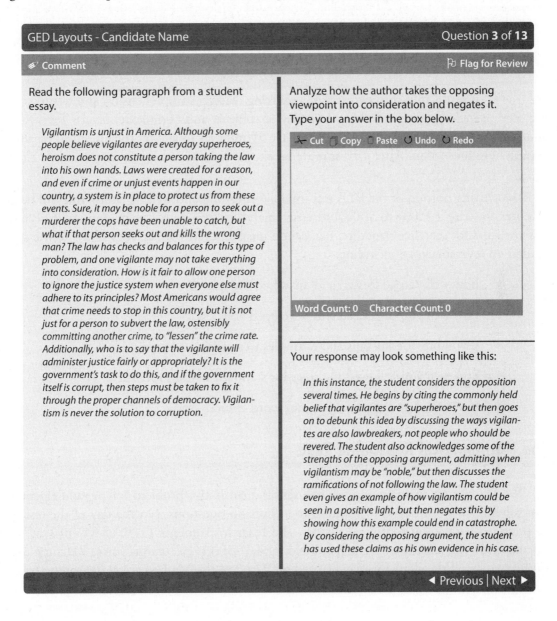

You can view more examples of all the types of GED® questions at *www.gedtestingservice.com/educators/itemsampler*.

Now that you know the array of questions you'll see on the GED® test, let's learn more about each test section. Later in the book, we'll delve deeper into each of the four GED® subjects.

The Reasoning Through Language Arts (RLA) Test

The Reasoning Through Language Arts test focuses on your ability to read closely, write clearly, and edit and understand the use of standard written English in context.

The RLA test is split into two sections covering reading comprehension and writing. The reading section includes texts reflecting a variety of subjects and complexity levels. Texts range from approximately 400 to 900 words. You will have 95 minutes to answer the questions on the reading comprehension section. After a 10-minute break, you will take the writing portion of the test.

The writing portion of the RLA test integrates reading and writing skills. You will be given 45 minutes to write a 3000- to 500-word essay analyzing two source texts. You are expected to follow the rules for sentence structure, usage, and mechanics in writing your essay. Your essay will be graded on several factors, including:

- how well you addressed and answered the question

- how well you organized and developed your essay

- if you provided details and examples to support your main idea

- how well you followed the rules for standard written English

- how varied and appropriate your word choices are

The Mathematical Reasoning Test

The Mathematical Reasoning test focuses on quantitative problem solving and algebraic problem solving. You will have 115 minutes to answer 46 questions. On the day of the test, you will be provided with an on-screen calculator—the Texas Instruments TI-30XS MultiView™ scientific calculator. If you already own the handheld model* of this calculator, you're welcome to bring it to the test site. This calculator may be used on Part 2 of the Mathematical Reasoning test. Here is a simplified picture of the calculator:

---

* Students who bring in a handheld Texas Instruments TI-30XS MultiView™ calculator must place it in their secure lockers before the start of the test. Once students complete Part 1 of the Math test, they will be able to go to their lockers during the three-minute break to get their handheld calculator to use for Part 2.

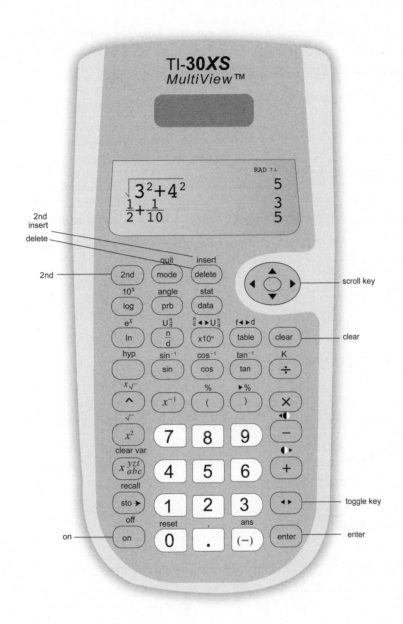

For more information about the calculator, visit: *www.gedtestingservice.com*.

The Science Test

The Science test focuses on science reasoning and three major domains:

- Life science (45% of questions)

- Physical science (35% of questions)

- Earth and space science (20% of questions)

The test is 90 minutes in length and features charts, figures, graphs, and information from which to answer the questions. Approximately half of the test is composed of problem-solving questions, and the other half presents conceptual-understanding questions.

The on-screen calculator is also available for the Science test, though, again, if you already own the handheld version, you're free to bring it.

The Social Studies Test

The Social Studies test focuses on the fundamentals of social studies reasoning and covers four major domains:

- Civics and government

- United States history

- Economics

- Geography and the world

The test is 70 minutes in length. Most of the questions are standard multiple-choice. But you'll also see special item types such as drag-and-drop, hot-spot, and fill-in-the-blank.

As with the Math and Science tests, the on-screen calculator or your own handheld TI-30XS MultiView™ version may be used for the Social Studies test.

Timing and the GED® Test

The GED® test is given in a computerized, timed format. You will have about seven and one-quarter hours to complete the full exam, but don't worry, you don't have to take the entire test in one day. Actually, most GED® test candidates don't take the whole test in one sitting!

Timing is everything, so it's crucial that you budget your time wisely. No matter what section of the test you're taking, you need to answer all the questions before time is up. Better yet, you should try to finish with time to spare so you can return to questions you weren't sure of or guessed on.

In fact, the GED® test is set up to help you do just that. The test's review feature allows you to flag questions so you can go back to them later. At the end of the test, the computer will show you which questions you flagged or didn't answer. Be sure to answer each question—even if you have to guess—because there is no penalty for guessing. If you work slowly or usually run out of time on tests, then you should practice your pacing.

What Score Do I Need to Pass the GED® Test?

The passing standard on each test section (or module) is 145 on a scaled score of 100 to 200. Therefore, you will need to score at least 145 on each section (for a total score of 580 across the battery of four tests) in order to receive your GED® test credential.

You will receive your scores the same day you take your test. The GED® test performance levels are:

- Performance Level 1: Below Passing (100–144 scaled score points)

- Performance Level 2: Pass/High School Equivalency (145–164 scaled score points)

- Performance Level 3: GED® College Ready (165–174 scaled score points)

- Performance Level 4: GED® College Ready + **Credit** (175–200 scaled score points)

Your transcript will contain standard scores and percentile ranks. The standard scores let you compare scores across tests and test forms. The percentile rank lets you compare your performance on each one of the tests with the performance of graduating high school seniors. The higher the percentile rank, the better your performance.

What Score Makes Me Eligible for College Credit?

GED® candidates are eligible for an ACE Credit Recommendation of up to 10 college credits (3 Math, 3 Science, 3 Humanities, and 1 Language Arts/English) when they score at least 175 on each GED® test subject. And after you earn your GED® credential, consider earning more college credit with qualifying scores on the College Board's CLEP exams. You can check out REA's targeted test prep for the CLEP exam series the next time you visit the GED Marketplace™, GED Testing Service's e-commerce site for adult learners, at *www.gedmarketplace.com*.

For more details about GED® scoring, visit the official GED Testing Service® website at *www.gedtestingservice.com*.

When Should the GED® Test Be Taken?

If you're currently enrolled in an adult education course, your teacher or advisor will give you feedback on when he or she thinks you're ready to take the test. If you're studying on your own, one of the best things you can do to get the ball rolling is to take a practice test and go from there (see our suggested study schedule on page 13). When you feel confident about your abilities and are ready to take the actual exam, go for it! Given the very nature of the GED® test, there's really no "best" time to take it.

When and Where is the Test Given?

The GED® test is administered year-round on computer at approximately 1,500 testing centers worldwide. The GED® test is offered in English and, at many locations, in Spanish as well. It is also available in French at a small number of testing centers mainly in Canada.

For more information on upcoming administrations of the GED® test, contact your local high school, adult education center, community college, or GED Testing Service® at 1-800-62 MY GED (1-800-626-9433) or visit *www.gedtestingservice.com*.

You can also locate a testing center near you by visiting *www.gedtestingservice.com* (search "testing centers").

How Do I Register for the Test and Is There a Registration Fee?

All registration for the GED® test is conducted online. You will have to register for the GED® test and pay a registration fee online. At the time of registration you will create an account and schedule your test.

For the most up-to-date information on registration, fees, and to view a tutorial about the registration process, visit *www.gedtestingservice.com*. You may also call Pearson VUE at 1-877-EXAM-GED or 1-877-392-6433, Monday through Friday, 7:00 a.m. to 7:00 p.m. CST with questions.

Can I Retake the Test?

Absolutely! If you don't do well on one section of the GED® test, don't panic! You can take it again, and in fact many candidates do. You don't have to retake the whole test in one sitting, and once you've passed a section of the test, you don't have to take it again.

Accommodations for Test-Takers with Disabilities

If you have special needs because of a physical or learning disability, accommodations may be available for you. Testing accommodations (such as an audio version of the test, extra testing time, or a separate testing room) will be made for test-takers with documented disabilities. For more information on testing accommodations, visit *www.gedtestingservice.com/testers/accommodations-for-disability*.

If you have questions, email: *accommodations@GEDtestingservice.com*.

Setting Up Your Study Plan

When Should I Start Studying?

Many people take the GED® test one test section at a time. Which test you take first is entirely up to you. Maybe you want to take the tests you feel more comfortable with first, or you might decide to tackle the "harder" tests to get them out of the way. Whatever you decide, it's never too early to start studying. The earlier you begin, the more time you will have to sharpen your skills.

Study Schedule

Although our study plan is designed to be used in the six weeks before you take each GED® test section, it can be condensed to three weeks by combining each two-week period into one. Or, if you need more time to study, expand the schedule to suit your needs.

Be sure to set aside enough time—at least two hours each day—to study. The more time you spend studying, the more prepared and relaxed you will feel on the day of the exam.

As you prepare for the GED® test, we recommend doing the following for each of the 4 test sections:

Suggested 6-Week Study Plan (for Each Subject)

WEEK	ACTIVITY
1	Take the Diagnostic Exam at the online REA Study Center. Your score report will identify topics where you need the most review.
2 to 4	Study the book, focusing on the topics you missed (or were unsure of) on the Diagnostic Exam.
5	Take Practice Test 1 in this book. Review your score and re-study any topics you missed.
6	Take Practice Test 2 in this book. See how much your score improves. If you still get a few questions wrong, go back to the review and study the topics you missed.

About the Official GED® Practice Tests

If you want even more practice before test day, GED Testing Service® provides free sample tests (not full-length) with limited functionality (go to *www.gedtestingservice.com* to find them). In addition, the official GED® practice test, called GED Ready®, is available for a nominal fee (go to *www.gedmarketplace.com*).

GED Testing Service® also provides a free computer skills tutorial that you can take prior to the actual testing appointment. Go to *www.gedtestingservice.com* and search for "computer tutorials."

Test-Taking Tips

Taking an important standardized test like the GED® test might make you nervous. These test tips will help alleviate your test-taking anxieties.

Become comfortable with the format ahead of time. When you are practicing to take the GED® test, use the same time constraints as you will have during the actual test. Stay calm, pace yourself, and pay attention to time as you practice. After simulating the test only a few times, you will boost your chances of doing well and you will be able to sit for the actual GED® test with greater confidence.

Become familiar with the directions. Make sure you read and understand the directions before you take the exam, to keep from wasting valuable testing time.

Know the format for each test section before you actually take the test. This will not only save you time, but will also ensure that you are familiar enough with the exam to avoid anxiety (and the mistakes that come from being anxious).

Work on the easier questions first. If you find yourself stuck on one question for too long, mark it using the FLAG FOR REVIEW button on-screen. When you have either answered or marked all of the questions, go back and answer any of the difficult questions you flagged for later review. Be sure your answer registers before you go to the next item. If your answer doesn't register, you won't get credit for that question.

Read all of the possible answers. Just because you think you have found the correct response or, as the case may be, multiple correct responses, do not automatically assume you've arrived at the best answer without checking your work. Read through the choices in context to be sure you are not making a mistake by jumping to conclusions.

Know how much time is allowed for each test section. Work at a steady pace and avoid focusing on any one question too long. (As a rule, don't linger on one question for more than 90 seconds.)

Use erasable noteboards to stay focused and on pace. You cannot use scratch paper, but the erasable noteboard you can request in the testing room is just as good. You can ask the test administrator for up to two more noteboards if you run out of space. Use the noteboards to jot down key ideas in your reading, to list hints and cues that help lead you to the correct answer, or to work a math problem.

If you don't know the answer to a question, guess! Eliminate answers you know are wrong, and then pick the best answer from the ones that remain. Even if you can't eliminate any answers, guess anyway! Remember that there is no penalty for guessing, and only correct answers are counted. This means that you should never leave an answer choice blank. If you guess correctly, you will increase your number of correct answers, and if you guess wrong, you will not lose any points.

Before the Test

Go to *www.gedtestingservice.com* and check your registration information so you'll know what time to arrive at the testing center. (Although you will receive this information when you register, be aware that the location, date, or time may change—so it's worth confirming.) Be sure you have all the documents you will need (admission ticket, proof of identification, etc.) to gain entrance to the testing center. You'll find a full list of the documentation you need in the registration booklet.

Be sure you know where the testing center is and make sure you arrive early. This will allow you to collect your thoughts and relax before the test, and it will also spare you the anguish that comes with being late. If you arrive late, you may not be admitted to the testing center.

Check the registration booklet for what you can (and cannot) bring with you on exam day. For example, electronic devices, watches, food, notebooks, and scratch paper are among the things that are *prohibited*. If an item is not permitted, don't bring it. You don't want to risk not being admitted or having your scores canceled.

The Day of the Test

On test day, dress comfortably so you are not distracted by being too hot or too cold while taking the test.

Procedures will be followed to maintain test security. Once you enter the testing center, follow all of the rules and instructions given by the test supervisor. If you do not, you risk being dismissed from the test and having your scores canceled. Note that an erasable note board will be provided at the testing center for use with any of the test sections; it will be collected at the end of the session.

After your test session, celebrate and relax—you deserve it!

Good luck on the GED® test!

Reasoning Through Language Arts

About the GED® Reasoning Through Language Arts Test

Although the GED® Reasoning Through Language Arts test assesses the fundamentals of reading and writing, the test's focus is actually on ensuring your mastery of language and its mechanics through your grasp of both fictional and non-fictional material. The breakdown of fictional versus non-fictional passages is approximately 25% and 75%, respectively, so you need to be prepared to read plenty of informational and persuasive writing! Today's test also places emphasis on synthesis through reading as opposed to rote reading comprehension; this means you'll need to pull together various strands—several main ideas, for instance—and either draw a conclusion or make a generalization. Let there be no doubt: The GED® Reasoning Through Language Arts test lives up to its name—you will be tested on your ability to **reason**, using text as your evidence and support.

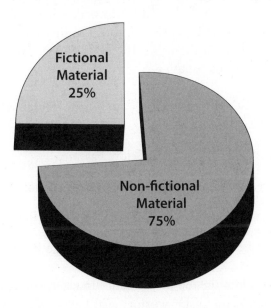

Fictional Material 25%

Non-fictional Material 75%

Question formats

The RLA test is 150 minutes long, including 45 minutes to write one essay. The test is made up of multiple-choice, drop-down, drag-and-drop, and extended-response (essay). The questions use several passage sets including texts running between 400 and 900 words. Each passage set has 6 to 8 associated test questions to determine your competency in the areas of reading comprehension, language, and writing in alignment with career- and college-readiness standards.

Every question on the RLA test is based on a source text or multiple source texts. There are no standalone questions. Drop-down items are actually embedded right in the texts; you'll be asked to move your cursor to the "select" button to reveal the available choices at different spots in the passage.

The GED® RLA test focuses on three essential skills:

1. The ability to read closely

2. The ability to write clearly

3. The ability to edit and understand the use of standard written English in context

This book covers each of these standards, as well as the related indicators (skills) for each one. This subject review discusses the implications and context of each standard, provides examples of possible questions modeled on the skills each standard seeks to measure, and offers feedback regarding correct answers.

Scoring

With a high enough score, today's GED® test makes it possible to earn college credit. GED® scoring is framed by Performance Level Descriptors. On the RLA test, performance levels are determined by the complexity level of the texts. The performance levels represent a sequence of skills, from the most basic to the most complex.

Your score on the GED® RLA test is based on where you fall relative to the four GED® Performance Level Descriptors:

- Performance Level 1 (< 145)—Below Passing

- Performance Level 2 (145-164)—Pass/High School Equivalency

- Performance Level 3 (165-174)—GED® College Ready

- Performance Level 4 (175-200)– GED® College Ready + Credit

If your score puts you into the top performance bracket, you may be eligible for undergraduate credit in English. For details on GED® scoring, visit *www.gedtestingservice.com*.

Now let's move on to the GED® RLA test's content areas.

Reading on the GED® Test

Essential Skills

GED Testing Service® uses seven assessment targets, or standards, in the reading comprehension component of the RLA test. Along with these standards, there are several skills the exam measures. This book will introduce each standard and thoroughly cover the skills related to it.

The first standard in Reading is:

Determine central ideas or themes of texts and analyze their development; summarize the key supporting details and ideas.

The questions assessing this standard are among the most straightforward reading questions you will see on the GED® test. Most of these questions ask you to read a passage and pull out key elements from it. In this standard, the GED® is measuring your ability to comprehend a text; later it will measure your ability to analyze, interpret, and evaluate texts.

The GED® test will assess some or all of these skills with questions relating to this standard:

- Comprehend explicit details and main ideas in text.

- Summarize details and ideas in text.

- Make sentence-level inferences about details that support main ideas.

- Infer implied main ideas in paragraphs or whole texts.

- Determine which detail(s) support(s) a main idea.

- Identify a theme, or identify which element(s) in a text support a theme.

- Make evidence-based generalizations or hypotheses based on details in text, including clarifications, extensions, or application of main ideas to new situations.

- Draw conclusions or make generalizations that require synthesis of multiple main ideas in text.

Let's look at each skill individually.

Comprehend explicit details and main ideas in text.

The first objective of any reading assignment is to understand what is happening in the text. This can be the fundamentals of the *plot* of a novel, the intended effect of an advertisement, or even the key parts of a *setting* of a play. When the GED® test measures your skills in comprehending the explicit details and main ideas in a text, it will test your **ability to read an excerpt and report back precisely what is taking place.** A question might look something like this:

EXAMPLE

Read the following excerpt from Olaudah Equiano's *The Interesting Narrative of Olaudah Equiano* and answer the question that follows.

We are almost a nation of dancers, musicians, and poets. Thus every great event, such as a triumphant return from battle, or other cause of public rejoicing, is celebrated in public dances, which are accompanied with songs and music suited to the occasion. The assembly is separated into four divisions, which dance either apart or in succession, and each with a character peculiar to itself. The first division contains the married men, who in their dances frequently exhibit feats of arms and the representation of a battle. To these succeed the married women, who dance in the second division. The young men occupy the third and the maidens the fourth. Each represents some interesting scene of real life, such as a great achievement, domestic employment, a pathetic story, or some rural sport and, as the subject is generally founded on some recent event, it is therefore ever new. This gives our dances a spirit and variety, which I have scarcely seen elsewhere. We have many musical instruments, particularly drums of different kinds, a piece of music that resembles a guitar, and another much like a stickado. These last are chiefly used by betrothed virgins, who play on them at all grand festivals.

(Project Gutenberg)

What is the main idea of this passage?

    A. The writer's love of dancing.

    B. The particular aspects, cultural influences, and traditions of dance in the author's country.

    C. The differences between how men and women dance in his culture.

    D. The best strategy to become a better dancer.

The correct answer is (B). Although most responses do address the main subject of the paragraph (dance), only answer (B) correctly identifies what the author truly means to address in the paragraph about dancing. He describes reasons people dance, the way they dance, the history behind dance, and adds a few descriptive details that embellish the paragraph and give it substance. In this way, the author's main idea is about appreciating the context of his culture, rather than simply reflecting about a love of dancing (A), considering the way men and women dance (C), or trying to improve one's dance (D).

In order to answer this question, you must study the details provided in the text, for they are the items which move you out of the superficial realm of response (A). Although (A) is a possible correct answer, (B) is a much better answer because it takes into account all aspects of the paragraph, not just the subject of dancing itself. This strategy will help to determine the difference between a subject and a main idea.

Another way this skill may be tested is to ask you questions about the explicit details. For example, you might be asked:

Which sentence contains a detail that best demonstrates Equiano's pride in his country's rich dancing tradition?

    A. "We are almost a nation of dancers, musicians, and poets."

    B. "The first division contains the married men, who in their dances frequently exhibit feats of arms and the representation of a battle."

    C. "Each represents some interesting scene of real life, such as a great achievement, domestic employment, a pathetic story, or some rural sport and, as the subject is generally founded on some recent event, it is therefore ever new."

    D. "We have many musical instruments, particularly drums of different kinds, a piece of music that resembles a guitar, and another much like a stickado."

In this case, the correct answer would be (C) because its specific details give exact reasons about why the author considers the dance tradition dynamic and impressive. As you approach questions on the GED® test that assess this skill, you must be careful you do not simply skim the passage and the answer choices, as you might be tempted to answer with options (B) or (D). Both of these options contain specific details about the text, but in choice (B) the detail is regarding the method of structure, while (D) addresses the musical instruments, rather than the dance itself. Your best choice in answering all reading comprehension questions is to read carefully and deliberately to determine not only what is being said, but why, and how often. It is possible a paragraph can say the word "dance" or its variation several times, but actually be about boxing!

For example:

> The two men danced around each other as they tried to find a way to break the tension. Their steps were in rhythm with each other, and until one broke stride, there would be no true action. The waltz was beautiful despite its impending violence, for the entire crowd knew that eventually there would be a knockout.

It would be very easy to skim this paragraph and assume the occasion was dancing, not boxing. Do not let these kinds of easy passages trip you up by not reading closely!

Summarize details and ideas in text.

Another important skill in reading comprehension is summarizing the key points in a text. This is a little different from simply identifying the ideas. For example, if you read a how-to book on the best ways to caulk a bathtub, you need to be able to summarize the steps, not just identify that the main idea is caulking a bathtub. Summarizing these ideas and details **requires you to completely understand the information** presented in a text, and have the clarity of thought to succinctly explain it.

EXAMPLE

Read the following guide about "Caring for a Betta Fish."

(1) Betta fish are amazing and delicate creatures. Not only do the males have beautiful, vivid fins, they are also astonishing parents! Did you know that the male betta fish is the main caregiver to the young, and the biggest job he has in his tank is to build a bubble nest?

(2) Bubble nests are created when a male betta fish "blows" bubbles in one corner of his tank, or, if he is in the wild, in a safe and protected location in his pond. This nest will house hundreds of fish eggs, and once the female has laid them, the male will drive her away to keep her from eating them. He is a very protective father, and he will help raise the baby bettas until they are strong enough to fend for themselves.

(3) It is very important that you create a tank for your betta that will make him feel safe and secure enough to blow his bubble nests, because it is your only indicator that he is healthy and happy. The first step you need to take to ensure your betta has a happy and comfortable environment is to change his water regularly. It is true that this may damage his nest, but do not worry; if he is happy, he will make another one tomorrow!

(4) You should complete a 100% water change twice a week. Make sure your betta is comfortable during the changes, as undue stress on your betta can cause his life to shorten. When you put in new water, the temperature should be between 78 and 82 degrees, and you must use a water-purifying agent to ward off toxic chemicals (to bettas) in tap water.

(5) Now that you have the water purification schedule down, feeding is the next key issue. You should feed your betta twice a day in very small amounts. Dried fish pellets can be purchased at your local pet store, but remember: your betta's stomach is only as big as his eye! Do not over feed, or it will lead to Swim Bladder Disorder. He would also love a few bloodworms or live miniature shrimp. He is a fighting fish, after all, and a little bit of hunting will do him good!

(6) Finally, make sure your betta's environment is cozy. Most people keep their bettas in small tanks, but that does not mean it cannot include a plant or fun sign! A betta has only one small space in which to live, so do all you can to make your fishy companion feel at home!

(7) In the end, if you follow these steps, you should be well on your way to a happy, healthy, and confident daddy-to-be, even if he never gets the chance to have babies in his bubble nest. Keep your betta's tank clean, and him well fed and happy, and he will blow you beautiful bubble nests every week!

Drag and drop the key steps this tutorial claims will help ensure your betta blows a bubble nest.

- A. Keep his colors vibrant.
- B. Perform biweekly, 100% full-tank water changes.
- C. Keep the water temperature between 78 and 82 degrees.
- D. Work on encouraging him to be aggressive so he can protect his young.
- E. Purify his water. Give him live bait every once in a while, but do not overfeed.
- F. Purchase fish pellets at a pet store.
- G. Feed twice a day with only a few pellets.
- H. Decorate his home with plants.

For this paper-and-pencil setting, simply place the letters for your selected answers below.

You should have selected these:

      B. Perform biweekly, 100% full tank water changes.

      C. Keep the water temperature between 78 and 82 degrees.

      E. Purify his water. Give him live bait every once in a while, but do not overfeed.

      G. Feed twice a day with only a few pellets.

      H. Decorate his home with plants.

This question asks you to read and summarize the main steps to maintaining a healthy betta fish and encouraging him to make bubble nests by eliminating the unnecessary information from the key steps. You must discern what is essential from what is extra. Some of the answers provided are referenced in the text, but they are not necessary for helping your fish blow the nest. For example, the colors indicate a healthy fish, but this is not a specific step that is explained in the text. Similarly, the text comments on the aggressiveness of the fish, but it is not an instruction. The article does suggest you purchase food from a pet store, but again, this does not directly correlate to the building of the nest. (However, feeding him twice a day does!) The GED® test raises the level of difficulty in this question, because drag-and-drop questions provide less room for error. You have to make sure you have identified all the correct steps—not just one. You also have to make sure you carefully separate information that is crucial to the question from information that is only tangential to the objective. To do this, you must read carefully!

Make sentence-level inferences about details that support main ideas.

When you make an inference, it means you are reading a little deeper than the words stated in the text. You could consider it "reading between the lines." For example, if a passage says that "the man had leathery hands, and paint splattered his overalls and tool belt," one can *infer* the character has some sort of carpentry job, although it is not explicitly stated in the text. You can make this inference because of the way the man is described ("paint splattered") and what he is wearing ("overalls and tool belt"). When you make sentence-level inferences about details that support main ideas in a text, you are simply reading a little deeper into the text and **drawing the connection between the details and the subject.**

Let's go back to the betta fish excerpt. Here is an example of a question you might receive with that passage that would test your ability to make inferences about details supporting the main idea.

What conclusions can you draw from the statement, ". . . your betta's stomach is only as big as his eye!" as it relates to the main idea of the passage?

- A. Betta fish have small stomachs.
- B. Too many pellets of food can injure your betta.
- C. Bettas tend to have eyes bigger than their stomachs.
- D. If a betta eats too much, his ensuing sickness can keep him from making bubble nests.

This question is much trickier than the ones that came before, because aside from answer (C), all the options are true statements, and that is what we have been trying to find until now. However, look at the wording of the question. You are asked to draw a conclusion, which means you cannot just state another fact—you have to reach some kind of new idea, or **draw a comparison** between two separate pieces of information (the detail and the main idea). The main idea in the passage is to instruct someone how to care for a betta fish so the fish will blow bubble nests, the best indicator of its health. Because you know this is the main idea, you have to find a way to connect the statement, ". . . your betta's stomach is only as big as his eye!" (a detail), to the main idea of the passage. Therefore, you must infer that the reason this relates is because his small stomach could easily lead to sickness, which will prevent him from blowing bubbles. Answer (D) is the correct response.

The best way to make sure the inference you are making is supported by the text is to finish this sentence: "I can prove the text indicates _____ because of the _____ example(s) I found in the text."

Infer implied main ideas in paragraphs or whole texts.

As discussed in the last section, inferring an idea is much more difficult than identifying an idea because oftentimes, an **inference requires you to make a leap between one piece of information and another.** When you are dealing with an implied main idea, you will have to be able to do two things:

1) Identify the subject.

2) Identify how that subject could be a statement about something else.

In literature, most authors use symbols. They use figurative language like metaphors and similes, and determining the purpose for this kind of writing is an inference skill. However, inferring that the play *The Crucible* (set in Salem during the witch hunt) is actually an extended metaphor, or allegory, for the hunt for Communists in America spurred on by McCarthyism during the Cold War requires that you have a bit more background knowledge, and the ability to connect parallel ideas. When you infer the main idea in a paragraph or a whole text, you must employ several factors in your inference: your reading comprehension, your background knowledge, and your common sense.

Let's take a look at a question that may test your ability to infer a main idea in a paragraph.

EXAMPLE

Read the following paragraph and answer the question:

Starbucks Coffee Company has been in existence for many years, and since its inception on the American West Coast, it has risen to the top of the consumer food chain. In its swift and deft approach to monopolized dominance of the coffee industry, Starbucks has managed to put thousands of independent coffeehouses out of business. These independent coffee shops have been the backbone of American creativity for decades, housing the Beat poets and chess champions of the world. Starbucks is interested in one thing, and one thing alone: making money. They need to get customers in and out of the door as quickly as possible, leaving no room for an environment that would engender community. Independent coffeehouses have always struggled financially, but they have provided a far greater service than Starbucks, on balance: they build communities and foster creativity. Starbucks is just one example of how America's money-hungry vision crushes all other visionaries.

This is the first paragraph of a student's paper. Infer the main idea of the rest of the essay from this paragraph.

- A. Starbucks ruins communities by running smaller coffee shops out of business.
- B. Greed in the American consumer market is overshadowing other important aspects of service.
- C. Corporations do not foster community.
- D. Starbucks and other corporations are too big for their own good.

The correct answer to this question is (B), although (A), (C), and (D) are also plausible answers. The difference is, once again, these answers are simply observations of the material stated in the paragraph; they do not go the next step in connecting this paragraph to the larger implications of the words themselves. To make an inference, you have to be able to look past the stated subject, which, in this instance is coffeehouses, and look towards what the author is using these coffeehouses to represent. The key line in determining the implied main idea in this paragraph is, "Starbucks is just one example. . . ." This leaves it to the rest of the paper to discuss the remainder of that sentence, "how America's money-hungry vision crushes all other visionaries." Because of this sentence, you can infer that the rest of the paper will discuss this main topic, and will likely use other examples of large corporations that have "crushed" the dreams of smaller companies and thus outweighed some of their more positive contributions.

Determine which detail(s) support(s) a main idea.

Many texts have superfluous details added to them in the name of style. It is important for you to **discern which details are necessary to the central idea**, and which are added for effect. To do this, you will have to determine or infer the main idea, and then distinguish which details lend support to this idea, and which simply embellish it.

EXAMPLE

Read the following excerpt from *Indoor and Outdoor Recreations for Girls* by Lina and Adelia Beard.

(1) ALMOST every girl at one time in her life has loved dearly to make mud-pies, and it is not strange, for her mother, grandmother, and many, many times great-great-grandmother before her delighted in making mud-pies. The last, the primitive women of our race, made them to some purpose, for they were the inventors of pottery. The home-making, housekeeping instinct was strong even in these women, who had no houses to keep, and they did their best with the material at hand.

(2) First they wove rude baskets for holding and carrying food; then they learned that cooked food was better than uncooked and could be preserved much longer, so they made baskets of a closer weave and cooked in them by means of water heated by hot stones; finally, they tried cooking over the fire in shallow baskets lined with clay. The clay came out of the basket baked and hard, and behold, they had a new kind of vessel — fireproof and water-proof.

(3) We may imagine with what joy they welcomed this addition to their meager store of home-making utensils and with what patient industry they strove to improve upon this discovery.

(4) They used their baskets as moulds to hold the soft clay, and they fashioned the clay without moulds into shapes suggested by natural objects. The seashells furnished inspiration and many vessels were made in their beautiful forms.

(5) The first potter was a woman, even as the first basket-maker was a woman, and, coming down to our own times, the important discovery of the production of exquisite colors and blending of colors in the Rookwood pottery was made by a woman.

(6) Discovered, developed, and still, in many cases, carried on by women, surely pottery is a woman's art, and as a girl inheriting the old instincts, you may find it the simplest and most natural means of expressing your individuality and love of the beautiful. Beginning as these gentle savages began, using their primitive method, you may be inspired to study deeper into the art, and perhaps become the discoverer of some new process that will give to the world a still more beautiful pottery.

(7) Even the smallest girls may do something in Coiled Pottery, for it is very simple and easy at first, growing more difficult only as one grows ambitious to attempt more intricate forms.

(Project Gutenberg)

Drag-and-drop the sentences that support the main idea.

    A. "ALMOST every girl at one time in her life has loved dearly to make mud-pies, and it is not strange, for her mother, grandmother, and many, many times great-great-grandmother before her delighted in making mud-pies."

    B. "First they wove rude baskets for holding and carrying food; then they learned that cooked food was better than uncooked and could be preserved much longer, so they made baskets of a closer weave and cooked in them by means of water heated by hot stones; finally, they tried cooking over the fire in shallow baskets lined with clay."

    C. "The sea-shells furnished inspiration and many vessels were made in their beautiful forms."

    D. "The first potter was a woman, even as the first basket-maker was a woman, and, coming down to our own times, the important discovery of the production of exquisite colors and blending of colors in the Rookwood pottery was made by a woman."

    E. "Discovered, developed, and still, in many cases, carried on by women, surely pottery is a woman's art, and as a girl inheriting the old instincts, you may find it the simplest and most natural means of expressing your individuality and love of the beautiful."

    F. "Even the smallest girls may do something in Coiled Pottery, for it is very simple and easy at first, growing more difficult only as one grows ambitious to attempt more intricate forms."

For this paper-and-pencil setting, simply place the letter for your selected answers below.

To answer this question correctly, you must first determine the main idea of this passage: Pottery is an art form that came about because of women's role in history. You should drag (B), (D), (E), and (F) to the answer blank. (A) and (C) are simply extra details that add color and commentary to the subject, and although they relate to the topic of women and pottery, they do not do their part to develop the main idea of the passage, which is the development of pottery as an art in women's experience.

As you approach questions like this one, make sure you are able to identify the pieces of information that are *essential* to the main idea, and which ones simply make it more interesting to read.

Identify a theme, or identify which element(s) in a text support a theme.

There is a small difference between a theme and a subject. A theme is usually some kind of **insightful statement about life in literature** that pervades the text. For example, "Love" is not a theme. "Love" is a *subject*. "Love drives us to do harmful things," is a *theme*. The best way to know if you are identifying a theme instead of a subject is to determine if it is a complete sentence that makes some observation you can apply elsewhere. If you are analyzing Shakespeare's *Othello*, for example, "Love kills," is a completely acceptable theme. "Jealousy changes a person's character," is also an astute theme; however, "jealousy" and "manipulation" are only subjects. While these portrayals of theme **may** present themselves on the GED® test as possible answers, always try to find the most insightful answer that is slightly more developed than one word or phrase if it is an option.

Let's see how well you can identify a theme in the following question.

EXAMPLE

Read the following passage from Antoine de Saint-Exupéry's *Wind, Sand and Stars*.*

(1) For how many of us had this old omnibus served as refuge in its day? Sixty? Eighty? I looked about me. Luminous points glowed in the darkness. Cigarettes punctuated the humble meditations of worn old clerks. How many of us had they escorted through the rain on a journey from which there was no coming back?

(2) I heard them talking to one another in murmurs and whispers. They talked about illness, money, shabby domestic cares. Their talk painted the walls of the dismal prison in which these men had locked themselves up. And suddenly I had a vision of the face of destiny.

(3) Old bureaucrat, my comrade, it is not you who are to blame. No one ever helped you to escape. You, like a termite, built your peace by blocking up with cement every chink and cranny through which the light might pierce. You rolled yourself up into a ball in your genteel security, in routine, in the stifling conventions of provincial life, raising a modest rampart against the winds and the tides and the stars. You have chosen not to be perturbed by great problems, having trouble enough to forget your own fate as man. You are not the dweller upon an errant planet and do not ask yourself questions to which there are no answers. You are a petty bourgeois of Toulouse. Nobody grasped you by the shoulder while there was still time. Now the clay of which you were shaped has dried and hardened, and naught in you will ever awaken the sleeping musician, the poet, the astronomer that possibly inhabited you in the beginning.

---

* Reprinted from Antoine de Saint-Exupéry, *Wind, Sand and Stars* (New York: Houghton Mifflin Harcourt, 2003). Copyright renewed 1967 by Lewis Galantiére.

What is the theme of this passage?

   A. People who are not artists are not as evolved as those that are creative, and people should strive to be more open-minded about their futures.

   B. Man versus Man

   C. The differences between the classes of people who work and those that are privileged

   D. No matter what a person might have the potential to become, he is the product of his environment.

The correct answer to this question is (D). It is true that (A) is a theme, but it is not the best theme for what the passage as a whole is trying to convey. Answer (A) creates a judgmental opinion, which would be okay if it were actually the tone of the author, but instead the author uses consoling words such as "it is not you who are to blame." Option (A) is a misread of the author's intentions. Option (B) and (C) would be viable if they were more fully developed ideas, but as they stand they are incomplete assessments of the text's intentions. In an instance such as this question, however, (D) is far more insightful into the text, and you should always choose the answer that encompasses the *most correct* answer.

This standard also asks you to identify which details in a text support a theme. You should employ the exact same skills you learned about identifying which details support a main idea. Once you have identified the theme itself, you should have no problems at all identifying which details support it.

So to use this same passage, you might come across a question that asks:

Which details support the theme that man is the product of his environment?

   A. How many of us had they escorted through the rain on a journey from which there was no coming back?

   B. Their talk painted the walls of the dismal prison in which these men had locked themselves up.

   C. Old bureaucrat, my comrade, it is not you who are to blame.

   D. Nobody grasped you by the shoulder while there was still time. Now the clay of which you were shaped has dried and hardened, and naught in you will ever awaken the sleeping musician, the poet, the astronomer that possibly inhabited you in the beginning.

In this example, the theme itself was given to you; you only need to identify which quote supports it. In this case, the answer to that is choice (D). This is the only example in which the author discusses man's environment and how it affects how a person turns out. Choice (A) does not discuss the theme at all, and although (B) might seem a good choice, this is more of a support for a theme that man makes his own fate. Choice (C) also tacitly supports the theme, but it is not nearly as direct as choice (D). (C) strikes a forgiving tone by painting man as a bit player in his environment.

Make evidence-based generalizations or hypotheses based on details in text, including clarifications, extensions, or applications of main ideas to new situations.

Making a hypothesis is very similar to making an inference, but this skill will require you to specifically **support the reasons why you made the inference** based on the textual evidence. Let's use one selection to demonstrate all these skills: clarification, extension, and application in a new situation.

EXAMPLE

Read the following passage from the collection of Eudora Welty's autobiographical essays, *One Writer's Beginnings*.

(1) I never knew anyone who'd grown up in Jackson without being afraid of Mrs. Calloway, our librarian. She ran the Library absolutely by herself, from the desk where she sat with her back to the books and facing the stairs, her dragon eye on the front door, where who knew what kind of person might come in from the public? **SILENCE** in big black letters was on signs tacked up everywhere. She herself spoke in her normally commanding voice; every word could be heard all over the Library above a steady seething sound coming from her electric fan; it was the only fan in the Library and stood on her desk, turned directly onto her steaming face.

(2) As you came in from the bright outside, if you were a girl, she sent her strong eyes down the stairway to test you; if she could see through your skirt she sent you straight back home: you could just put on another petticoat if you wanted a book that badly from the public library. I was willing; I would do anything to read.

(3) My mother was not afraid of Mrs. Calloway. She wished me to have my own library card to check out books for myself. She took me in to introduce me and I saw I had met a witch. "Eudora is nine years old and has my permission to read any book she wants from the shelves, children or adult," Mother said. "With the exception of Elsie Dinsmore," she added. Later she explained to me that she'd made this rule because Elsie the heroine, being made by her father to practice too long and hard at the piano, fainted and fell off the piano stool. "You're too impressionable, dear," she told me. "You'd read that and the very first thing you'd do, you'd fall off the piano stool." "Impressionable" was a new word. I never hear it yet without the image that comes with it of falling straight off the piano stool.

(4) Mrs. Calloway made her own rules about books. You could not take back a book to the Library on the same day you'd taken it out; it made no difference to her that you'd read every word in it and needed another to start. You could take out two books at a time and two only; this applied as long as you were a child and also for the rest of your life, to my mother as severely as to me. So two by two, I read library books as fast as I could go, rushing them home in the basket of my bicycle. From the minute I reached our house, I started to read. Every book I seized on, from Bunny Brown and His Sister Sue at Camp Rest-a-While to Twenty Thousand Leagues Under the Sea, stood for the devouring wish to read being instantly granted. I knew this was bliss, knew it at the time. Taste isn't nearly so important; it comes in its own time. I wanted to read immediately. The only fear was that of books coming to an end.

(5) My mother was very sharing of this feeling of insatiability. Now, I think of her as reading so much of the time while doing something else. In my mind's eye The Origin of Species is lying on the shelf in the pantry under a light dusting of flour—my mother was a bread baker; she'd pick it up, sit by the kitchen window and find her place, with one eye on the oven. I remember her picking up The Man in Lower Ten while my hair got dry enough to unroll from a load of kid curlers trying to make me like my idol, Mary Pickford. A generation later, when my brother Walter was away in the Navy and his two little girls often spent the day in our house, I remember Mother reading the new issue of Time magazine while taking the part of the wolf in a game of "Little Red Riding Hood" with the children. She'd just look up at the right time, long enough to answer — in character — "The better to eat you with, my dear," and go back to her place in the war news.

Clarification-type question: Here is an example of a clarification-type question, one of the ways in which the GED® test will ask you to make a generalization or form a hypothesis based on an excerpt from a passage.

Consider this sentence from the previous passage: "Taste isn't nearly so important; it comes in its own time." What is the main implication of this sentiment?

 A. It shows that readers need to choose their books carefully so they can become well-read.

 B. It demonstrates how an inexperienced reader does not need to be concerned with the types of text being read, because with exposure a taste will develop.

 C. It explains how none of us will become discerning readers until we read often. Therefore, it is an encouragement to read all the time.

 D. It is a metaphor for Welty's hunger to devour books, and shows her as an avid reader who will "eat" anything.

The correct answer to this question is (B). You are asked to use this sentence as a tool to clarify the larger message in the text. The message is that inevitably, with exposure to any kind of literature, taste, or critical judgment, will develop. Choice (B) best articulates this hypothesis. Answer choice (C) might have distracted you because it is a conclusion that can be inferred from the idea, but it is not the actual sentiment provided in the text. Choice (B) also provides a blanket negation, "none of us," which inverts Welty's commentary. Answer choice (A) is the opposite of the quotation's intention. Welty says that taste is not important. Taste is created through our choices, and (A) claims choosing carefully is important. Finally, (D) is an entertaining selection, but it misinterprets the text in context. "Taste" in this quotation is referring to a reader's preferences, not a need to consume or "devour" books. Your reading comprehension skills need to be employed carefully to answer this type of clarification question.

Extension-type question: Here is an example of an extension-type question, based on the same passage. This type of question asks you to respond by going beyond, or extending, what is said in the passage.

What kind of assessment can you make of Welty's mother's character?

A. Welty's mother was very intimidating, as indicated by the line, "My mother was not afraid of Mrs. Calloway."

B. Welty's mother was overbearing, as indicated by the line, "She wished me to have my own library card to check out books for myself."

C. Welty's mother, like Welty, cared little for the kind of book she read, as indicated by the line, "My mother was very sharing of this feeling of insatiability."

D. Welty's mother does not care about the well-being of her children, as indicated by the line, "She'd just look up at the right time, long enough to answer — in character—'The better to eat you with, my dear,' and go back to her place in the war news."

The correct answer to this question is (C). Were you to simply read the answers, you might guess randomly and incorrectly, because without reading the entire passage, each of these answers is a logical inference of the quote provided therein, especially option (D). You would have to read the entire work to make the extension that this quote indicates her love of reading, not her lack of interest in children. Indeed, her interest in children is indicated strongly at the beginning of the passage when she insists Welty read actively. This question tests your ability to determine subtle inferences and use your common sense. Just because a person is not afraid of someone else does not necessarily mean she is intimidating. Just because a mother wants her daughter to have freedom to check out books from the library does not mean she is overbearing; indeed, the text indicates the opposite. Make sure you read carefully!

Application of main idea to a new situation: Here is an example of an **application of the main idea to a new situation** question.

Based on this passage, what can you infer about Welty's life?

    A. Welty tapped into her love of reading as a child as she matured into a writer.

    B. Welty used her fear of the librarian to write exciting fiction works.

    C. Welty used ideas from *Twenty Thousand Leagues Under the Sea* in her papers in high school.

    D. Welty's mother was a constant source of material for Welty's fiction.

Each of these answer responses applies the main idea (or some version of it) to a new situation. However, only one of them is a completely logical response, and that is (A). You know this for one reason: the title of the piece. Do not forget about titles as you read! *One Writer's Beginnings* indicates this is a history of Welty's roots in writing, and although (D) may seem an equally plausible answer, you should look at the entirety of the main idea. Welty's mother, indeed, plays a major role in this work, but the focus of the text is Welty's own experience with reading, and though her mother is a large part of that, she is NOT what this piece is centrally about. Additionally, you are unable to tell from this piece if Welty ever wrote fictional pieces about her mother specifically. Answers (B) and (C) are entirely unsupported by the text. Be careful as you read, and be sure to make choices that are logical!

Draw conclusions or make generalizations that require synthesis of multiple main ideas in text.

Drawing conclusions from multiple main ideas in a work is a difficult reading skill to master, and it is the hardest skill in this standard. In order to do this, you must **make inferences based on several different ideas instead of just one.** Let's take a look at a few questions before we begin decoding what this means.

EXAMPLE

Read this passage from Lewis Lapham's *Money and Class in America.**

(1) I think it fair to say that the current ardor of the American faith in money easily surpasses the degrees of intensity achieved by other societies in other times and places. Money means so many things to us—spiritual as well as temporal—that we are at a loss to know how to hold its majesty at bay.

---

* Reprinted from Lewis Lapham, *Money and Class in America* (New York: Picador, 1988). Copyright © 1988 Picador.

(2) Henry Adams in his autobiography remarks that although the Americans weren't much good as materialists they had been so "deflected by the pursuit of money" that they could turn "in no other direction." The national distrust of the contemplative temperament arises less from an innate Philistinism than from a suspicion of anything that cannot be counted, stuffed, framed or mounted over the fireplace in the den. Men remain free to rise or fall in the world, and if they fail it must be because they willed it so. The visible signs of wealth testify to an inward state of grace, and without at least some of these talismans posted in one's house or on one's person an American loses all hope of demonstrating to himself the theorem of his happiness. Seeing is believing, and if an American success is to count for anything in the world it must be clothed in the raiment of property. As often as not it isn't the money itself that means anything; it is the use of money as the currency of the soul.

(3) Against the faith in money, other men in other times and places have raised up countervailing faiths in family, honor, religion, intellect and social class. New merchant princes of medieval Europe would have looked upon the American devotion as sterile cupidity; the ancient Greeks would have regarded it as a form of insanity. Even now, in the last decades of a century commonly defined as American, a good many societies both in Europe and Asia manage to balance the desire for wealth against the other claims of the human spirit. An Englishman of modest means can remain more or less content with the distinction of an aristocratic name or the consolation of a flourishing garden; the Germans show to obscure university professors the deference accorded by Americans only to celebrity; the Soviets honor the holding of political power; in France a rich man is a rich man, to whom everybody grants the substantial powers that his riches command but to whom nobody grants the respect due to a member of the National Academy. But in the United States a rich man is perceived as being necessarily both good and wise, which is an absurdity that would be seen as such not only by a Frenchman but also by a Russian. Not that the Americans are greedier than the French, or less intellectual than the Germans, or more venal than the Russians, but to what other tribunal can an anxious and supposedly egalitarian people submit their definitions of the good, the true and the beautiful if not to the judgment of the bottom line?

Drag-and-drop the conclusions or generalizations you can make from this passage.

  2 A. Americans are too in awe of money.

  1 B. Americans feel that they must have possessions to be successful.

  5 C. Americans without sufficient property are less intelligent than ones with it.

  3 D. Americans are less skilled at balancing wealth and other competing aspects of life as other countries.

  4 E. Wealthy Americans are neither good nor wise.

For this paper-and-pencil setting, simply place the letter for your selected answers below.

HeLP WitH DRoG + dROP

This is probably the most difficult of *any* reading passage you will see on the GED® test. Most passages will be at a slightly lower reading level. Do not let it scare you, just do your best to unlock it. This passage is simply a critique of America's obsession with money and wealth. The author suggests we should look to other nations as an example of a more holistic approach to life.

The correct answers to drag and drop are answer choices (A), (B), and (D). You can tell that the author feels Americans are "too in awe of money" by the quotation, ". . . we are at a loss to know how to hold its majesty at bay." This quotation indicates that we are puzzled about how to keep money's magnificence from ruling our lives, hence the generalization that we are "too in awe." The author levels criticism about our relationship with money. The generalization for choice (B) comes from the sentence, "Seeing is believing, and if an American success is to count for anything in the world it must be clothed in the raiment of property." Indeed, this answer choice is simply a restatement of the quotation itself, so you can select it as a generalization the author puts forth. Finally, you should have chosen answer choice (D). You must infer this from the final paragraph of the text, where the author compares and contrasts Americans' view on money to the views of other countries. The last paragraph indicates that we should take a hint from countries that are able to "balance the desire for wealth against the other claims of the human spirit." Although both choices (C) and (E) are discussed in the text, the generalizations drawn are incorrect readings of the author's intent. Choice (C), for example, is the fear which drives Americans to their disproportionate love of money. So even though the sentiment exists in the text, the author ultimately argues against it. Choice (E), too, is mentioned in the passage, but it is there only to point out our fallacious thinking as a country that equates wealth with virtue and intelligence. This is a generalization he contrasts with the French, for whom a rich man is simply a rich man, not a man who should necessarily be asked for counsel. Simply because the author uses this to point out America's flawed thinking does not mean that all wealthy Americans are bad or stupid, which choice (E) contends.

In this instance, you have had to synthesize a variety of information and evidence, each piece of which has its own small idea, and apply it to a larger argument. You also had to distinguish between generalizations the characters in the text may have versus the author's own conclusive statements. On the GED® test, you may encounter a twist on this, which asks you to draw a conclusion based on several different arguments. An example follows.

Drag-and-drop the sentences which support the idea that America has incorrectly put its "faith in money."

A. "I think it fair to say that the current ardor of the American faith in money easily surpasses the degrees of intensity achieved by other societies in other times and places."

B. "The national distrust of the contemplative temperament arises less from an innate Philistinism than from a suspicion of anything that cannot be counted, stuffed, framed or mounted over the fireplace in the den."

5   C. "As often as not it isn't the money itself that means anything; it is the use of money as the currency of the soul."

6   D. "New merchant princes of medieval Europe would have looked upon the American devotion as sterile cupidity; the ancient Greeks would have regarded it as a form of insanity."

2   E. "But in the United States a rich man is perceived as being necessarily both good and wise, which is an absurdity that would be seen as such not only by a Frenchman but also by a Russian."

4   F. "Not that the Americans are greedier than the French, or less intellectual than the Germans, or more venal than the Russians, but to what other tribunal can an anxious and supposedly egalitarian people submit their definitions of the good, the true and the beautiful if not to the judgment of the bottom line?"

For this paper-and-pencil setting, simply place the letter for your selected answers below.

The key to answering this question is the word "incorrectly." Because of this word, you must determine all the instances where the author passes judgment on the American "faith in money." In this case, the question has made the inference for you, and it is your job to find the multiple examples that support it. The correct items you should drag and drop are examples (C), (D), (E), and (F). In order to determine this, you must look for the author's negative tone and judgmental attitude. This is where your own inference comes into play. Answer (A) is simply an observation of America's behavior. Answer (B) certainly has negative connotations to it, but it does not also address the incorrect "faith in money" idea. While it is a judgment about America's desire to own and dominate, it does not have a *direct* comment about money itself. This quote is more of an explanation of how we got to where we are, rather than an argument against it. Answer (C) supports the idea because it suggests America's love of money trumps a great deal else in human experience, which is, in the author's mind, "incorrect." (D) is correct because it shows how other cultures view America's worship of money as "insane," (E) should be chosen because it uses the word "absurdity" to describe America's views about rich people. Both these choices pass extreme judgment, illuminating the incorrect approach America takes towards money. Answer (F) should also be selected due to its biting sarcasm (judgment), which builds off of the previous observations about the way other countries handle wealth.

In this instance, you have had to synthesize a variety of information and sources, each of which has its own small idea, and apply it to a larger argument. You may be asked to do this in a different manner by drawing a conclusion based on several different arguments. Here's an example:

EXAMPLE

Read the following paragraph:

The Clash, a British punk band, had excellent songwriting skills and produced a great many albums. Their proficiency on instruments showed greater talent than some of the other popular bands at the time, such as The Sex Pistols, who only seemed capable of a few chords on the guitar. The Clash provided relevant political observations about the state of the nation, which helped move people to action to speak out against injustices in the country. The Clash sold more albums than most other punk bands of its caliber, and made music for a longer stretch of time. Even today, most people know who The Clash is, but those same people would not be able to identify the American punk rock band, The Stooges, which performed punk before the genre had been named. The Clash has had its songs covered by pop singers like Annie Lennox, so its music has reached an even wider audience than punks.

What main conclusion can you draw from the various pieces of information presented in the paragraph?

    A. The Clash made more money than any other punk band.

    B. The Clash made better music than other punk bands.

    C. The Clash is arguably the most influential punk band in history.

    D. The Clash was responsible for changing the political climate in Britain.

The correct answer is (C). Although each of the other responses is mentioned in the paragraph, only choice (C) combines all these features into one general argument without ignoring any of the others. This question could have also been asked in short answer style, in which case you would have to draw that conclusion yourself. Give it a try with this passage:

EXAMPLE

Read the following paragraph:

What conclusion can you draw from this passage from D.H. Lawrence's *Why the Novel Matters?*

> In life, there is right and wrong, good and bad, all the time. But what is right in one case is wrong in another. And in the novel you see one man becoming a corpse, because of his so-called goodness, another going dead because of his so-called wickedness. Right and wrong is an instinct: but an instinct of the whole consciousness in a man, bodily, mental, spiritual at once. And only in the novel are *all* things given full play, or at least, they may be given full play, when we realize that life itself, and not inert safety, is the reason for living. For out of the full play of all things emerges the only thing that is anything, the wholeness of a man, the wholeness of a woman, man live, and live woman.

Lawrence brings up many ideas in this passage. How would you bring them into one strong, conclusive sentence? Perhaps you could say something like, "It is the object and the duty of the novel to consider all aspects of life, no matter how obscure or obscene."

Interpreting Text

Analyze how individuals, events, and ideas develop and interact over the course of a text.

Analysis is a little bit more complicated than reading comprehension and inference, which is what we studied earlier. Now you must take all your inferences and examine them in order to **explain** them. This means in this standard you will be discussing the way things (individuals, events, and ideas) grow or become richer as the text progresses. Most of the works that assess this skill will be fiction.

The GED® test will assess some or all of these skills with questions relating to this standard:

- Order sequences of events in texts.

- Make inferences about plot/sequence of events, characters/people, settings, or ideas in texts.

- Analyze relationships within texts, including how events are important in relation to plot or conflict; how people, ideas, or events are connected, developed, or distinguished; how events contribute to theme or relate to key ideas; or how a setting or context shapes structure and meaning.

- Infer relationships between ideas in a text (e.g., an implicit cause and effect, parallel, or contrasting relationship).

- Analyze the role that details play in complex literary or informational texts.

Let's look at each skill individually.

Order sequences of events in texts.

This is probably the least difficult task you will have to master in this standard. All this skill does is test your ability to **put things in the order they happened** in the piece. It is likely that all questions relating to this standard will be drag-and-drop in sequential order. Give it a try below.

EXAMPLE

Read this passage from Edgar Allan Poe's short story "The Angel of the Odd."

(1) My dreams were terrifically disturbed by visions of the Angel of the Odd. Methought he stood at the foot of the couch, drew aside the curtains, and, in the hollow, detestable tones of a rum-puncheon, menaced me with the bitterest vengeance for the contempt with which I had treated him. He concluded a long harangue by taking off his funnelcap, inserting the tube into my gullet, and thus deluging me with an ocean of Kirschenwasser, which he poured, in a continuous flood, from one of the long-necked bottles that stood him instead of an arm. My agony was at length insufferable, and I awoke just in time to perceive that a rat had run off with the lighted candle from the stand, but not in season to prevent his making his escape with it through the hole. Very soon, a strong suffocating odor assailed my nostrils; the house, I clearly perceived, was on fire. In a few minutes the blaze broke forth with violence, and in an incredibly brief period the entire building was wrapped in flames. All egress from my chamber, except through a window, was cut off. The crowd, however, quickly procured and raised a long ladder. By means of this I was descending rapidly, and in apparent safety, when a huge hog, about whose rotund stomach, and indeed about whose whole air and physiognomy, there was something which reminded me of the Angel of the Odd, —when this hog, I say, which hitherto had been quietly slumbering in the mud, took it suddenly into his head that his left shoulder needed scratching, and could find no more convenient rubbing post than that afforded by the foot of the ladder. In an instant I was precipitated, and had the misfortune to fracture my arm.

(2) This accident, with the loss of my insurance, and with the more serious loss of my hair, the whole of which had been singed off by the fire, predisposed me to serious impressions, so that, finally, I made up my mind to take a wife. There was a rich widow disconsolate for the loss of her seventh husband, and to her wounded spirit I offered the balm of my vows. She yielded a reluctant consent to my prayers. I knelt at her feet in gratitude and adoration. She blushed, and bowed her luxuriant tresse into close contact with those supplied me, temporarily, by Grandjean. I know not how the entanglement took place, but so it was. I arose with a shining pate, wigless, she in disdain and wrath, half buried in alien hair. Thus ended my hopes of the widow by an accident which could not have been anticipated, to be sure, but which the natural sequence of events had brought about.

(Project Gutenberg)

Drag-and-drop the events in the correct order:

   A. The narrator breaks his arm.

   B. The narrator loses his fiancée because she realizes he is wearing a wig.

   C. The narrator dreams the Angel of the Odd lectures him.

   D. The narrator's house catches on fire.

   E. The narrator loses his insurance.

   F. A hog knocks over the ladder upon which the narrator is standing.

> For this paper-and-pencil setting, simply place the letter for the events in the order in which they occurred.

The correct order is: (E), (C), (D), (F), (A), (B). The most difficult part of this question is determining where to place option E, because it is not directly stated in this part of the story when he lost his insurance; your only indication is the phrase, "This accident, with the loss of my insurance. . . ." You must use your common sense to order this as taking place *prior to* the events listed in this passage, which begin with (C). Ordering the rest is simply a matter of reading the passage and putting them in sequence.

Make inferences about plot/sequence of events, characters/people, settings, or ideas in texts.

You already know how to make inferences, so in this case, let's **apply your inference skills to these specific tasks**: plot/sequence, characters/people, settings and ideas. We can use the same short story by Poe to test each of these particular inference strategies.

Here is a question that will address the **plot and sequence** of the story.

What can you infer about what will happen next in this story, based on the passage you have been given?

   A. The narrator will find a new wife that loves him for who he is, not what his hair looks like.

   B. The narrator's luck will turn around and odd things will stop happening to him.

   C. The Angel of the Odd will decide he has committed enough peevish acts against the narrator and will leave him alone.

   D. The Angel of the Odd will continue to torment the narrator with strange events until the narrator makes some kind of change.

The correct answer to this question is (D). You can make this inference based on several key lines in the text: the fact that in his dream, the Angel of the Odd "menaced me with the bitterest vengeance for the contempt with which I had treated him," indicating the narrator has some relationship mending to do. Also relevant is that the hog which knocked over his ladder "reminded [him] of the Angel of the Odd." Finally, you should consider how the narrator describes the unforeseeable accident "which the natural sequence of events had brought about." These ideas foreshadow the facts that 1) the narrator has to make a change or receive the Angel's forgiveness, and that 2) the Angel is to blame for the unfortunate events that continue to happen to the narrator.

Here is a question that will address the skill of making an inference about the **character**.

Drag-and-drop the words you would use to describe the narrator.

    A. Cowardly

    B. Manipulative

    C. Unlucky

    D. Arrogant

    E. Victimized

    F. Desperate

For this paper-and-pencil setting, simply place the letter for your selected answers below.

Had you read the entire story, you might choose all of these words to describe the narrator; however, given just the passage you have before you, you should select (B), (C), (E), and (F). You have no reason to consider the narrator cowardly (A); in fact, you might think him rather brave since he climbed out of the window of a burning house. You also have no information in this passage to tell you he is arrogant (D); in fact, he almost seems humble in the opening lines during his dream. He may be consumed with his looks when he calls the loss of his hair worse than the loss of his home, but this does not necessarily mean he is arrogant. It could even be considered light-hearted, self-deprecating humor, and since it is impossible to tell this tone with so little context, again it is better to use textual evidence to be certain of your choices of inference. You can deduce that he is manipulative (B), however, because he decides to "take a wife," a "rich widow," to attempt to stave off the financial effects of his bad luck, and he deceives her by hiding his bald head with a wig. To this end, you can cross-apply that information to infer he is desperate (F). Obviously you can deduce that the narrator is unlucky (C) because of the events in the story (the burning of his house, the breaking of his arm, the loss of his fiancée). You can also deduce that he is victimized (E) for these exact same reasons; indeed there are times in the passage where we feel sorry for him as he is at the Angel's mercy.

Here is a question that will address the skill of making an inference about the **setting**.

What conclusions can you draw about the setting of this particular story?

    A. It is set in the future.

    B. It takes place over the course of one afternoon.

    C. It takes place in either a rural setting or a little further back in history than present day.

    D. It is set in Germany.

The answer to this question is (C), and the reason you can tell this is because of the inclusion of a hog in the middle of a "crowd" in a residential area. This leads you to believe it is either taking place in the country, or during a time when hogs were kept at nearly every home in a more metropolitan area. While this may be the future (A), there is no definitive text to support this, and you are better sticking with an answer you know you can prove. It is possible, though highly unlikely, that this takes place over the course of one day. However, once again you need to employ your common sense. Is it likely (can you infer) that a man can meet a woman, court her and plan a wedding all in one afternoon? Probably not. Again, unless there is some piece of text indicating this happened very quickly, stick with the more plausible answer. Finally, although the word "Kirschenwasser" sounds like it may be German, so does the word "Merlot" sound French (which it is). However, just because a story uses a word from another language, it does not mean the story is set in a country that uses this language. After all, there are plenty of Americans who drink Merlot in America. Do not make leaps in logic just because one part of the answer makes it sound could be a viable answer! Be sure you can point to a place in the text that supports any inference you make!

Here is a question that will address the skill of making inferences about an **idea**.

What is the lesson is Poe trying to teach with "The Angel of the Odd"?

    A. Always make sure you have insurance.

    B. You cannot avoid the unavoidable.

    C. Avoid alcohol.

    D. Faith can be a powerful factor in a person's life.

The answer to this question is (B), and you can infer this from several key aspects of the text. Mainly, we know that no matter what the narrator tries to do to improve his situation, something negative happens. For example, he tries to escape his burning house and he breaks his arm. He tries to marry a rich woman and his wig gets caught in her hair, exposing how undesirable he is. Whether this is a belief that personally resonates with you or not, it *is* something you can support by looking closely at the text. You cannot support, however, that Poe is trying to warn you to have insurance (A), because even if his home **was** insured, the narrator still would have broken his arm, and the events in the story would have unfolded in a similar way. He may not have needed to marry a rich widow, but he would have also lost his hair. Although alcohol (C) is a major factor in the rest of the story, it is barely mentioned in this passage, and so you can consider it mostly irrelevant to the lesson. Although (D) may be a true statement, it is unsubstantiated as a theme in this portion of the text. (Indeed, it is a theme for the entire short story, but not in this small section.) This section of the short story does not deal much with faith, so making an inference about it would be a jump in logic.

Analyze relationships within texts, including how events are important in relation to plot or conflict; how people, ideas, or events are connected, developed, or distinguished; how events contribute to theme or relate to key ideas; or how a setting or context shapes structure and meaning.

Many relationships are created in works of literature, not just relationships among the characters. This standard is pretty clear: you must be able to **analyze the interplay between two things**, be they people, ideas, or events. Once you understand how to analyze relationships, answering questions that measure this skill will be easy.

You must remember that, especially in works of fiction, rarely does an author write something that is not meaningful to another piece of the story, or to the story as a whole. Literature is full of inter-relations, and your job in this standard is to determine:

- how certain events lead to the outcome, how occasions cause characters to grow and develop,

- how events in a plot can stand for something larger than the event itself, and

- how the choices an author makes about setting can affect the message.

All of these ideas deal with how aspects of a story relate.

Let's discuss each of these ideas individually. Once again we will use one passage to consider them all.

EXAMPLE

Read this passage from Clifford Whittingham Beers' *A Mind that Found Itself, An Autobiography*.

(1) I am not telling the story of my life just to write a book. I tell it because it seems my plain duty to do so. A narrow escape from death and a seemingly miraculous return to health after an apparently fatal illness are enough to make a man ask himself: For what purpose was my life spared? That question I have asked myself, and this book is, in part, an answer. . . .

(2) The first years of my life were, in most ways, not unlike those of other American boys, except as a tendency to worry made them so. Though the fact is now difficult for me to believe, I was painfully shy. When first I put on short trousers, I felt that the eyes of the world were on me; and to escape them I hid behind convenient pieces of furniture while in the house and, so I am told, even sidled close to fences when I walked along the street. With my shyness there was a degree of self-consciousness which put me at a disadvantage in any family or social gathering. I talked little and was ill at ease when others spoke to me.

(3) Like many other sensitive and somewhat introspective children, I passed through a brief period of morbid righteousness. In a game of "one-old-cat," the side on which I played was defeated. On a piece of scantling which lay in the lot where the contest took place, I scratched the score. Afterwards it occurred to me that my inscription was perhaps misleading and would make my side appear to be the winner. I went back and corrected the ambiguity. On finding in an old tool chest at home a coin or medal, on which there appeared the text, "Put away the works of darkness and put on the armour of light," my sense of religious propriety was offended. It seemed a sacrilege to use in this way such a high sentiment, so I destroyed the coin.

(4) I early took upon myself, mentally at least, many of the cares and worries of those about me. Whether in this I was different from other youngsters who develop a ludicrous, though pathetic, sense of responsibility for the universe, I do not know. But in my case the most extreme instance occurred during a business depression, when the family resources were endangered. I began to fear that my father (than whom a more hopeful man never lived) might commit suicide.

(5) After all, I am not sure that the other side of my nature—the natural, healthy, boyish side—did not develop equally with these timid and morbid tendencies, which are not so very uncommon in childhood. Certainly the natural, boyish side was more in evidence on the surface. I was as good a sport as any of my playfellows in such games as appealed to me, and I went a-fishing when the chance offered. None of my associates thought of me as being shy or morose. But this was because I masked my troubles, though quite unconsciously, under a camouflage of sarcasm and sallies of wit, or, at least, what seemed to pass for wit among my immature acquaintances. With grown-ups, I was at times inclined to be pert, my degree of impudence depending no doubt upon how ill at ease I was and how perfectly at ease I wished to appear. Because of the constant need for appearing happier than I really was, I developed a knack for saying things in an amusing, sometimes an epigrammatic, way. I recall one remark made long before I could possibly have heard of Malthus or have understood his theory regarding birth rate and food supply. Ours being a large family of limited means and, among the five boys of the family, unlimited appetites, we often used the cheaper, though equally nutritious, cuts of meat. On one occasion when the steak was tougher than usual, I epitomized the Malthusian theory by remarking: "I believe in fewer children and better beefsteak!" . . .

(6) The last week of June, 1894, was an important one in my life. An event then occurred which undoubtedly changed my career completely. It was the direct cause of my mental collapse six years later, and of the distressing and, in some instances, strange and delightful experiences on which this book is based. The event was the illness of an older brother, who, late in June, 1894, was stricken with what was thought to be epilepsy. Few diseases can so disorganize a household

and distress its members. My brother had enjoyed perfect health up to the time he was stricken; and, as there had never been a suggestion of epilepsy, or any like disease, in either branch of the family, the affliction came as a bolt from a clear sky. Everything possible was done to effect a cure, but without avail. On July 4th, 1900, he died, after a six years' illness, two years of which were spent at home, one year in a trip around the world in a sailing vessel, and most of the remainder on a farm near Hartford. The doctors finally decided that a tumor at the base of the brain had caused his malady and his death.

(7) As I was in college when my brother was first stricken, I had more time at my disposal than the other members of the family, and for that reason spent much of it with him. Though his attacks during the first year occurred only at night, the fear that they might occur during the day, in public, affected my nerves from the beginning.

(8) Now, if a brother who had enjoyed perfect health all his life could be stricken with epilepsy, what was to prevent my being similarly afflicted? This was the thought that soon got possession of my mind. The more I considered it and him, the more nervous I became; and the more nervous, the more convinced that my own breakdown was only a matter of time. Doomed to what I then considered a living death, I thought of epilepsy, I dreamed epilepsy, until thousands of times during the six years that this disquieting idea persisted, my over-wrought imagination seemed to drag me to the very verge of an attack. Yet at no time during my life have these early fears been realized.

(Project Gutenberg)

How events are important in relation to plot or conflict

In this particular instance, the events are important to the conflict, which is the struggle for Clifford to reconcile the difficulties facing him as he grows up. There are several events in this passage which contribute to his internal conflict: his interaction with his schoolmates, his brother's illness, as well as his own.

Any question you might see on the GED® test dealing with this skill will measure your ability to determine the significance of the events in the text as they relate to either 1) what is happening or 2) what central struggle lies within the text. A sample question that measures this might be as simple as:

EXAMPLE

Determine which event does NOT contribute to Clifford's internal struggle.

    A. "None of my associates thought of me as being shy or morose."

    B. "I was painfully shy."

    C. "An event then occurred which undoubtedly changed my career completely."

D. "Because of the constant need for appearing happier than I really was, I developed a knack for saying things in an amusing, sometimes an epigrammatic, way."

In this case, it should be fairly easy for you to determine the correct answer is (A). Although the ease with which he associated with his friends was part of his "double life" it is the only one listed which does not directly affect the conflict. As always, make sure you read carefully and clearly so you can determine how one event affects another. This strategy will help you to determine and analyze relationships within the text.

How people, ideas, or events are connected, developed, or distinguished

The easiest relationship to look at when it comes to development is one between the characters. There is a great deal you can infer about the relationship between Clifford and his brother in this passage.

EXAMPLE

What can you infer about the relationship between Clifford and his brother?

A. They were close all through their early years.

B. Clifford felt responsible for his brother's illness.

C. Clifford believed that his own later sickness was a direct result of that of his brother's.

D. Clifford was jealous of the attention that his brother received.

Although (D) may be true, the correct answer is (C) because it directly analyzes Clifford's own problem since it appears as if most of what went on around Clifford was taken in as it affected him, and him alone. (D) might be correct, but there isn't any direct evidence pointing to this except as it might fall into the area of Clifford's narcissism. Clifford's brother isn't mentioned until that brother's illness so we don't know about any "closeness" (A). There is nothing in the text that can prove or disprove answer (B), though the writing indicates that (B) may be false, since Clifford didn't mention this when he spoke of caring for his brother.

How events contribute to theme or relate to key ideas

This particular skill is very similar to one we already covered, how events are important in relation to plot or conflict. This is because conflict is often a key idea in a work. To that end, the questions you will see here are very similar to the kinds you will see that address events relating to plot or conflict. Here is an example of a question about the relationship between theme and events.

What theme is created when Clifford's brother suddenly becomes ill?

    A. People who concentrate only on themselves can't turn to help others.

    B. Young people have to "grow up" when there is sickness in a family.

    C. Clifford's change to a more outgoing, caring person.

    D. Significance of the tension caused by sudden sickness in a family.

The correct answer is (D). Remember that a theme is a general truism about life generated through literature. That means it must be supported by the text in order to be a correct theme, and, in this instance, it must be created by the event in question. Because Clifford's brother suddenly became ill, his family was very concerned about his brother having an attack during the day, and Clifford became the person to care for him, it is safe to assume that "adversity" is a key factor in this event.

Clifford's entire purpose in writing is to analyze how he worked through with feeling drawn to two ways of living out his life's path with all that went on around him. His brother's illness was a huge event in his life therefore was one of the main themes throughout the text.

How a setting or context shapes structure and meaning

Let's look at **context** in this example, because it is a much larger factor in the passage than the setting itself. To find the context you must examine the influence of culture on the passage. That means you must look at the relationship between culture and meaning. You may be asked a question like this:

How would the meaning of this work change if Clifford were living today?

    A. There would be a heavier focus on Clifford's socioeconomic status.

    B. The focus would be more on his studies rather than on his personality issues.

    C. Clifford's brother would have been diagnosed more quickly and possibly healed.

    D. There would be no change.

The correct answer to this question is (C). It appears as if the doctors weren't able to do much for his brother at the time.

Therefore, (A) and (B) are based on suppositions that may be correct, but have no textual evidence to support them, and (D) is incorrect because it does not fully consider the impact of the context on the theme.

Infer relationships between ideas in a text (e.g., an implicit cause and effect, parallel, or contrasting relationship).

Once again we are going to look at relationships in a text, but this time you will have to **draw conclusions about the relationships between ideas using your inference skills.** This is a more advanced skill than the one you just mastered analyzing the interplay between things. However, it is also similar because it draws upon the same basic principle: determine the way one part of a text affects another. An idea is slightly more abstract than an event, the setting, or a character, which you learned to analyze in the previous skill section; but as long as you are able to identify ideas in a text, you should have no difficulty explaining how they **interact** with each other.

Let's take a look at a sample question as it relates to **implicit cause and effect.**

EXAMPLE

Read the following passage from "A Modest Proposal" by Jonathan Swift.

(1) Many other advantages might be enumerated. For instance, the addition of some thousand carcasses in our exportation of barrel'd beef: the propagation of swine's flesh, and improvement in the art of making good bacon, so much wanted among us by the great destruction of pigs, too frequent at our tables; which are no way comparable in taste or magnificence to a well grown, fat yearling child, which roasted whole will make a considerable figure at a Lord Mayor's feast, or any other publick entertainment. But this, and many others, I omit, being studious of brevity.

(2) Supposing that one thousand families in this city, would be constant customers for infant's flesh, besides others who might have it at merry meetings, particularly at weddings and christenings, I compute that Dublin would take off annually about twenty thousand carcasses; and the rest of the kingdom (where probably they will be sold somewhat cheaper) the remaining eighty thousand.

(3) I can think of no one objection, that will possibly be raised against this proposal, unless it should be urged, that the number of people will be thereby much lessened in the kingdom. This I freely own, and 'twas indeed one principal design in offering it to the world. I desire the reader will observe, that I calculate my remedy for this one individual Kingdom of Ireland, and for no other that ever was, is, or, I think, ever can be upon Earth. Therefore let no man talk to me of other expedients: Of taxing our absentees at five shillings a pound: Of using neither cloaths, nor houshold furniture, except what is of our own growth and manufacture: Of utterly rejecting the materials and instruments that promote foreign luxury: Of curing the expensiveness of pride, vanity, idleness, and gaming in our women: Of introducing a vein of parsimony, prudence and temperance: Of learning to love our country, wherein we differ even from Laplanders, and the inhabitants of Topinamboo: Of quitting our animosities and factions, nor acting any longer like the Jews, who were murdering one another at the very moment their city was taken: Of being a little cautious not to sell our country and consciences for nothing: Of teaching landlords to have at least one degree of mercy towards

their tenants. Lastly, of putting a spirit of honesty, industry, and skill into our shop-keepers, who, if a resolution could now be taken to buy only our native goods, would immediately unite to cheat and exact upon us in the price, the measure, and the goodness, nor could ever yet be brought to make one fair proposal of just dealing, though often and earnestly invited to it.

(4) Therefore I repeat, let no man talk to me of these and the like expedients, 'till he hath at least some glympse of hope, that there will ever be some hearty and sincere attempt to put them into practice.

(5) But, as to my self, having been wearied out for many years with offering vain, idle, visionary thoughts, and at length utterly despairing of success, I fortunately fell upon this proposal, which, as it is wholly new, so it hath something solid and real, of no expence and little trouble, full in our own power, and whereby we can incur no danger in disobliging England. For this kind of commodity will not bear exportation, and flesh being of too tender a consistence, to admit a long continuance in salt, although perhaps I could name a country, which would be glad to eat up our whole nation without it.

(6) After all, I am not so violently bent upon my own opinion, as to reject any offer, proposed by wise men, which shall be found equally innocent, cheap, easy, and effectual. But before something of that kind shall be advanced in contradiction to my scheme, and offering a better, I desire the author or authors will be pleased maturely to consider two points. First, As things now stand, how they will be able to find food and raiment for a hundred thousand useless mouths and backs. And secondly, There being a round million of creatures in humane figure throughout this kingdom, whose whole subsistence put into a common stock, would leave them in debt two million of pounds sterling, adding those who are beggars by profession, to the bulk of farmers, cottagers and labourers, with their wives and children, who are beggars in effect; I desire those politicians who dislike my overture, and may perhaps be so bold to attempt an answer, that they will first ask the parents of these mortals, whether they would not at this day think it a great happiness to have been sold for food at a year old, in the manner I prescribe, and thereby have avoided such a perpetual scene of misfortunes, as they have since gone through, by the oppression of landlords, the impossibility of paying rent without money or trade, the want of common sustenance, with neither house nor cloaths to cover them from the inclemencies of the weather, and the most inevitable prospect of intailing the like, or greater miseries, upon their breed for ever.

(7) I profess, in the sincerity of my heart, that I have not the least personal interest in endeavouring to promote this necessary work, having no other motive than the publick good of my country, by advancing our trade, providing for infants, relieving the poor, and giving some pleasure to the rich. I have no children, by which I can propose to get a single penny; the youngest being nine years old, and my wife past child-bearing.

(Project Gutenberg)

How would you best describe the relationship between the following two quotations from paragraphs 3 and 6, respectively?

"I can think of no one objection, that will possibly be raised against this proposal, unless it should be urged, that the number of people will be thereby much lessened in the kingdom."

AND

"First, As things now stand, how they will be able to find food and raiment for a hundred thousand useless mouths and backs."

    A. Swift creates a cause and effect.

    B. Swift creates a sequence of events.

    C. Swift shows the parallels between the two sentences.

    D. Swift shows the contrasts between the two sentences.

The correct answer is (A). This is a bit of a tricky question because these two quotations relate to each other as cause and effect, but in a more complex way than you might expect. The first quotation refers to the effect of his plan (which is to eat babies), and the second quotation is the cause for Swift's proposal of the plan in the first place (which is that there are too many people – "a hundred thousand useless mouths and backs"). So, the cause is that there are too many people, and in the end the effect is that there might be too few people. Not only is the order of these two ideas inverted chronologically, you have to be aware that the proposal is also being referenced. Do not be swayed by the word "First" in the second quotation. In context of the selection from which it was taken, it *is* a sequence. However, this is a sequence of consequences, not events. Furthermore, the nature of the two provided quotations is not sequential. You might also be swayed by choice (D) since one sentence is speaking about the huge number and one is speaking about lowering it. However, this is still ultimately better classified as a cause-and-effect relationship. Finally, though there may be parallels between these two quotations (C), these parallels are limited to the subject only, not the ideas.

Using the same passage, let's look at another question which would ask you to classify relationships.

Consider the following two quotations from paragraphs 1 and 5, respectively:

". . . which are no way comparable in taste or magnificence to a well grown, fat yearling child, which roasted whole will make a considerable figure at a Lord Mayor's feast, or any other publick entertainment."

AND

". . .and flesh being of too tender a consistence, to admit a long continuance in salt, although perhaps I could name a country, which would be glad to eat up our whole nation without it."

How can their relationship best be described?

    A. These quotations contrast each other

    B. The second quotation further explains the first.

    C. These quotations parallel each other.

    D. The first quotation is an effect of the first.

The correct answer is (C). You can draw this parallel by considering the words used to allude to eating people. A parallel is simply two people or things that are similar to each other. In this passage, these ideas parallel each other, as do the words in them: "taste," "roasted," "flesh," "salt," and "eat."

Now let's look at another kind of GED® question you might get that will ask you about a particular type of relationship within a passage. Let's stick with Swift's "A Modest Proposal."

When Swift lists the numerous problems Ireland has, why does he then say it has nothing to do with his solution?

    A. He wants to scare people in Ireland into eating babies so they will not starve.

    B. He wants to draw attention to the problems while using an outrageous solution to illustrate the lack of effort Ireland has put into solving these issues.

    C. He wants to contrast the problems of the rich with the problems of the poor, as well as the view the classes have of each other.

    D. He wants to stress the importance of his plan, and show how it will also cure all these additional problems in addition to the ones he's already addressed.

In order to answer this question you need to be able to analyze the contrast. In this section of the piece, Swift is contrasting the relationships between the problems, and what he perceives as insincere effort. To understand this question, it is imperative that you understand that "A Modest Proposal" is a satirical piece, which, in this case, means Swift is calling Ireland to action by satirizing the lack of earnest problem solving about the country's grievances. He implores his readers to look at what they have *not* done, and offers a ridiculous solution (eating children) to highlight this lack of effort. This, in its nature, is a form of contrast, but it requires you to draw inferences.

The correct answer is (B). Although (A), (C), and (D) look like viable answers, the question requires you to consider the piece as a whole. Choice (A) looks only at the superficial aspect of the text, and it does not analyze the contrast or understand the implications of satire. Choice (A) accepts the satire as fact, and misinterprets the work. Although choice (C) uses the word "contrast," do not let that fool you. Again, this choice only takes into account one single aspect of the text, and ignores the larger contrast inherent in the work as a whole. Though there is a real contrast between the rich and the poor, it ignores the contrast between Swift's solution (eating babies) and the actual nature of the problems facing Ireland. Answer choice (D) is on the right track in the second half of the answer; however, its first phrase makes the same error as choice (A): It assumes Swift is earnest in his proposal to eat children.

Questions that ask you to analyze the contrasting relationships in a piece are among the most difficult you will encounter in this reading standard. Your job, then, is to ensure you understand the piece as a whole, and then make sure you break down the smaller relationships to determine how they contrast each other without losing sight of the overall purpose of the work.

Analyze the roles that details play in complex literary or informational texts.

You can rightly assume this skill will require you to employ several skills you've already mastered: "complex texts" indicates complicated and difficult reading material, which will draw on your reading comprehension and inference skills. **Analyzing details** should not prove too difficult, but when that skill is being tested through complex texts, you will be challenged to ferret out details in lengthy or hard-to-follow passages.

EXAMPLE

Read this passage from _Stories of the Ships_, by Lewis R. Freeman.

(1) Of the countless stories of naval action which I have listened to in the course of the months I have spent with the Grand Fleet, I cannot recall a single one which was told as the consequence of being asked for with malice aforethought. I have never yet found a man of action who was enamoured of the sound of his own voice raised in the recital of his own exploits, and if there is one thing more than another calculated to throw an otherwise not untalkative British Naval Officer into a state of uncommunicativeness, in comparison with which the traditional silence of the sphinx or the proverbial close-mouthedness of the clam are alike sheer garrulity, it is to ask him, point blank, to tell you (for instance) how he took his submarine into the Baltic, or what his destroyer did at Jutland, or how he fought his cruiser at Dogger Bank, or something similar.

(2) The quiet-voiced but always interesting and often dramatic recitals of such things as these which I have heard have invariably been led up to quite incidentally—at dinner, on the bridge or quarter-deck, around the wardroom fire, or through something else that has just been told. Several times I have found in officers' diaries—little records never meant for other eyes than those of the writers' own friends or families—which have been turned over to me to verify some point regarding which I had inquired, laconic references to incidents and events of great human and even historic interest, and one of the most amusing and dramatic yarns I have ever listened to was told me in a "kite" balloon—plunging in the forty-mile wind against which it was being towed like a hooked salmon—by a man who had assured me before we went up that nothing really exciting had ever fallen to his experience.

(3) It was in this way—an anecdote now and then as this or that incident of the day recalled it to his mind—that Captain—came to tell me the story of the Cornwall during those eventful early months of the war when he commanded that now famous cruiser. He mentioned her first, I believe, one night in his cabin when, referring to a stormy midwinter month, most of which had been spent by his Division of the Grand Fleet on some sort of work at sea, I spoke of the "rather strenuous interval" we had experienced.

(Project Gutenberg)

What effect does the story of the "kite" balloon in paragraph 2 have on the narrative as a whole?

    A. It demonstrates the narrator's many exciting experiences.

    B. The Captain later refers to this story in his own "strenuous interval."

    C. The narrator uses this story as an example of a poor anecdote.

    D. The story serves to illustrate and develop the author's position about storytelling.

The correct answer is (D). The purpose of the "kite" balloon story is to show when and how an anecdote should be told by a "man of action." This is an example which supports his musing commentary about stories, and it specifically leads him into the story he is about to relate. Although (A) might be true, it does not fully consider the impact of the detail, and responds to the question on a superficial level. The narrator is not necessarily using his exciting and varied life as the basis for his writing. Answer choice (B) is irrelevant, because the Captain's story is not presented in this passage, and you cannot predict whether this anecdote will be referenced again. Finally, choice (C) is the inverse of the detail's purpose: The story is told to be a good example, not a poor one.

If you read this text in its entirety, you will find that the answer simply requires you to call upon your skills of reading comprehension in order to analyze the details. The text itself, however, is difficult to read, so take your time.

Chapter 3

Interpreting Words and Phrases

Interpret words and phrases that appear frequently in texts from a wide variety of disciplines, including determining connotative and figurative meanings from context and analyzing how specific word choices shape meaning or tone.

Interpretation is a more complicated skill than both analysis and comprehension, and in this particular standard you are being asked to interpret unfamiliar words and **determine how their meaning is constructed through context**. In order to do that, you have to be able to both comprehend and analyze. You are also going to be asked to consider how an author's diction (word choice) can inform your understanding of the piece's intent and the author's attitude toward that text.

The GED® test will assess some or all of these skills with questions relating to this standard:

- Determine the meaning of words and phrases as they are used in a text, including determining connotative and figurative meanings from context.

- Analyze how meaning or tone is affected when one word is replaced with another.

- Analyze the impact of specific words, phrases, or figurative language in text, with a focus on an author's intent to convey information or construct an argument.

Let's look at each skill individually.

Determine the meaning of words and phrases as they are used in a text, including determining connotative and figurative meanings from context.

This skill will require you to **understand an unfamiliar word or phrase** in a piece by relying on the other words in a sentence to get at the full meaning. This will include determining the **connotative definition** (an idea associated with the word, or a secondary meaning) and **the figurative meaning** (how the word is a substitute for something else). Let's look at all three aspects in one selection, the "Wheatsheaf" from *Soyer's Culinary Campaign* by Alexis Soyer.

(1) I slept that evening at the "Wheatsheaf;" I had given orders to be called the next morning at day-break, and was crossing the avenue of lime-trees leading to the lake, in anticipation of witnessing, as I was wont of a summer's morning, its interminable sheet of silvery waters and green moss velvet banks, sprinkled with myriads of daisies—or stars of the fields—intermixed with golden cups, covered with pearly dew, bordered also by mountainous trees forming a formidable forest; the glittering Chinese fishing temple, Corinthian ruin, the flag floating on the castle tower, "Royal George" frigate and barks, the swans, and the music of thousands of birds with their notes of freedom so wild and full of nature. Alas! all my illusions were dispelled, as I could scarcely see a yard before me; a thick veil, caused by a severe white frost, seemed to monopolise and wrap in its virgin folds the beauty of this lovely spot. Though greatly disappointed, I was returning to the humble country inn with my soul filled by sublime reminiscences of that charming spot, worthy of the enchanted gardens of Armida, when a deformed and awkward-looking lout of a stable-man, peeping from a clump of evergreens, thus accosted me: —"Will you take a red herring for breakfast, sir?"

(2) I leave my readers to imagine the effect produced upon my then exalted imagination. Pushing him violently from me, "Away with you! unsociable and ill-timed Quasimodo!" I said. Having thus unceremoniously repulsed my evil genius, and being by that electric shock entirely deprived of my appetite, I ordered a post-chaise in lieu of breakfast, and in a short time was at the turnpike-gate adjoining the inn, waiting for change to pay the toll. It was then about ten minutes to eight o'clock.

(3) In three-quarters of an hour the post-chaise took me to the railway station, and an hour after I was ascending my homely staircase, when the servant apprised me that many persons had called; some had left their cards, and a mounted groom had brought a letter, saying he would call at noon for an answer. Amongst the various letters I found upon my desk, I recognised one in the hand-writing of the Duchess of Sutherland. It was as follows:—

(4) The Duchess of Sutherland will be much pleased to see Monsieur Soyer at Stafford House at two o'clock this day; or ten to-morrow morning, if more convenient to Monsieur Soyer.

7th February, 1856.

(5) I had scarcely read this letter, when a double knock was heard at the street door. It was the footman from Stafford House, sent for an answer. I at once informed him I was going to wait upon her Grace; but as he was there, he might say that, at two o'clock precisely, I would do myself the honour of attending at Stafford House. Concluding, naturally enough, that the summons had reference to my letter, I immediately began to reflect how I should explain the plan I intended to adopt, in case my services were required. In the first place, I had decided that the most important question of all would be the entire freedom of my actions when I arrived at Scutari. This, of course, could not be granted, unless the Government, impressed with the importance of the subject, thought proper to do so. The active part would easily develop itself to my free and experienced mind.

(G. Routledge & Co., London, 1857)

Determine the meaning of a word or phrase.

What is the meaning of the word "exalted" as it is used in paragraph 2?

    A. angry

    B. weak

    C. fastidious

    D. grand

In order to determine the meaning of the word "exalted" in context, you should look at a few of the clues in the passage. In the preceding paragraph, the author uses words and phrases such as "illusions" and "sublime reminiscences" as well as the word "imagination" directly following the word "exalted." This should give you some clue that the correct answer to this question is (D), "grand." Although his daydreaming is interrupted by the "awkward-looking stableman," there is no reason to assume his imagination itself is "angry" (A), though he may be disappointed by the outcome of the interruption. In the same vein, there is no context at all to justify choosing the word "weak" to describe his imagination because the entire prior paragraph describes his fantasies as creative and lively. Finally, in order to rule out answer (C), you must know what the word "fastidious" means, which is fussy or finicky. There is no justification for this choice either. If you do not know the meaning of a word, you are better off choosing the word you *can* support with context clues, which in this case is (D), "grand."

Determine the connotation of a word or phrase.

What is the connotation of the idea of a "summer morning" in this passage?

    A. dull

    B. inviting

    C. hectic

    D. strenuous

When answering this question, you should be able to rule out choices (C) and (D) immediately because they are interchangeable synonyms. Any time a question gives you two answers that mean exactly the same thing, it would be impossible for you to choose one that is a better fit than the other. This is a trap many tests will use to make sure you are reading carefully. Ruling these two out will leave you with "dull" or "inviting," either of which is an acceptable answer, depending on *context*. For example, a student on summer vacation with nothing to do may consider a summer morning very dull, but another with a vivid imagination may consider it an invitation to adventure. It is up to you to determine the author's connotation implied when more than one exists. It should be fairly clear to you that in this instance, the connotation is (B), "inviting." This is because the narrator is excited to take a magical stroll through the countryside, and on his way he calls his environment "enchanted." In the event the author were to find it dull, you would be cued by his tone, which would be disengaged.

Determine the figurative meaning of a word.

This skill will call upon your ability to infer. Let's take a look at a question that might utilize this skill.

What is the meaning of the word "Quasimodo"?

    A. fine gentleman

    B. stableman

    C. crippled servant

    D. fool

If you have read *The Hunchback of Notre Dame*, you would be able to identify this allusion immediately and could answer it without considering the other answers, but if you have not, you will have to rely on the context clues in the passage to determine the meaning of the word "Quasimodo." The correct answer is (C), a "crippled servant." This is a difficult question because the person to whom the narrator is referring is, indeed, a stableman (B), which rules out (A). However, the figurative context hinges upon this phrase, ". . . a deformed and awkward-looking lout of a stableman." As always, in order to choose the correct answer, you should consider all the information you are given. "Fool" (D) may also be implied by the narrator's frustration, but the best answer is (C).

Analyze how meaning or tone is affected when one word is replaced with another.

This skill is simply asking you to determine how words construct meaning and tone. This is a relatively simple skill to master, because you should be able to **see how a work changes** when words are changed.

Let's go back to a different section of Jonathan Swift's "A Modest Proposal" to illustrate this point.

Write a short answer that rephrases the following sentence to show the horror of what Swift is proposing.

"Those who are more thrifty (as I must confess the times require) may flay the carcass; the skin of which, artificially dressed, will make admirable gloves for ladies and summer boots for fine gentlemen."

Your answer may look like this:

If you are poor, you can peel off the skin of the baby to make gloves and boots.

Can you see how Swift's diction (using words like "flay," "admirable," "fine") changes the tone of the sentence? When Swift uses those words, the proposal does not seem so odious, but when you rewrite it using gruesome language, you are using one of the tools of the trade at the author's disposal to shift the tone toward the horrific and disturbing.

Analyze the impact of specific words, phrases, or figurative language in text, with a focus on an author's intent to convey information or construct an argument.

Authors always choose their words carefully, as words are their only means of expression. We've already covered how changing one word can affect the meaning of a piece. Now let's discuss how these words or phrases are used by authors to convey information or construct an argument.

Let's first discuss conveying information, as that is a bit more straightforward than persuasion. When an author chooses words to convey information, he will employ them to best describe his subject. Sometimes this can be done through figurative language like similes or metaphors. Many words carry certain connotations along with them, which save the author extra steps. For example, if an author writes, "Her skin was like alabaster," several pieces of information have been conveyed to you by this choice. Alabaster is usually cold, smooth, and white. By choosing to incorporate this simile, the author has not only incorporated style, but has also conveyed all the previous information, perhaps even some inference—alabaster is stone, so the subject may also be stoic, unmoving, or solid. Carefully chosen words can have a big impact on the information presented in a piece.

When choosing words to construct an argument, the author has to be just as vigilant in selecting what words will best persuade an audience. Even though rhetoric will be covered later, the general rule of persuasion is this: Establish an emotional connection, establish a logical order, and establish credibility to be believable. This is why, in the previous section, Jonathan Swift chose nicer words to describe a horrible act: It is much more persuasive for his argument.

Let's take a look at a sample question you might see on the GED® test which will assess this skill.

Which of the following is NOT an impact of the word "evil-doers" in the following sentence?

We must stop the evil-doers from terrorizing our country.

A. It presents an emotional tone which engages the audience's sense of morality.

B. It conveys the information that the evil-doers are terrorists.

C. It strikes a particularly patriotic chord with the audience, as it excludes those who would harm us from "our country."

D. It indicates that our country is responsible for creating the evil-doers.

The correct answer is (D). This response is correct because the word "our" would indicate a separation between us and them. Additionally, the author's choice of word "the" before evil-doers further creates a separation between the two entities. This sentence takes no responsibility for any harm that may come to the country. Choices (A), (B), and (C) are each correct effects of the word in the sentence. In this instance, the word "evil-doers" has a major impact on the sentence, as it both conveys information and helps persuade the audience to take some kind of action. It unifies and motivates.

Can you see the considerable impact one single word can have on a sentence?

Analyzing the Structure of Texts

Analyze the structure of texts, including how specific sentences or paragraphs relate to each other and the whole.

This standard is going to require you to **consider** the construction, or **the *way* a piece is written**. In order to be successful in this area, you should consider the choices an author makes in *organization*. Additionally, you should think about how these choices affect each other, and the piece as a whole.

The GED® test will assess some or all of these skills with questions relating to this standard:

- Analyze how a particular sentence, paragraph, chapter, or section fits into the overall structure of a text and contributes to the development of the ideas.

- Analyze the structural relationship between adjacent sections of text (e.g., how one paragraph develops or refines a key concept or how one idea is distinguished from another).

- Analyze transitional language or signal words (words that indicate structural relationships, such as *consequently, nevertheless, otherwise*) and determine how they refine meaning, emphasize certain ideas, or reinforce an author's purpose.

- Analyze how the structure of a paragraph, section, or passage shapes meaning, emphasizes key ideas, or supports an author's purpose.

Let's look at each skill individually.

Analyze how a particular sentence, paragraph, chapter, or section fits into the overall structure of a text and contributes to the development of ideas.

This skill will apply in the same way whether it is a small section (a sentence), a larger section (a paragraph) or a very large section (a chapter); for our purposes we will focus on the smaller sections—the sentence and paragraph. As a practical matter, you will probably not see whole chapters on the GED® test because most reading passages on the test are not longer than about 900 words.

Here is an example of a question that will test your ability to analyze how a particular sentence fits into the overall structure of a text and contributes to the development of ideas.

EXAMPLE

Read this speech from Susan B. Anthony, delivered in 1873 after her conviction for voting without the right to vote in the 1872 presidential election.

(1) Friends and fellow citizens: I stand before you tonight under indictment for the alleged crime of having voted at the last presidential election, without having a lawful right to vote. It shall be my work this evening to prove to you that in thus voting, I not only committed no crime, but, instead, simply exercised my citizen's rights, guaranteed to me and all United States citizens by the National Constitution, beyond the power of any state to deny.

(2) The preamble of the Federal Constitution says:

(3) "We, the people of the United States, in order to form a more perfect union, establish justice, insure domestic tranquility, provide for the common defense, promote the general welfare, and secure the blessings of liberty to ourselves and our posterity, do ordain and establish this Constitution for the United States of America."

(4) It was we, the people; not we, the white male citizens; nor yet we, the male citizens; but we, the whole people, who formed the Union. And we formed it, not to give the blessings of liberty, but to secure them; not to the half of ourselves and the half of our posterity, but to the whole people—women as well as men. And it is a downright mockery to talk to women of their enjoyment of the blessings of liberty while they are denied the use of the only means of securing them provided by this democratic-republican government—the ballot.

(5) For any state to make sex a qualification that must ever result in the disfranchisement of one entire half of the people, is to pass a bill of attainder, or, an ex post facto law, and is therefore a violation of the supreme law of the land. By it the blessings of liberty are forever withheld from women and their female posterity.

(6) To them this government has no just powers derived from the consent of the governed. To them this government is not a democracy. It is not a republic. It is an odious aristocracy; a hateful oligarchy of sex; the most hateful aristocracy ever established on the face of the globe; an oligarchy of wealth, where the rich govern the poor. An oligarchy of learning, where the educated govern the ignorant, or even an oligarchy of race, where the Saxon rules the African, might be endured; but this oligarchy of sex, which makes father, brothers, husband, sons, the oligarchs over the mother and sisters, the wife and daughters, of every household—which ordains all men sovereigns, all women subjects, carries dissension, discord, and rebellion into every home of the nation.

(7) Webster, Worcester, and Bouvier all define a citizen to be a person in the United States, entitled to vote and hold office.

(8) The only question left to be settled now is: Are women persons? And I hardly believe any of our opponents will have the hardihood to say they are not. Being persons, then, women are citizens; and no state has a right to make any law, or to enforce any old law, that shall abridge their privileges or immunities. Hence, every discrimination against women in the constitutions and laws of the several states is today null and void, precisely as is every one against Negroes.

(Courtesy of "Gifts of Speech" collection, Sweet Briar College)

What is the purpose of the following sentence from paragraph 1 in the context of the overall speech?

"It shall be my work this evening to prove to you that in thus voting, I not only committed no crime, but, instead, simply exercised my citizen's rights, guaranteed to me and all United States citizens by the National Constitution, beyond the power of any state to deny."

A. It sets the agenda for what is to come in the following paragraphs.

B. It proves Anthony is innocent of a crime.

C. It uses cause and effect to explain how Anthony became a suffragette.

D. It provides the proof and evidence for her argument.

The correct answer is (A). In this sentence, Anthony identifies her "work," and tells her audience what she aims to accomplish: to convince them through proof that she was justified in voting. This sentence is the focus, or the goal, of the speech, and the rest of it is dedicated to providing this proof. Answer choice (B) is attractive because she does claim her innocence in the sentence, but it provides no actual proof. This comes later in the speech when she cites the U.S. Constitution. Instead of proving, this sentence is *arguing*. Choice (C) is incorrect because there is no cause and effect identifiable in the work, and there is no history regarding her decision to become a women's rights activist. Like (B), (D) is also incorrect because it fails to provide proof from the Constitution. Instead, it suggests that this proof will come later.

By answering this question, you have proven you know how a particular sentence fits into a work, and how it contributes to the development of ideas.

Now let's look at a question about how a whole paragraph can be analyzed in the same fashion.

How does paragraph 4, reproduced below, contribute to the work as a whole?

"It was we, the people; not we, the white male citizens; nor yet we, the male citizens; but we, the whole people, who formed the Union. And we formed it, not to give the blessings of liberty, but to secure them; not to the half of ourselves and the half of our posterity, but to the whole people—women as well as men. And it is a downright mockery to talk to women of their enjoyment of the blessings of liberty while they are denied the use of the only means of securing them provided by this democratic-republican government—the ballot."

A. It is a transitional paragraph which moves her away from the evidence in the Constitution into her argument about women's rights.

B. It is an inflammatory paragraph which is meant to offend her listeners into taking a stand for women's rights to vote.

C. It is an analysis of the effect created by the cause presented in the quotation from the Constitution.

D. It uses the language from the Constitution to establish a tone of sarcastic rebellion, which is the premise on which she bases the rest of her arguments.

The correct answer is (D). The language used here is exaggerated and hyperbolic, and it is employed for effect. Anthony means to point out how the interpretation of laws is in conflict with the guiding principles of the Constitution. Answer choice (A) is incorrect because it misinterprets what is actually happening. This paragraph relies upon the evidence presented immediately before it; Anthony uses it, she does not move away from it. Choice (B) is incorrect because Anthony's intention is not to offend her audience, but rather to rile them up by pointing out the offenses done to women. This is a fine line, and although her words may offend some people, these people would not be the ones she is trying to convince anyway. Choice (C) provides no real analysis of the paragraph's role in the total structure—the Constitution itself may be the cause for Anthony's subsequent musings, but the quotation provides no such cause directly.

In order to master this skill, you must not only employ your skills of reading comprehension and inference, but you must also be able to analyze the how and the why of an author's construction.

Analyze the structural relationship between adjacent sections of a text (e.g., how one paragraph develops or refines a key concept or how one idea is distinguished from another).

This skill is simply an extension of the previous skill. It asks you to **draw parallel relationships between two ideas** that immediately follow each other, or are *adjacent* to each other. When you are being tested on this skill, you will always be asked about the placement of two sequential sections (sentences or paragraphs) of a text. In this manner, it will test both reading comprehension and your ability to analyze structure. Let's look at an example of the type of question you might receive, again using Susan B. Anthony's speech as an example.

What is the relationship between paragraphs 7 and 8?

A. Paragraph 8 is an emotional extension of the ethical appeal provided in paragraph 7.

B. Paragraph 7 presents an idea, while paragraph 8 provides the details to support it.

C. Paragraph 8 uses the definition provided by paragraph 7 to prove that, by definition, women should have the right to vote.

D. The two paragraphs are set up to progress in a chronological format; first to define, then to apply the definition.

The correct answer is (C). Several of the answer choices have some merit to them, but (C) is the only one that best identifies the relationship between the two paragraphs. In paragraph 7, Anthony uses three sources to provide a definition of a citizen, and in paragraph 8, she shows that the current laws are not in accord with the accepted definition. Answer choice (A) may distract you because Anthony certainly uses an emotional appeal in paragraph 8 when she asks every household to consider its own power struggle; however, providing the definition is more of a logical statement than an ethical appeal. An ethical appeal must activate a sense of justice and trustworthiness of the speaker, but that argument is better seen in the paragraph 8 than paragraph 7. Answer choice (B) is also incorrect because it inverts the relationship. The idea is fleshed out in the final paragraph (No. 8), and the definition itself is the detail which sparks the idea to come, not the other way around. Finally, although answer choice (D) is partially correct (she does define a citizen, and then apply that definition through a rhetorical question), the word "chronological" relates to the sequential order of events, and there is no identifiable sequence being crafted in these two paragraphs. Choice (D) is not as precise a reading as choice (C).

Analyze transitional language or signal words (words that indicate structural relationships, such as *consequently*, *nevertheless*, *otherwise*) and determine how they refine meaning, emphasize certain ideas, or reinforce an author's purpose.

This skill asks you to analyze not only transitional words, but how those structural words play into an author's meaning. This is not a difficult skill to master, but it does require you to employ close reading skills and inference. Transitional language or **signal words** are ideas that shift a reader's thought process, either in a different direction or into the author's line of thinking—which might be new or persuasive.

EXAMPLE

Read the following paragraph from a student's essay about Susan B. Anthony's speech.

> Although Susan B. Anthony was an integral part of the women's right-to-vote movement, she was not the sole player in the cause. There were many other women who participated in the movement, but because of their more radical approaches to suffrage, they were largely ignored by history. Consequently, the only way students can find out more information about these integral women is often to research outside of traditional textbooks. History for the classroom is written, after all, not only by the victor, but with the idea of promoting proper behavior for those who would again attempt such radical changes.

Select all of the transitional or signal words or phrases in this paragraph.

A. Although

B. Integral

C. But

D. Suffrage

E. Consequently

F. After all

In this instance, you would drag and drop answers (A), (C), (E), and (F). All transitional words, save perhaps "after all," should be relatively clear to you, and the only way you can identify them is to become comfortable with them through close reading and frequent use in your own writing. Some examples are:

Above all	Finally	Meanwhile
Actually	First, Second, Third	Moreover
Afterward	First and foremost	Next
After all	For this reason	No doubt
All things considered	From here on	Of course
Accordingly	For instance/For example	On the other hand
Another	Furthermore	Otherwise
Arguably	However	Paradoxically
As a matter of fact	Incidentally	Presently
As a result	In addition	Presumably
At any rate	In any case	Regrettably
At the same time	In conclusion	Similarly
At this point	In fact	Still
Be that as it may	In my opinion	Strangely enough
By, but, and, or	In other words, as it were	Then
By and large	In the first place	Therefore
By the same token	In the meantime	Too, also
Consequently	In the same way	Ultimately
Even so	Ironically	

Beyond simply identifying these words, however, this skill also asks you to consider what role these words play in the larger meaning of the sentence or work as a whole. Here is a question that may test this skill.

What is implied by the student's choice of the phrase "after all"?

    A. This information may upset you.

    B. This information may surprise you.

    C. This information is contrary to what you believe.

    D. This is information you should already know.

The correct answer to this question is (B). In this instance, the student is providing you information you ought to consider, which indicates it may be a new or radical thought. In this instance, you are using the transitional word to identify the student's *tone* in writing, and he or she is imploring you to consider a new idea, which is a technique used frequently in persuasive writing.

Analyze how the structure of a paragraph, section, or passage shapes meaning, emphasizes key ideas, or supports an author's purpose.

This skill requires you to consider structural elements and how they communicate bigger ideas in a text. Some examples of structure that may be quizzed in this standard are **repetition** and **parallelism**. In those instances you will be asked to determine how an author constructs the piece and how that structure helps to relate his or her purpose.

EXAMPLE

Let's take a look at an excerpt from Martin Luther King Jr.'s "I Have a Dream"* speech as we approach this standard.

(1) I have a dream that one day on the red hills of Georgia the sons of former slaves and the sons of former slave owners will be able to sit down together at a table of brotherhood.

(2) I have a dream that one day even the state of Mississippi, a desert state, sweltering with the heat of injustice and oppression, will be transformed into an oasis of freedom and justice.

(3) I have a dream that my four children will one day live in a nation where they will not be judged by the color of their skin but by the content of their character.

(4) I have a dream today.

Do you see how the structure is repetitive in the beginning of each paragraph? This is called parallelism, and will be covered in more detail in the following chapters. In the meantime, however, let's look at the paragraphs themselves. Something you should notice immediately is that each paragraph is a single sentence. Though they are of varying length, each contains one singular idea. Why would King organize his speech in such a way? This is the type of question you will have to ask yourself on the GED® test, because it is exactly the kind of information you will have to analyze when presented with a question that measures this skill.

---

* "I Have a Dream" by Martin Luther King, Jr., reprinted by arrangement with the Estate of Martin Luther King, Jr., c/o Writers House as agent for the proprietor, New York, N.Y. Copyright © 1963 Martin Luther King, Jr., copyright renewed 1991 Coretta Scott King.

For example, a question on the GED® test might ask you:

What is accomplished by the structure of these four paragraphs in King's speech?

    A. King indicates that racism must end.

    B. King manages to tie together several different ideas into the same "dream."

    C. King uses succinct sentences in individual paragraphs to indicate that the dream is delineated in simple tasks.

    D. King indicates that the dream is closer to reality than one might expect.

The correct answer to this question is choice (C). By structuring his speech in this manner, King has managed to provide a list-like outline to his "dream." The characteristics of the dream are easy to follow, and by making his paragraphs short and to the point, he instills a rhythmic, easy-to-remember overview of this dream that any audience member can easily recall. While choice (A) is factually correct, this does not deal with the structure of the paragraphs themselves. Similarly, (B) is also true, but it is not as thorough an answer as choice (C). You should always choose the most correct, or best, answer. (D) may also be a factually correct observation relative to the message of the speech as a whole, but again, it does not address the particular structure of the passage and thus does not answer the question.

As you approach questions like this on the GED® test, you should always keep in mind that like word choice, sentence and paragraph structure are key tools employed by an author to convey a larger message. Sometimes you will find information in the structure of a piece that supports the message of the words themselves.

Chapter 5

Author's Purpose

Determine an author's purpose or point of view in a text and explain how it is conveyed and shapes the content and style of a text.

This skill is more difficult than it sounds because it is dealing with your ability to interpret an author's reasoning. At this point we have gone beyond what *you* think a text means, and you are now being asked to support your claims about what the author meant to convey. Beyond that, you must explain how this purpose or point of view affects the rest of the text in terms of what it says and how it is written. Even though this is slightly more complex than what you've done so far, that does not mean it is impossible! With a few techniques and some practice you should have no problem figuring out how the author feels and how that point of view shapes the text.

The GED® test will assess some or all of these skills with questions relating to this standard:

- Determine an author's point of view or purpose of a text.

- Analyze how the author distinguishes his or her position from that of others or how an author acknowledges and responds to conflicting evidence or viewpoints.

- Infer an author's implicit as well as explicit purposes based on details in text.

- Analyze how an author uses rhetorical techniques to advance his or her point of view or achieve a specific purpose (e.g., analogies, enumerations, repetition and parallelism, juxtaposition of opposites, qualifying statements).

Let's look at each skill individually.

Determine an author's point of view or purpose of a text.

When you are trying to determine an author's point of view or purpose of a text, you must read without your own personal bias. You must **look for key words that will inform you** of how the author feels, or what he or she is trying to say. Here is an example of a question that would test this skill.

EXAMPLE

Read the following passage from W.E.B. Du Bois's *The Souls of Black Folk*.

(1) After the Egyptian and Indian, the Greek and Roman, the Teuton and Mongolian, the Negro is a sort of seventh son, born with a veil, and gifted with second-sight in this American world,—a world which yields him no true self-consciousness, but only lets him see himself through the revelation of the other world. It is a peculiar sensation, this double-consciousness, this sense of always looking at one's self through the eyes of others, of measuring one's soul by the tape of a world that looks on in amused contempt and pity. One ever feels his twoness,—an American, a Negro; two souls, two thoughts, two unreconciled strivings; two warring ideals in one dark body, whose dogged strength alone keeps it from being torn asunder.

(2) The history of the American Negro is the history of this strife—this longing to attain self-conscious manhood, to merge his double self into a better and truer self. In this merging he wishes neither of the older selves to be lost. He would not Africanize America, for America has too much to teach the world and Africa. He would not bleach his Negro soul in a flood of white Americanism, for he knows that Negro blood has a message for the world. He simply wishes to make it possible for a man to be both a Negro and an American, without being cursed and spit upon by his fellows, without having the doors of Opportunity closed roughly in his face.

(3) This, then, is the end of his striving: to be a co-worker in the kingdom of culture, to escape both death and isolation, to husband and use his best powers and his latent genius. These powers of body and mind have in the past been strangely wasted, dispersed, or forgotten. The shadow of a mighty Negro past flits through the tale of Ethiopia the Shadowy and of Egypt the Sphinx. Through history, the powers of single black men flash here and there like falling stars, and die sometimes before the world has rightly gauged their brightness. Here in America, in the few days since Emancipation, the black man's turning hither and thither in hesitant and doubtful striving has often made his very strength to lose effectiveness, to seem like absence of power, like weakness. And yet it is not weakness,—it is the contradiction of double aims. The double-aimed struggle of the black artisan—on the one hand to escape white contempt for a nation of mere hewers of wood and drawers of water, and on the other hand to plough and nail and dig for a poverty-stricken horde—could only result in making him a poor craftsman, for he had but half

a heart in either cause. By the poverty and ignorance of his people, the Negro minister or doctor was tempted toward quackery and demagogy; and by the criticism of the other world, toward ideals that made him ashamed of his lowly tasks. The would-be black *savant* was confronted by the paradox that the knowledge his people needed was a twice-told tale to his white neighbors, while the knowledge which would teach the white world was Greek to his own flesh and blood. The innate love of harmony and beauty that set the ruder souls of his people a-dancing and a-singing raised but confusion and doubt in the soul of the black artist; for the beauty revealed to him was the soul-beauty of a race which his larger audience despised, and he could not articulate the message of another people. This waste of double aims, this seeking to satisfy two unreconciled ideals, has wrought sad havoc with the courage and faith and deeds of ten thousand thousand people—has sent them often wooing false gods and invoking false means of salvation, and at times has even seemed about to make them ashamed of themselves.

What is the author's purpose in this passage?

    A. Du Bois complains about the situation of black Americans and seeks to exact revenge for their struggles.

    B. Du Bois seeks to educate his audience about the split lives every black American must live and advocate for their freedom.

    C. Du Bois tries to call his audience to action on behalf of the black American initiative to gain the right to vote and work.

    D. Du Bois wants to use history as a precedent for the future of black Americans.

The correct answer to this question is (B). You can infer this from such lines in the text as "twoness," "double-consciousness," "it is the contradiction of double aims," and "This, then, is the end of his striving: to be a co-worker in the kingdom of culture, to escape both death and isolation, to husband and use his best powers and his latent genius." You can rule out answer choice (A) because there is nothing in the text that would give way to calling this text "complaint." In fact, Du Bois gives reason and logical construction for any shortcomings black Americans may have without placing blame. Choice (C) might seem a good selection, but this particular passage does not "call to action," especially about voting—though there is some information about the type of work and preparation the American blacks have had for those jobs. Although (D) is true to some extent (Du Bois does deal a lot with the history of black Americans), he does not necessarily use it as a framework to set the future; indeed he would like to *change* the future and uses the past as a justification for this change.

This skill merely asks you to apply your close reading skills to the mindset of the author. It is not a huge jump from the work you've already done.

Analyze how the author distinguishes his or her position from that of others or how an author acknowledges and responds to conflicting evidence or viewpoints.

This skill once again tests your ability to read closely. If you are able to **identify** when an author distinguishes his own ideas from those of his opponents, you should have no trouble **analyzing** why and how he accomplishes this task.

EXAMPLE

Read the following paragraph from a student essay.

> Vigilantism is unjust in America. Although some people believe vigilantes are everyday superheroes, heroism does not constitute a person taking the law into his own hands. Laws were created for a reason, and even if crime or unjust events happen in our country, a system is in place to protect us from these events. Sure, it may be noble for a person to seek out a murderer the cops have been unable to catch, but what if that person seeks out and kills the wrong man? The law has checks and balances for this type of problem, and one vigilante may not take everything into consideration. How is it fair to allow one person to ignore the justice system when everyone else must adhere to its principles? Most Americans would agree that crime needs to stop in this country, but it is not just for a person to avert the law, ostensibly committing another crime, to "lessen" the crime rate. Additionally, who is to say that the vigilante will administer justice fairly or appropriately? It is the government's task to do this, and if the government itself is corrupt, then steps must be taken to fix it through the proper channels of democracy. Vigilantism is never the solution to corruption.

Write a short answer that analyzes how the author takes the opposing viewpoint into consideration and negates it.

Your response may look something like this:

> In this instance, the student considers the opposition several times. He begins by citing the commonly held belief that vigilantes are "superheroes," but then goes on to debunk this idea by discussing the ways vigilantes are also lawbreakers, not people who should be revered. The student also acknowledges some of the strength of the opposing argument, admitting when vigilantism may be "noble," but then discusses the ramifications of not following the law. The student even gives an example of how vigilantism could be seen in a positive light, but then negates this by showing how this example could end in catastrophe. By considering the opposing argument, the student has used these claims as his own evidence in his case.

Now let's talk about how this particular passage distinguishes itself from conflicting viewpoints. This is mostly covered in the sample response to the student essay, but to strengthen it, the student might want to add in some information regarding the way his or her own position is different from the opposition. For example, the sample response might include a sentence or two that says something like this:

"Although the opposition is clearly delineated and negated in this paragraph, the student does his own argument justice by explaining how it is distinctively different from the opposing side. The student identifies how he believes vigilantism is 'unjust,' despite its errant popularity. In this manner, the student indicates that he is more interested in actual fairness, rather than the 'superhero' method of taking the law into one's own hands. Therefore, the student indicates his belief that laws must be followed in order for a society to maintain cohesive order."

Infer an author's implicit as well as explicit purposes based on details in text.

Before you can be successful on this skill, you must understand the **difference between an** *implicit* **and** *explicit* **purpose.** To be implicit, an idea should be implied or expressed indirectly, and to be explicit, an idea should be directly stated (or easily identified) in a text. This skill is simply an extension of skills you've already mastered: reading comprehension and inference, applied to the author's purpose.

Test yourself quickly on the difference between *implicit* and *explicit* by filling in the blanks below:

Alcohol labels give ⬚ warnings about the harms of consumption.

The students detected an ⬚ warning about plagiarism in the teacher's instructions about the paper.

If you answered **explicit** and **implicit**, respectively, then you have a good grasp of the meaning of these words.

EXAMPLE

Read the following paragraph from a student's persuasive essay.

All people should have the right to get married. As it is, teen suicide among the homosexual population is nearly triple that of heterosexual teens. When a country outwardly proclaims their bigotry by denying a minority of its citizens their basic human rights, we are contributing to the bullying and low self-esteem of our citizens. America's Declaration of Independence says all men are entitled to the "pursuit of happiness." Are our gay brothers and sisters not part of our people?

What is the explicit purpose of this paragraph?

    A. to stop teen suicide

    B. to stop bullying homosexuals

    C. to advocate for gay marriage

    D. to educate a population about the struggles of gay teens

The correct answer to this question is (C). Although the paragraph does mention suicide (A), bullying (B), and gay teens (D), the whole focus of this paragraph is to use bullying and suicide as an emotional appeal to a larger focus: to allow gay marriage (C). You should be able to identify this from the topic sentence of this paragraph, "All people should have the right to get married."

What is an implicit message in this paragraph?

    A. Denying gays the right to marry is un-American.

    B. Denying gays the right to marry is the reason for teen suicide.

    C. Bigotry destroys the institution of marriage.

    D. The U.S. Supreme Court's 2015 ruling that the Constitution guarantees a right to same-sex marriage was a welcome event.

The correct answer is (A). Choice (B) makes a faulty connection between two stated pieces of information; the author does not imply that teen suicide is caused by denying gays marriage rights, but that there is inherent prejudice which may contribute to depression. Choice (C) has no justification in the text at all, even if the words "bigotry" and "marriage" are used. Finally, (D) should be ruled out because the high court's decision is never even mentioned in the text, even if the author's agreement with it is implied.

Analyze how an author uses rhetorical techniques to advance his or her point of view or achieve a specific purpose (e.g., analogies, enumerations, repetition and parallelism, juxtaposition of opposites, qualifying statements).

Before we discuss this skill in depth, let's take a look at some definitions in this benchmark.

Analogy—A comparison between two things

Enumeration—A numbered list

Repetition (compare "parallelism)—Recurrent words or phrases

Parallelism (compare "repetition")—Successive grammatical construction in verbs, phrases, or sounds

Juxtaposition—An act or instance of placing items side by side

Qualifying statements—Modifying sentiments that refine an idea

This skill is very similar to one you've already mastered: "analyze how the structure of a paragraph, section, or passage shapes meaning, emphasizes key ideas, or supports an author's purpose." In this case, however, you are **looking individually at those rhetorical elements** (analogy, enumeration, etc.) to see how those techniques strengthen an argument.

Let's use a longer excerpt from Martin Luther King's "I Have a Dream"* speech to see which elements you can identify.

EXAMPLE

(1) Go back to Mississippi, go back to Alabama, go back to Georgia, go back to Louisiana, go back to the slums and ghettos of our northern cities, knowing that somehow this situation can and will be changed. Let us not wallow in the valley of despair.

(2) I say to you today, my friends, that in spite of the difficulties and frustrations of the moment, I still have a dream. It is a dream deeply rooted in the American dream.

(3) I have a dream that one day this nation will rise up and live out the true meaning of its creed: "We hold these truths to be self-evident: that all men are created equal."

(4) I have a dream that one day on the red hills of Georgia the sons of former slaves and the sons of former slave owners will be able to sit down together at a table of brotherhood.

(5) I have a dream that one day even the state of Mississippi, a desert state, sweltering with the heat of injustice and oppression, will be transformed into an oasis of freedom and justice.

(6) I have a dream that my four children will one day live in a nation where they will not be judged by the color of their skin but by the content of their character.

(7) I have a dream today.

(8) I have a dream that one day the state of Alabama, whose governor's lips are presently dripping with the words of interposition and nullification, will be transformed into a situation where little black boys and black girls will be able to join hands with little white boys and white girls and walk together as sisters and brothers.

---

* "I Have a Dream" by Martin Luther King, Jr., reprinted by arrangement with the Estate of Martin Luther King, Jr., c/o Writers House as agent for the proprietor, New York, N.Y. Copyright © 1963 Martin Luther King, Jr., copyright renewed 1991 Coretta Scott King.

(9) I have a dream today.

(10) I have a dream that one day every valley shall be exalted, every hill and mountain shall be made low, the rough places will be made plain, and the crooked places will be made straight, and the glory of the Lord shall be revealed, and all flesh shall see it together.

(11) This is our hope. This is the faith with which I return to the South. With this faith we will be able to hew out of the mountain of despair a stone of hope. With this faith we will be able to transform the jangling discords of our nation into a beautiful symphony of brotherhood. With this faith we will be able to work together, to pray together, to struggle together, to go to jail together, to stand up for freedom together, knowing that we will be free one day.

(12) This will be the day when all of God's children will be able to sing with a new meaning, "My country, 'tis of thee, sweet land of liberty, of thee I sing. Land where my fathers died, land of the pilgrim's pride, from every mountainside, let freedom ring."

(13) And if America is to be a great nation this must become true. So let freedom ring from the prodigious hilltops of New Hampshire. Let freedom ring from the mighty mountains of New York. Let freedom ring from the heightening Alleghenies of Pennsylvania!

(14) Let freedom ring from the snowcapped Rockies of Colorado!

(15) Let freedom ring from the curvaceous slopes of California!

(16) But not only that; let freedom ring from Stone Mountain of Georgia!

(17) Let freedom ring from Lookout Mountain of Tennessee!

(18) Let freedom ring from every hill and molehill of Mississippi, from every mountainside. Let freedom ring . . .

(19) When we allow freedom to ring—when we let it ring from every village and every hamlet, from every state and every city, we will be able to speed up that day when all of God's children, black men and white men, Jews and Gentiles, Protestants and Catholics, will be able to join hands and sing in the words of the old Negro spiritual, "Free at last! Free at last! thank God Almighty, We are free at last!"

First, can you identify which rhetorical structure King uses most frequently in this selection? If you said **repetition** and **parallelism**, you are absolutely correct. King consistently repeats certain phrases such as, "Go back to . . . ," "I have a dream," and "Let freedom ring."

Beyond this most obvious rhetorical strategy, King also uses the **juxtaposition** of opposing ideas when he says, "I say to you today, my friends, that in spite of the difficulties and frustrations of the moment, I still have a dream." King also uses **analogy** when he says, "I have a dream that one day even the state of Mississippi, a desert state, *sweltering* with the heat of injustice and oppression, will be transformed into an oasis of freedom and justice." Additionally, King uses **qualifying statements** throughout his speech, such as, "I have a dream that one day the state of Alabama, *whose governor's lips are presently dripping with the words of interposition and nullification*, will be transformed into a situation where little black boys and black girls will be able to join hands with little white boys and white girls and walk together as sisters and brothers."

When King employs all these rhetorical strategies in such a short selection of text, is it any wonder this speech is considered one of the most persuasive and memorable in American history?

Now that you are able to identify these rhetorical strategies in a text, analyzing how these specific strategies advance an author's purpose is simply a matter of revisiting the skill you learned previously.

EXAMPLE

What effect does King's use of parallelism and repetition have on the delivery of his message?

A. King uses these elements to make his speech seem like a poem.

B. King's message to spread and embody freedom is cemented in his audience's mind because the same language is used continuously.

C. King encourages his audience to reconsider their position regarding the way we treat each other, especially with regard to race.

D. King repeats himself so he can more easily remember what he is trying to convey.

The correct answer to this question is (B). You should be able to identify this relatively easily because it is the only response that takes into consideration all aspects of the question: how the structure conveys meaning. Response (A) deals only with the structural elements, and while it may be true, it's too narrowly construed: It does not delve into King's intended effect for composing the speech as he did. Similarly, (C) deals only with the message, not with the structure. Choice (D) is based on supposition — pure conjecture — and has no merit of fact to support it.

As you become more comfortable with your reading skills in preparation for the GED® test, you will begin to see that the same skills are used over and over; you simply have to know *when* to apply them in each particular situation.

Evaluating the Argument and Claims

Delineate and evaluate the argument and specific claims in a text, including the validity of the reasoning as well as the relevance and sufficiency of the evidence.

This standard in the GED® test is going to measure your ability to respond to persuasive works. To that end, you will need to decide if a piece is written with solid logic and whether or not the writer has done enough research to support the essay's claims. This work deals entirely with rhetoric and research, and this section of the guide will go into detail about both of these ideas. To begin, you might want to know the definition of **rhetoric**, which is simply **persuasive writing or speaking**. Usually authors employ three different types of appeal to persuade an audience: ethos, logos, and pathos. Those are fancy words for "ethical," "logical," and "emotional" persuasion, respectively. Every good piece of rhetoric uses all of these tactics!

The GED® test will assess some or all of these skills with questions relating to this standard:

- Delineate the specific steps of an argument the author puts forward, including how the argument's claims build on one another.

- Identify specific pieces of evidence the author uses in support of claims or conclusions.

- Evaluate the relevance and sufficiency of evidence offered in support of a claim.

- Distinguish claims that are supported by reasons and evidence from claims that are not.

- Assess whether the reasoning is valid; identify fallacious reasoning in an argument and evaluate its impact.

- Identify an underlying premise or assumption in an argument and evaluate the logical support and evidence provided.

Let's look at each skill individually.

Delineate the specific steps of an argument the author puts forward, including how the argument's claims build on one another.

This skill is asking you to outline the author's approach to an argument. Though it may sound difficult, this is actually a relatively simple skill to master. All you have to do is **read into the logic** an author employs to build his case, and then prove you are able to follow the steps he has taken to organize his thoughts. This also asks you to read into how one idea references and embodies a previous discussion.

EXAMPLE

Read the following essay, "Ideas" by Arthur Benson.

(1) There are certain great ideas which, if we have any intelligence and thoughtfulness at all, we cannot help coming across the track of, just as when we walk far into the deep country, in the time of the blossoming of flowers, we step for a moment into a waft of fragrance, cast upon the air from orchard or thicket or scented field of bloom.

(2) These ideas are very various in quality; some of them deliciously haunting and transporting, some grave and solemn, some painfully sad and strong. Some of them seem to hint at unseen beauty and joy, some have to do with problems of conduct and duty, some with the relation in which we wish to stand or are forced to stand with other human beings; some are questionings born of grief and pain, what the meaning of sorrow is, whether pain has a further intention, whether the spirit survives the life which is all that we can remember of existence; but the strange thing about all these ideas is that we find them suddenly in the mind and soul; we do not seem to invent them, though we cannot trace them; and even if we find them in books that we read or words that we hear, they do not seem wholly new to us; we recognize them as things that we have dimly felt and perceived, and the reason why they often have so mysterious an effect upon us is that they seem to take us outside of ourselves, further back than we can recollect, beyond the faint horizon, into something as wide and great as the illimitable sea or the depths of sunset sky.

(3) Some of these ideas have to do with the constitution of society, the combined and artificial peace in which human beings live, and then they are political ideas; or they deal with such things as numbers, curves, classes of animals and plants, the soil of the earth, the changes of the seasons,

the laws of weight and mass, and then they are scientific ideas; some have to do with right and wrong conduct, actions and qualities, and then they are religious or ethical ideas. But there is a class of thoughts which belong precisely to none of these things, but which are concerned with the perception of beauty, in forms and colours, musical sounds, human faces and limbs, words majestic or sweet; and this sense of beauty may go further, and may be discerned in qualities, regarded not from the point of view of their rightness and justice, but according as they are fine and noble, evoking our admiration and our desire; and these are poetical ideas.

(4) It is not of course possible exactly to classify ideas, because there is a great overlapping of them and a wide interchange. The thought of the slow progress of man from something rude and beastlike, the statement of the astronomer about the swarms of worlds swimming in space, may awaken the sense of poetry which is in its essence the sense of wonder. I shall not attempt in these few pages to limit and define the sense of poetry. I shall merely attempt to describe the kind of effect it has or may have in life, what our relation is or may be to it, what claim it may be said to have upon us, whether we can practice it, and whether we ought to do so.

Drag-and-drop the procession of the author's argument in the correct order.

    A. The author seeks to describe the effects poetry may have on our lives.

    B. The author references the roots of ideas.

    C. The author argues that some ideas merely come to us; they are not the products of our own effort of thought.

    D. The author argues that there is no new idea.

For this paper-and-pencil setting, simply place the letter for your selected answers below.

The correct sequence for this question is (C), (B), (D), (A). You can follow this by simply reading the text and pulling out key phrases in order. For example, "There are certain great ideas which . . . we cannot help coming across the track of . . ." (C) is in the first sentence. Then, by the author's use of parallelism and the repetition of the word "some" in the first section of the second paragraph (". . . some of them deliciously haunting and transporting, some grave and solemn, some painfully sad and strong. . ."), you can find the second argument about the roots of ideas, or how ideas come to us and from what places (B). Next, you can see that the author also makes reference to the fact that none of these ideas are completely original (D) when he says, "we find them suddenly in the mind and soul; we do not seem to invent them. . . ." Finally, the author makes direct reference to the sentiment about the effects of poetry in the concluding paragraph (No. 4) when he says, "I shall not attempt in these few pages to limit and define the sense of poetry. I shall merely attempt to describe the kind of effect it has or may have in life. . . ." As you can see, in order to delineate the construction of an author's progression of an argument, all you have to do is read closely.

To address the second part of this skill, you must also look at how the author builds the argument. You might see a question that will ask you how the author transitions into his new idea while taking the old one into consideration. A question along these lines would look something like this:

Which sentence indicates that the author will use his previous statements to begin his next argument, which is to describe the effect poetry has on life?

A. "It is not of course possible exactly to classify ideas, because there is a great overlapping of them and a wide interchange." (paragraph 4)

B. "Some of these ideas have to do with the constitution of society, the combined and artificial peace in which human beings live, and then they are political ideas; or they deal with such things as numbers, curves, classes of animals and plants, the soil of the earth, the changes of the seasons, the laws of weight and mass, and then they are scientific ideas; some have to do with right and wrong conduct, actions and qualities, and then they are religious or ethical ideas."(paragraph 3)

C. "There are certain great ideas which, if we have any intelligence and thoughtfulness at all, we cannot help coming across the track of, just as when we walk far into the deep country, in the time of the blossoming of flowers, we step for a moment into a waft of fragrance, cast upon the air from orchard or thicket or scented field of bloom."(paragraph 1)

D. "The thought of the slow progress of man from something rude and beast-like, the statement of the astronomer about the swarms of worlds swimming in space, may awaken the sense of poetry which is in its essence the sense of wonder."(paragraph 4)

The correct answer to this question is (A). You can see by the conditional phrase "of course," that the author is going to spring into a new idea by showing he is thinking about the consequences of what he has already stated. This phrase considers the arguments he has been making previously about how ideas come about, but also then launches into a clarifying idea, which is actually answer choice (D), the transitional sentence into the new idea. Do not let this fool you. The question asks you which sentence indicates his use of previous ideas, *not* which is the transitional sentence.

When you are answering questions that require you to delineate an author's line of argumentation, you must be careful to read the questions as carefully as you read the answers and the passages themselves. Oftentimes there may seem like more than one correct answer, but you can usually clear this up by looking at the specific requirements of the question itself.

Identify specific pieces of evidence the author uses in support of claims or conclusions.

This is another relatively simple skill that builds upon your previous work in reading comprehension. In this skill, most of your questions will ask you to simply identify what research or support an author gives in order to prove his point or make his case. Again, you will have to employ your reading comprehension skills to first determine the author's claims in order to point out the evidence he uses to support that argument, but you should be a whiz at that by now!

EXAMPLE

Read this excerpt from Vincent Carretta's book, *Phillis Wheatley: Biography of a Genius in Bondage*.

(1) The assertiveness that Phillis probably displayed in her dealings with Nathaniel Wheatley was anticipated more subtly in her Poems. Wheatley does not hesitate in Poems to proclaim her African heritage. Her opening poem, "To Maecenas," thanks her unnamed patron, loosely imitating Classical models such as Virgil and Horace's poems dedicated to Maecenas, the Roman politician and patron of the arts. Emphasizing in a footnote that the Classical Roman poet Terence "was an African by birth," Wheatley implies that her "Maecenas" has enabled her to claim a place in the Western literary tradition, which has included Africans since its beginning. Elsewhere in her poems, Wheatley appropriates the persona of authority or power normally associated with men and her social superiors. For example, in "To the University of Cambridge, in New-England," first composed when she was about fifteen years old, Wheatley speaks as a teacher to students, or a minister to his flock, in addressing the young men of what was to become Harvard University, many of whom were being trained there to become ministers themselves.

(2) Several of Wheatley's poems demonstrate a nuanced treatment of slavery unrecognized by some of her critics. For example, written in October 1772 to celebrate Dartmouth's appointment the previous August, "To the Right Honourable William, Earl of Dartmouth, His Majesty's Principal Secretary of State for North America, &c." is one of the most carefully crafted poems in the 1773 volume. In it Wheatley re-appropriates the concept of slavery from its common metaphorical use in the colonial rhetoric of discontent, which described any perceived limitation on colonial rights and liberty as an attempt by England to "enslave" (white) Americans.

Drag-and-drop the pieces of evidence that support the claim that Wheatley used her poetry as a vehicle for social mobility.

A. "The assertiveness that Phillis probably displayed in her dealings with Nathaniel Wheatley was anticipated more subtly in her Poems." (paragraph 1)

B. "Wheatley does not hesitate in Poems to proclaim her African heritage." (paragraph 1)

C. "Her opening poem, "To Maecenas," thanks her unnamed patron, loosely imitating Classical models such as Virgil and Horace's poems dedicated to Maecenas, the Roman politician and patron of the arts."(paragraph 1)

D. "Elsewhere in her poems, Wheatley appropriates the persona of authority or power normally associated with men and her social superiors."(paragraph 1)

E. "In it Wheatley re-appropriates the concept of slavery from its common metaphorical use in the colonial rhetoric of discontent, which described any perceived limitation on colonial rights and liberty as an attempt by England to "enslave" (white) Americans."(paragraph 2)

> **For this paper-and-pencil setting, simply place the letter for your selected answers below.**
>
>

You should have dragged responses (B), (C), and (E). You can rule out (A) and (D) because they are sub-claims of the larger argument outlined in the question, rather than evidence. Make sure you are able to differentiate between the two! A claim is its own argument, and the evidence is the material that supports that claim. You should be able to identify the claim in choice (A) by the word "probably." Also, in (D) you can see that by the word "elsewhere," the author will later provide the quotes that prove the sub-claim that Wheatley uses a man's superiority to claim her independence. When you are looking for evidence, look for quotes such as in (C) and (E), and observations about works as a whole, such as in (B).

Evaluate the relevance and sufficiency of evidence offered in support of a claim.

As you are mastering this particular skill, you will have to not only identify the claims and the evidence, but then determine whether they are relevant (helpful) or just added information (superfluous). Sometimes evidence is simply for our benefit or enjoyment, rather than for the purpose of beefing up the claim itself. It will be your job to consider the evidence to **determine if it is relevant and enough** (sufficient) to fully construct an argument.

Read the following excerpt from the essay "Upon Running After One's Hat" by G. K. Chesterton.

(1) For instance, there is a current impression that it is unpleasant to have to run after one's hat. Why should it be unpleasant to the well-ordered and pious mind? Not merely because it is running, and running exhausts one. The same people run much faster in games and sports. The same people run much more eagerly after an uninteresting, little leather ball than they will after a nice silk hat. There is an idea that it is humiliating to run after one's hat; and when people say it is humiliating they mean that it is comic. It certainly is comic; but man is a very comic creature, and most of the things he does are comic—eating, for instance. And the most comic things of all are exactly the things that are most worth doing—such as making love. A man running after a hat is not half so ridiculous as a man running after a wife.

(2) Now a man could, if he felt rightly in the matter, run after his hat with the manliest ardour and the most sacred joy. He might regard himself as a jolly huntsman pursuing a wild animal, for certainly no animal could be wilder. In fact, I am inclined to believe that hat-hunting on windy days will be the sport of the upper classes in the future. There will be a meet of ladies and gentlemen on some high ground on a gusty morning. They will be told that the professional attendants have started a hat in such-and-such a thicket, or whatever be the technical term. Notice that this employment will in the fullest degree combine sport with humanitarianism. The hunters would feel that they were not inflicting pain. Nay, they would feel that they were inflicting pleasure, rich, almost riotous pleasure, upon the people who were looking on. When last I saw an old gentleman running after his hat in Hyde Park, I told him that a heart so benevolent as his ought to be filled with peace and thanks at the thought of how much unaffected pleasure his every gesture and bodily attitude were at that moment giving to the crowd.

(3) The same principle can be applied to every other typical domestic worry. A gentleman trying to get a fly out of the milk or a piece of cork out of his glass of wine often imagines himself to be irritated. Let him think for a moment of the patience of anglers sitting by dark pools, and let his soul be immediately irradiated with gratification and repose. Again, I have known some people of very modern views driven by their distress to the use of theological terms to which they attached no doctrinal significance, merely because a drawer was jammed tight and they could not pull it out. A friend of mine was particularly afflicted in this way. Every day his drawer was jammed, and every day in consequence it was something else that rhymes to it. But I pointed out to him that this sense of wrong was really subjective and relative; it rested entirely upon the assumption that the drawer could, should, and would come out easily. "But if," I said, "you picture to yourself that you are pulling against some powerful and oppressive enemy, the struggle will become merely exciting and not exasperating. Imagine that you are tugging up a lifeboat out of the sea. Imagine that you are roping up a fellow-creature out of an Alpine crevass. Imagine even that you are a boy again and engaged in a tug-of-war between French and English." Shortly after saying this I left him; but I have no doubt at all that my words bore the best possible fruit. I have no doubt that every day of his life he hangs on to the handle of that drawer with a flushed face and eyes

bright with battle, uttering encouraging shouts to himself, and seeming to hear all round him the roar of an applauding ring.

(4) So I do not think that it is altogether fanciful or incredible to suppose that even the floods in London may be accepted and enjoyed poetically. Nothing beyond inconvenience seems really to have been caused by them; and inconvenience, as I have said, is only one aspect, and that the most unimaginative and accidental aspect of a really romantic situation. An adventure is only an inconvenience rightly considered. An inconvenience is only an adventure wrongly considered. The water that girdled the houses and shops of London must, if anything, have only increased their previous witchery and wonder. For as the Roman Catholic priest in the story said: "Wine is good with everything except water," and on a similar principle, water is good with everything except wine.

(Project Gutenberg)

Write a short answer that analyzes the sufficiency and relevance of the evidence provided in this passage to support the claim that in order to avoid frustration, man must consider every opportunity with a positive mindset.

Your answer may look something like this:

> In this essay, Chesterton employs several rhetorical strategies through his evidence. He first uses logical appeal when he draws a comparison between a man's irritation about chasing his hat when he would use far more energy for a sport, chasing an "uninteresting, little leather ball," which the author considers a thing of much less value. By using this comparison as evidence, Chesterton supports the claim that man must have a positive mindset and frame of reference. Next, Chesterton also employs good ethical appeal when he uses a real-world example of a friend's experience. When he relates a true story of a friend who changed his point of view regarding an annoying drawer, we see how Chesterton's argument is furthered by the successful playful mindset his friend used. Through these pieces of evidence, Chesterton best crafts an argument that we can all apply to our daily lives: every frustration is a misinterpreted adventure.

What is excellent about this response is its inclusion of the types of rhetorical appeal, ethos, and logos. The student who wrote this answer is not only fully aware of the claim itself, as evidenced by the reference to the text in the final statement, but has also selected two of the most powerful examples in the text which support this idea. The student has left out the anecdotal fancies of the author (the imagined sport of rich people chasing hats around) and has homed in on the real examples that best support the author's argument.

Distinguish claims that are supported by reasons and evidence from claims that are not.

In the Internet Age, opinions of all stripes are more readily accessible than at any time in the history of humankind. But the basis for many claims is either weak or totally lacking. This GED® skill requires you to tease apart mere opinion from *informed* opinion backed by evidence. The only prior skill you will need in this endeavor is the ability to **differentiate between a claim and evidence.** As you analyze persuasive texts, you should consider these words and definitions:

Claim: the argument presented

Evidence: facts, statistics, and corroborating examples

Warrant: reasoning that ties together the claim and the evidence

Knowing these terms will come in handy on the GED® test as you begin to write your own essays. Every good argument should include the claim, evidence, and warrant (justification). All these pieces make for a full statement, and without all three, your argument falls short.

Before we look at a question that will test this skill, let's take a quick look at an example of a claim, evidence, and warrant so it will make sense to you.

Claim: Smoking is bad.

Evidence: The American Cancer Society reported that smoking is the leading cause of lung cancer.

Warrant: Because the Cancer Society is the leader in cancer research, it is a credible source and proves (based on the weight of the evidence) that smoking, which is linked to lung cancer, is bad.

This may seem like common sense, but without the warrant, the claim and evidence are two unrelated pieces of information. The function of a warrant is to draw conclusions and relate information, successfully removing the need for the audience to have to think to understand a whole argument. The warrant is the **reasoning** this skill references. Although this particular example may be juvenile, it should help you understand the larger context of what this skill will ask in more complex situations. Any time authors make a claim, they should include evidence and a warrant to make their argument complete. This particular skill is asking you to identify when an author uses these three pieces together, and when they only make a bald claim.

Read the following excerpt from a student's paper.

(1) Teenagers need to make mistakes. Mistakes are an important part in a person's development, and as long as those mistakes are measured and done in a supportive environment, the benefits in learning outweigh the consequences of the risks. Teenagers should make mistakes before they become adults and leave their parents. In 1999, an honor student named Christopher Newport attended the University of Virginia in Charlottesville. All his life Christopher did what his parents wanted him to do, and followed every single rule. He never drank, he never sped in his car, he always came in by curfew, and he hung out with the right crowd. When Christopher got to college, he found himself surrounded by influences he had never before had to avoid because he had lived his entire previous life under the watchful eyes of his parents without ever doing anything wrong. In college everything was different. His dorm-mates threw wild parties, and Christopher found himself drinking too much. One night after a series of alcoholic beverages, Christopher decided to drive over to his girlfriend's sorority house, but on the way he ran into a school bus full of kindergarteners. He killed himself and three children.

(2) If Christopher had tried drinking when he was in high school and decided not to listen to his parents all the time, maybe he would have discovered all the reasons drinking is a bad idea before the consequences were so dire. If Christopher had let himself make a mistake before he became out of control, maybe he would still be alive and so would all those little kids. Not to mention, if Christopher had done this while he was in high school, he would have had his parents there to help him get through it before it was too late. Sure, it is possible that the same thing might have happened if Christopher was drinking in high school, but at least there would have been someone there to help him, unlike when he got to college and no one cared if he started to drive while he was drunk.

(3) A recent study done by Purdue University shows that the best way a person can learn to avoid a negative behavior is to suffer the consequences of that negative action. The drinking age should be lowered.

Which sentence from this essay is a claim unsupported by evidence and reasoning?

    A. "In 1999, an honor student named Christopher Newport attended the University of Virginia in Charlottesville."(paragraph 1)

    B. "His dorm-mates threw wild parties, and Christopher found himself drinking too much."(paragraph 1)

    C. "He killed himself and three children."(paragraph 1)

    D. "The drinking age should be lowered."(paragraph 3)

The correct answer is (D). Although it could be argued that this story lays the groundwork for making a case to lower the drinking age, it does not provide the warrant that would support it. The reader would have to make the connection that if the drinking age were lowered, perhaps Christopher would have learned to tolerate alcohol before he made such a huge, unsupervised mistake. Without this warrant, however, the last sentence of this passage is unsupported, unreasoned, and irrelevant to the rest of the paper. Answer choices (A), (B), and (C) are each examples of further evidence given to support the actual claim. None are arguments.

This is a difficult essay to analyze because it focuses more on a narrative than logical persuasion, and it moves into glorified storytelling early on. This essay focuses on emotional fallacies and ethical appeal rather than logical appeal. The essay has one main focus, though, which is its thesis statement: "Teenagers need to make mistakes." This idea is supported throughout by using an example of Christopher, a sheltered student who goes off to college and kills himself and others by making a tragic mistake.

As you answer questions on the GED® test that test this skill, be sure to look for complete arguments: claim, evidence, and warrant.

Assess whether the reasoning is valid; identify fallacious reasoning in an argument and evaluate its impact.

Let's start by defining a fallacy. A fallacy is simply a false argument; it can be accidental or purposefully manipulative. There are many different kinds of fallacies. Provided below is a list of **different types of fallacies** you may see in persuasive arguments and their definitions.

Ad Hominem Argument—attacking the opponent rather than the argument. "Would you trust the opinion of a man who did drugs in college?"

Appeal to Ignorance—this suggests that because no one has proven the argument wrong, it must be correct. Or, because no one has yet proven an argument that it is not true. "Martians are plotting to overthrow our planet. No scientific explanation has yet ruled out this idea."

Appeal to Pity—this is a misused emotional appeal seeking to manipulate the audience. The example of Christopher in the essay in the previous section was an appeal to pity.

Bandwagon Mentality—this is the implication that something can or cannot be true because the majority of people believe one way or another. This appeal manipulates an audience member's innate desire to be accepted. "All intelligent people know that Medicare is hiking up taxes for the middle class."

Bare Assertion—to deny an issue exists. "That's just how it is."

Begging the Question—assuming in the argument the point that needs to be proven. "We don't need these useless CDs when everyone has an iPod." The word "useless" begs the question.

Complex Question—a phrasing of a question that masks a more basic question. "Why can't we bring down these high food prices our corrupt corporations are charging?" This question ignores whether or not corporations are actually corrupt.

Either-Or Thinking—reduce all ideas to two extremes. "Either we go to war or we are attacked by terrorists and die."

False Analogy—this is an argument that A is bad (or good) because it is like B. "Do not bother voting in this election, this country is not a democracy, it's a communist dictatorship."

False Cause—if A comes before B, A must have caused B. "When the city unveiled the new metro station, crime rate increased in the area. It would have been better if the station was never built."

Hasty or Broad Generalization—this is a claim based on too little evidence. "Today's children spend too much time looking to "League of Legends" for inspiration rather than reading books."

Hypothesis Contrary to Fact—this fallacy indulges in "if only" thinking. "If only the U.S. Supreme Court hadn't pushed through the *Roe v. Wade* decision, innocent babies wouldn't be victims to irresponsible behavior."

Impressing with Numbers—although facts and statistics are often helpful to prove points, they can be misused or misleading, especially when the numbers are used out of context. "Only 3% of the taxpayers in Fairfax County, Virginia, are affected by the school system, which spends approximately $10,000 annually per student. In 2013, the Standards of Learning scores in Northern Virginia were approximately 6% higher than the passing rates of the other 94 counties in the state. The state should cut spending to the North of the state and supplement the South."

Misuse of Humor—humor can be very helpful for lightening a mood, but when it is used to mock, it undercuts an argument. It can also polarize the audience and have the opposite effect. For example, "People who drive hybrid cars are nothing but a bunch of granola-crunching hippies!"

Oversimplification—reduces complexity to simplicity.

Red Herring—this is an odd fallacy that puts the opponent "on the wrong track." For example, let's say the argument is about halting the opening of new drilling facilities in Alaska because of budgetary restrictions, and the writer begins with, "The massive oil spill off the coast of Louisiana led to horrific deaths of countless animals and diminished quality of life for thousands of Americans." This ignores the real issue of whether the budget allows for the expense.

Slippery Slope—this fallacy indicates that one step will unleash an unstoppable chain of events. "If we do not build a new road to alleviate traffic concerns, it will only be a matter of time before people bypass L.A. altogether, and we become a shadow of our former glory and Hollywood superpower."

Straw Man—the writer writes an argument against a claim that is easily refuted. "Those who oppose the War on Terror must believe that Americans deserve to be tortured."

Unreliable Testimony—this is an appeal to an authority that is not qualified in the proper field. "Eminem claims that gun control should not be a priority for the American political system." Although Eminem may feel this way and may reach a wide audience, he is not qualified to be an expert on this particular subject.

Use of Threats—this is an unethical way of sabotaging an argument, though they are often rhetorically effective. "If we do not pass the Obamacare Reform, we are killing off the poor!"

As long as you are able to identify these fallacies, you should have no problem identifying faulty reasoning in arguments on the GED® test.

Give it a try:

EXAMPLE

Read this passage from *The Book of Fallacies* by Jeremy Bentham.

(1) The present work confines itself to the examination and exposure of only one class of fallacies, which class is determined by the nature of the occasion in which they are employed.

(2) The occasion here in question is that of the formation of a decision procuring the adoption or rejection of some measure of *government*: including under the notion of a measure of government, a measure of legislation as well as of administration—two operations so intimately connected, that the drawing of a boundary line between them will in some *instances* be matter of no small difficulty, but for the distinguishing of which on the present occasion, and for the purpose of the present work, there will not be any need.

(3) Under the name of a *Treatise on Political Fallacies,* this work will possess the character, and, in so far as the character answers the design of it, have the effect of a treatise on *the art of government;*—having for its practical object and tendency, in the first place, the facilitating the introduction of such features of good government as remain to be introduced; in the next place giving them perpetuation—perpetuation, not by means of legislative clauses aiming directly at that object (an aim of which the inutility and mischievousness will come to be fully laid open to view in the course of this work), but by means of that instrument, viz. *reason,* by which alone the endeavour can be productive of any useful effect.

(4) Employed in this endeavour, there are two ways in which this instrument may be applied: one, the more direct, by showing, on the occasion of each proposed measure, in what way, by what probable consequences it tends to promote the accomplishment of the end or object which it professes to have particularly in view: the other, the less direct, by pointing out the irrelevancy, and thus anticipating and destroying the persuasive force, of such deceptious arguments as have been in use, or appear likely to be employed in the endeavour to oppose it, and to dissuade men from concurring in the establishment of it.

(5) Of these two different but harmonizing modes of applying this same instrument to its several purposes, the *more direct* is that of which a sample has, ever since the year 1802, been before the public, in that collection of unfinished papers on legislation, published at *Paris* in the French language, and which had the advantage of passing through the hands of Mr. Dumont, but for whose labours it would scarcely, in the author's lifetime at least, have seen the light. To exhibit the *less direct*, but in its application the more extensive mode, is the business of the present work.

(6) To give existence to good arguments was the object in that instance: to provide for the exposure of bad ones is the object in the present instance—to provide for the exposure of their real nature, and thence for the destruction of their pernicious force.

(7) Sophistry is a hydra, of which, if all the necks could be exposed, the force would be destroyed. In this work they have been diligently looked out for, and in the course of it the principal and most active of them have been brought to view.

(Project Gutenberg)

What type of fallacy is employed in the following sentence from paragraph 7?

Sophistry is a hydra, of which, if all the necks could be exposed, the force would be destroyed.

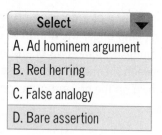

Select ▼
A. Ad hominem argument
B. Red herring
C. False analogy
D. Bare assertion

The correct answer is (C). Even if you did not know that "sophistry" means the use of fallacy, you can still see you're dealing with an analogy, as sophistry (whatever it may mean) is being compared to a mythical creature, the many-headed hydra. Although this may be an effective comparison, it is still a fallacy at its barest because it assumes all fallacies are stated on purpose, that they are prevalent in all works of persuasion, and that they must be destroyed. You can rule out (A) because no one is being attacked, (B) because it stays on topic and no deception is taking place, and (D) because the author advances a systematic case to expose fallacious arguments.

You may also be asked to identify why reasoning is fallible in an author's argument. Let's take a look at the kind of question on the GED® test that will address this skill.

EXAMPLE

Read the following sentence from a student's paper.

"We should avoid listening to someone who claims that we should be more aware of the dangers of not recycling when he himself wears a synthetic, polyester tie!"

Identify why the reasoning is fallacious.

    A. The student makes an incorrect assumption that synthetic materials are not recyclable.

    B. The student changes the scope of the argument from recycling to consumerism.

    C. The student attacks the speaker, not the subject.

    D. The student does not employ fallacious reasoning in this example.

The correct answer is (C). This is an example of an "ad hominem" argument, where the author attacks his opponent, rather than the issue at hand, which is recycling. Although the argument may have some merit (after all, synthetic material could indeed be made from recycled goods), there is no definitive connection provided in this sentence that would qualify this as a reasonable argument. This rules out choice (A), especially because it assumes the student's statement is incorrect, which is not provably so. Choice (B) is incorrect because it still keeps the subject at hand, which is recycling. The focus of the sentence does not shift, it is simply widened inappropriately.

Identify an underlying premise or assumption in an argument and evaluate the logical support and evidence provided.

This skill measures your ability to **fully analyze a persuasive argument**, synthesizing all of the skills you have learned in the standard thus far. Let's see if you can do it!

EXAMPLE

Read the following passage from the Mark Twain essay "Hygiene and Sentiment."

(1) For the rich, cremation would answer as well as burial; for the ceremonies connected with it could be made as costly and ostentatious as a Hindoo suttee; while for the poor, cremation would be better than burial, because so cheap (four or five dollars is the minimum cost)—so cheap until the poor got to imitating the rich, which they would do by and by. The adoption of cremation

would relieve us of a muck of threadbare burial-witticisms; but, on the other hand, it would resurrect a lot of mildewed old cremation-jokes that have had a rest for two thousand years.

(2) I have a colored acquaintance who earns his living by odd jobs and heavy manual labor. He never earns above four hundred dollars in a year, and as he has a wife and several young children, the closest scrimping is necessary to get him through to the end of the twelve months debtless. To such a man a funeral is a colossal financial disaster. While I was writing one of the preceding chapters, this man lost a little child. He walked the town over with a friend, trying to find a coffin that was within his means. He bought the very cheapest one he could find, plain wood, stained. It cost him twenty-six dollars. It would have cost less than four, probably, if it had been built to put something useful into. He and his family will feel that outlay a good many months.

What is the premise of this argument?

    A. The poor want to imitate the rich.

    B. Funerals are expensive.

    C. "Colored men" are poorer than white men.

    D. The poor should consider cremation as a way to ease the financial cost of funerals.

The answer to this question is (D). Although (A) is mentioned, it is not the premise of the entire argument. (B) may seem like a viable choice because it is true and mentioned, but it is not the **best** choice, because it is a fact or an observation, not an argument. (C) may also be true, but again it is not the focus of the work as a whole.

The GED® test may go on to measure your skill by then asking you something like this:

Drag-and-drop the evidence which supports the claim you selected.

    A. ". . . cremation would be better than burial, because so cheap . . ."

    B. . . . it would resurrect a lot of mildewed old cremation-jokes . . ."

    C. "I have a colored acquaintance who earns his living by odd jobs and heavy manual labor."

    D. "He never earns above four hundred dollars in a year . . ."

    E. "To such a man a funeral is a colossal financial disaster."

    F. "He and his family will feel that outlay a good many months."

For this paper-and-pencil setting, simply place the letter for your selected answers below.

You should drag and drop (A), (D), (E), and (F). All of these ideas support the idea that the poor should consider cremation as a way to ease the financial cost of funerals. (A) outlines that cremation is cheaper than burial, (D) shows Twain's acquaintance is poor, and both (E) and (F) support the notion that his friend will have debt as a result of a funeral. When you put all this together, you can come up with the logical conclusion that this friend, who is poor, should consider cremation as an alternative to burial. However, (B) is completely unrelated to the premise and is inserted as an anecdotal use of humor, and (C) is simply used to describe his friend further, but it fails to inform us matter-of-factly that his friend is poor. As you navigate your way through questions about rhetoric on the GED® exam, be sure to:

- Read closely and perceptively.

- Differentiate between fact and opinion.

- Remember the golden rule of persuasion: claim, evidence, warrant.

Chapter**7**

Analyzing Similar Themes or Topics

Analyze how two or more texts address similar themes or topics.

This standard is really rather self-explanatory, but as you work through it you must demonstrate your ability to read closely. You will also have to demonstrate stamina in reading, as well as perceptive analysis skills and a little bit of memory recall as you will be handling two separate texts at once. This is because you will have to draw comparisons and contrast between two separate pieces and distinguish how they are different or have different objectives.

The GED® test will assess some or all of these skills with questions relating to this standard:

- Draw specific comparisons between two texts that address similar themes or topics, or between information presented in different formats (e.g., between information presented in text and information or data summarized in a table or timeline).

- Compare two passages in similar or closely related genre that share ideas or themes, focusing on similarities and/or differences in perspective, tone, style, structure, purpose, or overall impact. (See also *Social Studies*, pp. 607–609.)

- Compare two argumentative passages on the same topic that present opposing claims (either main or supporting claims) and analyze how each text emphasizes different evidence or advances a different interpretation of facts. (See also *Extended Response*, pp. 159–167.)

- Analyze how data or quantitative and/or visual information extends, clarifies, or contradicts information in text, or determine how data supports an author's argument.

- Compare two passages that present related ideas or themes in different genres or formats (e.g., a feature article and an online FAQ or fact sheet) in order to evaluate differences in scope, purpose, emphasis, intended audience, or overall impact when comparing.

- Compare two passages that present related ideas or themes in different genre or formats in order to synthesize details, draw conclusions, or apply information to new situations.

Let's look at each one individually.

Draw specific comparisons between two texts that address similar themes or topics or between information presented in different formats (e.g., between information presented in text and information or data summarized in a table or timeline).

Notice that the standard says you will deal with different formats. This means you are going to have to draw out similarities and contrasts between two different types of writing—likely prose and something like a graph. When you approach questions like this, you might find yourself stretching your grasp of the material to **make connections**. It is good to think creatively, but always make sure you are able to identify which parts of the texts back up your assertions!

EXAMPLE

Read the following excerpt from William Osler's "The Student Life" and the graph that follows about unemployment.

The hardest conviction to get into the mind of a beginner is that the education upon which he is engaged is not a college course, not a medical course, but a life course, for which the work of a few years under teachers is but a preparation. Whether you will falter and fail in the race or whether you will be faithful to the end depends on the training before the start, and on your staying powers, points upon which I need not enlarge. You can all become good students, a few may become great students, and now and again one of you will be found who does easily and well what others cannot do at all, or very badly, which is John Ferriar's excellent definition of a genius.

(Reprinted from "A Way of Life" by Sir William Osler, London: Constable & Company, Ltd., 1913)

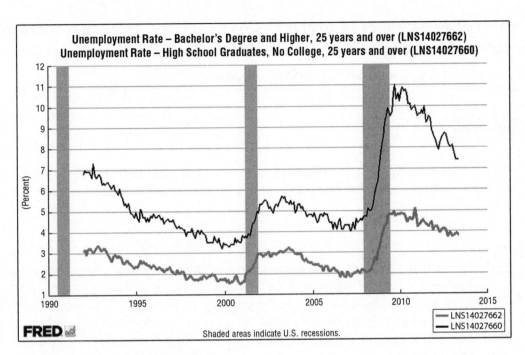

Courtesy of Federal Reserve Bank of St. Louis

What parallel can you draw between education and employment, based on these two pieces of information?

    A. The quality of education impacts the quality of the job one will land after finishing school.

    B. Education has no bearing on the likelihood of a career.

    C. Without a proper education, one is not equipped for life or the workforce.

    D. Recessions impact education.

The correct answer is (C). In order to answer this question you need to find the parallel between the information presented in both works. The paragraph is encouraging students to become the best students they are able because education is necessary for life, not just a career. The graph shows how much education matters in terms of a person's employability. Because of this, you should be able to draw the comparison (C) from your own personal experience. While (A) may be a true statement, it's not supported by either piece of information, while (C) is. (B) is actually negated by both pieces of information, and again, though (D) may be true, it is not information that is explicitly supported by both the text and the graph.

Sometimes the GED® test will select two seemingly unrelated pieces to present. <u>It is your job to look for connections and infer ideas as best you can.</u> Use your close reading skills and your powers of deduction, and you should have no trouble answering these questions.

Compare two passages in similar or closely related genre that share ideas or themes, focusing on similarities and/or differences in perspective, tone, style, structure, purpose, or overall impact.

EXAMPLE

To get a sense for this skill, let's look at two opinion pieces that address the environmental impact of highway construction. Read both selections and then answer the question that follows.

Passage #1

There's nothing more beautiful than observing animals running wild in their natural habitat. Anyone who has ever experienced the thrill of spotting a herd of deer cavorting on the edge of a forest will never forget the moment. Unfortunately, at the same time, people are wasting millions of hours mired in traffic. As our populations grow, this problem will only continue to increase. A few short tollways would go far to mitigate this problem. If we build carefully, we can cut down on the traffic problem and still protect our wildlife.

Passage #2

Highway congestion is one of the greatest problems plaguing urban areas in the United States today. Clearly, more roads could alleviate some of the trouble. But the more pavement there is, the more cars there are to fill it up. Is it really worth continuing to take away the remaining land available to our wildlife just to save a few person-hours? In the end, do we really want to know that we were the reason for the annihilation of some of our most beautiful animals?

Which of the following is the best characterization of how the two passages relate to each other?

    A. Passage 1 is an elaboration of Passage 2.

    B. Passage 2 is the antithesis of Passage 1.

    C. Passage 1 and 2 share similar solutions.

    D. Passage 1 serves as an introduction to Passage 2.

Choice (B) is the best answer: "Antithesis" means "opposite"; passages 1 and 2 advance nearly opposite viewpoints, but with a bit of a nuance. Passage 1 expresses the belief that highways can be engineered in a way sufficient to protect the animals that may live nearby. Passage 2 makes no such concession; its viewpoint is that the risk to wildlife is too high because highway construction and use are inherently – and irreversibly – dangerous to animals that live nearby. Nonetheless, the two passages do find some common ground in appreciating the beauty of wildlife. It's just that Passage 1 asserts the primacy of humans' needs over whatever consequences may befall the animal kingdom.

Compare two argumentative passages on the same topic that present opposing claims (either main or supporting claims) and analyze how each text emphasizes different evidence or advances a different interpretation of facts.

EXAMPLE

This skill is covered further in Chapter 10 when we discuss the Extended Response, which requires you to analyze arguments and marshal evidence in the course of writing an essay. For now, read two short passages that advance opposing arguments on how to view astrology. Then answer the question that follows.

Passage #1

The pseudo-science of astrology—not to be confused with the genuine science of astronomy—has been a bane of scientific thinking for untold generations. In the guise of a true science, complete with weighty books and complex chartings of planetary positions, astrology claims to be able to explain individual personality. No scientific study has ever been able to validate this claim. Indeed, attempts to test astrology's hypothesis have revealed just how nebulous that hypothesis is. The claim that being born under a particular sign makes an individual "creative" or "goal-oriented" can't really be tested, since the presence of such qualities in an individual is largely a matter of interpretation as well as degree.

Passage #2

In their understandable zeal to show that astrology is, indeed, a pseudo-science, critics of astrology have perhaps too vehemently dismissed the whole astrological project. Many early cultures independently developed sophisticated astrological systems that became the precursors of astronomy—indeed, for scientific investigation itself. Enticed by the predictive claims of astrology, Sir Isaac Newton studied geometry to learn how to cast horoscopes. This mathematical study would eventually lead to some of the greatest scientific discoveries of any age. Even psychology owes something to astrology and its emphasis on individual personality.

The author of Passage 2 would most likely react to the statement in Passage 1 that "astrology has been the bane of scientific thinking" by pointing out which of the following?

    A. Not all of astrology's claims have been disproved.

    B. Astrology has been a source of inspiration for science.

    C. Even genuine science has made unclear hypotheses.

    D. Science has been detrimental to astrology.

The correct answer is choice (B). This conclusion may be drawn from the author's statement crediting Newton with studying geometry "to learn how to cast horoscopes." In choosing to use Newton to help assert his claim, the author roots his case in the reputation of a highly regarded scientist.

Analyze how data or quantitative and/or visual information extends, clarifies, or contradicts information in text, or determine how data supports an author's argument.

Your task with this skill is again to **draw conclusions** using two different types of information: On the test it will most likely be visual data and written, or textual, data. You will need to show how this information either helps an author's argument or negates it.

EXAMPLE

Examine the chart below about seasonal vegetables and the excerpt from the essay "A Word for Autumn" by A. A. Milne. Use both the chart and the essay to answer the question that follows.

Legend: [SEEDS] Start Seeding Indoors   [shovel] Plant/Transplant Outdoors   [basket] Harvest

	Jan	Feb	Mar	Apr	May	Jun	Jul	Aug	Sep	Oct	Nov	Dec
Kale		Plant	Harvest					Plant			Harvest	
Lettuce		Plant			Harvest			Plant			Harvest	
Onions	Plant			Harvest								
Cabbage							Seeds	Plant				Harvest
Cauliflower								Seeds	Plant	Harvest		
Celery		Seeds				Plant		Harvest				
Spinach			Plant			Harvest		Plant				Harvest
Broccoli	Plant			Harvest				Plant			Harvest	
Sweet Potato					Plant			Harvest				
Tomato			Seeds	Plant			Harvest					

"A Word for Autumn" by A.A. Milne

(1) Last night the waiter put the celery on with the cheese, and I knew that summer was indeed dead. Other signs of autumn there may be—the reddening leaf, the chill in the early-morning air, the misty evenings—but none of these comes home to me so truly. There may be cool mornings in July; in a year of drought the leaves may change before their time; it is only with the first celery that summer is over.

(2) I knew all along that it would not last. Even in April I was saying that winter would soon be here. Yet somehow it had begun to seem possible lately that a miracle might happen, that summer might drift on and on through the months—a final upheaval to crown a wonderful year. The celery settled that. Last night with the celery autumn came into its own.

(3) There is a crispness about celery that is of the essence of October. It is as fresh and clean as a rainy day after a spell of heat. It crackles pleasantly in the mouth. Moreover it is excellent, I am told, for the complexion. One is always hearing of things which are good for the complexion, but there is no doubt that celery stands high on the list. After the burns and freckles of summer one is in need of something. How good that celery should be there at one's elbow.

(4) A week ago—("A little more cheese, waiter")—a week ago I grieved for the dying summer. I wondered how I could possibly bear the waiting—the eight long months till May. In vain to comfort myself with the thought that I could get through more work in the winter undistracted by thoughts of cricket grounds and country houses. In vain, equally, to tell myself that I could stay in bed later in the mornings. Even the thought of after-breakfast pipes in front of the fire left me cold. But now, suddenly, I am reconciled to autumn. I see quite clearly that all good things must come to an end. The summer has been splendid, but it has lasted long enough. This morning I welcomed the chill in the air; this morning I viewed the falling leaves with cheerfulness; and this morning I said to myself, "Why, of course, I'll have celery for lunch." ("More bread, waiter.")

(5) "Season of mists and mellow fruitfulness," said Keats, not actually picking out celery in so many words, but plainly including it in the general blessings of the autumn. Yet what an opportunity he missed by not concentrating on that precious root. Apples, grapes, nuts, and vegetable marrows he mentions specially—and how poor a selection! For apples and grapes are not typical of any month, so ubiquitous are they, vegetable marrows are vegetables *pour rire* and have no place in any serious consideration of the seasons, while as for nuts, have we not a national song which asserts distinctly, "Here we go gathering nuts in May"? Season of mists and mellow celery, then let it be. A pat of butter underneath the bough, a wedge of cheese, a loaf of bread and—Thou.

(6) How delicate are the tender shoots unfolded layer by layer. Of what a whiteness is the last baby one of all, of what a sweetness his flavor. It is well that this should be the last rite of the meal—*finis coronat opus*—so that we may go straight on to the business of the pipe. Celery demands a pipe rather than a cigar, and it can be eaten better in an inn or a London tavern than in the home. Yes, and it should be eaten alone, for it is the only food which one really wants to hear oneself eat. Besides, in company one may have to consider the wants of others. Celery is not a thing to share with any man. Alone in your country inn you may call for the celery; but if you are wise you will see that no other traveler wanders into the room, Take warning from one who

has learnt a lesson. One day I lunched alone at an inn, finishing with cheese and celery. Another traveler came in and lunched too. We did not speak—I was busy with my celery. From the other end of the table he reached across for the cheese. That was all right! it was the public cheese. But he also reached across for the celery—my private celery for which I owed. Foolishly—you know how one does—I had left the sweetest and crispest shoots till the last, tantalizing myself pleasantly with the thought of them. Horror! to see them snatched from me by a stranger. He realized later what he had done and apologized, but of what good is an apology in such circumstances? Yet at least the tragedy was not without its value. Now one remembers to lock the door.

(From the essay collection *Not That It Matters* by A. A. Milne, E.P. Dutton & Company, 1920)

What can be inferred about the essay from the chart?

    A. The author is actually writing about kale, not celery.

    B. The author lives in a different seasonal zone than this chart indicates.

    C. The author has confused October with July.

    D. The author is eating old celery.

The answer to this question is (B). The information presented in these two items is conflicting, rather than supporting; however, you should never make the assumption that either of them is incorrect. Indeed, the author is probably fully aware of the difference between celery and kale (A), especially since he has described celery in such depth. You can make the same assumption that (C) is incorrect because the season he is describing is very clearly autumnal, rather than a summer month, "July," which he makes reference to in his essay as a summer month. You can also rule out (D) when you read the clues about the freshness of the celery. However, you can choose (B) because neither the chart nor the essay state explicitly which seasonal area they are referencing. The author makes note of a national song, but does not clarify this nation. It is possible the author lives in Northern Ireland, and the chart is designed for Southwestern America.

As you approach questions such as these, make sure you consider all possibilities, and choose an answer that does not directly contradict the information provided in your examples, even if those examples contradict each other.

This standard also asks you to discuss how visual information may clarify or extend information presented in a text. Let's look at a question that would also address this part of the standard, using the same chart and essay.

How does the information in the chart support the following claim?

For apples and grapes are not typical of any month, so ubiquitous are they, vegetable marrows are vegetables *pour rire* and have no place in any serious consideration of the seasons, while as for nuts, have we not a national song which asserts distinctly, 'Here we go gathering nuts in May.'

A. Neither apples nor grapes are mentioned in the chart. This is likely because they have no specific growing season, which is stated in the sentence.

B. Apples and grapes likely do not grow in the area the chart reflects.

C. Nuts are not mentioned in the chart, which indicates that the author is incorrect in his assumption that they are harvested in May.

D. The vegetables *pour rire* are all the ones listed in the chart, which supports the idea that apples and grapes grow year round.

The correct answer is (A). Because the chart is a seasonal growth graph, it can be concluded that apples and grapes are excluded because, according to the passage, have no particular growing season. Choice (B) is an erroneous statement that would contradict, not support, the claim. Similarly, choice (C) negates the argument the author tries to make. Finally, unless you know for sure that all vegetables are "pour rire" (which means "to laugh"), you should not select choice (D). In this instance, though the quote itself makes sense, the answer selection does not.

Compare two passages that present related ideas or themes in different genres or formats (e.g., a feature article and an online FAQ or fact sheet) in order to evaluate differences in scope, purpose, emphasis, intended audience, or overall impact when comparing.

This skill requires you to evaluate how **different formats relaying similar information** may be used for varying reasons. Within this idea, you have to be able to identify the breadth of the topic (scope), the reason for the information (purpose), what is being highlighted (emphasis), to whom the information is addressed (audience), and effect (impact). This is simply an extension of the skills you have already mastered.

Let's look at a question that will test this skill.

EXAMPLE

Read the following excerpt from the essay, "My Garden" by Gail Hamilton, and the article, "Global Garden Report 2010: Survey Reveals Trends in U.S. Gardening." Analyze both the essay and the article to determine what the future may hold for the gardener. Use relevant and specific references to each text to support your response.

"My Garden"

(1) PARSNIPS.—They ran the race with an indescribable vehemence that fairly threw the beets into the shade. They trod so delicately at first that I was quite unprepared for such enthusiasm. Lacking the red veining, I could not distinguish them from the weeds with any certainty, and was

forced to let both grow together till the harvest. So both grew together, a perfect jungle. But the parsnips got ahead, and rushed up gloriously, magnificently, bacchanalianly,—as the winds come when forests are rended,—as the waves come when navies are stranded. I am, indeed, troubled with a suspicion that their vitality has all run to leaves, and that, when I go down into the depths of the earth for the parsnips, I shall find only bread of emptiness. It is a pleasing reflection that parsnips cannot be eaten till the second year. I am told that they must lie in the ground during the winter. Consequently it cannot be decided whether there are any or not till next spring. I shall in the mean time assume and assert, without hesitation or qualification, that there are as many tubers below the surface as there are leaves above it. I shall thereby enjoy a pleasant conscious-ness, and the respect of all, for the winter; and if disappointment awaits me in the spring, time will have blunted its keenness for me, and other people will have forgotten the whole subject. You may be sure I shall not remind them of it.

(2) CUCUMBERS.—The cucumbers came up so far, and stuck. It must have been innate depravity, for there was no shadow of reason why they should not keep on as they began. They did not. They stopped growing in the prime of life. Only three cucumbers developed, and they hid under the vines so that I did not see them till they were become ripe, yellow, soft, and worthless. They are an unwholesome fruit at best, and I bore their loss with great fortitude.

(3) TOMATOES.—Both dead. I had been instructed to protect them from the frost by night and from the sun by day. I intended to do so ultimately, but I did not suppose there was any emergency. A frost came the first night and killed them, and a hot sun the next day burned up all there was left. When they were both thoroughly dead, I took great pains to cover them every night and noon. No symptoms of revival appearing to reward my efforts, I left them to shift for themselves. I did not think there was any need of their dying in the first place; and if they would be so absurd as to die without provocation, I did not see the necessity of going into a decline about it. Besides, I never did value plants or animals that have to be nursed, and petted, and coaxed to live. If things want to die, I think they'd better die. Provoked by my indifference, one of the tomatoes flared up, and took a new start,—put forth leaves, shot out vines, and covered himself with fruit and glory. The chickens picked out the heart of all the tomatoes as soon as they ripened, which was of no consequence, however, as they had wasted so much time in the beginning that the autumn frosts came upon them unawares, and there wouldn't have been fruit enough ripe to be of any account, if no chicken had ever broken a shell.

(From the *Atlantic Monthly*, Vol. IX, 1862)

"Global Garden Report 2010: Survey Reveals Trends in U.S. Gardening"

(1) A "punk-rock" gardening revolution is occurring in the U.S., as found in Husqvarna and Gardena's annual Global Gardening Report 2010.

(2) Amateur gardeners reign supreme on the Internet, and the expert gardeners' expertise is being challenged through the blogosphere. Bloggers are less apt to follow the gardening experts and pave their own way, perhaps a result of a lingering "damn-the-man" mentality due to the eco-nomic slide and rise in unemployment in the U.S. Many amateurs are even sharing their foliage failures via blogs to show and educate other gardeners. With social networking continuing to rise, Americans throughout the blogosphere are showing that it takes a village to raise a rosebush.

(3) Urban farming is also prevalent in the U.S. A push for sustainability and green living has growers from Oregon to New York creating their own version of Eden in any small space available. This includes indoor growing of herbs and plants used in kitchens for cooking purposes. With a focus on fresh, local ingredients and self-reliance, urbanites are now more apt to pluck a leaf of basil from a pot in their kitchen than sprinkle dried-up plant crumbs on Wednesday night's chicken parmesan.

(4) Jay Dahlin, an urban gardener in Chicago, Ill., said that gardening, for him, is an obsession and addiction, noting that he thinks about it constantly from March to October. While growing mostly native plants in his garden, Dahlin says he likes to think that he is re-establishing a very small part of the lost prairie ecosystem.

(5) With spring right around the corner, weathered wintered minds around the U.S. are turning towards all things green. Husqvarna and Gardena, manufacturers of high-quality gardening equipment, identified trends in thirteen different countries after analyzing nearly 1.4 million blog posts worldwide. As experts in the gardening industry, they offer guidance on multiple types of agriculture from farm acres to flowerbeds. For more information on these companies and gardening trends, you can visit *www.gardena.com* and *www.husqvarna.com*.

(NewsUSA, Sept. 2010)

As you consider these passages, your objective is essentially to compare and contrast the two works to identify their differences. Since you have already mastered perspective, tone, style, structure, purpose, and impact in the previous skills, now all you have to do is apply those skills to two works at once and see how they differ, and what the different effects are on the intended audience.

Here's how the GED® test would pose a question about these excerpts.

What impact does the intended audience have on the works' construction?

A. Text A is a how-to guide on vegetable growing, whereas Text B seeks to persuade its audience to grow a backyard garden.

B. Text A uses more fictional elements (such as metaphor and visual imagery) in order to appeal to its readers, whereas Text B uses more nonfictional elements (such as listing and citation) in order to warn against adverse effects of growing your own food.

C. Text A is a persuasive argument which informs readers which vegetables ought to be grown, whereas Text B is an informative, instructive analysis which seeks to teach readers how to create their own gardens.

D. Text A is more of a personal reflection, and therefore has a diary-type construction. Text B is an article that seeks to inform and perhaps motivate its audience. This is, perhaps, why it offers further options for study.

The correct answer is (D). The audience of Text A seems to be the author herself, and she is taking notes regarding her successes and failures as a gardener. Text B is designed to educate its readers about current trends, and providing the websites for further study does, indeed, imply an appeal for readers to follow suit. Answer choice (A) is incorrect because even though Text B might persuade, the author of Text A does not provide any sort of instruction. Rather, Text A provides reflections of each attempt at growing vegetables. Although choice (B) makes correct observations about the techniques employed by both authors, it confuses the purpose of Text B, which encourages, rather than warns, growing food. Finally, choice (C) is incorrect because Text A provides very little persuasion, beyond personal assertion, and the "instructive analysis" in Text B is only suggested further reading. It is not provided by the text presented.

As you answer questions such as this, be sure to read carefully and think logically.

Compare two passages that present related ideas or themes in different genres or formats in order to synthesize details, draw conclusions, or apply information to new situations.

This skill builds on what you just mastered, except you now take the information presented in the texts to a new level. In order to answer questions such as these, you will have to **apply the information to a new idea**.

EXAMPLE

Review the graph, "Percentage of Women Employed in Professional Service Occupations 1870–1920," and the excerpt from "The Girls Who Make Boxes" by Nellie Bly.

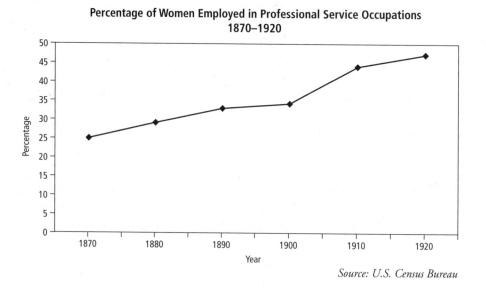

Source: U.S. Census Bureau

"The Girls Who Make Boxes"

(1) Very early the other morning I started out, not with the pleasure-seekers, but with those who toil the day long that they may live. Everybody was rushing—girls of all ages and appearances and hurrying men—and I went along, as one of the throng. I had often wondered at the tales of poor pay and cruel treatment that working girls tell. There was one way of getting at the truth, and I determined to try it. It was becoming myself a paper box factory girl. Accordingly, I started out in search of work without experience, reference, or aught to aid me.

(2) It was a tiresome search, to say the least. Had my living depended on it, it would have been discouraging, almost maddening. I went to a great number of factories in and around Bleecker and Grand streets and Sixth Avenue, where the workers number up into the hundreds. "Do you know how to do the work?" was the question asked by every one. When I replied that I did not, they gave me no further attention.

(3) "I am willing to work for nothing until I learn," I urged.

(4) "Work for nothing! Why, if you paid us for coming we wouldn't have you in our way," said one.

(5) "We don't run an establishment to teach women trades," said another, in answer to my plea for work.

(6) "Well, as they are not born with the knowledge, how do they ever learn?" I asked.

(7) "The girls always have some friend who wants to learn. If she wishes to lose time and money by teaching her, we don't object, for we get the work the beginner does for nothing."

(8) By no persuasion could I obtain an entree into the larger factories, so I concluded at last to try a smaller one at No. 196 Elm Street. Quite unlike the unkind, brusque men I had met at other factories, the man here was very polite. He said: "If you have never done the work, I don't think you will like it. It is dirty work and a girl has to spend years at it before she can make much money. Our beginners are girls about sixteen years old, and they do not get paid for two weeks after they come here."

(9) "What can they make afterward?"

(10) "We sometimes start them at week work—$1.50 a week. When they become competent they go on piecework—that is, they are paid by the hundred."

(11) "How much do they earn then?"

(12) "A good worker will earn from $5 to $9 a week."

(13) "Have you many girls here?"

(14) "We have about sixty in the building and a number who take work home. I have only been in this business for a few months, but if you think you would like to try it, I shall speak to my partner. He has had some of his girls for eleven years. Sit down until I find him."

(15) He left the office, and I soon heard him talking outside about me, and rather urging that I be given a chance. He soon returned, and with him a small man who spoke with a German accent. He stood by me without speaking, so I repeated by request. "Well, give your name to the gentleman at the desk, and come down on Monday morning, and we will see what we can do for you."

(From *Around the World in Seventy-Two Days and Other Writings* by Nellie Bly, The Pictorial Weeklies Company, 1890)

What can you infer from these two pieces of information?

A. It was very difficult for women to get work in the 19th century because they had to deal with sexist attitudes from men.

B. Women were not recorded as being part of the job force in the 19th century because they were working for free.

C. The reason the percentage of women workers was low in the 19th century was because it was difficult for women to receive training.

D. Women were not educated in the 19th century, but their tenacity to learn a skill in the workforce helped to raise the percentage of female workers.

The correct answer to this question is (C). Several of these answers are misleading, but you can come to this conclusion by studying the information presented in both pieces. Bly tells us that women had a hard time finding work if they were untrained, and that it was very difficult for a woman to receive this type of training. The graph shows us that the percentage was low, but rising during this time period. You can rule out (A) because Bly states that the last factory manager was quite kind to her. (B) is an interesting choice, but there is no definitive evidence to show that the unpaid workers were not documented as part of the percentage. (D) is also an attractive choice, but you have to be careful to pay attention to the exact wording of the response. The answer says women were not "educated," but the Bly excerpt discusses job training, not education, which indicates formal education such as a university or trade school. (C) is the correct answer because it is the only choice that properly synthesizes the information in both pieces of information.

As you approach questions such as this on the GED® test, be sure to employ your close reading skills.

Applying Rules of Standard English: Grammar and Usage

ESSENTIAL SKILL: The Ability to Write Clearly

What does it take to write clearly? For starters, you must be able to use standard English grammar, but perhaps more importantly, you must be able to edit written works to prove you are proficient in your knowledge of standard English. GED Testing Service® uses two assessment targets, or standards, for the language component of the RLA test. Here in Chapter 8, we'll cover the first standard, along with the skills related to it. Then, in Chapter 9, we'll look at the second standard as well as its related skills. Let's look at the ingredients needed for clear writing.

We'll start by considering the first standard for the RLA test's language component:

Demonstrate command of the conventions of standard English grammar and usage when writing or speaking.

This standard focuses on your editing skills. You will be presented with segments of text in order to prove that you know how to use correct vocabulary, and that you are generally able to employ the rules governing the English language. Most of the time this should not be too difficult for you, especially if you have a review of these rules! This guide will help you review most of the common grammatical rules in English, and it will focus specifically on the skills the GED® test will assess.

The GED® test will assess some or all of these skills with questions relating to this standard:

- Edit to correct errors involving frequently confused words and homonyms, including contractions (passed, past; two, too, to; there, their, they're; knew, new; it's, its).

- Edit to correct errors in straightforward subject-verb agreement.

- Edit to correct errors in subject-verb or pronoun antecedent agreement in more complicated situations (e.g., with compound subjects, interceding phrases, or collective nouns).

- Edit to correct errors in pronoun usage, including pronoun-antecedent agreement, unclear pronoun references, and pronoun case.

- Edit to eliminate non-standard or informal usage (e.g., correctly use "try to win the game" instead of "try and win the game").

- Edit to eliminate dangling or misplaced modifiers or illogical word order (e.g., correctly use "to meet almost all requirements" instead of "to almost meet all requirements").

- Edit to ensure parallelism and proper subordination and coordination.

- Edit to eliminate wordiness or awkward sentence construction.

- Edit to ensure effective use of transitional words, conjunctive adverbs, and other words and phrases that support logic and clarity.

Let's take a look at each skill individually.

Edit to correct errors involving frequently confused words and homonyms, including contractions.

The best way to hone this skill is to familiarize yourself with frequently confused words. If you do not already know these words, spend time acquainting yourself with them, as it may be the only way you will be able to identify and use them correctly. This section of the guide will give you a few key pointers for dealing with contractions by discussing the rules, but when it comes to regular homonyms, you will just have to memorize them.

Let's begin with a list of common homonyms and their definitions. **A homonym is one of two or more words that have the same pronunciation, but different spellings and meanings.** Although there are hundreds of homonyms in the English language, we will focus just on the ones you are most likely to see on the GED® test.

Common Homonyms		
✶ affect — change effect — result or consequence	bite — nibble byte — computer data	chord — musical tone cord — rope
air — atmosphere err — to make a mistake	blew — past tense of "blow" blue — color	cite — quote site — location sight — view
aisle — walkway I'll — I will isle — island	boar — pig bore — to cause boredom or disinterest bore — to drill	close — opposite of open clothes — clothing
allowed — permitted aloud — out loud	borough — area or district burrow — dig through burro — small donkey	✶ complement — to complete or make better compliment — praise
ant — a type of insect aunt — relative	bough — branch bow — bend or curtsy	council — committee counsel — guidance
ate — past tense of eat eight — number after seven	brake — stop pedal break — smash	creak — squeak creek — stream of water
bare — uncovered bear — animal	bread — bakery food bred — form of "breed"	crews — gangs cruise — ride
berry — fruit from a bush bury — to put underground	broach — mention brooch — pin	dear — darling deer — woodland animal
base — bottom bass — deep or low	brows — eyebrows browse — look around	dew — morning mist do — operate due — payable
be — to exist bee — buzzing insect	buy — purchase by — beside	die — cease to exist dye — color
beach — sandy shore beech — type of tree	cell — compartment sell — vend	doe — female deer dough — uncooked pastry or bread
beat — to pound beet — type of edible plant	cent — penny coin sent — past tense of send	dual — double duel — battle
berth — tie up birth — to be born	cereal — breakfast food serial — sequential	ewe — female sheep you — second-person personal pronoun

(continued)

Common Homonyms		
eye — sight organ I — me	hair — head covering hare — rabbit-like animal	know — have knowledge no — opposite of yes
fair — equal fare — price	hall — passageway haul — tow	lead — metal led — past tense of "lead"
fairy — elflike creature with wings ferry — boat	halve — cut in two parts have — possess	lessen — make smaller lesson — class
☞ faze — impact phase — stage	hay — animal food hey — interjection to get attention	loan — lend lone — solitary
feat — achievement feet — plural of foot	☞ heal — mend heel — back of foot	made — past tense of "make" maid — servant
fir — type of tree fur — animal hair	hi — hello high — up far	mail — postage male — opposite of female
flea — small biting insect flee — run	hoarse — croaky horse — riding animal	marry — to wed merry — very happy
flew — past tense of fly flu — illness	hole — opening whole — entire	meat — animal protein meet — encounter
flour — powdery, ground up grain flower — blooming plant	holey — full of holes holy — divine wholly — entirely	oar — boat paddle or — otherwise ore — mineral
for — on behalf of fore — front four — one more than three	hour — sixty minutes our — belonging to us	oh — expression of surprise or awe owe — obligated
forth — onward fourth — number four	knead — massage need — desire	one — single won — did win
knew — past tense of know new — not old	knight — feudal horseman night — evening	overdo — do too much overdue — past due date
groan — moan grown — form of grow	knot — tied rope not — negative	pail — bucket pale — not bright

(continued)

Common Homonyms

pain — hurt pane — window glass	ring — encircle wring — squeeze	toe — foot appendage tow — pull along
past — previous passed — went in front of	role — function roll — rotate	vary — differ very — much
peace — calm piece — segment	sail — move by wind power sale — bargain price	wail — howl whale — huge marine mammal
peak — highest point peek — glance	scene — landscape seen — viewed	waist — area below ribs waste — squander
plain — ordinary plane — flight machine plane — flat surface	sea — ocean segment see — observe with eyes	wait — to pause until something happens weight — measurable load
pole — post poll — survey	seam — joining edge seem — appear	war — battle wore — did wear
poor — opposite of rich pour — make flow	sew — connect with thread so — as a result sow — plant	warn — caution worn — used
pray — implore God prey — quarry	soar — ascend sore — hurt place	way — path weigh — measure mass
principal — most important principle — belief	sole — single soul — essence	we — us wee — tiny
rain — water from sky rein — bridle	some — a few sum — amount	weak — not strong week — period of seven days
rap — tap wrap — drape around	steal — swipe steel — alloy	weather — climate whether — if
real — factual reel — roll	tail — animal's appendage tale — story	which — that witch — sorcerer
right — correct; opposite of left (direction) write — scribble	to — toward too — also two — number after one	

Get to know that list!

Because some possessives and contractions sound alike (see chart below for examples), you have to pay close attention to the meaning you wish to convey.

The possessive/contraction pair "its" and "it's" are especially confusing because they not only sound alike but also contain the same letters. While adding *'s* usually forms the possessive form of a word, it's the reverse with the word "it." "Its" is the possessive form of "it," whereas "it's" is the contraction of "it is."

Fortunately, there's a simple way out of the confusion over "its" versus "it's." To determine which one you should use, just substitute "it is" into your phrasing. If "it is" works, use the contraction "it's." If not, use the possessive "its." This sentence uses both correctly: "<u>It's</u> (*contraction*) an undersea creature with eight sucker-covered arms attached to <u>its</u> (*possessive pronoun*) head."

Confusing Soundalikes	
Possessive Pronoun	**Contraction**
its	it's
their	they're
whose	who's
your	you're

Let's take a look at a sample question that might test this particular skill.

EXAMPLE

Read this letter of application for an intern position at a local zoo. As you read, consider each homonym and choose the correct word in context.

Dear Sir,

I am writing to express my interest in **you're** (A) program. I understand that you see thousands of applicants every day, and that my application needs to be outstanding in order to be considered.

The sciences, especially biology, have always been my favorite subjects in school. It is my dream in life to become a veterinarian, and I know that the internship in **your** (B) program will help me to achieve this goal. Feeding animals and caring for them while I am out of school for the summer will definitely help me **way** (C) the decision I have facing me about my college choices next year—should I go into large or small animal sciences? **Their** (D) are many factors in my future, and I believe that employing me as an intern at your zoo will help me determine my path. You see, **there** (E) are a lot of options for a teenager in terms of a summer job, and I know that even though this is unpaid, it is the program for me. I am very reliable and love animals very much. My scores in all my subjects have been **hi** (F), and I have not missed a day of school in three years. You can count on me!

Please see my attached résumé, and feel free to check my references.

Sincerely,

John Carmichael

Use the box below to show your answers.

In this instance, you would make the following adjustments: change (A) to "your" (possessive pronoun), (B) stays as is, (C) changes to "weigh" (consider), (D) to "there" (adverb), (E) stays as is, and (F) should change to "high" (measurement).

You can improve your ability to edit and correct mistakes such as these by memorizing these homonyms, reading for context, and simply reading as much as possible for pleasure. The more you are exposed to correct writing, the more you will be able to correct mistakes when you see them!

Next, we'll consider two related assessment targets at once.

Edit to correct errors in straightforward subject-verb agreement.

Edit to correct errors in subject-verb or pronoun antecedent agreement in more complicated situations (e.g., with compound subjects, interceding phrases, or collective nouns).

Before you can edit and correct errors in this area, you have to know the basic principle behind subject-verb agreement. Once you understand it, correcting errors dealing with it will be very simple!

The main idea is: **verbs vary based on the subject**. Singular subjects need to have singular verbs. Likewise, plural subjects need to have plural verbs. For example, "My mother **is** an Occupational Therapist." "My aunts **are** nurses." "Mother" is singular and receives a singular verb, while "aunts" is plural and receives a plural verb.

Most of the time you will be able to correct mistakes dealing with subject-verb agreement simply by reading the sentence aloud. If it sounds correct, it *usually* is. However, there are a few rules and exceptions that are not as typical and might throw you off.

- The indefinite pronouns *anyone, everyone, someone, no one, nobody* are always singular and, therefore, require singular verbs. For example, "Someone has left his phone on the desk." This may not sound correct to you because it is often misused in spoken communication. You just have to remember that these words are always singular. To help you remember this, notice that, with the exception of "nobody," each word has the word "one" embedded in it. You can also remember that "body" refers to just one.

- Certain indefinite pronouns, such as *all* or *some,* are singular or plural depending on what they are referencing. Ask yourself: Is this thing countable? For example, "Some of my juice **is** missing." "Some of the dogs **are** outside." Quantitative items are plural, but uncountable items are singular.

- When you encounter phrases such as *together with, as well as,* and *along with,* keep in mind that these are different from the word "and." These phrases modify the earlier word, but do not compound it, as "and" would do. For example, the sentence "The teacher, together with her students, is going to the capitol building" is the equivalent in meaning to: "The teacher and her students are going to the capitol building."

- The pronouns *neither* and *either* are singular and require singular verbs. This may confuse you because by nature they reference two things (a choice), but as you can see in the examples, "Neither of the students **is** going to pass this class," and "Either of these kittens **is** fine to take home to mother," the words "neither" and "either" discuss one of each at a time—not one of these students, and one of these kittens.

- The conjunction *or* does not compound as the word *and* does. When *nor* or *or* is used, the **subject closer to the verb** determines the number of the verb. For example, "Either the dog or the cats are going to win the battle of dominance in this house." "Neither the cats nor the dog is going to win the battle of dominance in this house; I will."

- The words *there* and *here* are never subjects. You must abide by the actual subject to determine if the verb needs to be singular or plural. For example, a plural subject using the word "there" might appear in a sentence like this: "There are 15 cats running around this room!" or, in the singular form, "There is one cat around here somewhere, and I must find him." For "here," you may see something like, "Here are the three cats I was hoping to find!" or, "Here is the cat I have been dreaming of my whole life!" In these cases (expletive constructions), the subject follows the verb, but still determines the singularity or plurality of the verb.

- Verbs in the present tense for third-person, singular subjects (*he, she, it,* and anything those words can stand for, such as cat, child, ladder, etc.) have *s*-endings. Other verbs do not add *s*-endings. "He loves. She loves. They love."

- Sometimes modifiers will come between a subject and its verb, but these modifiers must not confuse the agreement between the subject and its verb. "The *cat* I chose, who has a star over his left eye and 14 brothers and sisters, *is* the most adorable thing I've ever seen!"

- There are occasions when nouns may take unusual forms and appear to be plural when they are really singular, and vice versa. Words like "scissors," "pants," and "eyeglasses" are considered plural and receive plural verbs, unless those words are preceded by a modifier such as "pair of," in which case the word "pair" becomes the singular subject. For example, "The glasses *were* wire-framed." "The pair of glasses *was* atop the librarian's head."

These are the general rules surrounding subject-verb agreement. Let's take a look at the type of question you may see on the GED® test that would assess this skill.

EXAMPLE

Read the following passage from a rough draft of a student's paper on consumerism and waste. Correct the verbs that are not in agreement with their subjects. Show your work in the box below.

> The waste produced by the materials we consume **have** (A) to be cut down! As a culture, we **spend** (B) far too much money **buying** (C) things we do not need, and as a result our landfills **are** (D) filled with excessive trash that could be recycled or disposed of without taking up so much space. The mayor and his council **is** (E) beside themselves with the ramifications of this problem. We simply do not **know** (F) what to do with all of our "stuff." Big box companies such as Wal-Mart, the harbinger of all things evil, **is** (G) the culprit in this travesty. When you go to the store to buy a television, it **have been** (H) wrapped in a cardboard box and tons of Styrofoam. Though a television is delicate, there are (I) better ways to transport it without using non-biodegradable packing material. Better yet, here **are** (J) a solution. Go outside to play instead of watching television!

You should have selected (A), (E), (G), (H) and (J) to correct. In these instances, (A) would change to "has" because "waste" is singular; (E) should be changed to "are" because the word "and" creates a compound or plural subject; (G) should change to "are" because "companies" is plural; (H) should read "has been" because "television" is singular, and (J) should be changed to "is" because the subject of the sentence is "solution," which is singular.

Edit to correct errors in pronoun usage, including pronoun–antecedent agreement, unclear pronoun references, and pronoun case.

Before we begin addressing this particular skill, it is important that you understand the definitions of "pronoun" and "antecedent." A **pronoun** is simply a word that **replaces another word**. The **antecedent is the word** the pronoun **replaces**—typically a word that comes earlier in the text or sentence. Let's begin with a list of pronouns.

Pronouns		
All	Many	That
Another	Me	Their
Any	Mine	Theirs
Anybody	More	Them
Anyone	Most	Themselves
Anything	Much	These
Both	My	They
Each	Myself	This
Each other	Neither	Those
Either	No one	Us
Everybody	Nobody	We
Everyone	None	What
Everything	Nothing	Whatever
Few	One	Which
He	One another	Whichever
Her	Other	Who

(continued)

Pronouns		
Hers	Others	Whoever
Herself	Our	Whom
Him	Ours	Whomever
Himself	Ourselves	Whose
His	Several	You
I	She	Your
It	Some	Yours
Its	Somebody	Yourself
Itself	Someone	Yourselves
Little	Something	

Although this may seem like an exhaustive list, the list for antecedents would practically be never-ending. Consider, for example, how many words you could replace with the word "it"!

Now that you know what pronouns do, let's take a look at a pronoun in its simplest form. "When Brian came to dinner, he told me his mother was angry." This sentence employs two different pronouns, *he* and *his* to replace the antecedent, "Brian." If you did not use pronouns in this example, your sentence would read, "When Brian came to dinner, Brian told me Brian's mother was angry." Pronouns help us avoid overly wordy writing and speaking. It should not be too difficult for you to identify and edit for clarity, but there are several instances when pronoun-antecedent agreement can be tricky. There are a few rules you need to follow.

The first rule is that a pronoun **must agree in number** (that is, it must be singular or plural) with the word to which it refers. This is a very common mistake in grammar! To complicate matters, when dealing with people, gender is another factor to consider. Let's look at a sentence that is confusing for many people. "A student makes his own destiny." Believe it or not, this is the correct way to write this sentence. Many people would mistakenly write, "A student makes their own destiny," because the author rightly wants to invoke gender-neutral language. This can be tricky—you neither want to sound gimmicky nor do you want to undermine rules of grammar. The rub of it is this: "student" is always singular (one student), and "their" is plural, so the sentence written using the plural pronoun is incorrect. You could also write the sentence this way: "A student makes his or her own destiny." This avoids offending whichever gender you leave out, but it may also result in needlessly stilted phrasing. In this instance, you have another option; you could solve the problem by **pluralizing the subject** and write the sentence: "Students make their own destiny." The lesson here is always check the number of the subject. This is very similar to the work we just did in the previous section dealing with subject-verb agreement.

As we learned earlier, the indefinite pronouns "anyone," "anybody," "everyone," everybody," "someone," "somebody," "no one," and "nobody" are always singular. This is also true of "either" and "neither," which are always singular even though they seem to be referring to two things. For example, "Neither of these cameras is the one I want."

Another general rule about pronouns (especially "he," "her," "she," "him," "me," and "I") is that when they are compounded ("Fred and I," "Jennifer and me," "George and her," etc…) you should take the other item out of the sentence to determine which pronoun you need to use. For example, "Finding a good place to eat dinner is important to George and _____." Which pronoun would you use, "I" or "me"? Take out "George" and write that sentence again. "Finding a good place to eat dinner is important to ___." The answer is "me." To the same end, try the fill-in this way: "George and ___ like to find good restaurants." The answer is "I."

The pronoun "who" (and its forms) is often a source of frustration for many students. When do you select "who," "whose," "whom," "whoever," and "whomever"? In all cases, the number of the pronoun (singular or plural) and its verbs is determined by the antecedent. "Who" can replace a singular person or a group of people. The easiest way to decide which form of "who" to use is to compare it to the pronoun forms of "he," because they are similar. For example:

- When you would use "he," use "who."

- When you would use "his," use "whose."

- When you would use "him," use "whom."

- When you would use "they," use "who."

- When you would use "their," use "whose."

- When you would use "them," use "whom."

If you cannot remember this, rewrite the sentence to determine whether you would choose "he," "him" or "his." For example, "Who should pass this class?" might be rewritten as "Should he pass this class?" Similarly, "To whom does this bag belong?" might be reworked as "Does this bag belong to him?" Also, "Whose bag was left on the floor?" might be rewritten like this: "Is his bag on the floor?"

As you edit for pronouns, you may come across some writing that has unclear pronoun use. In these cases it will be your job to correctly write the sentence to clear up these errors. For example, "John and Ben went up to the cabin to see his grandfather. He said he was very stodgy." These sentences use the word "he" too much! Whom are we talking about? John? Ben?

The grandfather? The grandfather of which boy? To edit this sentence, you might have to say something like, "John and Ben went up to the cabin to see their grandfather. John said, 'He was very stodgy.'" It could also read, "John and Ben went up to the cabin to see Ben's grandfather, who was very stodgy." You will have a lot of options to take the sentence in the direction you choose. Generally, the interpretation you choose does not matter; it is only important that it makes sense and is clear about whom you are talking!

Personal pronouns come in three cases: **subjective**, **objective**, and **possessive**. Subjective pronouns are words such as: "I," "we," "you," "they," "he," "she," "it," and "who." Objective pronouns are words such as: "me," "you," "us," "them," "him," "her," "it," and "whom." Possessive pronouns are words such as: "my," "mine," "your," "yours," "his," "hers," "their," "theirs," "ours," and "whose." You can determine which case to use when you determine the pronoun's function in the sentence.

- Use the subjective case when the pronoun is the subject of a sentence: "I am the president!", or if it completes the subject: "The winner of the presidency is he."

- Use the objective case when the pronoun is the sentence's direct object: "Gatsby loves her."; the indirect object: "Gatsby asked her to fill the pool."; or the object of the preposition: "The decision was easy for her." *For* is the preposition.

- Use the possessive case pronouns with gerunds (a verb ending in *-ing* which serves as a noun). For example, "Their fighting upset Kristen."

Let's take a look at the type of question that would measure your ability to edit for pronoun-antecedent agreement.

Read the following letter and edit for correct pronoun usage.

Dear Sir or Madam,

I am writing to you because I have some complaints regarding **my** (A) neighbors' behavior. **They** (B) are constantly keeping me up late at night with **their** (C) wild parties, and I was not sure to **who** (D) I should direct my frustration. The gentleman, Rick Parkins, is the loudest person I have ever met. **His** (E) voice carries for miles. If you are looking for an emcee at a gathering of stampeding elephants, the person you want is **him** (F). Rick and his wife, Stephanie, have a two-year-old boy named Ethan. **He** (G) keeps me awake all night long, and **she** (H) is just as bad with her incessant shouting. Often **they** (I) fight over the television. **Their** (J) yelling is atrocious. Please help me by enforcing the noise ordinance. **Whomever** (K) fixes this is my hero!

You should edit (D), (F), (G), and (K). Remember when using *who* and *whom*, you should rewrite the sentence using the word *him*, so it would read, "I should direct my frustration to *him*." Therefore, you would change *who* to *whom*. You should correct (F) to *he* because it completes the subject of the clause, "he is the person you want." You should change (G) to either *Rick* or *Ethan* because it is not clear to which person the *he* refers. Finally, (K) should be adjusted to read *Whoever* because replacing *Whomever* with a *he* form gives us a sentence that reads "He fixes this." And that fixes our sentence!

Edit to eliminate non-standard or informal usage (e.g., correctly use "try to win the game" instead of "try and win the game").

This is perhaps the easiest and simultaneously most difficult skill you will meet on the GED® test. If you read often, you will be able to spot and correct informal usage immediately. If you are not exposed to a lot of examples of standard writing, however, you might have a difficult time determining what is standard and what is informal. The general rule is: **informal or non-standard language is used in spoken communication, while formal or standard language is used in written communication.** There are exceptions, of course, in both situations. For example, if you are giving a presentation to your boss, you need to speak in Standard English; however, if you are writing an email to your best friend about where you will meet her after school, your usage can be informal. Often, as you are editing for correct usage, you will be able to tell when the writing is informal if it is *unclear* or *misleading*. For example, "Try and win the game," is incorrect, unless you are talking about a game that only requires participation to win. "Try to win the game," is the correct way to write this, even though you will hear people say it the other way quite frequently!

As you are editing for informal language, remember that quotations in a text will often use dialect, slang, or informal construction, and this does *not* need to be edited! Direct quotations represent the exact words a person has said aloud (or written), and they should never be edited *unless* there is a typographical error in capitalization or punctuation. We will address this later in this guide.

Here is an example of two similar ideas expressed in formal and informal construction.

Formal: "When I considered all my options, I knew it was best to spend the additional forty dollars on the more reliable nanny than to gamble with my children's well-being on the inexperienced teenager."

Informal: "It was only forty bucks more to hire the good one, so I paid it instead of finding out later that the teenager ripped me off or left my kids alone while she talked to her boo."

Both ideas are quite possibly correct in the situation, but it should be obvious that the word choices of "bucks," "ripped off," and "boo" are far less formal than "additional," "gamble," and "inexperienced."

In Standard English, the expectation of correctness is higher. Some things are considered acceptable in spoken language, but completely incorrect in written form. For example, "I have made less mistakes" is informal, and "I have made fewer mistakes" is formal.

Can you identify which of the following is formal and informal?

"He likes it" versus "He's liking it."

"I feel real good" versus "I feel really good."

In formal construction, it is best to avoid contractions whenever possible. It is more formal to say "cannot" instead of "can't."

You can often identify informal language by a few of the techniques we often see in spoken English. For example, speakers use expressions to give themselves more time to think about what they are trying to communicate. "Well, if he had asked me he might have gotten a totally different answer, you know?" This is entirely correct, but it is not *formal*. To say this formally, one might say, "Had he asked me, I would have given him an entirely different response."

Additionally, speakers also often correct themselves as they work out their ideas. For example, "He's not right. I mean, he's not wrong, but his ideas are just not as good as they could be." Formally, one might say, "His ideas could be made more persuasive if he marshalled better evidence by sticking to the facts. Even so, he has laid the groundwork for what could be a worthwhile project."

Often in informal speech, speakers will also use qualifying expressions to indicate their thoughts are not entirely correct or complete. For example, "This whole Facebook thing is kind of getting boring." In formal expression one might say, "Mature social media sites like Facebook and Twitter risk becoming stodgy as more agile start-ups, with new ideas and less to lose, make inroads with younger audiences."

Let's take a look at the kind of question you might see on the GED® test that might test this skill.

Revise the following paragraph to eliminate informal usage.

> After the election, we had lots of arguments about who should've won. I wanted Obama to win because I think he's totally changed the system and given us hope for the way our country could be, you know? Without hate and prejudice. My girlfriend kept talking about how great Romney was, though. She'd say, "But Romney will fix all our economic problems. I mean, plus he was the governor of Massachusetts, after all, which is a real liberal state. They were the first to legalize gay marriage and it wasn't like he tried to change that!"

Your rewrite should look something like this:

> After the election, we had a great many arguments about who should have won the presidency. I was in favor of Obama's re-election because I believe he has initiated many programs that will benefit the United States in the long run. Additionally, Obama has changed the culture of our country to be more inclusive and give all our citizens the feeling that they could accomplish something, no matter how different they may be from each other. My girlfriend, however, was a great supporter of Romney. She would say, "But Romney will fix all our economic problems. I mean, plus he was the governor of Massachusetts, after all, which is a real liberal state. They were the first to legalize gay marriage and it wasn't like he tried to change that!"

As you write your response, be sure to clean up non-standard language by using more formal versions of what you're given. In the above version of the rewrite, the new paragraph eliminates the contractions "should've," "he's," and "she'd"; it also does away with a lot of the filler language such as "totally" and "you know?," which does nothing so much as distract (and delay) the reader. Notice, however, that informal language that is quoted must remain. Quotes cannot be changed because they convey literally what someone said or wrote. This rewrite specifies where the original is vague, but it does so without adding new information. It also eliminates the fragment. As you edit for errors in standard usage, try to avoid slang and informal statements you say in everyday conversation. Be clear, be thoughtful, and be appropriate.

Edit to eliminate dangling or misplaced modifiers or illogical word order (e.g., correctly use "to meet almost all requirements" instead of "to almost meet all requirements").

Let's start by defining a modifier. A modifier can be an adjective, adverb, phrase, or clause acting as an adjective or adverb. In every case, **the modifier adds information to another part of the sentence.** For example, in the sentence, "Nadine Gordimer, author of *The Pickup*, won the Nobel Prize for literature," the modifier is the phrase, "author of *The Pickup*." You know this because it gives you more information about the subject, Nadine Gordimer. With the modifying phrase, you know that she wrote the novel *The Pickup*. This serves as an adjective describing Nadine Gordimer.

As you are writing (or editing someone else's writing), you have options about where to place the modifier in a sentence. For example, the sentence, "We hiked up the hill tirelessly," can also be written: "We hiked tirelessly up the hill." Or, "Tirelessly we hiked up the hill." In all these cases, "tirelessly" is an adverb describing the verb, "hiked." As a general rule, you should put your modifier as close to the word it is modifying to avoid confusion from dangling or misplaced modifiers.

Here is an example of a misplaced modifier, "He was a very gifted teacher because after his lectures we could understand the complicated tenets of chemistry easily." Do we understand his lectures easily or chemistry easily? A revision that reads, "We could easily understand the tenets of chemistry" will help avoid this confusion.

You especially need to be careful of placing limiting modifiers where they belong, or you can skew the entire meaning of the sentence. Limiting modifiers are words "like," "nearly," "almost," "only," "just," etc. Consider this sentence, for example: "I nearly knocked over every can of soda on the table!" This sentence indicates that I came very close to knocking over every soda can (there could be fifty), but I did not actually knock any over. A different version of this sentence might read, "I knocked over nearly every can of soda on the table!" This sentence indicates that I knocked over almost all of the cans of soda. Which is it? Obviously, either could be correct, but it definitely matters where you put the modifier in the sentence. If the next sentence in the text read, "Everything was soaking wet and sticky from the cola," then you *know* the first sentence has a misplaced modifier.

This same standard should be applied to modifying phrases and clauses—put them as close to the item they are modifying as possible, otherwise you might have a very confusing sentence! This is what the GED® test standard means when it says, "logical word order."

Incorrect: Henry decided to poke the little girl with his finger in her eye.

Correct: Henry decided to poke the little girl in the eye with his finger.

Incorrect: After the wedding, Kat told me at the bachelorette party that she was finally going to be faithful.

Correct: Kat told me at the bachelorette party that she was finally going to be faithful after the wedding.

Incorrect: I heard you say that you are going to have a picnic while I was outside my window.

Correct: While I was outside my window, I heard you say that you are going to have a picnic.

A **dangling modifier** is often (though not always) at the beginning of a sentence. This modifier is often an adjective phrase that does not modify anything in the sentence, or an adjective that modifies the wrong word in a sentence. Consider these sentences:

Incorrect: Coming from the mine, it is natural to be covered in coal dust.

Correct: For a person coming from the mine, it is natural to be covered in coal dust.

In the first sentence, the modifier is referencing "it." What is it? The implied idea is "one" or a "person," but this is not explicitly stated, so the revision adjusts this problem of a random adjective phrase that does not provide further information about anything specifically in the sentence.

You could also write this sentence to read, "Coming from the mine, I am naturally covered in coal dust."

Let's take a look at a question you might see on the GED® test that will assess this skill.

Rewrite the following paragraph to correct the modifiers and word order.

> Raised in North Carolina, it is normal for me to be aggressively kind to strangers. I can nearly have a pleasant conversation with every single person I meet. In fact, I can almost predict the way I should interact with each person based on the way he carries himself when I get close. It is very rare that I misread a person's social cues.

Your revision may read,

> Raised in North Carolina, I am aggressively kind to strangers. I can have a pleasant conversation with nearly every single person I meet. In fact, I can predict the way I should interact with almost every person based on the way he carries himself when I get close. It is very rare that I misread a person's social cues.

If the last sentence were not there, the second to last sentence could remain the way it was, depending on your interpretation. However, because the last sentence clarifies the idea that the speaker can "predict" interactions with "almost" all of the people he meets, you know it should be rewritten in that way.

Edit to ensure parallelism and proper subordination and coordination.

This standard is dealing with **the way we join ideas in compound sentences.** First, let's discuss parallelism before we get into subordination and coordination. Parallelism means to use the same pattern of words to show that two or more ideas have the same level of importance in a sentence. This can happen with words, phrases, or clauses. (Parallel structure was used in that sentence!) The normal way to join parallel structures is to use the coordinating conjunctions, "and" or "or."

Here is an example of **parallelism** at the word level. "Jordan likes to cook, eat, bake, and sew."

At the phrase level: "Jordan likes to cook, to eat, to bake, and to sew."

At the clause level: "Jordan told her sisters that they should not call her during her baking time, that they should not bother her during her sewing, and that they should not disturb her while she was eating."

Do not mix these levels together!

Incorrect parallel structure would look like this: "Jordan likes cooking, eating, baking, and to sew."

Now let's take a look at **coordination**. Coordinating conjunctions are as follows: *for, and, nor, but, or, yet,* and *so.* This is an easily remembered acronym, "FANBOYS."

There are a few ways you can coordinate a sentence. First, let's look at the most traditional approach. You can conjoin two independent clauses to make a compound sentence by using a comma and a coordinating conjunction. For example, "I like peaches. Sylvia likes cherries." These two sentences can be compounded by rewriting, "I like peaches, but Sylvia likes cherries." You can easily identify when to use the comma and the conjunction by asking yourself: "Can these sentences work alone?" If the answer is yes, then the coordination is correct.

However, you can also coordinate with a coordinating conjunction without using the comma. For example, "I wanted more peaches. I did not want cherries." There are two ways you can rewrite this as one sentence. Let's try the way we just learned: "I wanted more peaches, but I did not want cherries." You could also write it this way: "I wanted more peaches but no cherries." The second option eliminates some of the wordiness. In the second instance, you should not use the comma. The comma is only needed to join two independent clauses, each of which must have a subject and a verb.

Now let's talk about **subordination**. The subordinating conjunctions are: "after," "although," "as," "as if," "because," "before," "even if," "even though," "if," "if only," "inasmuch," "just," "now since," "now that," "provided that," "rather than," "since," "supposing," "that," "though," "unless," "until," "when," "where," "whereas," "wherever," "whether," "whoever," "whomever," "which," and "while."

Subordinating conjunctions create complex sentences, which have an independent and a dependent clause. Subordinate clauses are also called dependent clauses. That should help you remember the difference between subordination and coordination. A subordinate clause means it depends on another part of the sentence to help it make sense.

For example, in the sentence, "I went to get more peaches after I threw out all the disgusting cherry pits," the subordinate clause is "after I threw out all the disgusting cherry pits." This idea cannot stand by itself, so you know it is dependent.

Usually the subordinate clause comes at the end of a sentence, but it is also correct to put it at the beginning of the sentence, as in, "After I threw out all the disgusting cherry pits, I went to get more peaches." Notice that when the subordinating clause comes at the beginning of the sentence, it is necessary to insert a comma before the independent clause.

Now that you understand parallel structure, subordination and coordination, let's take a look at a sample question you might see that will require you to use this skill on the GED® test.

Rewrite the following paragraph from a student's paper to ensure proper grammatical construction.

Benjamin Franklin became one of the greatest American leaders in the country, after establishing his business in Boston. Franklin is known for many things, including politics, writing, invention, and his playing of music. Franklin oversaw the implementation of a fire department. Franklin also oversaw the implementation of other civic organizations, like a university.

Your rewrite may look like this:

After establishing his business in Boston, Benjamin Franklin became one of the greatest American leaders in the country's history. Franklin is known for many things, including his involvement in politics, his love of writing, his many inventions, and his musical competence. Franklin oversaw the implementation of several civic organizations, such as a fire department and a university.

Once again, most of the work you will do with coordination, subordination, and parallel structure should fall into place when it seems to "sound" correct when read aloud. Usually that is true; just try to remember where to put the commas!

Edit to eliminate wordiness or awkward sentence construction.

Good writing is clear writing. Often, students interfere with the information they are trying to present by trying to sound more sophisticated than the situation requires. In doing so, they simply confuse the audience, and in that way they fail to communicate their ideas effectively. As you are editing for clarity on the GED® test, ask yourself: can I follow what is going on without too much effort? Is there a way to **say this more clearly?** We have already discussed some of the problems with awkward sentence construction, such as pronoun confusion and misplaced modifiers. So let's start with eliminating wordiness.

First off, you should begin by **omitting the filler phrases "it is," "there is," and "there are"** at the beginning of sentences; these often delay the sentence's subject and verb. For example, "It is difficult to stay in school," though a short sentence, is a bit stiff because it uses the passive voice. To eliminate this, rewrite the sentence to read, "Staying in school is difficult." The second sentence is concise but more engaging.

Next, **eliminate "this" from the beginning of a sentence** by combining it with the preceding sentence to make a compound or complex sentence. For example, "Kate has the best relationships with her students in the school. This is because she treats the kids like adults instead of children." To rewrite it without being wordy, the sentence would read, "Kate has the best relationships with her students because she treats the kids like adults instead of children."

Another thing you can do to eliminate wordiness is to **change "which" or "that" constructions to an "-ing" word**. For example, "The professional learning communities, which meet monthly, decide which standards should be emphasized in the classroom." To make this less wordy, you can rewrite the sentence, "The professional learning communities, meeting monthly, decide which standards should be emphasized in the classroom."

If you are able, **take out the words "which" or "that" entirely**. For example, "He knew that she would have a tough time forgiving him," could be written, "He knew she would have a tough time forgiving him."

It is helpful to **replace passive verbs with active verbs**. In passive voice, the subject of the sentence is being acted upon; in active voice, the subject is the actor. For example, "The students are being destroyed by mind-numbing smartphones," can be rewritten, "Mind-numbing smartphones are destroying the students."

Avoiding the overuse of **"is" or "was"** is another way to keep your writing from becoming too wordy. For example, "The test was passed by most of the class," can be rewritten to say, "Most of the class passed the test."

Replace "is," "are," "was," "were," or "have (and) an -ing word" with a simple present or past tense verb. For example, "Ms. Mac's class was experiencing some frustration with her lack of organization," can be rewritten to read, "Ms. Mac's class experienced frustration with her lack of organization."

Replace "should," "would," or "could" with more powerful verbs. For example, "The students could see several options to help her get organized," can be rewritten, "The students saw several options to help her get organized."

Similarly, you should **substitute strong verbs for "-tion" and "-sion" words** whenever possible. For example, "The school submitted a petition for more money," can be rewritten, "The school petitioned for more money."

Replace prepositional phrases with **one-word modifiers**. For example, "The President of the Student Council was in charge of refuting the claims of the principal," can be rewritten, "The Student Council President was in charge of refuting the principal's claims."

Use a colon to join two sentences (one of explanation and one of clarification), and leave out the beginning of the next sentence. For example, "The school offers three kinds of diplomas. These are standard, advanced, and International Baccalaureate," can be rewritten, "The school offers three kinds of diplomas: standard, advanced, and International Baccalaureate."

Combine two closely related short sentences by omitting part of one. For example, "Ms. Mac is concerned about problems. Usual problems are poor reporting, grammatical errors, and accountability," could be combined to read, "Ms. Mac is concerned about typical problems with poor reporting, grammatical errors, and accountability."

Let's take a look at a type of question on the GED® test that might assess your ability to edit for wordiness and awkward sentence construction.

EXAMPLE

Rewrite the following paragraph from a student's speech to ensure the clearest delivery.

> The President of the Student Council is perhaps the most important person in this school when it comes to our voice about how things are run around here. I believe I am the right person for this job. The reasons are because I have a lot of experience with advocating for our rights, speaking at public assemblies, and impressing teachers. I spoke to Tom Jones and John Edin about what they want from their school. He said he wants to see students given more freedom around this place! It is imperative that we elect me, Monica Morgan for Student Council President!

Your response may look something like this:

> The Student Council President is perhaps the most important person in school when it comes to our voice about how things are run around here. I am the best person for the job: I have a lot of experience advocating for our rights, speaking at public assemblies, and impressing teachers. I spoke to Tom Jones and John Edin about what they want from their school. John said he wants to see students given more freedom around this place! We must elect me, Monica Morgan, for Student Council President!

As you edit to demonstrate your command of the conventions of Standard English grammar and usage when writing or speaking, the best defense you will have is your common sense and your knowledge of the rules outlined in this section. Always check to make sure what you have said (or what you have corrected) is cohesive, thoughtful, clear, and correct.

Edit to ensure effective use of transitional words, conjunctive adverbs, and other words and phrases that support logic and clarity.

Transitional words and phrases have many uses, primarily:

- to show agreement, addition, or similarity; to show limitation, opposition, or contradiction;
- to show conditions or intentions; to provide examples, support, or emphasis;
- to show results, effects, or consequences;
- to summarize, conclude, or restate; or to show sequence, time, or chronology.

Before we begin editing, let's take a look at a very long list of transitional words and phrases and conjunctive adverbs grouped by specific use. (You can usually spot the conjunctive adverb by the "–ly" at the end.)

Transitional Words and Phrases, and Conjunctive Adverbs

Agreement, addition, or similarity		
in the first place	by the same token	too
not only . . . but also	again	moreover
as a matter of fact	to	as well as
in like manner	and	together with
in addition	also	of course
coupled with	then	likewise
in the same fashion/way	equally	comparatively
first, second, third	identically	correspondingly
in the light of	uniquely	similarly
not to mention	like	furthermore
to say nothing of	as	additionally
equally important		
Opposition, limitation, or contradiction		
although this may be true	above all	although
in contrast	in reality	instead
different from	after all	whereas
of course . . . , but	but	despite

(continued)

Opposition, limitation, or contradiction		
on the other hand	(and) still	conversely
on the contrary	unlike	otherwise
at the same time	or	however
in spite of	(and) yet	rather
even so / though	while	nevertheless
be that as it may	albeit	regardless
then again	besides	notwithstanding
Conditions or intentions		
in the event that	seeing / being that	while
granted (that)	in view of	lest
as/so long as	If . . . then	in case
on (the) condition (that)	unless	provided that
for the purpose of	when	given that
with this intention	whenever	only/even if
with this in mind	since	so that
in the hope that	while	so as to
to the end that	because of	owing to
for fear that	as	inasmuch as
in order to	since	due to
Examples, support, emphasis		
in other words	on the positive / negative side	surprisingly
to put it differently	with this in mind	frequently
for one thing	notably	significantly
as an illustration	including	in fact
in this case	like	in general
for this reason	to be sure	in particular
to put it another way	namely	in detail
that is to say	chiefly	for example
with attention to	truly	for instance
by all means	indeed	to demonstrate
important to realize	certainly	to emphasize
another key point	surely	to repeat
first thing to remember	markedly	to clarify
most compelling evidence	especially	to explain
must be remembered	specifically	to enumerate
point often overlooked	expressively	such as
to point out		

Results, effects, or consequences		
as a result	thus	therefore
under those circumstances	because the	thereupon
in that case	then	forthwith
for this reason	hence	accordingly
for	consequently	henceforth

Summation, conclusions, or restatements		
as can be seen	after all	overall
generally speaking	in fact	ordinarily
in the final analysis	in summary	usually
all things considered	in conclusion	by and large
as shown above	in short	to sum up
in the long run	in brief	on the whole
given these points	in essence	in any event
as has been noted	to summarize	in either case
in a word	on balance	all in all
for the most part	altogether	

Sequence, time, or chronology		
at the present time	finally	suddenly
from time to time	after	shortly
sooner or later	later	henceforth
at the same time	last	whenever
up to the present time	until	eventually
to begin with	since	meanwhile
in due time	then	further
until now	before	during
as soon as	hence	first, second
in the meantime	since	in time
in a moment	when	prior to
without delay	once	forthwith
in the first place	about	straightaway
all of a sudden	next	instantly
at this instant	now	presently
immediately	formerly	occasionally
quickly		

The **general rule** is to use a comma after the transitional word or phrase.

Additionally, one should consider asking one's parents for financial support.

Keep in mind that some of the words provided in these lists **require** you to finish the phrase before it is completely transitional. For example, "Whenever this happens, we find ourselves angry." You **cannot** simply state "Whenever," and expect it to be a complete transitional phrase.

You should use a semicolon and a comma when incorporating conjunctive adverbs between two independent clauses.

I wanted to go to the movies; nevertheless, I stayed home to babysit my little sister.

Now let's take a look at a question you might see on the GED® test that would test your ability to edit for the proper transitions.

EXAMPLE

Edit this student's paragraph to show logical order using transitional words and phrases.

Fashion has been a major part of people's lives since the beginning of human existence. We have always loved to show off our clothes and accessories. This can be a problem for us. In today's world we have become so consumed with how we look that sometimes we forget to behave humanely to each other. In order to fix this we need to stop being so obsessed with fashion. There are three things we can do to stop our reliance on fashion. We need to focus only on what we need rather than what we look like. We need to allow our interests to dictate our personalities, not our appearances. We need to reject the fashion industry's influence in our lives. The solution is not to become like animals. We should use clothing because we need it to keep us warm.

Technically, this paragraph is sound. However, you can improve it with a rewrite that may look something like this:

> Fashion has been a major part of people's lives since the beginning of human existence. We have always loved to show off our clothes and accessories; however, this can be a problem for us. In today's world we have become so consumed with how we look that sometimes we forget to behave humanely to each other. In order to fix this we need to stop being so obsessed with fashion. There are three things we can do to stop our reliance on fashion. First, we need to focus only on what we need rather than what we look like. Second, we need to allow our interests to dictate our personalities, not our appearances. Finally, we need to reject the fashion industry's influence in our lives. The solution is not to become like animals. After all, we should use clothing because we need it to keep us warm.

Do you see the difference in these two paragraphs? The rewritten draft shows a direction and provides an outline for the coming arguments in the paper. The first one does not accomplish this as logically or as orderly. Just a few transitional words and phrases can make a huge difference in the persuasive construction of a text!

Chapter 9

Applying Rules of Standard English: Capitalization and Punctuation

In Chapter 8, we discussed grammar and usage. Now, in Chapter 9, we'll move from how you write to how you *present* what you write, which brings us to capitalization and punctuation.

Demonstrate command of the conventions of standard English capitalization and punctuation when writing.

The only way to become really skilled at capitalization and punctuation is to learn the rules and practice how to apply them. The language component of the GED® RLA test deals with editing and correcting to get at this standard. Hopefully your exposure to correct writing mechanics in your extensive reading will help you to master this skill. This section of the guide will address the rules for capitalization and punctuation.

The GED® test will assess some or all of these skills with questions relating to this standard:

- Edit to ensure correct use of capitalization (e.g., proper nouns, titles, and beginnings of sentences).

- Edit to eliminate run-on sentences, fused sentences, or sentence fragments.

- Edit to ensure correct use of apostrophes with possessive nouns.

- Edit to ensure correct use of punctuation (e.g., commas in a series or in appositives and other non-essential elements, end marks, and appropriate punctuation for clause separation).

Edit to ensure correct use of capitalization.

Capitalization is a very important part of editing to ensure Standard English conventions. Capital letters indicate three things: proper nouns, titles, and the beginnings of sentences.

Let's begin with proper nouns. Simply put, a noun is a person, place, or thing. A proper noun is the official name of a particular person, place, or thing. You must always use a capital letter with a proper noun—except in the case of, say, quirky trademarks (e.g., eBay).

Here is a chart that shows an example of the difference between common nouns and proper nouns.

Common Nouns	Proper Nouns
country, city	United States, Cleveland
boy, man	Michael, Daniel
girl, woman	Alison, Sidney
shop, restaurant	Ace Hardware, Chipotle
book, film	*The Great Gatsby, Titanic*
company, corporation	Apple, Starbucks
month, day of the week	November, Wednesday

Can you identify the proper nouns in this sentence?

We went to the Kingstowne Theater to see the new film *Rise of the Guardians*.

You should have selected "Kingstowne Theater" and "*Rise of the Guardians.*" Now, let's see if you can do it on your own.

Capitalize all the proper nouns in this sentence by circling the letters that should be uppercase:

I went to macy's to buy a lot of costumes to use for a series of pictures I wanted to post on instagram.

You should have capitalized "Macy's" (because it is the name of a store) and "Instagram" because it is a corporation.

Let's talk about titles next. Capitalizing titles can be tricky because there are several different schools of thought regarding capitalization in titles (Chicago, AP, APA, MLA, etc.). The GED® test uses MLA title capitalization, so that is what you should learn. Here are the rules.

Capitalize the first and last word of the title and all principal words (which include: nouns, pronouns, verbs, adjectives, adverbs, and subordinating conjunctions). Do NOT capitalize the following parts of speech *when they fall in the middle of a title:* articles, prepositions, coordinating conjunctions, and the "to" in the infinitive form of a verb.

For example:

Flowers for Algernon ("Flowers" and "Algernon" are nouns, "for" is a preposition.)

What Is Literature (do not let the word "is" fool you. "Is" is a verb! Even short verbs are capitalized.)

Turbulent Indigo (Two nouns)

How to Play Parcheesi ("to" is part of the infinitive, "to play.")

The Calm between the Storm and the Hurricane ("between" is a preposition, "the" is an article, and "and" is a coordinating conjunction.)

Finally, you always need to capitalize the first word of any sentence, even a sentence in quotations in the middle of another sentence. There are no exceptions to this rule in formal prose.

Let's take a look at a question on the GED® test that would measure your ability to capitalize correctly.

Edit the following paragraph to show correct capitalization.

last night my friends and i went to see the play, *a streetcar named desire.* it was the greatest show i've ever seen! tennessee williams wrote it, but it's not set in tennessee; it's set in new orleans. i was so impressed by the lighting, the plot, and the acting that I couldn't stop talking about it. i am a big theater fan, and so is my best friend, matt. after the play we went to caribou coffee to talk about the differences in *a streetcar named desire* and a short play i really like called, *for whom the southern belle tolls* by christopher durang. *for whom the southern belle tolls* is a parody of a different tennessee williams play, *the glass menagerie.*

The correctly edited paragraph should look like this:

Last night my friends and I went to see the play, *A Streetcar Named Desire.* It was the greatest show I've ever seen! Tennessee Williams wrote it, but it's not set in Tennessee; it's set in New

Orleans. I was so impressed by the lighting, the plot, and the acting that we couldn't stop talking about it. I am a big theater fan, and so is my best friend Matt. After the play we went to Caribou Coffee to talk about the differences in *A Streetcar Named Desire* and a short play I really like called *For Whom the Southern Belle Tolls* by Christopher Durang. *For Whom the Southern Belle Tolls* is a parody of a different Tennessee Williams play, *The Glass Menagerie*.

As long as you remember the rules of capitalization, you should have no trouble editing for the proper case on the GED® test. Ask yourself: Does this look correct? If it does not, it probably is not.

Edit to eliminate run-on sentences, fused sentences, or sentence fragments.

There are three types of run-on sentences: a comma splice, a fused sentence, and a run-on. Let's look at each one individually.

A **comma splice** is a type of run-on that joins two independent clauses with only a comma between them. For example, the sentence, "I like iPads better than iPods, they have bigger faces," is an example of a comma splice.

A **fused sentence** is two sentences "fused" together without anything between them. Using the same problematic sentence from earlier, this would read, "I like iPads better than iPods they have bigger faces."

A **run-on sentence** is composed of two independent clauses with only a coordinating conjunction between them. "I like iPads better than iPods and they have bigger faces."

There are a few ways to correct any run-on sentence. In each instance, you could use a period to make it two separate sentences, "I like iPads better than iPods. They have bigger faces." You could use a semi-colon instead of a period, "I like iPads better than iPods; they have bigger faces." You could make a complex sentence using a subordinator, "I like iPads better than iPods <u>because</u> they have bigger faces."

A sentence fragment does not contain an independent clause. Every sentence must have a subject and a verb that can stand alone. For example, "Rue scratches" is a full sentence. It may be short, but it has a subject, "Rue," and a verb, "scratches." However, a longer idea might still be a fragment if it is missing the subject and verb. For example, "Rue, my beautiful and charming Siamese cat with her tail lopped off at the nub," is *not* a full sentence. In this instance, Rue is not doing anything because there is no verb.

A fragment **may** have a subject-verb relationship, but will remain fragmented if it is subordinated by a dependent word or idea. For example, "Even though she was adopted and was very clean," might sound like a full sentence because it has a subject, "she," and two relationships with the verb, "was." However, the fragment is dependent on a missing idea that is hinged upon the phrase, "even though." The sentence requires an independent clause to finish it up. For example,

"Even though she was adopted and very clean, Rue thought it was a good idea to scratch everyone she met."

Let's take a look at a sample question you might see on the GED® test that might assess this skill.

Rewrite this paragraph from a student's essay to ensure it demonstrates correct construction.

Greyhounds are the fastest dogs on the planet and they are very graceful, beautiful animals, too. Greyhounds make wonderful pets, adopting one is probably the best thing you can do for yourself! Even though greyhounds are large. They can still curl themselves up into small spaces and you would hardly even know they were around. Greyhounds are very clean and sensitive. They are also quiet. You will never even know your greyhound is there and he will bring so much joy to your life as you watch him lie around all day.

Your rewrite would look something like this:

Greyhounds are the fastest dogs on the planet, and they are very graceful, beautiful animals, too. Greyhounds make wonderful pets; adopting one is probably the best thing you can do for yourself! Even though greyhounds are large, they can still curl themselves up into small spaces. You would hardly even know they were around. Greyhounds are very clean, sensitive, and quiet. You will never even know your greyhound is there. He will bring so much joy to your life as you watch him lie around all day.

As you edit for run-ons and sentence fragments, remember that every sentence needs a subject and a verb. Dependent clauses (even with a subject and a verb) require an independent clause to make a complete sentence. Learn your comma rules, and you should have no problem editing these errors.

Edit to ensure correct use of apostrophes with possessive nouns.

There are only two reasons to use an apostrophe—to create a contraction between two words, or to show a noun's ownership. Most of the time this will be fairly easy for you, but as we have already learned, sometimes the English language will throw you a curve ball. For possession, this usually comes with plural nouns.

Let's begin with the basics. Any noun can show possession. For example, you could write about "France's Olympic Water Polo team," or "George's baseball collection." Even a common noun such as a cat can have ownership, as in, "the cat's paw." Inanimate objects, too, can have ownership, such as in the case of "the clock's dial" or the "window's latch."

An easy way to determine if you need to show possession through an apostrophe is to decide whether the word "of" would work in the sentence instead—as in "the Water Polo team of France," or "the baseball collection of George." **Any time there is a singular noun, the rule is to add an "'s" to the end of the noun.**

The unicorn's horn (the horn of the unicorn)

The tassel's sparkle (the sparkle of the tassel)

Christina's puppy (the puppy of Christina)

The rules change when you are dealing with **plural nouns**. With plural nouns (kids), you put the apostrophe *after* the "s." For example, you would write "the kids' messes" if you were discussing the messes of several kids. Similarly, you would write, "the lovers' kisses." You can change the meaning of the entire sentence if you misplace the apostrophe. For example, in the phrase "his lover's kisses," the position of the apostrophe indicates the subject has just one lover. However, if you write "his lovers' kisses," suddenly the subject has several people he is kissing! Be careful!

Most plural nouns in the English language end with the letter "s" already, so as you are dealing with their possession, you only have to remember to put the apostrophe at the end of the word.

You can also insert the word "of" into the phrase to make sure it is correct when you are dealing with plurals.

The trees' leaves (the leaves of the trees)

The bees' knees (the knees of the bees)

The states' constitutions (the constitutions of the states)

There are always exceptions. Sometimes plural nouns in the English language do not end in an "s." For example, the words "teeth," "women," "children," "mice," "deer," and many other words are plural, but they do not end in "s." There is no such thing as "teeths," any more than there is such a thing as "tooths. " In all of these instances, you have to **treat the plural noun as though it were singular.** There are such words as "tooth's" and "teeth's."

The children's coats (the coats of the children)

The men's room (the room of the men)

The geese's flock (the flock of the geese)

You may also run into confusion when the subject is compound. How many apostrophes do you use? Well, it depends on whether the pair owns the thing together or separately. If the item in question is owned by both of them, you treat the subject singularly on the last mentioned noun. If they each own it independently, they each get an " 's."

For example:

Herbert and Sarah's mother (only Sarah gets the " 's" because the children share the same mother)

Herbert's and Sarah's mothers (each of these children have a different mother—you can tell because the word "mother" is plural)

Herbert and Sarah's mothers (this phrase indicates the siblings share more than one mother, perhaps a stepmother or a mother-in-law)

Herbert and Sarah's wedding (they were married to each other and shared the wedding)

Herbert's and Sarah's weddings (they each had their own wedding)

Herbert and Sarah's weddings (they got married to each other several times)

Herbert's and Sarah's jackets (they each have their own jacket.)

You know the rule that a contraction takes precedence over possession, such as in the case of "its" and "it's." "Its" is a possessive noun, as in "Its tail flicked." "It's a sad occasion when a cat does not have a tail to flick." Interestingly enough, the possessive "yours" never takes an apostrophe.

Correct: You like that gun? It's yours.

Incorrect: You like that gun? Its your's.

Let's take a look at a question you might receive on the GED® test that will test this skill.

Rewrite the following paragraph from a student's paper.

Amanda Palmer and Neil Gaiman are one of the most interesting celebrity couple's these days. Palmer is a famous singer, and Gaiman is a very well-known author. Palmers' first band, The Dresden Dolls, had an immediate cult following with their punk-cabaret style. Gaimans' fame became mythic when his book, *Coraline*, was made into an animated film. Palmer's and Gaiman's wedding was small. Only a few people came to it, but now they help each others causes by bringing their own fan's attention to the work of their partner. When Gaiman was nominated for a Grammy, Palmer brought him a great deal of attention when she channeled her punk attitude on the red carpet's impressive history. Many people criticize Palmers personality, but it certainly helps bring notice to the issues she champion's, like internet-bullying and the future of music.

Your rewrite should look like this:

> Amanda Palmer and Neil Gaiman are one of the most interesting celebrity couples these days. Palmer is a famous singer, and Gaiman is a very well-known author. Palmer's first band, *The Dresden Dolls*, had an immediate cult following with their punk-cabaret style. Gaiman's fame became mythic when his book, *Coraline*, was made into an animated film. Palmer and Gaiman's wedding was small. Only a few people came to it, but now they help each other's causes by bringing their own fans' attention to the work of their partner. When Gaiman was nominated for a Grammy, Palmer brought him a great deal of attention when she channeled her punk attitude on the red carpet's impressive history. Many people criticize Palmer's personality, but it certainly helps bring notice to the issues she champions, like internet-bullying and the future of music.

You should not run into too many problems as you are editing for possession; just remember the basic rules!

Edit to ensure correct use of punctuation (e.g., commas in a series or in appositives and other non-essential elements, end marks, and appropriate punctuation for clause separation).

The English language has a variety of punctuation. To begin, let's look at a list of punctuation marks and what they mean.

Period (.)—full stop at the end of a sentence including commands or indirect questions; ALSO used for abbreviations.

> Maria went to work. She thought about the metro signs that told her which way to go. She wondered if there was a God.

Exclamation mark (!)—used at the end of an emphatic declaration, command, or interjection.

> Turn the wheel immediately or we will hit the tree! Do it now! "Oh my!" he exclaimed.

Question mark (?)—used at the end of a direct question.

> Is this the way to the Super Bowl?

Colon (:)—begins a list or an explanation preceded by an independent clause.

> I went to the store to buy these ingredients: eggs, milk, flour, and oil. There was only one thing to do now: bake a cake.

Semicolon (;) — joins two closely related independent clauses OR separates items in a complicated list.

> We knew we were in for something big at the conference; there were many great speakers listed on the brochure. Among them were: Jeremy Brighton, Professor of Mathematics; Elizabeth Carlton, Nuclear Physicist; Erin Nelson, Director of Calculus at the University of Mississippi; and Earl Dietrich, Master of Ceremonies.

Quotation marks ("") — indicates the title of a small piece of a work (poem, short story, article, song, etc.) OR indicates spoken words or direct quotations.

> When I told the class that "The Love Song of J. Alfred Prufrock" is my favorite poem, Julie said, "I hate Eliot!"

Apostrophe (') — shows possession OR indicates the place from which a letter has been removed to create a conjunction; occasionally will be used to create plurals or to indicate a quotation within a quotation.

> I was reading Joseph's essay, but I didn't like it. He got straight As in English class, but when I read his paper it said, "I went to see Mrs. Jones last night, and she said, 'Whoa! Back off!'" What kind of sentence is that? It isn't even interesting.

Hyphen (-) — used to compound words.

> My ex-husband was using an out-of-date textbook. The thing only had ninety-nine pages in it!

Dash (–) — indicates a longer break than a comma, used in place of a comma when a parenthetical idea contains internal punctuation OR shows an interruption in dialogue.

> It was awkwardly silent in the room—no one said anything for six full minutes. All three of the girls—Jordan, Daisy, and Myrtle—were surprised when Gatsby entered the room. "Excuse me ladies, I didn't mean to—'Get out!'" Myrtle screamed.

Parentheses (()) — indicates a less important clarifying thought OR used to show citation of sources.

> I was about to close my MacBook (which is far superior to a PC) when I noticed a quote I wanted to include in my research paper, ". . . The laws that laid down who could be loved and how much" (Roy 28).

Ellipsis (. . .) — creates a break in the flow of a sentence OR indicates part of a quotation has been omitted.

> Justin thought and thought about what to say to break up with his girlfriend . . . then he thought some more. She had said to him last night, "I want us to get married . . . you'd make a great father."

Comma (,) — joins sentences, introduces modifiers and quotations, or differentiates items in a list.

> He was an educated fellow, and he always cut me with his sharp remarks. Although he was tall, articulate, and handsome, I knew he was not the man for me. His biting, caustic insults of others were too much for my fragile ego. One time he told me, "You're a smart girl, Alyssa. Don't say such stupid things." For days I was wounded, but we still manage to remain friends.

Brackets ([]) — indicate something in a quotation has been changed to ensure proper grammatical structure.

> Geoffrey was convinced Martin Luther King's speech was the greatest oration in the world; after all, he "[had] a dream."

Slash (/) — indicates a choice between the words it separates OR it can indicate a break in a line of quoted poetry.

> Whenever a person writes poetry, he/she should consider the greatest poet of all time, Sylvia Plath. Plath's poem "Lady Lazarus" was brilliant. Consider the first stanza, "I have done it again. / One year in every ten / I manage it --"

If you can learn when these punctuation marks are used, you will be able to correctly punctuate any sentence you will see on the GED® test, even when dealing with more difficult ideas.

Let's take a look at a sample question you might see that will test your ability to punctuate properly.

Place the correct punctuation marks in the following paragraph.

> Forests are amazing beautiful essential parts of our world Did you know that a forest spreads It's true On the edge of nearly every forest in America you will find pine trees Pines are fast growing trees that help establish the boundaries of forests As the pines spread the rest of the forests hardwoods can grow safely because the pines have created a kind of haven for saplings Hermann Hesse once said that For him trees have always been the most penetrating preachers It is important for us to recognize the importance of forests If a person has grown up in this world without seeing a forest he she is missing out on one of the greatest experiences life has to offer It is grand to walk through a forest and see redwoods evergreens maples birches and junipers.

Your punctuation should look like this:

Forests are amazing, beautiful, essential parts of our world. Did you know that a forest spreads? It's true! On the edge of nearly every forest in America you will find pine trees. Pines are fast-growing trees that help establish the boundaries of forests. As the pines spread, the rest of the forest's hardwoods can grow safely because the pines have created a kind of haven for saplings. Herman Hesse once said that, "For [him] trees have always been the most penetrating preachers." It is important for us to recognize the importance of forests. If a person has grown up in this world without seeing a forest, he/she is missing out on one of the greatest experiences life has to offer. It is grand to walk through a forest and see redwoods, evergreens, maples, birches, and junipers.

Written English in Context: Extended Response

Approaching the Extended-Response Question

After you complete Section 1 of the GED® RLA test, you will be presented with a single extended-response question. This task requires you to write a probing essay that analyzes two source texts. The texts together will total no more than 650 words.

Your essay need not be perfect, says GED Testing Service®, but it does need to be solid and thoughtful. To achieve this, put time on your side by dividing it up smartly. You will have a total of 45 minutes. Set aside about 10 minutes to read and analyze the source documents; 10 minutes to pull out the quotes you'll use to build your argument; another 10 minutes to prepare a rough draft; and 15 minutes to refine and proofread your work. If you stay reasonably within the target zone for each piece of the task, you'll need to be able to keyboard about 25 words a minute to produce a 300- to 500-word essay. Very doable!

Your essay score will hinge on your ability to:

1. Analyze arguments and gather evidence found in the source texts to support your position.

2. Develop and organize your writing.

3. Demonstrate fluency with the conventions of Edited American English.*

---

*For more on Edited American English, search the term at the Purdue Online Writing Lab (OWL) at *https://owl.english. purdue.edu.*

To do well on the essay, you'll need a plan of attack. Here's a 7-point plan to follow. Use this plan in combination with official GED Testing Service® guidelines on the following pages in this chapter.

Basic Steps for Acing the Extended-Response Question (45 minutes)

1. Read the source text or texts and the question (a.k.a. the prompt) that follows.

2. Pick out key words in the question.

3. Recast the question as your thesis statement.

4. Use relevant details from the source text—but don't go overboard with quotes; paraphrase (use your own words) instead.

5. Outline and organize the details logically, tying them to your main points. Use your erasable noteboard to map it out.

6. Draft an answer.

7. Review your work and edit/revise the answer, ensuring that you respond to everything the question asks.

On test day, the extended-response task will be presented to you on a split computer screen. On the left, you'll see the passages; use the tabs at the top left of your screen to move from page to page of the passages. On the right side of the screen, you'll see the question or prompt as well as instructions. Under the instructions will be a box for you to type your response.

Heads up! The 10-minute break that follows the extended response is managed by the computer, so you must be sure to return to your testing station in time for Section 3 of the RLA test to begin.

Next we'll take an inside look at the extended-response task courtesy of GED Testing Service®. The content in the next several pages, drawn from the September 2015 release of the testing service's "Extended Response Resource Guide" and used by REA with permission, takes you through all the elements of the task, including a sampling of top-scoring essays from actual GED® candidates. The testing service's annotations shine a light on how real essays are graded. We provide the ER scoring rubric in the back of the book.

GED Testing Service® Guidelines/Directions for the Extended Response[†]

Please use the guidelines below as you answer the Extended Response question on the Reasoning Through Language Arts test. Following these guidelines as closely as possible will ensure that you provide the best response.

1. Please note that this task must be completed in no more than 45 minutes. However, don't rush through your response. Be sure to read through the passage(s) and the prompt. Then think about the message you want to convey in your response. Be sure to plan your response before you begin writing. Draft your response and revise it as needed.

2. Fully answering an ER prompt often requires 4 to 7 paragraphs of 3 to 7 sentences each—that can quickly add up to 300 to 500 words of writing! A response that is significantly shorter could put you in danger of scoring a 0 just for not showing enough of your writing skills.

3. As you read, think carefully about the argumentation presented in the passage(s). "Argumentation" refers to the assumptions, claims, support, reasoning, and credibility on which a position is based. Pay close attention to how the author(s) use(s) these strategies to convey his or her positions.

4. When you write your essay, be sure to:

    •   Determine which position presented in the passage(s) is better supported by evidence from the passage(s).

    •   Explain why the position you chose is the better-supported one.

    •   Remember, the better-supported position is not necessarily the position you agree with.

    •   Defend your assertions with multiple pieces of evidence from the passage(s).

    •   Build your main points thoroughly.

    •   Put your main points in logical order and tie your details to your main points.

    •   Organize your response carefully and consider your audience, message, and purpose.

    •   Use transitional words and phrases to connect sentences, paragraphs, and ideas.

    •   Choose words carefully to express your ideas clearly.

    •   Vary your sentence structure to enhance the flow and clarity of your response.

    •   Reread and revise your response to correct any errors in grammar, usage, or punctuation.

Taxation and Revenue Stimulus Passage #1

Press Release from the Office of U.S. Representative Melody Walls
United States House of Representatives, Washington, DC

Representative Walls Announces Economic Boost for 12th District

July 17, 2013

Washington, DC—Representative Melody Walls announced that Congress passed the highway and transit bill today.

"This bill funds the expansion of Highway 17 from a two-lane highway to a four-lane thoroughfare. It will positively affect the town of Oak Falls," Walls said. As part of the expansion, Highway 17 will move two miles east of the town of Oak Falls. The bill will ease traffic congestion and create job opportunities during and after construction.

Last year, Representative Walls held town hall meetings to gather opinions from her constituents about revitalizing the economy in the 12th District. Two years ago, Turnaround Motors and Bell Camera closed their factory doors. The result has been high unemployment with no immediate prospects for new businesses. Representative Walls heard residents' concerns for jobs in the district.

Improving the highway means jobs for local construction workers. Once completed, the highway will bring more long-distance travelers into the area. Some officials anticipate a 30% increase in highway traffic due to the ease of traveling on the improved Highway 17. An increase in travelers will attract national motel and restaurant chains along the highway route. These national businesses will mean permanent jobs for residents.

In the future, historical features in Oak Falls and Gaston, such as brick streets built by early settlers and the old wheat mill, will likely become popular tourist attractions. More visitors will increase business for local shops and restaurants.

The improved highway will eliminate eighteen-wheeler traffic through towns, a major source of traffic congestion and noise. A 2001 study in Texas showed that bypasses reduce traffic through towns by as much as 75%. Eliminating eighteen-wheeler traffic will also reduce road maintenance costs.

The improvement of Highway 17, funded by federal tax allocations, is an important investment in the area.

Taxation and Revenue Stimulus Passage #2

Oak Falls Gazette
Letter to the Editor

I am a small-business owner living in Representative Walls's congressional district. A bill has been passed to expand Highway 17 from a two-lane highway to a four-lane thoroughfare. This change includes plans to move Highway 17 two miles to the east, which means it will now bypass our town completely. I find this unacceptable.

The *Gazette* reports that because Highway 17 runs through six states, construction will be paid for with federal road funds. That means some of our federal taxes will pay for a road that I believe will harm our town. I also believe that few residents of Oak Falls will use the road. Our town and district will lose money as a result of this highway bypass paid for by our tax dollars.

The road construction jobs are only a temporary bandage on the wound made by our two manufacturers closing their doors. Once the road construction is finished, only minimum wage jobs will remain.

In fact, the highway will bypass four cities in our district alone. Each of these towns will lose business because fewer travelers will pass through them and eat, stay overnight, or purchase gas. There is no guarantee that tourists will drive an extra two miles into our town if national chain motels and restaurants are built at the highway exits. The 2001 study Representative Walls references does show that bypasses reduce traffic and noise in towns, but the study also shows they have a negative impact on local businesses.

If this project were paid for with state tax money alone, angry voters would have struck it down. Representative Walls held town hall meetings to hear residents' opinions about the local economy, but obviously she did not listen to the concerns they voiced. Please consider local concerns about this federal project.

Taxation and Revenue Prompt

Analyze the arguments presented in the press release and the letter to the editor.

In your response, develop an argument in which you explain how one position is better supported than the other. Incorporate relevant and specific evidence from both sources to support your argument.

Remember, the better-argued position is not necessarily the position with which you agree. This task should take approximately 45 minutes to complete. Your response should contain 4 to 7 paragraphs of 3 to 7 sentences each, about 300 to 500 words.

Sample Response A

Representative Melody Walls' announcement was more strongly supported than the letter to the Oak Falls Gazette Editor by Alice Jenkins. The letter to the newspaper editor was a strong letter, however, it was pumped full of opinions and very few facts. The announcement by Representative Walls had a vast assortment of facts ranging from job opportunities and noise in the town to traffic congestion.

Representative Melody Walls begins her announcement regarding the highway by pointing out a crucial fact: Turnaround Motors and Bell Camera closed their factory doors. Melody then further explains the devastating effect this had on the town of Oak Falls; high unemployment and no immediate prospects for new businesses. By introducing this fact to the audience first, Melody is then able to turn it back around to the highway and transit bill that was passed and show the positive effects it will have on this suffering town.

The most obvious positive effect this new transit bill will have would be that it will provide immediate jobs to construction workers while Highway 17 is being expanded. Not only does Representative Walls point out the unemployment decrease while the highway is being worked on, but also brings up the fact that if there is an increase in traffic on the highway, it will most likely result in an increase of foreign travelers which means more business for the town.

The highway expansion also will produce more jobs, not only for the construction workers while it is being worked on, but also for the rest of the townsfolk in Oak Falls. Melody states that the increase in travelers will attract national motel and restaurant chains and who would they hire to run those businesses? The residents of Oak Falls, producing even more job opportunities.

Conclusively, Melody Walls expresses that with an improved highway eliminating 18-wheeler traffic through the town, there will be much less traffic congestion as well a noise. As if that isn't enough, less 18-wheeler traffic also means there will be less road maintenance for the town.

Representative Melody Walls' announcement was crammed with positive facts regarding how this highway and transit bill will benefit their town of Oak Falls; While the letter from Alice Jenkins is full of nothing but opinions.

The letter written by Alice Jenkins was, as I said earlier, a strong letter. However, the only paragraph that contains hard hitting facts is the first one that states the bill was passed to expand Highway 17 from a two-lane highway to a four-lane highway. The rest of her letter is, basically, Alice expressing her grievance regarding this new bill that was passed. Several different excerpts can be listed from Alice Jenkins' letter to show the overwhelming opinions given: "I find this unacceptable", "I also believe that few residents of Oak Falls will use the road", "[federal] taxes will pay for a road that I believe will harm our town", "Our town and district will lose money", etc. etc. These are just a few examples of the opinions expressed in Alice Jenkins letter.

Consequently, the announcement by Representative Melody Walls was more creditable, trustworthy and reputable due to the facts that were presented within the speech.

Annotations for Sample Response A

Trait 1: Score Point 2

- The writer builds a text-based argument by evaluating the argumentation of each author's message. The writer argues that Walls's press release is the stronger argument because it includes a *"vast assortment of facts* [and] *was more creditable, trustworthy* and *reputable due to the facts."* In contrast, the writer argues that the letter to the newspaper editor *"was pumped full of opinions and very few facts."*

- The response includes specific details from the text.

- The writer evaluates the details to show the strength in the argumentation and distinguishes claims (. . . Melody is then able to turn it back around . . . and show the positive effects it will have on this suffering *town).*

- The writer makes inferences based on the argumentation (. . . it will most likely result in an increase . . . which means more business for the town).

- In addition to demonstrating the strengths of Walls's arguments, the writer includes relevant evidence to show the weaknesses in Jenkins' argument (Several different excerpts can be listed . . . to show *overwhelming opinions given).*

- Overall, the writer maintains a purpose connected to the prompt and a text-based argument by citing relevant evidence and evaluating the validity of the two authors' arguments.

- The response earns a score of 2 for Trait 1.

Trait 2: Score Point 2

- The response contains well-developed ideas, most of which the writer has elaborated upon. The opening paragraph states the writer's position, followed by the line of argument he/she intends to use in the rest of the response, contrasting the *"vast assortment of facts"* used by Rep. Walls with the *"opinions"* offered by Alice Jenkins.

- The next four paragraphs address specific points made by Rep. Walls, demonstrating a logical progression from one to the next. The writer then makes a transition between Rep. Walls's press release being "*crammed with positive facts*" to Alice Jenkins's letter, which is "*full of nothing but opinions.*"

- Using specific examples from Jenkins's letter, the writer then supports this viewpoint, ending the response with a concluding summary statement.

- Although there is some informality in tone (the writer repeatedly refers to Rep. Walls by her first name), overall, the organization of the response clearly conveys its message and purpose.

- Therefore, Response A earns a score of 2 for Trait 2.

Trait 3: Score Point 2

- Despite occasional errors in punctuation, primarily with comma use, the writer demonstrates a clear command of the conventions of standard English. The errors do not interfere with comprehension (*The letter to the newspaper editor was a strong letter, however, it was pumped full of opinions and very few facts*).

- The response contains a variety of sentence types and avoids wordy or awkward sentences.

- There are no apparent problems with subject-verb agreement, pronoun use, or capitalization.

- Standard usage is at a level appropriate for on-demand draft writing.

- Therefore, Response A earns a score of 2 for Trait 3.

Sample Response B

I have just read two different accounts of a highway bypass and expansion. One side argues that this expansion will create jobs, reduce maintenence costs for the local roads, reduce traffic noise in town, reduce traffic in town by 75% and attract national hotel and business chains to create permanant jobs. The other side argues that taxpayer money is paying for it, that moving the highway 2 miles outside of town will deter people from going into town to shop at the local businesses and it would make them suffer. They also stated that the local concerns were not addressed, and that the highway would bypass four cities in its district.

The first account was from U.S. Representative, Melody Walls. In her press release, she outlined many ways that the expansion of the highway would be good for the town. She expressed that in building the expansion, it would create construction jobs for the local people. While these jobs are temporary, after the project is complete, it would attract national hotels and businesses to pop up along the way, creating permanant jobs for the locals.

Walls also expressed that with the new bypass, it would ease traffic congestion and noise throughout the town. She also stated, "A 2001 study in Texas showed that bypasses reduce traffic through towns as much as 75%. Eliminating eighteen-wheeler traffic will also reduce road maintenance costs." This is very true. Semi-trucks and their cargo weigh a lot, and tend to ruin normal roads. Walls spoke about brick streets that were built by settlers in Oak Falls, and Gaston which would attract tourists. If the big trucks and all that traffic were traveling on those roads for a long time, then it would ruin the historical value of those brick streets that were built by the settlers.

Walls provided studies and numbers to support her position. She stated that she held meetings in the towns for the bypass, and knew that they were hurting for jobs. This is a way to give the people more jobs, and a hope for a better future.

The other side was argued by Alice Jenkins, of the Oak Falls Antiques. She is a small business owner, and feels that without all of the in-town traffic, her business will suffer. She gave a few points to outline her concerns, but had no evidence to back it up. There was no background information, no references, and no facts like Walls had. Jenkins stated that the highway expansion would only create temporary jobs for construction, and leave the minimum wage jobs behind. Yes, the construction jobs are temporary. However, with the bypass happening, and attracting other businesses out there, it would create more jobs in the long run, jobs that are permanant and are not going anywhere. Jenkins also expressed concern about how the townspeople would not even use the new highway and how the travelers would not want to go two miles out of the way to fill up on gasoline or to stay the night at one of the local hotels. She also said that Walls did not listen to the locals' concerns about the issue.

Walls had a better point, and a better way of saying it. She backed up her main points with evidence and facts. She included numbers and studies. Jenkins did not reference a specific study or point out any numbers at all. She has a biased opinion based on the fact that she herself is a small business owner, and is afraid that she may be affected. The truth of the matter is, that the same people will still be going to her store, but with the new highway, it would attract more tourists into town to want to shop there. Jenkins simply did not back up her information as well as Walls did. Jenkins seemed not to even consider that eliminating the eighteen-wheelers through town would reduce the maintenance costs, therefore reducing the local taxes for them. She also did not consider that hotels and other national businesses are not minimum wage jobs, they are permanant and they do pay very well.

Credibility is also something to take into consideration here. Walls is a Representative of the state, and Jenkins is a small business owner. Walls has a job description to do what is best for her district and her state, and Jenkins just lives in it. Walls has tough decisions to make all of the time about the good of the people, taxes, and the good of the state. All Jenkins has to worry about is whether she is getting business or not. These are two very different points of view, but Walls argued a better point that benefits everyone, rather than just one group of people.

Annotations for Sample Response B

Trait 1: Score Point 2

- The writer generates a text-based argument for the highway expansion. Although the response includes unsupported claims, the writer makes reasonable inferences about assumptions from the argument (If the big trucks . . . were traveling on the roads for a long time . . . then it would ruin the historical *value of those brick streets*).

- The writer distinguishes between claims by highlighting unsupported claims in Jenkins's argument ([Jenkins] *gave a few points to outline her concerns, but had no evidence to back it up* [and] . . . did not *reference a specific study or point out any numbers at all)* and supported claims in Walls's argument ([Walls] *backed up her main points with evidence and facts)*.

- The writer also evaluates the credibility of the sources *(Walls is a Representative of the state, and* Jenkins is a small business owner. Walls has a job . . . to do what is best for her district . . . .All Jenkins has *to worry about is whether she is getting business or not)*.

- Overall, the writer generates a text-based argument with evidence to support the evaluation.

- As a result, the response earns a score of 2 for Trait 1.

Trait 2: Score Point 2

- The writer has established an organizational structure that clearly conveys his or her message. The response begins with an introduction to the issue of the highway expansion and to the two opposing positions.

- The paragraphs that follow spell out each position in detail and analyze the strength of each.

- The final two paragraphs evaluate the presentation of the two positions and the credibility of the two writers.

- The ideas follow logically from one another, and the writer has used transitional devices to lead the reader from one topic to the next (*Yes, the construction jobs are temporary. However, with the bypass* happening . . .).

- Overall, the tone is appropriate to the purpose of the task.

- Therefore, Response B earns a score of 2 for Trait 2.

Trait 3: Score Point 2

- With some minor exceptions, the response shows a command of standard English conventions that demonstrates the writer's ability to express him- or herself coherently.

- Sentence structure is varied, apostrophes are used correctly, parallelism is maintained, and transitional devices are employed usefully.

- There are several instances of vague pronoun-antecedent references and incorrect comma use, but these do not interfere with comprehension.

- Standard usage is at a level appropriate for on-demand draft writing.

- Therefore, Response B earns a score of 2 for Trait 3.

Responses A and B are part of a larger sequence of actual candidate responses available from GED Testing Service® at *www.gedtestingservice.com*. Search "RLA Extended Response Resource Guide." Candidate responses are reproduced here exactly as produced.

Mathematical Reasoning

About the GED® Mathematical Reasoning Test

GED Testing Service® consistently finds that the GED® Mathematical Reasoning test is the toughest of the four tests. But take heart: Studies show that GED® students who practice the kind of math they'll face on the test do better than their peers who don't. The key is to get in the groove and stay there.

Standardized math tests breed anxiety. We get that. But here's the good news: The GED® Mathematical Reasoning test is grounded in the stuff of the real world. That means you'll be using real-world problem-solving skills rather than just applying rote memorization.

This all-in-one prep provides you with extensive review and practice in strict alignment with the GED® test objectives. Still, some GED® candidates need more practice. If that's you, we recommend consulting our *GED® Math Test Tutor*, which is available at your neighborhood bookstore or GED Marketplace™, GED Testing Service's e-commerce site for adult learners. While you're at GED Marketplace™, we also recommend purchasing the GED Ready™ official GED® math practice test.

The 115-minute math test is divided into two parts with no break between them. The first part contains just 5 questions for which no calculator is allowed. The second part contains approximately 41 questions for which a calculator. You will be provided with an on-screen calculator (the Texas Instruments TI-30XS Multiview™ scientific calculator) but are welcome to use your own hand-held TI-30XS if you wish. If you bring your own calculator, you will be able to get it from your locker to use on the second part of the test. You will also be given a mathematics formula sheet, so any formulas you need will be at your fingertips, not jamming your memory. Be sure to download a copy beforehand at *GED.com*.

The Mathematical Reasoning Test at a Glance

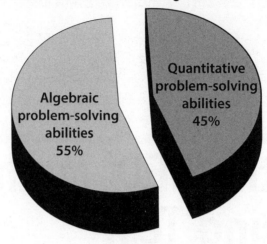

Question formats

The test includes these item types:

- Standard multiple-choice items, which you've probably seen on other tests, featuring four choices from which you will select your answer.

- Drag-and-drop items. For such questions you will drag small images, words, or numerical expressions and drop them in the appropriate place. This will allow you to create expressions, equations, and inequalities; to classify or sort data; or to show the steps in a process or solution, or to match items from two sets.

- Drop-down items. These questions are a bit like multiple-choice items except that the choices are embedded right in the text. Such items will test your command of math vocabulary or ask you to select a numerical value to complete a statement.

- Hot-spot items. This kind of question has you click within a set range on an image. When you click on the image, a marker will appear showing the area selected. Here you will plot points on grids, number lines, or scatter plots, among other things.

- Fill-in-the-blank items. These questions will present you with an empty field where you will enter a numerical answer or an equation.

Scoring

Each question on the math test is worth 1 raw point except for instances where two drop-down selections are embedded in a single question; such questions are worth 2 points. As with all the GED® subject tests, your score will be converted to a scaled score. The scale goes from 100 to 200.

With a high enough score, today's GED® test makes it possible to earn college credit.

Your score on the GED® Mathematical Reasoning test is based on where you fall relative to the four GED® Performance Level Descriptors:

- Performance Level 1 (< 145) — Below Passing

- Performance Level 2 (145–164) — Pass/High School Equivalency

- Performance Level 3 (165–174) — GED® College Ready

- Performance Level 4 (175–200) — GED® College Ready + Credit

If your score puts you into the top performance bracket, you may be eligible for three undergraduate credits in college algebra. For details on GED® scoring, visit *www.gedtestingservice.com*.

Now let's discuss what you need to know to excel on the GED® Mathematical Reasoning test.

Operations with Real Numbers

In this first chapter on the Mathematical Reasoning test, we will review:

- The Real Number System

- Adding, Subtracting, Multiplying, and Dividing Real Numbers

- Signed Numbers

- Absolute Value

- Exponents

- Order of Operations

- Scientific Notation

The Real Number System

The math questions on the GED® test work with numbers that are members of the *real number system*. Numbers in the real number system are comprised of the following:

- Natural or counting numbers: 1, 2, 3, 4 . . .

- Whole numbers: 0, 1, 2, 3, 4 . . .

- Integers: . . . –2, –1, 0, 1, 2 . . .

- Rational numbers: the quotients of two integers in the form of $\frac{a}{b}$. Rational numbers can be in the form of fractions such as:

$$\frac{1}{2}, \frac{9}{7}, 3\frac{5}{8}, \frac{6}{1}$$

or decimals that terminate:

0.6, 2.7, 0.0004

Any decimal that is infinite but repeats a pattern is also considered a rational number:

3.333..., 0.142561425614256...

Rational numbers that do not terminate but repeat a pattern are often expressed with a decimal bar:

$5.276276... = 5.\overline{276}$

- Irrational numbers: numbers that cannot be written as the quotient of two integers. Some examples are:

$5.2351758..., \pi, \sqrt{17}$

The symbol π, pronounced "pi," has a value equal to 3.141592653...

$\sqrt{17}$, pronounced "the square root of 17," equals 4.123105626...

There is another set of numbers, the complex number system, that you will study in college. However, GED® math questions will use values that are solely part of the real number system.

Adding, Subtracting, Multiplying, and Dividing Real Numbers

The GED® math test features the use of an on-screen calculator. Many operations with real numbers, such as addition, subtraction, multiplication and division, can be done quickly on the calculator. Let's review the mechanics of each of the four operations, first *without* a calculator and then *with* one.

Addition

The solution to an addition question is called the sum. Find the sum of the following numbers:

271 + 843 + 977 =

Answer: You can add the numbers vertically:

$$
\begin{array}{r}
271 \\
843 \\
+977 \\
\hline
2,091
\end{array}
$$

Use the TI-30XS MultiView™ scientific calculator to check your work.

$$271 + 843 + 977 = 2,091$$

Subtraction

The answer to a subtraction question is called the difference. Find the difference of the following numbers:

$$892 - 437 =$$

Answer: Place the two numbers above and below each other with 892 on top:

```
    8
  8 9̷ 2
 -4 3 7
 ──────
   455
```

[handwritten: DON'T UNDERSTAND]

```
   1
  892
 -437
 ────
  455
```

Now try the same problem on the calculator:

$$892 - 437 = 455$$

Multiplication

The answer to a multiplication question is called the product. Find the product in the example below.

$$437 \times 26 =$$

[handwritten work]

Answer: Place the two numbers on top of each other with 437 on the top.

```
    437
 ×   26
 ──────
   2622
 + 8740
 ──────
 11,362
```

Now try the example with a calculator:

$$437 \times 26 = 11{,}362$$

Division

The answer to a division example is called the quotient. Find the quotient of the following two numbers.

$$27{,}063 \div 31 =$$

Answer: Create a division problem with the dividend, 27,063, inside the division symbol and the divisor, 31, to the side.

```
       873
   ┌──────
31 ) 27063
     248
     ───
      226
      217
      ───
       93
       93
       ──
        0
```

Now divide the numbers using your calculator.

$$27{,}063 \div 31 = 873$$

Signed Numbers

If a number has no negative sign to its left, it is considered to be a positive number. For example, the numbers 9 and 231 are both positive numbers because there is no negative sign that precedes either. The numbers –8 and –407 are both negative numbers because each is preceded by a negative sign. All negative numbers have a value that is less than 0. In our everyday lives we use negative numbers to designate temperatures below zero, overdrawn bank accounts and elevations that are lower than sea level.

Positive and negative numbers can be displayed using a number line.

Numbers to the right of a number on a number line are larger than that number, and numbers to the left of that number are smaller. For example, 3 is less than 8 because it is to the left of 8 on a number line. However, 3 is larger than –27 because it is to right of –27 on a number line.

We can use inequality signs to show the following relationships:

–27 < 3 and 3 < 8 so –27< 3 < 8.

The GED® test-taker must be well versed in his/her understanding of operations with signed numbers. Although the test's on-screen calculator will be a useful instrument for solving problems with signed numbers, let's first understand these operations without one.

Addition

A number line is a useful aid to visualize how to add with signed numbers.

Example: 6 + 5 = ?

EXAMPLE

12 + –15 = ?

Note: It is important to note that the subtraction sign on the GED® on-screen calculator is **not** to be used as a negative sign. The bottom row of the calculator has a symbol "(–)" that must be used to designate a negative number.

Subtraction

When subtracting numbers, simply change the subtraction sign to an addition sign and change the sign of the number being subtracted.

EXAMPLE

9 – 4 =

9 – 4 = 9 + –4 = 5

EXAMPLE

15 – 31 =

15 – 31 = 15 + –31 = –16

EXAMPLE

29 – (–14) =

29 + (14) = 43

Multiplication and Division

When multiplying or dividing numbers with negative signs, count the number of negatives.

- If the number of negatives is an even number, the product or quotient is positive.
- If the number of negatives is an odd number, the product or quotient is negative.

EXAMPLE

(9)(–14) =

There is only one negative sign and since one is an odd number, the answer is negative.

$9 \times -14 = -126$

$-15 \times -12 =$

There are two negative signs; since two is an even number, the answer is positive.

$-15 \times -12 = 180$

$-144 \div -18 =$

There are two negative signs and since two is an even number, the answer is positive.

$-144 \div -18 = 8$

$$-\frac{-96}{-16} =$$

There are three negative signs, so the answer is negative.

$$-\frac{-96}{-16} = -6$$

Absolute Value

The absolute value of a number is its distance from 0.

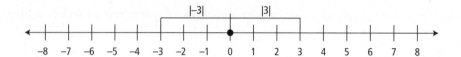

The symbol for absolute value is "$|\;\;|$". Regardless of the sign of the number within the absolute value, the value is always positive.

EXAMPLE

$|3| = 3$

$|-3| = 3$

EXAMPLE

$|-5| > 4$ True or False?

True. $|-5| = 5$ and $5 > 4$, so $|-5| > 4$.

EXAMPLE

$-|-3| > 2$ True or False?

False. Although $|-3| = 3$, the negative sign preceding the absolute value means $-|-3| = -(3) = -3$. Since -3 is not greater than 2, the statement $-|-3| > 2$ is false.

Exponents

Exponents, also called powers, are the number of times a base number is multiplied by itself. For example, $3^3 = 3 \times 3 \times 3 = 27$.

EXAMPLE

125 × 4 × 1

$5^3 \times 2^2 \times 1^4 = ?$

$5^3 \times 2^2 \times 1^4 = 5 \times 5 \times 5 \times 2 \times 2 \times 1 \times 1 \times 1 \times 1 = 500$ *EXPANDED form*

Notice that 1 raised to any power is always 1.

EXAMPLE

$(-4)^3 \times (-2)^2 = ?$

Remember to use the rules of multiplying with signed numbers.

$(-4)^3 \times (-2)^2 = -4 \times -4 \times -4 \times -2 \times -2$

Since five of the numbers are negative, and five is odd, the answer is negative.

$(-4)^3 \times (-2)^2 = -4 \times -4 \times -4 \times -2 \times -2 = -256$

The on-screen calculator on the GED® test is useful in quickly resolving numbers with exponents. Use the x^y button to simplify the following.

$12^3 = 12 \; x^y \; 3 = 1{,}728$

There are properties of exponents that facilitate their use.

$2^2 \times 2^4 = (2 \times 2)(2 \times 2 \times 2 \times 2) = 4 \times 16 = 64$

 Note that $2^6 = 64$; when multiplying numbers with the same base, add the exponents.

$2^2 \times 2^4 = 2^{2+4} = 2^6 = 64$

$$(2 \times 2 \times 2) \times 2 = (8)^2$$

When raising one exponent to another, multiply the exponents.

$$(2^3)^2 = (8)^2 = 64$$

$$(2^3)^2 = 2^{3 \times 2} = 2^6 = 64$$

When dividing numbers that have the same base, subtract the exponents.

$$5^4 \div 5^2 = 625 \div 25 = 25$$

$$5^4 \div 5^2 = 5^{4-2} = 5^2 = 25$$

Order of Operations

Consider the following example:

$$6 + 2 \times 7$$

Is the answer 56 or is it 20? Do we simply proceed from left to right or do we prioritize certain operations in arithmetic? The answer, 20, is the result of using the order of operations.

The order of operations is a system that sequences operations in mathematics. The order is:

Parentheses

Exponents

Multiplication

Division

Addition

Subtraction

The acronym PEMDAS is useful in remembering the precise order of operations (some students also use the expression "Please Excuse My Dear Aunt Sally" as an alternate method of remembering the order of operations). Regardless of which method you use to remember the order of operations, it is important to note that multiplications and division are considered equivalent operations and addition and subtraction are considered equivalent operations. When encountering a line of math that is solely multiplication and division or solely addition and subtraction, proceed from left to right to make the correct calculation.

1. $12 \times 4 \div 6 = ?$

2. $9 \div 3 \times 4 = ?$

3. $12 + 8 - 10 = ?$

4. $9 - 4 + 6 = ?$

SOLUTIONS

1. 8

The example contains both multiplication and division, so proceed from left to right:

$$12 \times 4 \div 6 = 48 \div 6 = 8$$

2. 12

The example contains both multiplication and division, so proceed from left to right:

$$9 \div 3 \times 4 = 3 \times 4 = 12$$

3. 10

The example contains both addition and subtraction, so proceed from left to right:

$$12 + 8 - 10 = 20 - 10 = 10$$

4. 11

The example contains both addition and subtraction, so proceed from left to right:

$$9 - 4 + 6 = 5 + 6 = 11$$

Let's try a more challenging example:

$$3(2 - 5)^3 - (-12) = ?$$

[handwritten: PARENTHIS FIRST 2-5 = -3]

- Simplify the parentheses first:

$$3(2 - 5)^3 - (-12) = 3(-3)^3 - (-12)$$

- Work with exponents next:

$$3(-3)^3 - (-12) = 3(-27) - (-12)$$

- Multiply:

$$3(-27) - (-12) = -81 - (-12)$$

- Subtract:

$$-81 - (-12) = -81 + 12 = -69$$

Scientific Notation

Scientific notation is a tool that makes managing large numbers more efficient. A number expressed in scientific notation is the product of two numbers:

1. A number greater than or equal to 1 and less than 10 ($1 \leq n < 10$).

2. 10 raised to some power.

The quantity 2.756×10^5 is in scientific notation because $1 \leq 2.756 < 10$ and its multiplier 10 is raised to the power of 5. A number, such as 432.7, is shown here in standard form, but can be converted to scientific notation by relocating the decimal point just to the right of the units digit. Count the number of places you moved the decimal point: if you moved the decimal point to the left, add that many powers to the multiplier 10. If you moved the decimal point to the right, subtract that many powers to the multiplier 10.

$$432.7 = 4.327 \times 10^2$$
$$0.0435 = 4.35 \times 10^{-2}$$

Notice how a cumbersome math problem is facilitated by using scientific notation.

A light-year, the distance light travels in a year, is approximately 6,000,000,000,000 miles. The distance to the Andromeda Galaxy is 2,200,000 light-years. How many miles distant is the Andromeda Galaxy from the Earth? (Express your answer in scientific notation.)

- Convert miles in a light-year to scientific notation:

  $6,000,000,000,000 = 6.0 \times 10^{12}$

- Next, convert the light-years to the Andromeda Galaxy to scientific notation.

  $2,200,000 = 2.2 \times 10^{6}$

- Multiply 6.0×10^{12} and 2.2×10^{6} to find the number of miles to the Andromeda Galaxy.

  $(6.0 \times 10^{12})(2.2 \times 10^{6}) = 13.2 \times 10^{18}$

- The product is not in scientific notation because 13.2 is not between 1 and 10. Move the decimal point one place to the left and increase the power of 10 by 1.

  $13.2 \times 10^{18} = 1.32 \times 10^{19}$

PRACTICE!

Questions 1 and 2: Classify each number as natural, whole, integer, rational or irrational.

1. 4,613

    A. rational only

    B. rational and whole

    C. whole and integer

    D. natural, whole, integer and rational

    E. irrational only

2. $\sqrt{39}$

    A. irrational only

    B. rational only

    C. whole, integer and rational

    D. rational and whole

    E. irrational, integer and natural

3. Add the following numbers without using a calculator. Verify the sum with a calculator.

$$
\begin{array}{r}
726 \\
547 \\
981 \\
+1764 \\
\hline
\end{array}
$$

4. Find the difference of the two numbers below without using a calculator. Verify your answer using a calculator.

$$
\begin{array}{r}
7{,}016 \\
-4{,}233 \\
\hline
\end{array}
$$

5. Find the product of the two numbers below without using a calculator. Verify the product using a calculator.

$$
\begin{array}{r}
746 \\
\times\ 38 \\
\hline
\end{array}
$$

6. Find the quotient of the numbers below without using a calculator. Check your solution with a calculator.

$$56\overline{)38{,}248}$$

7. $|-17| = ?$

    A. -17

    B. 17

    C. 17 and -17

    D. 34

    E. -34

8. Simplify the following:

$(-7)^3(-4)^3 = ?$

    A. 70

    B. −252

    C. 252

    D. 21,952

    E. −21,952

9. Simplify the following:

$12 - 2(-3 + 5)^2 - |-5| = ?$

    A. −2

    B. −1

    C. 0

    D. 3

    E. 17

10. Simplify the following:

$-8 \times 5^3 \div -10 \times -5 + 6 = ?$

    A. 506

    B. 500

    C. −494

    D. 66

    E. 72

11. Simplify the quantity below and express your answer in scientific notation.

$$\frac{(81.9 \times 10^9)(3.69 \times 10^{-4})}{(2.73 \times 10^3)}$$

    A. 11.07×10^2

    B. 1.107×10^3

    C. 1.107×10^2

    D. 0.1107×10^4

    E. 0.1107×10^3

MATH PRACTICE 1 ANSWERS

1. **D.**

   Remember, 4,613 is also rational because it can be expressed as $\dfrac{4,613}{1}$, which is the ratio of two integers.

2. **A.**

   $\sqrt{39}$ = 6.244997... The decimal neither terminates nor repeats a pattern so $\sqrt{39}$ is irrational.

3. **4,018**

$$
\begin{array}{r}
\overset{3\,2\,1}{726} \\
547 \\
981 \\
+\,1764 \\
\hline
4,018
\end{array}
$$

4. **2,783**

$$
\begin{array}{r}
\overset{6\ \ 9\,1}{\cancel{7,016}} \\
-\,4,233 \\
\hline
2,783
\end{array}
$$

5. **28,348**

$$
\begin{array}{r}
746 \\
\times\quad 38 \\
\hline
5968 \\
2238 \\
\hline
28,348
\end{array}
$$

6. **683**

$$56\overline{)38248}$$
$$\underline{336}$$
$$464$$
$$\underline{448}$$
$$168$$
$$\underline{168}$$
$$0$$

7. **B.**

A number's absolute value is its distance from 0 on a number line.

$$|-17| = 17$$

8. **D.**

$$(-7)^3(-4)^3 = -7 \times -7 \times -7 \times -4 \times -4 \times -4$$

There are six negative signs. Since six is an even number, the answer is positive.

$$(-7)^3(-4)^3 = -7 \times -7 \times \ -7 \times -4 \times -4 \times -4 = 21{,}952$$

9. **B.**

Use the order of operations to simplify the example.

Parentheses:

$$12 - 2(-3 +5)^2 - |-5| =$$
$$12 - 2(2)^2 - |-5|$$

Exponents:

$$12 - 2(2)^2 - |-5| =$$
$$12 - 2(4) - |-5|$$

Multiplication:

$$12 - 2(4) - |-5| =$$
$$12 - 8 - |-5|$$

Subtract:

$$12 - 8 - |-5| =$$
$$12 - 8 - 5 = -1$$

10. **C.**

Use the order of operations to simplify the example.

Exponents:

$$-8 \times 5^3 \div -10 \times -5 + 6 =$$

$$-8 \times 125 \div -10 \times -5 + 6$$

Multiplication and division from left to right:

$$-8 \times 125 \div -10 \times -5 + 6 =$$

$$-1000 \div -10 \times -5 + 6 =$$

$$100 \times -5 + 6 =$$

$$-500 + 6$$

Add:

$$-500 + 6 = -494$$

11. **B.**

Multiply and divide the first numbers in each parentheses.

$$(81.9 \times 3.69) \div 27.3 = 11.07$$

Multiply and divide the 10's:

$$(10^9 \times 10^{-4}) \div 10^3 = 10^{(9+(-4))-3} = 10^2$$

$$\frac{(81.9 \times 10^9)(3.69 \times 10^{-4})}{(2.73 \times 10^3)} = 11.07 \times 10^2$$

Convert the number to scientific notation by moving the decimal point one place to the left and adding 1 to the power of 10.

$$11.07 \times 10^2 = 1.107 \times 10^3$$

Fractions, Percents, and Decimals

We will review the following topics in this chapter:

- Basics of fractions

- Operations with fractions

- Basics of decimals

- Operations with decimals

- Comparing Fractions and Decimals

- Arranging Fractions and Decimals on a Number Line

- Basics of percents

- Simple interest problems

Virtually all of the math questions on the GED® test probe your knowledge of fractions, decimals, and percents. The GED® test features an on-screen scientific calculator that will help you quickly and accurately answer questions. In this chapter we will briefly discuss operations with fractions, decimals, and percents. We will then proceed with instructions on how to use the calculator to perform many of the calculations.

Fractions

A fraction is the comparison of two integers in the form of $\frac{x}{y}$. The number above the fraction bar is called the numerator and the number below is the denominator. There are three types of fractions:

Proper fraction: A proper fraction is one in which the denominator is greater than the numerator. $\dfrac{7}{11}$ and $\dfrac{74}{107}$ are examples of proper fractions.

Improper fraction: An improper fraction is one in which the numerator is equal to or greater than the denominator. $\dfrac{11}{9}$ and $\dfrac{49}{6}$ are examples of improper fractions.

Mixed number (also called mixed fraction): A mixed number has an integer component and a fraction component. $7\dfrac{2}{3}$ and $-14\dfrac{5}{7}$ are examples of mixed numbers.

Let's try to enter all three types of fractions into your TI-30XS calculator. (Note: The TI-30XS calculator is the calculator that appears on-screen during the GED® test. No other Texas Instruments calculator should be used during your studies.)

Proper and improper fractions: Enter the numerator followed by the $\dfrac{n}{d}$ button followed by the denominator. Try entering $\dfrac{27}{11}$ by pressing 27 $\dfrac{n}{d}$ 11 into your key pad.

Mixed number: Enter [2*nd*] and the $U\dfrac{n}{d}$ buttons followed by the whole number component. Press the right cursor and enter the numerator, then the down cursor and the denominator. Try entering $7\dfrac{5}{8}$ by entering [2*nd*] and then 7. Move the right cursor and enter 5 followed by the down cursor and enter 8. Practice entering a few mixed numbers until you feel comfortable with the process.

Operations with Fractions

Adding, subtracting, multiplying and dividing fractions is easy with the on-screen calculator. Although we will briefly discuss the mechanics of each operation, the test-taker is strongly advised to perform most of these operations using the calculator.

Addition and Subtraction

When adding and subtracting fractions with the same denominator, add the numerators while keeping the denominator the same. For example:

$$\dfrac{2}{7} + \dfrac{3}{7} = \dfrac{5}{7}$$

Sometimes adding two proper fractions results in a sum that is an improper fraction.

$$\frac{5}{8} + \frac{4}{8} = \frac{9}{8}$$

The answer choices may be in the form of an improper fraction or a mixed number. You can convert $\frac{9}{8}$ to a mixed number by dividing 9 by 8.

$$\begin{array}{r} 1\frac{1}{8} \\ 8\overline{)9} \\ -8 \\ \hline 1 \end{array}$$

When adding or subtracting fractions with different denominators, find a common denominator.

$$\frac{3}{8} - \frac{1}{6} = ?$$

Find the smallest number which 8 and 6 divide into evenly (this number is called the least common multiple or LCM). Begin by multiplying each number by 1, 2, 3 . . .

6: 6, 12, 18, **24**, 30, 36 . . .

8: 8, 16, **24**, 32, 40 . . .

Since 24 is the LCM, it is also the lowest common denominator (LCD). Multiply $\frac{3}{8}$ by $\frac{3}{3}$ and $\frac{1}{6}$ by $\frac{4}{4}$ to express both as equivalent fractions.

$$\frac{3}{8} \times \frac{3}{3} = \frac{9}{24}$$

$$\frac{1}{6} \times \frac{4}{4} = \frac{4}{24}$$

Now subtract the fractions as you normally would:

$$\frac{9}{24} - \frac{4}{24} = \frac{5}{24}$$

Now try adding $\frac{7}{11}$ and $\frac{2}{9}$ on your calculator.

$$\frac{7}{11} + \frac{2}{9} = \frac{85}{99}$$

The calculator automatically expresses every result in simplest terms; there is no need to simplify.

Adding and Subtracting Mixed Numbers

Once a tedious task, adding and subtracting mixed numbers is easy when using the calculator. Consider the following example:

$$7\frac{2}{23} - 5\frac{7}{11} = ?$$

Enter $[2nd]\ U\frac{n}{d}\ 7\frac{2}{23} - [2nd]\ U\frac{n}{d}\ 5\frac{7}{11}$ and then press the enter button.

$$7\frac{2}{23} - 5\frac{7}{11} = \frac{367}{253}$$

You can express $\frac{367}{253}$ as a mixed number by pressing $[2nd]\frac{n}{d}\ \triangleleft\triangleright\ U\frac{n}{d}$. You will see the following on your calculator: $\frac{367}{253}[2nd]\frac{n}{d}\ \triangleleft\triangleright\ U\frac{n}{d}1\frac{114}{253}$. The calculator will easily convert improper fractions into mixed numbers with just a few key strokes on the calculator's keypad. Practice a few examples on your own until you feel comfortable adding and subtracting mixed numbers with your calculator.

Multiplying and Dividing Fractions

When multiplying fractions, simply multiply numerators and denominators; there is no need for common denominators.

$$\frac{3}{7} \times \frac{4}{13} = \frac{12}{91}$$

Sometimes it is easier to simplify the product by cross-dividing first:

$$\frac{18}{35} \times \frac{14}{27} = \frac{252}{945} \div \frac{63}{63} = \frac{4}{15}$$

Notice how much easier it is to cross-divide the fractions first.

$$\frac{\overset{2}{\cancel{18}}}{\underset{5}{\cancel{35}}} \times \frac{\overset{2}{\cancel{14}}}{\underset{3}{\cancel{27}}} = \frac{4}{15}$$

By dividing 18 and 27 by 9 and then 14 and 35 by 7, the product, $\frac{4}{15}$, is assured to be expressed in simplest form. The calculator makes this process even easier:

$$\frac{18}{35} \times \frac{14}{27} = ?$$

Press $\frac{n}{d}$ and enter 18 and 35 for the numerator and denominator, respectively. Next, press the multiplication sign followed by $\frac{n}{d}$ again. Now enter 14 and 27 for the numerator and denominator, respectively. When you press [*enter*], you will see $\frac{4}{15}$ on your screen.

When multiplying mixed numbers, convert each to an improper fraction. Follow these steps to change a mixed number into an improper fraction:

1. Multiply the denominator of the fraction by the whole number.

2. Add that value to the original numerator to create a new numerator. Keep the original denominator.

EXAMPLE

Change $7\dfrac{5}{8}$ to an improper fraction.

$$\frac{(8 \times 7) + 5}{8} = \frac{61}{8}$$

After converting a mixed number into an improper fraction, multiply and cross-divide as needed.

EXAMPLE

$$3\frac{1}{3} \times 1\frac{4}{5} =$$

$$\frac{\overset{2}{\cancel{10}}}{\underset{1}{\cancel{3}}} \times \frac{\overset{3}{\cancel{9}}}{\underset{1}{\cancel{5}}} = 6$$

Note how easily this is done on the calculator.

$$5\frac{3}{7} \times 4\frac{1}{4} = ?$$

Press $U\dfrac{n}{d}\ 5\dfrac{3}{7} \times 4\dfrac{1}{4}$, then press [*enter*]. The improper fraction $\dfrac{323}{14}$ appears on the screen.

Now press $\left[2nd\right]\dfrac{n}{d}\ \vartriangleleft\vartriangleright\ U\dfrac{n}{d}$ and [*enter*]. The answer, $23\dfrac{1}{14}$, appears on your screen.

When dividing fractions, change the division sign to multiplication and invert the values in the numerator and the denominator of the second fraction. This new fraction is called the *reciprocal* of the original.

$$\frac{3}{8} \div \frac{11}{16} = \frac{3}{8} \times \frac{16}{11} = \frac{6}{11}$$

The calculator relieves us of the need to multiply by the reciprocal. Enter the original fractions as a division problem directly into your calculator.

$$\frac{7}{9} \div \frac{12}{13} = ?$$

The quotient, $\frac{91}{108}$, appears on the screen.

Dividing mixed numbers in the calculator uses the same procedure as multiplying them, but replace × with ÷:

$$9\frac{11}{15} \div 4\frac{6}{7} = \frac{511}{255} = 2\frac{1}{255}$$

Decimals

A "decimal" refers to one or more digits to the right of a decimal point. In the number 148.768, .768 is the decimal.

Each value in a decimal is $\frac{1}{10}$ the value of the number to its left. Consider the following number:

235.0749

2 is in the hundreds place
3 is in the tens place
5 is in the ones (or units) place

0 is in the tenths place $\frac{1}{10}$

7 is in the hundredths place $\frac{1}{100}$

4 is in the thousandths place $\dfrac{1}{1000}$

9 is in the ten thousandths place $\dfrac{1}{10,000}$

In our daily lives, we say a normal body temperature is "ninety-eight point six degrees" (98.6). Mathematically we say "ninety-eight and six tenths degrees"; the point is referred to by the word "and."

Rounding Decimals

When rounding decimals, follow these steps.

1. Identify the number to be rounded.

2. Look to that number's immediate right. If that number is 5 or greater, increase the number to be rounded by 1. If the number is less than 5, the number to be rounded remains the same. Any numbers to the right should be rounded to zero, then dropped.

EXAMPLE

Round 19.278 to the nearest hundredth.

1. 7 is the number in the hundredths place.

2. The number to its right, 8, is larger than 5, so round up.

19.278 rounded to the nearest hundredth is 19.28.

Operations with Decimals

Adding Decimals

When adding decimals, align the decimal points and add as you normally would.

EXAMPLE

5.1 + 7.0003 + 8.35 = ?

Some students find it useful to add zero place holders.

$$5.1000$$
$$7.0003$$
$$+\ 8.3500$$
$$\overline{20.4503}$$

The on-screen calculator makes adding decimals effortless.

$$7.071 + 9.5555 + 6.17 = ?$$

Enter the numbers into the calculator, making sure to enter the decimal point as needed.

$$7.071 + 9.5555 + 6.17 = 22.7965$$

Subtracting Decimals

When subtracting decimals, align the decimal points and subtract as you normally would. You may wish to use zero place holders as a visual aid.

$$11.12 - 3.051 = ?$$

$$11.120$$
$$-\ 3.051$$
$$\overline{8.069}$$

The on-screen calculator makes subtracting decimals effortless.

$$13.1 - 8.0071 = ?$$

Enter the numbers into the calculator, making sure to place the decimal point in the correct place.

$$13.1 - 8.0071 = 5.0929$$

Multiplying Decimals

There is no need to align the decimal points when multiplying decimals. There are three steps to follow:

1. Count the number of decimal places in both numbers.

2. Ignore the decimal points and multiply the numbers as you normally would.

3. Go to your product and, starting from the right-most digit, move the decimal point to the left as many places as you counted in step 1.

EXAMPLE

$15.367 \times 14.602 = ?$

1. Multiply the numbers as you normally would, ignoring the decimal points.

$15,367 \times 14,602 = 224,388,934$

2. Since 15.367 and 14.602 contain a total of six decimal places, count six places from the right of 224,388,934.

$15.367 \times 14.602 = 224.388934$

The online calculator makes multiplying decimals effortless.

$5.886 \times 3.41 = ?$

Enter the numbers as you normally would, making sure to enter the decimal point.

$5.886 \times 3.41 = 20.07126$

Dividing Decimals

$$4.22\overline{)143.902} = ?$$

When dividing by a decimal, follow these steps.

1. Move the decimal point in the divisor, in this case 4.22, to the right as many places as needed to create an integer.

2. Move the decimal point in the dividend, in this case 143.902, an equal number of places. If a decimal remains, align the decimal point in the quotient.

$$4.22\overline{)143.902} = 422\overline{)14390.2}^{\;34.1}$$

The on-screen calculator makes dividing decimals effortless.

$$148.55603 \div 36.89 = ?$$

Enter the numbers as you normally would, making sure to enter the decimal point as needed.

$$148.55603 \div 36.89 = 4.027$$

Comparing Fractions and Decimals

A fraction can be converted to a decimal by dividing the numerator by the denominator.

EXAMPLE

Convert $\dfrac{5}{8}$ to a decimal: $8\overline{)5.000}^{\;0.625}$

Thus, $\dfrac{5}{8}$ expressed as a decimal is 0.625

You can easily compare fractions by converting each to a decimal.

Place $\dfrac{5}{8}$, $\dfrac{2}{5}$ and $\dfrac{13}{20}$ in ascending order.

Convert the fractions into decimals:

$$\dfrac{5}{8} = 0.625$$

$$\dfrac{2}{5} = 0.40$$

$$\dfrac{13}{20} = 0.65$$

$$0.40 < 0.625 < 0.65$$

$$\dfrac{2}{5} < \dfrac{5}{8} < \dfrac{13}{20}$$

Arranging Fractions and Decimals on a Number Line

The GED® test-taker may be asked to arrange fractions and decimals on a number line.

EXAMPLE

Arrange the following numbers in order on a number line.

$$\dfrac{5}{8} \quad -1.3 \quad 2\dfrac{4}{5} \quad 3.7$$

ANSWER

The quickest way to discern the order of the values is to convert each to a decimal.

$$\dfrac{5}{8} = 0.625$$

$$2\dfrac{4}{5} = 2.8$$

Now arrange all of the decimals in ascending order.

$$-1.3 < 0.625 < 2.8 < 3.7$$

And finally, covert back to fractions as needed.

$$-1.3 < \frac{5}{8} < 2\frac{4}{5} < 3.7$$

Place all of the values in order on a number line.

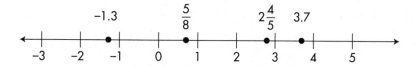

Percents

Percents mean "by the hundred." Percents are a useful way of expressing values as some fraction of a hundred. For example, we can find 11% of $250.00 by multiplying 250 by $\frac{11}{100}$:

$$\frac{11}{100} \times 250 = 27.50.$$

11% of $250.00 is $27.50

We will have more to say about percents in our discussion of ratios and proportions. In this section, we will discuss applications of percents using decimals.

We can change any percentage into a decimal by moving the decimal point two places to the left.

14.7% = 0.147

9.3% = 0.093

5% = 0.05

If a number has no decimal point, it can be added to the end because 14 = 14.0 = 14.000, and so on.

When we are asked what is 37.1% of 89.2, we convert 37.1% into a decimal and multiply it by 89.2 (remember that "of" means multiplication).

37.1% = 0.371

0.371 × 89.2 = 33.0932

37.1% of 89.2 is 33.0932

Decimals can be converted into percents. To convert a decimal into a percent, move the decimal point two places to the right.

0.412 = 41.2%

You can use the formula $\dfrac{\text{part}}{\text{whole}} \times 100$ to find a percent.

EXAMPLE

During a recent math test, 13 of the 25 students received a grade of B or A. What percent of the students received a B or an A?

Define your terms:

Part = 13

Whole = 25

$$\dfrac{\text{part}}{\text{whole}} \times 100$$

$$\dfrac{13}{25} = 0.52$$
$$0.52 \times 100 = 52$$

52% of the students who took the math test received a B or an A.

Simple Interest Problems

Interest is the earnings gained by placing a lump sum of money, called the principal, in a bank. For example, if you placed $500 in a certificate of deposit (CD) for some agreed-upon period of time, you would expect to find more money in that account at the end of the term.

The formula used to calculate interest is I = PRT, where P, R, and T are multiplied and they represent:

I = interest earned

P = principal

R= rate of interest expressed as a percent

T = time, always in years or parts of years

EXAMPLE

Michelle deposited $2,500 in a CD for two years. If the rate of earnings is 7.5%, how much will Michelle have earned at the end of the term? What will her account balance be after two years?

Use the formula I = PRT, where

I = interest earned

P = $2,500

R = 7.5%

T = two years

I = (2,500)(.075)(2) = 375

Michelle will have earned $375 on her deposit in two years. To find her account balance after two years, add her interest to the principal she initially deposited.

$2,500 + $375 = $2,875

PRACTICE!

Use the TI-30XS calculator on the following questions.

1. $\dfrac{5}{8} + \dfrac{3}{17} = ?$

2. $\dfrac{2}{7} - \dfrac{5}{9} = ?$

3. $2\dfrac{2}{3} \times \dfrac{5}{8} = ?$

4. $5\dfrac{1}{3} \div 7\dfrac{4}{9} = ?$

5. $1.113 + 0.5 + 38.06 = ?$

6. $59.1 - 11.683 = ?$

7. $3.007 \times 15.63 = ?$

8. $697.79016 \div 19.003 = ?$

9. Find 14.3% of 96.

    A.   137.28

    B.   13.728

    C.   1.3728

    D.   1.0728

10. Round 41.4068 to the nearest thousandth.

    A. 42.00

    B. 41.41

    C. 41.407

    D. 41.4

11. Nina has $5\frac{1}{8}$ yards of rope and Josh has $3\frac{5}{12}$ yards of rope. How much longer is Nina's rope than Josh's?

    A. $1\frac{1}{2}$

    B. $1\frac{17}{24}$

    C. $8\frac{13}{24}$

    D. $17\frac{49}{96}$

12. Kathy has 30 pounds of candy to distribute on Halloween. If she groups the candy into $\frac{3}{10}$ pound servings, how many servings will she have?

    A. 9

    B. 30

    C. $30\frac{3}{10}$

    D. 100

13. 87.5% of 6,400 homeowners surveyed indicate that they have cable television. How many of the families have cable television?

    A. 5,600

    B. 560

    C. 56

    D. 54

14. Multiply the two quantities and express the product in scientific notation.

$$(41.9 \times 10^4)(6.75 \times 10^2) = ?$$

    A. 282.825×10^6

    B. 28.2825×10^7

    C. 2.82825×10^8

    D. 2.82825×10^{10}

15. Alice needs to earn at least $400 on her certificate of deposit (CD). She places $4,000 in her account at the rate of 5.75% for 2.5 years. Will she earn the $400 she needs?

16. Arrange the fractions into ascending order.

$$\frac{7}{8}, \frac{4}{5}, \frac{17}{20}$$

    A. $\frac{7}{8}, \frac{4}{5}, \frac{17}{20}$

    B. $\frac{4}{5}, \frac{17}{20}, \frac{7}{8}$

    C. $\frac{7}{8}, \frac{17}{20}, \frac{4}{5}$

    D. $\frac{17}{20}, \frac{7}{8}, \frac{4}{5}$

Math Practice 2 Answers

1. $\dfrac{109}{136}$

2. $-\dfrac{17}{63}$

3. $\dfrac{5}{3}$ or $1\dfrac{2}{3}$

4. $\dfrac{48}{67}$

5. 39.673

6. 47.417

7. 46.99941

8. 36.72

9. **B.**

"Of" means multiply. Convert 14.3% into a decimal by moving the decimal point two places to the left.

$$14.3\% = 0.143$$
$$0.143 \times 96 = 13.728$$

10. **C.**

The number in the thousandths place is 6. The number to its right, 8, is larger than 5, so we round the 6 to 7. Thus, 41.4068 yields 41.407 when rounded to the nearest thousandth.

11. **B.**

Nina's rope is longer than Josh's. To find the the difference, subtract $3\frac{5}{12}$ from $5\frac{1}{8}$.

$$5\frac{1}{8} - 3\frac{5}{12} = 1\frac{17}{24}$$

12. **D.**

The word "grouped" means divide, so divide 30 by $\frac{3}{10}$.

$$30 \div \frac{3}{10} = 100$$

13. A.

Convert 87.5% into a decimal and multiply it by 6,400.

$$87.5\% = 0.875$$
$$0.875 \times 6,400 = 5,600$$

14. **C.**

First multiply 41.9 by 6.75.

$$41.9 \times 6.75 = 282.825$$

Next, when multiplying numbers with the same base, add the exponents.

$$10^4 \times 10^2 = 10^{4+2} = 10^6$$

A number expressed in scientific notation is the product of a number greater than or equal to 1 and less than 10 ($1 \leq n < 10$) and a multiplier of 10 to some power. Next, express our new product, 282.825×10^6, in scientific notation by moving the decimal point in 282.825 two places to the left while adding 2 to the power of 10.

$$282.825 \times 10^6 = 2.82825 \times 10^8$$

15. Alice will earn more than the $400 she wants from her CD. Use the formula I = PRT to calculate her interest.

I = interest

P = $4,000

R = 5.75%

T = 2.5

I = (4,000)(0.0575)(2.5) = 575

Alice will earn $575 on her CD.

16. **B.**

Convert each fraction into a decimal and arrange in ascending order.

$$\frac{7}{8} = 0.875$$

$$\frac{4}{5} = 0.80$$

$$\frac{17}{20} = 0.85$$

$$0.80 < 0.85 < 0.875$$

$$\frac{4}{5} < \frac{17}{20} < \frac{7}{8}$$

Algebraic Expressions and Equations

In this chapter, we will review the following topics:

- Algebraic terms and expressions

- Equations

- Inequalities

- Square and cube roots

- Quadratic expressions and equations

Think about a see-saw with a seventy-pound child on each side. The see-saw will balance because the same weight is on each of its sides. What will happen when a fifty-pound child sits on the same side as one of the seventy-pound children? Since the weight on one side is now 120 pounds (70 + 50), the see-saw will no longer be balanced. The see-saw can resume its balance, however, if another fifty-pound child joins the other seventy-pound child.

The image of a see-saw provides a useful visual tool in our discussion of algebra. To keep an equation balanced, we must always perform the same operation on both sides. Before we begin our discussion of equations, we must first review the building blocks of algebra: terms and expressions.

Terms and Expressions

A term is a number, a variable, or a quotient or product of a real number and one or more variables, sometimes raised to exponents (also called powers). A variable is an unknown quantity, usually symbolized by a letter, such as x or n. The following are examples of terms:

$$213 \quad \pi \quad 25q \quad \frac{1}{4} \quad 2x^3 \quad -7n^2 \quad \frac{2}{3}x^3y \quad 5r^{-2}$$

An exponent that is not expressly noted is understood to be 1. The term $7x$ is understood to be $7x^1$. A number that directly precedes a variable multiplies that variable. The multiplying number is called a coefficient. If no coefficient is shown, it is also understood to be 1. Thus the variable, x, can be understood as $1x^1$.

Any collection of terms joined by addition or subtraction is called an expression. The following are examples of expressions, each containing two terms:

$$-7x + 5y \quad 2.8x^3y - 3.2x \quad 9xy - 5mn$$

Order of Operations

In the first chapter, we discussed the order of operations. A brief review follows.

The order of operations is a system that sequences operations in mathematics. The order is:

Parentheses

Exponents

Multiplication

Division

Addition

Subtraction

We are ready to simplify some expressions that contain variables using the order of operations.

Find $-3x^3y^2 - \dfrac{2\,yz^3}{x}$ if $x = -1$, $y = 2$, and $z = -2$

1. Substitute the value for each variable:

$$-3(-1)^3(2)^2 - \frac{2(2)(-2)^3}{-1}$$

2. Since all the parentheses are simplified, proceed to the exponents.

$$-3(-1)^3(2)^2 - \frac{2(2)(-2)^3}{-1} = -3(-1)(4) - \frac{(2)(2)(-8)}{-1}$$

3. Multiply and divide, proceeding from left to right.

$$-3(-1)(4) - \frac{(2)(2)(-8)}{-1} =$$
$$12 - \left(\frac{-32}{-1}\right) =$$
$$12 - 32 = -20$$

Expressions with Like Terms

Expressions can be simplified if they contain "like terms." Like terms are those that possess the same variable raised to the same power. Consider the following expression:

$3x + 5y + 6x$

The like terms in this expression are $3x$ and $6x$. They can be combined as follows:

$3x + 5y + 6x = 9x + 5y$

When combining like terms, add or subtract the coefficients but leave the variables and exponents the same. In this example, $5y$ is not a like term because it contains a y, not an x, and cannot be combined with $9x$.

Let's try a more challenging example:

$7xy + 2x^2y - xy + 3xy^2$

Notice that each term contains both x and y, yet not every term is a like term. In order for terms to be like terms, the variables *and* the exponents must be identical. Therefore, in the expression $7xy + 2x^2y - xy + 3xy^2$ only $7xy$ and xy can be combined with subtraction (remember: $xy = 1xy$) to create:

$$7xy + 2x^2y - xy + 3xy^2 = 6xy + 2x^2y + 3xy^2$$

Expressions with Undefined Terms

Dividing by 0 is undefined in the real number system. Although $0 \div 9 = 0$, there is no quotient for the expression $9 \div 0$. A term cannot have a divisor that equals 0.

EXAMPLE

For what value is the term $\dfrac{9}{b - 8}$ undefined?

In order to find the value for b that renders the term undefined, set the denominator equal to zero and solve for the variable:

$$b - 8 = 0$$

$$b = 8$$

When b equals 8, the term $\dfrac{9}{b - 8}$ is undefined. *many terms in a expression*

GED® test-takers need to be able to work with polynomials. A polynomial is an expression that contains terms with variables and exponents that are added, subtracted, divided or multiplied. The following are examples of polynomials:

$$5x^2 + 7x + 3 \qquad -7mn - 4mn^2 \qquad 3b + 11d - 13.2z$$

Polynomials can be used to model everyday situations.

EXAMPLE

Create a polynomial that represents each situation.

1. The sum of c cookies and g glasses of milk.

2. The cost of m adult tickets and k children tickets if their costs are \$7.00 and \$4.00 respectively.

3. The size of a single study group if r students are divided into n study groups.

SOLUTIONS:

1. $c + g$

2. $7a + 4k$

3. $\dfrac{r}{n}$ or $r \div n$

Using Expressions to Model Everyday Situations

Expressions can be used to calculate outcomes in everyday life.

EXAMPLE

The sixth grade class is visiting a wildlife park on a hot summer day. The chaperones need to divide the 60 bottles of water for each group of students. Use the expression $\dfrac{60}{g}$ to represent the various groupings that are possible. Let g be the set of numbers that include: 2, 4, 10, 20, and 30

SOLUTION: Divide 60 by each of the values that are represented by the variable g.

$$\frac{60}{2} = 30$$

$$\frac{60}{4} = 15$$

$$\frac{60}{10} = 6$$

$$\frac{60}{20} = 3$$

$$\frac{60}{30} = 2$$

For the set of values g, the 60 bottles of water will be divided into groups of 30, 15, 6, 3, and 2.

Equations

At the outset of the chapter, we discussed the idea of a see-saw in balance. As long as each side of the see-saw possessed the same weight, the see-saw would balance. Let's see how this concept relates to algebra.

An equation results when two quantities are set equal to one another. The following are examples of equations:

$$7 = 7$$

ASK Helen

$$9 + 5 = 14$$

$$8 + 9 = 10 + 7$$

+2 -2

Some equations contain variables.

$$-2n - 11 = 14 + 3n$$

?

$$7n^2 = 15$$

$$\sqrt{2n} = 71$$

Consider the following equation:

$$n + 3 = 8$$

It is obvious that $n = 5$ because $5 + 3 = 8$. However, in the following equation $r - 79 = -43$, the value of r is not readily apparent. There are two simple rules for solving any equation, regardless of its complexity:

Rule #1: In order to isolate a variable, perform an opposite operation.

Rule #2: Any operation performed on one side of an equation must be performed on the other side as well.

Let's use our new skills to solve a few examples.

EXAMPLE

Solve for n: $n + 19 = 97$

SOLUTION: Since 19 is being added to n, subtract 19 from each side of the equation to isolate the variable.

$$n + 19 - 19 = 97 - 19$$
$$n = 78$$

You can check to see if your answer is correct by substituting 78 for n in the original equation:

$$78 + 19 = 97$$
$$97 = 97 \quad \checkmark$$

EXAMPLE

Solve for x: $x - 72 = -48$

SOLUTION: Since 72 is being subtracted from x, add 72 to both sides of the equation to isolate the variable:

$$x - 72 + 72 = -48 + 72$$
$$x = 24$$

Check your answer by substituting 24 for x in the original equation:

$$24 - 72 = -48$$
$$-48 = -48 \quad \checkmark$$

EXAMPLE

Solve for r: $3r = -729$

SOLUTION: Since r is being multiplied by 3, divide each side by 3 to isolate the variable:

$$\frac{3r}{3} = \frac{-729}{3}$$
$$r = -243$$

Check your answer by substituting –243 for r in the original equation:

$$3(-243) = -729$$

$$-729 = -729 \quad \checkmark$$

EXAMPLE

Solve for m: $\dfrac{m}{11} = 11$

SOLUTION: Since m is being divided by 11, multiply both sides of the equation by 11 to isolate the variable:

$$11 \, \frac{m}{11} = (11)(11)$$
$$m = 121$$

Check your answer by substituting 121 for m in the original equation:

$$\frac{121}{11} = 11$$
$$11 = 11 \quad \checkmark$$

Multi-Step Equations

Some equations require several steps to solve for a variable.

EXAMPLE

Solve for n: $3n - 12 = -48$

SOLUTION: In this example, 12 is being subtracted from $3n$. In order to isolate n, begin by adding 12 to both sides of the equation.

$$3n - 12 + 12 = -48 + 12$$
$$3n = -36$$

Next, since *n* is being multiplied by 3, divide both sides of the equation by 3.

$$\frac{3n}{3} = \frac{-36}{3}$$
$$n = -12$$

Check your solution by replacing –12 for *n* in the original equation:

$$3(-12) - 12 = -48$$
$$-36 - 12 = -48$$
$$-48 = -48 \quad \checkmark$$

EXAMPLE

Solve for *m*: $\frac{3}{2}m + 6 = -13$

SOLUTION: In this example, 6 is being added to $\frac{3}{2}m$ so subtract 6 from both sides of the equation.

$$\frac{3}{2}m + 6 - 6 = -13 - 6$$

$$\frac{3}{2}m = -19$$

In the second step, since *m* is being multiplied by $\frac{3}{2}$, we can divide both sides of the equation by $\frac{3}{2}$. There is an easier way to isolate the variable, however. Rather than dividing both sides of the equation by $\frac{3}{2}$ (resulting in complex fractions), we can multiply both sides of the equation by its reciprocal, $\frac{2}{3}$.

$$\frac{2}{3} \quad \frac{3}{2}m = (-19) \quad \frac{2}{3}$$

$$m = -\frac{38}{3} \ or -12\frac{2}{3}$$

Check your answer by replacing m with $-\dfrac{38}{3}$.

$$\frac{3}{2} \quad -\frac{38}{3} \quad + 6 = -13$$

$$-19 + 6 = -13$$

$$-13 = -13 \quad \checkmark$$

Equations with Multiple Variables

Sometimes an equation contains a variable in more than one location.

EXAMPLE

Solve for x:

$$2x - 11 + 5x = 3x + 14$$

SOLUTION:

Step #1: Combine like terms.

$$2x - 11 + 5x = 3x + 14$$

$$7x - 11 = 3x + 14$$

Step #2: Add 11 to both sides of the equation.

$$7x - 11 + 11 = 3x + 14 + 11$$

$$7x = 3x + 25$$

Step #3: Subtract $3x$ from both sides of the equation to place the variable on one side of the equation.

$$7x - 3x = 3x + 25 - 3x$$

$$4x = 25$$

Step #4:   Divide both sides of the equation by 4 to isolate the variable.

$$\frac{4x}{4} = \frac{25}{4}$$

$$x = \frac{25}{4} \text{ or } 6\frac{1}{4}$$

Check your answer by substituting $\frac{25}{4}$ into the original equation.

$$2\frac{25}{4} - 11 + 5\frac{25}{4} = 3\frac{25}{4} + 14$$

$$\frac{50}{4} - 11 + \frac{125}{4} = \frac{75}{4} + 14$$

$$\frac{131}{4} = \frac{131}{4}$$

Let's try a more challenging problem.

$$-4(-n + 6n - 5) = 12 - 11n + 3$$

SOLUTION:

Step #1:   Using the order of operations, simplify the values in the parentheses.

$$-4(-n + 6n - 5) = 12 - 11n + 3$$

$$-4(5n - 5) = 12 - 11n + 3$$

Step #2:   Since there are no exponents, proceed to multiplication.

$$-4(5n - 5) = 12 - 11n + 3$$

$$-20n + 20 = 12 - 11n + 3$$

Step #3:   Next perform addition to combine like terms.

$$-20n + 20 = 12 - 11n + 3$$

$$-20n + 20 = 15 - 11n$$

Step #4: Begin to isolate the variable by subtracting 20 from both sides of the equation.

$$-20n + 20 = 15 - 11n$$

$$-20n + 20 - 20 = 15 - 11n - 20$$

$$-20n = -5 - 11n$$

Step #5: Continue isolating the variable by adding $11n$ to both sides of the equation.

$$-20n = -5 - 11n$$

$$-20n + 11n = -5 - 11n + 11n$$

$$-9n = -5$$

Step #6: Divide both sides of the equation by –9.

$$-9n = -5$$

$$\frac{-9n}{-9} = \frac{-5}{-9}$$

$$n = \frac{5}{9}$$

We will leave the checking of this solution to you.

Solving a System of Equations

A system of equations is a set of two or more equations with two or more variables. Systems of equations can be solved algebraically or by graphing.

When solving a system of equations algebraically, we can use the substitution method or the linear combination method (also known as the addition-subtraction method or the elimination method).

EXAMPLE

Solve the system of equations by using the substitution method.

$$y = x + 1$$

$$2x + y = 4$$

SOLUTION: Substitute, the value of y, $x + 1$, into the second equation.

$$2x + (x + 1) = 4$$

$$3x + 1 = 4$$

$$3x + 1 - 1 = 4 - 1$$

$$3x = 3$$

$$\frac{3x}{3} = \frac{3}{3}$$

$$x = 1$$

Now solve for y by inputting 1 into either equation for x.

$$2(1) + y = 4$$

$$2 + y = 4$$

$$2 + y - 2 = 4 - 2$$

$$y = 2$$

The solution set for the system of equations is (1, 2).

We can solve the same system of equations using the linear combination method.

First we must make sure that both equations are in standard form ($ax + by = c$).

$$y = x + 1$$

$$-x + y = x + 1 - x$$

$$-x + y = 1$$

$$-1(-x + y = 1)$$

$$x - y = -1$$

Place both equations, one over the other, and add downward.

$$x - y = -1$$
$$+ 2x + y = 4$$
$$\overline{3x = 3}$$
$$\frac{3x}{3} = \frac{3}{3}$$
$$x = 1$$

Substitute 1 for x in either equation.

$$2(1) + y = 4$$

$$2 + y = 4$$

$$2 - 2 + y = 4 - 2$$

$$y = 2$$

We arrive at the same solution as we did using the substitution method, (1,2).

Using Equations in Word Problems

Equations are very useful in solving everyday problems. Before we begin to use equations to model real-life situations, let's first review how words translate into algebraic expressions.

Word or Expression	Operation
more than	Addition
greater than	Addition
increased by	Addition
decreased by	Subtraction
less than	Subtraction
times	Multiplication
double, triple, etc.	Multiplication
split	Division
grouped	Division

There are specific names for the answers to problems using mathematical operations.

Operation	Result
Addition	Sum
Subtraction	Difference
Multiplication	Product
Division	Quotient

Our knowledge of terms and expressions helps us model everyday situations.

EXAMPLE

Create an expression to model each situation.

1. A number n is increased by four.

2. Paul has twice as many quarters as Gina and eighteen fewer than Jake.

3. Seven less a number squared.

4. A number of pies, p, divided equally among eleven friends.

SOLUTIONS:

1. $n + 4$

2. Gina is g

   Paul is $2g$

   Jake is $2g + 18$

3. $7 - x^2$

4. $\dfrac{n}{7}$ or $n \div 7$

Let's use this knowledge to solve a word problem.

Maria and Josh walked a total of 48 miles in one week. If Maria walked 14 miles more than Josh walked, how many miles did each of them walk?

Whenever using equations to model real-life situations in a word problem, use a five-step process.

Step #1: Define the variable.

Step #2: Create an equation that models the situation in the word problem.

Step #3: Solve the equation.

Step #4: Answer the question posed in the word problem.

Step #5: Assess the validity of your answer.

We will use the five-step process to answer the word problem about Maria and Josh.

Step #1: Define the variable.

We can define either Josh's or Maria's walking distance as a variable. Let's choose n to represent Josh's walking distance.

Let n = Josh's walking distance.

Since Maria walked 14 miles farther than Josh, we can say:

Let $n + 14$ = Maria's walking distance.

Step #2: Create an equation that models the situation.

Josh's distance + Maria's distance = 48 miles

$$n \quad + \quad (n + 14) \quad = 48$$

$$n + (n + 14) = 48$$

Step #3:   Solve the equation.

$$n + (n + 14) = 48$$

$$2n + 14 = 48$$

$$2n + 14 - 14 = 48 - 14$$

$$2n = 34$$

$$\frac{2n}{2} = \frac{34}{2}$$

$$n = 17$$

Step #4:   Answer the question posed in the problem.

Although we have successfully solved for the variable, the question asks how many miles *each person* (Maria and Josh) walked.

Josh: $n = 17$ miles, so Josh walked 17 miles

Maria: $n + 14 = 17 + 14 = 31$ miles

Step #5:   Assess the validity of your answer.

The problem states that Maria walked 14 miles farther than Josh and that the sum of their distances is 48.

Did Maria's distance exceed Josh's by 14 miles?

$$31 - 17 = 14$$

$$14 = 14 \quad \checkmark$$

Do Maria's and Josh's distances add to 48 miles?

$$31 + 17 = 48$$

$$48 = 48$$

Let's try another word problem, this time using ratios.

A local businesswoman donated $192,000 to three charities: the Girl Scouts, the Boy Scouts and the Girls' Club. The ratio of the contributions to the Girl Scouts, the Boy Scouts and the Girls' Club was 5:2:1, respectively. What amount was donated to the Boy Scouts?

Step #1: Define the variable.

Although any of the charities can be symbolized by the variable, it would be wise to let the smallest donation be the variable. Thus:

Let x = the donation to the Girls' Club

Let $2x$ = the donation to the Boy Scouts

Let $5x$ = the donation to the Girl Scouts

Step #2: Create an equation that models the situation.

Girl Scouts + Boy Scouts + Girls' Club = $192,000

$$5x \quad + \quad 2x \quad + \quad x \quad = 192,000$$

Step #3: Solve the equation.

$$5x + 2x + x = 192,000$$

$$8x = 192,000$$

$$\frac{8x}{8} = \frac{192,000}{8}$$

$$x = 24,000$$

Step #4: Answer the question posed in the problem.

Since the Boy Scouts contribution is represented by the term $2x$, multiply 24,000 by 2 to find the contribution made to the Boy Scouts.

$$(2)(24,000) = \$48,000$$

Step 5: Decide if the answer makes sense.

Substitute 24,000 for x in the original equation.

$$5(24,000) + 2(24,000) + 1(24,000) = 192,000$$

$$120,000 + 48,000 + 24,000 = 192,000$$

$$192,000 = 192,000 \quad \checkmark$$

Since our calculations are correct, we conclude that the contribution to the Boy Scouts was $48,000.

Inequalities

An inequality states that one quantity is greater than another.

$m > n$ means "m is greater than n"

$-3 < -1$ means "-3 is less than -1"

$12r \geq -5.3$ means "$12r$ is greater than or equal to -5.3"

$-\dfrac{2}{3}x \leq 7$ means "$\dfrac{-2}{3}x$ is less than or equal to 7"

Inequalities share many of the same properties as equations.

EXAMPLE

Solve for c:

$$4c + 12 \leq 16$$

SOLUTION: Subtract 12 from both sides of the inequality:

$$4c + 12 - 12 \leq 16 - 12$$

Simplify: $4c \text{ " } 4$

Divide both sides of the inequality by 4:

$$\frac{4c}{4} \text{ " } \frac{4}{4}$$

Simplify: $c \leq 1$

It is important to note that when dividing or multiplying an inequality by a negative number, you must reverse the inequality sign.

EXAMPLE

Solve for p: $\dfrac{-2}{3}p > -12$

SOLUTION: Multiply both sides of the equation by $\dfrac{-3}{2}$. Remember to reverse the inequality sign:

$$\dfrac{-3}{2}\ \dfrac{-2}{3}p\ < (-12)\ \dfrac{-3}{2}$$

Simplify: $p > 18$

Inequalities can be used to model real-life situations.

EXAMPLE

Julia needs at least $20 to cover the cost of materials for a puppet show. The cost is to be shared equally among the nine other students in the class. What is the least amount of money each student must spend?

SOLUTION: Create an inequality that models the situation:

Let n equal the least amount of money each student needs to spend. Since 10 students will share the cost, use the inequality

$10n \geq 20$

Simplify: $\dfrac{10}{10}n \geq \dfrac{20}{10}$

$n \geq 2$

We used the $\geq$ sign because the cost could have been $2 or more per student.

Square Roots and Cube Roots

The product of two equal quantities is called a square. 81 is a square because $9 \times 9 = 81$. Fractions can be squares, too. $\frac{36}{49}$ is a square because $\frac{6}{7} \times \frac{6}{7} = \frac{36}{49}$. The opposite of a square is a square root. Since 81 is the square of 9 (9^2), then 9 is the square root of 81. The symbol for finding the square root of a number is "$\sqrt{}$" and is called a radical. Thus, $\sqrt{81} = 9$.

It is helpful to remember a few squares and square roots:

$0^2 = 0$

$1^2 = 1$	$6^2 = 36$	$11^2 = 121$
$2^2 = 4$	$7^2 = 49$	$12^2 = 144$
$3^2 = 9$	$8^2 = 64$	$13^2 = 169$
$4^2 = 16$	$9^2 = 81$	$14^2 = 196$
$5^2 = 25$	$10^2 = 100$	$15^2 = 225$
$\sqrt{0} = 0$	$\sqrt{36} = 6$	$\sqrt{144} = 12$
$\sqrt{1} = 1$	$\sqrt{49} = 7$	$\sqrt{169} = 13$
$\sqrt{4} = 2$	$\sqrt{64} = 8$	$\sqrt{196} = 14$
$\sqrt{9} = 3$	$\sqrt{81} = 9$	$\sqrt{225} = 15$
$\sqrt{16} = 4$	$\sqrt{100} = 10$	
$\sqrt{25} = 5$	$\sqrt{121} = 11$	

Simplifying Square Roots

Some square roots, though irrational, can still be simplified.

EXAMPLE

Simplify $\sqrt{18}$

SOLUTION: $\sqrt{18} = \sqrt{9} \times \sqrt{2} = 3\sqrt{2}$

Simplifying some square root problems can be more challenging.

EXAMPLE

Simplify $\sqrt{147}$

SOLUTION: Use a factor tree to identify squares.

$$147$$
$$49 \times 3$$

$$\sqrt{147} = \sqrt{49} \times \sqrt{3} = 7\sqrt{3}$$

Adding and Subtracting Square Roots

Square roots can be added or subtracted if the number under the radical is the same.

EXAMPLE

Simplify $6\sqrt{7} - 5\sqrt{7} + \sqrt{7}$

SOLUTION: $6\sqrt{7} - 5\sqrt{7} + \sqrt{7} = 2\sqrt{7}$

It is important to note that $\sqrt{7}$ is the same as $1\sqrt{7}$, though the 1 rarely appears.

Multiplying and Dividing Square Roots

When multiplying square roots, simply multiply the numbers under the radicals and simplify as needed.

EXAMPLE

$\sqrt{8} \times \sqrt{18} = ?$

SOLUTION: $\sqrt{8} \times \sqrt{18} = \sqrt{144} = 12$

EXAMPLE

$\sqrt{8} \times \sqrt{6} = ?$

SOLUTION: $\sqrt{8} \times \sqrt{6} = \sqrt{48} = \sqrt{16} \times \sqrt{3} = 4\sqrt{3}$

When dividing square roots, divide the numbers under the radicals.

EXAMPLE

$$\sqrt{192} \div \sqrt{3} = ?$$

SOLUTION: $\sqrt{192} \div \sqrt{3} = \sqrt{64} = 8$

Cube Roots

A cube is a number raised to the third power. 27 is a cube because $3 \times 3 \times 3 = 27$ (27 can also be expressed as 3^3). Conversely, we can say 3 is the cube root of 27 and can express it as $\sqrt[3]{27} = 3$. It will be helpful to know a few cubes and cube roots before taking the GED® test.

$0^3 = 0$	$\sqrt[3]{0} = 0$
$1^3 = 1$	$\sqrt[3]{1} = 1$
$2^3 = 8$	$\sqrt[3]{8} = 2$
$3^3 = 27$	$\sqrt[3]{27} = 3$
$4^3 = 64$	$\sqrt[3]{64} = 4$
$5^3 = 125$	$\sqrt[3]{125} = 5$
$6^3 = 216$	$\sqrt[3]{216} = 6$

Although you will not be asked to work extensively with cubes and cube roots on the GED® test, it is worth knowing how to simplify them. When simplifying square roots, we extracted perfect squares; when simplifying cube roots, we extract perfect cubes.

EXAMPLE

Simplify $\sqrt[3]{108}$

The largest perfect cube that is a factor of 108 is 27 because $27 \times 4 = 108$. Thus we get:

$$\sqrt[3]{108} = \sqrt[3]{27} \times \sqrt[3]{4} = 3\sqrt[3]{4}$$

Equations with Exponents and Square Roots

Some equations contain exponents and square roots.

$$3x^2 = 75$$

$$\sqrt{2x} = 8$$

As we learned earlier, whenever we wish to isolate a variable, we perform the opposite operation on both sides of the equation. In this case, squares and square roots are opposite operations.

EXAMPLE

Solve for n.

$$\sqrt{2n} = 6$$

SOLUTION: Isolate the variable by squaring both sides of the equation.

$$\sqrt{2n} = 6$$

$$(\sqrt{2n})^2 = 6^2$$

$$2n = 36$$

$$\frac{2n}{2} = \frac{36}{2}$$

$$n = 18$$

Check your answer by replacing n with 18 in the original equation.

$$\sqrt{(2)(18)} = 6$$

$$\sqrt{36} = 6$$

$$6 = 6 \quad \checkmark$$

Let's try another example:

EXAMPLE

Solve for x.

$$x^2 = 961$$

SOLUTION: Isolate the variable by performing the opposite operation on both sides of the equation.

$$x^2 = 961$$

$$\sqrt{x^2} = \sqrt{961}$$

$$x = 31$$

Check your answer by replacing x with 31 in the original equation.

$$31^2 = 961$$

$$961 = 961 \quad \checkmark$$

Equations with Exponents and Square Roots

In this final section of the chapter, we will integrate squares and square roots into our knowledge of equation solving.

EXAMPLE

Solve for n.

$$3n^2 - 11 = 136$$

SOLUTION:

Step #1: Begin isolating the variable by adding 11 to both sides of the equation.

$$3n^2 - 11 + 11 = 136 + 11$$

$$3n^2 = 147$$

Step #2: Continue to isolate the variable by dividing both sides of the equation by 3.

$$\frac{3n^2}{3} = \frac{147}{3}$$

$$n^2 = 49$$

Step #3: Isolate the variable by taking the square root of each side of the equation.

$$\sqrt{n^2} = \sqrt{49}$$

$$n = 7$$

You can check your answer by substituting 7 for n in the original equation.

$$3(7)^2 - 11 = 136$$

$$3(49) - 11 = 136$$

$$147 - 11 = 136$$

$$136 = 136 \quad \checkmark$$

EXAMPLE

Solve for x.

$$\sqrt{2x + 1} - 3 = 6$$

SOLUTION:

Step #1: In order to isolate the variable, we must first isolate the radical. Add 3 to both sides of the equation.

$$\sqrt{2x + 1} - 3 + 3 = 6 + 3$$

$$\sqrt{2x + 1} = 9$$

Step #2: Isolate the expression, $2x + 1$, by squaring both sides of the equation.

$$(\sqrt{2x + 1})^2 = 9^2$$

$$2x + 1 = 81$$

Step #3: Finish the calculations as you would for any equation.

$$2x + 1 = 81$$

$$2x + 1 - 1 = 81 - 1$$

$$2x = 80$$

$$\frac{2x}{2} = \frac{80}{2}$$

$$x = 40$$

Check your answer by replacing x with 40.

$$\sqrt{2(40) + 1} - 3 = 6$$

$$\sqrt{81} - 3 = 6$$

$$9 - 3 = 6$$

$$6 = 6 \quad \checkmark$$

Quadratic Expressions and Equations

A quadratic expression has a power or exponent of two. The following are examples of quadratic expressions:

$$2x^2 + 6x - 7$$

$$-5x^2 + 3x$$

$$\frac{1}{2}x^2 - 2x - 11$$

Questions on the GED® test ask you to multiply quantities that create quadratic expressions. In the following example, a monomial (one term) must multiply a binomial (two terms).

EXAMPLE

Find the product of $(3x)(2x - 7)$.

SOLUTION: Use the distributive property to multiply the terms:

$$(3x)(2x) - (3x)(7)$$

Remember to add the exponents when multiplying like terms.

$$(3x)(2x) - (3x)(7) = 6x^2 - 21x.$$

Some examples ask you to multiply two binomials. To find the product, you can use a method called "FOIL." FOIL is an acronym that means:

F: First terms get multiplied

O: Outer terms get multiplied

I: Inner terms get multiplied

L: Last terms get multiplied

EXAMPLE

Find the product of $(2x + 3)(x - 5)$

SOLUTION: Use FOIL to find the product.

First: $(2x)(x) = 2x^2$

Outer: $(2x)(-5) = -10x$

Inner: $(3)(x) = 3x$

Last: $(3)(-5) = -15$

List the terms in descending order of exponent and simplify.

$$2x^2 - 10x + 3x - 15 = 2x^2 - 7x - 15$$

Factoring Quadratic Expressions

Conversely, quadratic expressions can be factored (broken down into smaller terms) by extracting the greatest common factor (GCF).

EXAMPLE

Factor $3x^2 + 9x$

SOLUTION: The GCF of $3x^2 + 9x$ is $3x$. Divide each term by $3x$.

$$3x^2 + 9x = 3x(x + 3)$$

You can verify that the expression is correctly factored by multiplying $3x$ by the terms in the parentheses.

$$3x(x + 3) = (3x)(x) + (3x)(3) = 3x^2 + 9x$$

Some quadratic expressions use a more sophisticated form of factoring.

EXAMPLE

Factor $x^2 + 9x + 20$

SOLUTION: By inspection, we see the expression does not have a GCF other than 1. When the leading coefficient is 1, we ask: What two numbers have a product of the last term (in this case, 20) and a sum of the middle coefficient (in this case, 9)?

$2 \times 10 = 20$	$2 + 10 = 12$
$1 \times 20 = 20$	$1 + 20 = 21$
$4 \times 5 = 20$	$4 + 5 = 9$

4 and 5 have a sum of 9 and a product of 20, so they are most likely the desired factors. Place each one inside a parentheses with the variable, as follows:

$$(x + 4)(x + 5)$$

These factors in parentheses are the answers requested, but still use FOIL to check your work.

First:	$(x)(x) = x^2$
Outer:	$(x)(5) = 5x$
Inner:	$(4)(x) = 4x$
Last:	$(4)(5) = 20$

Array the terms and simplify to be sure the factors generate your original expression.

$$x^2 + 5x + 4x + 20 = x^2 + 9x + 20$$

Let's try a few more.

Factor the following quadratic expressions.

1. $x^2 + 7x + 12$

2. $x^2 + 2x - 8$

3. $x^2 - x - 56$

SOLUTIONS:

1. $x^2 + 7x + 12 = (x + 4)(x + 3)$
2. $x^2 + 2x - 8 = (x + 4)(x - 2)$
3. $x^2 - x - 56 = (x + 7)(x - 8)$

Remember, the coefficient of $-x$ in problem 3 above $(x^2 - x - 56)$ is -1.

Quadratic Equations

Solving quadratic equations is easy once you have mastered factoring quadratic expressions.

EXAMPLE

Solve $2x^2 - 22x = 0$

SOLUTION: Factor the left side of the equation.

$$2x^2 - 22x = 0$$

$$2x(x - 11) = 0$$

Since $2x(x - 11) = 0$, one of the parenthesized quantities must equal 0. Set each quantity equal to 0 and solve.

Either $(2x = 0)$ or $(x - 11) = 0$

Therefore, either $x = 0$ or $x = 11$

You can check each value to verify its accuracy.

If $x = 11$, then: $2(11)^2 - 22(11) = 0$

$242 - 242 = 0$ ✓

Or, if $x = 0$, then: $2(0)^2 - 22(0) = 0$

$0 - 0 = 0$ ✓

EXAMPLE

Solve $x^2 - 6x - 72 = 0$

SOLUTION: Factor the left side of the equation:

$x^2 - 6x - 72 = 0$

$(x - 12)(x + 6) = 0$

Then either $(x - 12) = 0$ or $(x + 6) = 0$

Therefore, $x = 12$ or $x = -6$

The Quadratic Formula

The general form for a quadratic formula is $ax^2 + bx + c = 0$, where a and b are coefficients of x^2 and x. The third term, c, is called a constant (a number). Earlier we learned how to solve a quadratic equation by factoring. Look at the example we used in the last section.

$x^2 - 6x - 72 = 0$

$(x - 12)(x + 6) = 0$

Then either $(x - 12) = 0$ or $(x + 6) = 0$

And so, $x = 12$ or $x = -6$

Another way to solve quadratic equations is by using the quadratic equation formula.

$$x = \frac{-b \pm \sqrt{b^2 - 4ac}}{2a}$$

Although the quadratic equation formula is provided in the reference section on the GED® test, it is a useful formula to remember for your future math classes. From the equation $x^2 - 6x - 72 = 0$, we get $a = 1$, $b = -6$ and $c = -72$. Place each value in the quadratic equation and solve:

$$x = \frac{-b \pm \sqrt{b^2 - 4ac}}{2a}$$

$$x = \frac{-(-6) \pm \sqrt{(-6)^2 - 4(1)(-72)}}{2(1)}$$

$$x = \frac{6 \pm \sqrt{(36) - (-288)}}{2}$$

$$x = \frac{6 \pm 18}{2}$$

$$x = 12 \text{ or } x = -6$$

The quadratic formula is useful if you find factoring difficult, and it always works. Consider the following equation:

$$x^2 + 4x - 6 = 0$$

There are no values that have a product of –6 and a sum of 4. Use the quadratic equation formula to solve.

$$a = 1, b = 4, c = -6$$

$$x = \frac{-4 \pm \sqrt{(4)^2 - 4(1)(-6)}}{2(1)}$$

$$x = \frac{-4 \pm \sqrt{40}}{2}$$

$$x = \frac{-4 \pm 2\sqrt{10}}{2}$$

$$x = -2 \pm \sqrt{10}$$

The two solutions are irrational and could not have been derived with factoring, so it is clear that the formula can be quite useful in such cases.

PRACTICE!

1. $5m^2n - 2mn - 3$ is an example of an

    A.   algebraic term

    B.   algebraic equation

    C.   order of operation

    D.   algebraic expression

2. Simplify: $2(3 - 6)^2 + 12 \div 6$

    A.   20

    B.   8

    C.   5

    D.   2

3. Simplify $\dfrac{-3xy^2 - z}{-3xz}$ if $x = 2$, $y = -2$ and $z = 4$

    A. 7

    B. 6

    C. $\dfrac{7}{6}$

    D. -6

4. Simplify the following:

    $-4xy^2 - 2xy + xy - 8mn + mn$

    A. $-5x^3y^3 - 8m^2n^2$

    B. $-5x^3y - 7m^2n^2$

    C. $-32y - 8$

    D. $-4xy^2 - xy - 7mn$

5. Solve for n:

    $n + 27 = -83$

    A. 110

    B. 56

    C. -34

    D. -110

6. Solve for m:

    $3m - 15 = 99$

    A. 51

    B. 38

    C. 19

    D. 0

7. Solve for r:

$$-2(5 - 3r) = 12 - 3(5 - r)$$

    A. $\dfrac{7}{3}$

    B. $\dfrac{7}{6}$

    C. 0

    D. $\dfrac{-7}{6}$

8. If the product of 5 and an integer, n, is increased by 12, the result is -13. What is the value of n?

    A. 25

    B. 5

    C. $\dfrac{1}{5}$

    D. -5

9. Simplify the expression:

$$\sqrt{3}(\sqrt{6} - 3\sqrt{2})$$

    A. $3 - 3\sqrt{6}$

    B. $3 + 3\sqrt{6}$

    C. $3\sqrt{2} - 3\sqrt{6}$

    D. $9 - \sqrt{2}$

10. Simplify the expression.

$$\sqrt[3]{192}$$

    A. $4\sqrt[3]{3}$

    B. $3\sqrt[3]{4}$

    C. $4\sqrt{3}$

    D. $3\sqrt{4}$

11. Solve for the positive value of b.

$$9b^2 - 11 = 718$$

    A. 12

    B. 9

    C. 6

    D. 3

12. Find the value of x. Write your answer in the box below.

$$\sqrt{10x + 1} - 2 = 17$$

```
┌─────────────────────┐
│                     │
│                     │
└─────────────────────┘
```

13. Sal has deposited $17,500 in a certificate of deposit at the rate of 5.2%. If the interest he earned is $6,142.50, how long did the funds remain in the account?

    A. 4.75 years

    B. 5.2 years

    C. 6.25 years

    D. 6.75 years

14. Solve $x^2 + x - 30 = 0$

    A. 6, –5

    B. –6, 5

    C. $\sqrt{30}$

    D. 11

15. Solve the system of equations using the substitution method.

$$y = 2x - 1$$

$$2x + 3y = 21$$

    A. $x = 3, y = 5$

    B. $x = 5, y = 3$

    C. $x = 7, y = 2$

    D. $x = 2, y = 7$

16. Solve for x:

   $-4x - 4 > 14$

   A. $x > -4.5$

   B. $x < -4.5$

   C. $x \leq 4.5$

   D. $x \geq -4.5$

Math Practice 3 Answers

1. **D.**

   $-5m^2n$, $-2mn$ and -3 are all examples of terms. A collection of terms joined by addition or subtraction, such as $5m^2n - 2mn - 3$, is called an **expression**.

2. **A.**

   Use the order of operations to simplify the expression.

   Simplify parentheses: $2(3 - 6)^2 + 12 \div 6 =$

   $2(-3)^2 + 12 \div 6.$

   Simplify exponents: $2(-3)^2 + 12 \div 6 =$

   $2(9) + 12 \div 6$

   Multiply and divide, proceeding from left to right.

   $2(9) + 12 \div 6 =$

   $18 + 2$

   Add: $18 + 2 = 20$

3. **C.**

   Input the values for each variable, then use the order of operations to simplify.

   $$\frac{-3(2)(-2)^2 - 4}{-3(2)(4)}$$

All of the values in the parentheses are expressed in simplest form, so proceed with working with the exponents.

$$\frac{-3(2)(-2)^2 - 4}{-3(2)(4)} =$$

$$\frac{-3(2)(4) - 4}{-3(2)(4)}$$

Next, multiply the quantities in the numerator and the denominator:

$$\frac{-3(2)(4) - 4}{-3(2)(4)} =$$

$$\frac{-24 - 4}{-24}$$

Use subtraction to simplify the numerator.

$$\frac{-24 - 4}{-24} = \frac{-28}{-24}$$

Finally, simplify the numerator and the denominator by dividing each by –4.

$$\frac{-28 \div -4}{-24 \div -4} = \frac{7}{6}$$

4. **D.**

Combine like terms by adding and subtracting the coefficients. Like terms are those that contain the same variable(s) raised to the same power(s). In this example, the following are the like terms:

$-2xy$, xy and $-8mn$ and mn

$-4xy^2 - 2xy + xy - 8mn + mn =$

$-4x^2y - xy - 7mn$

Remember, a term such as mn is understood to have a coefficient of 1.

5. **D.**

Isolate the variable by subtracting 27 from each side of the equation.

$n + 27 = -83$

$n + 27 - 27 = -83 - 27$

$n = -110$

Check your solution by replacing n with -110 in the original equation.

$$-110 + 27 = -83$$
$$-83 = -83 \quad \checkmark$$

6. **B.**

Begin isolating the variable by adding 15 to both sides of the equation.

$$3m - 15 = 99$$
$$3m - 15 + 15 = 99 + 15$$
$$3m = 114$$

Continue isolating the variable by dividing both sides of the equation by 3.

$$3m = 114$$
$$\frac{3m}{3} = \frac{114}{3}$$
$$m = 38$$

Check your solution by replacing m with 38 in the original equation.

$$3(38) - 15 = 99$$
$$114 - 15 = 99$$
$$99 = 99 \quad \checkmark$$

7. **A.**

Use the order of operations to isolate the variable. The parentheses are in simplest form and there are no exponents, so proceed to multiplication.

$$-2(5 - 3r) = 12 - 3(5 - r)$$
$$-10 + 6r = 12 - 15 + 3r$$

Next, add the like terms.

$$-10 + 6r = 12 - 15 + 3r =$$
$$-10 + 6r = -3 + 3r$$

Add 10 to both sides of the equation.

$$-10 + 6r = -3 + 3r$$
$$-10 + 10 + 6r = -3 + 3r + 10$$
$$6r = 3r + 7$$

Subtract $3r$ from both sides of the equation.

$$6r = 3r + 7$$

$$6r - r = 3r + 7 - 3r$$

$$3r = 7$$

Divide both sides of the equation by 3 to isolate the variable.

$$3r = 7$$

$$\frac{3r}{3} = \frac{7}{3}$$

$$r = \frac{7}{3}$$

Check your solution by replacing r with $\frac{7}{3}$ in the original equation.

$$-2\left(5 - 3\left(\frac{7}{3}\right)\right) = 12 - 3\left(5 - \frac{7}{3}\right)$$

$$-2(5 - 7) = 12 - 3\left(\frac{8}{3}\right)$$

$$-2(-2) = 12 - 8$$

$$4 = 4 \quad \checkmark$$

8. **D.**

Let n = the integer

The product of two values is the result of multiplying them. "Increased by" means use addition. We therefore arrive at the equation:

$$5n + 12 = -13$$

Begin isolating the variable by subtracting 12 from both sides of the equation.

$$5n + 12 - 12 = -13 - 12$$

$$5n = -25$$

Complete the problem by dividing both sides of the equation by 5.

$$\frac{5n}{5} = -\frac{25}{5}$$

$$n = -5$$

Check your solution by replacing *n* with –5 in the equation we have created.

$$5(-5) + 12 = -13$$
$$-25 + 12 = -13$$
$$-13 = -13 \quad ✓$$

9. **C.**

Multiply $\sqrt{3}$ by both terms in the parentheses.

$$\sqrt{3}\left(\sqrt{6} - 3\sqrt{2}\right) =$$
$$\sqrt{18} - 3\sqrt{6} =$$
$$\sqrt{9} \times \sqrt{2} - 3\sqrt{6} =$$
$$3\sqrt{2} - 3\sqrt{6}$$

10. **A.**

Extract the largest cube from $\sqrt[3]{192}$

$$\sqrt[3]{192} = \sqrt[3]{64} \times \sqrt[3]{3} = 4\sqrt[3]{3}$$

11. **B.**

Step #1: Begin isolating the variable by adding 11 to both sides of the equation.

$$9b^2 - 11 + 11 = 718 + 11$$

$$9b^2 = 729$$

Step #2: Divide both sides of the equation by 9.

$$\frac{9b^2}{9} = \frac{729}{9}$$

$$b^2 = 81$$

Step #3: Find the square root of both sides of the equation.

$$\sqrt{b^2} = \sqrt{81}$$

$$b = 9$$

Check your solution by replacing 9 for b in the original equation.

$$9(9)^2 - 11 = 718$$

$$9(81) - 11 = 718$$

$$729 - 11 = 718$$

$$718 = 718 \quad \checkmark$$

12. **36**

Step #1: Isolate the radical by adding 2 to both sides of the equation.

$$\sqrt{10x + 1} - 2 = 17$$

$$\sqrt{10x + 1} - 2 + 2 = 17 + 2$$

$$\sqrt{10x + 1} = 19$$

Step #2: Begin to isolate the variable by squaring both sides of the equation.

$$(\sqrt{10x + 1})^2 = 19^2$$

$$10x + 1 = 361$$

Step #3: Finish solving for the variable.

$$10x + 1 - 1 = 361 - 1$$

$$10x = 360$$

$$\frac{10x}{10} = \frac{360}{10}$$

$$x = 36$$

Check your solution by replacing x with 36.

$$\sqrt{10(36) + 1} - 2 = 17$$

$$\sqrt{361} - 2 = 17$$

$$19 - 2 = 17$$

$$17 = 17 \quad \checkmark$$

13. **D.**

Use the formula I = PRT and solve for T.

I = $6,142.5

P = $17,500

R = 5.2 %

T = time in years

$6,142.5 = (17,500)(0.052)(T)

$6,142.5 = 910T

6.75 = T

Sal earned his interest in the CD over a period of 6.75 years.

14. **B.**

Solve by factoring

$x^2 + x - 30 = 0$

$(x + 6)(x - 5) = 0$

Either $(x + 6) = 0$ or $(x - 5) = 0$

Therefore, $x = -6$ or $x = 5$

15. **A.**

Substitute $2x - 1$ for y in the other equation.

$2x + 3(2x - 1) = 21$

$2x + 6x - 3 = 21$

$8x - 3 = 21$

$8x - 3 + 3 = 21 + 3$

$8x = 24$

$\dfrac{8x}{8} = \dfrac{24}{8}$

$x = 3$

Substitute 3 for x in either equation.

$$y = 2(3) - 1$$
$$y = 5$$

16. **B.**

$$-4x - 4 > 14$$
$$-4x - 4 + 4 > 14 + 4$$
$$-4x > 18$$
$$\frac{-4x}{-4} < \frac{18}{-4}$$
$$x < -4.5$$

Chapter **4**

Ratios and Proportions

In this chapter, we will review the following topics:

- Definition of a ratio

- Applications of ratios

- Definition of a proportion

- Applications of proportions

- Percents as proportions

Definition of Ratio

A ratio is the comparison of two numbers or quantities. When you travel at a rate of 60 miles per hour (mph), your rate is a ratio: It compares distance (miles) to time (hours). Other examples of ratios include:

Price per pound: compares money to weight

Annual gym membership fees: compares money (your dues) to time (a year)

Scale on maps: compares distance (in inches) to distance (in miles)

A ratio can be expressed three ways. The ratio of 7 grapefruits for $3.00 can be expressed as follows:

$$7 \text{ to } 3 \qquad 7:3 \qquad \frac{7}{3}$$

Applications of Ratios

A ratio can be a useful tool when comparing prices.

EXAMPLE

A store offers 4 cans of soup for $5.00 while another store offers 5 cans of soup for the same price. Which is the better deal?

If the cans of soup are of the same quality, then 5 cans of soup for $5.00 is preferred over 4 cans for the same price. We can see this comparison mathematically.

$$\frac{\$5.00}{4 \ cans} = \$1.25 \ per \ can$$

$$\frac{\$5.00}{5 \ cans} = \$1.00 \ per \ can$$

Sometimes we cannot make a logical comparison between options because the units of measure are not equivalent.

EXAMPLE

Sam can buy a six-ounce hamburger for $1.99 or a one-half-pound hamburger for $2.99. Which is the better deal?

Notice that one hamburger has its weight expressed in ounces while the other is expressed in pounds. Unless both weights are expressed in equivalent units, we cannot accurately gauge which is the preferred option. Although we can express both options in pounds or ounces, it is usually easier to convert to the smaller unit.

Option #1: The 6-ounce hamburger: $\dfrac{\$1.99}{6 \ ounces}$ = about $0.33 per ounce

Option #2: Convert pounds into ounces: Since 1 pound = 16 ounces, then $\dfrac{1}{2}$ pound equals 8 ounces ($\dfrac{1}{2} \times 16 = 8$).

$\dfrac{\$2.99}{8 \ ounces}$ = about $0.37 per ounce

If the quality of both hamburgers is equivalent, it is wiser to buy the 6-ounce hamburger.

Definition of Proportion

A proportion is a statement that two ratios are equal. For example, $\frac{1}{2} = \frac{8}{16}$ is a proportion because $\frac{1}{2}$ and $\frac{8}{16}$ are equal ratios. You can test if two ratios are equal by cross-multiplying the two fractions.

EXAMPLE

Prove that $\frac{1}{2} = \frac{8}{16}$ by cross-multiplying the two fractions.

$$\frac{1}{2} = \frac{8}{16}$$

$$1 \times 16 = 2 \times 8$$

$$16 = 16$$

EXAMPLE

Show that $\frac{7}{19}$ and $\frac{12}{23}$ do not create a proportion.

$$\frac{7}{19} = \frac{12}{23}$$

$$7 \times 23 = 12 \times 19$$

$$161 \neq 228$$

Since their cross-products are not equal, $\frac{7}{19}$ and $\frac{12}{23}$ do not form a proportion.

Applications of Proportions

We can use the fact that a proportion's cross-products are equal to solve many problems.

EXAMPLE

If 3 pizzas will feed 11 students, how many pizzas are needed to feed 14 students?

(Round any decimal/fraction remainder up to the nearest whole pizza.)

Solve this problem by using the proportion $\dfrac{\text{pizzas}}{\text{students}} = \dfrac{\text{pizzas}}{\text{students}}$

We can let a variable, p, represent the unknown number of pizzas needed to feed 14 students.

$$\frac{3}{11} = \frac{p}{14}$$

Cross-multiply fractions and solve for p.

$$\frac{3}{11} = \frac{p}{14}$$

$$11 \times p = 3 \times 14$$

$$11p = 42$$

$$\frac{11}{11}p = \frac{42}{11}$$

$$p = 3\frac{9}{11}$$

The question asks us to round any fraction of a pizza up to the nearest whole pizza, so we must purchase 4 pizzas to feed 14 students.

Let's try one more example—a common one—using a map.

One common use of proportions is to compare items of different scale. Perhaps you have noticed the following on the legend of a map:

1 inch = 25 miles.

This useful tool compares two different scales: inches on a map to the actual miles they represent.

EXAMPLE

The legend on a state map of California indicates that 1 inch = 47 miles. If the distance on the map between San Diego and Los Angeles is 2.8 inches, what is the actual distance between the two cities?

Use the proportion $\dfrac{\text{map distance}}{\text{actual distance}} = \dfrac{\text{map distance}}{\text{actual distance}}$. Since the actual distance between San Diego and Los Angeles is unknown, we will use a variable, d, to represent that distance.

$$\frac{1}{47} = \frac{2.8}{d}$$

Cross-multiply the fractions and solve for d.

$$1 \times d = 2.8 \times 47$$

$$d = 131.6$$

The distance between San Diego and Los Angeles is 131.6 miles.

Percents as Proportions

Earlier we discussed how percent problems can be solved using decimals. In this section we will show how percents can also be calculated using proportions.

We can solve any type of percent problem using the following proportion: $\dfrac{\text{part}}{\text{whole}} = \dfrac{n}{100}$, where n stands for the unknown percent.

If 17 of 25 people in the theater program are actors, what percent are actors?

Use $\dfrac{\text{part}}{\text{whole}} = \dfrac{n}{100}$ to solve the problem.

$$\dfrac{17}{25} = \dfrac{n}{100}$$

Solve for n:

$$\dfrac{17}{25} = \dfrac{n}{100}$$

$$17 \times 100 = 25 \times n$$

$$1{,}700 = 25n$$

$$\dfrac{1{,}700}{25} = \dfrac{25}{25}n$$

$$68 = n$$

In the theater group, 68% of the members are actors.

Sometimes the percent is known but the part is not.

EXAMPLE

A cooking class has 20 students. If 35% of the students in the cooking class are male, how many males are in the class?

In this class, the percent is known but the number of males is not. Use the variable m to represent the part of the whole class that is male.

$$\frac{\text{part}}{\text{whole}} = \frac{n}{100}$$

$$\frac{m}{20} = \frac{35}{100}$$

$$20 \times 35 = m \times 100$$

$$700 = 100m$$

$$\frac{700}{100} = \frac{100}{100}m$$

$$7 = m$$

There are 7 males in a cooking class made up of 20 students.

We can also use the proportion $\frac{\text{part}}{\text{whole}} = \frac{n}{100}$ to solve problems in which the percent and part are known, but the whole is not.

EXAMPLE

In a recent survey of tire users, 69 of the respondents use Big Discount Tire brand. If the 69 users of those tires represent 37.5% of the respondents, how many tire users were surveyed?

$$\frac{\text{part}}{\text{whole}} = \frac{n}{100}$$

$$\frac{69}{t} = \frac{37.5}{100}$$

$$t \times 37.5 = 69 \times 100$$

$$37.5t = 6,900$$

$$\frac{37.5}{37.5}t = \frac{6,900}{37.5}$$

$$t = 184$$

A total of 184 tire users were surveyed.

PRACTICE!

1. If a class has 9 men and 13 women, what is the ratio of men to the class?

    A. 9:13

    B. 13 to 9

    C. $\dfrac{13}{22}$

    D. $\dfrac{9}{22}$

2. If apples cost $3.20 per pound, what is the cost of a 3-ounce apple (1 pound = 16 ounces)?

    A. $3.20

    B. $2.40

    C. $1.20

    D. $0.60

3. Licorice costs $2.70 per yard or $0.11 per inch. Which is the better deal? (1 yard = 3 feet = 36 inches).

    A. $0.11 per inch

    B. $2.70 per yard

    C. Both deals are the same.

    D. It cannot be determined from the information provided.

4. Which of the following ratio pairs forms a proportion?

    A. $\dfrac{1}{3} = \dfrac{17}{51}$

    B. $\dfrac{17}{20} = \dfrac{84}{100}$

    C. $\dfrac{5}{8} = \dfrac{16}{25}$

    D. $\dfrac{2}{5} = \dfrac{7}{16}$

5. The legend on a map shows that 1 inch = 80 miles. The distance on the map shows that St. Louis and Little Rock are 5.05 inches apart. What is the actual distance?

    A. 80 miles

    B. 205 miles

    C. 395 miles

    D. 404 miles

6. Which proportion can be used to find 17% of 95?

    A. $\dfrac{95}{n} = \dfrac{17}{100}$

    B. $\dfrac{17}{95} = \dfrac{n}{100}$

    C. $\dfrac{n}{95} = \dfrac{17}{100}$

    D. $\dfrac{95}{100} = \dfrac{n}{17}$

7. The 35 members of a committee represent 28% of a school's students. How many students attend the school?

    A. 125

    B. 75

    C. 49

    D. 35

8. A machine produces 4,200 metal brackets every hour. On the average, if 56 brackets each hour are defective, what percent are defective (round your answer to the nearest tenth of a percent)?

    A. 13.3%

    B. 4.4%

    C. 1.3%

    D. 0.13%

9. A store has discounted its running shoes by 12.5%. If the original price of the shoes was $88.00, what is the sale price?

    A. $11.00

    B. $55.00

    C. $75.50

    D. $77.00

10. A retailer purchases sunglasses for $16 per pair and sells them for $30 in her store. What is her profit margin (also known as a markup)?

    A. 87.5%

    B. 125%

    C. 144%

    D. 187.5%

Math Practice 4 Answers

1. **D.**

Since there are 9 men and 13 women in the class, the class roster consists of 22 students. The ratio of men to the class is $\dfrac{9}{22}$ (or 9 to 22, or 9:22).

2. **D.**

Convert pounds to ounces to find the cost of apples per ounce.

$$\frac{\$3.20}{1\,\text{pound}} = \frac{\$3.20}{16\,\text{ounces}} = \$0.20 \text{ per ounce}$$

Multiply $0.20 per ounce by 3 to get the cost of a 3-ounce apple.

$$3 \times \$0.20 = \$0.60$$

3. **B.**

Convert the cost of licorice per yard into licorice per inch.

$$\frac{\$2.70}{\text{yard}} = \frac{\$2.70}{36\,\text{inches}} = \$0.075 \text{ per inch}$$

$0.075 per inch is more economical than $0.11 per inch.

4. **A.**

Two ratios form a proportion when their cross-products are equal.

$$\frac{1}{3} = \frac{17}{51}$$

$1 \times 51 = 3 \times 17$

$51 = 51$

5. **D.**

Use the proportion $\dfrac{\text{map distance}}{\text{actual distance}} = \dfrac{\text{map distance}}{\text{actual distance}}$ to answer the question.

$$\frac{1}{80} = \frac{5.05}{d}$$

$1 \times d = 80 \times 5.05$

$d = 404$

6. **C.**

Use the proportion $\dfrac{\text{part}}{\text{whole}} = \dfrac{n}{100}$ to find 17% of 95. The whole, 95, is known but the part is not.

$$\frac{n}{95} = \frac{17}{100}$$

7. **A.**

Use the formula $\dfrac{\text{part}}{\text{whole}} = \dfrac{n}{100}$ and input the known information.

$$\frac{35}{n} = \frac{28}{100}$$

$35 \times 100 = 28 \times n$

$3{,}500 = 28n$

$$\frac{3{,}500}{28} = \frac{28}{28}n$$

$125 = n$

8. **C.**

Use the formula $\dfrac{\text{part}}{\text{whole}} = \dfrac{n}{100}$ and input the known information.

$$\dfrac{56}{4,200} = \dfrac{n}{100}$$

$$56 \times 100 = 4,200 \times n$$

$$5,600 = 4,200n$$

$$\dfrac{5,600}{4,200} = \dfrac{4,200}{4,200}n$$

$$1.333\ldots\% = n$$

1.333...% rounded to the nearest tenth of percent is 1.3%.

9. **D.**

Use the formula $\dfrac{\text{part}}{\text{whole}} = \dfrac{n}{100}$ to calculate the discount.

$$\dfrac{n}{88} = \dfrac{12.5}{100}$$

$$100 \times n = 12.5 \times 88$$

$$100n = 1,100$$

$$\dfrac{100}{100}n = \dfrac{1,100}{100}$$

$$n = \$11.00$$

Subtract the discount, $11.00, from the original price of the shoes to find the sale price.

$88.00 - 11.00 = \$77.00$

10. **A.**

Use the formula $\dfrac{\text{part}}{\text{whole}} = \dfrac{n}{100}$ to find the store owner's profit margin.

profit = selling price − purchase price

$30.00 − 16.00 = $14.00

$$\frac{14}{16} = \frac{n}{100}$$

$16 \times n = 14 \times 100$

$16n = 1,400$

$$\frac{16}{16}n = \frac{1,400}{16}$$

$n = 87.5\%$

Chapter 5

Linear Equations and the Coordinate Plane

In this chapter we will review:

- Relations

- Functions

- Functional Notation

- The Coordinate Plane

- Slopes of Lines

- Linear Equations

- Linear Inequalities

- Applications of Linear Models

- Quadratic Functions

Relations

A **relation** is any set of ordered pairs. The following is a relation.

$$(2, 0) \qquad (-3, 5) \qquad (7, 4) \qquad (-2, -5)$$

We can express the relation in an input-output table.

Input	Output
2	0
−2	−5
7	4
−3	5

The set of all inputs is called the **domain**. The set of all outputs is called the **range**. The domain for the relation above is −3, −2, 2, and 7. The range for the relation is −5, 0, 4, and 5.

Functions

A **function** is a relation that establishes a relationship between inputs and outputs. It is important to note that for any input there is exactly one output.

EXAMPLE

Does the following input-output table express a function?

Input	Output
6	−3
12	−6
18	−9
24	−12
30	−15

SOLUTION: The input-output table expresses a function because each input has exactly one output.

The following input-output table does NOT express a function.

Input	Output
7	2
3	8
5	−3
7	−7

Notice that the input, 7, has two outputs, 2 and –7. *Each input in a function can only have one output.*

EXAMPLE

Does the following input-output table express a function?

Input	Output
7	3
8	3
9	3
23	3

SOLUTION: Although the outputs are identical, each input has only one output. Therefore, the input-output table expresses a function.

Functions are useful in our everyday lives. Consider the following situation.

EXAMPLE

Elena earns a certain dollar amount per hour. Below is table of the hours she worked and the pay she received.

Hours Worked	Pay Earned ($)
6	72
4	48
5	60
9	108
11	132

1. Does the table represent a function?

2. What is Elena's predicted pay for a 15-hour work week?

SOLUTION:

1. The table represents a function. Each input (the hours worked) yields solely one output, the pay earned for those hours. The function can be visualized as

    (6, 72), (4, 48), (5, 60), (9, 108), (11, 132)

2. Dividing each output by each input, we derive an hourly pay of $12.00 per hour. Thus, a 15-hour work week will yield $180.00 because $12 \times 15 = 180$

Functional Notation

Functions use the notation $f(x)$ which means "the function of x." Although any letter can be used, we usually see most functions expressed using the letter f. We can find any member of the range of the function simply by inputting values into the domain.

EXAMPLE

If $f(x) = 9x^2 - 2x$, find the value of $f(-2)$.

SOLUTION: Substitute -2 for x in the function.

$$f(-2) = 9(-2)^2 - 2(-2) = (9)(4) + 4 = 40$$

Thus $f(-2) = 40$

The Coordinate Plane

The coordinate plane consists of an x- and y-axis. Each axis is composed of negative and positive values. The point at which the two axes intersect is called the **origin**.

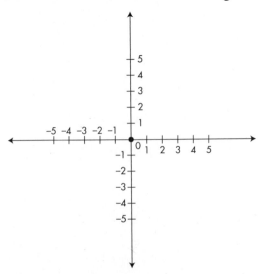

Each point on the coordinate plane is designated by an x and y value; each value is called a **coordinate**.

A point on the coordinate plane is represented by a coordinate pair in the form of (x, y). A coordinate plane is shown below with certain points described by their coordinate pairs.

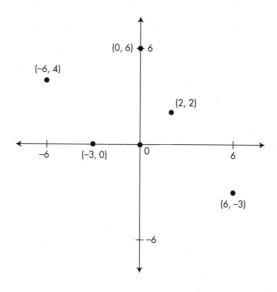

Slopes of Lines

A line can be drawn between any two points on the coordinate plane. Look at the line drawn between the points (1,2) and (5,8).

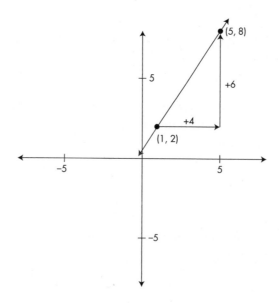

To move from (1, 2) to (5, 8), we move up 6 units and to the right 4 units. The slope of this line, defined as $\dfrac{\text{rise}}{\text{run}}$, is $\dfrac{6}{4}$ which simplifies to $\dfrac{3}{2}$.

The slope of a line can be found without graphing using the formula $m = \dfrac{y_2 - y_1}{x_2 - x_1}$ where m represents the slope of a line connecting (x_1, y_1) and (x_2, y_2). Using the slope formula and the coordinates from the previous example we get:

$(x_1, y_1) = (1, 2)$

$(x_2, y_2) = (5, 8)$

$m = \dfrac{y_2 - y_1}{x_2 - x_1} = \dfrac{8 - 2}{5 - 1} = \dfrac{6}{4} = \dfrac{3}{2}$

EXAMPLE

Without graphing, calculate the slope of the line that connects (7, –5) and (–4, –6).

SOLUTION: Use the slope formula $m = \dfrac{y_2 - y_1}{x_2 - x_1}$ and input the coordinates.

$(x_1, y_1) = (7, -5)$

$(x_2, y_2) = (-4, -6)$

$m = \dfrac{-6 - (-5)}{-4 - 7} = \dfrac{-1}{-11} = \dfrac{1}{11}$

Note what happens when we swap the values of points 1 and 2 so that we consider (x_1, y_1) to be (–4, –6) and (x_2, y_2) to be (7, –5), respectively.

$m = \dfrac{-5 - (-6)}{7 - (-4)} = \dfrac{1}{11}$

Regardless of which point is designated (x_1, y_1) and (x_2, y_2) , the result will be the same.

The Slope-Intercept Form of a Line

Any equation of a line is called a **linear equation**. A line in the form of $y = mx + b$ is called the slope-intercept form of a line. In this general equation, m represents the slope of the line and b stands for the line's y-intercept. The y-intercept of a line is the point at which the line intersects the y-axis.

EXAMPLE

In the equation $y = -\dfrac{2}{3}x - 3$, what is the line's slope and y-intercept?

SOLUTION: The slope, m, is $-\dfrac{2}{3}$ and the y-intercept, b, is -3.

The slope-intercept form of a line is a useful tool for quickly graphing a line. Let's graph the equation $y = -\dfrac{2}{3}x - 3$ by first plotting points individually. Start by choosing random values for x.

Let $x = -6$, so $y = -\dfrac{2}{3}(-6) - 3 = 1$

Let $x = -3$, so $y = -\dfrac{2}{3}(-3) - 3 = -1$

Let $x = 0$, so $y = -\dfrac{2}{3}(0) - 3 = -3$

Let $x = 3$, so $y = -\dfrac{2}{3}(3) - 3 = -5$

Let $x = 6$, so $y = -\dfrac{2}{3}(6) - 3 = -7$

We can summarize our findings with the following chart.

x	y
–6	1
–3	–1
0	–3
3	–5
6	–7

Plot the points (–6, 1), (–3, –1), (0, –3), (3, –5), and (6, –7).

Draw the line that connects the points.

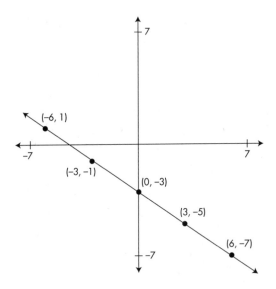

Now we'll graph the line using the slope-intercept form of a line.

In the equation $y = -\dfrac{2}{3}x - 3$, the slope is $-\dfrac{2}{3}$ and –3 is the y-intercept. Follow these two steps to graph the line.

1. Place a dot at –3 on the y-axis.

2. Slope is defined as $\dfrac{\text{rise}}{\text{run}}$. From the point $(0, -3)$, move down 2 units and to the right 3 units. Repeat this process a few times, each time making a dot. Connect all the dots, making a straight line that covers a large portion of the graph.

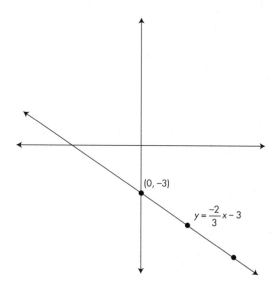

Graphing a line using the slope-intercept form is easier and quicker than plotting points. Notice in the chart that when $x = 0$, $y = -3$, which is the y-intercept. A line's y-intercept is found by letting the x-coordinate equal 0.

Deriving the Equation of a Line

We can derive the equation of a line in slope-intercept form using only two points.

EXAMPLE

What is the equation of a line in slope-intercept form that connects the points $(6, -8)$ and $(5, -12)$?

SOLUTION: Follow these steps to derive the equation of the line.

Step 1. Find the slope m through the points (x_1, y_1) and (x_2, y_2) by using the formula

$$m = \frac{y_2 - y_1}{x_2 - x_1}$$

$$\frac{-12 - (-8)}{5 - 6} = \frac{-4}{-1} = 4$$

Step 2. Replace m with 4 in the general equation of a line.

$$y = mx + b \qquad y = 4x + b$$

Step 3. To find b, substitute for x and y one of the coordinate pairs. In this example, we will use $(6, -8)$.

$$y = 4x + b$$

$$-8 = 4(6) + b$$

$$-8 = 24 + b$$

$$-32 = b$$

Step 4. Put the slope and the y-intercept into the general formula to get $y = 4x - 32$.

The Point-Slope Form of a Line

The point-slope form of a line can be found when the slope of a line and a point on that line are known. The general formula for a line in point-slope form is $y - y_1 = m(x - x_1)$.

EXAMPLE

What is the point-slope form of a line with slope of $-\dfrac{5}{8}$ that passes through $(2, -8)$?

SOLUTION: Use the formula $y - y_1 = m(x - x_1)$ and input the known data.

$$y - (-8) = -\frac{5}{8}(x - 2)$$

$$y + 8 = -\frac{5}{8}(x - 2)$$

Linear Inequalities

An **inequality** is a mathematical expression indicating that one value is greater than another. The symbols $<$ and $>$ mean "less than" and "greater than," respectively; likewise, the symbols $\leq$ $\geq$ mean "less than or equal to" and "greater than or equal to."

Which of the following statements can be true?

    A. $9 > -2$

    B. $-2 < -3$

    C. $2 \leq 2$

SOLUTION:

    A. True. $9 > -2$ because 9 lies to the right of -2 on a number line.

    B. False. -2 is not less than -3 because -2 lies to the right of -3 on a number line.

    C. True. $2 \leq 2$. Although 2 is not less than 2, it is equal to 2. Only one condition, greater than **or** equal to needs to be true to make the statement true.

We can use principles of algebra to solve many inequalities. In the example below, we will review the basics of solving an algebraic inequality.

$$4x - 16 > 20$$

Solve the inequality as you would normally solve an algebraic equation.

$$4x - 16 > 20$$

$$4x - 16 + 16 > 20 + 16$$

$$4x > 36$$

$$\frac{4}{4}x > \frac{36}{4}$$

$$x > 9$$

The solution can be graphed on a number line.

We darken the values greater than 9 on the number line. There is an open circle at 9 because 9 is not included in the solution. If the equation was $4x - 16 \geq 20$, the solution would be $x \geq 9$. The new solution is graphed below.

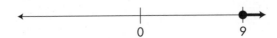

The circle is darkened at 9 denoting that 9 is part of the solution set.

When multiplying or dividing an inequality by a negative number, reverse the direction of the inequality sign.

EXAMPLE

Solve and graph $-2x + 8 < 12$.

SOLUTION:

$$-2x + 8 < 12$$

$$-2x + 8 - 8 < 12 - 8$$

$$-2x < 4$$

$$\frac{-2}{-2}x < \frac{4}{-2}$$

$$x > -2$$

When we multiplied the inequality by -2, the direction of the inequality sign needed to be reversed. We can check our solution with an included value. If $x > -2$, we can substitute 1 for x because $1 > -2$.

$$-2(1) + 8 < 12$$

$$-2 + 8 < 12$$

$$6 < 12$$

Our solution set, $x > -2$, is verified by replacing x with 1. The graph of the inequality is shown below.

Modeling Situations with Linear Inequalities

Linear inequalities are useful to model situations in our everyday lives. Let's review some inequality signs along with standard verbiage to represent theses signs.

$\leq$ $\geq$ means:

— at least

— at most

— not less than

— not greater than/cannot exceed

— up to

$<$ $>$ means:

— less than

— greater than

— more than

Let's use this information to model and solve a real-life event.

Marla wants to purchase several gallons of beige paint. The cost per gallon is $18.00 and Marla has a budget of $160.00. What is the greatest number of gallons she can purchase? (Assume only whole gallons can be purchased.)

SOLUTION: Let g represent the maximum number of gallons of paint Marla can purchase.

Since Marla must pay $18.00 per gallon, the cost of her purchase is $18g$. She can spend up to $160.00 so we arrive at the inequality:

$$18g \leq 160$$

$$g \leq 8.89$$

Marla has enough money to purchase 8.89 gallons of paint. Since paint can only be purchased in whole gallons, Marla can purchase 8 gallons of paint.

Graphing Linear Inequalities

The rules of graphing inequalities also apply to graphing linear inequalities. Earlier in the chapter we learned about the slope-intercept form of a line. This format can be used to graph linear inequalities as well.

EXAMPLE

Graph the following inequality:

$$y \geq -\frac{2}{3}x + 4$$

SOLUTION: First, graph the line $y = -\frac{2}{3}x + 4$

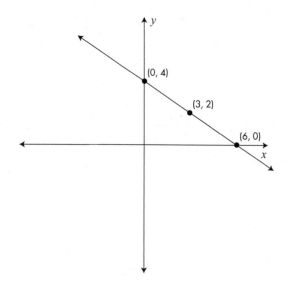

Next, choose a point on either side of the line and input the coordinates for *x* and *y*. If the test point satisfies the inequality, shade its side of the line. If it does not satisfy the inequality, shade the other side of the line. Unless (0,0) is on the line, it is usually the easiest point to test.

$$y \geq -\frac{2}{3}x + 4$$

$$0 \geq -\frac{2}{3}(0) + 4$$

$$0 \geq 4$$

0 is not greater than or equal to 4, so (0, 0) does not satisfy the inequality. Thus the area above the line is shaded.

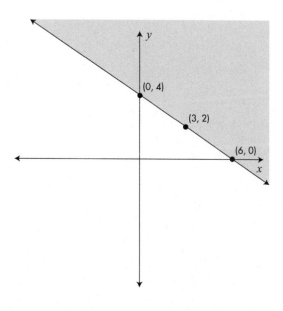

Graph $y < \dfrac{1}{4}x - 2$

SOLUTION: Notice that the inequality sign is "<" not "≤." This means the line, $y = \dfrac{1}{4}x - 2$, is not part of the graph. We show this by drawing the line dotted rather than solid.

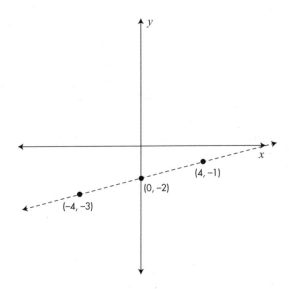

Use a test point to determine where to shade. Since (0,0) is not on the line, it will serve as the test point again.

$$y < \dfrac{1}{4}x - 2$$

$$0 < \dfrac{1}{4}(0) - 2$$

$$0 < -2$$

Since 0 is not less than −2, shade below the line.

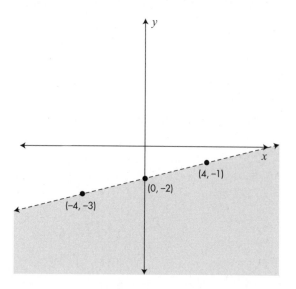

More than one inequality can be graphed on the same coordinate plane.

Graph $y \geq 4x - 7$ and $y < -\dfrac{2}{3}x + 3$ on the same coordinate plane.

SOLUTION: 1. Graph $y = 4x - 7$ first. Remember that the slope, 4, can be thought of as $\dfrac{4}{1}$, so starting at –7, the y-intercept, move up four spaces and to the right one. Repeat this procedure a few times and connect the dots with a solid line.

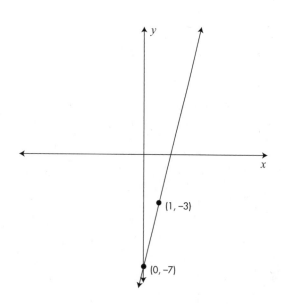

Use the point (0, 0) to decide which side of the line to shade.

$$0 \geq 4(0) - 7$$

$$0 \geq -7$$

0 is greater than or equal to –7, so shade above the line.

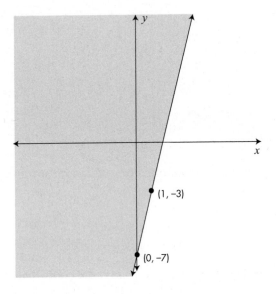

Now graph $y < -\dfrac{2}{3}x + 3$. Remember the line in this graph is dotted, not solid.

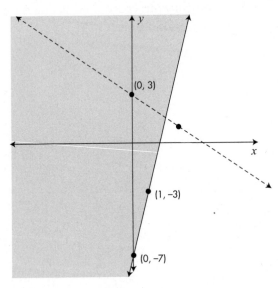

Use (0,0) to assess which side of the line should be shaded.

$$0 < -\frac{2}{3}(0) + 3$$

$$0 < 3$$

$0 < 3$ is a true statement so shade below the line.

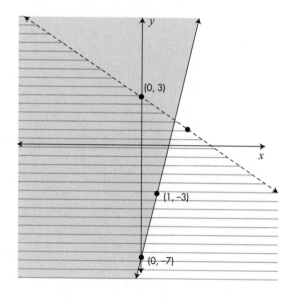

The solution to the problem is the area in which the shading from each line overlaps.

Parallel and Perpendicular Lines

Parallel lines do not intersect in the coordinate plane. Perpendicular lines intersect such that they create four right angles.

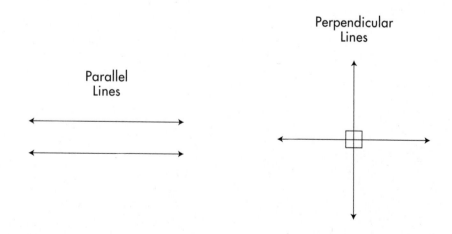

Lines that are parallel have the same slope but different intercepts. Look at the equations and their graphs below.

$$y = \frac{3}{4}x + 2$$

$$y = \frac{3}{4}x - 2$$

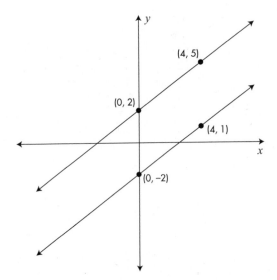

Perpendicular lines have slopes that are the opposite reciprocal of one another. For example, if a line has a slope of $\frac{3}{5}$, a line perpendicular to it would have a slope of $-\frac{5}{3}$.

Below are the equations of perpendicular lines and their graphs.

$$y = \frac{3}{5}x - 2$$

$$y = -\frac{5}{3}x + 4$$

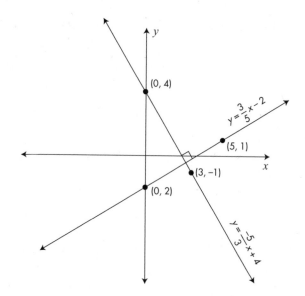

Lines can be discerned to be parallel, perpendicular or neither, simply by inspecting their slopes.

EXAMPLE

Classify each of the following pairs of lines as parallel, perpendicular or neither.

A. $y = 3x - 5$

$y = -\dfrac{1}{3}x + 2$

B. $y = \dfrac{2}{3}x - 5$

$2x - 3y = -4$

C. $y = 5x - 3$

$4x + 2y = 7$

SOLUTION:

A. The lines are perpendicular because $\dfrac{3}{1}$ and $-\dfrac{1}{3}$ are opposite reciprocals of one another.

B. The lines are parallel. Convert the second equation to the slope-intercept form of a line.

$$2x - 3y = -4$$

$$2x - 3y - 2x = -2x - 4$$

$$-3y = -2x - 4$$

$$\dfrac{-3}{-3}y = \dfrac{-2}{-3}x - \dfrac{4}{-3}$$

$$y = \dfrac{2}{3}x + \dfrac{4}{3}$$

Both lines have the same slope, $\dfrac{2}{3}$, so the lines are parallel.

C. The lines are neither parallel nor perpendicular. Convert the second equation to the slope-intercept form of a line.

$$4x + 2y = 7$$

$$4x + 2y - 4x = -4x + 7$$

$$2y = -4x + 7$$

$$\dfrac{2}{2}y = \dfrac{-4}{2}x + \dfrac{7}{2}$$

$$y = -2x + \dfrac{7}{2}$$

The slopes of the two lines, −2 and 5, are neither equal nor the opposite reciprocals of one another. Therefore the lines are neither parallel nor perpendicular.

Applications of Linear Models

Real-life situations can be modeled using linear equations.

EXAMPLE

The third grade class at a local school is raising funds for a school field trip. The class plans to raise funds for eight weeks with the intent of earning $750, the amount needed for the trip. After two weeks, the class raised $180 and after five weeks, it had $540. If the class continues raising money at the same rate, will it have enough money after eight weeks?

SOLUTION: The expression "... continues raising money at the *same rate* ..." means that a linear model is needed to answer the question. Let x represent time (in weeks) and y represents the money raised. Thus, we have the points $(2,180)$ and $(5,540)$. Find the equation of a line that connects these two points.

$$m = \frac{y_2 - y_1}{x_2 - x_1} = \frac{540 - 180}{5 - 2} = \frac{360}{3} = 120$$

Replace m with 120 in the general form of the line.

$$y = 120x + b$$

Solve for b by replacing x and y with one of the two points.

$$180 = 2 \times 120 + b$$
$$180 = 240 + b$$
$$-60 = b$$

The equation of the line connecting $(2,180)$ and $(5,540)$ is $y = 120x - 60$. Replace x with 8 to see if the class will raise at least $750 for the field trip.

$$y = 120(8) - 60$$
$$y = \$900.$$

The class will raise $900, which is more than the $750 needed.

There are other applications of the linear model in our everyday lives. Consider the following.

EXAMPLE

Sarah is considering two car rental agencies for an upcoming business trip. Rent Today offers the following daily rate:

$20 per day plus $.15 per mile

Always Autos, the other automobile rental agency, offers the following daily rate:

$30 per day plus $.05 per mile

What number of miles would Sarah have to drive to make the two deals equal in cost?

SOLUTION: Use a linear model in the form of $y = mx + b$ where:

x = the number of miles for the two rates to be the same

y = the combined cost of the daily rate plus the mileage fee

We therefore arrive at the following linear models.

Rent Today: $y = .15x + 20$

Always Autos: $y = .05x + 30$

Notice that each of the linear models is equal to y, the combined cost of the daily rental. Since we want both of the costs to be equal, we can assume that y in each equation has the same value. Therefore we can set $(.15x + 20)$ and $(.05x + 30)$ equal to one another to find the value of x.

$.15x + 20 = .05x + 30$

$.10x = 10$

$x = 100$

The cost for the rentals from both agencies is the same when Sarah drives 100 miles.

Quadratic Functions

A quadratic function is a function that uses the model $f(x) = ax^2 + bx + c$ where a, b, and c are called constants. For example, the outputs of the function $f(x) = 2x^2 - 6x + 8$ for the following inputs –3, 0.5, and 7 are:

$$f(-3) = (2)(-3)^2 - (6)(-3) + 8 = 44$$

$$f(0.5) = (2)(0.5)^2 - (6)(0.5) + 8 = 5.5$$

$$f(7) = (2)(7)^2 - (6)(7) + 8 = 64$$

The quadratic function can be expressed using the following input/output table.

x	$f(x)$
–3	44
0.5	5.5
7	64

Graphing Quadratic Functions

In chapter 3 we learned to solve quadratic equations in the form of $ax^2 + bx + c = 0$

EXAMPLE

Solve the quadratic equation $x^2 + 2x - 24 = 0$

$$x^2 + 2x - 24 = 0$$

$$(x + 6)(x - 4) = 0$$

$$x + 6 = 0 \text{ or } x - 4 = 0$$

$$x = -6 \text{ or } x = 4.$$

Quadratic equations in the form of $y = ax^2 + bx + c$ can be graphed in the coordinate plane. The graph of a quadratic equation is called a **parabola** and can take several forms. On the GED® test, you need to know the following forms of a parabola.

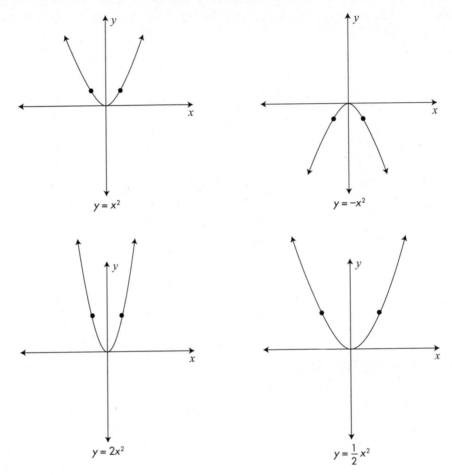

$y = x^2$

$y = -x^2$

$y = 2x^2$

$y = \frac{1}{2}x^2$

When the coefficient of x^2 is negative, the parabola opens downward; when the coefficient of x^2 is positive, the parabola opens upward. Further, larger coefficients of x^2 narrow the opening of the parabola while smaller ones widen it.

A parabola always has a vertex and an axis of symmetry. The vertex is the minimum value of y when the parabola is in the form of $y = ax^2$ and the maximum value when the form of the graph is $y = -ax^2$. The **axis of symmetry**, usually shown as a dotted line, separates the halves of the parabola. Many parabolas contain x- and y-intercepts.

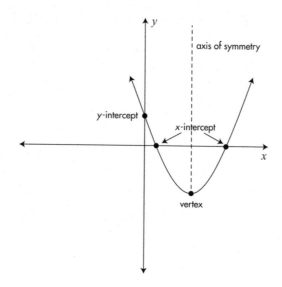

Follow these steps when graphing a parabola.

EXAMPLE

Graph $y = x^2 - 8x + 12$

SOLUTION:

Step 1:   Find the axis of symmetry by using the formula $x = -\dfrac{b}{2a}$.

$$y = x^2 - 8x + 12$$

$$a = 1, \ b = -8, \ c = 12$$

$$x = -\frac{(-8)}{2(1)} = 4$$

Step 2:   Find the vertex by replacing x with the value of the axis of symmetry.

$$y = (-4)^2 - 8(4) + 12 = -4$$

The coordinates of the vertex are $(4, -4)$.

Step 3: Finding the x-intercepts by letting $y = 0$ in the original equation.

$$0 = x^2 - 8x + 12$$

$$0 = (x - 6)(x - 2)$$

$$x - 6 = 0 \quad x - 2 = 0$$

$$x = 6, \, x = 2$$

The x-intercepts are $(6,0)$ and $(2,0)$.

Step 4: Find the y-intercept by letting $x = 0$.

$$y = (0)^2 - (8 \times 0) + 12 = 12$$

The y-intercept is $(0,12)$.

Graph the axis of symmetry, vertex and, x- and y-intercepts to get an idea of the graph's shape.

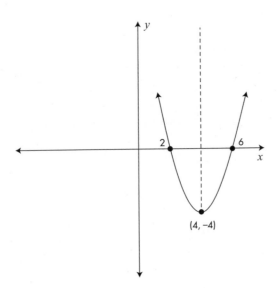

Add some other values of x and y to get a better idea of the parabola's shape.

$$y = x^2 - 8x + 12$$

x	y
1	5
3	-3
7	5

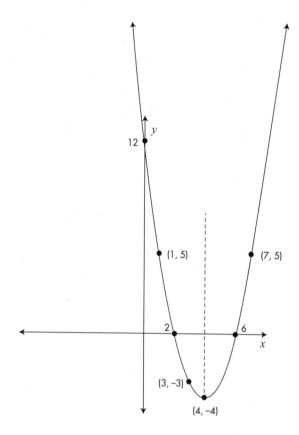

Using Quadratic Equations in Everyday Life

Imagine throwing a softball to a friend. The arc of your throw can be modeled with a quadratic equation; the ball rises and falls in the shape of a parabola. Businesses often use quadratic models to aid in maximizing profits.

EXAMPLE

A manufacturer of athletic socks uses the following quadratic function for a single production run:

$$P(x) = -.04x^2 + 6x - 611$$

Where:

x = the most profitable number of socks (in pairs) to produce during the production run

$P(x)$ = the greatest profit earned during the production run

What is the most profitable number of socks to produce? What is the greatest profit that can be earned?

SOLUTION: The lead term of $-.04x^2 + 6x - 11$ is negative so the parabola opens down. The vertex, then, is a maximum with the following properties:

- The x-coordinate is the most profitable number of pairs of socks to produce.

- The y-coordinate (in this case, the value of $P(x)$) is the maximum profit earned.

Find the x-coordinate by using the formula $x = -\dfrac{b}{2a}$.

$$P(x) = -.04x^2 + 6x - 11$$

$$a = -.04 \qquad b = 6$$

$$x = -\dfrac{6}{(2)(-.04)} = 75$$

The most profitable quantity of socks to produce is 75 pairs. Replace x with 75 to find the greatest profit from the production run.

$$P(x) = (-.04)(75^2) + (6)(75) + 11 = 214$$

When the manufacturer produces 75 pairs of socks, it will generate \$214 in profit.

The graph of the profit function is shown below.

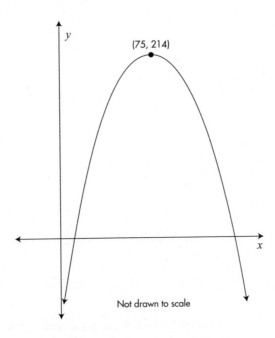

(75, 214)

Not drawn to scale

PRACTICE!

1. The line connecting the points (2, –5) and (–8, 3) has slope

   A. $-\dfrac{11}{7}$

   B. $-\dfrac{5}{4}$

   C. $-\dfrac{4}{5}$

   D. $\dfrac{4}{5}$

2. A line with the coordinates $(x, 7)$ and $(-4, -2)$ has slope $\dfrac{2}{3}$. What is the value of x?

   A. 9.5

   B. 6

   C. –6

   D. –9.5

3. What is the equation of a line in slope-intercept form that contains the points (7, –4) and (–5,0)?

   A. $y = \dfrac{5}{3}x - \dfrac{1}{3}$

   B. $y = -\dfrac{1}{3}x + \dfrac{5}{3}$

   C. $y = -\dfrac{1}{3}x - \dfrac{5}{3}$

   D. $3x - 12$

4. What is the equation in point-slope form of a line with slope 6 passing though (6, 7)?

   A. $y = 6x - 6$

   B. $y - 6 = 6(x - 7)$

   C. $y - 7 = 6(x - 6)$

   D. $2x + 6y = 7$

5. What is the graph of the inequality $5 - 3x \geq -7$?

A.
![number line with closed circle at 4, shaded left]
-4 -3 -2 -1 0 1 2 3 4 5 6

B.
![number line with open circle at 4, shaded left]
-4 -3 -2 -1 0 1 2 3 4 5 6

C.
![number line with closed circle at 4, shaded right]
-4 -3 -2 -1 0 1 2 3 4 5 6

D.
![number line with open circle at 4, shaded right]
-4 -3 -2 -1 0 1 2 3 4 5 6

6. Which of the following is the graph of $y < -\dfrac{3}{4}x + 7$?

A.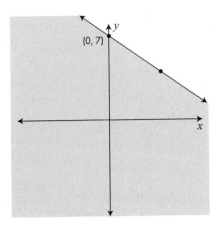

C.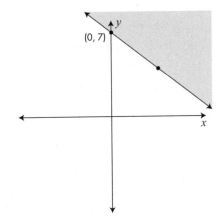

B.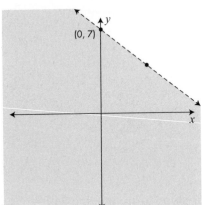

D.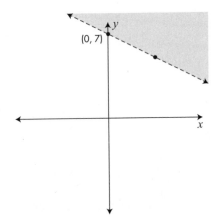

7. Graph the inequalities $y \geq 4x - 2$ and $y < -\dfrac{1}{2}x + 3$ on the same coordinate plane.

8. $y = \dfrac{2}{5}x - 3$

$2x - 5y = 7$

These linear equations form lines that are

    A. Parallel

    B. Perpendicular

    C. Parallel and perpendicular

    D. Neither parallel nor perpendicular

9. $y = \dfrac{5}{3}x - 7$

$y = -\dfrac{5}{3}x + 7$

The two equations form lines that are

    A. Parallel

    B. Perpendicular

    C. Parallel and perpendicular

    D. Neither parallel nor perpendicular

10. An auto garage charges $48.00 to inspect a car and $75.00 per hour subsequently for every hour of labor. What linear model represents the fee schedule? (Disregard the cost of parts.)

    A. $48x + 75y = 123$

    B. $y = 75x + 48$

    C. $y = 48x + 75$

    D. $y = 75x - 48$

11. A family began saving for its oldest child's education. At the end of two years, it had saved $4,500 and at the end of seven years, it had saved $18,600. How much money will the family have saved after 10 years if it saved at the same rate?

    A. $ 2,820

    B. $11,400

    C. $21,440

    D. $27,060

12. In the equation $y = -x^2 + 6x - 12$, what are the coordinates of the vertex? Does the graph open up or down?

A. (−3, 3) opens down

B. (−3, 3) opens up

C. (3, −3) opens down

D. (3, −3) opens up

13. Which of the following functions represents the input/output table below?

x	f(x)
−2	−17
0	−11
6	17

A. $f(x) = 2x + 5$

B. $f(x) = -x + 11$

C. $f(x) = 3x - 11$

D. $f(x) = -3x + 11$

Math Practice 5 Answers

1. **C.**

   Use the formula $m = \dfrac{y_2 - y_1}{x_2 - x_1}$ to find the slope.

   $$\frac{3 - (-5)}{-8 - 2} = -\frac{8}{10} = -\frac{4}{5}$$

2. **A.**

   Place the known values into the slope formula and solve for x.

   $$\frac{-2 - 7}{-4 - x} = \frac{2}{3}$$

   $$\frac{-9}{-4 - x} = \frac{2}{3}$$

Cross multiply and solve for x.

$$-9(3) = 2(-4 - x)$$

$$-27 = -8 - 2x$$

$$-19 = -2x$$

$$\frac{-19}{-2} = \frac{-2}{-2}x$$

$$9.5 = x$$

3. **C.**

Find the slope of the line connecting $(7, -4)$ and $(-5, 0)$.

$$\frac{0 - (-4)}{-5 - 7} = -\frac{4}{12} = -\frac{1}{3}$$

Replace x and y with one of the coordinate pairs.

$$0 = -\frac{1}{3}(-5) = b$$

$$0 = \frac{5}{3} + b$$

$$-\frac{5}{3} = b$$

The equation of the line in slope-intercept form that connects $(7, -4)$ and $(-5, 0)$ is $y = -\frac{1}{3}x - \frac{5}{3}$.

4. **C.**

The point-slope form of a line is $y - y_1 = m(x - x_1)$ where x_1 and y_1 are the coordinates of the point. Thus we get $y - 7 = 6(x - 6)$.

5. **A.**

Solve the inequality.

$$5 - 3x \geq -7$$

$$-3x \geq -12$$

$$x \leq 4$$

(Remember to reverse the direction of the inequality sign when dividing by -3. Also, note that the graph includes -4, so -4 is darkened on the number line.)

6. **B.**

Draw the dotted line representing $y = -\frac{3}{4}x + 7$. Use $(0, 0)$ as a test to determining which side of line will be shaded.

$$0 < -\frac{3}{4}(0) + 7$$

$$0 < 7$$

Since 0 is less than 7, the point $(0, 0)$ satisfies the inequality. Thus, shade below the line.

7. Graph the line $y = 4x - 2$, making sure it is a solid line. Use $(0, 0)$ to test which area to shade.

$$0 \geq 4(0) - 2$$

$$0 \geq -2$$

0 is greater than or equal to –2, so shade above the line.

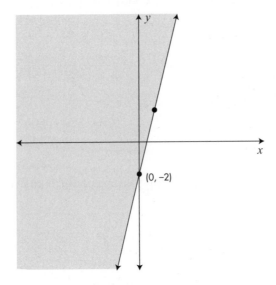

Next graph $y = -\frac{1}{2}x + 3$, making sure to draw a dotted line. Use $(0, 0)$ to test which area to shade.

$$0 < -\frac{1}{2}(0) + 3$$

$$0 < 3$$

0 is less than 3, so shade below the line.

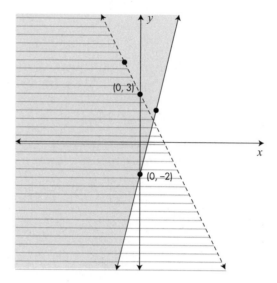

The correct solution is to shade the area that is the intersection of the two inequalities.

8. **A.**

Parallel lines have the same slope. Convert the second equation into slope-intercept form to compare the slope of the equations.

$$2x - 5y = -3$$

$$-5y = -2x - 3$$

$$\frac{-5}{-5}y = \frac{-2}{-5}x - \frac{3}{-5}$$

$$y = \frac{2}{5}x + \frac{3}{5}$$

The slope of both lines is $\frac{2}{5}$, so the lines are parallel.

9. **D.**

The slopes of parallel lines are equal. The slopes of perpendicular lines are the opposite reciprocals of another. $\frac{5}{3}$ and $-\frac{5}{3}$ are neither equal nor the opposite reciprocal of one another. Thus, the lines are neither perpendicular nor parallel.

10. B.

The fixed cost, $48.00, is the *y*-intercept; it does not vary. The cost of labor, $75.00 per hour, varies according to the number of hours worked. Thus, $75 is the slope. The linear model that represents this fee schedule is $y = 75x + 48$.

11. D.

Since all saving is done at the same rate, use a linear model to answer the question.

Find the slope of the line containing the points (2, 4,500) and (7, 18,600).

$$\frac{18,600 - 4,500}{7 - 2} = \frac{14,100}{5} = 2,820$$

The slope of the linear model is 2,820.

$$y = 2,820x + b$$

Find *b* by replacing *x* and *y* with one of the points.

$$4,500 = 2,820 \, (2) + b$$

$$4,500 = 5,640 + b$$

$$-1,140 = b$$

The linear model's equation is $y = 2,820x - 1140$. Replace *x* with 10 to see how much the family would save after ten years.

$$y = 2,820(10) - 1140$$

$$y = 27,060$$

After ten years, the family will have saved $27,060 for its oldest child.

12. C.

Use the formula $x = -\dfrac{b}{2a}$ to find the axis of symmetry.

$$y = -x^2 + 6x - 12$$

$$a = -1, b = 6, c = -12$$

$$x = -\frac{6}{2(-1)} = 3$$

The *x*-coordinate of the vertex is 3. Find the *y* coordinate of the vertex by replacing *x* with 3 in the original equation.

$$y = -(3)^2 + 6(3) - 12 = -3$$

The vertex is (3, −3). Since the coefficient of the x^2 term is −1, the parabola opens down.

13. **C.**

Input each value of the domain and verify that it corresponds to the range.

$(3)(-2) - 11 = -17$

$(3)(0) - 11 = -11$

$(3)(6) - 11 = 7$

Measurement and Geometric Figures

In this chapter we will review the following:

- Units of Measure

- Geometry: Points, Lines, and Planes

- The Distance and Midpoint Formulas

- Angles

- Triangles

- Parallel Lines

- Quadrilaterals

- Circles

Units of Measure

Questions on the GED® math test require an understanding of U.S. and metric units of measure. You must be proficient in converting units within each system. However, you are not required to convert units of measure between the two systems.

The U.S. System

Below is a list of U.S. measurements used in GED® test questions.

Length
1 foot = 12 inches
3 feet = 1 yard
36 inches = 1 yard

Liquid Measure
1 cup = 8 ounces (oz.)
1 pint = 2 cups = 16 oz.
1 quart = 32 oz.
1 gallon = 4 quarts

Time
60 seconds = 1 minute
60 minutes = 1 hour
24 hours = 1 day
7 days = 1 week
52 weeks = 1 year
Also: 12 months = 1 year

Weight
1 pound (lb) = 16 ounces (oz)
1 ton = 2,000 lbs.

Two rules are used to convert from one unit to another:

Rule #1: When converting from larger units to smaller units, multiply by the conversion factor.

Rule #2: When converting from smaller units to larger units, divide by the conversion factor.

Examples of Rule #1:

EXAMPLE

Convert 8 pounds into ounces.

SOLUTION: Pounds are greater than ounces, so multiply 8 by 16, the number of ounces in a pound.

$$8 \times 16 = 128$$

8 pounds is equivalent to 128 ounces.

Sometimes more than one conversion (more than one step) is needed.

EXAMPLE

Convert 7.5 tons into ounces.

SOLUTION: Although a direct conversion from tons to ounces may not be readily apparent, it can be derived. Multiply the number of ounces in a pound, 16, by the number of pounds in a ton, 2,000.

$$16 \times 2,000 = 32,000$$

Now multiply 32,000 by 7.5 to find the number of ounces in 7.5 tons.

$$7.5 \times 32,000 = 240,000$$

There are 240,000 ounces in 7.5 tons.

Let's try a few examples of Rule #2, converting smaller units to larger ones.

EXAMPLE

Convert 1,080 inches into yards.

SOLUTION: Inches are smaller than yards, so divide 1,080 by 36, the number of inches in a yard.

$$1,080 \div 36 = 30$$

1,080 is equal to 30 yards.

Convert 5,184 minutes into days.

SOLUTION: Although we do not have a direct conversion factor from minutes to days, we can derive it.

1 day = 24 hours; 1 hour = 60 minutes

Multiply 24 by 60 to find the number of minutes in one day.

$24 \times 60 = 1,440$

Finally, divide 5,184 by 1,440 to find the number of days that are equal to 5,184 minutes.

$5,184 \div 1,440 = 3.6$

There are 5,184 minutes in 3.6 days.

The Metric System

There are three standard units of measure in the metric system.

Gram: a unit of weight (about the weight of a U.S. dime)

Liter: a liquid measure (about 1.4 ounces more than a quart)

Meter: a measure of distance (about 39.3 inches; a little more than a yard)

The GED® math test requires you to know the following prefixes for units of metric measure:

milli-: $\dfrac{1}{1,000}$ of a standard unit

cent-: $\dfrac{1}{100}$ of a standard unit

deci-: $\dfrac{1}{10}$ of a standard unit

deka-: 10 times a standard unit

hecto-: 100 times a standard unit

kilo-: 1000 times a standard unit

The two rules for U.S. unit conversion also apply to metric conversion:

Rule #1: When converting larger units to smaller units, multiply by the conversion factor.

Rule #2: When converting smaller units to larger units, divide by the conversion factor.

Examples for Rule #1, converting larger units to smaller ones:

EXAMPLE

Convert 7.7 kilometers into meters.

SOLUTION: Kilometers are larger than meters, so multiply 7.7 by 1,000, the number of meters in a kilometer.

$$7.7 \times 1,000 = 7,700$$

There are 7,700 meters in 7.7 kilometers.

Sometimes more than one conversion (more than one step) is needed.

EXAMPLE

Convert 511.2 hectograms into centigrams.

SOLUTION: Although a direct conversion from hectograms to centigrams is not readily apparent, it can be derived. There are 100 centigrams in every gram and 100 grams make a hectogram. Multiply 100 by 100 by 511.2 to find the number of centigrams that are equal to 511.2 hectograms.

$$100 \times 100 \times 511.2 = 5,112,000$$

There are 5,112,000 (5.112×10^6) centigrams in 511.2 hectograms.

These are examples of Rule #2, converting smaller units to larger.

EXAMPLE

Convert 471 liters into kiloliters.

SOLUTION: Liters are smaller than kiloliters, so divide 471 by 1,000, the number of liters in a kiloliter. This can be accomplished easily by moving the decimal point three units to the left.

$$471 \div 1,000 = 0.471$$

EXAMPLE

Convert 97.2 decimeters into dekameters.

SOLUTION: A direct conversion from decimeters to dekameters can be derived. There are 10 decimeters in a meter and 10 meters make a dekameter, so multiply 10 by 10 to find the number of decimeters in a dekameter:

$$10 \times 10 = 100.$$

Next, divide 97.2 by 100 to find how many dekameters is 97.2 decimeters.

$$97.2 \div 100 = 0.972$$

97.2 decimeters is equal to 0.972 dekameters.

Geometry: Points, Lines, and Planes

The building blocks of geometry are points, lines and planes.

Point: represented by a dot, a point has no dimension.

> • *A* is called point *A*

Line: Through any two points, a line can be drawn. A line has one dimension and extends infinitely in opposite directions.

The line above can be labeled as $\overleftrightarrow{AB}$ (called line *AB*) or $\overleftrightarrow{BA}$.

The line above can also be labeled by a lowercase letter, such as ℓ.

If three or more points lie on the same line, they are called **collinear points**. Points that do not lie on the same line are called **non-collinear points**.

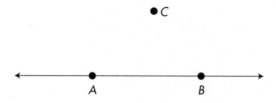

Plane: A plane extends indefinitely in two dimensions. A minimum of three non-collinear points determine a plane. Points that lie in the same plane are called co-planar points. Planes can be drawn using three co-planar points or using an uppercase letter.

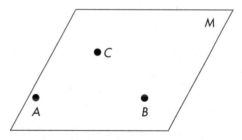

The intersection of two lines is a **point**, and the intersection of two planes is a **line**.

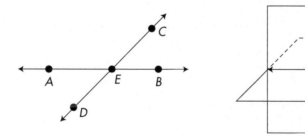

A part of a line that begins at one point (called an endpoint) and extends infinitely in the opposite direction is called a ray. A **ray** is shown below.

Since the endpoint is *A*, the ray is labeled $\overrightarrow{AB}$. It is important to note that the ray cannot be labeled $\overrightarrow{BA}$; the endpoint must always come first.

A part of a line that has a beginning and end is called a **line segment**.

This line segment can be labeled $\overline{AB}$ or $\overline{BA}$.

The Distance Formula

On a coordinate plane, the distance formula is used to determine the length of a segment. The formula is shown below.

$$\text{Distance} = \sqrt{(x_1 - x_2)^2 + (y_1 - y_2)^2}$$

EXAMPLE

Find the length of $\overline{AB}$ if the coordinates of *A* are (2, –4) and *B* (2, –12).

SOLUTION: Input the coordinates into the distance formula.

$$x_1 : 2$$

$$x_2 : 2$$

$$y_1 : -4$$

$$y_2 : -12$$

$$\text{Distance} = \sqrt{(2 - 2)^2 + (-4 - (-12))^2} = \sqrt{64} = 8$$

Either point can be designated (x_1, y_1); the results will still be the same.

The Midpoint Formula

All line segments have a mid-point. The formula to calculate a midpoint of a segment is:

$$\frac{x_1 + x_2}{2}, \frac{y_1 + y_2}{2}$$

EXAMPLE

Find the midpoint of a segment with endpoints $(8, -3)$ and $(7, -1)$.

SOLUTION: Use the midpoint formula to find the midpoint.

$$\frac{8 + 7}{2}, \frac{-3 + -1}{2}$$

$$\frac{15}{2}, -2$$

Angles

A pair of rays with a common endpoint is called an **angle**.

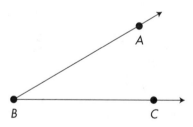

This angle can be named in several ways:

$$\angle ABC, \angle CBA, \text{ or } \angle B$$

Note that an angle can be named solely by its vertex (in this figure, B). However, in the case of adjacent angles, three letters must be used.

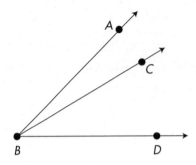

In the above diagram, referring to $\angle B$ is confusing. The reader cannot discern if $\angle B$ in the diagram is $\angle ABC$, $\angle CBD$, or $\angle ABD$.

Angles are measured in units called **degrees** which are indicated by the symbol "°". Angles are classified as:

Acute: measures less than 90°

Obtuse: measures more than 90°

Right: measures exactly 90°

Straight: measures exactly 180°

Special Angle Pairs

Two angles with measures that add to 90° are called **complementary angles**.

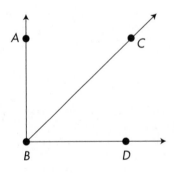

$\angle ABC$ and $\angle CBD$ are complementary angles.

Two angles with measures that add to 180° are called **supplementary angles**.

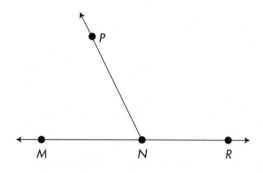

$\angle MNP$ and $\angle PNR$ are supplementary angles.

$\angle ABC$ and $\angle CBD$ are complementary angles. If $m\angle ABC$ (pronounced "the measure of angle ABC") is 67.2°, what is $m\angle CBD$?

SOLUTION: Complementary angles have a sum of 90°. Subtract 67.2° from 90° to find $m\angle CBD$.

$90 - 67.2° = 22.8°$.

$m\angle CBD = 22.8°$

Find the value of x in the diagram below.

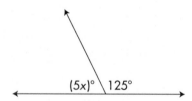

SOLUTION: The two angles are supplementary because they create a straight angle; their sum will equal 180°.

$5x + 125 = 180$

$5x = 55$

$x = 11$

Parallel Lines

Parallel lines are lines in the same plane that do not intersect.

The addition of more arrowheads on the lines denotes that the lines are parallel. We could also show parallelism by indicating $l \parallel m$, where the symbol "$\parallel$" means "is parallel to."

When parallel lines are intersected by another line (called a **transversal**), several angle relationships are created.

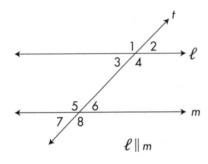

Corresponding angles are shown below.

$$m\angle 1 = m\angle 5$$

$$m\angle 3 = m\angle 7$$

$$m\angle 2 = m\angle 6$$

$$m\angle 4 = m\angle 8$$

Alternate interior angles are shown below.

$$m\angle 3 = m\angle 6$$

$$m\angle 4 = m\angle 5$$

Alternate exterior angles are shown below.

$$m\angle 2 = m\angle 7$$

$$m\angle 1 = m\angle 8$$

Vertical angles are shown below.

$$m\angle 1 = m\angle 4$$

$$m\angle 3 = m\angle 2$$

$$m\angle 5 = m\angle 8$$

$$m\angle 7 = m\angle 6$$

All other angle pairs not listed above are supplementary.

Triangles

A **triangle** is a closed figure composed of three sides and three angles. Two sides of a triangle meet to form a vertex.

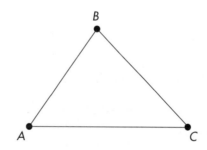

Sides: $\overline{AB}, \overline{BC}, \overline{AC}$

Angles: $\angle A, \angle B, \angle C$

The sum of the measures of the angles in a triangle is 180°. Triangles can be classified by sides:

Equilateral: all sides have equal measures

Isosceles: two sides have equal measures

Scalene: no sides have equal measures

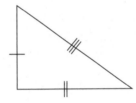

Triangles can be classified by angle measure:

Acute: all angles measure less than 90°

Right: contains one right angle

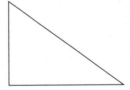

Obtuse: contains one angle greater than 90° but less than 180°.

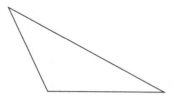

Angle-Side Relationship

In a triangle, the largest angle is opposite the longest side. Similarly, the middle and smallest angles are opposite the middle and smallest sides, respectively.

EXAMPLE

List the sides from greatest to least in $\triangle ABC$.

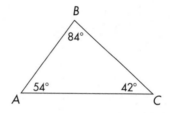

SOLUTION: $\overline{AC} > \overline{BC} > \overline{AB}$

Similarly, the longest side is opposite the largest angle.

EXAMPLE

List the angles from greatest to least.

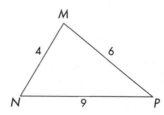

SOLUTION: $\angle M > \angle N > \angle P$

Exterior Angles

An **exterior angle** to a triangle is the sum of the two remote interior angles.

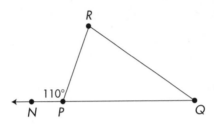

In $\triangle PRQ$, if the measure of exterior angle $\angle RPN$ is 110°, then the sum of the measures of $\angle R$ and $\angle Q$ is also 110°. You can see this more vividly with another look at $\triangle PRQ$.

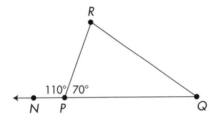

$\angle RPN$ and $\angle RPQ$ are supplementary angles. Thus, if $m\angle RPN$ is 110°, then $m\angle RPQ$ is 70° because 180 − 110 = 70. Input the measure of $\angle RPQ$ to solve the measure of the sum of $\angle R$ and $\angle Q$.

$$70 + m\angle R + m\angle Q = 180$$

$$m\angle R + m\angle Q = 110$$

The Pythagorean Theorem

When two sides of a right triangle are known, the Pythagorean theorem can be used to calculate the measure of the third.

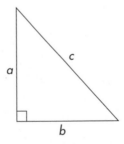

The formula for the Pythagorean theorem is $a^2 + b^2 = c^2$ where a and b are the shorter sides of the triangle (called **legs**). The longest side, c, is called the **hypotenuse**.

EXAMPLE

Find the length of the hypotenuse in $\triangle LMN$.

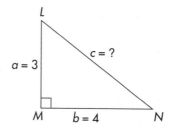

SOLUTION: Use the Pythagorean theorem, $a^2 + b^2 = c^2$, to find c.

$$3^2 + 4^2 = c^2$$

$$9 + 16 = c^2$$

$$25 = c^2$$

$$\sqrt{25} = \sqrt{c^2}$$

$$5 = c$$

The sides 3, 4, and 5 are known as a **Pythagorean triple**. A triple exists when all the sides of the triangle are whole numbers. Below are additional triples worth knowing for the GED® test:

5-12-13

8-15-17

7-24-25

All multiples of triples are triples as well. If 3-4-5 is a triple, then so are 6-8-10, 9-12-15, 30-40-50, and so on. Use your knowledge of triples to quickly solve the triangle below without resorting to the Pythagorean theorem.

Find the perimeter of △BCD.

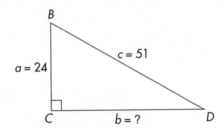

SOLUTION: Perimeter is the distance around a figure. To find the perimeter, you must first determine the length of side b. Notice that two of the sides are multiples of the triple "8-15-17" by a factor of 3. ($24 = 8 \times 3$, and $51 = 17 \times 3$), so the missing side must be 15×3, or 45. We have used a multiple of the 8-15-17 triple to find the missing side.

Finally, add the three sides to find the perimeter: $24 + 45 + 51 = 120$ feet.

(Note: Not all questions using the Pythagorean theorem use whole numbers.)

In the triangle below, what is the length of $\overline{BC}$?

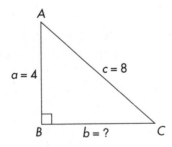

SOLUTION: Using the Pythagorean theorem we get:

$$4^2 + b^2 = 8^2$$

$$16 + b^2 = 64$$

$$b^2 = 48$$

$$b = 4\sqrt{3}$$

Quadrilaterals

A **quadrilateral** is a closed, four-sided figure. The sum of the measures of the four angles is 360°. A list of common quadrilaterals is shown below:

Trapezoid: Exactly two parallel sides

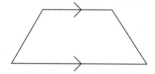

Square: four right angles and four equal sides

Rectangle: four right angles and opposite sides have equal lengths

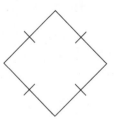

Rhombus: four equal sides

Parallelogram: opposite sides parallel and have equal length

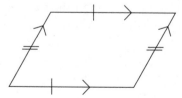

Circles

A **circle** is the set of points equidistant from a given point. A circle measures 360°.

Below are some features of a circle.

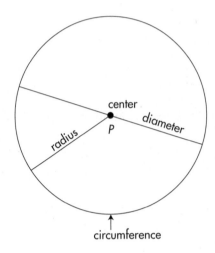

The perimeter of a circle is called the **circumference**. The formulas for the circumference are:

$$C = 2\pi r$$

$$C = \pi D$$

In the circumference formulas, r is the radius and D is the diameter. The formulas are equivalent because two radii are equal to one diameter. The symbol π (spelled and pronounced "pi") is approximately equal to 3.14 or $\dfrac{22}{7}$.

EXAMPLE

A circle has a radius that measures 6 feet. To the nearest foot, what is its circumference?

SOLUTION: The circle provides the radius, 6 feet, so use the formula $C = 2\pi r$. Some questions will permit you to leave π in your answer. However, when a question asks for a measure to the nearest unit, use $\pi = 3.14$ or $\dfrac{22}{7}$.

$$C = 2\pi r$$

$$C = 2(3.14)(6) = 37.68 \text{ feet}$$

Rounded to the nearest foot, the circumference of the circle is 38 feet.

Arcs of a Circle

In the diagram below, O is the center of a circle and $m\angle AOP = 72°$. When the vertex of an angle is located in the center of a circle, the angle is called a **central angle**. The measure of a central angle and its intercepted arc are equal.

> ## EXAMPLE

What is the measure of $\overset{\frown}{AB}$ (pronounced "arc AB")?

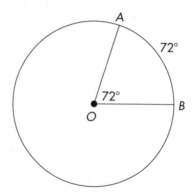

SOLUTION: A central angle equals its intercepted arc, so $m\overset{\frown}{AB}$ is also 72°.

Finding the length of an arc relates to the ratio of the central angle to 360°, the number of degrees in a circle. Find the length of an arc by using the formula: arc length = $\dfrac{m}{360}(2\neq r)$, where m represents the measure of a central angle.

In the circle with center P (represented by "$\odot P$"), find the length of $\overset{\frown}{AB}$ (express your answer in terms of π).

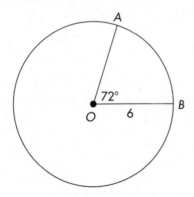

SOLUTION: Use the formula arc length $= \dfrac{m}{360}(2\pi r)$ to find the length of $\overset{\frown}{AB}$.

$$\frac{72}{360}(2 \times \pi \times 6) = 2.4\pi$$

The length of $\overset{\frown}{AB}$ equals 2.4π.

PRACTICE!

1. 17 pints is equal to how many gallons?

    A. 6.625

    B. 4.375

    C. 2.125

    D. 1.875

2. 9.71 grams equals how many milligrams?

    A. 9,710

    B. 971

    C. 97.1

    D. 0.971

Questions 3 and 4 refer to $\overleftrightarrow{AM}$.

3. $\overleftrightarrow{AM}$ is called a

    A. line segment

    B. line

    C. ray segment

    D. ray

4. $\overrightarrow{AM}$ is called a

    A. ray

    B. ray segment

    C. line

    D. line segment

5. Three non-collinear points determine a

    A. line

    B. ray

    C. line segment

    D. plane

6. $\overline{AB}$ has its endpoints at $A(-6, 2)$ and $B(4, -8)$. What is the length of $\overline{AB}$?

    A. 200

    B. $2\sqrt{10}$

    C. $10\sqrt{2}$

    D. $\sqrt{20}$

7. A segment has endpoints $(5, -4)$ and $(3, -8)$. What are the coordinates of the segment's midpoint?

    A. $(4, -6)$

    B. $(-4, 6)$

    C. $(4, 6)$

    D. $(-4, -6)$

8. Two supplementary angles have measures of $(7x)°$ and $(5x)°$. What is the measure of the smaller angle?

    A. $180°$

    B. $105°$

    C. $75°$

    D. $15°$

9.

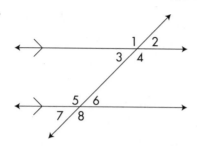

$m\angle 2 = (6x)°$ and $m\angle 6 = (4x + 40)°$. What is the value of x?

    A. 20

    B. 30

    C. 40

    D. 60

10.

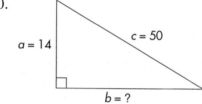

What is the length of the unknown leg?

    A. 24

    B. 36

    C. 48

    D. 60

11. In ⊙*P*, what is the length of $\overset{\frown}{AB}$?

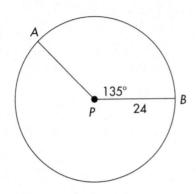

A. 6π

B. 12π

C. 18π

D. 24π

Math Practice 6 Answers

1. **C.**

   4 quarts = 1 gallon and 2 pints equal one quart. Thus, there are 8 pints in a gallon. Divide 17 by 8 to find how many gallons are equivalent to 17 pints.

   $$17 \div 8 = 2.125$$

2. **A.**

   1,000 milligrams = 1 gram. When converting from larger units to smaller units, grams to milligrams, multiply by the conversion factor.

   $$9.71 \times 1,000 = 9,710$$

3. **B.**

   $\overleftrightarrow{AM}$ refers to the line that passes through points *A* and *M*.

4. **A.**

   $\overrightarrow{AM}$ is called a ray. A ray has an endpoint, in this case *A*, and passes through *M* to extend indefinitely.

5. **D.**

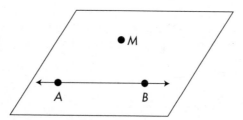

Points *A*, *B*, and *M* are non-collinear points because they do not all lie on the same line. A minimum of three non-collinear points are needed to determine a plane. Since non-collinear points determine a plane, they are also called coplanar points.

6. **C.**

Use the distance formula to calculate the length of $\overline{AB}$.

$$\text{Distance} = \sqrt{(x_1 - x_2)^2 + (y_1 - y_2)^2}$$
$$\text{Distance} = \sqrt{(-6 - 4)^2 + (2 - (-8))^2} = \sqrt{200} = 10\sqrt{2}$$

7. **A.**

Use the midpoint formula to calculate the midpoint.

$$\frac{x_1 + x_2}{2}, \frac{y_1 + y_2}{2}$$

$$\frac{5 + 3}{2}, \frac{-4 + -8}{2}$$

$$(4, -6)$$

8. **C.**

Supplementary angles are angle pairs with sum of 180°. Add the two angle measures and solve for *x*.

$$5x + 7x = 180$$

$$12x = 180$$

$$x = 15$$

The question requires the measure of the smaller angle, so multiply 5 and 15.

$$5 \times 15 = 75$$

9. **A.**

   $\angle 2$ and $\angle 6$ are corresponding angles. When lines are parallel, corresponding angles have equal measures. Set $6x$ equal to $4x + 40$ to find the value of x.

   $$6x = 4x + 40$$
   $$2x = 40$$
   $$x = 20$$

10. **C.**

    Use the Pythagorean theorem, $a^2 + b^2 = c^2$, to calculate the value of b.

    $$14^2 + b^2 = 50^2$$
    $$196 + b^2 = 2{,}500$$
    $$b^2 = 2{,}304$$
    $$b = 48$$

    A quicker route to calculating b would be to use the Pythagorean triple $7 - 24 - 25$. Since $7 \times 2 = 14$ and $25 \times 2 = 50$, then the missing side is $24 \times 2 = 48$.

11. **C.**

    Use the formula arc length $= \dfrac{m}{360}(2\pi r)$ to find the length of $\overset{\frown}{AB}$.

    Arc length $= \dfrac{135}{360}(2 \times \pi \times 24) = 18\pi$.

Chapter 7

Area, Surface Area, and Volume

In this chapter we will review the following topics:

- Area of plane figures

- Surface area

- Volume

- Composite solids

- Similarity

This chapter discusses the area of plane figures and the surface area and volume of solids. The GED® reference chart provides several formulas to calculate these measures. Many other formulas, however, are expected to be committed to memory prior to taking the GED® test. This chapter will help you to master all of these formulas.

The GED® test also requires the test-taker to master a special skill: finding a dimension (such as length or width) when an area or volume is provided. The instruction provided in this chapter will also help you to master this skill.

Area

Area is the region contained within a plane figure. In our daily lives, we encounter terms such as square feet, square yards, etc. These square units are measures of area. If the unit of measure is not provided, then areas are listed as square "units." Measures of area can be shown as, for example, "square feet," "feet²," or abbreviated: "ft²."

The GED® math test provides the following formulas for area in a handy reference sheet:

Parallelogram: base × height ($A = bh$)

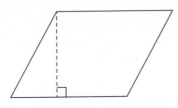

Trapezoid: $\dfrac{1}{2}$ × height × (base$_1$ + base$_2$)

$$A = \dfrac{1}{2}h(b_1 + b_2)$$

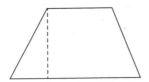

The following area formulas are expected to have been mastered before you sit for the test:

Rectangle: length × width ($A = l \times w$)

Circle: π × radius × radius ($A = \pi r^2$)

Square: side × side ($A = s^2$)

Let's apply these formulas to some practice questions.

EXAMPLE

Find the area of a circle with a diameter that measures 28.6 meters.

SOLUTION: The area of a circle is found by using the formula $A = \pi r^2$. The question provides the diameter, so divide 28.6 by 2 to find the radius.

$$28.6 \div 2 = 14.3.$$

$A = \pi(14.3)^2 = 204.49\pi$ (approximately 642.1 square meters).

The GED® test may ask you to compute the measure of a radius or diameter, given that the area is known.

EXAMPLE

$\odot P$ has an area that measures 361π. What is the measure of the diameter?

SOLUTION: The area of a circle is found by using the formula Area $= \pi r^2$. Input the known data and solve for r, the radius.

$$\pi r^2 = 361\pi$$
$$r^2 = 361$$
$$r = 19$$

The question asked for the diameter, which is twice the radius. Multiply 19 by 2 to find the length of the diameter.

$$(19)(2) = 38$$

Earlier we learned the area of a square is found by using the formula $A = s^2$. We can use this formula to calculate the perimeter of a square as well.

EXAMPLE

The area of a square is 289 square inches. What is the perimeter of the square?

SOLUTION: Input the known information into the area formula and solve for s.

$$A = s^2$$
$$289 = s^2$$
$$\sqrt{289} = \sqrt{s}$$
$$17 = s$$

Use the perimeter formula, $P = 4s$, to find the perimeter of the square.

$$P = 4s$$

$$P = (4)(17) = 68$$

A square with an area that measures 289 square inches has a perimeter that measures 68 inches.

Knowing the perimeter of a square can be useful for finding the length of a single side.

EXAMPLE

The perimeter of a square is 264 meters. What is the measure of one of the sides of the square?

SOLUTION: Using the formula $P = 4s$, input the known information to find the length of one side.

$$P = 4s$$

$$264 = 4s$$

$$66 = s$$

A square with a perimeter that measures 264 meters has sides that measure 66 meters.

EXAMPLE

The area of the trapezoid pictured below is 66 in². What is the length of b_1?

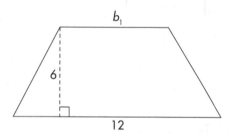

SOLUTION: The area formula for a trapezoid is $A = \dfrac{1}{2}h(b_1 + b_2)$. Input the known information to solve for b_1.

$$66 = \frac{1}{2}(6)(b_1 + 12)$$

$$66 = 3(b_1 + 12)$$

$$66 = 3b_1 + 36$$

$$30 = 3b_1$$

$$10 = b_1$$

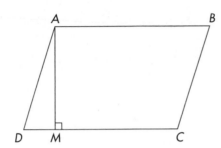

Parallelogram ABCD is pictured above. If the slope of $\overline{AB}$ is $\frac{7}{3}$, what is the slope of $\overline{CD}$? What is the slope of altitude $\overline{AM}$?

SOLUTION: The opposite sides of a parallelogram are parallel. We learned earlier that parallel lines have the same slope. Thus, if the slope of $\overline{AB}$ is $\frac{7}{3}$, then the slope of $\overline{CD}$ is also $\frac{7}{3}$. The altitude of a parallelogram, as pictured above, connects the bases to form a right angle. Since the altitude $\overline{AM}$ forms a right angle with $\overline{CD}$, we can say that $\overline{AM}$ and $\overline{CD}$ are perpendicular to one another. We learned earlier that perpendicular lines have slopes that are the opposite reciprocals of one another. Therefore if the slope of $\overline{AB}$ and $\overline{CD}$ is $\frac{7}{3}$, then the slope of altitude $\overline{AM}$ is $-\frac{3}{7}$.

Surface Area

Surface area (SA) is the region that spans the outside of a solid object. Similar to the area of plane figures, surface area is measured in square units.

The GED® Mathematical Reasoning test reference guide provides most of the formulas needed to pass the test. These formulas are provided in the shaded box at the right. Let's look at how surface area is computed for solid objects.

r = radius

p = perimeter of base

s = slant height

h = height

B = base area

π = 3.14

Right prism: $SA = ph + 2B$

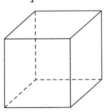

Lateral Area + $2B$ (where B is the base area).
Lateral area: ph (h = height and p = perimeter of the base)

Cylinder: $\quad SA = 2\pi rh + 2\pi r^2$

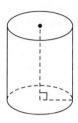

Pyramid: $\quad SA = \dfrac{1}{2}ps + B$

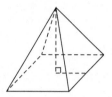

Cone: $\quad SA = \pi rs + \pi r^2$

Sphere: $\quad SA = 4\pi r^2$

Although a **cube** falls into the rectangular solid category, an easy formula to remember is $SA = 6e^2$, where e represents the length of an edge.

EXAMPLE

What is the surface area of the cone below? (Round your answer to the nearest square foot.)

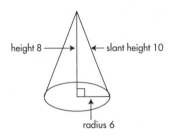

height 8 → ← slant height 10

radius 6

SOLUTION: Use the formula SA = $2\pi rh + 2\pi r^2$

SA = $(3.14)(6)(8) + (3.14)(6^2) = 263.76$

Rounded to the nearest square foot, the cone's surface area is 264 ft².

EXAMPLE

The rectangular prism pictured below has surface area measuring 268 square inches. The length and width of the base are 11 and 6 inches, respectively. What is the height of the rectangular solid?

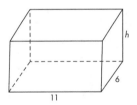

h

6

11

SOLUTION: Use the formula SA = LA + 2B to find the surface area of the rectangular prism.

LA = hp

$p = 6 + 6 + 11 + 11 = 34$

LA = $34h$

$2B = (2)(6)(11) = 132$

Input the known data and solve for h.

$$268 = 34h + 132$$

$$136 = 34h$$

$$4 = h$$

EXAMPLE

A sphere has a surface area of 288π cm². What is the measure of its radius?

SOLUTION: Use the formula $SA = 4\pi r^2$ to calculate the measure of the radius.

$$288\pi = 4\pi r^2$$

$$\frac{288\pi}{4\pi} = \frac{4\pi r^2}{4\pi}$$

$$72 = r^2$$

$$\sqrt{72} = \sqrt{r^2}$$

$$6\sqrt{2} = r$$

The radius measures $6\sqrt{2}$ (approximately 8.5 cm).

Volume

Volume is the measure of the region within a solid object. Volume is measured in cubic units such as cubic inches, cubic meters, etc. Cubic units are labeled as follows:

cubic feet or feet³ or ft³.

The GED® test provides the following volume formulas as seen in the shaded box at right:

Rectangular solid/rectangular prism/right prism: $V = Bh$

    Cylinder: $V = \pi r^2 h$

    Pyramid: $\frac{1}{3}Bh$

r = radius

B = base area

r = radius

h = height

π = 3.14

Cone: $\dfrac{1}{3}\pi r^2 h$

Sphere: $V = \dfrac{4}{3}\pi r^3$

A **cube** is a rectangular prism, but an easier formula to use is $V = e^3$, where e is the length of an edge.

EXAMPLE

What is the volume of the cone shown below? (Leave π in your answer.)

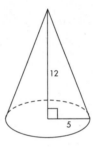

SOLUTION: Use the formula $V = \dfrac{1}{3}\pi r^2 h$ to calculate the volume.

$$V = \dfrac{1}{3}\pi(5^2)(12)$$

$$V = \dfrac{1}{3}(\pi)(300)$$

$$V = 100\pi \text{ units}^3$$

EXAMPLE

A square pyramid has a volume of $391.08\overline{3}$ inches³. If the height of the pyramid is 13 inches, what is the perimeter of the base?

SOLUTION: Use the formula $V = \dfrac{1}{3}Bh$ and input the known data.

$$391.08\overline{3} = \frac{1}{3}(B)13$$

$$391.08\overline{3} = \frac{13}{3}B$$

$$\frac{3}{13} \quad 391.08\overline{3} = \quad \frac{13}{3} \quad (B) \quad \frac{3}{13}$$

$$90.25 = B$$

The base area, B, is the area of a square. Find the square root of 90.25 to find the length of one side.

$$\sqrt{90.25} = 9.5$$

One side of the square base is 9.5. Multiply 9.5 by 4 to find the perimeter.

$$9.5 \times 4 = 38$$

The perimeter of the base of the pyramid is 38 inches.

EXAMPLE

The volume of a sphere is 288π feet³. What is the surface area of the sphere (leave π in your answer)?

SOLUTION: The volume of a sphere is found by using the formula $V = \frac{4}{3}\pi r^3$. Use the formula to calculate the radius, then input that value into the formula for the surface area of a sphere, $SA = 4\pi r^2$.

$$288\pi = \frac{4}{3}\pi r^3$$

$$\frac{3}{4\pi}\,(288\pi) = \frac{4}{3}\pi r^3\,\frac{3}{4\pi}$$

$$216 = r^3$$

$$\sqrt[3]{216} = \sqrt[3]{r^3}$$

$$6 = r$$

$$SA = 4\pi r^2$$

$$SA = 4\pi(6^2) = 144\pi$$

EXAMPLE

The surface area of a sphere is 324π units^2. What is the radius of the sphere?

SOLUTION: The surface area of a sphere is found by using the formula $A = 4\pi r^2$ where r represents the length of the radius. Input the known data and solve for r.

$$324\pi = 4\pi r^2$$

$$81 = r^2$$

$$9 = r$$

The radius of a sphere that has a surface area that measures 324π is 9 units.

EXAMPLE

A cube has a volume that measures 216 cm^3. Find the length of one of its edges and calculate its surface area.

SOLUTION: Use the formula $V = e^3$ to find the measure of one of the edges.

$$V = e^3$$

$$216 = e^3$$

$$\sqrt[3]{216} = \sqrt[3]{e^3}$$

$$6 = e$$

The measure of one of the edges of the cube is 6 cm. Use the formula Surface Area = $6e^3$ to find the surface area of the cube.

$$SA = 6e^2$$

$$SA = (6)(6^2) = 216$$

A cube with a volume that measures 216 cm³ has an edge that measures 6 cm and surface area that measures 216 cm².

Given the volume of a cylinder, you may be asked to calculate the measure of the height or the length of the radius.

EXAMPLE

The volume of a cylinder is 337 inches³. If the height is 7.5 inches, find the measure of the radius (use $\pi = 3.14$).

SOLUTION: The formula for the volume of a cylinder is $V = \pi r^2 h$ where r is the radius and h is the height. Input the known data and solve for r.

$$337 = (3.14)(r^2)(7.5)$$

$$337 = 23.55r^2$$

$$14.31 = r^2$$

$$3.78 = r$$

A cylinder that has a volume of 337 inches³ and height of 7.5 inches has a radius that measures 3.78 inches.

The GED® test may ask you to calculate the measure of a side or slant height of a pyramid given the surface area.

EXAMPLE

A certain pyramid has a square base. If each side of the base is 12 feet and the surface area is 384 square feet, what is the measure of the slant height?

SOLUTION: The formula for the surface area of pyramid is found by using the formula

$$SA = \frac{1}{2}ps + B, \text{ where}$$

p is the perimeter of the base

s is the slant height of the pyramid

B is the area of the base

Input the known data and solve for s, the measure of the slant height. Remember the pyramid has a square base, each side with a measure of 12 feet. Therefore the perimeter of the base is $4 \times 12 = 48$ and the area of the base is $12 \times 12 = 144$ square feet

$$384 = \left(\frac{1}{2}\right)(48)(s) + 144$$

$$384 = 24s + 144$$

$$240 = 24s$$

$$10 = s$$

The slant height of the pyramid is 10 feet.

Composite Solids

There will be one or two questions on the GED® test requiring you to compute the volume or surface area of a composite solid figure. A composite solid figure is composed of two or more solids combined to function as a whole. For example, the gumball dispenser you see in many supermarkets is a composite solid figure. The spherical bowl contains the gumballs and rests on a cubical base. Other common examples of composite solids include:

- House: the roof, a triangular prism, rests on the house, a rectangular solid.

- Grain silo: a cylinder topped by a hemisphere

- Snow cone: a cone embedded with a sphere of flavored ice

This last example, a snow cone, serves as a useful example to illustrate the process of measuring a composite solid.

EXAMPLE

Maria is a vendor of snow cones. She will be purchasing a promotional tool, a large plastic snow cone that will rest on the roof of her store. The plastic snow cone is shown below with some of its dimensions, in feet.

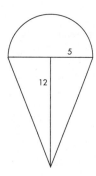

What are the surface area and volume of the plastic snow cone?

SOLUTION: When calculating measures of a composite geometric solid, use the following three-part process:

1. **Create a strategy:** Identify the component parts of the composite solid to be measured.

2. **Assess the formulas:** Identify which formulas are needed to find the surface area or volume. Make sure that the formulas are amended as needed to accurately measure each part of the figure.

3. Calculate the measures of each component, adding or subtracting values as needed.

Let's use the three-step plan to calculate the surface area and volume of the plastic snow cone.

Surface area:

1. **Strategy:** The base of the cone is in its interior and is not included in the surface area. Solely one-half of the sphere contributes to the surface area of this composite figure.

2. **Formulas:**

Surface area of the cone: $\pi r^2 + \pi r s$ where r is the radius of the base and s is the slant height.

The slant height is not known but can be calculated using the Pythagorean theorem.

$$12^2 + 5^2 = c^2$$

$$169 = c^2$$

$$13 = c = s$$

Deleting the circular base we get:

$$\pi r s = (\pi)(5)(13) = 65\pi \text{ square feet}$$

Surface area of a sphere: $4\pi r^2$

Since we are dealing with only $\dfrac{1}{2}$ of the sphere (a hemisphere) multiply the surface area formula by $\dfrac{1}{2}$

$$\left(\dfrac{1}{2}\right)(4\pi r^2) = 2\pi r^2$$

$$2\pi r^2 = (2)(\pi)(5^2) = 50\pi \text{ square feet}$$

3. Calculate total surface area: $65\pi + 50\pi = 115\pi$ (approximately 361.1 square feet).

Volume:

1. **Strategy:** The entire volume of the cone is included in the volume of the composite figure. Only one-half, however, of the sphere's volume is included in the volume of the composite figure.

2. **Formulas:** The volume of a cone is found by using the formula $V = \dfrac{1}{3}(\pi)(r^2)(h)$ where r is the radius of the circular base and h is the height of the cone.

$$\text{Volume: } \dfrac{1}{3}(\pi)(5^2)(12) = 100\pi \text{ cubic feet}$$

The volume of a sphere is found by using the formula $V = (4/3)(\pi)(r^3)$ where r is the radius of the sphere. Multiply the formula by $\dfrac{1}{2}$ to find the volume of the hemisphere: $\dfrac{1}{2}\ \dfrac{4}{3}(\pi)(r^3) = \dfrac{2}{3}(\pi)(r^3)$.

$$\text{Volume} = \left(\frac{2}{3}\right)(\pi)(5^3) = 83\frac{1}{3}\pi \text{ cubic feet}$$

3. **Calculate:** Add the volume of the cone and the hemisphere to find the volume of the composite figure.

$$100\pi + 83\frac{1}{3}\pi = 183\frac{1}{3}\pi \text{ (approximately 576) cubic feet.}$$

Similarity

Similar geometric figures have the same shape, but are different sizes. In order for figures to be similar, all of their angles must have equal measures and their sides must be proportional. Triangles ABC and DEF are similar because their angles are equal and their sides are proportional.

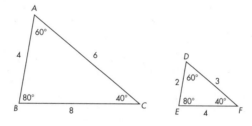

$$\frac{AB}{DE} = \frac{4}{2} = \frac{2}{1}$$

$$\frac{BC}{EF} = \frac{8}{4} = \frac{2}{1}$$

$$\frac{AC}{DF} = \frac{6}{3} = \frac{2}{1}$$

The symbol "$\sim$" means "is similar to." In the triangles above, $\triangle ABC \sim \triangle DEF$.

EXAMPLE

$\triangle CDE \sim \triangle FGH$. If $CD = 12$, $CE = 8$ and $FG = 5$, what is the measure of FH?

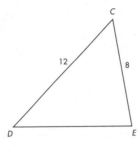 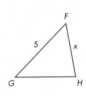

SOLUTION: Use the fact that similar triangles have sides that are proportional to solve for x. Use the proportion

$$\frac{\text{side } 1_{\text{larger triangle}}}{\text{side } 1_{\text{smaller triangle}}} = \frac{\text{side } 2_{\text{larger triangle}}}{\text{side } 2_{\text{smaller triangle}}}.$$

$$\frac{12}{5} = \frac{8}{x}$$

$$12x = 40$$

$$x = 3\frac{1}{3}$$

EXAMPLE

Rectangle $ABCD \sim$ rectangle $EFGH$. What is the ratio of the areas of rectangle $ABCD$ to rectangle $EFGH$?

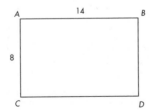

SOLUTION: The area of a rectangle is found by using the formula $A = lw$. Although the length and width of *ABCD* are known, the length of *EFGH* is not. Similar figures are proportional; use a proportion to find *EF*.

$$\frac{14}{x} = \frac{8}{4}$$

$$56 = 8x$$

$$7 = x$$

Find the area of each rectangle by inputting the known data into the area formula.

Area *ABCD*: $14 \times 8 = 112$ units^2

Area *EFGH*: $7 \times 4 = 28$

Find the ratio of the area of rectangle *ABCD* to rectangle *EFGH*:

$$\frac{112}{28} = \frac{4}{1}$$

A quicker way to answer this question is to square the ratio of corresponding sides.

$$\frac{AC}{EG} = \frac{8}{4} = \frac{2}{1}$$

$$\frac{2}{1}^2 = \frac{4}{1}$$

1. What is the height of a triangle with an area equal to 108.8 in² and a base that equals 12.8 inches?

    A. 34

    B. 21.6

    C. 17

    D. 14.4

2. A circle is inscribed in square *ABCD*. If the perimeter of the square is 64 ft, what is the area of the shaded portion?

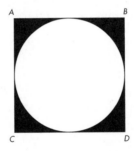

    A. 256 ft²

    B. 200.96 ft²

    C. 110.08 ft²

    D. 55.04 ft²

3. What is the surface area of a cube with a volume that equals 216 mm³?

    A. 6 mm²

    B. 36 mm²

    C. 216 mm²

    D. 432 mm²

4. A rectangular solid has a volume of 720 cubic inches. If the rectangular base has a length of 8 inches and width 6 inches, what is the height of the solid?

    A. 15

    B. 20

    C. 36

    D. 72

5. $\overline{OA}$ measures 4 meters and $\overline{OB}$ 8 meters. What is the area of the shaded ring? (Retain π in your answer.)

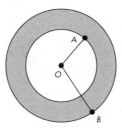

    A. 64π

    B. 48 π

    C. 32 π

    D. 16 π

6. What is the ratio of the volume of a sphere with a radius of 8 units to a sphere with a radius of 3 units?

    A. $\dfrac{9}{512}$

    B. $\dfrac{27}{64}$

    C. $\dfrac{216}{169}$

    D. $\dfrac{512}{27}$

7. The two trapezoids below are similar. What is the height of the smaller trapezoid?

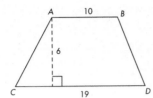 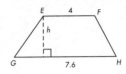

    A. 47.5

    B. 26.4

    C. 4.8

    D. 2.4

8. An aquarium in the shape of a rectangular solid is 6 feet long, 2 feet wide, and 4 feet high. Water is poured into the aquarium and rises to a height of 1.5 feet. The water is poured into another aquarium that is 5 feet long, 3 feet wide, and 4 feet high. What will be the height of the water in the second aquarium?

    A. 1 foot

    B. 1.2 feet

    C. 1.8 feet

    D. 2.1 feet

Math Practice 7 Answers

1. **C.**

    Use the formula $A = \frac{1}{2}bh$, the formula for the area of a triangle, and input the known data.

    $$108.8 = \frac{1}{2}(12.8)h$$

    $$108.8 = 6.4h$$

    $$17 = h$$

2. **D.**

    Find the area of the circle and subtract it from the area of the square. The area of the square is found by using the formula $A = s^2$ where s is the side length of the square. Find the length of a side by dividing the perimeter by 4.

    $$64 \div 4 = 16$$

    $$A = s^2$$

    $$A = 16^2 = 256$$

    The area of a circle is found by using the formula $A = \pi r^2$. Note that the side of the square is equal to the circle's diameter. The radius can be found by dividing one side of the square by 2 to get $r = 8$.

    $$A = \pi(8)^2 = 64\pi = 200.96$$

    Subtract the area of the circle from the area of the square.

    $$256 - 200.96 = 55.04 \text{ ft}^2$$

3. **C.**

    Use the formula $V = e^3$, where e is the measure of an edge. Once the edge's value is known, put it in the formula $SA = 6e^2$.

    $$216 = e^3$$

    $$\sqrt[3]{216} = \sqrt[3]{e^3}$$

    $$6 = e$$

    $$SA = 6e^2$$

    $$SA = 216 \text{ mm}^2$$

4. **A.**

The volume of a rectangular solid is found by using the formula $V = Bh$. Find B by finding the area of the rectangle.

$A = lw$

$A = 6 \times 8 = 48$ inches^2

Input 48 for B in the volume formula.

$720 = 48h$

15 inches $= h$

5. **B.**

Find the area of the larger circle with radius $\overline{OB}$ and subtract the area of the smaller circle with radius $\overline{OA}$. Use the formula $A = \pi r^2$ to find the area of both circles.

Larger circle: $A = \pi(8)^2 = 64\pi$

Smaller circle: $A = \pi(4)^2 = 16\pi$

$64\pi - 16\pi = 48\pi$

6. **D.**

Compute each volume and compare the measures. Use the formula $V = \dfrac{4}{3}\pi r^3$.

8 unit radius: $\dfrac{4}{3}\pi(8)^3 = \dfrac{2048}{3}\pi$

3 unit radius: $\dfrac{4}{3}\pi(3)^3 = 36\pi$

$\dfrac{2048}{3} \times \dfrac{1}{36} = \dfrac{2048}{108} = \dfrac{512}{27}$

All spheres are similar; an easier way to do this problem is to cube the ratio of the radii:

$\dfrac{8}{3}^{3} = \dfrac{512}{27}$

7. **D.**

Similar figures have sides that are proportional. Use the proportion $\dfrac{AB}{EF} = \dfrac{h_{ABCD}}{h_{EFGH}}$.

$$\frac{10}{4} = \frac{6}{h}$$

$$10h = 24$$

$$h = 2.4$$

8. **B.**

Find the volume of the water by using the formula $V = Bh$.

$B = 6 \times 2 = 12$ square feet

$h = 1.5$ feet

$V = 12 \times 1.5 = 18$ feet³

The same 18 feet³ of water is poured into the new aquarium.

$V = Bh$

$18 = (5 \times 3)h$

$18 = 15\,h$

$1.2 = h$

Chapter 8

Statistics and Data Analysis

In this chapter, we will review the following topics:

- Measures of Central Tendency

- The Mean

- The Median

- The Mode

- The Range

- Data Analysis

- Probability

- The Counting Principle

- Combinations and Permutations

Measures of Central Tendency

Any group of data, such as your monthly checking account balances or the national daily temperatures, can be collected and analyzed. Each data set can be used to calculate the following statistics: mean, median, mode, and range. Taken together, these four statistics are called measures of central tendency. These measures are useful for drawing conclusions quickly about large sets of data.

The Mean

The **mean**, also known as the average, is the sum of a group of numbers divided by that quantity of numbers. For example, if a bowler rolled scores of 213, 186 and 234, her mean score would be calculated as follows:

$$\frac{213 + 186 + 234}{3} = \frac{633}{3} = 211$$

The mean score of the bowler's three games is 211.

When the mean of a series of numbers is known, specific data points can be calculated.

EXAMPLE

Diego needs an average of 80% on his three exams to earn a B grade in math. On his first two exams he received grades of 65% and 75%. What score must he receive to get an 80% average for the three exams?

SOLUTION: Let x = the score needed on the third test to raise his average to 80%.

$$\frac{65 + 75 + x}{3} = 80$$

$$\frac{140 + x}{3} = 80$$

$$(3)\frac{140 + x}{3} = 80(3)$$

$$140 + x = 240$$

$$x = 100$$

Diego needs to score 100% on his third test to average 80% for the three exams.

Consider the incomes of four families (incomes in thousands of dollars).

$$47.6 \qquad 71.3 \qquad 62.4 \qquad 611.2$$

What do you notice when we calculate the average income of the four families?

$$\frac{47.6 + 71.3 + 62.4 + 611.2}{4} = 198.1$$

The average income of the four families is \$198,100 per year, which is much greater than three of the four families. The family with an annual income of \$611,200 greatly skewed the data set to yield an average that doesn't truly represent most of the group. This large input value, called an **outlier**, is the reason we cannot solely rely on the mean as a representative statistic of a data set. Often, using several of the measures of central tendency is needed to accurately represent the group.

The Median

The **median** is the middle value in a data set when the values are arranged in order. In the set of numbers {2, 4, 6, 8, 10}, 6 is the median because it is the value in the middle. In the data set {4, 11, 6, 7, 9}, the median is not immediately apparent because the numbers are not in order. When arranged in ascending order, {4, 6, 7, 9, 11}, it is clear that 7 is the median.

Some data sets have two numbers in the middle. For example, in the data set {4, 9, 11, 17, 20, 26}, 11 and 17 are the middle values. In this case, find the mean of the two numbers to get the median.

$$\frac{11 + 17}{2} = \frac{28}{2} = 14$$

The median of the data set {4, 9, 11, 17, 20, 26} is 14. Sometimes the median of a data set is not a member of the group.

In the next example, we will see how the median can represent a data set better than a mean.

The following are the weights (in pounds) of fish caught off of a pier during a one-hour period.

6, 93, 11, 16, 24, 13

Find the median and the mean of the weights of the fish.

SOLUTION: Find the median by arranging the weights in ascending order.

6   11   13   16   24   93

There are two weights in the middle, 13 and 16, so find their mean.

$$\frac{13 + 16}{2} = \frac{29}{2} = 14.5$$

Now find the mean weight of all the fish.

$$\frac{6 + 11 + 13 + 16 + 24 + 93}{6} = \frac{163}{6} \approx 27.2$$

The median, 14.5, is a useful statistic to represent the data set. Three of the weights are below 14.5 pounds and three are above. The mean, 27.2, is greater than five of the six values in the data set. The greatest weight of any of the fish, 93 pounds, is an outlier and it skewed the mean toward a higher value. In this situation, the median is a better representative of the data set than is the mean.

The Mode

The **mode** is the value that occurs most frequently in a data set. In the following group of numbers {7, 8, 8, 11, 15}, 8 is the mode because it appears two times while the rest of the numbers appear only once.

Some data sets have no mode. In the set {22, 33, 44, 55}, no number appears more frequently than the rest. Thus, this collection of numbers has no mode.

Some data sets have more than one mode. In the group {1, 7.4, 7.4, 9.2, 11.6, 11.6, 13}, 7.4 and 11.6 appear twice while all of the other numbers show up only once. Thus, 7.4 and 11.6 are modes of this group.

The Range

In a group of numbers, the difference between the least and greatest values is called the **range**. In the data set {15.2, 17.4, 22.4, 46.2}, the range is 31 because 46.2 − 15.2 = 31.

EXAMPLE

In the data set {17.6, 19.1, 56.3, x}, the range is 74.9. Assuming that the values are in ascending order, what is the value of x?

SOLUTION: The range is found by calculating the difference between the least and greatest values. Use the given assumption that x must be the greatest value of the set to find its value.

$$x - 17.6 = 74.9$$

$$x = 92.5$$

Data Analysis

Many questions on the GED® math test will be answered by referring to graphs and charts. The graphs may be in the form of tables, bar graphs, pie charts, or line graphs. Let's take a look at each to see what kinds of questions you can expect.

Tables

Some GED® math test questions will require you to compute and analyze information presented in tables. Look at the table below and answer the question that follows.

EXAMPLE

Soda Sale

Quantity	Price
24-pack	$7.29
6-pack	$2.25
Single cans	$0.60

What is the lowest cost for 32 sodas?

SOLUTION: To minimize the cost of 32 sodas, find the cost per soda for the 24-pack and the 6-pack.

$$\$7.29 \div 24 \approx \$0.30 \text{ per can}$$

$$\$2.25 \div 6 \approx \$0.38 \text{ per can}$$

The lowest cost for 32 cans is found by maximizing the number of 24-packs purchased and minimizing the number of individual cans purchased. Thus, the following quantities should be purchased:

1 24-pack at $7.29

1 6-pack at $2.25

2 individual cans: $2 \times \$0.60 = \$1.20$

Total: $10.74

The lowest cost for 32 cans of soda is $10.74

Bar Graphs

Bar graphs, also known as histograms, convey information by using adjacent rectangular bars.

EXAMPLE

The chart below shows the number of aluminum cans collected for recycling by a local grade school.

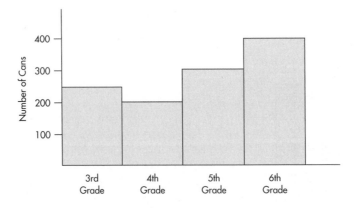

The sixth and fourth grades collected how many more cans than did the third and fifth grades?

SOLUTION: Find the sum of the third and fifth grade collections and subtract that value from the collections of the sixth and fourth graders.

6th and 4th grades: 400 + 200 = 600

5th and 3rd grades: 300 + 250 = 550

600 − 550 = 50

The sixth and fourth grades collected 50 more cans than did the fifth and third grades.

Pie Charts

A **pie chart** gets its name because it displays data in a circular graph. A pie chart is useful because it portrays data in a way that is simple and visually appealing.

EXAMPLE

The chart below shows the percentage of students who attend each grade at a local high school. The total enrollment of students in the school is 800.

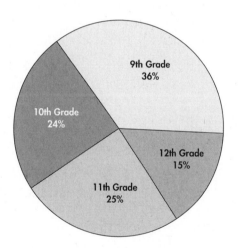

1. How many more ninth graders attend the school than do eleventh graders?

2. What is the measure of the central angle formed by the twelfth graders?

SOLUTION:

1. The ninth grade class represents 36% of the 800 students.

    (0.36)(800) = 288

    The eleventh grade class represents 25% of the 800 students.

    (0.25)(800) = 200

    288 – 200 = 88.

    There are 88 more ninth graders attending the school than eleventh graders.

2. A circle measures 360°. Find 15% of 360 to get the measure of the central angle formed by the twelfth graders at the school.

    (0.15)(360) = 54°.

    The central angle formed by the twelfth graders in the pie chart measures 54°.

Line Graphs

Line graphs may remind you of graphs in the coordinate plane. Line graphs on the GED® math test may be used to convey different functions simultaneously. In the example below, the line graphs show levels of costs and revenues generated over time.

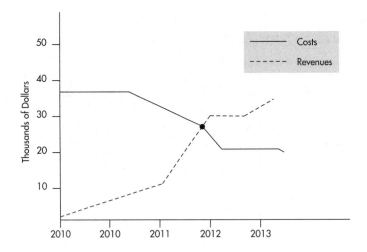

EXAMPLE

1. In what year were the costs at the maximum value above the revenues? Why do you suppose there was such a difference at this time?

2. In what year were the revenues at the highest value above the costs? Why do you suppose there was such a difference at this time?

3. What is the significance of the point in which the two lines intersect?

SOLUTION:

1. In 2009, costs exceeded revenues by the greatest degree (about $38,000). It is likely the business owner had start-up costs that needed to be paid before any money could be earned.

2. In 2013, revenues exceeded costs the most (about $15,000). It is likely the business had begun to succeed, bringing in revenues while incurring fewer costs.

3. The lines intersect when revenues and costs were equal. In business, this is known as the **break-even point**.

Creating Data Displays

Earlier we mentioned the different types of data displays that appear on the GED® math test: tables, bar graphs, pie charts, and line graphs. The GED® test may ask you questions about how to set up data displays.

EXAMPLE

The sales staff at Hallmark Camera Sales competed in a one-day sales contest. The contest logged the following number of cameras sold (by sales representative):

Wong: 13

Garcia: 17

Jensen: 9

Minton: 23

Parrish: 17

Create a bar graph to display the results of the contest. What would be the label of the horizontal axis? What would be the label of the vertical axis? What would be suitable increments of sales to display the number of cameras sold by each salesperson?

SOLUTION: Bar graphs usually feature a category in the horizontal axis (in this case, the individual salesperson) and some output for the vertical axis (in this case, the number of cameras sold). The number of cameras sold ranges from a minimum of 9 (Jensen) to a maximum of 23 (Minton). We could illustrate the sales by using increments of 5 or increments of individual sale.

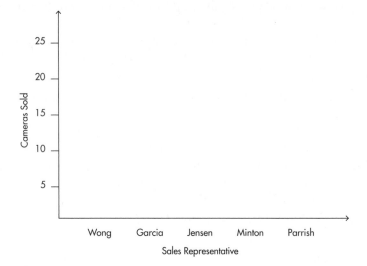

Remember to keep adequate space in the horizontal axis to record the performance of the individual salespeople.

Next, input the data from the sales report to finish the data display.

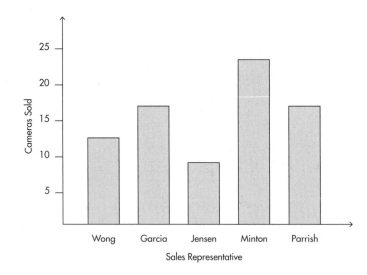

Notice how the data display offers a powerful visual tool that conveys the following data:

- The sales volume of each individual salesperson

- The difference between the highest and lowest number of sales

- The range of sales numbers (i.e., from 9 to 23 units sold)

Histograms

A histogram looks like a bar graph with prominent bars rising from the horizontal axis. However, the data along the horizontal axis is no longer a category but rather some frequency. Remember the exercise earlier about the sales contest? Each bar represented the sales of a particular salesperson. Notice the difference between a histogram and a bar graph in the example below.

EXAMPLE

Thirty football players on a certain professional football team wrote down their weights on a note card. The following numbers were collected:

Weight class	Number of players
160–179	4
180–199	7
200–219	10
220–249	7
>250	2

Create a histogram that depicts the number of players in each weight in class.

SOLUTION: Create a vertical axis that shows the number of players of a certain weight class. Given that the greatest number of players at any weight class is 10, we can show increments of single players. The horizontal axis will show the weight classes that define the players.

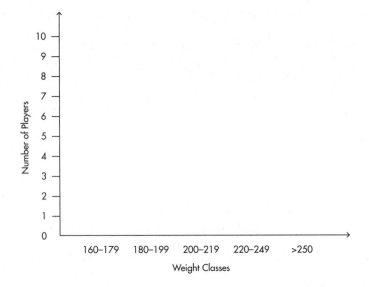

Next, fill in the data as described by the table above.

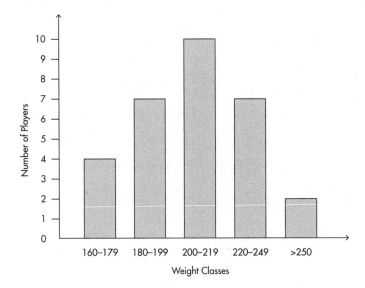

The histogram provides a powerful visual tool to demonstrate at a glance the values of each weight class. For example, it is obvious that the smallest number of players in any weight class are those weighing greater than 250 pounds, with just 2 players.

Scatter Plots

Scatter plots are groups of numbers graphed in the coordinate plane. Scatter plots can assume many forms:

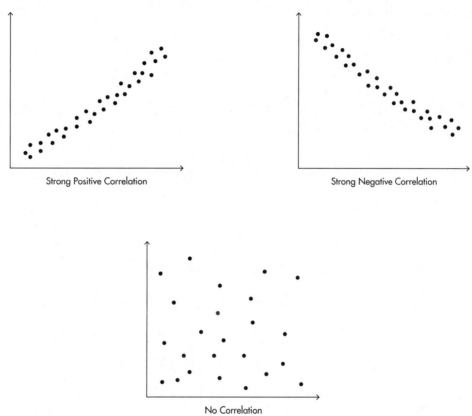

Scatter plots can also display weak positive or negative correlation. Examples of each are shown below.

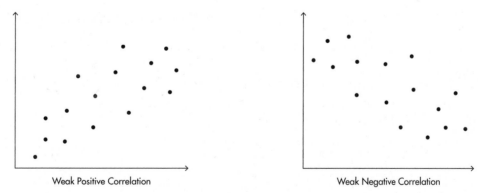

Although the data points seem to rise (weak positive correlation) and fall (weak negative correlation), the coherency among the data points is less pronounced than in the two strong models.

Line of Best Fit

When data points on a coordinate plane demonstrate strong correlation, a line of best fit can be used to predict future events. A line of best fit is drawn within the center of the points, perhaps connecting many of them.

EXAMPLE

Astronomers catalogued the number of meteors observed during the first seven hours of a meteor shower. The results are displayed below.

Hour	# of meteors observed
1	24
2	30
3	36
4	40
5	43
6	46
7	53

Graph the data in the chart and draw a line of best fit. Create a linear model from the data and use it to predict the number of meteors that are predicted to be seen in the ninth hour.

SOLUTION:

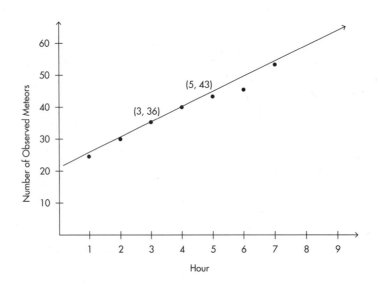

The data show a strong correlation; most of the data points are near or on the line. Choose two data points that are on the line to derive a linear model.

The points (3, 36) and (5, 43) appear to be on the line of best fit. Find the slope of the line connecting these two points.

$$m = \frac{43 - 36}{5 - 3} = \frac{7}{2} = 3.5$$

In the linear model, $y = mx + b$, replace m with 3.5.

$y = 3.5x + b$

Next, substitute either point for x and y to find b.

$36 = 3.5(3) + b$

$25.5 = b$

$y = 3.5x + 25.5$

Finally, replace x with 9 to predict the number of meteors expected to be seen in the ninth hour of the meteor shower.

$y = 3.5(9) + 25.5 = 57$

The line of best fit predicts 57 meteors will be observed at hour 9.

Probability

When you enter a raffle for a prize, you are experiencing an example of **probability**. How many tickets did you buy? How many were sold? These questions affect the probability of your winning the raffle. Probability can be expressed using the formula $\frac{\text{favored outcomes}}{\text{all outcomes}}$.

EXAMPLE

Michael purchased a package of baseball trading cards. He knows among the ten cards in the package, there is one Chipper Jones card. What is the probability he will draw the Chipper Jones card on the first draw?

SOLUTION:

$$\frac{\text{favored outcomes}}{\text{all outcomes}} = \frac{1}{10}$$

The answer, $\frac{1}{10}$, may also be expressed in decimal form, 0.1.

We can use our knowledge of probability to calculate the probability of two independent events occurring.

EXAMPLE

Jamie flips a coin and then rolls a die. What is the probability that the coin will land on heads and the die will land on an even number?

SOLUTION: Calculate the probabilities of both events occurring and multiply those probabilities.

Probability of a coin landing on heads: $\frac{1}{2}$

Probability of a die landing on an even number: $\frac{3}{6} = \frac{1}{2}$

Multiply the probabilities: $\frac{1}{2} \times \frac{1}{2} = \frac{1}{4}$

There is a $\frac{1}{4}$ probability (0.25) of a coin landing on heads and a die landing on an even number.

The Counting Principle

If a school lunch menu offers 2 different types of sandwiches, 3 different side orders and 2 different beverages, how many different combinations of sandwich, side order, and beverage are available? One way we can express the answer is by using a **tree diagram**.

S = Sandwich
SO = Side Order
D = Drinks

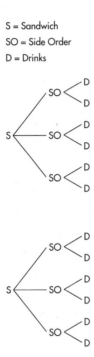

The tree diagram is a useful visual aid to demonstrate that there are a total of 12 different combinations of sandwich, side order, and beverage. However, we ought not draw a tree diagram for every problem of this sort. An easier to way to calculate the number of combinations of lunch options is to multiply all the possibilities.

$$2 \quad \times \quad 3 \quad \times \quad 2 \quad = \quad 12$$

sandwiches × side orders × drinks = combinations of lunches

Multiplying the number of sandwiches, side orders, and drinks is an example of the counting principle. A variation on the counting principle is the **factorial**, represented by the symbol "!". Any integer that precedes the factorial symbol is multiplied by all the positive smaller integers. For example, 6! means $6 \times 5 \times 4 \times 3 \times 2 \times 1 = 720$. The factorial is used to form combinations and permutations, the subject of our next section.

Combinations and Permutations

A **combination** is the number of groups that can be made from a larger group of elements. The formula for a combination is $\dfrac{n!}{r!(n-r)!}$ where n represents the larger set of numbers from which the smaller groups, r, are derived.

EXAMPLE

How many committees of three students can be made from a group of ten students?

SOLUTION: $\quad n = 10$

$\quad r = 3$

$$\frac{10!}{3!(10-3)!} = \frac{10 \times 9 \times 8 \times 7 \times 6 \times 5 \times 4 \times 3 \times 2 \times 1}{3 \times 2 \times 1 \times 7 \times 6 \times 5 \times 4 \times 3 \times 2 \times 1} = 120$$

Thus, there are 120 different groups of three that can be created from a group of ten students.

These calculations can be done in seconds using the on-screen calculator. Using the same problem, type in 10 followed by $[\,prb\,]$ followed by nCr followed by 3 and [enter].

$\qquad$ 10 nCr 3 = 120

In the preceding situation, the order in which the students were selected was unimportant. A committee that contained Billy, Maria and Juan is the same committee that contains Juan, Maria and Billy. In this case order did not matter, which is a feature of combinations. However, sometimes order does matter.

EXAMPLE

In a race that features 6 runners, how many ways can the competitors come in first, second, and third?

SOLUTION: If Billy came in first, followed by Maria in second and Juan in third, it would not be the same as Maria coming in first followed by Juan and Billy. The order mattered in this case. When order matters, we use a **permutation**.

The formula for a permutation is $\dfrac{n!}{(n-r)!}$, where n represents the larger group and r the smaller. Using the situation above we get:

$$\frac{6!}{(6-3)!} = \frac{6 \times 5 \times 4 \times 3 \times 2 \times 1}{3 \times 2 \times 1} = 120$$

Permutations, like combinations can be quickly calculated in the on-screen calculator. Using the same problem, type in 6 followed by $[\,prb\,]$ followed by nPr followed by 3 and [enter].

$$6 \text{ nPr } 3 = 120$$

PRACTICE!

Questions 1–4 refer to the data set below.

| 11.43 | 19.76 | 14.41 | 3.86 | 7.86 | 17.68 |

1. What is the mean of the data set?

    A. 12.5

    B. 12.92

    C. 15.9

    D. 19.76

2. What is the median of the data set?

    A. 12.5

    B. 12.92

    C. 15.9

    D. 19.76

3. What is the range of the data set?

    A. 12.5

    B. 12.92

    C. 15.9

    D. 19.76

4. What is the mode of the data set?

    A. 12.5

    B. 12.92

    C. Each number is a mode

    D. There is no mode.

Questions 5–6 refer to the histogram below.

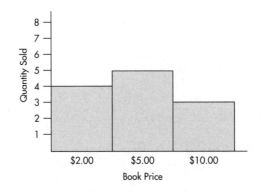

5. What is the median cost of the books sold?

    A. $2.00

    B. $5.00

    C. $7.50

    D. $10.00

6. What is the mean cost of the books sold?

    A. $9.95

    B. $7.35

    C. $6.45

    D. $5.25

7. What is the mean sale price of the cars shown in the chart below? (Round to the nearest dollar.)

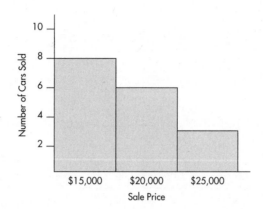

A. $18,529

B. $19,488

C. $21,121

D. $23,632

Questions 8–9 refer to the chart below.

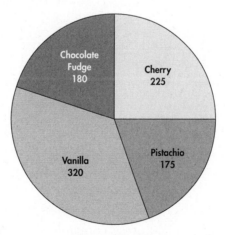

Ice Cream Cones Sold

8. What percent of sales is represented by pistachio ice cream?

A. 16.2%

B. 19.4%

C. 20.0%

D. 35.6%

9. What is the measure of the central angle formed by the vanilla sales in the pie chart (round your answer to the nearest degree)?

    A. 124°

    B. 128°

    C. 164°

    D. 178°

10. After a chapter test, the following scores were recorded for the class:

60%	70%	80%	90%	100%
X	X	X	X	X
X		X	X	

What score must a ninth student earn for the median and mode to have equivalent values?

    A. 70

    B. 80

    C. 90

    D. 100

11. A restaurant offers 5 salads, each with a choice of 3 different types of lettuce and 4 different salad toppings. How many different kinds of salads are available at the restaurant?

    A. 12

    B. 24

    C. 32

    D. 60

12. How many groups of committees containing 7 students can be formed from a pool of 12 students?

    A. 792

    B. 488

    C. 84

    D. 19

13. Calculate the value of 9 nPr 6 on your on-screen calculator.

    A. 54

    B. 108

    C. 1,728

    D. 60,480

Math Practice 8 Answers

1. **A.**

   The mean is the average of the numbers. Find the sum of the numbers and divide by 6.

   $(11.43 + 19.76 + 14.41 + 3.86 + 7.86 + 17.68) \div 6 = 12.5$

2. **B.**

   The median is the number in the middle. Arrange the numbers in ascending order to identify the median.

       3.86   7.86   11.43   14.41   17.68   19.76

   Both 11.43 and 14.41 are the middle values. In this case, the median is the mean of the middle numbers.

   $(11.43 + 14.41) \div 2 = 12.92$

3. **C.**

   The range of a group of numbers is the difference between the greatest and least values.

   $19.76 - 3.86 = 15.9$

4. **D.**

   The mode is the value that occurs most frequently. Each number in the group appears the same number of times, once, so there is no mode.

5. **B.**

Array the number of books sold; there are four $2 books, five $5 books and three $10 books.

$$2 \quad 2 \quad 2 \quad 2 \quad 5 \quad 5 \quad 5 \quad 5 \quad 5 \quad 10 \quad 10 \quad 10$$

The middle numbers are both 5's, so find their mean.

$$(5 + 5) \div 2 = 5$$

6. **D.**

Add the costs of the books and divide the sum by 12.

$$(2 + 2 + 2 + 2 + 5 + 5 + 5 + 5 + 5 + 10 + 10 + 10) \div 12 = 63 \div 12 = 5.25$$

7. **A.**

First, find the total sales volume.

$$8 \times \$15{,}000 = \$120{,}000$$

$$6 \times \$20{,}000 = \$120{,}000$$

$$3 \times \$25{,}000 = \$75{,}000$$

Total: $315,000

Divide the sales volume by 17 to get the mean sale price of the cars.

$$\$315{,}000 \div 17 = \$18{,}529$$

8. **B.**

Use the formula $\dfrac{\text{part}}{\text{whole}} = \dfrac{n}{100}$ to find the percent.

$$\frac{175}{175 + 225 + 320 + 180} = \frac{n}{100}$$

$$\frac{175}{900} = \frac{n}{100}$$

$$175 \times 100 = 900 \times n$$

$$17{,}500 = 900n$$

$$19.4 = n$$

9. **B.**

The central angle is a percent of 360°. Find the percent of sales comprised by vanilla ice cream.

$$\frac{\text{part}}{\text{whole}} = \frac{n}{100}$$

$$\frac{320}{900} = \frac{n}{100}$$

$$900n = 32,000$$

$$n = 35.55\%$$

Find 35.55% of 360°.

$$0.3555 \times 360 \approx 128$$

10. **B.**

Array the scores from least to greatest.

| 60 | 60 | 70 | 80 | 80 | 90 | 90 | 100 |

The median score is 80 and the modes are 60, 80, and 90. When another student scores an 80% on the test, the scores are:

| 60 | 60 | 70 | 80 | 80 | 80 | 90 | 90 | 100 |

The median remains 80, but only a third score of 80 yields an equivalent mode of 80.

11. **D.**

Use the counting principle to find the number of salads:

(5 salads) × (3 types of lettuce) × (4 salad toppings) = 60

12. **A.**

The order of the students does not matter, so use combinations.

12 C 7 = 792

13. **D.**

Type in 9 nPr 6 on your calculator to arrive at 60,480.

Real-World Applications of Mathematical Models

In this chapter we will review the following topics:

- Pathways to Problem Solving

- Modeling Real-Life Situations

- Representing Real-Life Situations Visually

- Using Logic to Solve Real-World Problems

- Graphing Real-World Functions

- Logic and Counterexamples

Pathways to Problem Solving

The content and format of mathematics as it is taught in schools is evolving. In the past, high school math teachers taught algebra, geometry, trigonometry and advanced math in that order. Today, math teachers use a more integrated approach; students will attempt to solve problems using several disciplines simultaneously. This process of problem solving is the main feature of the Common Core movement in education.

The GED® test requires you to use the following techniques when answering some questions:

- Recognize the scope of a problem and the pathway to its solution

- Plan the pathway that will be used to solve the problem

- Recognize any information that is needed to solve the problem

- Use mathematical techniques to solve the problem

Let's try to solve a problem using these methods.

EXAMPLE

Pauline has a job interview in a city in a nearby county. She starts her trip to the meeting by driving 16 miles due south from her home. Her GPS map indicates she must now begin driving 30 miles due west to arrive at the site. When she arrives at her destination, what will be her distance from her home?

In order to answer this question, do the following:

1. Devise a plan to answer this question.

2. Indicate a solution pathway or a line of reasoning to answer the question.

3. Identify any missing information needed to solve the problem.

4. Identify mathematical techniques used to answer the question.

5. Find the solution.

SOLUTION:

1. Pauline has driven two legs, south and west, of a right triangle. Using geometry and algebra knowledge, calculate the measure of the hypotenuse of the triangle.

2. When the measures of two sides of a right triangle are known, use $a^2 + b^2 = c^2$, the Pythagorean theorem, to calculate the measure of the hypotenuse.

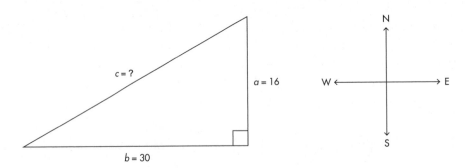

3. The missing information is *c*, the measure of the hypotenuse.

4. Input the known data, $a = 16$ and $b = 30$ to calculate c^2. Once c^2 is known, square root that value to find the measure of the hypotenuse.

5. Calculate:

$$16^2 + 30^2 = c^2$$

$$256 + 900 = c^2$$

$$1156 = c^2$$

$$\sqrt{1156} = \sqrt{c^2}$$

$$34 = c$$

Pauline is 34 miles away from her home when she arrives for her interview.

You may have noticed that 16-30-34 is a multiple of the 8-15-17 Pythagorean triple we learned about in Chapter 6.

Modeling Real-Life Situations

Most mathematics tests traditionally require carefully calculated solutions. Some questions on the GED® Mathematical Reasoning test may ask you *how* a problem can be framed.

EXAMPLE

Use algebraic equations and inequalities to model each situation.

1. The cost of three watermelons cannot exceed $7.50.

2. The cost of 5 apples and 7 oranges is $4.30.

3. The difference between the costs of two insurance policies must be more than $85.

SOLUTIONS:

1. $3w \leq 7.5$

2. $5x + 7y = 4.3$

3. $x - y > 85$

Representing Real-Life Situations Visually

Earlier in the book we learned how to use pie charts, tables, and graphs to draw conclusions. The GED® math test may also ask you to discern which data display better reflects a certain situation.

EXAMPLE

Kari is asked to persuade a parents' group to raise funds for a new bleacher section to be constructed in the school gym. The purchase price is $14,500. She researched funding for the project and her findings are shown below:

Funding Sources for the Bleacher Project

Parents' Group: $1,160

School District: $4,250

State Funding: $3,880

Private Sponsors: $ 3,000

Basketball Team Funds: $2,255

Kari needs to set up a PowerPoint presentation for the group. She knows the parents' group has few funds and many competing projects to consider supporting. Should Kari use a pie chart or a table chart for her presentation?

SOLUTION: Visual data displays can be powerful tools when trying to persuade the viewer. Note how the data looks in a table:

Group	Funding ($)
Parents' Group	1,160
School District	4,205
State Funds	3,880
Private Sponsors	3,000
Basketball Team	2,255

Now, notice how the data appear in a pie chart.

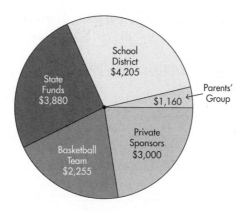

Bleacher Project Funding

The pie chart demonstrates, at a glance, that the parents' group has to provide a small portion of the total funding (8% of the pie). Using a pie chart is a more effective visual display than is the simple table. It is always important to have one's data at hand but displaying that data effectively may be just as important.

Using Logic to Solve Real-World Problems

Many GED® questions require the test-taker to calculate precise answers. There will be some questions, however, that require logic to arrive at accurate answers more quickly. Consider the following example.

EXAMPLE

In 1908 an object exploded above Tunguska, Russia. The explosion occurred 8.5 kilometers above the Earth's surface but nonetheless leveled trees for miles around. All of the scientists agree that the item that exploded was between 10 and 100 meters in diameter. One group of scientists believes the object that exploded was a comet while another group indicated that item was a meteor. Which of the following would disprove one of the scientist group's assertions as to the object's nature?

A. Meteors rarely exceed 15 meters in diameter.

B. Comets can explode at altitudes greater than 8.5 kilometers.

C. Comets are always larger than 100 meters.

D. Comets never reach the surface but meteors do reach the surface about 35% of the time.

SOLUTION: Let's look at each assertion to see if that information disproves the fact that the object was a comet or a meteor.

A. Meteors rarely exceed 15 meters in diameter.

   Both scientific camps agree that the item was between 10 and 100 meters in diameter. Although meteors rarely exceed 15 meters in diameter, 15 is within the range of 10 to 100 meters. Choice (A) does not disprove that the object was a meteor.

B. Comets can explode at altitudes greater than 8.5 kilometers.

   Although comets can explode at an altitude higher than 8.5 kilometers, that does not disprove the fact that a comet can explode at 8.5 kilometers. Choice (B) does not disprove the fact that the object could have been a comet.

C. Comets are always larger than 100 meters.

   Both scientific camps agree that the object was between 10 and 100 meters in diameter. If comets are larger than 100 meters in diameter, then the object could not have been a comet. Choice (C) disproves the idea that the object that exploded over Tunguska could have been a comet.

D. Comets never reach the Earth's surface but meteors do reach the surface about 35% of the time.

   Both camps agree the object exploded above the Earth's surface. Comets never collide with the Earth's surface and meteors also explode in the atmosphere most of the time (65% of the time). Thus, choice (D) does not disprove that the object was a comet or a meteor.

Graphing Real-World Functions

Earlier we learned how to display data in meaningful ways using:

—Pie charts

—Histograms

—Bar charts

—Line graphs

You should be prepared to graph real-world functions as well. We will illustrate this point below.

EXAMPLE

Chuck is a plumber who uses the following fee schedule:

Home visit fee: $50

Hourly rate: $40 per hour

Sara contacts Chuck because her shower won't drain properly. She is familiar with Chuck's fee schedule and needs to know what her 4-hour appointment will cost.

Find Sara's cost for plumbing work by doing the following:

1. Create a table showing that Chuck's fee schedule is a function.

2. Find the cost of Sara's 4-hour appointment.

3. Graph the function in a coordinate plane.

4. Demonstrate graphically that Chuck's fee schedule is a function.

SOLUTION: The table below illustrates the costs of Chuck's appointments. Let x be the input, the number of hours Chuck works, and y be the output, the visit's total cost. Remember, the output is the sum of the home visit and the hours spent at the site.

Hours (x)	Total cost (y)
1	90
2	130
3	170
4	210
5	250

Next, demonstrate that the chart represents a function. Shown as ordered pairs, the inputs and outputs are:

$$(1, 90) \ (2, 130) \ (3, 170) \ (4, 210) \ (5, 250)$$

1. The ordered pairs shown in the table model a function because each input has only one output.

2. Using the chart above, Sara's 4-hour appointment will cost her $210.

3. Use the function f(x) = 40x + 50 to graph the data points shown above.

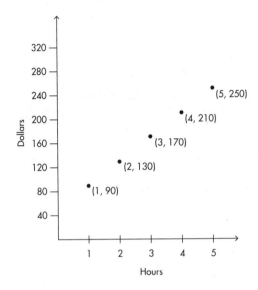

Use the vertical line test to show the graph represents a function.

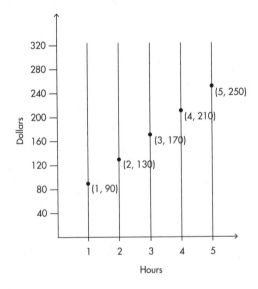

The vertical lines pass through only one point at a time, so the graph represents a function.

Logic and Counterexamples

Imagine trying to locate an old friend from high school. She is a young adult, just starting out in her career. Although you know the name of the small town she lives in, you do not know her exact address. What can you do to limit unnecessary searching? Your friend certainly lives in the residential part of town so investigating the commercial areas would be a waste of time. Since she is young and just starting out in her career, it's likely she does not live in the upscale part of town. Perhaps you should begin your search in a series of modest apartment complexes you've just seen.

The above example shows how logic can be used to find solutions to problems more quickly. The GED® test-taker is expected to do the following on the exam:

- Identify information required to evaluate a line of reasoning.

- Recognize and use counterexamples.

- Recognize flaws in others' reasoning.

EXAMPLE

Aaron and Elizabeth were reading the following question in the logic section of their math quiz:

Given that all men in the Endicott family are over six feet tall, which of the following must be true?

A. No man under six feet tall is in the Endicott family.

B. All men over six feet tall are in the Endicott family.

C. There is one man under six feet tall who is a member of the Endicott family.

D. Every member of the Endicott family who is taller than six feet is a man.

SOLUTION: Elizabeth says, "I know the answer is not (B); my uncle Woody is over six feet tall and he is not a member of the Endicott family. I am leaning toward answer (D)." Aaron responds, "I don't think that's correct, Elizabeth. Don't you think it's possible that a woman in the Endicott family could be over six feet tall?" Elizabeth agrees, leaving the two with options (A) and (C). Elizabeth correctly points out that the problem starts out by stating that every man in the Endicott family is over six feet tall, so choice (C) cannot be correct; if a man is under six feet tall, he cannot be an Endicott. Aaron and Elizabeth both agree the correct answer is (A): if you are a man and you under six feet tall, you cannot be a member of the Endicott family.

PRACTICE!

Mark will purchase 6 pairs of pants and y pairs of socks. The cost of the pants is $25 and the cost of the socks is $7. If the total cost of his purchase is between $178 and $185, how many pairs of socks can Mark purchase?

Answer these five questions needed to solve this problem:

1. Devise a plan to answer this question.

2. Indicate a solution pathway or a line of reasoning to answer the question.

3. Identify any missing information needed to solve the problem.

4. Identify mathematical techniques used to answer the question.

5. Find the solution.

6. A political candidate wants to show how his opponent has outspent him in the ratio of 10 to 1. Which of the following data displays will be useful in making his point?

    A. A bar chart

    B. A line graph

    C. A pie chart

    D. All of the above

7. Squares are rectangles and rectangles are parallelograms. Which of the following can logically be deduced?

    A. Parallelograms are squares.

    B. Rectangles are squares and parallelograms.

    C. Squares are parallelograms.

    D. Parallelograms are also rectangles or squares.

8. Julio danced with Cara. Cara danced with Sam. Sam danced with Fehra and Julio also danced with Fehra. If we displayed this information in a table, would the table represent a function?

    A. Yes, because all inputs have only one output.

    B. Yes, because one input has two different outputs.

    C. No, because each input has only one output.

    D. No, because one input has more than one output.

9. All males are either men or boys. Which of the following is a counterexample that disproves the above statement.

    A. My sister Sheena is not a male.

    B. My father is a male.

    C. My mother is not a male.

    D. My dog Max is a male

10. Carla is using a pie chart to demonstrate that 40% of her school's student body was born in a neighboring state. What would be the measure of the central angle formed by that portion of the pie chart?

    A. 144°

    B. 160°

    C. 172°

    D. 180°

Math Practice 9 Answers

1. Find the solution to $178 \leq 6$ pants $+ y$ socks ≤ 185.

2. Multiply 6 by 25 to find the total cost of the pants. Add that figure to the cost of y socks, each pair costing $7, and apply those values to the inequality $178 \leq 6$ pants $+ y$ socks ≤ 185.

3. The missing information is the number of pairs of socks. Be aware that there may be more than one correct solution to the problem.

4. Create two equations to find the solution:

$178 = (6 \cdot 25) + 7y$ and $(6 \cdot 25) + 7y = 185$

5. Solve:

First equation

$178 = (6 \cdot 25) + 7y$

$178 = 150 + 7y$

$28 = 7y$

$y = 4$

Second equation

$185 = (6 \cdot 25) + 7y$

$185 = 150 + 7y$

$35 = 7y$

$5 = y$

Mark can afford to purchase 4 or 5 pairs of socks.

6. **D.**

A bar chart, a line graph, and a pie chart will all be powerful visual aids to demonstrate that the candidate's opponent has outspent him 10 to 1.

7. **C.**

Use the following logical sequence:

If $A = B$ and $B = C$, then $A = C$. This called the transitive property.

Let A = squares B = rectangles C = parallelograms

$A = B$: squares are rectangles

$B = C$: rectangles are parallelograms

$A = C$: squares are parallelograms

8. **D.**

Arrange the different dancers in ordered pairs:

(Julio, Cara) (Cara, Sam) (Sam, Fehra) (Julio, Fehra)

A relation of data points is only a function if each input has solely one output. The ordered pairs above do not represent a function because the input Julio has two outputs, Cara and Fehra.

9. **D.**

The statement indicates that all males are either men or boys. But a dog (or any other animal) can also be a male which disproves the statement "All males are either men or boys."

10. **A.**

Use the proportion $\dfrac{\text{percent}}{100} = \dfrac{m}{360}$ where m represents the measure of the central angle of the pie chart.

$$\frac{40}{100} = \frac{m}{360}$$

$$14,400 = 100m$$

$$144 = m$$

Science

About the GED® Science Test

To succeed on the GED® Science test, you need to know the fundamentals of how science works. This means not just being familiar with the key ideas in the field but also knowing how to make observations, gather evidence, and conduct experiments. Though you certainly should be comfortable with science vocabulary, realize that the test will never ask you to define a term without the question itself providing "contextual support," as GED Testing Service® puts it.

As with the test itself, the following sections take you through three major content areas:

- Life Science
    - Human Body and Health
    - Relationship Between Life Functions and Energy Intake
    - Energy Flows in Ecologic Networks (Ecosystems)
    - Organization of Life (Structure and Function of Life)
    - Molecular Basis for Heredity
    - Evolution
- Physical Science
    - Conservation, Transformation, and Flow of Energy
    - Work, Motion, and Forces
    - Chemical Properties and Reactions Related to Living Systems

- Earth and Space Science

  — Interactions Between Earth's Systems and Living Things

  — Earth and its System Components and Interactions

  — Structures and Organization of the Cosmos

The test features approximately 40 questions. About half of them are self-contained, while the other half are grouped in scenarios. This means that the test will often present you with two or three items based on a single prompt, or stimulus. The stimulus could be a text or graphic, or sometimes both. The stimulus will give you the details you need to be able to answer the questions.

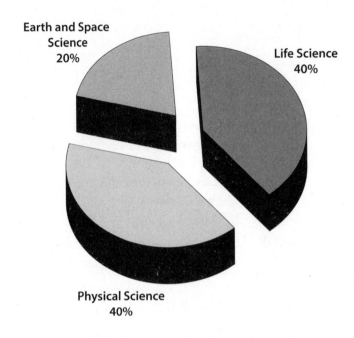

Question formats

The Science test includes these item types, several of which are technology-driven in light of the fact that the GED® test is given on computer:

- Standard multiple-choice items, just like you've probably seen on many other tests

- Fill-in-the-blank items

- Drag-and-drop items

- Drop-down items

- Hot-spot items

- Short-answer items

Each question is worth one point except for the two short-answer items, which are scored on a three-point scale. You can earn the points in one of two ways on each such item. Some have you pick up points based on your ability, as GED Testing Service® puts it, "to identify or analyze up to three specific details or correct answers." This means that you earn as you go in the item. In other items, you are scored holistically, or in terms of the entirety of your answer. Such holistic items zero in on your skill at either summarizing or synthesizing information. Synthesizing hinges on your ability to pick out what's important and then organize it in a way that makes it meaningful to you.

Scoring

With a high enough score, today's GED® test makes it possible to earn college credit.

Your score on the GED® Science test is based on where you fall relative to the four GED® Performance Level Descriptors:

- Performance Level 1 (< 145) – Below Passing

- Performance Level 2 (145–164) – Pass/High School Equivalency

- Performance Level 3 (165–174) – GED® College Ready

- Performance Level 4 (175–200)– GED® College Ready + Credit

If your score puts you into the top performance bracket, you may be eligible for three undergraduate credits in introductory physical science. For details on GED® scoring, visit *www.gedtestingservice.com.*

Now let's move on to the Science test's three content areas. Studying the following review thoroughly will give you the leg up you need to excel on the GED® Science test.

Life Science

Human Body and Health

Body systems (e.g., muscular, endocrine, nervous systems) and how they work together to perform a function (e.g., muscular and skeletal work to move the body)

Systems

The human body is an integration of several complex systems that perform specific functions while also interacting with each other as a complete healthy body. Human body systems include the digestive, circulatory, respiratory (gas exchange), excretory, immune, skeletal, muscular, nervous, endocrine, and reproductive systems.

Digestive System

The digestive system (see Science Fig. 1-1) serves to process ingested food so that it becomes useful for energy at the cellular level. The human digestive system encompasses the processes of ingestion (food intake), digestion (breaking down of ingested particles into molecules that can be absorbed by the body), and egestion (the elimination of indigestible materials). The digestive organs are divided into two categories—the gastrointestinal (GI) tract, and the accessory organs. The GI tract includes the mouth, pharynx, esophagus, stomach, small intestine, large intestine, rectum, and anus. These are the organs through which food directly passes. The accessory organs perform functions along the GI tract and include the teeth, tongue, salivary glands, liver, gallbladder, and pancreas.

Let's take a look at each organ and its function as we consider Figure 1-1.

The **mouth** (oral cavity, 1) is the organ of ingestion and the first organ in the GI tract. The first step in digestion occurs as food is chewed with the aid of the teeth and tongue. Chewing is the initial step in breaking down food into particles of manageable size. Chewing also increases the surface area of the food and mixes it with saliva, which contains the starch-digesting enzyme amylase. Saliva is secreted by the salivary glands (2). Chewed food is then swallowed and moved toward the stomach (3) by peristalsis (muscle contraction) of the esophagus (4). The **stomach** is a muscular organ that stores incompletely digested food. The stomach continues the mechanical and chemical breakdown of food particles begun by the chewing process. The lining of the stomach secretes mucous to protect it from the strong digestive chemicals necessary in the digestive process. The stomach also secretes digestive enzymes and hydrochloric acid, which continue the digestive process to the point of producing a watery soup of nutrients, which then proceed into the small intestine.

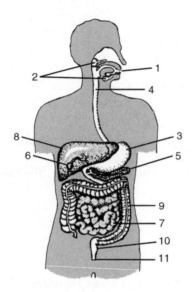

Fig. 1-1. Human Digestive System

The **pancreas** (5) and **gallbladder** (6) release more enzymes into the small intestine, the site where the final steps of digestion, along with most absorption, occurs. The cells lining the **small intestine** (7) have protrusions called villi that extent out into the intestine. Villi provide a large surface area for absorption of nutrients. Nutrients move into the capillaries through or between the cells making up the villi. The enriched blood travels to the **liver** (8), where some sugars are removed and stored. The liver produces bile from broken-down pigments and chemicals (often from pollutants and medications) and secretes it into the small intestine, where it proceeds to the large intestine and is expelled in the feces. The liver also breaks down some nitrogenous molecules (including some proteins), excreting them into the bloodstream as urea. The indigestible food moves from the small intestine to the **large intestine** (9), where water is absorbed back into the body. The waste (feces) is then passed through the **rectum** (10) and excreted from the **anus** (11).

Circulatory System

The circulatory system is the conduit for delivering nutrients and gases to all cells and for removing waste products from them. Circulation of nutrients, gases, and wastes occurs with the essential body fluid, blood. Blood consists of a composite of several types of cells suspended in liquid plasma. Plasma makes up more than half the volume of blood and consists of mostly water, but also carries various nutrients, proteins, clotting factors, hormones, and waste products. Suspended within the plasma are three types of blood cells:

- **Red blood cells**—contain protein molecules called hemoglobin that bind to oxygen at the lungs and carry it to cells throughout the body

- **White blood cells** (leukocytes)—fight infections and invasions to the body of various forms; there are several types of white blood cells that fight different infections

- **Platelets**—small cells that help with clotting blood when necessary

Fig. 1-2. A scanning electron microscope image of normal circulating human blood. In addition to the irregularly shaped leukocytes, both red blood cells and many small disc-shaped platelets are visible.

Blood flows throughout the circulatory system within vessels. **Vessels** include arteries, veins, and capillaries. The pumping action of the heart (a hollow, muscular organ) forces blood in one direction throughout the system. Valves within the heart, and some of the vessels in limbs, keep blood from flowing backwards (being pulled downward by gravity). Blood carries many products to cells throughout the body, including minerals, infection-fighting white blood cells, nutrients, proteins, hormones, and metabolites. Blood also carries dissolved gases (particularly oxygen) to cells and waste gases (mainly carbon dioxide) away from cells.

The process of **cellular metabolism** is a fundamental process of life and cannot proceed without a continuous supply of oxygen to every living cell within the body. **Oxygen** is carried by hemoglobin (containing iron) in red blood cells. Oxygen enters the blood in the lungs and travels to the heart, then through arteries (larger vessels that carry blood away from the heart), to arterioles (small arteries), and to capillaries. **Capillaries** (tiny vessels) surround all tissues of the body and exchange carbon dioxide for oxygen. The blood picks up carbon dioxide waste from the cells and carries it through capillaries, then **venules** (small veins), and **veins** (vessels that carry blood toward the heart), back to the heart and on to the lungs. *Thus, blood is continually cycled.*

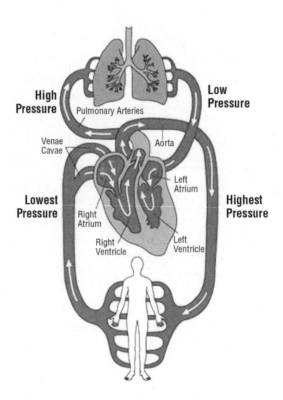

Fig. 1-3. The heart pumps blood through the lungs (where oxygen is picked up and waste products are released) and out to the body organs and limbs.

Respiratory System

The **respiratory system** (see Fig. 1-4) is responsible for the intake and processing of oxygen required by all cells in the human body, and for expelling CO_2 produced as a waste product, as well as any other unused gases. Air is taken in primarily through the nose (although gases may be inhaled through the mouth, the nose is better at filtering out pollutants in the air). The **nasal passages** (1) have a mucous lining to capture foreign particles. This lining is surrounded by epithelial tissue with embedded capillaries, which serve to warm the entering air. Air then passes through the **pharynx** (2) and into the **trachea** (3). The trachea includes the windpipe or larynx in its upper portion, and the glottis, an opening allowing gases to pass into the two branches known as the bronchi. The glottis is guarded by a flap of tissue, the epiglottis, which prevents food particles from entering the bronchial tubes. The **bronchi** (4) lead to the two **lungs** (5) where they branch out in all directions into smaller tubules known as **bronchioles** (6). The bronchioles end in **alveoli** (7), thin-walled air sacs, which are the site of gas exchange. The bronchioles are surrounded by capillaries, which bring blood with a high density of carbon dioxide and a low concentration of oxygen from the pulmonary arteries. At the alveoli, the carbon dioxide diffuses from the blood into the alveoli and oxygen diffuses from the alveoli into the blood. The oxygenated blood is carried away to tissues throughout the body.

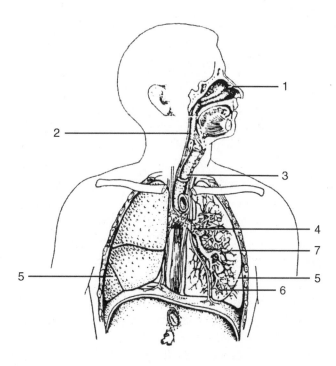

Fig. 1-4. Human Respiratory System

The respiratory system and the circulatory system work in concert to perform the two essential functions of

1. taking in oxygen from the surrounding atmosphere and delivering it to all cells throughout the human body for use in cellular metabolism, and

2. picking up and emptying gaseous waste products back into the atmosphere.

If and when these two essential functions are impaired, the human body is unable to function.

Excretory System

The **excretory system** is responsible for collecting waste materials and transporting them to organs that expel them from the body. There are many types of waste that must be expelled from the body, and there are many organs involved in this process.

The primary excretory organs of the human body are the **kidneys**. The kidneys filter metabolic wastes from the blood and excrete them as urine into the urinary tract. The **urinary tract** carries the fluid that is eventually expelled from the body to the bladder. The **bladder** holds urine until it is expelled. Urine is typically 95% water, and also contains urea (formed from the breakdown of proteins), uric acid (formed from breaking down nucleic acids), creatinine (a byproduct of muscle contraction), and various minerals and hormones.

While the excretory system organs are the kidneys and bladder, there are several other organs that reside in other organ systems that serve excretory functions. The excretory system works together with several other systems to maintain a balance of healthy substances in the body. The **lungs** are the site of excretion for carbon dioxide during respiration. The **skin** is the site of the excretion of salts, urea, and other wastes along with water from sweat glands in the skin. The **colon** and **anus** are the location of excretion of feces from the digestive system.

Immune System

The **immune system** functions to defend the body from infection by bacteria, viruses, and any other foreign pathogens. The lymphatic system is the principal infection-fighting component of the immune system. The organs of the lymphatic system in humans include: the lymph, lymph nodes, spleen, thymus, and tonsils. **Lymph** is a collection of excess fluid that is absorbed from between cells into a system of vessels, which circulates through the lymphatic system and finally dumps into the bloodstream. Lymph also collects plasma proteins that have leaked into interstitial fluids.

Lymph nodes are small masses of lymph tissue that function to filter lymph and produce lymphocytes. **Lymphocytes** and other cells are involved in the immune system. Lymphocytes begin in bone marrow as stem cells and are collected and distributed via the lymph nodes. There are two classes of lymphocytes—B cells, and T cells. B cells emerge from the bone marrow mature, and produce antibodies, which enter the bloodstream. These antibodies find and attach themselves to foreign antigens (toxins, bacteria, foreign cells, etc.). The attachment of an antibody to an antigen marks the pair for destruction.

The **spleen** contains some lymphatic tissue, and is located in the abdomen. It filters larger volumes of lymph than nodes can handle. The **tonsils** are a group of lymph cells connected together and located in the throat.

The **thymus** is another mass of lymph tissue, which is active only through the teen years, fighting infection and producing T cells. T cells mature in the thymus gland. Some T cells (similar to B cells) patrol the blood for antigens, but T cells are also equipped to destroy antigens themselves. T cells also regulate the body's immune responses.

Skeletal System

The **skeletal system** provides the body with structure, stability, and—together with the muscular system—the ability to move. The human skeletal system is comprised of **206 bones**. The skeleton provides protection for the soft internal organs, as well as structure and stability allowing for upright stature and movement. **Bones** also perform the important function of storing calcium and phosphates, and producing red blood cells within the bone marrow. The 206 bones forming the human skeleton are linked with movable joints, and joined by muscle systems controlling movement.

Muscular System

The **muscular system** is comprised of joints, ligaments, cartilage, and muscle groups. **Smooth muscle** lines most internal organs, protecting their contents and function, and generally contracting without conscious intent. For instance, the involuntary (automatic) contraction of smooth muscle in the esophagus and lungs facilitates digestion and respiration. **Cardiac muscle** is unique to the heart. It is involuntary muscle (like smooth muscle), but cardiac muscle also has unique features, which cause it to "beat" rhythmically. Cardiac muscle cells have branched endings that interlock with each other, keeping the muscle fibers from ripping apart during their strong contractions. In addition, electrical impulses travel in waves from cell to cell in cardiac muscle, causing the muscle to contract in a coordinated way with a rhythmic pace. **Skeletal muscles** are voluntary—they are activated by command in cooperation with the nervous system and work to move the bones of the skeletal system, resulting in body movement.

Nervous System

The **nervous system** is a communication network that connects the entire body and provides control over bodily functions and actions. The nervous system allows the body to sense stimuli and conditions in the environment and respond with necessary reactions. **Sensory organs**—skin, eyes, nose, ears, etc.—transmit signals in response to environmental stimuli to the **brain**, which then conveys messages via nerves to glands and muscles, which produce the necessary response.

The human nervous system is anatomically divided into two systems: the central nervous system, and the peripheral nervous system. The **Central Nervous System** (CNS) has two main components: the **brain** and the **spinal cord**. These organs control all other organs and systems of the body. The **Peripheral Nervous System** (PNS) is a network of nerves throughout the body. It includes sensory nerves that carry impulses from organs to the CNS and motor nerves that carry messages back to the body organs and muscles. The nervous system is highly sophisticated, providing conscious response and unconscious controls.

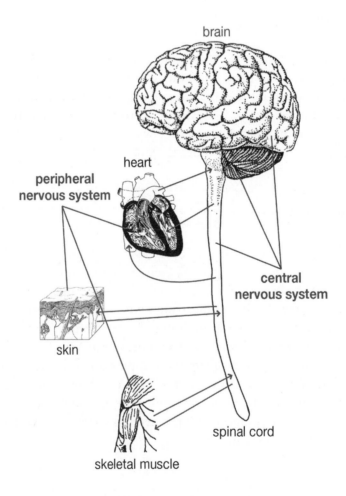

Fig. 1-5. Human Nervous System

Endocrine System

The **endocrine system** regulates various body functions through the secretion of chemicals that serve as "messengers" known as hormones. **Hormones** are made within specialized clusters of cells called endocrine glands. Whereas other glands in the body, such as digestive glands, have ducts carrying products to their target, endocrine glands are generally ductless, secreting hormones directly into the bloodstream. Secreted hormones travel through the bloodstream to targeted organs where they perform various important functions.

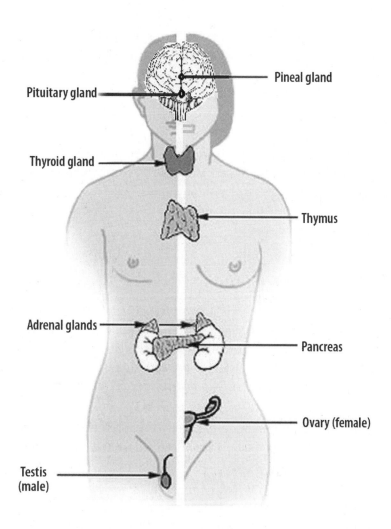

Fig. 1-6. Major Endocrine Organs

Examples of hormones include insulin and estrogen. **Insulin** is a hormone secreted by the pancreas whose function is to regulate blood sugar. Like all hormones, the shape of the insulin molecule is recognized by hormone receptor cells (insulin receptor cells) that impact the liver's control of blood sugar level. Each hormone's shape is specific and can be recognized by the corresponding target cells. The binding sites on the target cells are called **hormone receptors**. Many hormones come in antagonistic pairs that have opposite effects on the target organs. For example, insulin and glucagon have opposite effects on the liver's control of blood sugar level. Insulin lowers the blood sugar level by signaling the liver to take glucose out of circulation and store it, while glucagon signals the liver to release some of its stored sugar supply to raise the blood sugar level. Much hormonal regulation depends on feedback loops to maintain balance and homeostasis.

Hormones control many physiological functions, from digestion, to conscious responses and thinking, to reproduction. For instance, women of childbearing age have a continuous cycle of hormones. The hormone cycle causes the release of eggs at specific times. If the egg is fertilized, a different combination of hormones stimulates a chain of events that promotes the development of the embryo.

The glands of the endocrine system include the **hypothalamus** and the **pituitary gland**. These two glands are considered to be the master glands in the human body since they perform so many regulatory functions. The thyroid, adrenal, and pineal glands—as well as the gonads and pancreas—are all additional organs that provide various hormones which are necessary to keep the body functioning and in homeostasis.

Reproductive System

Preservation of the human species is accomplished through reproduction, which requires the preparation of gametes (the female egg and male sperm sex cells) within the reproductive organs of a female and male adult and then the fertilization of the egg through the act of intercourse. Thanks to modern technology, it is now possible for the egg to be fertilized outside the body through *in vitro* **fertilization** (literally "in glass," or in a test-tube fertilization).

The **organs of reproduction** include the internal gonads (female ovaries and male testes) that produce gametes, the internal female organs of gestation and birth (uterus and vagina), and the external genitalia (penis and vulva).

The reproductive system works with the endocrine system to time and execute the complex functions of egg release, sperm production, sexual libido, etc., through the release and coordination of hormones.

Homeostasis, feedback methods that maintain homeostasis (e.g., sweating to maintain internal temperature), and effects of changes in the external environment on living things (e.g., hypothermia, injury)

Homeostatic Mechanisms

All human cells, tissues, and organs must maintain a tight range of physical and chemical conditions in order to live and thrive. Conditions such as temperature, pH, water balance, sugar levels, etc., must be monitored and controlled in order to keep them within the accepted ranges that will not inhibit life. When conditions are within acceptable ranges, the body is said to be in **homeostasis**. The body has a special set of mechanisms that serve to keep it in homeostasis. Homeostasis is a state of dynamic equilibrium, which balances forces tending toward change and forces acceptable for life functions.

Homeostasis is achieved mostly by actions of the sympathetic and parasympathetic nervous systems by a process known as feedback control. For instance, when the body undergoes physical activity, muscle action causes a rise in temperature. Unchecked, rising temperature can destroy cells. In this instance, the nervous system detects rising temperature and reacts with a response that causes sweat glands to produce **sweat**. The evaporation of sweat cools the body.

There are many instances of feedback control. These take effect when any situation arises that may drive levels out of the normal acceptable range. In other words, the homeostatic mechanism is a reaction to a stimulus. This reaction, called a feedback response, is the production of some counterforce that levels the system.

External environmental conditions can cause feedback responses within the body to attempt to maintain homeostasis. For example, if an individual is exposed to extreme cold, the body will react by constricting blood vessels near the surface of the skin, which causes shivering. **Shivering** is meant to produce heat and to warm the body back up when the internal temperature begins to drop. If the body core temperature continues to drop, a condition known as **hypothermia** will occur, metabolic systems will begin to slow down, the heart pumps slower and brain functions become sluggish. If a warm-up does not occur, hypothermia will lead to death. However, the metabolic slow-down preserves organs for a time in hopes of a rescue. In fact, inducing hypothermic states is now used in some lengthy surgeries to maintain the health of organs during high-stress situations.

An **injury** is an assault on the body's homeostatic mechanisms. When any type of injury occurs, homeostatic mechanisms within the body will set about to make the situation right. For example, if bleeding is occurring, feedback mechanisms go to work that release clotting factors to stop bleeding at the injury site. While the immune system moves to fight infection, homeostatic mechanisms will work to regulate body temperature, chemical concentrations needed for cellular metabolism, etc.

Sources of nutrients (e.g., foods, symbiotic organisms) and concepts in nutrition (e.g., calories, vitamins, minerals)

Nutrition

All living things require sustenance to replenish and maintain growing, multiplying, or damaged organelles, cells, tissues, and organs. Depending on the organism, the nutrients needed vary greatly. There are **seven types of nutrients** needed by living things and generally categorized into two major groups—macronutrients and micronutrients. **Macronutrients** include carbohydrates, fats, and proteins. These substances are found within structural components of organisms such as cell membranes, tissues, and energy storage features. They are also essential to cellular and organismal functions (e.g., metabolism, respiration, etc.). The **micronutrients** are a range of vitamins and minerals that include a variety of molecules that perform specified functions in cellular reactions. They are micronutrients since—unlike proteins, carbohydrates, and fats—they are needed in only limited quantity. Still, micronutrients are absolutely essential to health. Not all organisms need the same micronutrients. There are 13 vitamins known to be needed by humans for growth and development along with a host of minerals (including sodium, iron, magnesium, etc.). In addition to macro- and micronutrients, all organisms need water, and some animals need dietary fiber.

The function of nutrition is twofold: (1) to provide **molecular components** needed for structural support of organismal regeneration and reproduction, and (2) to provide **energy** for organismal function. Some nutrients provide both, while others provide just one or the other. Water and the micronutrients do not provide energy. The macronutrients—fats and proteins—provide both energy and molecular nutrients, while carbohydrates provide only energy.

Energy is provided through nutrients in the form of kilocalories, commonly designated with the term *Calories* (capital *C*)*. Each gram of carbohydrate or protein provides approximately 4 Calories, while a gram of fat provides 37 Calories. All functions of organisms from the cellular level to the body level require energy. Nutrient Calories provide energy for consumer organisms. Consumers that take in more Calories than are used immediately for energy store Calories in the bonds of fat tissue. It is, therefore, important for a healthy balance of caloric intake and energy usage to be established through patterns of intake and exercise.

Organisms such as mammals that require fiber do not use it for its molecular components nor for energy. Fiber is indigestible carbohydrate that provides bulk that assists in the digestive process.

Each type of nutrient has a particular structure that provides a specific nutritive role:

- **Carbohydrates**—Carbohydrates are made of varying combinations of only carbon, hydrogen, and oxygen. The ratio of hydrogen to oxygen in carbohydrates is always

---

* The spelling distinguishes the calorie used as food energy in daily life from the metric energy unit (lowercase *c*).

2:1, just as in water (H_2O)—thus the name *carbohydrate* (carbon plus water). Sugars and starches are both forms of carbohydrates. Plants synthesize glucose and store them as polysaccharides known as starches. This energy is then used throughout the food chain as the basic source of food energy in the form of sugar and starch carbohydrates. Carbohydrates store energy within the chemical bonds between molecules that provide the energy for all life functions. Carbohydrates are macronutrients that provide energy through Calories.

- **Fats**—Fats are highly efficient lipid molecules used for long-term energy storage. When an organism takes in more carbohydrates than are necessary for its current energy use, the excess energy is stored in fat molecules. The energy is stored in chemical bonds between the atoms of lipid molecules. When these bonds are broken, energy is released. In addition to storing energy, fats also function in organisms to provide a protective layer that insulates internal organs and maintains heat within the body. Considering fat as a nutrient, while the body creates its own fat, it is also important to ingest certain types of fat because there are certain essential fatty acids, vitamins, and hormones that are fat soluble and only available when ingested with the intake of some types of oils and fats. Fats are macronutrients that provide energy through Calories as well as molecular components for structural regeneration and reproduction.

- **Proteins**—Proteins are present in every living cell. Proteins are large un-branched chains of amino acids. There are 20 common amino acids that can combine in various sequences to form thousands of different proteins. Proteins found in living things may have dozens or hundreds of amino acids. Since the human body is made of a complex number of proteins that are synthesized from a variety of 21 amino acids, protein is an important nutrient to a healthy diet. Proteins are macronutrients that provide energy through Calories as well as molecular components for structural regeneration and reproduction.

- **Vitamins**—Vitamins are organic compounds that are essential to structural regeneration and/or regeneration of an organism and that the organism cannot produce in sufficient supply on its own, although these nutrients are generally needed in small amounts. A dietary deficiency of any vitamin can cause a disease. Some vitamins are fat-soluble and others water-soluble. Fat-soluble vitamins can only be obtained through fatty food sources and are stored in fatty body organs. Water-soluble vitamins are not as easily stored in the body. There are 13 vitamins that are used by humans. Vitamins are micronutrients that provide molecular components for structural regeneration and reproduction.

- **Minerals**—Minerals are elemental micronutrients that provide molecular components for structural regeneration and reproduction. The elements calcium, phosphorus, potassium, sulfur, sodium, chlorine, and magnesium are the seven most common minerals found in the human body in order of abundance. In addition to these, trace minerals are also necessary in smaller amounts for mammals including iron, cobalt, copper, zinc, molybdenum, iodine, and selenium.

- **Dietary Fiber**—Dietary fiber for the human diet may be either soluble or insoluble. In either case it is not digested but functions in regulation of digestion as well as aiding with regulation of blood chemicals such as sugar and some lipoproteins.

- **Water**—Water is the most necessary chemical to life. In humans it makes up 70-75% of the body and provides the environmental basis for chemical structure and function of cells and tissues. The body cannot function without water.

Food sources generally contain a mixture of macro- and micronutrients. A varied diet is necessary to ensure that all types of necessary nutrients are included.

In some cases two or more species of organisms live in a symbiotic relationship that provides either a portion or all of the nutrition for one of the organisms in the relationship. **Symbiosis** is a close and potentially long-term biological relationship between species. For example, lichens are a composite of a fungus and an alga. The mutualistic symbiotic relationship exists as the green alga provides energy through the process of photosynthesis and the fungus provides minerals.

Fig. 1-7. Example of a Nutritional Symbiont—Lichen: Xanthoparmelia sp.

Another example of a symbiotic relationship involved in a nutritive situation is the **lactobacilli bacteria** that lives in the human gut. These bacteria survive on milk sugar and provide the essential function to humans of breaking down milk sugar into digestible form for the human system.

Transmission of disease and pathogens (e.g., airborne, bloodborne), effects of disease or pathogens on populations (e.g., demographics change, extinction), and disease prevention methods (e.g., vaccination, sanitation)

Though the human body is protected by an extensive immune system, there are still microbial threats known as **pathogens** that may overwhelm the immune system, causing disease and sometimes death. Pathogens such as bacteria, viruses, fungi, or protozoa may be transmitted through the environment directly or from person to person via the air, surfaces, or body fluids.

Airborne pathogens are spread when viruses, bacteria, or fungi are suspended in the air (for example, through tiny particles spread through a sneeze) and breathed into the respiratory tract of the unknowing victim. An infection occurs if the immune system cannot overcome the growth and attack of the pathogen. The common cold, influenza (the flu), and chicken pox are some of the many well known viruses that spread in this manner. Bacterial pneumonia, tuberculosis, and bacterial meningitis are all forms of serious diseases that are transmitted via airborne bacteria. There are also forms of chronic sinusitis that are caused by airborne fungi (molds). While initial infection of an airborne pathogen may occur directly from a fungal, bacterial, or viral source in the environment, there is danger to larger human populations as the disease spreads from person to person exponentially through families, communities, and further. The prevalence and ease of travel options has increased the dissemination of these easily spread (communicable) diseases in the past 50 years.

Bloodborne pathogens are spread when an individual comes in contact with the blood or bodily fluids containing blood products of an infected human or animal. In some cases the blood may be in dried form and still infectious, so items such as dirty laundry, intravenous needles, or other items that have remains of infected blood may be sources of infection as well as direct contact with the body fluids of an infected person or animal. Bloodborne infectious diseases include viruses such as Human Immunodeficiency Virus (HIV) that leads to AIDS and Hepatitis B (HPV). These viruses are both highly contagious through sexual contact or blood contact (needle sharing or other accidental contact) and have extremely serious symptomatic consequences on the human body. Rabies is a viral bloodborne pathogen that is transmitted by contact with infected animals.

Malaria is a bloodborne disease transmitted by a mosquito bite that introduces a protist (protozoan) into the human bloodstream. According to the World Health Organization (WHO), almost half of the world's population lives in an area at risk for malaria transmission. According to WHO estimates, 438,000 people died from maleria in 2015. The highest areas at risk of malaria infection are African countries, where heat and moisture encourage mosquito growth and human demographic features of poverty and poor living conditions make protection from mosquito bites difficult.

In extreme cases, diseases can cause dramatic impacts on populations. In human history this has happened during episodes of infestation of the plague. **Plague** is a disease caused by a bacterial pathogen that is carried by rodents and spread by fleas that bite rodents and then humans. Plague is particularly deadly because once spread to humans it can transform into an airborne, bloodborne, or surface-borne pathogen. Throughout history there have been times when episodes of plague have wiped out large populations in huge geographic areas of the world. For example, in the 6th–7th centuries c.e. Europe's population was reduced by 50% by the bubonic plague.

In addition to human diseases, animal and plant populations can be impacted and devastated by disease. **Dutch Elm Disease** is spread by the elm bark beetle, which infects Elms with the fungi Ascomycota. The fungus spread through several continents being passed back and forth via shipping of logs. The latest strains have driven the North American population of Elm trees very near to extinction. Botanists have managed to save a very limited number of Elms in hopes of regrowing a population that will be resistant to the disease, having survived the latest outbreak and developed immune factors for protection.

There is only one case of extinction thought to have been potentially caused by disease amongst mammals—that of the black rat. However, some other species, including amphibians, have succumbed to extinction by disease. In most cases, disease may heavily impact populations and may completely wipe out isolated populations (such as on islands). However, there are usually a number of resistant individuals that preserve the species and allow for regrowth unless other environmental factors are also at play (lack of food, predation, etc.).

In modern times, since an understanding of microbial life and sanitation has developed, the **spread of disease has become easier to limit**. Hygienic practices include washing hands often with soap and water, washing fruits and vegetables before eating them, having clean water to drink, and protecting living spaces from insects and rodents. Simple hygiene has significantly lowered the incidence of infectious disease in much of the world. So demographics may play a role. A locality's sanitation practices and access to clean water heavily impact the incidence of disease in a given area. Outbreaks of disease are much more likely to occur in poverty-stricken areas that lack sanitation facilities for clean water to drink, proper drainage for sewage, and/or where insects and rodents are not controlled.

In addition, there are now **antimicrobial agents** used in cleaning and health products available to fight infection on skin and surfaces in hospitals and in surgical areas that significantly lower the spread of viruses and bacteria. In addition, medications have been developed that can be taken internally or used topically (on the skin) that will kill the invading species. These antibiotics, antivirals, antifungals, etc., are essential to medical care and disease treatment and containment.

It is important to use these agents with care, however, since microbes are living organisms and also resist extinction. Not every organism is necessarily killed by these agents and only the resistant organisms survive and multiply. This has, in some cases, resulted in proliferation of "superbugs" that are resistant to antimicrobials.

Vaccination is another way to stop the spread of infectious diseases. Vaccination is the process of purposely and artificially exposing a patient to a disease in a weakened, killed, or small dose in order to induce immunity to the disease. Vaccines have been successfully used since the 1800's and have even wiped out deadly diseases such as smallpox. There are vaccines now in use for many worldwide diseases including forms of hepatitis, some cancers, measles, pneumonia, and forms of the influenza virus.

Relationship between Life Functions and Energy Intake

Energy for life functions (e.g., photosynthesis, respiration, fermentation)

Life functions of organisms occur through several processes of cellular metabolism, which includes respiration, growth, movement, etc. Energy transforms as chemicals are broken apart or synthesized within the cell. Cells constantly build molecules and store energy (in the form of chemical bonds) and also break down molecules and release stored energy through several essential processes.

Photosynthesis

Producer organisms contain special structures known as chloroplasts that are the site of photosynthesis. **Photosynthesis** is the process of turning light energy into chemical energy stored in the bonds of carbohydrate molecules. Producers use the converted energy for their own life processes, and also store energy that they may use later or that may be used by organisms that consume them. The process of photosynthesis includes a crucial set of reactions. These reactions convert the light energy of the Sun into chemical energy usable by living things.

Although the process of photosynthesis actually occurs through many small steps, the entire process can be summed up with the following equation:

$$6CO_2 + 6H_2O + \text{light energy} \rightarrow C_6H_{12}O_6 + 6O_2$$

(carbon dioxide + water → glucose + oxygen)

Chlorophyll is a green pigment. A pigment is a substance that absorbs light energy. Photosynthesis occurs in the presence of chlorophyll, as the chlorophyll is able to absorb a photon of light. Chlorophyll is contained in the grana of the chloroplast found in cells of plants, algae, and some protists. Photosynthesis can only occur where chlorophyll is present. While it is not used up in the photosynthetic process, it must be present for the reactions to occur.

There are two phases of the photosynthetic process: the light reaction, or photolysis, and the dark reaction, or CO_2 fixation. During photolysis, the chlorophyll pigment absorbs a photon of light, leaving the chlorophyll in an excited (higher energy) state.

The **light reaction** is a decomposition reaction, which separates water molecules into hydrogen and oxygen atoms, utilizing the energy from the excited chlorophyll pigment. Oxygen, which is not needed by the cell, combines to form O_2 (gas) and is released into the environment. The free hydrogen is grabbed and held by a specialized molecule (called the hydrogen acceptor) until it is needed. The excited chlorophyll also supplies energy to a series of reactions that produce ATP from ADP and inorganic phosphate (Pi).

The **dark reaction** (CO_2 fixation) then occurs in the stroma of the chloroplast. This second phase of photosynthesis does not require light; however, it does require the use of the products (hydrogen and ATP) of photolysis. In this phase, six CO_2 molecules are linked with hydrogen (produced in photolysis) forming glucose (a six-carbon sugar). This is a multi-step process, which requires the ATP produced in the photolysis phase. Glucose molecules can link to form polysaccharides (starch or sugar), which are then stored in the cell.

Energy from the Sun is transformed by photosynthetic organisms into chemical energy in the form of ATP. ATP (adenosine triphosphate) is known as the energy currency of cellular activity. While energy is stored in the form of carbohydrates, fats, and proteins, the amount of energy contained within the bonds of any of these substances would overwhelm (and thus kill) a cell if released at once. In order for the energy to be released in small packets usable to a cell, large molecules need to be broken down in steps. ATP is an efficient storage molecule for the energy needed for cellular processes.

Cellular Respiration

Unlike photosynthesis (which occurs only in photosynthetic cells), respiration occurs in all cells. **Respiration** is the process that releases energy for use by the cell. There are several steps involved in cellular respiration. Some require oxygen (that is, they are aerobic) and some do not (that is, they are anaerobic reactions).

Glycolysis is the process that breaks down six-carbon sugar (glucose) molecules into smaller carbon-containing molecules yielding ATP (glyco = sugar, lysis = breakdown). It is the first step in all respiration pathways and occurs in the cytoplasm of all living cells. Each molecule of glucose (six carbons) is broken down into two molecules of pyruvic acid (or pyruvate with three carbons each), two ATP molecules, and two hydrogen atoms (attached to NADH, nicotinamide adenine dinucleotide). This is an anaerobic reaction (no oxygen is required). After glycolysis has occurred, respiration will continue on one of two pathways, depending upon whether oxygen is present or not. The process of glycolysis is summarized by the following chemical equation:

glucose (6 C) + 2ADP + 2 Pi + 2NAD$^+$ $\rightarrow$ 2 pyruvic acid (3 C each) + 2ATP + 2NADH + 2H$^+$

Aerobic respiration (in the presence of oxygen) begins with glycolysis and proceeds through two major steps—the Krebs cycle (also known as the citric acid cycle) and electron transport. The first step, the Krebs cycle, occurs in the matrix of a cell's mitochondria and breaks down pyruvic acid molecules (three carbons each) into CO_2 molecules, H^+ (protons), and 2 ATP molecules. The Krebs cycle also liberates electrons, which then enter the next step.

The second step occurs along the **electron transport system**, or ETS, which captures the energy (in the form of electrons) released by the Krebs cycle. The ETS is a series of cytochromes, which exist on the cristae of the mitochondria. Cytochromes are pigment molecules, which include a protein and a heme (iron containing) group. The iron in heme groups may be either oxidized (loses electron to form Fe^{+3}) or reduced (gains electron to form Fe^{+2}) as electrons are passed along the ETS. As electrons pass from one cytochrome to another, energy is given off. Some of this energy is lost as heat; the rest is stored in molecules of ATP. This process can produce the most ATP molecules per cycle, 32 ATPs per glucose molecule. The final step of the electron transport chain occurs when the last electron carrier transfers two electrons to an oxygen atom that simultaneously combines with two protons from the surrounding medium to produce water.

Fermentation

If no oxygen is present within the cell, respiration will proceed anaerobically after glycolysis. Anaerobic respiration is also called **fermentation**. Anaerobic respiration breaks down the two pyruvic acid molecules (three carbons each) into end products (such as ethyl alcohol, C_2H_6O or lactic acid $C_3H_6O_3$), plus carbon dioxide (CO_2). The net gain from anaerobic respiration is two ATP molecules per glucose molecule. Fermentation is not as efficient as aerobic respiration; it uses only a small part of the energy available in a glucose molecule.

Energy Flows in Ecologic Networks (Ecosystems)

Flow of energy in ecosystems (e.g., energy pyramids), conservation of energy in an ecosystem (e.g., energy lost as heat, energy passed on to other organisms) and sources of energy (e.g., sunlight, producers, lower lever consumer)

Energy Cycle (Food Chain)

Since all life requires the input of energy, the **energy cycles** within the ecosystem are central to its well-being. On Earth, the **Sun** provides the energy that is the basis of life in most ecosystems. (An exception is the hydrothermal vent communities that derive their energy from the heat of Earth's core.) Without the constant influx of solar energy into our planetary ecosystem, most life would cease to exist. Energy generally flows through the entire ecosystem in one direction—from producers to consumers and on to decomposers (consumers may also consume decomposers) through the food chain.

Photosynthetic organisms—such as plants, some protists, and some bacteria—are the first link in most food chains; they use the energy of sunlight to combine carbon dioxide and water into sugars, releasing oxygen gas (O_2). Photosynthetic organisms are called **producers**, since they synthesize sugar and starch molecules using the Sun's energy to link the carbons in carbon dioxide. **Primary consumers** (also known as herbivores) are species that eat photosynthetic organisms. Consumers utilize sugars and starches stored in cells or tissues for energy. **Secondary consumers** feed on primary consumers, and on the chain goes, (tertiary, quaternary, etc.). Finally, **decomposers** (bacteria, fungi, some animals) are species that recycle the organic material found in dead plants and animals back into the food chain.

Animals that feed only on other animals are called **carnivores** (meat-eaters), whereas those that consume both photosynthetic organisms and other animals are known as **omnivores**.

The energy cycle of the food chain is subject to the laws of thermodynamics. Energy can neither be created nor destroyed. However, every use of energy is less than 100% efficient, with about 10% lost as heat. When we call photosynthetic organisms "producers," we mean that they produce food, using the Sun's energy to form chemical bonds in sugars and other biomolecules. Other organisms can use the energy stored in the bonds of these biomolecules.

The steps in the food chain are also known as trophic levels.

Flow of matter in ecosystems (e.g., food webs and chains, positions of organisms in the web or chain) and the effects of change in communities or environment on food webs

Consider the pyramid diagram (Fig. 1-8) as one example of a food chain with many trophic levels. **Grasses** are on the bottom of the pyramid; they are the producers, the first trophic level. Producers are also known as autotrophs, as they produce their own food ("auto," the same root found in "autograph," means "self"). Each trophic level is greater in biomass (total mass of organisms) than the level above it.

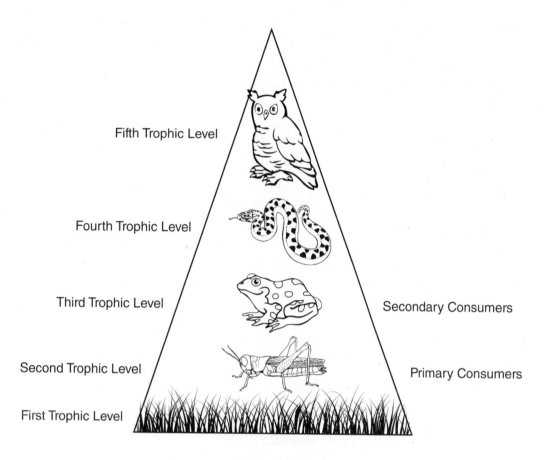

Fig. 1-8. Food Chain

Grasshoppers represent the second trophic level, or primary consumers in this example of a food chain. Grasshoppers consume plants and are consumed (in this example) by toads, the secondary consumers, which represent the third trophic level. Snakes consume toads, and are in turn consumed by owls—making these the fourth and fifth trophic levels. In this example, bacteria are the decomposers that recycle some of the nutrients from dead owls (and other levels) to be reused by the first trophic level.

The pyramid illustrates a food chain; however, in nature it is never actually as simple as shown. Owls consume snakes, but they may also consume toads (a lower level in the pyramid) and fish (from an entirely different pyramid). Thus, within every ecosystem there may be numerous food chains interacting in varying ways to form what is truly a food web. Furthermore, all organisms produce waste products that feed decomposers.

A food web (Fig. 1-9) represents the cycling and recycling of both energy and nutrients within the ecosystem. The productivity of the entire web is dependent upon the amount of photosynthesis carried out by producers. The food web is also the main agent for cycling matter throughout the ecosystem that provides the nutrient resources for life.

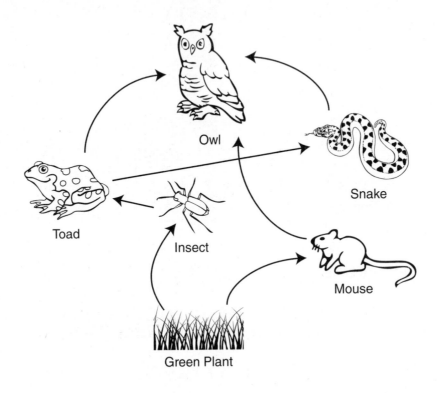

Fig.1-9. Food Web

Nitrogen Cycle

Nitrogen is essential to life processes, since it is a key component of amino acids (components of proteins) and nucleic acids. Nitrogen is the most plentiful gas in the atmosphere, making up 78% of the air. However, neither photosynthetic organisms nor animals are able to use nitrogen gas (N_2), which does not readily react with other compounds, directly from the air. Instead, a process known as nitrogen fixing makes nitrogen available for absorption by the roots of plants. **Nitrogen fixing** is the process of combining nitrogen with either hydrogen or oxygen, mostly by nitrogen-fixing bacteria, or to a small degree by the action of lightning.

Nitrogen-fixing bacteria live in the soil and perform the task of combining gaseous nitrogen from the atmosphere with hydrogen, forming ammonium (NH_4^+ ions). (Some cyanobacteria, also called blue-green bacteria, are also active in this process.) Ammonium ions are then absorbed and used by plants. Other types of nitrogen-fixing bacteria live in symbiosis on the nodules of the roots of legumes (beans, peas, clover, etc.), supplying the roots with a direct source of ammonia.

Some plants are unable to use ammonia; instead, they use nitrates. Some bacteria perform nitrification, a process which further breaks down ammonia into nitrites (NO_2^-), and yet again by other bacteria that convert nitrites into nitrates (NO_3^-).

Nitrogen compounds (such as ammonia and nitrates) are also produced by natural, physical processes such as volcanic activity. Another source of usable nitrogen is lightning, which reacts with atmospheric nitrogen to form nitrates.

In addition, nitrogen passes along through the food chain, and is recycled through decomposition processes. When plants are consumed, the amino acids are recombined and used, a process that passes the nitrogen-containing molecules on through the food chain or web. Animal waste products, such as urine, release nitrogen compounds (primarily ammonia) back into the environment, yet another source of nitrogen. Finally, large amounts of nitrogen are returned to the Earth by bacteria and fungi, which decompose dead plant and animal matter into ammonia (and other substances), a process known as **ammonification**.

Various species of bacteria and fungi are also responsible for breaking down excess nitrates, a process known as **denitrification**, which releases nitrogen gas back into the air. The nitrogen cycle involves cycling nitrogen through both living and non-living entities.

Carbon Cycle

Carbon is an important element contained in the cells of all species. Earth's atmosphere contains large amounts of carbon in the form of carbon dioxide (CO_2). Photosynthetic organisms require the intake of carbon dioxide for the process of photosynthesis, which is the foundation of the food chain. Most of the carbon within organisms is derived from the production of carbohydrates in photosynthetic organisms through photosynthesis. The process of photosynthesis also releases oxygen molecules (O_2), which are necessary to animal respiration. Animal respiration releases carbon dioxide back into the atmosphere in large quantities.

Since plant cells consist of molecules containing carbon, animals that consume photosynthetic organisms are consuming and using carbon from the photosynthetic organisms. Carbon is passed along the food chain as these animals are then consumed. When animals and photosynthetic organisms die, decomposers, including the detritus feeders, bacteria, and fungi, break down the organic matter. Detritus feeders include worms, mites, insects, and crustaceans, which feed on dead organic matter, returning carbon to the cycle through chemical breakdown and respiration.

Carbon dioxide (CO_2) is also dissolved directly into the oceans, where it is combined with calcium to form calcium carbonate, which is used by mollusks to form their shells. When mollusks die, the shells break down and often form limestone. Limestone is then dissolved by water over time and some carbon may be released back into the atmosphere as CO_2, or used by new ocean species.

Finally, organic matter that is left to decay may, under conditions of heat and pressure, be transformed into coal, oil, or natural gas (the fossil fuels). When fossil fuels are burned for energy, the combustion process releases carbon dioxide back into the atmosphere, where it is available to plants for photosynthesis.

Phosphorus Cycle

Phosphorus* is another mineral required by living things. Unlike carbon and nitrogen, which cycle through the atmosphere in gaseous form, phosphorus is only found in solid form, within rocks and soil. Phosphorus is a key component in ATP, NADP (a molecule that, like ATP, stores energy in its chemical bonds), and many other molecular compounds essential to life.

Phosphorus is found within rocks and is released by the process of **erosion**. Water dissolves phosphorus from rocks, and carries it into rivers and streams. Here, phosphorus and oxygen react to form phosphates that end up in bodies of water. **Phosphates** are absorbed by photosynthetic organisms in and near the water and are used in the synthesis of organic molecules. As in the carbon and nitrogen cycles, phosphorus is then passed up the food chain and returned through animal wastes and organic decay.

New phosphorus enters the cycle as undersea sedimentary rocks are thrust up during the shifting of the Earth's tectonic plates. New rock containing phosphorus is then exposed to erosion and enters the cycling process.

Any change in the population of one organism in the food web can have an impact on the entire system. For example, in the example above, if a disease impacts the snake population, it will impact the entire web by causing an overpopulation of grasshoppers that can in turn cause a depletion in the grasses. This will then eventually limit the food source for grasshoppers and cause damage to that population. Meanwhile, the owl population will be affected by the lack of food source from snakes. The complexities do not end there.

Carrying capacity, changes in carrying capacity based on changes in populations and environmental effects and limiting resources necessary for growth

Many factors, both temporary and permanent, affect the life of an ecosystem. Populations within an ecosystem will be affected by changes in the environment including abiotic resources (physical, non-living factors such as fire, pollution, sunlight, soil, light, precipitation, availability of oxygen, water conditions, and temperature) and biotic resources (biological factors, including availability of food, competition, predator-prey relationships, symbiosis, and overpopulation).

---

* *Phosphorus* is widely misspelled as "phosphorous." The only correct spelling of the element is "phosphorus."

These biotic and abiotic resources are known as **limiting factors** since they will determine how much a particular population within a community will be able to grow. For instance, the resource in shortest supply in an ecosystem may limit population growth. As an example, we know that photosynthetic organisms require phosphorus in order to thrive, so the population growth will be limited by the amount of phosphorus readily available in the environment. On the other hand, growth may be limited by having more of an element (such as heat or water) than it can tolerate. For example, plants need carbon dioxide to grow; however, a large concentration of carbon dioxide in the atmosphere is toxic. The ecosystem can support only a limited number of organisms—known as the **carrying capacity** (usually designated by the letter **K**). Once the carrying capacity (K) is reached, a competition for resources ensues.

Limiting factors interact with each other and generally produce a situation within the ecosystem that supports homeostasis (a balanced condition). **Homeostasis** is achieved within an ecosystem that is functioning at its optimum level. Homeostasis is the tendency of the ecological community to stay the same. However, the balance of the ecosystem can be disturbed by the removal, or decrease, of a single resource or by the addition, or increase, of a resource.

Populations are rarely governed by the effect of a single limiting factor; instead, *many factors interact to control population size*. Changes in limiting factors have a domino effect in an ecosystem, as the change in population size of one species will change the dynamics of the entire community. The number of individuals of a particular species living in a particular area is called the population density (number of organisms per area).

Both abiotic- and biotic-limiting factors exist in a single community; however, one may be dominant over the other. Abiotic limiting factors are generally not dependent on population density of organisms. **Pollution** is a major abiotic factor in the health of ecosystems. Pollution is usually a byproduct of human endeavors and affects the air or water quality of an ecosystem with secondary effects. In addition to producing pollution, humans may deliberately utilize chemicals such as pesticides or herbicides to limit growth of particular species. Such chemicals can damage the homeostatic mechanisms within a community, causing a long-term upset in the balance of an ecosystem.

In other situations, populations of organisms, biotic factors, will impact the ecosystem overall. Within a given area, there is a maximum level the population may reach at which it will continue to thrive. This is known as the carrying capacity of the environment. When an organism has reached the carrying capacity of the ecosystem, the population growth rate will level off and show no net growth. Populations also occupy a particular geographic area with suitable conditions. This total area occupied by a species is known as the **range**. Typically, populations will have the greatest density in the center of their range, and lower density at the edges. The area outside the range is known as the area of intolerance for that species, since it is not able to survive there. Environmental changes will affect the size and location of the range, making it a dynamic characteristic.

Symbiosis (e.g., mutualism, parasitism, commensalism) and predator/prey relationships (e.g., changes in one population affecting another population)

There are some relationships within ecosystems that seem simple. For example, a predator is simply an organism that eats another and the organism that is eaten is known as the prey. The **predator/prey relationship** is one of the most important features of an ecosystem. As seen in our study of the energy cycle, energy is passed from lower trophic levels to higher trophic levels, as one animal is consumed by another. This relationship not only provides transfer of energy up the food chain, but it also is a population-control factor for the prey species. In situations where natural predators are removed from a region, the overpopulation occurring amongst the prey species can cause problems in the population and community. For instance, the hunting and trapping of wolves in the United States has led to an overpopulation of deer (the prey of wolves), which in turn has caused a shortage of food for deer in some areas, causing these deer populations to starve.

There are also relationships that are more complex. When two species interact with each other within the same range, it is known as **symbiosis**. **Amensalism** is one type of symbiosis where one species is neither helped nor harmed while it inhibits the growth of another species. **Mutualism** is another form of symbiosis where both species benefit, while **commensalism** is where one organism benefits and the other is neither helped nor harmed. **Parasitism** is symbiosis in which one species benefits, but the other is harmed. (Parasites are not predators, since the parasitic action takes a long period of time and may not actually kill the host.)

Disruption of ecosystems (e.g., invasive species, flooding, habitat destruction, desertification) and extinction (e.g., causes [human and natural] and effects)

Community Growth and Disruption

Over time, species may move in or out of a particular area through **emigration** (permanent one-way movement out of the original range), **immigration** (permanent one-way movement into a new range), and **migration** (temporary movement out of one range into another, and back). Migration is an important process to many species and communities, since it allows animals that might not survive year round in a particular ecosystem to temporarily relocate for a portion of the year. Therefore, migration gives the opportunity for greater diversity of species in an ecosystem.

Two or more species living within the same area and that overlap niches (their function in the food chain) are said to be in competition if the resource they both require is in limited supply. If the niche overlap is minimal (other sources of food are available) then both species may survive. In some cases, one of the species may be wiped out in an area due to competition, a situation called **competitive exclusion**. This is a rare but plausible occurrence.

When the entire population of a particular species is eliminated, it is known as extinction. **Extinction** may be a local phenomenon, the elimination of a population of one species from one area. However, species extinction is a worldwide phenomenon, where all members of all populations of a species die.

The extinction of a single species may also cause a chain reaction of secondary extinctions if other species depend on the extinct species. Conversely, the introduction of a new species into an area can also have a profound effect on other populations within that area. This new species may compete for the niche of native population or upset a predator/prey balance. For example, the brown tree snake (native to Australia) was introduced into islands in the Pacific years ago. (They probably migrated on ships.) The brown snake was an invasive species that caused the extinction of several species of birds on those Pacific islands. The bird populations could not withstand the introduction of this new predator. Invasive species are those that disrupt the ecosystem by dominating over the native populations. Invasive species are usually non-native introduced species that take over resources needed by native populations, sometimes threatening native populations with extinction.

Fig. 1-10. Invasive Species: Kudzu vines on trees in Atlanta, Georgia.

Ultimately, the survival of a particular population is dependent on maintaining a minimal viable population size. When a population is significantly diminished in size, it becomes highly susceptible to breeding problems and environmental changes that may result in extinction.

Community structure refers to the characteristics of a specified community, including the types of species that dominate, major climatic trends of the region, and whether the community is open or closed. A **closed community** is one whose populations occupy essentially the same range with very similar distributions of density. These types of communities have sharp boundaries called **ecotones** (such as a pond aquatic ecosystem that ends at the shore). An open community has indefinite boundaries, and its populations have varying ranges and densities (such as a forest). In an open community, the species are more widely distributed and animals may actually travel in and out of the area.

An **open community** is often more able to respond to calamity and may therefore be more resilient. Since the boundaries are subtler, the populations of a forest, for instance, may be able to move as necessary to avoid a fire. If, however, a closed community is affected by a traumatic event (for example, a pond being polluted over a short period of time) it may be completely wiped out.

Communities do grow and change over time. Some communities are able to maintain their basic structure with only minor variations for very long periods of time. Others are much more dynamic, changing significantly over time from one type of ecosystem to another. When one community completely replaces another over time in a given area, it is called **succession**. Succession occurs both in terrestrial and aquatic biomes.

Succession may occur because of small changes over time in climate or conditions, the immigration of a new species, disease, or other slow-acting factors. It may also occur in direct response to cataclysmic events such as fire, flood, or human intervention (for example, clearing a forest for farmland). The first populations that move back into a disturbed ecosystem tend to be hardy species that can survive in bleak conditions. These are known as **pioneer communities**.

An example of terrestrial succession occurs when a fire wipes out a forest community. The first new colonization will come from quick-growing species such as grasses, which will over time produce a grassland ecosystem. The decay of grasses will enrich the soil, providing fertile ground for germination of seeds for shrubs brought in by wind or animals. The shrubs will further prepare the soil for germination of larger species of trees, which over time will take over the shrub-land and produce a forest community once again.

When succession ends in a stable community, the community is known as the **climax community**. The climax community is the one best suited to the climate and soil conditions, and one that achieves a homeostasis. Generally, the climax community will remain in an area until a catastrophic event (fire, flood, etc.) destroys it.

Habitat destruction may occur on a broad scale such as with a catastrophic event such as fire or flooding, or with an event such as the spread of disease, which may wipe out a tree species and thus destroy the habitat for a symbiotic bird species. Habitat destruction can also occur more gradually as in the case of desertification, the process of fertile land losing the ability to sustain vegetation and wildlife. Desertification may happen due to the removal of vegetation, such as through human intervention in cases of deforestation or aggressive agricultural practices (e.g., overgrazing, overtill-age). It may also occur as a result of natural processes such as climatic shifts, drought, or fire. Since vegetation plays a major role in supplying nutrients to soil for the basis of a healthy food chain, human interventions in ecological reintroduction of vegetation and nutritive supplements and water into these areas usually provide the only hope for renewing a desertified (made into a desert) area into a productive ecosystem.

Organization of Life (Structure and Function of Life)

Essential functions of life (e.g., chemical reactions, reproduction, metabolism) and cellular components that assist the functions of life (e.g., cell membranes, enzymes, energy)

Essential Life Functions

Chemical Reactions

Within cells, it is the process of chemical reactions that keep the functions of life ongoing. **Chemical reactions** occur when molecules interact with each other to form one or more molecules of another type. Chemical reactions that occur within cells provide energy, nutrients, and other products that allow the organism to function.

There are several categories of chemical reactions. Chemical reactions are symbolized by an equation where the reacting molecules (reactants) are shown on one side and the newly formed molecules (products) on the other, with an arrow between indicating the direction of the reaction. Some chemical reactions are simple, such as the breakdown of a compound into its components, (a decomposition reaction):

$$AB \rightarrow A + B$$

A simple combination reaction is the reverse of decomposition:

$$A + B \rightarrow AB$$

When one compound breaks apart and forms a new compound with a free reactant, it is called a replacement reaction:

$$AB + C \rightarrow AC + B$$

Chemical reactions may require an input of energy or they may release energy. Reactions that require energy are called **endothermic** reactions. Reactions that release energy are termed **exothermic**.

In a study of biology, it is crucial to understand endothermic and exothermic reactions. It is through endothermic reactions on the cellular level that living things are able to store energy in the form of chemical bonds.

All chemical reactions are subject to the **laws of thermodynamics**.

The first law of thermodynamics (also known as the law of conservation of matter and energy) states that matter and energy can neither be created nor destroyed. In other words, the sum of matter and energy of the reactants must equal that of the products.

The second law of thermodynamics, or the law of increasing disorder (or entropy), asserts that all reactions spread energy, which tends to diminish its availability.

So, although we know from the first law that the energy must be equal on both sides of a reaction equation, reaction processes also tend to degrade the potential energy into a form that cannot perform any cellular work.

Reproduction

The process of cell reproduction is called **cell division**. The process of cell division centers on the replication and separation of strands of DNA.

When a cell is going to divide, it progresses through a sequence of events ending in cell division, producing two daughter cells. This is known as the cell cycle. The time taken to progress through the cell cycle differs with different types of cells, but the sequence is the same. Cells in many tissues never divide.

There are two major periods within the cell cycle: interphase and mitosis (also called the M phase or cell division phase). **Interphase** is the period when the cell is active in carrying on its function. Interphase is divided into three phases. During the first phase, the G1 phase, metabolism and protein synthesis are occurring at a high rate, and most of the growth of the cell occurs at this time. The cell organelles are produced (as necessary) and undergo growth during this phase. During the second phase, the S phase, the cell begins to prepare for cell division by replicating the DNA and proteins necessary to form a new set of chromosomes. In the final phase, the G2 phase, more proteins are produced, which will be necessary for cell division, and the centrioles (which are integral to the division process) are replicated as well. Cell growth and function occur through all the stages of interphase.

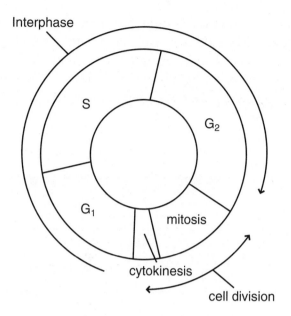

Fig. 1-11. The Stages of the Cell Cycle of Reproduction

A **gene** is a length of DNA that encodes a particular protein. Each protein the cell synthesizes performs a specific function in the cell. The function of one protein, or the function of a group of proteins, is called a **trait**.

Metabolism

Cellular metabolism is a general term, which includes all types of energy transformation processes, including photosynthesis, respiration, growth, movement, etc. Energy transformations occur as chemicals are broken apart or synthesized within the cell. The process whereby cells build molecules and store energy (in the form of chemical bonds) is called **anabolism**. **Catabolism** is the process of breaking down molecules and releasing stored energy. The individual processes of photosynthesis, respiration, growth, and movement are discussed elsewhere in this section.

Cellular Components

Cell Membrane

All cells are enclosed within the cell membrane (or plasma membrane). Near the center of each eukaryotic cell is the **nucleus**, which contains the chromosomes. Between the nucleus and the cell membrane, the cell contains a region called the **cytoplasm**. Since all of the organelles outside the nucleus but within the cell membrane exist within the cytoplasm, they are all called **cytoplasmic organelles**.

The cell membrane encloses the cell and separates it from the environment. This membrane is composed of a double layer (bilayer) of phospholipids with globular proteins embedded within the layers. The membrane is extremely thin (about 80 angstroms; 10 million angstroms = 1 millimeter) and elastic. The combination of the lipid bilayer and the proteins embedded within it allow the cell to determine what molecules and ions can enter and leave the cell, and regulate the rate at which they enter and leave.

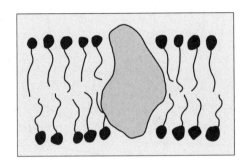

Fig. 1-12. Cell Membrane. A phospholipid bilayer with embedded globular proteins.

The cell membrane is an especially important cell organelle with a unique structure, which allows it to control movement of substances into and out of the cell. Made up of a fluid phospholipid bilayer, proteins, and carbohydrates, this extremely thin (approximately 80 angstroms) membrane can only be seen clearly with an electron microscope. The cell membrane manages the concentration of substances within the cell. Substances can cross the cell membrane by passive transport, facilitated diffusion, and active transport. During passive transport, substances freely pass across the membrane without the cell expending any energy. Facilitated diffusion does not require added energy, but it requires the help of specialized proteins. Active transport requires energy output from the cell.

Simple diffusion is one type of passive transport. **Diffusion** is the process whereby molecules and ions flow through the cell membrane from an area of higher concentration to an area of lower concentration (thus tending to equalize concentrations). Where the substance exists in higher concentration, collisions occur, which tend to propel them away toward lower concentrations. Diffusion generally is the means of transport for ions and molecules that can slip between the lipid molecules of the membrane. Diffusion requires no added energy to propel substances through a membrane.

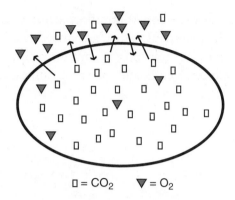

□ = CO₂ ▼ = O₂

Fig. 1-13. Diffusion. CO_2 diffuses out of the cell since its concentration is higher inside the cell. O_2 diffuses into the cell because its concentration is higher outside. Molecules diffuse from areas of high concentration to areas of lower concentration. This process is also referred to as "moving down the gradient."

Osmosis is a mode of passive transport that occurs only with water; it does not require the addition of any energy, but occurs when the water concentration inside a cell differs from the concentration outside the cell. The water on the side of the membrane with the highest water concentration will move through the membrane until the concentration is equalized on both sides. When water concentration is equal inside and outside the cell, the cell is considered **isotonic**. For instance, a cell placed in a salty solution will tend to lose water until the solution outside the cell has the same concentration of water molecules as the cytoplasm (the solution inside the cell).

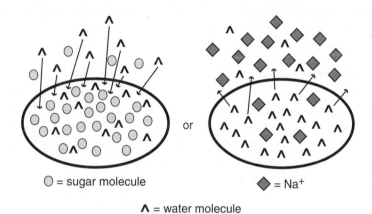

○ = sugar molecule ◆ = Na⁺

∧ = water molecule

Fig. 1-14. Osmosis. Water crosses the membrane into a cell that has a higher concentration of sugar molecules than the surrounding solution. Water crosses the membrane to leave the cell when there is a higher concentration of Na⁺ ions outside the cell than inside the cell.

Facilitated diffusion is another method of transport across the cell membrane that requires the help of specialized proteins. These proteins, which are embedded in the cell membrane, are able to pick up specific molecules or ions and transport them through the membrane. The special protein molecules allow the diffusion of molecules and ions that cannot otherwise pass through the lipid bilayer.

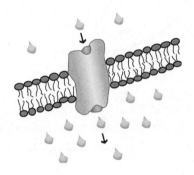

Fig. 1-15. Facilitated Diffusion. Specialized proteins embedded in the cell membrane permit passage of substances of a particular shape and size.

Active transport, like facilitated diffusion, requires membrane-bound proteins. Unlike facilitated diffusion, active transport uses energy to move molecules across a cell membrane against a concentration gradient (in the opposite direction than they would go under normal diffusion circumstances). With the addition of the energy obtained from ATP, a protein molecule embedded in the membrane changes shape and moves a molecule across the membrane against the concentration gradient.

Large molecules are not able to pass through the cell membrane, but may be engulfed by the cell membrane. **Endocytosis** is the process whereby large molecules (i.e., some sugars or proteins) are taken up into a pocket of membrane. The pocket pinches off, delivering the molecules, still inside a membrane sack, into the cytoplasm. This process, for instance, is used by white blood cells to engulf bacteria. Exocytosis is the reverse process, exporting substances from the cell.

Enzymes

Enzymes are protein molecules that act as catalysts for organic reactions. (A catalyst is a substance that lowers the activation energy of a reaction. A catalyst is not consumed in the reaction.) Enzymes do not make reactions possible that would not otherwise occur under the right energy conditions, but they lower the activation energy, which increases the rate of the reaction.

Enzymes are named ending with the letters *-ase*, and usually begin with a syllable describing the catalyzed reaction (i.e., hydrolase catalyzes hydrolysis reactions, lactase catalyzes the breakdown of the sugar lactose). Thousands of reactions occur within cells, each controlled by one or more enzymes. Enzymes are synthesized within the cell at the ribosomes, as all proteins are.

Enzymes are effective catalysts because of their unique shapes. Each enzyme has a uniquely shaped area, called its active site. For each enzyme, there is a particular substance known as its substrate, which fits within the active site (like a hand in a glove). When the substrate is seated in the active site, the combination of two molecules is called the enzyme-substrate complex. An enzyme can bind to two substrates and catalyze the formation of a new chemical bond, linking the two substrates. An enzyme may also bind to a single substrate and catalyze the breaking of a chemical bond, releasing two products. Once the reaction has taken place, the unchanged enzyme is released.

The operation of enzymes lowers the energy needed to initiate cellular reactions. However, the completion of the reaction may either require or release energy. Reactions requiring energy are called endothermic reactions. Reactions that release energy are called exothermic reactions. Endothermic reactions can take place in a cell by being coupled to the breakdown of ATP or a similar molecule. Exothermic reactions are coupled to the production of ATP or another molecule with high-energy chemical bonds.

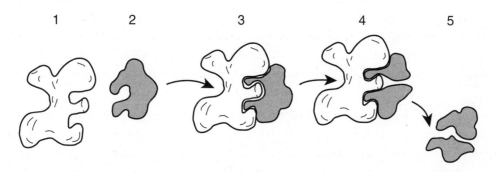

Fig.1-16. Enzyme Reaction. 1—enzyme; 2—substrate; 3&4—enzyme-substrate complex; 5—products.

Energy

The currency of energy within cells is **ATP**, which is synthesized in the process of cellular respiration in the mitochondria. Cellular respiration is the process of breaking up covalent bonds within sugar molecules with the intake of oxygen and release of ATP, adenosine tri-phosphate. ATP molecules store energy that is later used in cell processes. Mitochondria (plural of *mitochondrion*) are organelles present in nearly all cells and more numerous in cells requiring more energy (muscle, etc.). Mitochondria are self-replicating, containing their own DNA, RNA, and ribosomes. Mitochondria have a double membrane; the internal membrane is folded. Cellular respiration reactions occur along the folds of the internal membrane (called *cristae*).

Cell theory (e.g., cells come from cells, cells are the smallest unit of living things), specialized cells and tissues (e.g., muscles, nerve, etc.) and cellular levels of organization (e.g., cells, tissues, organs, systems)

Cells are the basic structures of life and understanding them is fundamental to understanding biology. The cell theory is central to our understanding of the basic components of life:

1. All living things are made up of one or more cells.

2. Cells are the smallest units of living things.

3. All cells come from pre-existing cells.

There are two main types of cells: prokaryotic and eukaryotic. **Prokaryotes** have no nucleus or any other membrane-bound organelles (cell components that perform particular functions). The DNA in prokaryotic cells usually forms a single chromosome, which floats within the cytoplasm. Prokaryotic organisms have only one cell and include all bacteria. Plant, fungi, and animal cells, as well as protists, are eukaryotic. **Eukaryotic cells** contain membrane-bound intracellular organelles, including a nucleus. The DNA within eukaryotes is organized into chromosomes.

A single organism can be **unicellular** (consisting of just one cell), or **multicellular** (consisting of many cells). A multicellular organism may have many different types of cells that differ in structure to serve different functions. Individual cells may contain organelles that assist them with specialized functions. For example, muscle cells tend to contain more mitochondria (organelles that make energy available to the cells) since muscle requires the use of extra energy.

Animal cells differ in structure and function from photosynthetic cells, which are found in plants, some bacteria, and some protists. Photosynthetic cells have the added job of producing food, so they are equipped with specialized photosynthetic organelles. Plant cells also have a central vacuole and cell walls, structures not found in animal cells.

Cells may be specialized to perform a wide variety of functions. A collection of similarly specialized cells form **tissue**. All multicellular organisms, plants and animals alike contain several kinds of tissues, made up of different cell types. Differentiated cells may organize into specialized tissues performing particular functions. There are eight major types of animal tissue:

1. **Epithelial tissue** consists of thin layers of cells. Epithelial tissue makes up the layers of skin, lines ducts and the intestine, and covers the inside of the body cavity. Epithelial tissue forms the barrier between the environment and the interior of the body.

2. **Connective tissue** covers internal organs and composes ligaments and tendons. This tissue holds tissues and organs together, stabilizing the body structure.

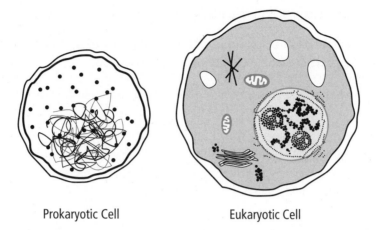

Prokaryotic Cell   Eukaryotic Cell

Fig. 1-17. The prokaryotic cell has no nucleus or other membrane-bound organelles and is approximately 1–10 micrometers in diameter. The eukaryotic cell has membrane-bound organelles, including a nucleus containing the chromosomes. Eukaryotic cells are approximately 10–100 micrometers in diameter.

3. **Muscle tissue** is divided into three types—smooth, skeletal, and cardiac. Smooth muscle makes up the walls of internal organs and functions in involuntary movement (breathing, etc.). Skeletal muscle attaches bones of the skeleton to each other and surrounding tissues. Skeletal muscle's function is to enable voluntary movement. Cardiac muscle is the tissue forming the walls of the heart. Its strength and electrical properties are vital to the heart's ability to pump blood.

4. **Bone tissue** is found in the skeleton and provides support, protection for internal organs, and the ability to move as muscles pull against bones.

5. **Cartilage tissue** reduces friction between bones, and supports and connects them. For example, it is found at the ends of bones and in the ears and nose.

6. **Adipose tissue** is found beneath the skin and around organs providing cushioning, insulation, and fat storage.

7. **Nerve tissue** is found in the brain, spinal cord, nerves, and ganglion. It carries electrical and chemical impulses to and from organs and limbs to the brain. Nerve tissue in the brain receives these impulses and sustains mental activity.

8. **Blood tissue** consists of several cell types in a fluid called plasma. It flows through the blood vessels and heart, and is essential for carrying oxygen to cells, fighting infection, and carrying nutrients and wastes to and from cells. Blood also has clotting capabilities, which preserve the body's functions in case of injury.

Plant tissues include:

1. **Meristem tissue** consists of undifferentiated cells capable of quick growth and specialization existing at the end of roots and stems.

2. **Stem tissue** is made of vascular tissue, including two varieties—xylem and phloem.

3. **Epidermal tissue** made up of parenchyma cells that makes up the coverings of leaves and stems, this tissue protects and keeps water in.

4. **Ground tissue** makes up the bulk of stems, roots, and leaves.

Tissues are organized into organs, and organs function together to form systems, which support the life of an organism. Many different body plans exist amongst animals, and each type of body plan includes systems necessary for the organism to live.

Mitosis, meiosis (e.g., process and purpose)

Mitosis and Meiosis are the two processes of cell reproduction. In **mitosis** a cell produces two identical daughter cells by distributing duplicated chromosomes to each daughter cell so that each has a full set of chromosomes. Mitosis progresses through four phases: prophase, metaphase, anaphase, and telophase. **Meiosis** is the process of producing four gamete cells required for sexual reproduction, each with single unduplicated chromosomes (haploid). The parent cell is diploid, that is, it has a normal set of paired chromosomes. Meiosis goes through a two-stage process resulting in four new cells, rather than two (as in mitosis). Each daughter cell has half the chromosomes of the parent. Meiosis occurs in reproductive organs only, and the resultant four haploid cells are called gametes (egg and sperm).

Mitosis occurs as shown in Figure 1-18.

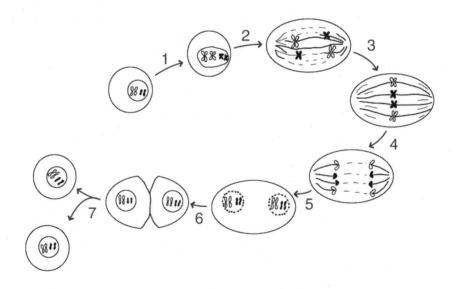

Fig. 1-18. Mitosis. See explanations of numbered steps in text.

During prophase (1, 2), the first stage of mitosis, the chromatin condenses into chromosomes within the nucleus and becomes visible through a light microscope. The centrioles move to opposite ends of the cell, and spindle fibers begin to extend from the centromeres of each chromosome toward the center of the cell. At this point, although the chromosomes become visible, the nucleolus no longer is. During the second part of prophase, the nuclear membrane dissolves and the spindle fibers attach to the centromeres forming a junction called a kinetochore. The chromosomes then begin moving in preparation for the next step, metaphase.

During metaphase (3), the spindle fibers pull the chromosomes into alignment along the equatorial plane of the cell, creating the metaphase plate. This arrangement ensures that one copy of each chromosome is distributed to each daughter cell.

During anaphase (4), the chromatids are separated from each other when the centromere divides. Each former chromatid is now called a chromosome. The two identical chromosomes move along the spindle fibers to opposite ends of the cell. Telophase (5) occurs as nuclear membranes form around the chromosomes. The chromosomes disperse through the new nucleoplasm, and are no longer visible as chromosomes under a standard microscope. The spindle fibers disappear. After telophase, the process of cytokinesis (6) produces two separate cells (7).

Cytokinesis differs somewhat in plants and animals. In animal cells, a ring made of the protein actin surrounds the center of the cell and contracts. As the actin ring contracts, it pinches the cytoplasm into two separate compartments. Each cell's plasma membrane closes, making two distinct daughter cells. In plant cells, a cell plate forms across the center of the cell and extends out towards the edges of the cell. When this plate reaches the edges, a cell wall forms on either side of the plate, and the original cell then splits into two.

Mitosis produces two nearly identical daughter cells. (Cells may differ in distribution of mitochondria or because of DNA replication errors, for example.) Organisms (such as bacteria) that reproduce asexually, do so through the process of mitosis.

Meiosis produces four gamete cells—eggs or sperm—for sexual reproduction. When two haploid gametes fuse during the process of fertilization, the resultant cell has one chromosome set from each parent, and is diploid. This process allows for the huge genetic diversity available among species.

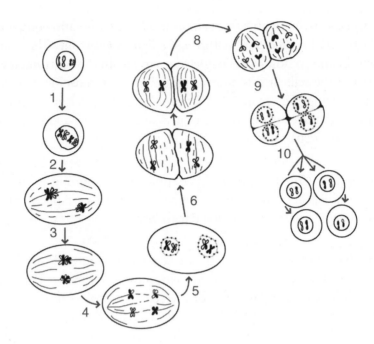

Fig. 1-19. Meiosis. See explanations of numbered steps in the text.

Two distinct nuclear divisions occur during meiosis, **reduction** (or meiosis 1, steps 1 to 5 in Fig. 1-19), and **division** (or meiosis 2, steps 6 to 10). Reduction affects the ploidy (referring to haploid or diploid) level, reducing it from 2n to n (i.e., diploid to haploid). Division then distributes the remaining set of chromosomes in a mitosis-like process.

The phases of meiosis 1 are similar to the phases of mitosis, with some notable differences. As in mitosis, chromosome replication (1) occurs before prophase; then during prophase 1 (2), homologous chromosomes pair up and join at a point called a synapse (this happens only in meiosis). The attached chromosomes are now termed a tetrad, a dense four-stranded structure composed of the four chromatids from the original chromosomes. At this point, some portions of the chromatid may break off and reattach to another chromatid in the tetrad. This process, known as crossing over, results in an even wider array of final genetic possibilities.

The nuclear membrane disappears during late prophase. Each chromosome (rather than each chromatid) develops a kinetochore, and as the spindle fibers attach to each chromosome, they begin to move.

In metaphase 1 (3), the two chromosomes (a total of four chromatids per pair) align themselves along the equatorial plane of the cell. Each homologous pair of chromosomes contains one chromosome from the mother and one from the father from the original sexual production of that organism. When the homologous pairs orient at the cell's center in preparation for separating, the chromosomes randomly sort. The resulting cells from this meiotic division will have a mixture of chromosomes from each parent. This increases the possibilities for variety among descendent cells.

Anaphase 1 (4) occurs next as the chromosomes move to separate ends of the cell. This phase differs from the anaphase of mitosis where one of each chromosome pair (rather than one chromatid) separates. In telophase 1 (5), the nuclear envelope may or may not form, depending on the type of organism. In either case, the cell then proceeds to meiosis 2.

The nuclear envelopes dissolve (if they have formed) during prophase 2 (6) and spindle fibers form again. Everything else proceeds as in mitosis, through metaphase 2 (7), anaphase 2 (8), and telophase 2 (9). Again, as in mitosis, each chromosome splits into two chromatids. The process ends with cytokinesis (10), forming four distinct gamete cells.

Molecular Basis for Heredity

Central dogma of molecular biology, the mechanism of inheritance (e.g., DNA) and chromosomes (e.g., description, chromosome splitting during meiosis)

Structure of Chromosomes

Chromosomes are long chains of subunits called nucleosomes. Each nucleosome is composed of a short length of DNA wrapped around a core of small proteins called histones. The combination of DNA with histones is called chromatin. Each nucleosome is about 11 nm in diameter (a nanometer is one billionth of a meter) and contains a central core of eight histones with the DNA double helix wrapped around them. Each gene spans dozens of nucleosomes. (A **gene** is a specific length of DNA that codes for a particular protein corresponding to a version of an identifiable inheritable trait.) DNA plus histone strings are then tightly packed and coiled, forming chromatin.

In a cell that is getting ready to divide, each strand of chromatin is duplicated. The two identical strands (called chromatids) remain attached to each other at a point called the centromere. During cell division, the chromatin strands become more tightly coiled and packed, forming a chromosome, which is visible in a light microscope. At this stage, a chromosome consists of two identical chromatids, held together at the centromere, giving each chromosome an X shape.

Within the nucleus, each chromosome pairs with another of similar size and shape. These pairs are called homologs. Each set of homologous chromosomes has a similar genetic constitution, but the genes are not necessarily identical. Different forms of corresponding genes are called alleles.

Reproduction of cells and/or organelles is constantly necessary in the function of all organisms for repair, replacement, and growth. In order to replicate, a portion of a DNA molecule unwinds, separating the two halves of the double helix. (This separation is aided by the enzyme helicase.) Another enzyme (DNA polymerase) binds to each strand and moves along them as it collects nucleotides using the original DNA strands as templates. The new strand is complementary to the original template and forms a new double helix with one of the parent strands. If no errors occur during DNA synthesis, the result is two identical double-helix molecules of DNA.

The process of DNA replication, however, is occasionally subject to a mistake known as a mutation. All the DNA of every cell of every organism is copied repeatedly to form new cells for growth, repair, and reproduction. A **mutation** can result from an error that randomly occurs during replication. Mutations can also result from damage to DNA caused by exposure to certain chemicals, such as some solvents or the chemicals in cigarette smoke, or by radiation, such as ultraviolet radiation in sunlight or x-rays. Cells have built-in mechanisms for finding and repairing most DNA errors; however, they do not fix them all. The result of a DNA error—a mutation—expresses itself in a change (small or large) in the cell structure and function.

DNA carries the information for making all the proteins a cell can make. The DNA information for making a particular protein can be called the gene for that protein. Genetic traits are expressed, and specialization of cells occurs, as a result of the combination of proteins encoded by the DNA of a cell.

In some cases the DNA strand "unzips" and corresponds with individual RNA nucleotides which are strung together to match the DNA sequence. In the processed RNA, each unit of three nucleotides, known as a codon, encodes a particular amino acid. Amino acids are coded and strung together at the ribosomes, forming proteins that are fitted for particular functions in the cell.

Genes encode proteins of two varieties. Structural genes code proteins that form organs and structural characteristics. Regulatory genes code proteins that determine functional or physiological events, such as growth. These proteins regulate when other genes start or stop encoding proteins, which in turn produce specific traits.

Genotypes, phenotypes and the probability of traits in close relatives (e.g., Punnett squares, pedigree charts)

The process by which characteristics pass from one generation to another is known as **inheritance**. The study of the principles of heredity (now called genetics) advanced greatly through the experimental work (c. 1865) of **Gregor Mendel**. Mendel studied the relationships between traits expressed in parents and offspring, and the hereditary factors that caused expression of traits.

Mendel systematically bred pea plants to determine how certain hereditary traits passed from generation to generation. First, he established true-breeding plants, which produce offspring with the same traits as the parents. For example, the seeds of pea plants with yellow seeds would grow into plants that produced yellow seeds. Green seeds grew into plants that produced green seeds. Mendel named this first generation of true-breeding plants the parent, or P1, generation; he then bred the plant with yellow seeds and the plant with green seeds. Mendel called the first generation of offspring the F1 generation. The F1 generation of Mendel's yellow seed/green seed crosses contained only yellow seed offspring.

Mendel continued his experiment by crossing two individuals of the F1 generation to produce an F2 generation. In this generation, he found that some of the plants (one out of four) produced green seeds. Mendel performed hundreds of such crosses, studying some 10,000 pea plants, and was able to establish the rules of inheritance from them. The following are Mendel's main discoveries:

- Parents transmit hereditary factors (now called genes) to offspring. Genes then produce a characteristic, such as seed-coat color.

- Each individual carries two copies of a gene, and the copies may differ.

- The two genes an individual carries act independently, and the effect of one may mask the effect of the other. Mendel coined the terms geneticists still use: "dominant" and "recessive."

We now know that chromosomes carry all the genetic information in most organisms. Most organisms have corresponding pairs of chromosomes that carry genes for the same traits. These pairs are known as homologous chromosomes. Genes that produce a given trait exist at the same position (or locus) on homologous chromosomes. Each gene may have different forms, known as alleles. For instance, yellow seeds and green seeds arise from different alleles of the same gene. A gene can have two or more alleles, which differ in their nucleotide sequence. That difference can translate into proteins that function differently, resulting in variations of the trait.

Sexual reproduction (meiosis) produces gamete cells with one-half the genetic information of the parents (paired chromosomes are separated and sorted independently). Therefore, each gamete may receive one of any number of combinations of each parent's chromosomes.

In addition, a trait may arise from one or more genes. (However, because one-gene traits are easiest to understand, we will use them for most of our examples.) If a trait is produced from a gene or genes with varying alleles, several possibilities for traits exist. The combination of alleles that make a particular trait is the **genotype**, while the trait expressed is the **phenotype**.

An allele is considered dominant if it masks the effect of its partner allele. The allele that does not produce its trait when present with a dominant allele is recessive. That is, when a dominant allele pairs with a recessive allele, the expressed trait is that of the dominant allele.

A **Punnett square** is a notation that allows us to easily predict the results of a genetic cross. In a Punnett square, a letter is assigned to each gene. Uppercase letters represent dominant traits, while lower case letters represent recessive traits. The possible alleles from each parent are noted across the top and side of a box diagram; then the possible offspring are represented within the internal boxes. If we assign the allele that produces yellow seeds the letter Y, and the allele that produces green seeds y, we can represent the cross between homozygous yellow and green pea plants (YY × yy) by the following Punnett square:

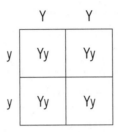

	Y	Y
y	Yy	Yy
y	Yy	Yy

One can deduce the genotypes of the parents and offspring by knowing the phenotypes of both. The offspring pea plants were all green (green is the phenotype), so these cannot have any of the dominant genes for yellow (Y), and the genotype must be yy. If the second parent had one allele for yellow (Y) which is dominant with the other green then some of the offspring would have inherited two genes for green. Since the offspring were all yellow, the second parent must have been homozygous YY.

When both alleles for a given gene are the same in an individual (such as YY or yy), that individual is homozygous for that trait. Furthermore, the individual's genotype is called homozygous. Both of the above parents (P1) were homozygous. The offspring in the F1 generation all have one dominant gene (Y) and one recessive gene (y), their phenotype is yellow, and their genotype is Yy. When the two alleles for a given gene are different in an individual (Yy), that individual is said to be heterozygous for that trait; that is, its genotype is heterozygous.

Breeding two F1 offspring from the example above produces the following Punnett square of a double heterozygous (both parents Yy) cross:

	Y	y
Y	YY	Yy
y	Yy	yy

Through this Punnett square, we can determine that three-fourths of the offspring will produce yellow seeds. However, there are two different genotypes represented among the yellow seed offspring. One-half of the offspring were heterozygous yellow (Yy), while one-fourth is homozygous yellow (YY).

The example above shows a monohybrid cross—a cross between two individuals where only one trait is considered.

Pedigree charts can be used to keep track of the frequency and occurrence of a particular phenotype (a particular gene) in an organism from one generation to the next. Pedigree charts are useful in everything from charting diseases in family trees to breeding strains of hardy plants that can withstand cold weather.

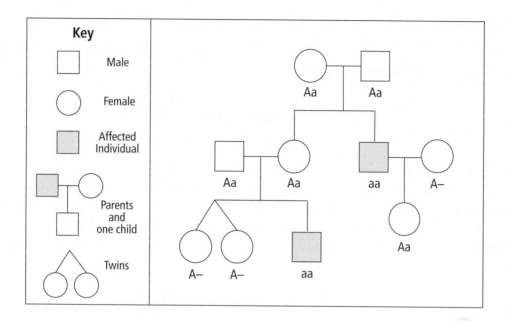

Fig. 1-20. Pedigree chart tracking the occurrence of a homozygous recessive genotype that manifests a phenotype of a fatal disease. In this chart, the dash after A indicates that it is undetermined whether the genotype is AA or Aa. The phenotype, however, indicates that the disease is not evident in the individual.

The availability of DNA testing has made it easier to fill in information in pedigree charts more fully and accurately then was possible historically. DNA testing allows for genotypes to be determined other than through inferring from the phenotype.

Pedigree charts are used in selective breeding of special strains of vegetables as well as purebred dogs, cats, horses, etc.

Photo by Stephen Ausm

Fig. 1-21. Researchers have selectively bred carrots with pigments that reflect almost all colors of the rainbow. More importantly, though, they're very good for your health.

New alleles, assortment of alleles (e.g., mutations, crossing over), environmental altering of traits, and expression of traits (e.g., epigenetics, color-points of Siamese cats)

When two possible alleles exist in a species, the genotype will be a combination of those two alleles. There are some cases where more than two choices of alleles are present. For example, for human blood types there is a dominant allele for type A blood, another dominant allele for type B blood, as well as a recessive allele for neither A nor B, known as O blood. There are three different alleles and they may combine in any way. In multiple-allele crosses, it is conventional to denote the chromosome by a letter (in this case I for dominant, i for recessive), with a subscript letter representing the allele types (in this case A, B, or O). The alleles for A and B blood are co-dominant, while the allele for O blood is recessive. The possible genotypes and phenotypes, then, are as follows:

Genotype	Phenotype
$I^A I^A$	Type A Blood
$I^B I^B$	Type B Blood
$I^A i^O$	Type A Blood
$I^B i^O$	Type B Blood
$I^A I^B$	Type AB Blood
$i^O i^O$	Type O Blood

Note: There is another gene responsible for the Rh factor that adds the + or − to the blood type.

In studying fruit flies it was found that some traits are always inherited together; they are not independently sorted. Traits that are inherited together are said to be linked. Genes are portions of chromosomes, so most traits produced by genes on the same chromosome are inherited together. (The chromosomes are independently sorted, not the individual genes.)

However, an exception to this rule complicates the issue. During metaphase of meiosis I, when homologous chromosomes line up along the center of the dividing cell, some pieces of the chromosomes break off and move from one chromosome to another (change places). This random breaking and reforming of homologous chromosomes allows genes to change the chromosome to which they are linked, thus changing the genome of that chromosome. This process, known as crossing over, adds even more possibility of variation of traits among species. It is more likely for crossing over to occur between genes that do not lie close together on a chromosome than between those that lie close together.

Gender is determined in an organism by a particular homologous pair of chromosomes. The symbols X and Y denote the sex chromosomes. In mammals and many insects, the male has an X and Y chromosome (XY), while the female has two X's (XX). Genes that are located on the gender chromosome Y will only be seen in males. It would be considered a sex-limited trait. An example of a sex-limited trait is bar coloring in chickens which occurs only in males.

Some traits are sex-linked. In sex-linked traits, more males (XY) develop the trait because males have only one copy of the X chromosome. Females have a second X gene, which may carry a gene coding for a functional protein for the trait in question that may counteract a recessive trait. These traits (for example, hemophilia and colorblindness) occur much more often in males than females.

Still other traits may be sex-influenced. In this case, the trait is known as autosomal—it only requires one recessive gene to be expressed if there is no counteracting dominant gene. A male with one recessive allele will develop the trait, whereas a female would require two recessive genes to develop it. An example of a sex-influenced trait is male-pattern baldness.

While the best-studied genetic traits arise from alleles of a single gene, most traits, such as height and skin color, are produced from the expression of more than one set of genes. Traits produced from the interaction of multiple sets of genes are known as polygenic traits. Polygenic traits are difficult to map and difficult to predict because of the varied effects of the different genes for a specific trait.

Sometimes genetic material in chromosomes is damaged by chemicals in the body, radiation from the Sun, or an assortment of other possible methods. When this happens, mutations can occur which are permanent changes in the DNA and therefore the genes of an organism. This changes the protein coding and causes a change in traits.

Every cell in a single organism carries identical DNA, except in the case where a mutation has occurred in a particular area (for example, an area of skin). However, portions of DNA are expressed differently in cells throughout the body allowing for varying tissues and organs to carry out their functions. This altering of the functioning of DNA is called cell differentiation and the study of it is called epigenetics. There are many ways in which cell differentiation occurs, through the action of various chemicals on the cells, and even by environmental factors. The study of epigenetics is very complex.

Fig. 1-22. The coloring in Siamese cats comes from a mutation that causes pigment (dark color) to be produced according to body temperature. Colder areas of the body (called *points*) produce darker hair.

Evolution

Evolutionary concepts are the foundation of much of the current study in biology. The term **evolution** refers to the gradual change of characteristics within a population, producing a change in species over time.

Common ancestry (e.g., evidence) and cladograms (e.g., drawing, creating, interpreting)

The preeminent idea of evolution is that all life on Earth has evolved from a single source, a common ancestry. Evidence of this can be shown by the existence of shared characteristics throughout a variety of organisms of many species and the development of characteristics along a developmental line. The study of connections between species can be shown on special diagrams called cladograms. **Cladograms** show how species relate to a common ancestor (see Fig. 1-23).

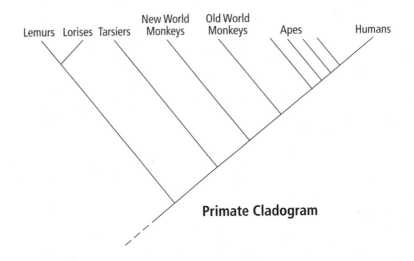

Fig. 1-23. Cladogram

It is possible to create a cladogram with a given group of organisms by analyzing their characteristics. In the past this was done by looking at morphology (what an organism looked like) only, but with advances in genetic mapping, it is now possible to produce cladograms based on advanced understanding of an organism's DNA. Organisms are arranged on the cladogram with the derived characteristics, those that are innovations of evolution in increasing order going away from the end of the branch where the common ancestor is indicated. In the example above, lemurs and lorises have the least derived characteristics and humans the most.

Selection (e.g., natural selection, artificial selection, evidence) and the requirements for selection (e.g., variation in traits, differential survivability)

Within every population, there is variation among traits. Individuals who win the competition for resources pass successful traits on to their offspring. Only the surviving competitors reproduce successfully generation after generation. Therefore, traits providing the competitive edge will be represented most often in succeeding generations.

The modern concept of natural selection emerged from Darwin's original ideas, focusing on the concept that evolution is a process of gradual (over thousands or hundreds of thousands of generations) adaptive change in traits among populations.

All evolution is dependent upon genetic change. The entire collection of genes within a given population is known as its gene pool. Individuals in the population will have only one pair of alleles for a particular single-gene trait. Yet the gene pool may contain dozens or hundreds of alleles for this trait. Evolution does not occur through changes from individual to individual, but rather as the gene pool changes through one of a number of possible mechanisms.

One mechanism that drives the changing of traits over time in a population is differential reproduction. Natural selection assumes some individuals within a population are more suited for survival, given environmental conditions. Differential reproduction takes this supposition one step further by proposing that those individuals within a population that are most adapted to the environment are also the most likely individuals to reproduce successfully. Therefore, the reproductive processes tend to strengthen the frequency of expression of desirable traits across the population. Differential reproduction increases the number of alleles for desirable traits in the gene pool. This trend will be established and strengthened gradually over time, eventually producing a population where the desirable trait becomes dominant, if environmental conditions remain the same.

Another mechanism of genetic change is mutation. A **mutation** is a change of the DNA sequence of a gene, resulting in a change of the trait. Although a mutation can cause a very swift change in the genotype (genetic code) and possibly phenotype (expressed trait) of the offspring, mutations do not necessarily produce a trait desirable for a particular environment. *Mutation is a much more random occurrence than differential reproduction.*

Although mutations occur quickly, the change in the gene pool is minimal, so change in the population occurs very slowly (over multiple generations). Mutation does provide a vehicle for introducing new genetic possibilities; genetic traits, which did not exist in the original gene pool, can be introduced through mutation.

A gene pool (particularly in a small population) may experience a change in frequency of particular genes simply due to chance fluctuations. In a finite population, the gene pool may not reflect the entire number of genetic possibilities of the larger genetic pool of the species population. Over time, the genetic pool within this finite population changes, and evolution occurs. This genetic drift, as it is called, has no particular tie to environmental conditions, and thus the random change in gene frequency is unpredictable. The change of gene frequency may produce a small or a large change, depending on what traits are affected. The process of genetic drift, as opposed to mutation, actually causes a *reduction* in genetic variety.

In addition to natural selection, **artificial selection** may also occur. This is the process of selective breeding of species by human intervention in the laboratory or through plant propagation or animal husbandry.

Adaptation, selection pressure, and speciation

The most basic function of evolutionary change is **adaptation**. This idea is what comes to mind when we think of Darwin's idea of survival of the fittest. Adaptation occurs when a species gains or loses a trait gradually over the course of many generations in order to be fit for its ecological situation. Ultimately this is the basis of the idea of natural selection: Those species most fit for their environment are those that would theoretically be the ones that would be most likely fit to procreate and therefore pass on their genetic traits through their DNA.

Selection pressure occurs due to the fact that as change occurs in the genetic information of an organism so does the overall viability of the organism. If the changes produced in a genetic change cause that particular adaptation to be even slightly less viable than there is an added factor that enters into the situation to determine whether that adaptation will be retained over time.

Genetic drift occurs within finite separated populations, allowing that population to develop its own distinct gene pool. However, occasionally an individual from an adjacent population of the same species may immigrate and breed with a member of the previously locally isolated group. The introduction of new genes from the immigrant results in a change of the gene pool, known as gene migration. Gene migration is also occasionally successful between members of different, but related, species. The resultant hybrids succeed in adding increased variability to the gene pool.

The study of genetics shows that in a situation where random mating is occurring within a population (which is in equilibrium with its environment), gene frequencies and genotype ratios will remain constant from generation to generation. This law is known as the **Hardy-Weinberg Law of Equilibrium**, named after the two men (G.H. Hardy and Wilhelm Weinberg, c. 1909) who first studied this principle in mathematical studies of genetics. The Hardy-Weinberg Law is a mathematical formula that shows why recessive genes do not disappear over time from a population.

Speciation

A **species** is an interbreeding population that shares a common gene pool and produces viable offspring. Up to this point we have been considering mechanisms that produce variation within species. It is apparent that to explain evolution on a broad scale we must understand how genetic change produces new species. There are two mechanisms that produce separate species, allopatric speciation and sympatric speciation.

In order for a new species to develop, substantial genetic changes must occur between populations which prohibit them from interbreeding. These genetic changes may result from genetic drift or from mutation that take place separately in the two populations. **Allopatric speciation** occurs when two populations are geographically isolated from each other. For instance, a population of squirrels may be geographically separated by a catastrophic event such as a volcanic eruption. Two populations (separated by the volcanic flow) continue to reproduce and experience genetic drift and/or mutation over time. This limits each population's gene pool and produces changes in expressed traits. Later, the geographical separation may be eliminated as the volcanic flow subsides; even so, the two populations have now experienced too much change to allow them to successfully interbreed again. The result is the production of two separate species.

Speciation may also occur without a geographic separation when a population develops members with a genetic difference, which prevents successful reproduction with the original species. The genetically different members reproduce with each other, producing a population, which is separate from the original species. This process is called **sympatric speciation**.

As populations of an organism in a given area grow, some will move into new geographic areas looking for new resources or to escape predators. (In this case, a natural event does not separate the population; instead, part of the population moves.) Some of these adventurers will discover new niches and advantageous conditions. Traits possessed by this traveling population will grow more common over several generations through the process of natural selection. Over time the species will specially adapt to live more effectively in the new environment. Through this process, known as **adaptive radiation**, a single species can develop into several diverse species over time. If the separated populations merge again and are able to successfully interbreed, then by definition new species have not been developed. Adaptive radiation is proven to have occurred when the species remerge and do not interbreed successfully.

All of the above evolutionary mechanisms are dependent upon reproduction of organisms over a long period of time, a very gradual process. Punctuated equilibrium is an entirely different method of explaining speciation. **Punctuated equilibrium** is a scientific model that proposes that adaptations of species arise suddenly and rapidly. Punctuated equilibrium states that species undergo a long period of equilibrium, which at some point is upset by environmental forces causing a short period of quick mutation and change.

Punctuated equilibrium was first proposed as paleontologists studied the fossil record. Gradualism would produce slowly changing and adapting species over many generations. However, the fossil record seems to show that organisms in general survive many generations in many areas with very little change over long periods of geologic time. New species appear in the fossils suddenly, without transitional forms, though "sudden" in this context needs to be understood on a geologic time scale.

Scientists still do not agree on the degree to which gradualism, punctuated equilibrium, or a combination of these processes is responsible for speciation.

PRACTICE!

1. Which of the following statements is TRUE?

    A. Primary consumers are mostly carnivores.

    B. Bacteria recycle nutrients from organisms they decompose.

    C. Secondary consumers are mostly herbivores.

    D. Omnivores eat more than one type of animal but no plants.

2. Which of the following are contained within both plant and animal cells?

    A. Chloroplasts

    B. Ribosomes

    C. Cell wall

    D. Grana

3. Which system is only found in vertebrates?

    A. Gas exchange (respiratory) system

    B. Circulatory system

    C. Skeletal system

    D. Nervous system

4. Which of the following is NOT part of a DNA molecule?

    A. Nucleotide

    B. Sugar

    C. Phosphate group

    D. An alcohol

5. ATP (adenosine triphosphate) is known as the energy currency of cellular activity because

    I. The amount of energy stored in a carbohydrate molecule is more than is usable by a single cell.

    II. ATP can be broken down into ADP plus a phosphate group yielding a small packet of energy usable by a cell.

    III. ATP contains three high-energy bonds making it an efficient energy storage molecule.

    IV. Green plants produce ATP molecules during photosynthesis.

  A. I, II, III, IV

  B. II

  C. II and III

  D. IV

6. The modern concept of evolution stresses that it

  A. represents gradual change in traits across populations.

  B. is only seen over millions of years.

  C. may occur in bursts over a short period of time.

  D. represents the presence of acquired characteristics in individuals.

7. In the diagram below, step No. 3 represents _____.

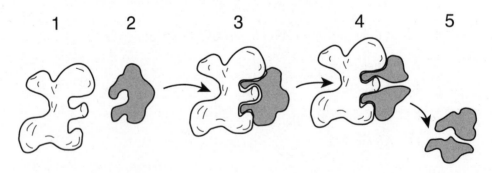

  A. a substrate

  B. an enzyme

  C. the products

  D. the enzyme-substrate complex

Questions 8–9.

In snapdragons, a red flower crossed with a white flower produces a pink flower. In this illustration, R stands for red color and W for white color. The Punnett square for a cross between a white snapdragon and a red snapdragon is shown here:

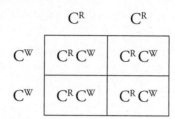

8. Which of the following statements about this cross MUST be true?

   A. Both parents of the red snapdragon must have had the genotype $C^R C^R$.

   B. One of the parents of the red snapdragon must have had the genotype $C^R C^R$.

   C. Both parents of the red snapdragon must have been pink.

   D. Neither parent of the red snapdragon could be white.

9. If two of the heterozygous offspring ($C^R C^W$) of this cross are bred, what will be the ratio of phenotypes of the offspring?

   A. 1 red: 2 pink: 1 white

   B. 2 red: 2 pink: 0 white

   C. 1 red: 1 pink: 1 white

   D. 2 red: 0 pink: 2 white

10. After a forest fire, a meadow community develops and is later replaced by a temperate forest community. This process is called

   A. commensalism.

   B. succession.

   C. dynamic equilibrium.

   D. alternation of generations.

Science Practice 1 Answers

1. **B.**

   The only true statement is this: Bacteria are decomposers that recycle some of the nutrients from dead organisms to be reused by plants. Primary consumers are *mostly* herbivores. Secondary consumers are *mostly* carnivores. No food chain has exactly a certain number of levels. Omnivores eat both plants and animals.

2. **B.**

   Grana are parts of the chloroplasts. These and cell walls are features of plant cells, but not animal cells. Ribosomes are essential to both plant and animal cell function as they are the site of protein synthesis.

3. **C.**

   The skeletal system provides the body with structure, stability, and the ability to move. By definition, the skeletal system is unique to vertebrates, although some invertebrates (such as mollusks and insects) have external support structures (exoskeletons) and muscle. Invertebrates *may* have a gas exchange system, a circulatory system, a nervous system, and/ or an excretory system.

4. **D.**

   A DNA molecule is a long chain of nucleotides, each of which is composed of a sugar, a phosphate group, and a nitrogen base. Alcohol is not a component of DNA.

5. **A.**

   Energy from the Sun is transformed by green plants into chemical energy in the form of ATP. ATP (adenosine triphosphate) is known as the energy currency of cellular activity. While energy is stored in the form of carbohydrates, in order to be used by cells, the energy must be released in small packets. Since ATP contains three high-energy bonds, it is an efficient storage molecule for the energy needed for cellular processes. ATP consists of a base (adenine), a simple sugar (ribose), and three phosphate groups. When a cellular process requires energy, a molecule of ATP can be broken down into ADP (adenosine diphosphate) plus a phosphate group. The energy that was stored in the bond between the phosphate and ADP is released into the cell and is available to fuel other reactions. Even more energy is released when ATP is decomposed into AMP (adenosine mono-phosphate) and two phosphate groups.

6. **A.**

Modern evolution focuses on the process of gradual adaptive change in traits across populations of species. The concept of acquired characteristics (Lamarck's theory that animals adapted within their lifetimes) was discredited. The timespan of the evolution of any trait varies.

7. **D.**

Step No. 3 shows the enzyme and substrate joined to become the enzyme-substrate complex. No. 1 is the enzyme, No. 2 the substrate, and No. 5 the products.

8. **D.**

While choices (A), (B), and (C) could have been true, a red snapdragon could have been produced by any of those choices. However, a white snapdragon cannot produce a red snapdragon as an offspring even if paired with a red.

9. **A.**

If two of the heterozygous offspring of an incomplete dominant trait are bred, the Punnett square would be:

	C^R	C^W
C^R	$C^R C^R$	$C^R C^W$
C^W	$C^R C^W$	$C^W C^W$

The phenotypic ratio of the offspring then is one-fourth red, one-half pink, and one-fourth white, a 1:2:1 ratio—1 red: 2 pink: 1 white.

10. **B.**

Succession occurs when one community completely replaces another over time in a given area. Commensalism is a type of symbiosis in which one organism is helped and the other is neither helped nor harmed. Dynamic equilibrium refers to chemical reactions or homeostatic mechanisms in animals. Alternation of generations is a feature of plant life cycles. Competition occurs when one organism's niche overlaps another in the same community.

Physical Science

Conservation, Transformation, and Flow of Energy

Heat, temperature, the flow of heat results in work and the transfer of heat (e.g., conduction, convection)

Heat is energy that flows from an object that is warm to an object that is cooler. It is important to understand the difference between heat and temperature. **Temperature** is the measure of the average kinetic energy of a substance. The atoms and molecules of all substances are constantly in motion. The energy of the motion of the atoms and molecules in a substance is called its kinetic energy. Temperature is a measure of that energy. The faster the particles in a substance move, the higher the temperature will be (more energy). The slower the particles move, the lower the temperature (less energy).

The theoretical temperature at which particle motion stops is called **absolute zero** (or 0 Kelvin). This temperature has never been reached by any known substance.

When substances come in contact, the hotter substance (greater energy) transfers kinetic energy to the cooler one (lower energy) and heat has been expended. It can also be said that work was done. Heat is measured in calories or joules.

Energy (including heat) may be transferred from one object to another by three processes: radiation, conduction, and convection. **Radiation** is the transfer of energy via waves. Radiation can occur through matter or without any matter present. Radiation from the Sun passes through space, where there is a very low density of matter, until it reaches Earth. **Convection** involves the movement of energy by the movement of matter, usually through currents. For instance, convection moves warm air up, while cool air sinks. In a fluid, the heat will move with the fluid. **Conduction** is movement of energy by transfer from particle to particle. Conduction can only occur when objects are touching. A pan on a stove heats water by conduction. An oven cooks by convection, warming food by movement of hot air. A microwave cooks by radiation, waves travel into food adding kinetic energy.

Endothermic and exothermic reactions

Chemical reactions may require an input of energy or they may release energy. Reactions that require energy are called **endothermic** reactions. Reactions that release energy are termed **exothermic**. Endothermic reactions are useful for storing energy within the chemical bonds of molecules. An example of this is the photosynthetic reaction that stores energy in the bonds of carbohydrates. Exothermic reactions release the energy that is stored in bonds usually in the form of heat, light, or movement. An example of an exothermic reaction is cellular metabolism that uses energy in the cell to perform work like moving a muscle.

Types of energy (e.g., kinetic, chemical, mechanical) and transformations between types of energy (e.g., chemical energy [sugar] to kinetic energy [motion of body])

Energy exists in multiple forms and can be transformed between these forms for varying uses. Kinetic energy is energy of motion. The energy of the motion of the atoms and molecules in a substance is **kinetic energy**. Kinetic energy also includes any type of energy of motion such as a moving ball or car. **Chemical** energy is energy that is stored in chemical bonds of molecules. This energy can be released when the bonds are broken. **Mechanical energy** is the total energy of a system including stored energy and kinetic energy. For example, a wagon at the top of a hill has mechanical energy that includes the positional energy from the gravitational pull on it and the kinetic energy as it begins to move down the hill.

Energy is constantly being changed in form all over the Earth. Energy is defined as the ability to do work, and work is constantly being done and needing to be done. For example, as we live, our body cells consume chemical energy in the form of sugar by breaking the bonds in sugar molecules and converting that energy into mechanical energy to move our muscles and allow us to breathe and move. As a car travels down the road, the bonds between gasoline molecules are burned and the motor propels the car forward. Meanwhile, plants are harvesting the solar energy of the Sun and putting together molecular bonds that contain energy.

Sources of energy (e.g., Sun, fossil fuels, nuclear) and the relationships between different sources (e.g., level of pollutions, amount of energy produced)

Energy that is used for human utility comes from a limited number of resources that can be classified into renewable and nonrenewable resources. **Renewable resources** are not used up with use. These include solar energy (from the Sun), wind energy, geothermal energy, and hydropower (from moving water).

Nonrenewable resources are resources that are being used more quickly than they can be replaced. Examples of nonrenewable resources include oil, coal, natural gas, and nuclear. Oil, coal, and natural gas are called fossil fuels because they are made of dead plants and animals. They have been formed over millions of years by pressure and heat within the Earth. Fossil fuels and nuclear power are the most common fuels used to make electricity. Fossil fuels produce the most pollution when they are used as they are burned. Solar energy is somewhat less efficient but it is very clean (produces no pollution). Water power is very efficient and produces little pollution but only is available near large water sources. Wind power requires large amounts of land for wind farms that are not pleasing to the eye. All forms of energy production have their limitations and advantages and the search for more efficient energy forms is a constant scientific endeavor.

Types of waves, parts of waves (e.g., frequency, wavelength), types of electromagnetic radiation, transfer of energy by waves, and the uses and dangers of electromagnetic radiation (e.g., radio transmission, UV light and sunburns)

Waves

A **wave** is movement within a medium, a disturbance that does not cause the medium itself to move significantly. A wave has no mass and causes no permanent movement of the medium. There are different types of waves with different types of movement. Light and ocean waves travel in transverse waves. A **transverse wave** causes particles to move perpendicular to the wave motion—for example, up and down if the wave is moving forward relative to you. Sound and some earthquake waves travel as longitudinal (compression) waves. In a **longitudinal wave** the particles move back and forth but parallel with (in the same direction) as the wave motion.

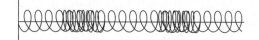

Fig. 2-1. Longitudinal Waves

Fig. 2-2. Transverse Wave

The **wavelength of a wave** is defined as the distance over which the wave's shape repeats. It is usually measured from one crest (or top) of a wave to the next crest, but can be measured from one point of the wave to the corresponding point on the next wave. The **frequency of a wave** is the number of wavelengths that pass a point in one second. Frequency is measured in Hertz (hz), which stands for cycles per second. If a particular wave passes a given point 50 times in a second, its frequency is 50 hz.

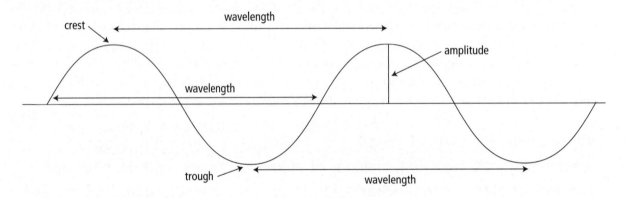

Fig. 2-3. Wavelength in Transverse Waves

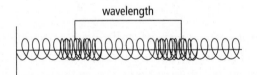

Fig. 2-4. Wavelength in Longitudinal Waves

Sound travels in longitudinal waves. **Sound waves** are made when an object vibrates and causes air molecules to take on a compression wave motion. This motion is picked up by our eardrums and translated in our brains into sounds. Changes in amplitude account for volume changes, while changes in frequency result in pitch changes.

Electromagnetic Radiation

Much of the energy of the universe is in the form of electromagnetic radiation. **Electromagnetic radiation** consists of waves of energy connected to magnetic and electric fields that result from acceleration of electrons. Electromagnetic radiation exists across a spectrum of wavelengths and frequencies. The electromagnetic spectrum (EMS) spans from radio waves with very long wavelengths and low frequency to gamma waves with very short wavelength and high frequency. Figure 2-5 shows the variety of types of waves that exist along the EMS. The varying frequency and wavelength give each type of wave different properties. Radio waves are able to carry voice transmissions throughout space allowing communication on varying frequencies as we know it on AM, FM, short wave, etc. Light as we know it is the visible portion of the electromagnetic spectrum. This visible portion of the EMS includes wavelengths that together produce white light but that can be broken down into red, orange, yellow, green, blue, and violet. Just past the visible light spectrum is ultraviolet (UV) radiation, which, with a higher frequency and shorter wavelength, is very dangerous to organisms as it can burn flesh (sunburn) and even alter DNA, causing mutations (cancer). X-rays and gamma rays are also damaging, but the atmosphere filters most of these out before they can reach us. The same is true of microwaves. Most of the waves that pass through the atmosphere are radio and visible light waves.

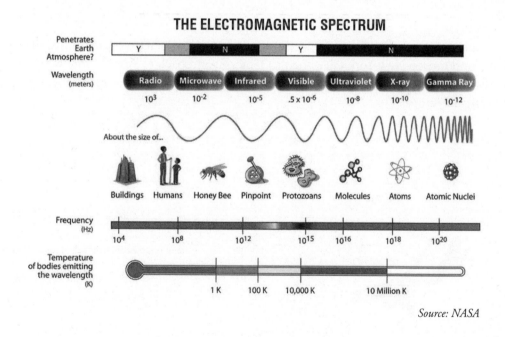

Source: NASA

Fig. 2-5. Electromagnetic Spectrum

Work, Motion, and Forces

Speed, velocity, acceleration, momentum, and collisions (e.g., inertia in a car accident, momentum transfer between two objects)

Speed is the rate of change of an object's position. An object traveling at high speed (going fast) will have a greater change in position (go farther) in a shorter period of time. Therefore, we can say that:

$$\text{speed} = \frac{\text{distance}}{\text{time}} \qquad s = \frac{d}{t}$$

Velocity is the rate of change of displacement, and includes both speed and direction whereas speed does not take direction into consideration. So we say that:

$$\text{velocity} = \frac{\text{displacement}}{\text{time}} \qquad v = \frac{^{+/-}d}{t}$$

To demonstrate the difference between speed and velocity, consider this: If a plane leaves Atlanta and flies to New York City, then to Chicago and back to Atlanta following the plan below, what is the difference between the plane's average speed and average velocity for the entire trip, not including any stops?

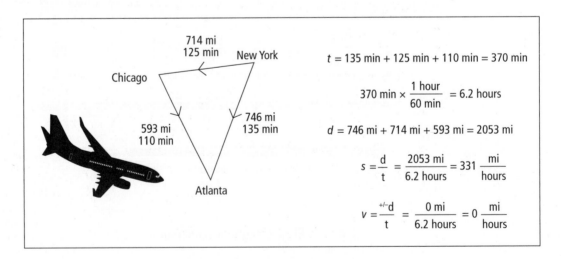

Fig. 2-6. Speed and Velocity

As you can see, to figure the speed you find the total distance and the total time, then divide the total distance by the total time to get the speed of 331 mi/hr. However, since velocity takes into account total displacement, and since the plane returned to its original position in Atlanta, the total displacement is 0. It returned to its starting position, canceling out all positive motion with equivalent negative motion. Therefore, the average velocity is 0 for the trip.

Friction is the rubbing force that acts against motion between two surfaces in contact. In a frictionless environment, there is nothing to stop a forward force unless another type of force, such as a collision acts on a moving body. Friction may come from air or any type of surface.

Acceleration is the rate of change of velocity and can act in the direction of motion, at an angle, or opposite to the direction of motion. Acceleration may be constant or it may change. To find acceleration for a given body use the following:

$$\text{average acceleration} = \frac{\text{change in velocity}}{\text{time}} \qquad a = \frac{v_2 - v_1}{t}$$

Momentum is the product of mass and velocity, the quantity of motion for an object. The greater the mass and/or velocity is, the greater the momentum. This is demonstrated by a snowball going downhill. As the snowball gains snow, it gains mass, and as it travels downhill it gains speed until it reaches terminal velocity. It gains momentum as it goes and becomes harder to stop, meaning it will take greater force to stop as it goes.

Inertia is an object's resistance to change in velocity—in other words, the tendency for an object at rest to stay at rest and an object in motion to stay in motion. In general, the greater the mass of an object, the more inertia it has.

When two objects, such as cars collide, several forces occur at once. For example, if a car traveling 40 mph goes through a red light and hits a vehicle traveling 5 mph crossing in front of it, the inertia of the driver's body in the car will cause him to move forward, even though the car is suddenly stopped by solid frictional force (metal on metal). Hopefully, he will be stopped by a seat belt and an air bag. Since momentum can be transferred from one object to another, the momentum of the 40 mph car will be transferred to the slower-moving car and it will be pushed with that force, causing forceful movement to the passenger within as well.

Force, Newton's Laws, gravity, acceleration due to Gravity (e.g., free fall, law of gravitational attraction), mass and weight

Force is the push or pull exerted on an object. Newton's Laws of Motion form the basis of our understanding of forces and things in motion. These three laws are:

- **Newton's First Law—Law of Inertia:** A particle at rest will stay at rest and a particle in motion will stay in motion until acted upon by an outside force.

- **Newton's Second Law—Law of Force versus Mass:** The rate of change of a particle is directly proportional to its mass and the force that is exerted on it, or

  $$F = m \times a \text{ or } F = ma$$

  (where F is force, m is mass, and a is acceleration)

- **Newton's Third Law—Law of Action and Reaction:** For every action there is an equal and opposite reaction.

Gravity

The **mass of an object** refers to the amount of matter that is contained by the object; however, the **weight of an object** is the force of gravity acting upon that object. Mass is related to how much stuff is there, while weight refers to the pull of the Earth (or any other planet or object) upon that stuff.

The mass of an object (measured in kg) will be the same no matter where in the universe the object is located. Mass is never altered by location, the pull of gravity, speed or even the existence of other forces. A 51 kg object will have a mass of 51 kg whether it is located on Earth, the Moon, or anywhere else. The amount of mass and the force of gravity from the Earth (or the Moon, etc.) gives an object its weight. The weight of an object, though, will vary according to where in the universe the object is. Weight depends upon the mass of the object that is exerting the gravitational force and the distance from the gravitational force.

Gravity is a property of all matter; all matter exerts a gravitational force on all other matter. Gravity acts at a distance and attracts bodies of matter toward each other. The gravity of the Moon affects the water in the Earth's oceans, causing the tides. In the study of atomic particles, there is even a weak force of gravity between all particles.

The amount of matter in an object is called its **mass**. The force of gravity is dependent on the amount of mass a body has. That means that the gravity on Earth is greater than the gravity on the Moon, since the Earth has much more matter or mass than the Moon. The force of gravity on an object caused by the mass of the Earth equals the mass of the object (m) times the acceleration caused by gravity (g). The equation is:

$$F = mg$$

This acceleration caused by gravity on Earth (more commonly called the acceleration of gravity) equals 9.8 m/s^2 in the metric system and 32 ft/s^2 in the English system. The weight of an object is the measurement of the force of gravity on that object. You weigh something on a scale, according to the force with which the Earth pulls it down. Thus, the weight is actually the force of gravity on that object:

$$\text{Weight} = mg$$

The mass of the Moon is less than the mass of the Earth, so the acceleration of gravity (g) is less on the Moon than the Earth. If you put the same object on the Moon and weighed it, its weight would be one-sixth the weight on Earth. In other words, a 180-pound man would only weigh 30 pounds on the Moon.

$$F = G\frac{Mm}{r^2}$$

Mass is measured in grams in the metric system. To get the weight of an object in the metric system, you multiply the mass in kilograms by the acceleration of gravity (9.8 m/s^2), resulting in the units of Newton. The universal law of gravitational attraction states that the force of gravity between two objects is proportional to the product of the masses of the objects and inversely proportional to the square of the distance between them—in simple English—as objects get further apart, the effect of gravity drops dramatically. The equation below shows this relationship . . . the mass of one body is designated as M, the mass of a second as m, and the distance between them is r; the force of attraction between the two bodies is F and G is the universal gravitational constant $G = 6.67 \times 10^{-11}$ N(m^2/kg^2) (Newton-meter squared per kilogram squared).

If you drop an object relatively near the Earth, it will speed up according to the acceleration of gravity (g). When you let go of the object, its velocity is zero.

Since g = 32 ft/s² = 9.8 m/s², the velocity will be 32 ft/s (9.8 m/s²) after one second. Because the object is accelerating, the velocity after 2 seconds will be 2 × 32 ft/s² = 64 ft/s² (19.6 m/s²). After 10 seconds, the velocity will be 10 × 32 ft/s² = 320 ft/s² or 98 m/s².

Although a free-falling object will continue to accelerate until it is made to stop (hits the ground), air resistance will slow down that acceleration. Air resistance is approximately proportional to the square of the velocity, so as the object falls faster, the air resistance increases until it equals the force of gravity. The point at which these forces are equal is called its **terminal velocity**. For instance, a falling baseball reaches 94 miles per hour or 42 meters/second; it would remain at the velocity and no longer accelerate. A penny dropped from a high building will accelerate until it reaches around 230 mph.

The acceleration of force of gravity on falling bodies is independent of the mass of the falling object. Therefore, a 15-pound weight would fall at the same rate as a 2-pound weight and would hit the ground at the same time if dropped from the same height. In addition, gravity of the mass of an object is also independent of the velocity of the object parallel to the ground. Therefore, a bullet shot from a gun will hit the ground at the same time as one that was simply dropped from the same height.

Since force = mass times acceleration, the universal gravity equation implies that as objects are attracted and get closer together, the force increases and the acceleration between them also increases.

Work, simple machines (types and functions), mechanical advantages (force, distance, and simple machines), and power

Work is the movement of a mass over a distance. All manner of work, whether tending a garden or building a structure requires movement of materials and lifting of items, needs to be accomplished daily. Since the beginning of time, humans have sought to simplify work processes with the use of machines.

$$\text{Work} = \text{Force} \times \text{Distance}$$

$$\text{W} = F \times d \text{ or W} = Fd$$

Simple machines give advantage to the worker by changing the magnitude or direction of a force using some manner of mechanical device. Mechanical advantage is also defined as leverage. And in fact, the simplest of simple machines is the lever.

Each of these simple machines has a specific movement or mechanism that increases the power or leverage of a human action. These can be combined in various formats to form more complex machinery.

Table 2-1. Simple Machines

Classic Simple Machine	Examples	Use
Lever	Bottle openers, baseball bats, see-saws	Uses a fulcrum to magnify the force along a surface
Wheel and Axle	Tire, rolling pin	Is a simple machine that is able to move mass over distance with greatly reduced work
Pulley	Clotheslines, cargo lifter on ships	Is able to distribute mass over distance, allowing work to be done with greater advantage
Inclined plane	Ramp in a factory, ramp for wheelchair use	Is commonly used to lighten the workload when moving boxes or even walking from one place to another up a steep slope
Wedge	Common knife, axe	Is a double-inclined plane that acts to separate objects
Screw	Common screw used in construction, type of entrance, exit in some tall parking garages	Is a shaft with an inclined groove along its surface. Its structure allows for it to firmly grasp two surfaces together or even to elevate a substance such as water from a lower to a higher elevation.

Power is the rate at which work is done. Machines, therefore, generally increase the power we have available to us for doing work.

Chemical Properties and Reactions Related to Living Systems

Structure of Matter

Matter—Atoms, Elements, Molecules

The study of matter is known as **chemistry**. All matter is made up of atoms. The properties of matter are a result of the structure of atoms and their interaction with each other. An **element** is a substance that cannot be broken down into any other substances. The simplest unit of an element that retains the element's characteristics is known as an **atom**. Each atom of a given element has a nucleus containing a unique number of protons and about the same number of neutrons. The number of neutrons can vary and still be the same element, however. The nucleus is surrounded by electrons.

Elements are listed by atomic number on the periodic table of the elements. The atomic number is the number of protons found in the nucleus of an atom of that element. In an uncharged atom, the number of protons is equal to the number of electrons, so for an uncharged atom, the atomic number gives you the number of protons and the number of electrons.

Electrons have a charge of $^-1$, while protons have a charge of $^+1$. Neutrons have no charge. The number of protons in the nucleus of an atom carries a positive charge equal to this number; that is, if an atom's nucleus contains 4 protons, the charge is $^+4$. Since positive and negative charges attract, the positive charges of the nucleus attract an equal number of negatively charged electrons. According to the Periodic Table of the Elements, an atom with 4 protons is Beryllium.

Be   Beryllium

Atomic Number = 4
Atomic Mass = 9.01

Electrons have no discernible mass, and the mass of each proton is 1 atomic mass unit (AMU). Neutrons also have an atomic mass of 1 AMU. We know Be has 4 protons so that leaves 5.01 AMUs for protons. The reason the number is not a whole number is that 5.01 is an average of all the forms of Beryllium found in natural state. When atoms of the same element have different numbers of neutrons they are called isotopes. Beryllium has isotopes containing 1–13 neutrons, but only one is stable, the one with 5 neutrons, so most Be is in that form. Thus, the average atomic mass of Be is very close to 9 or 9.01. No single atom of Be will have a partial neutron and no atom's atomic mass includes the mass of an electron or any such thing. The atomic mass equals the number of protons plus the average number of neutrons for all isotopes of that element.

Electrons travel freely in a three-dimensional space that may be called an electron cloud, an electron shell, or an orbital. Current models of the atom follow the principles of quantum mechanics, which predict the probabilities of an electron being in a certain area at a certain time. Although the term "orbital" is used, electrons do not orbit the nucleus like a planet orbiting a sun. The orbital (or electron cloud, or electron shell) represents a probability of finding an electron at a particular location.

Each orbital has a particular amount of energy related to it, and is therefore also referred to as an energy level. Energy levels are named utilizing a quantum number and a letter designation (i.e., 1s, 2s, 2p, etc.). The quantum number of the energy level closest to the nucleus is 1, and progresses as the levels get farther from the nucleus (2, 3, etc.). The letter designation indicates the shape of that particular energy level. The energy level closest to the nucleus has the least energy related to it; the farthest has the most. Each energy level has a limited capacity for holding electrons and each energy level requires a different number of electrons to fill it. Lower energy levels (closer to the nucleus) have less capacity for electrons than those farther from the nucleus.

Since electrons are attracted to the nucleus, electrons fill the electron orbitals closest to the nucleus (lowest energy levels) first. Once a given level is full, electrons start filling the next level out. The outermost occupied energy level of an element is called the valence orbital. The number of electrons in the valence orbital will determine the combinations that this atom will be likely to make with other atoms. Atoms are more stable when every electron is paired and are most stable when their valence shell is full. The tendency for an atom toward stability means that elements having unpaired or partially filled valence shells will easily gain or lose electrons in order to obtain the most efficient configuration.

Chemical Bonds

Valence properties of atoms provide opportunities for them to bond with other atoms. A covalent bond between atoms is formed when atoms share electrons. For instance, hydrogen has only one electron, which is unpaired, leaving the 1s valence shell one electron short of full. Oxygen has 6 electrons in the valence shell; it needs 2 more electrons in the valence shell for that shell to be full. It is easy for 2 hydrogen atoms to share their electrons with the oxygen, making the effective valence shells of each full. Covalent bonds are the strongest type of chemical bond.

A molecule is two or more atoms held together by shared electrons (covalent bonds). *A compound is formed when two or more different atoms bond together chemically to form a unique substance (ex. H_2O, CH_4).*

Charged atoms are called ions. An atom that loses one or more electrons becomes a positively charged particle, or a positive ion. An atom that gains one or more electrons becomes a negative ion. Positive and negative ions are attracted to each other in a bond called an ionic bond. An ionic bond is weaker than a covalent bond. Na^+Cl^- (sodium chloride or table salt) is an example of a substance held together by ionic bonds.

Some molecules have a weak, partial negative charge at one region of the molecule and a partial positive charge in another region. Molecules that have regions of partial charge are called polar molecules. For instance, water molecules (which have a net charge of 0) have a partial negative charge near the oxygen atom and a partial positive charge near each of the hydrogen atoms. Thus, when water molecules are close together, their positive regions are attracted to the negatively charged regions of nearby molecules; the negative regions are attracted to the positively charged regions of nearby molecules. The force of attraction between water molecules is called a hydrogen bond. A hydrogen bond is a weak chemical bond.

Properties of Water

Water exhibits unique characteristics that affect the processes of life. Water is able to dissolve many types of organic and inorganic substances. This property promotes several biological processes such as muscle contraction, nerve stimulation, and transport across membranes (permeability).

Because water molecules are polar, certain types of chemicals dissociate in water. Some chemicals yield protons and others accept protons when dissolved in water. An **acid** is a chemical that donates protons (H+ ions) when dissolved in water. Acidity then, is a measure of the concentration of H+ ions in a solution. A chemical that accepts protons (H+ ions) when dissolved in water is a **base**. The pH (standing for potential of hydrogen) scale is a measurement of H+ ions in solution. The pH of a substance can range from 0–14. A pH of 7 is neutral (as is pure water). A pH below 7 is acidic and a pH above 7 is basic (or alkaline). Acids and bases tend to neutralize each other when dissolved together in water. The neutralization of an acidic solution with a basic solution produces a salt (an ionic compound) and water. Acids, bases, and salts are important chemicals to many life processes.

The transparent quality of water keeps it from disturbing processes within cells that require light (such as in photosynthetic and light-sensing cells). Water also exhibits unique responses to temperature change. Most substances contract upon becoming a solid; however, water expands as it solidifies (a process we call freezing), forming a loose lattice structure (crystal). This crystalline form also makes frozen water (ice) less dense than liquid water. This accounts for lakes and other bodies of water freezing on the top first (insulating the water and organisms below from harsh temperature changes).

Water has a high specific heat; it resists changes in temperature. The presence of water in an environment will tend to moderate the effect of harsh temperature changes.

Hydrogen bonds between water molecules also give water a high surface tension, allowing small particles, and even some organisms (such as the water strider) to rest on the surface. This surface tension also causes liquid water in air to form drops (rain).

Physical and chemical properties, changes of state, and density

All matter has physical properties that can be observed. These properties affect the way substances react with each other under various conditions. **Physical properties** include color, odor, taste, strength, hardness, density and state. Physical properties arise from the nature of the element, the number of protons, neutrons, and electrons of a substance plus any chemical bonds that might occur between atoms. The uniqueness of any substance is due in total to the unlimited ways that atoms are able to be arranged. This can cause colors, odors, electrical properties like conductivity, etc.

Solids, Liquids, Gases, Plasma

Matter exists in one of several states at any given time. The most common of these are solid liquid, gas, or plasma. Under most conditions elements will be in the solid, liquid, or gas state.

Plasma exists in the case of extreme heat and ionization such as on the surface of stars. In this state, ions and electrons move about freely, giving plasma properties different from the other three states. There are other states that can be reached in extreme conditions and some that are theorized, but we consider only those commonly encountered in basic science.

A **solid** has molecules in fixed positions giving the substance definite shape. Solids have a definite volume. In a solid the molecules are packed and bonded together. The strength of the bonds determines the strength of the solid and its melting point. When heat energy is applied to the bonds, they break apart, the molecules can move about, and the substance becomes a liquid.

A **liquid** has definite volume but not definite shape since the molecules are loosely attracted. The loose attractions between molecules allow for the shape of the substance to mold to its surroundings. When a liquid is cooled the molecules become bonded and the substance becomes a solid. Heat energy is lost since the molecules are moving less. When heat energy is added to a liquid the weak attractions holding the molecules together break apart causing the molecules to move about randomly and the liquid becomes a gas.

A **gas** is a substance with relatively (relative to solids and liquids) large distances and little attraction between molecules. The molecules are free to move about randomly. Gases have no definite shape or volume. Temperature and pressure directly impact their density.

Different substances have different conditions under which they exist in a solid, liquid, or gas. The state that a substance exists in at room temperature depends on how the molecules are bonded together.

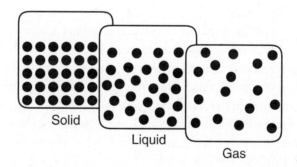

Fig. 2-7. Solids, liquids, and gases differ in the arrangement and density of molecules.

The following are some terms that are important to know related to substances and their states:

- melting point—temperature at which a substance changes from solid to liquid form

- boiling point—temperature at which a substance changes from liquid to gas

- evaporation—escape of individual particles of a substance into gaseous form

- condensation—change of a gaseous substance to liquid form

Changing from one state to another does not change the nature of the substance; it still remains the same element or compound. Substances also have unique chemical properties such as flammability and toxicity that arise from the chemical structure. When the chemical structure changes a chemical change takes place and a new substance is formed.

Density

Density is the measure of how much matter exists in a given volume. The density of a substance is determined by measuring the mass of a substance and dividing it by the volume ($D = m/v$). Substances that are less dense will float when placed in a more dense substance. More dense substances will sink in a less dense liquid. It is important to understand that density is a function of mass (amount of matter), not weight (attraction of gravity on mass). Density has to do with how tightly packed the atoms in a substance are.

Consider this: Which weighs more, a pound of lead or a pound of feathers? Neither. A pound is a pound; but the *volume* of a pound of feathers will be much greater than that of a pound of lead.

Pressure is a measure of the amount of force applied per unit of area. Pressure exerted on a gas may affect its density, by compressing its volume. Liquids and solids are much less responsive to pressure. Pascal's principle states that the pressure exerted on any point of a confined fluid is transmitted unchanged throughout the fluid. Therefore, if you exert pressure on a liquid it will exert that same pressure on its surroundings. Archimedes' principle states that when an object is placed in a fluid the object will have a buoyant force equal to the weight of the displaced fluid. Archimedes' principle states that buoyancy (the tendency to float) is a decrease in the measured apparent weight of an object in a fluid due to the net upward force caused by the displaced fluid. This apparent decrease in weight of the object is a result of the force of the displaced fluid acting in an upward direction opposing the object.

Balancing chemical equations and different types of chemical equations, conservation of mass in balanced chemical equations and limiting reactants

Chemical Reactions and Equations

Chemical reactions occur when molecules interact with each other to form one or more molecules of another type. Chemical reactions that occur within cells provide energy, nutrients, and other products that allow the organism to function.

There are several categories of chemical reactions. Chemical reactions are symbolized by an equation where the reacting molecules (reactants) are shown on one side and the newly formed molecules (products) on the other, with an arrow between indicating the direction of the reaction. Some chemical reactions are simple, such as the breakdown of a compound into its components, (a decomposition reaction):

$$AB \rightarrow A + B$$

A simple combination reaction is the reverse of decomposition:

$$A + B \rightarrow AB$$

When one compound breaks apart and forms a new compound with a free reactant, it is called a replacement reaction:

$$AB + C \rightarrow AC + B$$

Chemical reactions may require an input of energy or they may release energy. Reactions that require energy are called **endothermic** reactions. Reactions that release energy are termed **exothermic**.

All chemical reactions are subject to the laws of thermodynamics. The first law of thermodynamics (also known as the law of conservation of matter and energy) states that matter and energy can neither be created nor destroyed. In other words, the sum of matter and energy of the reactants must equal that of the products. The second law of thermodynamics, or the law of increasing disorder (or entropy), asserts that all reactions spread energy, which tends to diminish its availability. So, although we know from the first law that the energy must be equal on both sides of a reaction equation, reaction processes also tend to degrade the potential energy into a form that cannot perform any cellular work.

The fact that the amount of matter must be equal on both sides of a chemical reaction (equation) means that we can mathematically balance chemical equations knowing that the number of atoms of each element must be the same on each side. The process of balancing chemical equations helps us understand chemical reactions.

Balancing Chemical Equations

To balance chemical reactions, use the following steps:

- The same number of like atoms must exist both as reactants and products.

- To balance reactions, alter only the coefficients; do not change the formula.

- In general, when balancing reactions, balance the hydrogen and oxygen atoms last.

- When faced with an unbalanced reaction that involves the combustion (breaking up) of a hydrocarbon, look for the following:

  1. First match the number of carbons in the hydrocarbon in the reactants by adjusting the coefficient of carbon dioxide in the product.

     $$C_3H_8 + O_2 \rightarrow 3CO_2 + H_2O$$

     There are three carbon atoms on both sides.

  2. Then balance the hydrogen atoms by adding a coefficient to water in the product so that the hydrogen atoms equal the number of hydrogen atoms in the reactant hydrocarbon.

     $$C_3H_8 + 5O_2 \rightarrow 3CO_2 + 4H_2O$$

     Now there are eight hydrogen atoms on both sides.

  3. Finally, add up the oxygen atoms in the products (carbon dioxide and water) and adjust the coefficient for the oxygen molecule in the reactants so that all oxygen atoms balance.

     $$C_3H_8 + 5O_2 \rightarrow 3CO_2 + 4H_2O$$

     Now there are ten oxygen atoms on both sides. The equation is balanced.

In nature when chemical reactions are occurring, they will keep occurring as long as there are enough reactants and the conditions are right for the reaction to take place. However, as soon as one of the reactants runs out, the reaction stops. That reactant that is completely consumed in a reaction is called the **limiting reactant** because it controls or limits how long the reaction can continue. For example, for the equation balanced above,

$$C_3H_8 + 5O_2 \rightarrow 3CO_2 + 4H_2O$$

if you have an unlimited supply of O_2 and 10 grams of C_3H_8, the production of $3CO_2 + 4H_2O$ will be limited by the amount of C_3H_8 on hand.

Parts in solutions, general rules of solubility (e.g., hotter solvents allow more solute to dissolve), saturation and the differences between weak and strong solutions.

When working with chemical reactions it is important to have a basic understanding of how chemicals are going to behave when mixed before you attempt the reaction. Of course, knowing if a chemical reaction will produce a highly exothermic reaction (an explosion) is important and generally there are warnings on chemical containers to let one know if a chemical component is dangerous when mixed in particular ways. However, it is also useful to have knowledge of how compounds react in other ways, and one of the most important is solubility. Knowing whether a compound is soluble in an aqueous solution is useful for predicting whether a reaction might involve formation of a precipitate (an insoluble compound that drops to the bottom) or not.

There are two parts that make up a solution: the **solvent** which is the liquid that accommodates the **solute** which dissolves in the solvent. A **precipitate** is any of the compound that is added to the solvent that does not dissolve, but falls to the bottom of the mixture. **Solubility** refers to the characteristic of the solute to dissolve in the solute, whether it dissolves under a particular set of circumstances or not.

While no substance is completely insoluble, a substance is considered insoluble if it forms a precipitate when equal volumes of 0.1 M solutions of its components are combined. There are general rules of solubility that chemists have determined regarding varying substances. The following set of rules concerns which chemicals are considered insoluble according to the standard above. They are given in an order that can help you remember them as you study; however, there is no particular order in which they need to be learned.

Compound Solubility Rules
(NAAGGS except PMS and CaBS)

Soluble Chemicals:

Nitrates (NO_3^-)

Acetates ($C_2H_3O_2^-$)

Ammonium (NH_4^+)

Group 1 (Li^+, Na^+, etc.)

Group 17 (F^-, CL^-, Br^-, etc.) except #

Sulfates (SO_4^{-2}) except *#

Exceptions (2 groups)

#PMS P = Pb^{+2} (lead) M = Mercury

(Hg_2^{+2}) S = Silver (AG^+)

*CaBS Ca = Ca^{+2} (calcium) B = Ba^{+2}

(barium) S = Sr^{+2} (strontium)

In addition to the compound solubility rules, other factors can impact the rate of solubility of compounds. For example, since a rise in temperature is an increase in the motion of molecules, the rate of a compound dissolving will increase as well. Hotter solvents (what the compound is dissolved in) will also allow more solute to be accommodated without becoming saturated. The saturation point is when no more solute can be dissolved and a precipitate is formed. Stirring and mixing can also increase the rate of dissolving and the amount of solute that will dissolve.

In an aqueous solution (the solvent is water), the number of ions of a solute is related to the number of moles of that solute per concentration of the substance in the aqueous solution. **Molarity** is the number of moles of a solute (n) divided by the total volume (V) of the solution:

$$M = n/V$$

A weak solution is one where there is low molarity (low n) and a strong solution has high molarity, one where the solution is nearing the point of precipitate formation.

 PRACTICE!

1. An athlete with a sore shoulder places a warm compress on it to soothe the muscle. This is an example of what type of energy transfer?

    A. Radiation

    B. Convection

    C. Irradiation

    D. Conduction

2. The conversion of light energy into chemical energy is accomplished by

    A. photosynthesis.

    B. oxidative phosphorylation.

    C. metabolism.

    D. catabolism.

3. A wave does not carry along the medium through which it travels. Thus, it follows that

    A. molecules of water in the ocean are pushed to shore by waves.

    B. the ocean's water molecules are thoroughly mixed each day by waves.

    C. debris in the ocean is washed ashore by waves.

    D. individual water molecules do not travel toward shore, but wave peaks do.

4. According to Newton's laws of motion, the greater the mass of an object, the greater the force necessary to change its

    A. position.

    B. force.

    C. state of motion.

    D. shape.

5. An astronaut is traveling in a spacecraft that is slowing down. To the astronaut inside the spacecraft, the apparent force inside the craft is directed

    A. backward.

    B. forward.

    C. sideways.

    D. nowhere because there is no force.

6. The discoveries of Galileo Galilei (1564–1642) and Isaac Newton (1642–1727) precipitated the scientific revolution of the seventeenth century. Stressing the use of detailed measurements during experimentation enabled them to frame several universal laws of nature and to overthrow many of Aristotle's (384–322 B.C.E.) erroneous ideas about motion, which were based on reasoning alone. One of these universal laws is now known as the law of inertia or Newton's first law of motion. According to this law, objects in motion tend to stay in motion and objects at rest tend to stay at rest unless acted upon by an external force. The more mass (inertia) an object has, the more resistance it offers to changes in its state of motion. According to the law of inertia, which of the following would offer the greatest resistance to a change in its motion?

    A. A pellet of lead shot

    B. A golf ball

    C. A large watermelon

    D. A feather

7. As you go down the periodic table and to the left, which of the following traits increases?

    A. Atomic radius

    B. Electronegativity

    C. Electron affinity

    D. Ionization energy

8. Which state of matter does NOT have a definite shape or a definite volume?

    A. Liquid

    B. Gas

    C. Plasma

    D. Both (B) and (C)

9. Which of the following statements is true about electrons?

    A. Electrons have a positive charge.

    B. Electrons have less mass than protons and neutrons.

    C. Electrons are found within the nucleus of atoms.

    D. The number of electrons is equal to the number of protons in an ion.

10. Water molecules are attracted to each other due to which of the following?

    A. Polarity; partial positive charge near hydrogen atoms; partial negative charge near oxygen atoms

    B. Inert properties of hydrogen and oxygen

    C. Ionic bonds between hydrogen and oxygen

    D. The crystal structure of ice

Science Practice 2 Answers

1. **D.**

The compress is an example of conduction, the transfer of energy from molecule to molecule by collisions, passing heat through one material into another. Radiation is the movement of energy without a medium while convection is the movement of energy through movement of hot air. Irradiation is infusing a medium with radiation.

2. **A.**

The process of photosynthesis is the crucial reaction that converts the light energy of the Sun into chemical energy that is usable by living things. Metabolism breaks down molecules for energy and catabolism breaks down chemicals into smaller parts. Oxidative phosphorylation is the process of forming ATP in cells.

3. **D.**

The water molecules, which are the medium, are not carried but the wave peaks do move toward shore. Molecules of water in the ocean are not pushed to shore by waves. Although the ocean is somewhat mixed each day, this mixing is due to turbulence and currents, not waves. Similarly, debris washes ashore by turbulence and currents—not wave action. Currents and turbulence are responsible for moving both the water and swimmers.

4. **C.**

The greater the mass of an object, the greater the force necessary to change its state of motion. Newton's first law of motion states that an object in motion will stay in motion and an object at rest will stay at rest until acted upon by an outside force. Since Newton's second law of motion states that Force = (mass × acceleration), then in order to change its motion, as the object increases in mass, more force will be necessary to alter its acceleration. Its position may be changed slightly with the same amount of force as might be applied to a smaller object, so changing its position is not the correct answer. Greater force may not change its shape at all.

5. **B.**

The astronaut will feel as if he is being pushed forward toward the front of the space-craft. The others are incorrect directions of motion. There is a negative acceleration (deceleration) and thus a negative force occurring since the vehicle is slowing down.

6. **C.**

The property of an object that determines the object's resistance to motion is its mass. A large watermelon has a far greater mass than the pellet of lead shot, the golf ball, or the feather. The mass of an object never changes. Its mass is equal to the object's weight divided by the acceleration due to gravity (g) at its current position in space.

7. **A.**

Only the size of the atom increases as you move down and to the left in the periodic table.

8. **D.**

Both gas and plasma have no defined shape or volume. A liquid holds the shape of its container and thus has a definite volume.

9. **B.**

Electrons have very little mass, much less than either protons or neutrons. They are found orbiting in a cloud surrounding the nucleus. Electrons are negatively charged. An ion is an atom with a greater or fewer number of electrons than the standard atom for the element, causing a charge of positive or negative due to the unequal number of protons and electrons.

10. **A.**

The hydrogen atoms in water molecules have a partial positive charge, while the oxygen atoms in water have a partial negative charge, causing polarity. This polarity allows the oxygen of one water molecule to attract the hydrogen of another. The partial charges attract other opposite partial charges of other water molecules, allowing for weak (hydrogen) bonds between the molecules. *Inert* means non-reactive; it does not explain the attraction between H and O. There are no ionic bonds within water molecules, only covalent bonds. A crystal structure forms in ice because of the attraction of hydrogen bonds; the crystal structure does not cause the attraction.

Chapter 3

Earth and Space Science

Interactions between Earth's Systems and Living Things

Interactions of matter between living and non-living things (e.g., cycles of matter) and the location, uses and dangers of fossil fuels

On Earth, matter is constantly being cycled between living and non-living things. Just as chemical equations are balanced in keeping with the law of conservation of matter, matter is also conserved on a much larger scale of the Earth and the universe. There are several cycles that we can observe happening that account for different elements or substances being passed, used, and passed on in Earth's environment. Other substances are formed on Earth and then combusted (used up). While matter and energy must be conserved, they may be converted into less usable forms. This occurs when fossil fuels are used.

Water Cycle

The availability of water is crucial to the survival of all living things. Water vapor circulates through the biosphere in a process called the hydrologic cycle. Water is evaporated via solar radiation from the ocean and other bodies of water into clouds. Water is also released into the atmosphere from vegetation (leaves) by transpiration. Some water is also evaporated directly from soil, but most water in the ground flows into underground aquifers, which eventually empty into the oceans. Water above ground flows into waterways, which also eventually flow into the ocean (a process known as runoff). Water vapor is then redistributed over land (and back into oceans as well) via clouds, which release water as precipitation.

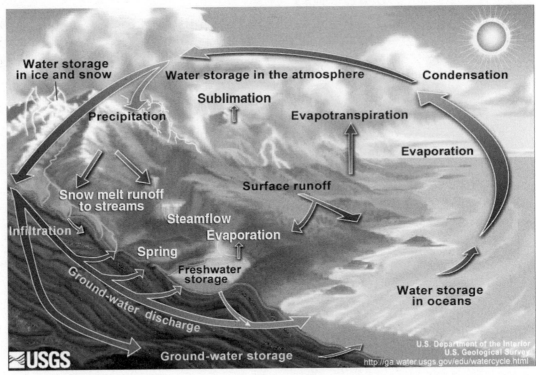

Fig. 3-1. The Water Cycle

The water cycle also has a profound effect on Earth's climate. Clouds reflect the sun's radiation away from Earth, causing cool weather. Water vapor in the air also acts as a greenhouse gas, reflecting radiation back toward Earth, and therefore trapping heat. The water cycle also intersects nearly all the other cycles of elements and nutrients.

Nitrogen Cycle

Nitrogen is another substance essential to life processes, since it is a key component of amino acids (components of proteins) and nucleic acids (DNA, RNA). The nitrogen cycle recycles nitrogen. Nitrogen is the most plentiful gas in the atmosphere, making up 78% of the air. However, neither photosynthetic organisms nor animals are able to use nitrogen gas (N_2)—which does not readily react with other compounds—directly from the air. Instead, a process known as nitrogen fixing makes nitrogen available for absorption by the roots of plants. Nitrogen fixing is the process of combining nitrogen with either hydrogen or oxygen, mostly by nitrogen-fixing bacteria, or, to a small degree, by the action of lightning.

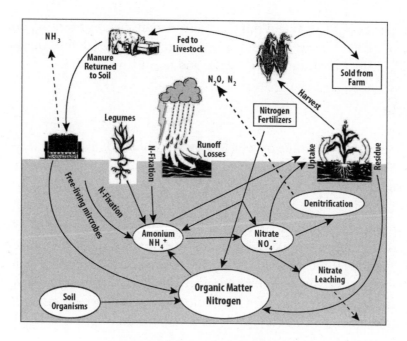

Fig. 3-2. The Nitrogen Cycle

Nitrogen-fixing bacteria live in the soil and perform the task of combining gaseous nitrogen from the atmosphere with hydrogen, forming ammonium (NH^{4+} ions). (Some cyanobacteria, also called blue-green bacteria, are active in this process as well.) Ammonium ions are then absorbed and used by plants. Other types of nitrogen-fixing bacteria live in symbiosis on the nodules of the roots of legumes (beans, peas, clover, etc.), supplying the roots with a direct source of ammonia.

Some plants are unable to use ammonia; instead, they use nitrates. Some bacteria perform nitrification, a process which further breaks down ammonia into nitrites (NO^{2-}), and yet again by another bacterium, which converts nitrites into nitrates (NO^{3-}).

Nitrogen compounds (such as ammonia and nitrates) are also produced by natural, physical processes such as volcanic activity. Another source of usable nitrogen is lightning, which reacts with atmospheric nitrogen to form nitrates.

In addition, nitrogen passes along through the food chain, and is recycled through decomposition processes. When plants are consumed, the amino acids are recombined and used, a process that passes the nitrogen-containing molecules on through the food chain or web. Animal waste products, such as urine, release nitrogen compounds (primarily ammonia) back into the environment, being yet another source of nitrogen. Finally, large amounts of nitrogen are returned to the soil by bacteria and fungi, which decompose dead plant and animal matter into ammonia (and other substances), a process known as ammonification.

Various species of bacteria and fungi are also responsible for breaking down excess nitrates, a process known as denitrification, which releases nitrogen gas back into the air. The nitrogen cycle involves cycling nitrogen through both living and non-living entities.

Carbon Cycle

The **carbon cycle** is the route by which carbon is obtained, used, and recycled by living things. Carbon is an important element contained in the cells of all species. The study of organic chemistry is the study of carbon-based molecules.

Earth's atmosphere contains large amounts of carbon in the form of carbon dioxide (CO_2). Photosynthetic organisms require the intake of carbon dioxide for the process of photosynthesis, which is the foundation of the food chain. Most of the carbon within organisms is derived from the production of carbohydrates in photosynthetic organisms through photosynthesis. The process of photosynthesis also releases oxygen molecules (O_2), which are necessary to animal respiration. Animal respiration releases carbon dioxide back into the atmosphere in large quantities.

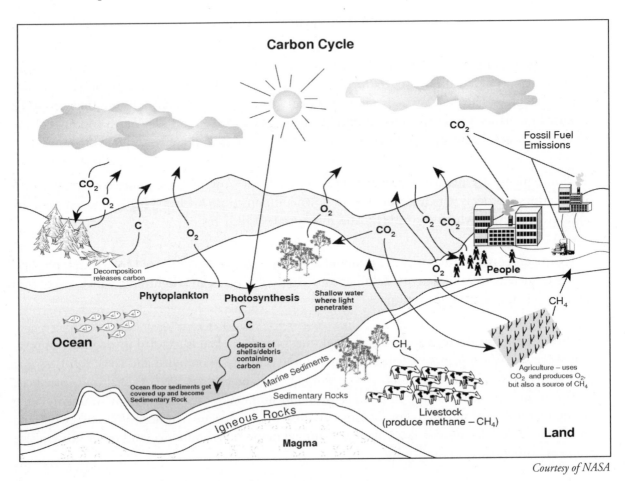

Courtesy of NASA

Fig. 3-3. The Carbon Cycle

Since plant cells consist of molecules containing carbon, animals that consume photosynthetic organisms are consuming and using carbon from the photosynthetic organisms. Carbon is passed along the food chain as these animals are then consumed. When animals and photosynthetic organisms die, decomposers, including the detritus feeders, bacteria, and fungi, break down the organic matter. Detritus feeders include worms, mites, insects, and crustaceans, which feed on dead organic matter, returning carbon to the cycle through chemical breakdown and respiration.

Carbon dioxide (CO_2) is also dissolved directly into the oceans, where it is combined with calcium to form calcium carbonate, which is used by mollusks to form their shells. When mollusks die, the shells break down and often form limestone. Limestone is then dissolved by water over time and some carbon may be released back into the atmosphere as CO_2, or used by new ocean species.

Finally, organic matter that is left to decay, may, under conditions of heat and pressure be transformed into coal, oil, or natural gas (the fossil fuels). When fossil fuels are burned for energy, the combustion process releases carbon dioxide back into the atmosphere, where it is available to plants for photosynthesis.

Phosphorous Cycle

Phosphorous is another mineral required by living things. Unlike carbon and nitrogen, which cycle through the atmosphere in gaseous form, phosphorous is only found in solid form, within rocks and soil. Phosphorous is a key component in ATP, NADP (a molecule that, like ATP, stores energy in its chemical bonds), and many other molecular compounds essential to life.

Phosphorous is found within rocks and is released by the process of erosion. Water dissolves phosphorous from rocks, and carries it into rivers and streams. Here phosphorous and oxygen react to form phosphates that end up in bodies of water. Phosphates are absorbed by photosynthetic organisms in and near the water and are used in the synthesis of organic molecules. As in the carbon and nitrogen cycles, phosphorous is then passed up the food chain and returned through animal wastes and organic decay.

New phosphorous enters the cycle as undersea sedimentary rocks are thrust up during the shifting of the Earth's tectonic plates. New rock containing phosphorous is then exposed to erosion and enters the cycling process.

Fossil Fuels

Oil, coal, and natural gas are called **fossil fuels** because they are made of dead plants and animals, organisms that can be fossilized but that also when subjected to heat and pressure over time form substances rich in energy holding chemical bonds. We use fossil fuels to make electricity and to power our vehicles (gasoline and diesel) and heat our homes and power factories. At the moment, mankind is highly dependent on fossil fuels. Burning fossil fuels comes at a price since it generally takes millions of years for them to form, making them non-renewable resources. Fossil fuels are buried deep underground and must be either mined or drilled and piped to the surface. When they run out, there is no new supply. Additionally, burning fossil fuels for energy gives off byproducts including CO_2 gas and other pollutants that cause harm to the ozone layer of our atmosphere, resulting in potential global warming as well as air pollution.

Natural hazards (e.g., earthquakes, hurricanes, etc.), their effects (e.g., frequency, severity, and short-and long-term effects), and mitigation thereof (e.g., dikes, storm shelters, building practices)

The world is full of hazards—those that are nature-induced (or natural hazards) and those that are human-induced (or man-made). In the case of natural hazards, they are usually most detrimental when they are catastrophic—that is, when they have a sudden and unpredictable onset. Earthquakes and wildfires are usually unpredictable and are an example of natural hazards. Hurricanes are more predictable weather-related hazards. Natural hazards can have long-lasting biological and ecological impacts beyond the short-term damaging effects that they generally cause.

Some natural hazards such as earthquakes are difficult to predict, while others may give some warning (hurricanes, volcanoes, etc.). In recent years the world has suffered notably and publicly from earthquakes, tsunamis (byproducts of undersea earthquakes), hurricanes, widespread wildfires, tornadoes, volcanoes, widespread floods, and widespread droughts. These weather- and Earth-related issues lead to secondary human issues such as famine and outbreak of disease. Some of these events are weather-related (e.g., hurricanes, tornadoes, droughts, wildfires due to lightning, floods) and some are seemingly not (earthquakes, volcanoes, tsunamis).

Earthquakes happen all over the world, although they are more common along fault lines. When fault lines (breaks between rock layers or sections) rub together or move above, below, or laterally next to each other, the energy released from rocks causes all the ground adjacent to the epicenter to move violently—resulting in an earthquake. The strength of an earthquake depends on how much movement occurs. The amount of damage that occurs to humans and man-made structures depends on where the epicenter of the quake occurs, how deep it was, how strong it was, and how far from a populated area it was. Some areas (e.g., the San Francisco Bay Area) are located on known fault lines where repeated earthquakes are known to occur. Over the years, governments in vulnerable areas have put building codes in place to ensure that all construction of buildings is done with special care to be able to withstand strong earthquakes. There are also special emergency plans in place in high-earthquake-frequency areas so that in the event of an earthquake people know where to go for shelter and medical care. There are special shelters designated for emergency purposes.

Over the long term, earthquakes can change the shape of the landscape permanently.

Volcanoes are generally found only where tectonic plates meet (see Fig. 3-4). Active volcanoes must be watched and are moderately predictable as a hazard.

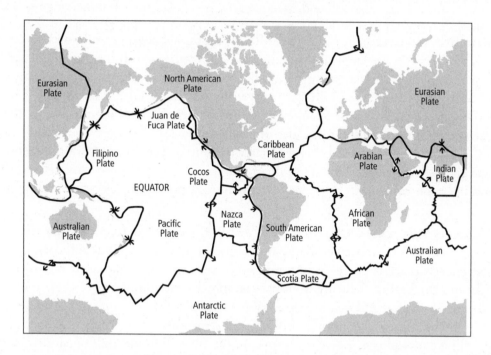

Fig. 3-4. Tectonic Plates. Volcanoes are likely to occur along the boundaries of these plates.

Hurricanes are weather-related hazards that can be partially predictable. Meteorologists can track hurricanes with some accuracy, allowing residents and government agencies to prepare in advance for a storm's arrival. Still, there is not absolute certainty to these predictions, and even with preparations, a hurricane can bring devastating effects through high winds, flooding, and erosion. There is a yearly hurricane season on both the Atlantic and Pacific U.S. coasts and equivalent types of storms on other shorelines throughout the world. Areas that are prone to hurricanes such as the Eastern and Gulf coasts have complex emergency plans in place with storm shelters and building codes to ensure that any new buildings are built to withstand hurricane force winds. After recent large storm flooding events in large cities, the possibilities of building storm walls, dikes, and levees that would more thoroughly protect cities from storm surge and flood waters are becoming bigger priorities in more places.

The recent worldwide disasters that have been weather-related, along with research that has noted changing weather patterns over the past one hundred years has sparked a debate regarding a potential concern regarding worldwide climate change. Many scientists posit that there is an overall change in our world climate that is occurring with the destruction of our atmospheric layering and even the slight rise in global temperatures over time. This hazard is thought to impact our globe with catastrophic effects of melting glacial ice, flooding continental areas, and long-range change in global weather patterns.

Extraction and use of natural resources, renewable vs. non-renewable resources, and sustainability

Resources can be classified into two different types—renewable and nonrenewable resources. Renewable resources can be used over and over again without running out. **Renewable** resources used for energy include solar energy (from the Sun) wind energy, geothermal energy (from inside the Earth), and hydropower (from moving water). Renewable energy sources are generally readily available but require extensive manpower and machinery to convert into usable energy such as electricity. Dams must be built in order to use hydropower. Vast solar arrays and wind farms are needed to capture solar or wind energy in large quantities. Special capture equipment is needed to harness geothermal energy. Still, all of these sources are good potential sources for future energy. Renewable resources tend to be cleaner energy sources, producing less waste and pollutants.

Nonrenewable resources are resources that are being used more quickly than they can be replaced. Examples of nonrenewable resources used for energy include oil, coal, natural gas, and nuclear energy. Nuclear energy is non-renewable because it uses radioactive elements, which are mined from the Earth. These are in limited supply. Extraction of any of these resources requires drilling and/or mining and then transport of the raw materials and sometimes refining those materials into useful forms. The mining, drilling, and transport can be dangerous since accidents such as oil spills are possible (as seen, for example, in the BP spill in the Gulf of Mexico in 2010). Since oil is not a natural part of any above ground habitat, an oil spill can destroy food sources and living habitats for generations unless it can be cleaned up. Mining can also leave land and habitats irrevocable damaged. These are trade-offs that are made when we gather non-renewable resources from the Earth to be used for energy.

Earth and Its System Components and Interactions

Characteristics of the atmosphere, including its layers, gasses and their effects on the Earth and its organisms, including climate change

Atmosphere

The atmosphere is comprised of several layers of gases immediately surrounding the Earth. Earth's atmosphere is an essential feature that allows our planet to sustain life. It extends approximately 560 km (350 miles) from the surface of the Earth, though the actual thickness varies from place to place. Our atmosphere makes Earth a habitable planet for people, plants, and animals by absorbing the Sun's energy, recycling and preserving water and chemicals needed for life, and by moderating our weather patterns. The atmosphere is attracted and maintained by the force of gravity of the Earth.

Without the protection of our atmosphere, Earth would be subjected to the extreme freezing temperatures found in the vacuum of space. The Earth would also be bombarded by dangerous amounts of radiant energy from the Sun. Earth's atmosphere (Fig. 3-5) is made up of about 78% nitrogen, 21% oxygen, slightly less than 1% argon, plus trace amounts of carbon dioxide, helium, hydrogen, krypton, methane, neon, nitrogen dioxide, nitrous oxide, ozone, sulfur dioxide, water vapor, and xenon.

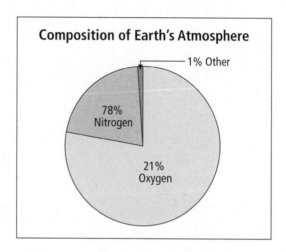

Fig. 3-5. Atmospheric Composition.

We identify five distinct layers (called strata) of Earth's atmosphere: the troposphere, stratosphere, mesosphere, thermosphere, and exosphere. Each layer differs from the others by its temperature, density, and chemical composition. Four transition zones separate the four atmospheric layers: the tropopause, stratopause, mesopause, and thermopause.

The **troposphere** is the atmospheric layer closest to the Earth's surface. It extends to an altitude of approximately 8 to 15 kilometers (5 to 9 miles). The force of gravity is strongest nearest the surface of the Earth, thus the number of gas molecules per area (density) is greatest at the lowest altitudes. In addition, the density of gas molecules decreases as altitude increases. Therefore, the troposphere is the densest atmospheric layer, accounting for most of the mass of the atmosphere.

The troposphere contains 99% of the water vapor found in the atmosphere. Water vapor in the air absorbs solar energy and absorbs heat that radiates back from the Earth's surface. The water vapor concentration within the troposphere is greatest near the equator and lowest at the poles.

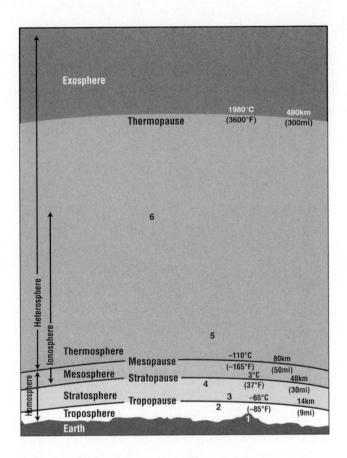

Fig. 3-6. Layers of the atmosphere.
1: Mt. Everest; 2: Commercial Jet; 3: Fighter Jet; 4: Ozone Layer; 5: Auroras; 6: Space Shuttle.

Nearly all weather phenomena experienced on Earth are caused by the interactions of gases (including water vapor) within the troposphere. The temperature of the troposphere decreases as altitude increases from about 16°C (60°F) nearest the Earth's surface to –65°C (–85°F) at the tropopause. (Temperatures are averages of all the temperatures over the surface of the Earth and across all seasons.) For every kilometer in altitude above the Earth, the temperature drops approximately 6°C within the troposphere.

The troposphere is separated from the next layer (the stratosphere) by the tropopause.

The **stratosphere** is above the troposphere. The stratosphere extends from the tropopause (found approximately 14 km or 9 miles above the Earth's surface) to approximately 48 km (30 miles) above the Earth's surface. The stratosphere contains much less water vapor than the troposphere. The gases of the stratosphere are much less dense than in the troposphere as well.

The temperature within the lower stratosphere (up to about 25km altitude) is mostly constant. In the upper stratosphere, the temperature rises gradually with increased altitude to a temperature of approximately 3°C. The rising temperatures are caused by the absorption of ultraviolet radiation from the Sun by ozone molecules.

Ozone (0_3) molecules form the ozone layer at the upper ranges of the stratosphere. Ozone molecules absorb solar ultraviolet radiation, which is converted to kinetic energy (heat). This process accounts for the increased temperature levels as altitude increases within the stratosphere. The ozone layer also performs the crucial function of protecting organisms from the harmful effects of too much ultraviolet radiation. The ozone layer can be depleted by interference of so-called greenhouse gases such as an excess of CO_2 and other hydrocarbons that build up in the atmosphere and trigger excess warming of the Earth. This is the proposed cause behind the theory of global warming—considered to be a potential source of recent climate change issues and a threat of more serious global climate change issues in the future.

The stratosphere is separated from the next atmospheric layer (the mesosphere) by the stratopause.

The **mesosphere** is the atmospheric layer found at approximately 50–80 km altitude. The mesosphere is characterized by temperatures decreasing with increased altitude from about 3°C at the stratopause to −110°C at 80km. The mesosphere has a low density of molecules with very little ozone or water vapor. The atmospheric gases of the upper mesosphere separate into layers of gases according to molecular mass. This phenomenon is caused by the weakened effects of gravity on the gas molecules (because of distance from Earth). Lighter (low molecular mass) gases are found at the higher altitudes.

The mesopause separates the stratosphere from the next layer, the thermosphere.

The **thermosphere** is found at altitudes of approximately 80 to 480 kilometers. Gas molecules of the thermosphere are widely separated, resulting in very low gas density. The absorption of solar radiation by oxygen molecules in the thermosphere causes the temperature to rise to approximately 1980°C at the upper levels of the thermosphere.

The final layer, the **exosphere** extends from the thermopause at approximately 480km to an altitude of 960 to 1000 kilometers. The exosphere, however, is difficult to define and is more of a transitional area between Earth and space than a distinct layer. The low gravitational forces at this altitude hold only the lightest molecules, mostly hydrogen and helium. Even these are at very low densities.

In addition to the names of the five atmospheric layers, some other terms describe various levels of the atmosphere. The troposphere and tropopause together are sometimes referred to as the "lower atmosphere." The stratosphere and mesosphere are sometimes called the "middle atmosphere," while the thermosphere and exosphere are together known as the "upper atmosphere." Still other scientists describe the troposphere, mesosphere, and stratosphere together as the "homosphere," and the thermosphere and exosphere as the "heterosphere."

The ionosphere includes portions of the mesosphere and thermosphere. The term **ionosphere** refers to the portion of the atmosphere where ultraviolet radiation causes excitation of atoms resulting in extreme temperatures. Under extreme temperature conditions, electrons are actually separated from the atoms. The highly excited atoms are left with a positive charge. Charged atoms (ions) form layers within the thermosphere. The charged layers are referred to as the ionosphere. The charged particles within the ionosphere deflect some radio signals. While some radio frequencies are not affected by the ionosphere, others are. This reflection of some radio signals causes some radio frequencies (particularly AM transmissions) to be received far from their origination point—often hundreds of miles.

Solar flares create magnetic storms in the thermosphere near Earth's poles. These storms temporarily strip electrons from atoms. When the electrons rejoin the atoms, brilliant light (in green and red) is emitted as they return to their normal state. These lights are called auroras, or the Northern and Southern lights.

The total weight of the atmosphere exerts force on the Earth. This force is known as **atmospheric pressure** and can be measured with a barometer.

Characteristics of the oceans (e.g., salt water, currents, coral reefs) and their effects on Earth and organisms

Oceans cover more than 70% of the Earth's surface. The impact of oceans on Earth's climate, habitats, weather, and the ability to sustain life is huge. Oceans are filled with salt water, meaning the composition is H_2O mixed with positive and negative ions and other trace minerals (see Fig. 3-7).

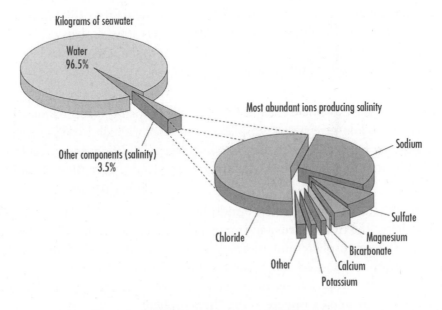

Fig. 3-7. Chemical Composition of Ocean Water

Since the oceans cover an expanse from pole to pole, there is a wide range of temperatures of ocean waters at all times. There is also variation in temperatures caused by the depth of the ocean, with the surface receiving sunlight and the depths being dark, and some areas being near hydrothermal hot vents and others near icy glaciers. Temperature gradients induce movement of water that stirs and causes currents to flow. There are large regular current systems in the world's oceans, such as the Gulf Stream, that carry streams of warm water through otherwise cool or cold regions of ocean.

Currents may also be caused by gradients (differences) in salinity. Entire habitats may live in a particular current system or in an area of a particular temperature, such as a hydrothermal vent community. (Sea water in a hydrothermal vent is heated by hot magma, reaching temperatures of over 700°F, yet it doesn't boil because of the extreme pressure at the lowest depths.) Other habitats, such as coral reefs, exist in calm shallow waters in tropical climate zones. Reef structures are built from coral polyps; when the living polyps die, their calcium carbonate shells are left behind to serve as a structure for other plants and animals to live in and on. The living coral continue to build on the shells of the prior coral and a myriad of fish, mollusks, turtles, worms, sea plants, and other sea species make their home in the coral complex.

Fig. 3-8. Coral reef near Bermuda.

The algae (phytoplankton) in the ocean is responsible for about 70% of the current oxygen production on Earth. The temperature of the Earth is moderated by the vast amount of ocean surface, and much of Earth's weather patterns are derived from marine weather systems.

Interactions between Earth's systems (e.g., weathering caused by wind or water on rock, wind caused by high/low pressure and Earth rotation, etc.)

The Earth as a whole acts as a **closed system** where the oceans and land masses interact in ways that cause repeating cycles of weather patterns of seasons with occasional unusual weather events. Warming of air masses in one place causes differences in air temperature, which induces movement. When air is heated, it expands, becomes lighter and rises. Cooler, heavier air falls back toward the Earth and replaces the warmer, rising air. The cooler air is heated at Earth's surface and rises again as it is warmed. The movement of warmer, lighter air and cooler, heavier air forms a cycle of air movement. This cycle is called wind.

The weight of the air pressing down on the Earth is called **air pressure**. Air pressure decreases as you move higher and higher away from land since there is less air above pressing down.

Air pressure also increases and decreases depending on weather conditions. High pressure is generally associated with good weather and low pressure is generally associated with deteriorating weather conditions. Colder air is more dense, and warmer air less dense.

In addition to air pressure and temperature affecting air movement, the Earth is also rotating, causing actual movement and frictional forces of air molecules against each other and the Earth as it rotates.

Therefore, *the atmosphere is in constant motion*. Weather changes as wind moves large bodies of air from one location to another according to how the factors of rotation, air pressure, and temperature are interacting at any given time. Large bodies of air share about the same temperature, humidity (moisture), and pressure throughout. If there were no wind, then weather would stay the same.

Wind, in turn, causes waves and some of the movement of water. Other types of water movement, like tides, is caused by gravitational pull from the Moon and Sun, or runoff by gravity (moving downhill). The force of both water and wind movement can cause weathering, the wearing down of rock.

Fig. 3-9. Weathered Rock

Interior structure of the Earth (e.g., core, mantle, crust, tectonic plates) and its effects (e.g., volcanoes, earthquakes, etc.) and major landforms of the Earth (e.g., mountains, ocean basins, continental shelves, etc.)

Layers of the Earth

The Earth consists of layers, from the outer crust down to the inner core, separated according to density and temperature. There are two ways to classify the composition of the Earth's layers:

1. chemically, into crust, mantle, and core, or

2. functionally, into lithosphere and asthenosphere.

The density of the Earth averages three times that of water. This density varies depending upon the layer of the Earth being considered. The crust is the outermost layer of what we think of as "the Earth." It includes the mountains, valleys, continents, continental shelves, ocean basins, etc. The crust is rich in oxygen, silicon, and aluminum, with lesser amounts of other elements like iron, nickel, etc. It has low density (2.5 to 3.5 gm/cm^3), that allows it to float on the denser mantle. It is brittle and breaks relatively easily. It is made up mostly of sedimentary rocks resting on a base of igneous rocks. Several separate tectonic plates float beneath it on the surface of the mantle. The tectonic plates touch but magma can leak between the plates, at times causing volcanoes or the formation of under ocean ridges of new rock. The brittleness of the crust rocks allows for breakage and slipping between large portions of plates of rock along fault lines, causing earthquakes that can shake large regions. Many of Earth's major landforms are features that occurred due to tectonic plates hitting each other causing folding of rock into mountains or slipping of one plate under another forming a continental shelf. Careful study of the tectonic plates and the land formations between them will reveal how the formations came to be.

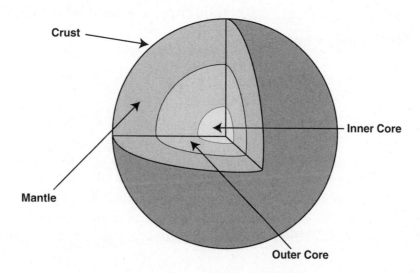

Fig. 3-10. Layers of the Earth.

It is estimated that the entire surface of the Earth can reform in about 500 million years through erosion and subsequent recreation through tectonic activity.

The **mantle** is the complex middle layer of the geosphere. It is a broad layer of dense rock and metal oxides that lies between the molten core and the crust and extends to a depth of between 40 to 2,900 kilometers. It accounts for around 82% of the Earth's volume and is thought to be made up mostly of iron, magnesium, silicon, and oxygen. From the study of earthquake waves we know that the mantle consists of rigid and plastic zones.

The **core** is the innermost layer composed of mostly iron and nickel. It extends from a depth of about 2,900 kilometers to nearly 6,400 kilometers (1,800 to 3,900 miles). It is extremely hot, even after millions of years of cooling. The core has two layers, the liquid outer core, and the solid iron inner core at the Earth's center. Even with the high temperatures at the center (up to 7,500 K, hotter than the Sun's surface), this layer is solid due to the immense pressure of the overlying layers. The material that makes up the Earth's interior is similar to that of liquid steel.

Another way to classify the layers is into the lithosphere and asthenosphere. The rigid outermost layer is called the **lithosphere**. The upper layer of the lithosphere is the crust. Beneath the crust is a layer of rigid mantle. The **asthenosphere** is the molten plastic outer mantle of hot silicate rock beneath the lithosphere.

Structures and Organization of the Cosmos

Structures in the universe (e.g., galaxies, stars, constellations, solar systems), the age and development of the universe, and the age and development of stars (e.g., main sequence, stellar development, deaths of stars [black hole, white dwarf])

Galaxies

A **galaxy** is a system that contains stars, star systems (like our solar system), dust, and any other objects within range of the gravitation of its star systems. While all galaxies are massive in scale, the galaxy our solar system resides in, the Milky Way, is thought to be average in size. It is known to contain hundreds of billions of stars including our Sun. Galaxies come in a myriad of shapes and take on various overall colors, but ours is a rotating spiral of milky white. It is theorized that at the center of most galaxies is a black hole. Recent data from space probes and telescopes has given us important insight into the nature of black holes. Scientists theorize that these incredibly dense areas of matter arise from remnants of a large star (or the collision of stars) that implodes after a supernova explosion. Once the mass of the star becomes large enough it collapses under the force of its own gravity. As it collapses, the surface of the star nears an imaginary surface called the "event horizon," as time there on the star becomes slower than the time kept by observers far away. When the surface reaches the event horizon, time stands still, and the star can collapse no more. This object contains gravity enough to pull entire star systems into its grasp.

Photo courtesy of NASA

Fig. 3-11. Center of Milky Way Galaxy orbiting a black hole.

Stars

The core of our Sun, along with most stars, begins with hydrogen. With the core temperature of stars being over 10 million Kelvin, and given the tremendous pressures they contain, protons can fuse together to produce helium, gamma ray energy, positrons and neutrinos. These neutrinos are nearly massless and charge-less. They do not interact with other matter very much and flow almost unimpeded throughout the universe. It is speculated that neutrinos produced in the center of the Sun sweep through the average human's body here on Earth at a rate of billions per second.

Stars are huge masses of plasma with colossal amounts of energy and gravity. Many stars are held in by magnetic fields, but particles slip through occasional holes in the fields. The atoms are so hot, the protons, neutrons, and electrons move rapidly and react with each other, thus releasing energy. This energy moves out from stars in electromagnetic waves producing heat and light. We are too far from most stars to notice their heat, but their light still reaches us.

The stars consist of incredible amounts of matter. Since we know all matter has gravity, stars have very large gravitational forces. Many stars have their own systems, like our solar system, with planets, asteroids, and moons orbiting them.

The stars are arrayed in the sky in patterns that ancient peoples named for various creatures and objects (scales, scorpions, archers, etc.). We call these the **zodiac**. Travelers have used the zodiac for navigation since biblical times. In addition, Polaris, the North Star, sits directly over our North Pole so it can be used to determine directions on the Earth.

Current scientific theory including the **theory** of the **Big Bang**, describes the birth of our universe as a massive explosion occurring approximately fifteen billion years ago. The matter and energy that became the universe was compacted into an infinitely small area then began an expansion process at an explosive rate that slowed down over time but that is theorized to still be occurring. The simplest components of matter, protons, neutrons, electrons, came into being and over time condensed into particles of matter. Over hundreds of thousands of years of expansion and cooling, gases condensed and stars were formed, then galaxies, and much later solar systems.

Since the beginning of the universe stars have been forming and dying. Stars begin as large masses of dust and cosmic gasses that collapse together due to gravitational forces. This process of collapse may take millions of years, and during this time the mass is called a **nebulae** or a proto-star. Over time a process of nuclear fusion of hydrogen (and later helium) atoms begins to power the star at its core, and this will fuel it as a main sequence star for the rest of its life. As the star grows in size, powered by the nuclear fusion reactor at its core, it eventually reaches a **red giant** phase. Our sun is a red giant. Eventually the star will consume its supply of nuclear fuel, and the core will collapse on itself due to its own gravity. At this point it is called a **white dwarf**. Very large stars may explode into supernovas, then coalesce into a dense neutron star or a black hole.

Sun, planets, moons (e.g., types of planets, comets, asteroids), the motion of the Earth and the interactions within the Earth's solar system (e.g., tides, eclipses)

The Sun

Our Sun is a star of mid-size that emits heat and light energy. There are stars much larger than our Sun, and stars that are smaller. Our star, the Sun, is about ten times more massive than the largest planet in the solar system (Jupiter) and 109 times larger than the Earth's diameter.

The Sun releases incredible amounts of energy as protons interact with each other (nuclear fusion). The energy is in the form of heat and light radiation, providing heat and light for life on Earth.

The Solar System

Our **solar system** consists of all of the common celestial bodies such as planets, moons, asteroids, and various types of space debris that orbit our star, the Sun.

A **planet** is a celestial body that (a) is in orbit around the Sun, (b) has sufficient mass for its self-gravity to assume a nearly round shape, and (c) has cleared the neighborhood around its orbit.

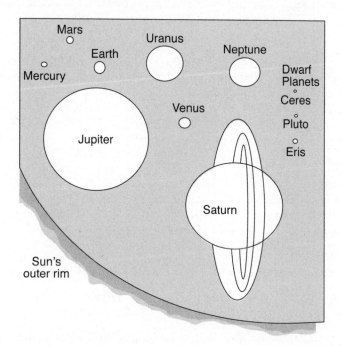

Fig. 3-12. Approximate relative sizes of planets and dwarf planets in relation to the Sun.

The characteristics of the planets vary greatly because of their size, composition, and distance from the Sun. It is easy to remember the eight planets in order, starting with the closest to the Sun, by learning the following mnemonic sentence: My Very Educated Mother Just Served Us Noodles. The beginning letter of each word in this sentence is the first letter of a planet's name (Mercury, Venus, Earth, Mars, Jupiter, Saturn, Uranus, and Neptune).

Planet	Type of Planet	Size (to nearest thousand)	Average Distance from Sun (in Miles/Km)	Number of Moons
Mercury	Terrestrial	3,000 mi (5,000 km)	36 million miles (58 million km)	0
Venus	Terrestrial	8,000 mi (12,000 km)	67 million miles (108 million km)	0
Earth	Terrestrial	8,000 mi (13,000 km)	93 million mi. (150 million km)	1
Mars	Terrestrial	4,000 mi (7,000 km)	142 million mi. (228 million km.)	2
Jupiter	Gas Giant	89,000 mi (143,000 km)	483 million mi. (778 million km.)	67
Saturn	Gas Giant	75,000 mi (120,000 km)	885 million mi. (1,426 million km.)	62
Uranus	Gas Giant	32,000 mi (51,000 km)	1,787 million mi. (2,877 milion km.)	27
Neptune	Gas Giant	31,000 mi (50,000 km)	2,800 million mi. (4.508 million km.)	13

Table 3-1. Our Solar System

From the table above you can note several trends about the planets of our solar system. The terrestrial planets are so named because they are made composed of solid elements. As distance from the Sun increases, so does the size of the planet, and from that information you can infer that the mass of the planet also increases. The planets inside the asteroid belt (which lies outside Mars's orbit) are significantly larger and have more mass. The composition of these planets is also different. Being farther from the Sun, they are much colder and are composed of mostly gases with huge atmospheric layers. They are called the Gas Giants. Their distance from the Sun means their orbital around the Sun is much longer, making their year much longer. These planets also have much stronger gravitational attraction, since gravity is a function of mass. Therefore they have captured many more moons into their orbit than the smaller terrestrial planets.

In addition to the planets orbiting our Sun, our solar system also has asteroids and several other minor planets and other space objects. Asteroids are irregular masses of rock and metal that are smaller than planets. There is an asteroid belt between Mars and Jupiter and another beyond the orbit of Neptune.

The outer Solar System is home to comets—masses of frozen gas that travel in orbital patterns. At times comets travel near the Sun, where the tail of the comet begins to melt and form a stream of gas which gives them a long, extended look.

Courtesy of NASA

Fig. 3-13. Halley's Comet

Our calendar year is a measure of the time the Earth takes in orbiting the Sun. Each year Earth completes one trip around the Sun in about 365 days. The seasons we experience are a result of the inclination of the Earth on its axis. That is, if you draw a line through the Earth's poles, this line is not perpendicular with its orbit around the Sun (see Fig. 3-14).

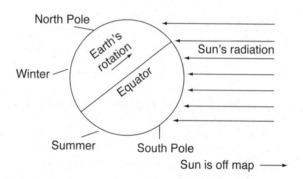

Fig. 3-14. Tilt of the Earth and seasons.

The Earth's axis tilts at an angle of twenty-three and one-half degrees with its orbit. The tilt means that the Northern Hemisphere will be tilted toward the Sun for half the orbit, and the Southern Hemisphere will be tilted for the other half (half-a-year). The hemisphere tilted toward the Sun absorbs more of the solar radiation during that half of the year and experiences summer. The hemisphere tilted away from the Sun experiences winter.

The orbit of the Moon around the Earth occurs approximately every twenty-nine days. This is the origin of our months. A day is the time the Earth takes to rotate one time on its axis. An hour is simply a division of the rotation of the Earth (one day) obtained by taking the globe and dividing it into twenty-four time zones.

The Moon

Our view of the Moon is constantly changing as the Moon orbits Earth and as Earth rotates on its axis. Our daily view of the Moon changes as it moves around Earth along its regular orbital path. The changes we see in the shape and location of the Moon are regular in their occurrence because of the regular nature of the rotation and orbit. The Moon orbits around the Earth once approximately every twenty nine days (one lunar month). The Moon's rotation on its axis is synchronous with its orbit, so we always see the same side of the Moon reflecting the sunlight.

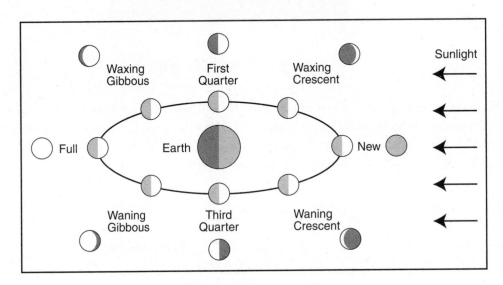

Fig. 3-15. The Phases of Earth's Moon.

The Moon does not emit any of its own light, but reflects the light from the Sun. Our daily view of the Moon changes during its orbit of the Earth. The phases that we see are a result of the angle between the Earth, Moon, and Sun as viewed by us from Earth.

A new moon occurs when the Moon is directly between the Earth and the Sun. At this point, the Moon will rise at about 6:00 a.m. and set at about 6:00 p.m. (on standard, not daylight saving, time). The lighted side of the Moon is toward the Sun, so our view is of the dark side only (we don't see it at all).

Following the new moon, the Moon (continuing its orbit) moves so that we see an increasing portion of the lit side each night. We call this the waxing crescent moon.

In about a week's time, the angle between the Earth, Sun, and Moon is 90°, allowing us to see half the Moon's lighted surface, the first quarter. This 90° angle means the Moon rises halfway through the day at about noon, and sets at about midnight.

For the following week, we see more of the Moon's surface each night (waxing gibbous) until the full moon, which marks the middle of the lunar orbit (and the lunar month).

During the full moon, the Earth/Moon/Sun angle is 180°, meaning the Earth is between the Sun and the Moon so we see the entire bright half of its surface. The full moon rises near sundown and sets near sunrise, opposite the Sun (see Fig. 3-16).

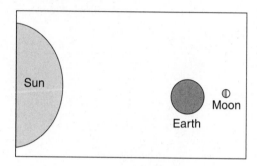

Fig. 3-16. Positioning of Full Moon.

During the remaining two weeks of the lunar month, the Moon wanes through another gibbous moon to the third quarter (the other half of the Moon's lit surface is visible rising around midnight and setting at noon). It wanes through another crescent moon until it returns to the beginning of the orbital—the new moon.

We view the Moon "rising" in the east and "setting" in the west as the Earth rotates on its axis. The Moon's orbit is nearly in the same plane as the orbits of the planets around the Sun, so we view the Moon near that plane in the sky called the **ecliptic**. The tilt of the Earth on its axis means the ecliptic is visible (to those in the northern hemisphere of the Earth) in the southern sky at varying heights through the seasons.

At most times, the angle between the Sun, Moon, and Earth at full and new moon is such that there is no blockage of the view of the Moon or Sun. However, when it happens during a full moon that the Earth lies directly in the path between the Earth viewer and the Moon, it is called a lunar eclipse, since the Earth will exactly block the light of the Sun from reaching the Moon for a period of time.

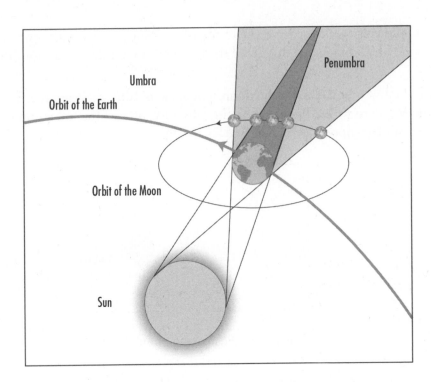

Fig. 3-17. Lunar eclipse positions of Earth, Sun, Moon.

During a new moon, on occasion, the Moon falls in direct line between the Sun and Earth so that it causes a shaded area on the Earth. That portion of the Earth then experiences a solar eclipse where the Sun's light is temporarily blocked by the Moon. Because the Sun is so much larger than the Moon, the area of a Solar eclipse is very small in relation to the entire Earth. Schedules for solar eclipses, where and when they will occur, can be determined and found on various sites on the Internet.

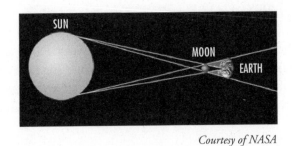

Courtesy of NASA

Fig. 3-18. Solar eclipse positions of Earth, Sun, Moon.

The Moon is 1/4 the diameter of the Earth with about 1/80th the mass of the Earth. The gravity from the Moon pulls the ocean causing it to bulge and rise on one side while it lowers on the other as the Earth rotates and the Moon orbits forming tides. The Sun has some gravitational effect on tides, but not as much as the Moon. Tides rise and fall daily with the rotation of the Earth and especially high (spring tides) occur during full and new moons while especially low (neap tides) occur during first and third quarters (see Fig. 3-19).

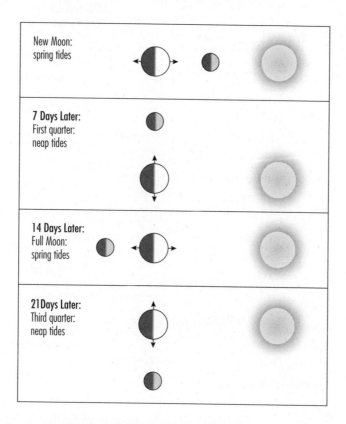

Fig. 3-19. Spring and Neap Tide position of Earth, Sun, and Moon.

The age of the Earth, including radiometrics, fossils, and landforms

The Geologic column is the layers of the Earth near the surface that contain fossils and various types of sediment. The layers are categorized by Eras, Periods, and Epochs. The estimated age of Earth, determined by radiometric dating and geological estimates, is about 4.6 billion years.

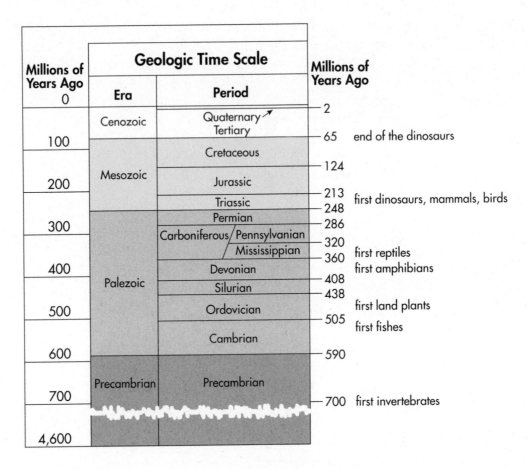

Fig. 3-20. Geologic History of Earth

The ages of each layer are determined using radiometric dating methods, by determining the amount of certain radioactive elements that have decayed in a given sample from their originating elements. By extrapolating backward, scientists can estimate the age of the rock they are testing. In addition, geologists can study landforms and how sediments are laid down and what fossils they contain to determine their age. If a layer of sediment contains only invertebrates then it is likely Precambrian. See the Geologic Time Scale chart for details of the various geologic Eras, the time spans, and dominant fossil life for that period.

PRACTICE!

1. Why is stratospheric ozone depletion (destruction of the ozone layer) a serious concern?

    A. It is a major cause of the "greenhouse effect."

    B. It will increase the amount of ultraviolet radiation reaching the ground.

    C. It causes acid rain.

    D. It leads to global warming as more radiation enters through the hole in the atmosphere.

2. If the Moon completely covers the Sun as seen by an earthbound observer, there is a

    A. total lunar eclipse.

    B. total solar eclipse.

    C. partial lunar eclipse.

    D. partial solar eclipse.

3. A light-year represents the

    A. total amount of light energy that travels past a point on Earth in one year.

    B. total distance that an object travels in space in one year.

    C. total amount of time that a photon of light travels in order to reach a star, planet, or other extraterrestrial object.

    D. distance that a photon of light travels in a year.

4. Which of the following statements is TRUE?

    A. Despite the contraction of space, galaxies appear to be static relative to each other when observed.

    B. The expansion of space makes galaxies appear to be moving apart, causing the color of their spectral lines to shift when observed.

    C. Galaxies themselves are moving apart from each other.

    D. Hubble's law states that the redshift in light coming from a distant galaxy is inversely proportional to its distance from Earth.

5. Mountain and valley breezes form because of

    A. gravity and the pressure gradient force.

    B. the pressure gradient force and heating.

    C. gravity and heating.

    D. the pressure gradient force and the Coriolis force.

Science Practice 3 Answers

1. **B.**

    The "greenhouse effect" is the result of radiation being blocked from leaving the atmosphere because of the ozone layer. Depletion of the ozone layer would impact the "greenhouse effect," not cause it. The "greenhouse effect" is also believed to be caused mainly by other atmospheric gases such as water vapor and carbon dioxide. This depletion will increase radiation because the hole in the ozone layer will get larger. Acid rain is primarily caused by oxides of sulfur and nitrogen due to pollution. Photochemical reactions involving oxides of nitrogen and chloro-fluorocarbons play a major role in ozone destruction. These chemicals react with ozone and lead to a net decrease in ozone concentration in the stratosphere. Since ozone is a strong absorber of incoming ultraviolet (UV) radiation, any decrease in ozone concentration will increase the amount of UV radiation reaching the surface. This will, in turn, significantly increase the risk of skin cancer from exposure to the Sun.

2. **B.**

    The eclipse must be a solar eclipse because the Moon is between the Earth and the Sun. The solar eclipse is total because the Moon's disk covers the Sun from our view completely.

3. **D.**

    A light-year is a distance, not a speed or velocity. It is also not a time measurement. A light-year represents the distance light (a photon) travels in one year.

4. **B.**

    Although it appears that galaxies are moving apart, Hubble's law explains that this apparent motion is the expansion of the space between them, not the motion of the galaxies themselves. Hubble's law states that the redshift in light coming from a distant galaxy is directly and linearly proportional to its distance from Earth.

5. **C.**

The pressure gradient force plays no significant role in vertical air circulations. Since temperature decreases with height, as the valley air warms during the day, it becomes less dense than the air along the adjacent hillsides and begins to flow up the surrounding slopes. At night, air in the hills cools faster than the air in the valleys. Gravity pulls the cooler, denser air down the hillsides into the valleys. It is low pressure near the top of the mountain that forces breezes up from the valley.

Chapter 4

Science Practices

In addition to the three content areas of Life Science, Physical Science, and Earth and Space Science, the GED® test assesses knowledge of Science Practices. Each question on the GED® Science test incorporates one Science Practice skill along with one or more of the content areas. This chapter provides an explanation of the Science Practice skills and ideas that you should know to perform well on the GED® test.

Comprehending Scientific Presentations

Understand and explain textual scientific presentations.

You should be prepared to be able to understand text that explains scientific information. In addition to understanding the review material in the content sections of this book, it would be very valuable if you took the time to read some articles in current science magazines as well. These will prepare you for up to date understanding of science material, vocabulary, and practices.

Determine the meaning of symbols, terms, and phrases as they are used in scientific presentations.

While reading scientific text, you should be able to recognize common scientific textual tools such as symbols in chemical and physics equations, scientific terms, degree and other symbols, and phrases that are commonly used in science. The content review of this book is designed to familiarize you with these tools.

Examples of symbols would include those in this chemical equation:

$$CH_4 + 2O_2 \rightarrow CO_2 + 2H_2O$$

In this equation the letters stand for elements in the **Periodic Table of the Elements** (see page 527), the subscript numbers tell how many atoms of the element directly previous, and the coefficient number (large number before) tells the number of molecules of the compound. The plus signs mean "combine" and the arrow means "yield" or "combines to make."

Symbols are also used throughout science to represent concepts that are able to be manipulated by equations. For example, let's look at the following equation:

$$v = f\lambda$$

v = velocity (speed) of a wave; f = frequency of the wave; and λ = wavelength

There are terms that are used in a unique way in science, different than they are used in the everyday world. You should be able to distinguish meanings of these terms when reading scientific text. For example, the term "control" has a specific meaning in a scientific context that is different from the colloquial definition of control. In science, the control is that portion of an experiment for which the outcome is known and can be compared to the treatment group. Consider the term "polar," which in science generally refers to having oppositely charged ends, not the existence of a cold climate.

There are also many phrases that are meaningful only in a scientific context, such as "absolute zero" (the theoretical temperature at which all molecular movement would stop, zero K) and "continental drift" (the very slow movement of continents away from the upwelling of lava under the Atlantic Ocean).

Understand and explain a non-textual scientific presentation.

You should be prepared to explain scientific charts, graphs, diagrams, pictures, etc. The examples in the text and in the practice questions in this book should help you with this. For instance, scientific data is often presented in chart form that is then converted to a graph. In the example that follows, we see temperature graphed by day in the form of variables—where the independent variable is the day (the thing that is considered changing as the test variable) and the dependent variable (that which is being recorded as the response to the test). Once the data is collected on the chart, it can be graphed.

PERIODIC TABLE
Atomic Properties of the Elements

NIST
National Institute of Standards and Technology
U.S. Department of Commerce

Physics Laboratory
physics.nist.gov

Standard Reference Data
www.nist.gov/srd

Frequently used fundamental physical constants

For the most accurate values of these and other constants, visit physics.nist.gov/constants
1 second = 9 192 631 770 periods of radiation corresponding to the transition between the two hyperfine levels of the ground state of ^{133}Cs

speed of light in vacuum	c	299 792 458 m s^{-1}	(exact)
Planck constant	h	6.6261×10^{-34} J s	($\hbar = h/2\pi$)
elementary charge	e	1.6022×10^{-19} C	
electron mass	m_e	9.1094×10^{-31} kg	
	$m_e c^2$	0.5110 MeV	
proton mass	m_p	1.6726×10^{-27} kg	
fine-structure constant	α	1/137.036	
Rydberg constant	R_∞	10 973 732 m^{-1}	
	$R_\infty c$	$3.289 842 \times 10^{15}$ Hz	
	$R_\infty hc$	13.6057 eV	
Boltzmann constant	k	1.3807×10^{-23} J K^{-1}	

Legend: Solids, Liquids, Gases, Artificially Prepared

Legend (key example)
- Atomic Number: 58
- Symbol: Ce
- Name: Cerium
- Atomic Weight†: 140.116
- Ground-state Configuration: [Xe]4f5d6s^2
- Ground-state Level: $^1G_4°$
- Ionization Energy (eV): 5.5387

Group 1 / IA
1 — H — Hydrogen — 1.00794 — 1s — 13.5984 — $^2S_{1/2}$

Group 2 / IIA
- 3 Li Lithium 6.941 1s^{2}2s 5.3917 $^2S_{1/2}$
- 4 Be Beryllium 9.012182 1s^{2}2s^2 9.3227 $^1S_0$
- 11 Na Sodium 22.98976928 [Ne]3s 5.1391 $^2S_{1/2}$
- 12 Mg Magnesium 24.3050 [Ne]3s^2 7.6462 $^1S_0$
- 19 K Potassium 39.0983 [Ar]4s 4.3407 $^2S_{1/2}$
- 20 Ca Calcium 40.078 [Ar]4s^2 6.1132 $^1S_0$
- 37 Rb Rubidium 85.4678 [Kr]5s 4.1771 $^2S_{1/2}$
- 38 Sr Strontium 87.62 [Kr]5s^2 5.6949 $^1S_0$
- 55 Cs Cesium 132.9054519 [Xe]6s 3.8939 $^2S_{1/2}$
- 56 Ba Barium 137.327 [Xe]6s^2 5.2117 $^1S_0$
- 87 Fr Francium (223) [Rn]7s 4.0727 $^2S_{1/2}$
- 88 Ra Radium (226) [Rn]7s^2 5.2784 $^1S_0$

Group 3 / IIIB
- 21 Sc Scandium 44.955912 [Ar]3d4s^2 6.5615 $^2D_{3/2}$
- 39 Y Yttrium 88.90585 [Kr]4d5s^2 6.2173 $^2D_{3/2}$

Group 4 / IVB
- 22 Ti Titanium 47.867 [Ar]3d^{2}4s^2 6.8281 $^3F_2$
- 40 Zr Zirconium 91.224 [Kr]4d^{2}5s^2 6.6339 $^3F_2$
- 72 Hf Hafnium 178.49 [Xe]4f^{14}5d^{2}6s^2 6.8251 $^3F_2$
- 104 Rf Rutherfordium (265) [Rn]5f^{14}6d^{2}7s^2 6.0? $^3F_2$

Group 5 / VB
- 23 V Vanadium 50.9415 [Ar]3d^{3}4s^2 6.7462 $^4F_{3/2}$
- 41 Nb Niobium 92.90638 [Kr]4d^{4}5s 6.7589 $^6D_{1/2}$
- 73 Ta Tantalum 180.94788 [Xe]4f^{14}5d^{3}6s^2 7.5496 $^4F_{3/2}$
- 105 Db Dubnium (268)

Group 6 / VIB
- 24 Cr Chromium 51.9961 [Ar]3d^{5}4s 6.7665 $^7S_3$
- 42 Mo Molybdenum 95.96 [Kr]4d^{5}5s 7.0924 $^7S_3$
- 74 W Tungsten 183.84 [Xe]4f^{14}5d^{4}6s^2 7.8640 $^5D_0$
- 106 Sg Seaborgium (271)

Group 7 / VIIB
- 25 Mn Manganese 54.938045 [Ar]3d^{5}4s^2 7.4340 $^6S_{5/2}$
- 43 Tc Technetium (98) [Kr]4d^{5}5s^2 7.28 $^6S_{5/2}$
- 75 Re Rhenium 186.207 [Xe]4f^{14}5d^{5}6s^2 7.8335 $^6S_{5/2}$
- 107 Bh Bohrium (272)

Group 8 / VIII
- 26 Fe Iron 55.845 [Ar]3d^{6}4s^2 7.9024 $^5D_4$
- 44 Ru Ruthenium 101.07 [Kr]4d^{7}5s 7.3605 $^5F_5$
- 76 Os Osmium 190.23 [Xe]4f^{14}5d^{6}6s^2 8.4382 $^5D_4$
- 108 Hs Hassium (277)

Group 9 / VIII
- 27 Co Cobalt 58.933195 [Ar]3d^{7}4s^2 7.8810 $^4F_{9/2}$
- 45 Rh Rhodium 102.90550 [Kr]4d^{8}5s 7.4589 $^4F_{9/2}$
- 77 Ir Iridium 192.217 [Xe]4f^{14}5d^{7}6s^2 8.9670 $^4F_{9/2}$
- 109 Mt Meitnerium (276)

Group 10 / VIII
- 28 Ni Nickel 58.6934 [Ar]3d^{8}4s^2 7.6399 $^3F_4$
- 46 Pd Palladium 106.42 [Kr]4d^{10} 8.3369 $^1S_0$
- 78 Pt Platinum 195.084 [Xe]4f^{14}5d^{9}6s 8.9588 $^3D_3$
- 110 Ds Darmstadtium (281)

Group 11 / IB
- 29 Cu Copper 63.546 [Ar]3d^{10}4s 7.7264 $^2S_{1/2}$
- 47 Ag Silver 107.8682 [Kr]4d^{10}5s 7.5762 $^2S_{1/2}$
- 79 Au Gold 196.966569 [Xe]4f^{14}5d^{10}6s 9.2255 $^2S_{1/2}$
- 111 Rg Roentgenium (280)

Group 12 / IIB
- 30 Zn Zinc 65.38 [Ar]3d^{10}4s^2 9.3942 $^1S_0$
- 48 Cd Cadmium 112.411 [Kr]4d^{10}5s^2 8.9938 $^1S_0$
- 80 Hg Mercury 200.59 [Xe]4f^{14}5d^{10}6s^2 10.4375 $^1S_0$
- 112 Cn Copernicium (285)

Group 13 / IIIA
- 5 B Boron 10.811 1s^{2}2s^{2}2p 8.2980 $^2P_{1/2}°$
- 13 Al Aluminum 26.9815386 [Ne]3s^{2}3p 5.9858 $^2P_{1/2}°$
- 31 Ga Gallium 69.723 [Ar]3d^{10}4s^{2}4p 5.9993 $^2P_{1/2}°$
- 49 In Indium 114.818 [Kr]4d^{10}5s^{2}5p 5.7864 $^2P_{1/2}°$
- 81 Tl Thallium 204.3833 [Xe]4f^{14}5d^{10}6s^{2}6p 6.1082 $^2P_{1/2}°$
- 113 Uut Ununtrium (284)

Group 14 / IVA
- 6 C Carbon 12.0107 1s^{2}2s^{2}2p^2 11.2603 $^3P_0$
- 14 Si Silicon 28.0855 [Ne]3s^{2}3p^2 8.1517 $^3P_0$
- 32 Ge Germanium 72.64 [Ar]3d^{10}4s^{2}4p^2 7.8994 $^3P_0$
- 50 Sn Tin 118.710 [Kr]4d^{10}5s^{2}5p^2 7.3439 $^3P_0$
- 82 Pb Lead 207.2 [Xe]4f^{14}5d^{10}6s^{2}6p^2 7.4167 $^3P_0$
- 114 Uuq Ununquadium (289)

Group 15 / VA
- 7 N Nitrogen 14.0067 1s^{2}2s^{2}2p^3 14.5341 $^4S_{3/2}°$
- 15 P Phosphorus 30.973762 [Ne]3s^{2}3p^3 10.4867 $^4S_{3/2}°$
- 33 As Arsenic 74.92160 [Ar]3d^{10}4s^{2}4p^3 9.7886 $^4S_{3/2}°$
- 51 Sb Antimony 121.760 [Kr]4d^{10}5s^{2}5p^3 8.6084 $^4S_{3/2}°$
- 83 Bi Bismuth 208.98040 [Xe]4f^{14}5d^{10}6s^{2}6p^3 7.2855 $^4S_{3/2}°$
- 115 Uup Ununpentium (288)

Group 16 / VIA
- 8 O Oxygen 15.9994 1s^{2}2s^{2}2p^4 13.6181 $^3P_2$
- 16 S Sulfur 32.065 [Ne]3s^{2}3p^4 10.3600 $^3P_2$
- 34 Se Selenium 78.96 [Ar]3d^{10}4s^{2}4p^4 9.7524 $^3P_2$
- 52 Te Tellurium 127.60 [Kr]4d^{10}5s^{2}5p^4 9.0096 $^3P_2$
- 84 Po Polonium (209) [Hg]6p^4 8.414 $^3P_2$
- 116 Uuh Ununhexium (293)

Group 17 / VIIA
- 9 F Fluorine 18.9984032 1s^{2}2s^{2}2p^5 17.4228 $^2P_{3/2}°$
- 17 Cl Chlorine 35.453 [Ne]3s^{2}3p^5 12.9676 $^2P_{3/2}°$
- 35 Br Bromine 79.904 [Ar]3d^{10}4s^{2}4p^5 11.8138 $^2P_{3/2}°$
- 53 I Iodine 126.90447 [Kr]4d^{10}5s^{2}5p^5 10.4513 $^2P_{3/2}°$
- 85 At Astatine (210) [Hg]6p^5 $^2P_{3/2}°$
- 117 Uus Ununseptium (294)

Group 18 / VIIIA
- 2 He Helium 4.002602 1s^2 24.5874 $^1S_0$
- 10 Ne Neon 20.1797 1s^{2}2s^{2}2p^6 21.5645 $^1S_0$
- 18 Ar Argon 39.948 [Ne]3s^{2}3p^6 15.7596 $^1S_0$
- 36 Kr Krypton 83.798 [Ar]3d^{10}4s^{2}4p^6 13.9996 $^1S_0$
- 54 Xe Xenon 131.293 [Kr]4d^{10}5s^{2}5p^6 12.1298 $^1S_0$
- 86 Rn Radon (222) [Hg]6p^6 10.7485 $^1S_0$
- 118 Uuo Ununoctium (294)

Lanthanides
- 57 La Lanthanum 138.90547 [Xe]5d6s^2 5.5769 $^2D_{3/2}$
- 58 Ce Cerium 140.116 [Xe]4f5d6s^2 5.5387 $^1G_4°$
- 59 Pr Praseodymium 140.90765 [Xe]4f^{3}6s^2 5.473 $^4I_{9/2}°$
- 60 Nd Neodymium 144.242 [Xe]4f^{4}6s^2 5.5250 $^5I_4$
- 61 Pm Promethium (145) [Xe]4f^{5}6s^2 5.582 $^6H_{5/2}°$
- 62 Sm Samarium 150.36 [Xe]4f^{6}6s^2 5.6437 $^7F_0$
- 63 Eu Europium 151.964 [Xe]4f^{7}6s^2 5.6704 $^8S_{7/2}°$
- 64 Gd Gadolinium 157.25 [Xe]4f^{7}5d6s^2 6.1498 $^9D_2°$
- 65 Tb Terbium 158.92535 [Xe]4f^{9}6s^2 5.8638 $^6H_{15/2}°$
- 66 Dy Dysprosium 162.500 [Xe]4f^{10}6s^2 5.9389 $^5I_8$
- 67 Ho Holmium 164.93032 [Xe]4f^{11}6s^2 6.0215 $^4I_{15/2}°$
- 68 Er Erbium 167.259 [Xe]4f^{12}6s^2 6.1077 $^3H_6$
- 69 Tm Thulium 168.93421 [Xe]4f^{13}6s^2 6.1843 $^2F_{7/2}°$
- 70 Yb Ytterbium 173.054 [Xe]4f^{14}6s^2 6.2542 $^1S_0$
- 71 Lu Lutetium 174.9668 [Xe]4f^{14}5d6s^2 5.4259 $^2D_{3/2}$

Actinides
- 89 Ac Actinium (227) [Rn]6d7s^2 5.3807 $^2D_{3/2}$
- 90 Th Thorium 232.03806 [Rn]6d^{2}7s^2 6.3067 $^3F_2$
- 91 Pa Protactinium 231.03588 [Rn]5f^{2}6d7s^2 5.89 $^4K_{11/2}$
- 92 U Uranium 238.02891 [Rn]5f^{3}6d7s^2 6.1939 $^5L_6°$
- 93 Np Neptunium (237) [Rn]5f^{4}6d7s^2 6.2657 $^6L_{11/2}$
- 94 Pu Plutonium (244) [Rn]5f^{6}7s^2 6.0260 $^7F_0$
- 95 Am Americium (243) [Rn]5f^{7}7s^2 5.9738 $^8S_{7/2}°$
- 96 Cm Curium (247) [Rn]5f^{7}6d7s^2 5.9914 $^9D_2°$
- 97 Bk Berkelium (247) [Rn]5f^{9}7s^2 6.1979 $^6H_{15/2}°$
- 98 Cf Californium (251) [Rn]5f^{10}7s^2 6.2817 $^5I_8$
- 99 Es Einsteinium (252) [Rn]5f^{11}7s^2 6.3676 $^4I_{15/2}°$
- 100 Fm Fermium (257) [Rn]5f^{12}7s^2 6.50 $^3H_6$
- 101 Md Mendelevium (258) [Rn]5f^{13}7s^2 6.58 $^2F_{7/2}°$
- 102 No Nobelium (259) [Rn]5f^{14}7s^2 6.65 $^1S_0$
- 103 Lr Lawrencium (262) [Rn]5f^{14}7s^{2}7p? 4.9? $^2P_{1/2}°$

†Based upon ^{12}C. ( ) indicates the mass number of the longest-lived isotope.

For a description of the data, visit physics.nist.gov/data

NIST SP 966 (September 2010)

Table 4-1. Periodic Table of the Elements

Day	Temperature in Degrees Celsius
1	−7.5
2	−2.4
3	5.0
4	−0.9
5	−5.9
6	6.0
7	6.5
8	18.0
9	5.5
10	5.9

Table 4-2.

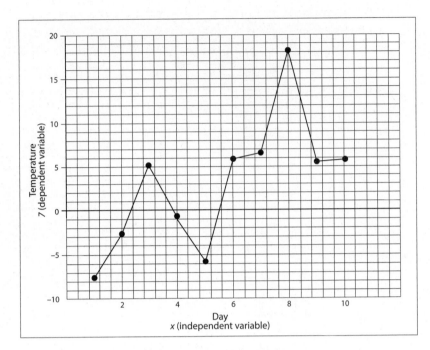

Fig. 4-1. Graph of Day versus Temperature

Sometimes scientific data is represented in pictorial form such as the representation below of Earth's tectonic plates. In this case, by studying the key and the symbols and labels in the picture, the reader can answer questions and gain information about this topic more easily than with text or other forms of graphics.

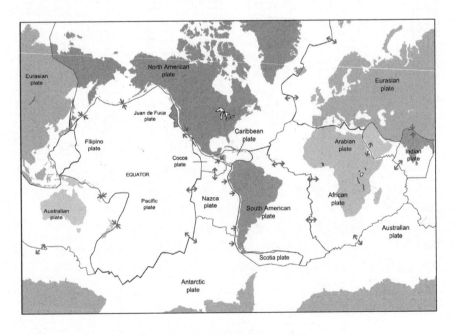

Fig. 4-2. Earth's Tectonic Plates

Next we'll turn to how you should identify possible sources of error in the course of your investigation. Let's examine this in the context of a physical science, life science or earth or space science content question. The practice test questions will help you prepare for this.

Identify possible sources of error and alter the design of an investigation to ameliorate the error.

How, then, should you begin your hunt for errors? Let's look at the common types of errors that can exist in the design of an investigation in any area of science. These need to be identified either before or during testing and remedied before final data is recorded. Such errors include:

1. **Material**—using incorrect materials, impure samples, contaminated cultures, etc.

2. **Procedure**—improper experimental protocol; improper technique; misconstruction (misreading of phenomenon by observer—placebo effect); not differentiating similar phenomena in control.

3. **Observational**—insufficient control to establish solid data and observations; unclear instrument of measure; perceptual bias (seeing what you want or expect to see).

4. **Sampling**—not enough samples to justify statistical significance; flaw in reasoning; mistaking correlation for causation, incomplete evidence.

Any errors (these are just some examples) in investigational design must be rethought and the design rebuilt before final data is collected in order for an investigation to be scientific, accurate, and viable. For example, for example No. 3 it may be necessary to establish a more clear and extensive control sample in order to clearly differentiate between the control variable and the test variable. If as in No. 4 the statistical sample is not large enough, the investigation should be postponed until enough samples are obtained.

Identify and refine hypotheses for scientific investigations.

To generate a hypothesis is to explain why and how a situation in the natural world occurs. At this point in an investigation, you have researched and learned some information about your question, and you should have some ideas about what the phenomenon you're investigating entails. Thus, the hypothesis should be based on some specifics and should be relatively sharp and focused. Good hypotheses address the main source of the question and propose details of a possible answer. Hypotheses should also be proposed in a way that can be tested.

To refine the hypothesis is to evaluate its credibility. There are two approaches you can use, depending on the nature of your data:

1. Comparison of the hypotheses with established facts, and

2. Analytic processing, which allows you to test your hypotheses

You would use the first method when your evidence is so strong that the hypothesis does not need to be tested. A 1991 investigation of an outbreak of vitamin D intoxication in Massachusetts is a good example. In that case, all the people affected had drunk milk delivered to their homes by the same local dairy. Investigators hypothesized that the dairy was the source, and the milk was the vehicle of excess vitamin D. Upon visiting the dairy, they quickly recognized that far more than the recommended dose of vitamin D was inadvertently being added to the milk. Thus, in this case, no further analysis was necessary.

The second method—analytic processing—is used when the cause is less clear. With this method, you test your hypotheses by using a comparison group to quantify relationships between the hypotheses.

Identify the strength and weaknesses of one or more scientific investigation (i.e., experimental or observational) designs.

It is important to identify and compare the strengths and weaknesses of experimental designs to ensure that the design being used is the most appropriate for the question being studied. For example, developing a design that is implemented in a lab gives the strength of being able to control the greatest number of variables, but it may not be the most generalizable method in terms of being applied to a question that occurs in nature (for example). A design that is repeatable is preferable to one that is able to be tested only once (due to cost or rarity of materials, for example). These considerations require study and thought as one determines the best experimental design.

Design a scientific investigation.

Experimental design does not happen in rigid steps of the scientific method, but it does follow a logical pattern. Various scientists adapt their method to suit unique aspects of their study, but there are constants in the process that allow new discoveries to be presented for peer consideration. When scientists want to share a new discovery, they report it to their peers in a journal article or a presentation at a conference, so their methods must be understood by all scientists. The general scheme of an experimental design in science will be to:

1. Pose a question about the natural world.

2. Develop a prediction or a hypothesis.

3. Gather information from prior tests, research, books, and any other resources to see what is already known.

4. Plan an investigation, a fair test for the possible variables, keeping all other things constant. (Identify an independent variable—the factor that you will test or change, and a dependent variable—the thing you are seeking to measure, and be sure to control all other factors in the experiment.) Where appropriate, use a test group and a control group. The control group is subjected to all the same factors that the test group is subjected to *except* for the one variable that is being tested (the dependent variable).

5. Gather, analyze, and interpret data using tools to measure.

6. Describe results, pose answers, and provide explanations.

7. Use evidence to support conclusions.

8. Communicate results to peers.

9. Accept and analyze peer comment and review.

There are many scientific situations for which experimental design is simply not possible (having a control situation with defined variables, etc.). For example, it is impossible to assign variables to planetary motion. When studying animals (for example, gorillas) in the wild in their habitat, you cannot manipulate variables to conduct a formal experiment. Further, sometimes it is unethical in cases involving animals and humans to use variables and controls. In these situations, an observational investigation design is appropriate. An observational study would consist of making careful, consistent observations of the system in question as it functions in its natural state. There are limitations for this type of study as to what it can show in terms of cause and effect or correlation, but carefully planned, long-term observational studies can yield important and accurate scientific data. It is observational studies that have taught us about the orbit and rotation of celestial bodies, the action of weather patterns throughout the world, the ecology of plants and animals, and much more in science.

Identify and interpret independent and dependent variables in scientific investigations.

In an experimental study, a testable hypothesis is developed. The experiment will try to establish an answer to the hypothesis, in most cases a causal relationship between variables. This is done by manipulating an independent variable to assess the effect upon a dependent variable, while keeping all other factors controlled. For example, if a researcher hypothesizes that grasshoppers that eat flax seeds will chirp louder than grasshopper that eat grass seeds, then the independent variable is the type of seed (it is the variable that is manipulated) and the dependent variable is the loudness of chirping (in decibels). The controls would be the number of grasshoppers, the type, the location, the time of day, the instrument of measuring decibels, etc.

Reasoning from Data

The ability to look at data and draw logical conclusions is central to the practice of science. Every experiment should have a purposeful design. The question should have a reason to be asked and the answer to the hypothesis, whether supported or not supported, should lead to a process of thinking, reasoning about what is happening in the tested system. Conclusions should be able to be drawn. Perhaps the conclusion is that more testing needs be done. Perhaps the results are clear. Whatever the results of the data, you should be able to interpret, analyze, and present it in a way that allows you to reason through what happened in your experiment, along with why, how, and what should be done next.

You should be prepared to use your knowledge in any of the content areas and apply it by completing any of the following tasks involving data:

Cite a specific textual evidence to support a finding or conclusion.

When given data or evidence for a particular study, you should be able to reason by forming a conclusion or selecting the correct conclusion from a set of answer options.

Reason from data or evidence to a conclusion.

These tasks will likely give you a passage to read, or a chart, graph, figure, or list of data concerning one of the GED® content areas. You will then either be given a multiple-choice question or set of questions asking you to identify the evidence for a conclusion or requiring you to write a short paragraph giving evidence from the passage to support the finding or conclusion.

Make a prediction based upon data or evidence.

Sometimes the task will be to read a prompt such as a passage, or a chart, graph, figure, or list of data concerning one of the GED® content areas and then make a prediction or hypothesis based on the prompt. Consider the following example from NASA's Earth Observatory website at *http:// earthobservatory.nasa.gov*.

Forecasting the Future of the Amazon

As counterintuitive as a "good" dry season might seem, that response is perfectly in tune with research about the soil-water-tapping potential of mature rainforest trees. Since the early 1990s, field studies and soil-moisture modeling research have been accumulating evidence that in the undisturbed rainforest, roots extend as far as 20 meters (more than 60 feet) into the soil, where the wet-season rains are stored. Rather than being a time of stress, the normal dry season may be the forests' most productive time of year because the rain clouds clear up, and more sunlight reaches the forest.

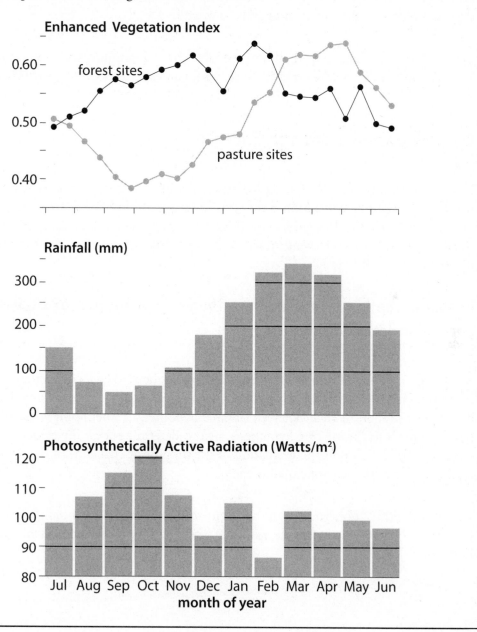

Courtesy of NASA

Fig. 4-3. Making a Prediction based on a Prompt

From the previous information, predict what month(s) would likely have the most forest site vegetation in the following year.* (The answer is below).

Use sampling techniques to answer scientific questions

Many scientific investigations rely on sampling techniques for a research design. For example, it is impossible to test every liter of water in a pond to find what organisms exist in it. However, it is possible to take several samples from varying places in the pond and determine the organisms in these samples, giving a survey of organisms overall.

The GED® test may provide charts and tables from a sampling technique from an investigation and ask you to evaluate the experiment or design an experiment using a sampling technique.

Evaluating Conclusions with Evidence

When making a conclusion regarding a scientific question, hypothesis, or theory, the key to making it a scientific conclusion is that it is carefully and fully based on evidence. Evidence is the foundation of science. This is why experimental testing is key to gathering evidence. Now it is time to take that evidence and arrange it in a way that brings sense and clarity to the question, whether it supports or challenges it.

Evaluate whether a conclusion or theory is supported or challenged by particular data or evidence.

The point of your testing and/or investigation has been to collect data that will support or challenge your testable hypothesis. Now it is time to conclude whether your evidence from your test does in fact support or challenge your original hypothesis. Either result is acceptable as you should never set forth to "prove" any hypothesis, just to determine what the evidence will support. Your writing of the conclusion and evaluation of the support or challenge of the hypothesis at this time is a key point in the scientific methodology.

On the GED® test, you will be asked to read a passage and/or look at charts, tables, and/or graphics and consider whether the evidence provided supports the theory or conclusion presented in the question.

*Answer: October.

Working with Findings

Reconcile multiple findings, conclusions, or theories.

Once data in an experiment or test is gathered, analyzed, and summarized, it may be found that there are discrepancies in which some data or evidence supports the hypothesis while other data seems to challenge it (or vice versa). At this point of evaluation it is time to look deeper into techniques used and any situational differences in the data discovery phase that may account for a given discrepancy and report it in your notes. If none seem to exist, then your conclusions will be straightforward. However, often discrepancies of some sort exist.

Sometimes there are just a few points of data that fall outside the normal curve of a data plot. Look at the following chart:

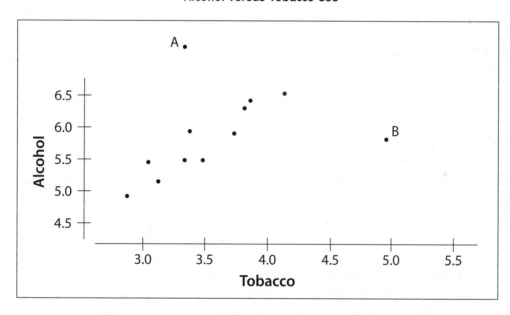

Fig. 4-4. Interpreting Data

In this graph of tobacco use versus alcohol use there is a clear correlation of increased alcohol use with increased tobacco use except with points A and B, which fall outside the curve. These are considered outliers; while they should be reported, they should be explained as being outliers to the preponderance of data. If you know a potential reason why these outliers could have occurred, you may mention it, but it is not necessary.

You may need to reconcile your findings with those of another study that went about things a little differently. It is important to be able to find the baseline similarities: What was that study ultimately testing for? Did the investigators use a different method to test the same thing? Did they get corresponding findings? If not, what reasons could be given for findings that don't match?

The same is true for conclusions or theories. Did the other tests get similar results but reach different conclusions? If not, why not? Use reasoning to examine both experiments to consider and make a reasoned explanation for why one conclusion or theory is the most supported by the *evidence*.

This type of reasoning may form the basis for an entire GED® question or portion of a question that focuses on the findings of an experiment and asks you to explain an aspect related the findings by either answering multiple-choice questions or writing a sentence or paragraph.

Expressing Scientific Information

There are numerous ways to express scientific information. Let's look at several that are important to understand, and to be able to use. The following specific approaches are necessary for all science students to comprehend.

Express scientific information or findings visually.

Visual representation of scientific information may include graphs, pictures, tables, figures, etc. For example, when data is gathered and placed in a table for easy reading it should then be natural to express that data in graphic form.

The following data on children per household in a given area shows a table of data transformed into a bar graph.

Number of children	Number of households
1	4
2	7
3	11
4	4
5	3
6	0
7	1
Total	30

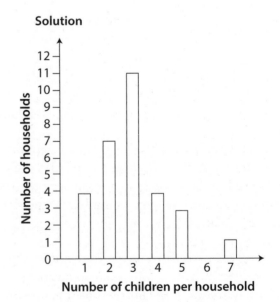

Fig. 4-5.   Fig. 4-6.

Express scientific information or findings numerically or symbolically.

In some cases you would want to express findings purely in numbers (possibly with units), or with symbols: as in chemical symbols, electrical symbols in physics, equations, etc. The question and hypothesis with which you are working and the data you produce will dictate what type of expression you will use in communicating your findings. On the GED® test, you may gain critical score points for being open to a chemical equation (as seen in the chemistry section, for example) as a potential finding in a scientific test.

Express scientific information or findings verbally.

Clearly, for all of the above scenarios, there may be a portion of scientific information or findings expressed verbally to accompany visual or numeric/symbolic expressions. In some cases, *only* verbal findings will be given. Verbal findings may be as small as the type of information exchanged in a meeting with co-workers or as large as a presentation at a major scientific convention. Verbal reports of findings can be key in communicating with peers the latest in the fields of research on important topics. Verbal presentations should always be well-prepared, organized, and complete in representing all steps in the process, explaining any hurdles, or discrepancies, and fully presenting any conclusions alongside any questions that remain.

Your familiarity with these expectations will be tested with either multiple-choice questions or a question asking you to write out the explanation of findings or scientific information. Your knowledge may also be tested with questions that ask you to complete information on a graph or table since the GED® test is indeed interactive.

Scientific Theories

Conducting scientific inquiry also includes the process of identifying and avoiding bias as completely as possible. In addition, an important goal of scientific inquiry is to structure scientific knowledge in the form of theories and laws. Both of these terms have very specific definitions in the scientific world. Scientific laws are universal generalizations related to an aspect of how the natural world behaves under certain conditions. A scientific law must be testable, internally consistent, and compatible with available evidence and known phenomena. For example, Newton's Laws of Motion are well established as scientific laws. A theory is an explanation of a particular phenomenon of the natural world. Theories explain aspects of laws, but not all laws have corresponding theories. Theories do not become laws with increasing testing or evidence. Rather, theories are a separate type of explanation.

It is the nature of scientific pursuit to search for the best theory to fit the observations available. Therefore, as more information becomes available, whether through more testing, developing technology, or increased access, theories may develop and change. Therefore, no matter how well a theory may fit a given set of observations, a new theory may be developed that fits as well or better or that may fit with a greater set of observations.

Understand and apply scientific models, theories and processes.

There are many valuable ways to investigate the natural world in a scientific manner through methods such as direct observation, modeling, testing hypotheses, etc. The socio-scientific methods of gathering knowledge are subject to careful scrutiny by the body of knowledgeable individuals that belong to the scientific community. While there is no one set of steps that defines the one scientific method, there are general methods and acceptable practices that characterize a scientific approach. These practices include a foundation of reliance on empirical observations, testing, healthy skepticism, and naturalistic explanations.

Apply formulas from scientific theories.

Knowledge and application of formulas from previously developed scientific theories is crucial to expedient use of the scientific method. Examples of such formulas include these:

$$C_6H_{12}O_6 \qquad E = mc^2 \qquad V = RI$$

Students should be proficient at finding and using appropriate formulas to the problem at hand.

Probability and Statistics

Statistics is the science of manipulating data in a manner that can make it more easily understood and by which discrepancies and trends can more easily be seen and understood. Statistics is widely used in scientific experimentation to explain and generalize the results of an experiment. There are many tools available within the field of statistics that can make the presentation of data more understandable.

A representation of probability is the ratio of the number of expected results of a test to the total number of results in a given experiment. For example, if you are testing how many purple offspring you get from a double hybrid cross of purple flowers in a genetic experiment (Pp × Pp) and your results are 3 purple and 1 white, the probability is 3(purple) over 4(total) or ¾ or 0.75.

Describe a data set statistically

Many scientific studies yield large amounts of data that can be arranged into data sets such as the following example of climate data from NASA. This data is used to chart climate change in various areas of Earth over a long time period. It can be subjected to a number of statistical tests via computer programs since it is arranged and labeled according to a standard method of presenting data.

Generally, investigations that yield large amounts of data are registered via computer and set up to be manipulated via a number of data set types and multiple software applications.

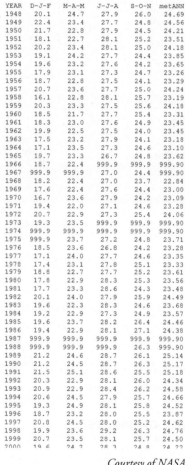

YEAR	D-J-F	M-A-M	J-J-A	S-O-N	metANN
1948	20.1	24.7	27.9	26.0	24.69
1949	22.4	23.4	27.7	24.8	24.56
1950	21.7	22.8	27.9	24.5	24.21
1951	18.1	22.7	28.1	25.2	23.51
1952	20.2	23.4	28.1	25.0	24.18
1953	19.1	24.2	27.7	24.4	23.85
1954	19.6	23.2	27.6	24.2	23.65
1955	17.9	23.1	27.3	24.7	23.26
1956	18.7	22.8	27.5	24.1	23.29
1957	20.7	23.6	27.7	25.0	24.24
1958	16.1	22.8	28.1	25.7	23.19
1959	20.3	23.3	27.5	25.6	24.18
1960	18.5	21.7	27.7	25.4	23.31
1961	18.3	23.0	27.6	24.9	23.45
1962	19.9	22.5	27.5	24.0	23.45
1963	17.5	23.2	27.9	24.1	23.18
1964	17.1	23.5	27.3	24.6	23.10
1965	19.7	23.3	26.7	24.8	23.62
1966	18.7	22.4	999.9	999.9	999.90
1967	999.9	999.9	27.0	24.4	999.90
1968	18.2	22.4	27.0	23.7	22.84
1969	17.6	22.4	27.6	24.4	23.00
1970	16.7	23.6	27.9	24.2	23.09
1971	19.4	22.0	27.1	24.6	23.28
1972	20.7	22.9	27.3	25.4	24.06
1973	19.3	23.5	999.9	999.9	999.90
1974	999.9	999.9	999.9	999.9	999.90
1975	999.9	23.7	27.2	24.8	23.71
1976	18.5	23.6	26.8	24.2	23.28
1977	17.1	24.0	27.7	24.6	23.35
1978	17.4	23.1	27.8	25.1	23.33
1979	18.8	22.7	27.7	25.2	23.61
1980	17.8	22.9	28.3	25.3	23.56
1981	17.7	23.3	28.6	24.3	23.48
1982	20.1	24.0	27.9	25.9	24.49
1983	19.6	22.3	28.3	24.6	23.68
1984	19.2	22.9	27.3	24.9	23.57
1985	19.6	23.7	28.2	26.4	24.46
1986	19.4	22.9	28.1	27.1	24.38
1987	999.9	999.9	999.9	999.9	999.90
1988	999.9	999.9	999.9	26.3	999.90
1989	21.2	24.6	28.7	26.1	25.14
1990	21.2	24.5	28.7	26.3	25.17
1991	21.5	25.1	28.6	25.5	25.18
1992	20.3	22.9	28.1	26.0	24.34
1993	20.9	22.9	28.4	26.2	24.58
1994	20.6	24.5	27.9	25.7	24.66
1995	19.3	24.9	28.1	25.8	24.52
1996	18.7	23.2	28.0	25.5	23.87
1997	20.8	24.5	28.0	25.2	24.62
1998	19.9	23.6	29.2	26.3	24.76
1999	20.7	23.5	28.1	25.7	24.50
2000	19.6	24.2	28.3	24.8	24.22

Courtesy of NASA

Fig. 4-7. Large Data Set

Use counting and permutations to solve scientific problems.

One example of using counting in a scientific problem is population microbiology. The following image shows direct counting using the grid method of determining the number of bacterial colonies growing on a streak plate.

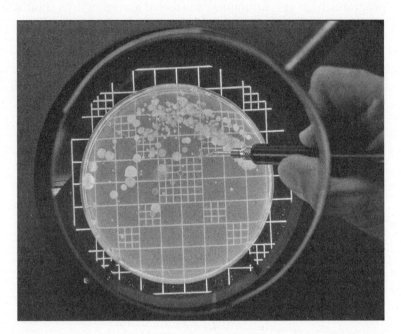

EPA Gulf Breeze Laboratory, the Micro-Biology Lab

Fig. 4-8. Taking A Bacteria Colony Count - Nara - 546274.

Permutations are various ways of combining material pieces of data to provide several variations in which a set or number of things can be arranged. For example if you have four possible alleles (Y, y, G, or g) available for a three-gene polygenic trait there are many permutations possible for that trait (YYY, GGG, yyy, ggg, YyG, YYy, GgY, etc.). Statistical software can be used to determine all possible permutations.

Determine the probability of events.

Statistics are also used to determine the probability of events. For example, in the prior paragraph the permutations of alleles for a polygenic trait were considered. To determine the probability of any one of those permutations to occur at a given time, a statistical analysis can be performed that takes into account the availability of each allele and the likelihood of that gene to be formed under certain conditions.

PRACTICE!

Use the following diagram to answer questions 1–5.

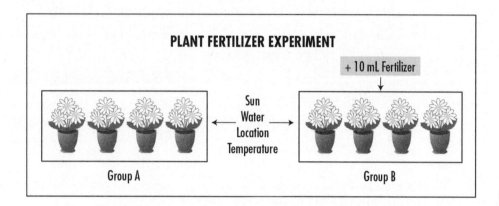

PLANT FERTILIZER EXPERIMENT

+ 10 mL Fertilizer

Sun
Water
Location
Temperature

Group A   Group B

1. In the experiment pictured above, what is Group A called?

    A. dependent variable

    B. independent variable

    C. control group

    D. test group

2. Which of the following is the most important factor to keep constant between the two groups?

    A. temperature

    B. amount of fertilizer

    C. size of pot

    D. number of plants

3. What is the independent variable in this experiment?

    A. amount of fertilizer

    B. location

    C. the types of plants

    D. Group A

4. The experimenter predicted that the Group B plants will grow faster and higher. The plants were started as seedlings and Group B was treated with the fertilizer on the 5th day. After 30 days the average plant height for Group B was 8.3 cm while the average plant height for Group A was 8.1 cm. What would be the best next step for the experimenter?

    A. Continue to let the plants keep growing for another 30 days and gather more data on the growth patterns.

    B. Add fertilizer to Group A and check growth of both groups in 10 days for patterns of faster and higher growth.

    C. Analyze the data of each plant to see if there is a pattern of faster and higher growth in Group B.

    D. Redo the experiment with a different amount of fertilizer and different types of plants.

5. What would be the most appropriate way to express and analyze the measurements of the dependent variable for this experiment?

    A. a picture of the plants over time

    B. a graph of days the fertilizer was added and how much

    C. a paragraph explaining what happened during the experiment

    D. a graph of time and how much the plants have grown

6. How do scientists most commonly share the results of their experimentation?

    A. Other scientists ask for information about the results.

    B. The results of the experiment are published in an article for review by peers.

    C. The results are written into textbooks.

    D. They ask other scientists to try the experiment.

7. Not all scientific investigations proceed according to the same set of steps. If an investigation begins with observations that then lead to a question that is testable (potentially after some research on the topic), what is the next step to consider in the process of experimentation?

    A. Develop a test that will give a yes or no answer to the question.

    B. Do more research on the topic to ensure understanding.

    C. Check with peers to see if this question has already been tested.

    D. Develop a hypothesis that answers the question.

8. Miguel and Anna have set up an experiment to test their hypothesis that a dihybrid cross made by pairing male flies that were homozygous for vestigial wings and rosy eyes with female flies that were homozygous wild type for both traits would result in a F^1 generation of all heterozygous for each trait although wild type in phenotype. They will test a cross of 10 males with 10 females. Which of the following is NOT true?

    A. Their hypothesized result for offspring is accurate.

    B. The plan appears free from any error in sampling. 10 males and 10 females are enough crosses to provide a large enough number for a statistical sample.

    C. They should continue the cross with the F^1 generation to confirm the heterozygous genotype.

    D. The plan appears free from error in material and procedure.

Science Practice 4 Answers:

1. **C.**

Group A is the control group since it is subjected to the same factors except for the treatment: the fertilizer. The independent variable is the fertilizer while the dependent variable is what is being measured: plant growth over time. Group B is the test group since it is being treated with the fertilizer.

2. **A.**

It is necessary to keep temperature constant between the groups as well as the location and the amount of sunlight and water and any other environmental variables. The amount of fertilizer is what is being tested so it should not be the same between the groups. The size of the pot is not likely to impact this investigation. The number of plants used has to do with the number of times the investigation is repeated, so each plant represents one trial of the investigation. The more plants tested, the more reliable the results. However, it is not necessary to keep the number of plants constant between the groups.

3. **A.**

The independent variable in this experiment is the amount of fertilizer. This is the variable that is being changed. The location and types of plants are kept constant. Group A is the control group that is there to see what happens when there is no treatment.

4. **C.**

The correct response is to analyze the data of each plant to see if there is a pattern of faster and higher growth in Group B. Since the data given was the average growth and it did show that the plants in Group B did grow higher, though not by a lot, it would be important to analyze the data further and consider if any plants in Group A grew faster or higher than in Group B or if they were all similar to each other. Were all the plants in group B higher than those in Group A or were some smaller? This is important information to determine if the fertilizer was effective or if more testing is necessary. Then it might be possible to determine whether it would be helpful to either continue to let the plants keep growing for another 30 days or gather more data on the growth patterns. Adding fertilizer to Group A and checking the growth of both groups in 10 days for patterns of faster and higher growth would not be appropriate in any circumstance since Group A is the control. It would be appropriate to redo the experiment once you have drawn some conclusions, and you could decide to vary the amount of fertilizer. However, using different types of plants would be a different investigation entirely.

5. **D.**

A graph of how much time has passed and how much the plants have grown is the best way to analyze and report the dependent variable of this experiment. From this you could then write a paragraph explaining the data on the graph, but the graph is essential. Pictures would be useful to show the methods, but not for analyzing data. Listing the amount and date of fertilizer addition is important for information of how the experimental method was done.

6. **B.**

Scientists most commonly share the results of their experimentation by publishing an article for review by peers. Then other scientists can try the experiment and send comments or questions back to the experimenter.

7. **D.**

The most general steps in a basic scientific investigation include to: (1) Pose a question about the natural world; (2) Develop a prediction or a hypothesis; (3) Gather information from prior tests, research, books, and any other resources to see what is already known, etc.

8. **B.**

Choice (B) is the only statement that is NOT true since 10 flies of each gender is not enough to show a statistical pattern. The sample needs to be much larger. Choices (A), (C), (D) are all true.

Social Studies

About the GED® Social Studies Test

For the GED® Social Studies test, it's as important to understand what topics are covered as it is to know the skills the test will require of you. The majority of Social Studies test questions focus on either civics and government (50%) or United States history (20%). The rest of the coverage is split down the middle between economics (15%) and geography and the world (15%). More than anything, the test assesses your ability to reason based either on a passage or other form of text, or a data or visual display (e.g., charts, cartoons, tables, or maps). What sort of text will be on the test? It will either be primary or secondary sources. A primary source is an artifact (i.e., historical object), document, or some other source of information created or authored by someone with firsthand knowledge of an issue. A secondary source is a document or other source of information that quotes, refers to, or relies upon a primary source—and is produced after the event, period, or issue in history to which it connects.

Question Formats

The GED® Social Studies test is 70 minutes long. Apart from the typical multiple-choice questions you may have seen on other tests, the test also uses drag-and-drop, hot-spot, and fill-in-the-blank questions.

Half of the test questions are presented in scenarios in which two or three items are based on one prompt (e.g., textual, graphic, or a combination of both); the other half of the test uses self-contained standalone questions.

The reasoning skills you'll need to demonstrate include analysis, evaluation, and inference. Though the test expects that you "should be able to recognize and understand" certain key social studies topics in context, you will not be expected to have detailed knowledge of any subtopic. Thus, rest assured that the test will give you all the details you'll need to make judgments about figures, events, processes, or ideas. Nor will you have to give a definition for a term without being offered choices from which to select the definition.

The Social Studies Test at a Glance

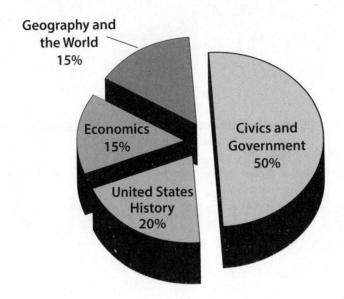

Geography and the World 15%

Economics 15%

United States History 20%

Civics and Government 50%

Scoring

With a high enough score, today's GED® test makes it possible to earn college credit. GED® scoring is framed by Performance Level Descriptors. On the RLA test, performance levels are determined by the complexity level of the texts. The performance levels represent a sequence of skills, from the most basic to the most complex.

Your score on the GED® Social Studies test is based on where you fall relative to the four GED® Performance Level Descriptors:

Performance Level 1 (< 145)—Below Passing

Performance Level 2 (145-164)—Pass/High School Equivalency

Performance Level 3 (165-174)—GED® College Ready

Performance Level 4 (175-200)—GED® College Ready + Credit

If your score puts you into the top performance bracket, you may be eligible for up to three undergraduate credits in Social Studies. For details on GED® scoring, visit *www.gedtestingservice.com*.

Now let's move on to the GED® Social Studies test's content areas.

Civics and Government

Since Civics and Government account for 50% of the questions on the GED® Social Studies test, it is a good idea to spend some time reading and recalling the various main points about governments. Understanding what government really is and memorizing the types of modern and historical governments is important. You'll need to know what types of governments existed in various time periods and how and why they changed over time. All this may seem like a lot to take in, but this chapter has simplified it and placed the focus where you most need it. Let's review government.

Definition of Government

A body of people that sets and administers public policy, and exercises executive, political, and sovereign power through customs, institutions, and laws within a state.[1]

The above definition may seem vague, but, in fact, it is the definition of government. We cannot really understand the meaning unless we look at the many types and forms of government. Governments can be classified in several ways. Some are based on the type of rule, others are based on social systems, and still others are based on economic systems. Let's look at the most common.

---

[1] *http://www.businessdictionary.com*

Types of government

Example I

Type of Government	Type of Ruler	Title of Ruler	Nature of Government
Monarchy	single person who inherited this role	Queen or King	**Aristocracy** ruled by elites
Dictatorship	single leader or small group of leaders	Most do not admit they are dictators but instead claim to be leaders of democracies.	**Authoritarian** controlled by unelected ruler(s) who rule by threat of force
Representative Democracy	elected by the people to represent them in decision making	President or Prime Minister	**Democracy** elected by the people
Theocracy	religious leaders who claim they get power directly from God	the Pope a Caliph	Religious leaders (of the dominant religion in the country) make ruling decisions based on their notion of religious law or (claimed) divine guidance.

Here's another way to classify types of governments:

Example II

Governments can be classified into several types. Some of the more common types of governments are:[2]

1. **Democracy**

   The word "democracy" literally means "rule by the people" (from the Greek words *demos* meaning "citizen" and *kratos* meaning "power" or "rules"). In a democracy, the people govern.

2. **Republic**

   A literal democracy (where the people rule directly) is impossible in a political system containing more than a few people. All "democracies" are really *republics*. In a republic, the people elect representatives to make and enforce laws.

---

[2] *http://depts.alverno.edu*

3. **Monarchy**

   A **monarchy** is ruled by a king or queen. Sometimes a king is called an "emperor," especially if there is a large empire, such as China before 1911. There are no large monarchies today. The United Kingdom, which has a queen, is really a republic, because the queen has virtually no political power.

4. **Aristocracy**

   An aristocracy is ruled by the aristocrats. **Aristocrats are** typically wealthy, educated people. They are regarded in their society as the highest social class, typically claiming to be related by blood to the nobility of the country (i.e., the hereditary rulers, who hold office by virtue of being the birth descendants of previous rulers). Aristocrats generally are regarded by themselves and the society in which they are established as the best qualified to rule their country, because of both their noble birth and their claimed inherent superiority to lower social classes. Many monarchies have really been ruled by aristocrats. Today the term "aristocracy" is typically used negatively to assert that a republic of being dominated by rich people—for example, "The United States has become an aristocracy."

5. **Dictatorship**

   A **dictatorship** is ruled by one person or a group of people. Very few dictators admit they are dictators; they almost always claim to be leaders of democracies. The dictator may be one person, such as Castro in Cuba or Hitler in Germany, or a group of people, such as the Communist Party in China.

6. **Democratic Republic**

   Usually, a **democratic republic** is neither democratic nor a republic. In fact, a government that officially calls itself a "democratic republic" is usually a dictatorship. Communist dictatorships have been especially prone to use this term. For example, the official name of North Vietnam was "The Democratic Republic of Vietnam." China uses a variant: "The People's Republic of China."

Yet another way to examine forms of government is by socioeconomic attributes:

Example III

Capitalism—free-market economy.

Communism—government owns all the businesses and farms and provides its people healthcare, education, and welfare.

Socialism—government owns many large industries and provides education, health, and welfare services.

Welfare state—protects and promotes the economic and social well-being of its citizens based on distribution of wealth and public responsibility.

You can see that there are many ways to classify governments, and most fit into more than one category. A typical GED® Social Studies test question will provide you with a table like Example I or a set of definitions like Examples II or III, then ask you to make connections with examples of government services, well-known countries, or typical situations in this type of government.

Presidential Democracy	Parliamentary Democracy
Stable, democratic	Stable, democratic, and protective of minority interests
Two strong political parties	Separation of power
Elections—vote for the party not the leader	Strong executive department
Parliament can dismiss the leader (Prime Minister)	Set terms for the executive (President)
	Direct elections of the candidate

EXAMPLE

Here's a sample question about types of government:

Under which of the following systems would traditional authority, based on inheritance or birthright, most likely occur?

    A. A socialist republic

    B. A communist state

    C. A monarchy

    D. A dictatorship

ANSWER: A monarchy (C) is the correct answer, since it is based on the inheritance of rule.

How government has changed over time

Another way to connect governments to countries is to think about the reasons they changed. The United States is a great example. Settlers from other countries came to the Americas either escaping something or looking for something (escaping religious persecution, looking for gold, etc.). Once settled, they established colonies of their homeland (still under their original government), and they could become embroiled in wars between their homeland and other countries that had (or claimed) colonies in America. Some people also wanted to spread their religion, government, or way of life.

EXAMPLE

All of the following are reasons the settlers came to the New World *EXCEPT*:

    A. religious freedom.

    B. economic wealth.

    C. political stability.

    D. missionary work.

ANSWER: (C)

Although settlers may have been unhappy with the political situation in their homeland, they could not be certain that matters would be any more politically stable in the New World than they were back in Europe. In fact, the situation could be even more unstable, since the stabilizing influence of a strong government might be absent in their New World settlements.

After a while, the colonists wanted to become independent of other countries in order to form their own country.

All of the following describe reasons the colonists wanted to be independent:

- Control by a distant ruler

- Control by foreigners

- Restrictions on trade

- Taxed by others

- No representation in the government

Structure of government

Structure of government is also a big part of the exam. A typical question follows. It gives you the definition of each of the three branches of the United States government and asks you to match some duties to the appropriate branch.

EXAMPLE

Below is the definition of each of the three branches of the United States government.

Executive Branch

The executive branch of the government is responsible for enforcing the laws of the land. The president, vice president, department heads (cabinet members), and heads of independent agencies carry out this mission.

Judicial Branch

Courts decide arguments about the meaning of laws and how they are applied. They also decide if laws violate the U.S. Constitution—which is known as judicial review, and it is how federal courts provide checks and balances on the legislative and executive branches.

Legislative Branch

Article I of the U.S. Constitution establishes the legislative, or law-making, branch of government. It has a two-branch Congress—the Senate and the House of Representatives—and agencies that support Congress.

Drag-and-drop the following duties under the appropriate heading in the chart below:

- Enacts taxes, authorizes borrowing, and sets the budget.

- Has power to grant pardons to convicted persons, except in cases of impeachment.

- Sets up federal courts.

- Determines how a law acts to compel testimony and the production of evidence.

- Determines how a law acts to determine the disposition of prisoners.

- May override presidential vetoes.

Executive Branch	Judicial Branch	Legislative Branch

ANSWER: Your answer table should look like this:

Executive Branch	Judicial Branch	Legislative Branch
• Has power to grant pardons to convicted persons, except in cases of impeachment. • Sets up federal courts.	• Determines how a law acts to compel testimony and the production of evidence. • Determines how a law acts to determine the disposition of prisoners.	• Enacts taxes, authorizes borrowing, and sets the budget. • May override presidential vetoes.

Checks and balances

The system of **checks and balances** is part of the structure of the government and is crucial to understanding how the government works. One way a question might be presented on the system of checks and balances is in a flow chart of the steps in the process. Here is an example:

EXECUTIVE
• Proposes laws
• Appoints federal judges

LEGISLATIVE
• Passes legislation
• Can impeach and remove a president

JUDICIAL
• Interprets the law
• Can declare legislation unconstitutional
• Can declare executive actions unconstitutional

One of the functions of the government is to make and enforce laws. The steps in this process are illustrated in the flow chart that follows.

In the U.S. Congress, legislation may begin in either chamber.
Similar proposals are often introduced in both chambers.

HOUSE
• Measure introduced in the House
↓
• Measure referred to committee, which holds hearings and reports measure to the House
↓
• House debates and can amend measures
↓
• House passes measure

SENATE
• Measure introduced in the Senate
↓
• Measure referred to committee, which holds hearings and reports measure to the Senate
↓
• Senate debates and can amend measures
↓
• Senate passes measure

(continued)

(continued)

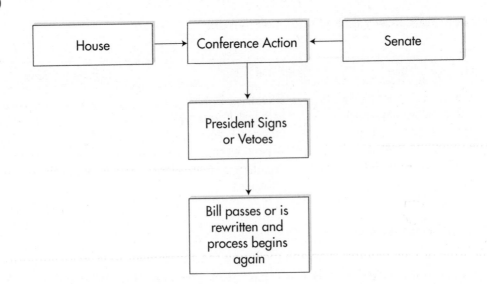

A typical question might leave some of the steps blank and ask you to drag and drop the missing steps into the appropriate box. For example, the United States Constitution is described as a living and timeless document. It can be changed and added to as time goes by and events make it necessary. Amendments are changes or additions made to the Constitution. To date, 27 amendments have been added to the Constitution. There is a process that must be followed in order to make these changes possible. How the Constitution is amended could very well be part of the GED® Social Studies test. You may be given a paragraph or passage that explains this process. Then, you might have a chart with missing parts. You would add the missing steps in the process.

In 1776–1778, Americans needed a system to manage economic and political relationships between states. Political leaders knew some type of union or confederation was needed in order to reach their goals. In 1776 a set of resolutions was introduced in the Congress. One of those resolutions called for a form of government. The Articles of Confederation was the resulting document. General George Washington, a strong leader during the American Revolution, was a member of the new Congress. He was elected the Chief Commander and later the President when the Articles of Confederation were dissolved and the United States Constitution became the source document of government.

Eight Parts of the U.S. Constitution

It is a good idea to be familiar with the U.S. Constitution and its most important amendments. The document has eight parts. The first part is the Preamble, which discusses the goals of the Constitution. There were six main principles that the authors of the document believed were important.

1. Popular sovereignty

2. Limited government

3. Separation of powers

4. Checks and balances

5. Judicial review

6. Federalism

The following parts are the first seven articles, which describe the way government works, how the states should interact, and the powers of the government. Article Six is called the Supremacy Law. It includes an explanation of how the states, all government officials, and the citizens must obey the Constitution. Article Seven explains how the Constitution must be ratified in order to become the law of the land.

The Rule of Law requires everyone including the government to exercise authority under law. Every citizen is subject to law. This was part of the natural rights theory. The majority (most of the people) has no power to vote away or otherwise abridge the natural rights of political, ethnic, religious, and/or other minorities. This was a statement taken from the Federalist papers written by the leaders of the nation. This idea is one that is the basis for the Bill of Rights.

Bill of Rights

When the Founding Fathers wrote and approved the Constitution, there was much discussion about what it was missing and the problems that might occur as a result. One of the main problems was that there were no provisions to guarantee individual rights. As a result, the **Bill of Rights** was added. The Bill of Rights is the first ten Amendments made to the Constitution. This addition did not change the Constitution, but instead made it more powerful in that it clarified the rights the government should and must protect. For example, the government cannot tell people what religion to follow. The Bill of Rights was added with three purposes in mind. Those three goals were (1) to protect the freedoms of the people, (2) to prevent the abuse of power by the government, and (3) to protect people accused of a crime.

Amendments to the U.S. Constitution

Ever the pragmatists, the Founding Fathers knew they needed to allow for some mechanism to change the Constitution to meet an evolving nation's needs over time. But they didn't want this mechanism to be too easy. They devised a process whereby amendments could be proposed either of two ways. The first way is for Congress to propose an amendment with a two-thirds majority vote in both the House of Representatives and the Senate. The second way is for two-thirds of the states to call a convention to consider proposing an amendment. None of the 27 amendments we have today were added the second way.

There are also two ways constitutional amendments can be ratified by the states. The more frequently used method is for three-fourths of the state legislatures to approve the amendment under consideration. Ratification can be complicated by the requirement in some state constitutions for a supermajority of the state legislature to pass an amendment to the U.S. Constitution. The second path requires the approval of three-fourths of state conventions specially selected to review the amendment. Though similar to the way in which the Constitution was originally ratified, this process has been used only once, to deal with the Twenty-first Amendment, which repealed the federal prohibition of alcohol put in place by the Eighteenth Amendment.

Given the high hurdle created by the need for supermajorities to achieve ratification, it is unsurprising that many amendments have been proposed but relatively few have passed.

You can expect to see questions about the **Amendments to the U.S. Constitution** on the GED® test. These questions may give you a passage to read and then an example in which you identify the Amendment that fits that situation. The question may have you classify circumstances, then match the circumstance to the appropriate Amendment. In any case, examining the Amendments should be part of your study plan. The following is a list and general explanation of some of the most important Amendments:

Key Amendments to the U.S. Constitution

First Amendment	Protects the five freedoms: religion, speech and press, assembly, petitioning
Fifth and Sixth Amendments	Protect the rights of the accused: speaking against oneself, due process, double jeopardy, fair and speedy jury trial
Thirteenth, Fourteenth, and Fifteenth Amendments	The Civil War Amendments: prohibit slavery, define citizenship, ensure voting rights for African Americans
Nineteenth Amendment	Women's Suffrage (right to vote)
Twenty-second Amendment	Limits the term of the president.
Twenty-sixth Amendment	Sets age for voting rights at 18 years old.

Executive Branch of the U.S. Government

In addition to **the president**, the executive branch is made up of **the executive departments.** These departments form the largest part of the executive branch and are responsible for carrying out the laws of Congress. The presidential cabinet is made up of the secretaries from each executive department. The following is a table of the department names, agencies, and responsibilities:[3]

---

[3] Source: *USA.gov.*

The President's Cabinet: Agencies and Their Roles

Department	Major Agencies	Responsibility
Agriculture	Food Safety and Inspection Food and Nutrition Service Commodity Credit Corporation	Inspects dairy, meat, and poultry School lunches and food stamps program Farmer assistance
Commerce	International Trade Administration Census Bureau Patent and Trademark Office National Weather Service	Promotes international trade Conducts census Issues patents Issues weather-related warnings to protect life and property; enhances economic growth
Defense	Joint Chiefs of Staff Departments of Armed Forces	Advises the president on security and military affairs Maintains armed forces Builds military bases
Education	Elementary and Secondary Education Educational Research and Improvement	Studies problems in education Advises the president about education programs
Energy	Conservation and Renewable Energy Nuclear Energy	Finds sources of energy Protects the energy supply Controls the use of nuclear energy
Health and Human Services	Social Security Administration Food and Drug Administration Public Health Services	Manages Social Security and Medicare Programs Approves new medicines Manages health and welfare programs
Housing and Urban Development	Housing Public Housing and Indian Housing	Assists state and local governments with urban problems Provides housing for low-income people
Homeland Security	Federal Emergency Management Transportation Security Administration U.S. Immigration and Customs Enforcement U.S. Coast Guard Customs and Border Protection Secret Service	Enhances domestic security Enforces laws concerning terrorism, immigration, travel Enforces border control, customs, trade, and immigration Protects U.S. borders along the sea coast, polices maritime trade, and saves those in peril on the sea Protects against entry into the country by illegal immigrants, illegal drugs, terrorists, and terrorist weapons Safeguards the nation's financial infrastructure and payment systems, and protects national leaders, visiting heads of state, and government-designated sites

(continued)

Department	Major Agencies	Responsibility
Justice	Alcohol, Tobacco, Firearms, and Explosives	Enforces drug, immigrations, and customs laws
	Drug Enforcement Administration	Protects against import, manufacture, and sale of illegal drugs
	Federal Bureau of Investigation (FBI)	Protects against terrorist and foreign intelligence threats, and uphold federal criminal laws
	U.S. Parole Commission	Supervises paroled criminal offenders
	U.S. Marshals Service	Protects federal courts and judges, transport prison inmates, carry out arrests and other police functions for courts
	INTERPOL Washington	Facilitates law enforcement cooperation with police agencies of other nations
Labor	OSHA (Occupational Safety and Health Administration)	Enforces labor laws and safety laws
	VETS	Aids military veterans to find employment
	Bureau of Labor Statistics	Provides data on employment, wages, inflation, productivity, and many other topics
State	Arms Control Global Affairs Public Diplomacy U.S. mission to the United Nations	Develops and implements foreign policy
Interior	Indian Affairs Land Management Fish and Wildlife Geological Parks Mining	Protects and provides access to national, natural, and cultural heritage
Treasury	Engraving and Printing Internal Revenue Service (IRS) U.S. Mint	Maintains and monitors financial well-being
Transportation	Federal Aviation Administration (FAA) National Transportation Safety Board	Develops and provides for the safety of transportation
Veterans Affairs	Veterans Benefits Administration (VBA) Veterans Health Administration (VHA) National Cemetery Association (NCA)	The department's mission is to serve U.S. veterans and their families comprehensively—as their principal advocate in ensuring that they receive medical care, benefits, and social support; and to promote the health, welfare, and dignity of all veterans in recognition of their service to the nation.

Test questions about the executive departments may include a table like the one above. After reading the table, you may be asked to find information concerning a department's duties, or match an agency to a department. You may be given a scenario and asked to identify which department would handle this situation.

Besides executive departments, there also are many independent departments. Some of the independent departments and agencies will be familiar to you. If they are not, often it is not difficult to determine what the agency does just by the title. For example, the Environmental Protection Agency enforces laws to protect the air, land, and water.

Classifying Information

Classifying is a part of the GED® test. Classifying is also a strategy for organizing information. The test might ask you to put things in the correct category or identify the category of a group of items. This will require you to examine the information and the items. Then, compare and contrast in order to fit the items together or not.

EXAMPLE

These words, phrases, or items are part of one executive department. Determine which department they would best match.

1. Food stamps, free lunches, free corn seeds

2. Collect taxes, arrest counterfeiters, destroy old money

3. Build interstate highway, inspect airplanes, make regulations for waterways

4. Manage Indian reservations, decide areas for mines, develop national parklands

ANSWER: You should have answered based on the information in the table:

1. Department of Agriculture

2. Department of the Treasury

3. Department of Transportation

4. Department of the Interior

Another way to classify is to determine what does NOT belong under the category.

1. Department of Energy—Nuclear fuel reserves, coal and oil reserves, solar power devices, National Council for Teachers of Mathematics.

2. Department of Education—Elementary school curriculum, school charters, school lunches, secondary school standards.

3. Department of Health and Human Services—SSA, FDA, IRS, PHS.

You should have answered, based on the information in the table:

1. National Council for Teachers of Mathematics does not fit.

2. School lunches is not part of this department.

3. The IRS is not part of the Department of Health and Human Services.

Democracies often have several political parties. Political parties are groups of people with the same ideologies who join together to nominate and support a candidate. The United States is dominated by two major parties. Nonetheless, other parties have existed and influenced voters throughout the years. Many people believe there is little difference between the parties; however, a careful comparison reveals many differences between and among parties. Below is a chart of some of the influential parties in the United States over the years.

Influential U.S. Political Parties

Political Party	Period and leaders	Ideologies and platform
Federalists	1789–1820, Alexander Hamilton	National bank, tariffs, bankers, and businessmen
Anti-Federalists	1789–1792, Patrick Henry	Against central, powerful government
Democratic-Republican	1791–1793, James Madison, Thomas Jefferson	Against big business and a national bank
Whigs	1833–1856, Daniel Webster	Opposed Andrew Jackson Supported Congress over the president
Free-Soilers	1848–1855	Anti-slavery
Progressive Party	1912, Theodore Roosevelt	Reforms
Black Panther Party	1966–1970s	Equality for African Americans
Workers World Party	1959–Present	Workers' rights Affirmative action
Green Party	1984–Present	Environmental and social justice
Tea Party	2004–Present	Generally opposes government intervention in the private sector while supporting lower taxation and stronger immigration controls

This list is just some of the political parties that were popular at one time, though some remain active. However, the major political parties remain the Republicans and the Democrats. Both nominate and campaign for major candidates in all elections in the United States on the local, state, and federal levels.

Specialist groups, also known as special interest groups, are people, companies, organizations that attempt to influence politicians and their political parties. These groups use lobbying as a tactic to convenience the politicians and parties to support their ideas or concerns. Over the years, special interest groups and political parties have shaped public policy. Below is a list of some contemporary issues that are favorites of lobbyists:

Death Penalty	Drug Trafficking
Gun Control	Abortion
Budget and Taxes	Education Reforms
Environmental Concerns	Campaign Finance
Social Security	Defense Spending
Health Insurance Reform	Agriculture Policy (Farm Bill)

One of the most misunderstood processes in the United States system of government is the **Electoral College**. The average American voter does not understand why this system exists or how it works. It is in place to serve as a check and balance against unsound decisions made by the voters. Recently, the utility of the electoral system has been questioned. To understand better why it is criticized, it is important to understand how it works.

Electoral College

The Electoral College requires candidates to win electors, as opposed to winning the popular vote nationally. Each state has a number of electors, based on population. For example, California has 55 electors, while North Dakota only has three. (The District of Columbia is allocated three electors, which gives it the status of a state.) In the case of almost all the states, the candidate who wins the majority of popular votes in that state wins all of the electoral votes for that state. Therefore, if candidate Mr. Smith wins 51% of the popular vote in Florida, while candidate Mrs. Jones wins 49% of the popular vote, then Mr. Smith wins all 29 of the electoral votes for Florida. Maine and Nebraska are exceptions to this "winner-take-all" rule, as they split the electoral votes in certain circumstances. There are a total of 538 electors nationally. The candidate who wins 270 electoral votes is declared the winner of the general election.

Election of 2000

The Electoral College has come under fire, especially after the election of 2000. That year, the winner of the popular vote overall in the United States did not win enough electoral votes to win the general election. This was only the fourth time in U.S. history that the winner of the election was not the winner of the popular vote. George W. Bush won 47.9% of the popular vote, in comparison to Al Gore's 48.4%, yet Bush won 271 electoral votes to Gore's 266.

Below is a map of the results of the Election of 2000 showing how the states awarded electoral votes to the candidates.

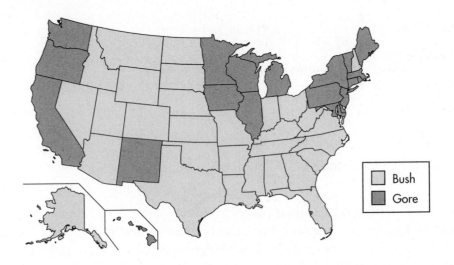

Bush
Gore

Gore won the dark states, while Bush won the lighter states. Compare this to the graph below:

Popular Votes

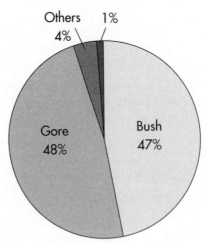

Others 4%   1%

Gore 48%   Bush 47%

PRACTICE!

Based on the map and the graph on the previous page, choose the correct answer to the following questions.

1. Based on the electoral map, which one of these statements is true?

    A. The candidates were equal in electoral votes.

    B. Each candidate carried states in the South.

    C. Gore won New York and California.

    D. Gore won his home state of Tennessee.

2. Based on the pie graph, which one of these statements is true?

    A. 1% of the vote was not counted.

    B. Gore won the popular vote.

    C. Bush won the popular vote.

    D. Neither candidate was very popular.

3. Based on the map, pie graph, and related information, which of these statements best summarizes the Election of 2000?

    A. The popular vote is not as important as the electoral vote.

    B. The electoral vote must be 270-plus in order for the candidate to be declared a winner.

    C. The popular vote alone is enough to select a winner.

    D. Gore should have won the 2000 election since he is a good person.

Social Studies Practice 1 Answers

1. C.

Gore won New York and California. The map indicates the dark states were won by Gore. California and New York are dark states. Options A and B are not information found on the map. To answer this question incorrectly would be to confuse the shades of color on the map. It is very important to read and consider all the information provided in the text.

2. **B.**

Gore won the popular vote. Option A (1%) does not say what it represents. Option C would be to confuse the shades of color again. Option D is an opinion and cannot be supported by the map or graph.

3. **B.**

Electoral vote must be 270-plus in order for the candidate to be declared a winner. The passage supports answer choice B. Option A is not true nor is it supported by any of the information given. Option C is not based on facts given. Option D is an opinion and cannot be supported by the information provided.

The Election of 1800

There have been many controversial elections in the United States. For example, the election of 1800, which some historians called the "Revolution of 1800," was very different from previous elections. It started out similar to the elections the country had seen before, with John Adams running for re-election as the Federalist candidate and Thomas Jefferson as the Republican. However, the campaign took an unprecedented turn. It was the first of its kind with mudslinging and radical accusations. The election finally came to a tie in electoral votes, which left the decision to the House of Representatives. At first there was a strong deadlock on the vote. Finally, Jefferson was elected president, marking the first peaceful transfer of power between parties.

The Election of 1828

The Election of 1828 was also an unusual campaign. By this time, the two-party system was in place. Incumbent John Quincy Adams ran against Andrew Jackson. This campaign went as far as to accuse war hero Jackson of murder. But nonetheless, Jackson won by 56% of the popular vote and 83 electoral votes. This made the election of 1828 the most decisive in United States history up to that point.

The Election of 1860

In 1860, the ballot was divided among four candidates because important issues had divided the country. Slavery and the railroad made this election explosive.

The Election of 1912

The election of 1912 has been called one of the most unusual in United States history. Why? Two Republican presidents ran against one another. William Howard Taft was the incumbent, and his predecessor, Theodore Roosevelt, was the challenger. However, a break in one party's loyalty historically opened the door for the other party. In 1912, Woodrow Wilson, the Democratic candidate, won with approximately 42% of the popular vote. In addition to two Republicans and one Democrat, a Socialist, Eugene V. Debs, received 6% of the vote. Below is an image illustrating the states carried by each candidate.

1912 ELECTORAL MAP
How Each State Voted

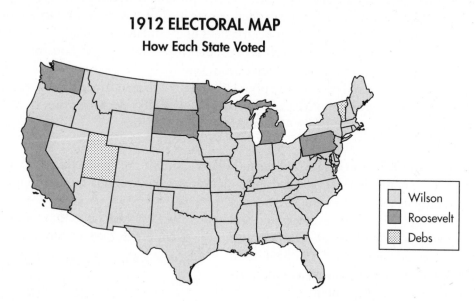

Watergate Scandal

Richard M. Nixon became the president in 1969. It was a troubled time in the United States, with many changes taking place in society on the cultural, political, and economic fronts. Nixon faced a hostile Democratic Congress and a nation in an unpopular war in Vietnam, but his greatest downfall was the **Watergate scandal.**

The Watergate incident (1972) involved a break-in at the offices of the Democratic National Committee by five men attempting to plant wiretapping equipment. It was discovered that the men worked for the Committee for the Re-Election of the President. It was later revealed that President Nixon was part of a cover-up, which sparked an investigation and media blitz.

In the end, the U.S. Supreme Court ruled against Nixon on the issue of whether he had to turn over incriminating evidence to an investigative committee. The evidence included tape-recorded telephone conversations and discussions in the White House that indicated he had knowledge of attempts by his subordinates to cover up the break-in. On August 9, 1974, Nixon resigned as president before articles of **impeachment** could be brought against him by the U.S. House of Representatives. After Nixon **resigned**, Vice President Gerald Ford took office. The new president gave his predecessor a full pardon for "any offenses against the United States, which he . . . has committed or may have committed while in office." The result of the Watergate scandal was a loss of faith in the American political system and the government.

In Focus: Elections of 2008 and 2016

The Election of 2008 was unusual in many ways. For example, it was the first campaign since 1952 not to include an **incumbent** president or vice president. In addition, the election saw the Republicans nominate, for the first time in their party's history, a woman for vice president (Sarah Palin, then governor of Alaska). The Democratic field of candidates included Senator Hillary Rodham Clinton of New York, the wife of former President Bill Clinton, and Senator Barack Obama of Illinois. The Democrats nominated Obama, who went on to receive more votes than any candidate in history as he garnered 53% of the popular vote. In a first in American history, he defeated a fellow sitting U.S. senator, John McCain of Arizona, with 365 electoral votes to McCain's 173. Obama thus became the nation's first African American president.

In 2016, with Obama in his second term, Hillary Clinton ran again, this time becoming the first woman to be nominated for president by a major party. Following a bitterly fought campaign, however, Republican (and onetime Democrat) Donald J. Trump, a real estate developer and political novice who had never held elective office, was elected the 45th U.S. president. Trump's election was widely viewed as a repudiation of the so-called **establishment**.

Bear in mind that American presidential elections *always* follow the same electoral procedures, even amidst unique twists and turns. On the GED® Social Studies test, be sure to closely read the information and examine any graphics provided. Maps, charts, and campaign advertisements are the sorts of things with which you may be presented. Be sure to stick to the facts before you.

Victoria Woodhull, the first woman to run for the presidency, arguing for woman suffrage before the House Judiciary Committee in 1871. Illustration from *Frank Leslie's Illustrated Newspaper* (vol. 31, no. 801). *Library of Congress.*

The First Woman to Run for President Could Not Cast a Ballot for Herself

Though Hillary Clinton became the first woman to be named as a major party's nominee for President of the United States in 2016, she is far from the first woman to run for the nation's highest office. That distinction goes to Victoria Claflin Woodhull.

- Ran in the 1872 election as the Equal Rights Party nominee.

- Abolitionist Frederick Douglass was chosen as her running mate, but he never acknowledged the campaign.

- Promoted allowing women to vote (they could not yet do so under the Constitution) as well as reforms for workers.

- Could not legally vote for herself, and at 34 years old would have been a year shy of being eligible for the presidency.

- Backed by financier Cornelius Vanderbilt, she and her sister opened the first Wall Street brokerage firm run by women.

- Died in England on June 9, 1927, just under seven years after women in the U.S. gained the right to vote.

(Adapted from the Voice of America, "First Female Candidate for U.S. President Ran in 1872," July 27, 2016, by Chris Hannas.)

Drawing Conclusions and Making Inferences

The GED® Social Studies test will require you to be able to make inferences and draw conclusions based on information you are given. Making a logical **inference** means making an educated guess based on the evidence in front of you. **Drawing conclusions** refers to information that is implied, but is not clearly stated. Writers often tell you more than they say literally or explicitly. They provide hints and clues that help you to get the idea of what they are saying. It is not a matter of guessing. It really means taking the information provided and going deeper into its meaning. You can use your logic or prior knowledge to understand what the writer is leading the audience to understand.

Drawing conclusions and making inferences are closely related. **Drawing a conclusion** is the result of making an inference. For example, suppose you are in your room studying. Suddenly, you hear tires screeching and a loud crash. Next, you hear sirens. You saw nothing, but by using the facts of what you heard, prior knowledge, and logic, you can infer that there was a car accident on the street outside your building. Though it may turn out not to be *exactly* how you pictured it, your conclusion is reasonable and logical. Making inferences and drawing conclusions means choosing the most likely explanation based on the facts you know and the situation with which you are presented.

There are several ways to help you draw conclusions.

When the meaning of a word is implied, it is used in a context that will provide the word's general meaning. This will help you understand the meaning of the unknown word. For instance, the following sentence implies the meaning of the word "licit."

> There are several licit standards used in all court proceedings and trials in the United States.

Since trials and court proceedings have to do with lawyers, judges, and courtrooms, it is logical that "licit" does too. **Standards** mean rules or standards of practice, so you can infer that "licit" means legal, lawful, sets of regulations. Replace the word "licit" with "legal" and it is an understandable sentence.

Practice using inference to draw conclusions with the following questions on government.

 PRACTICE!

Read the passages and answer the questions.

The Framers of the United States Constitution in 1787 knew the Constitution had to be ratified quickly. Earlier, in 1777, 13 states were required for ratification of the Articles of Confederation. It took a long time and was difficult for the states to reach agreement. Therefore, in order to ratify the U.S. Constitution more easily and quickly, the Framers decided that only nine states would be needed for ratification. Nine states was a clear majority. In a democracy, the majority is used to make decisions.

1. What are the facts in this paragraph?

   _____

   _____

   _____

   _____

   _____

   _____

2. What does the word **ratify** mean?

   A. to change

   B. to approve

   C. to neglect

   D. to reject

3. What conclusion can you draw from this passage?

   A. The Constitution was a long document and difficult to read.

   B. The Framers of the Constitution could not agree on anything.

   C. The Framers decided that a majority vote would make it easier to obtain ratification of the Constitution by the states.

   D. The Articles of Confederation were more important than the Constitution.

Read the following passage and answer the questions.

The duty of the United States Congress is to make new laws. Both the senators and representatives meet to write and pass new bills during their terms. They meet for at least two regular sessions, which last several months of the year. When both the House and Senate agree that they have finished their work for the year, the session is adjourned. At this point, the members of Congress return to their home states to work with their constituents (i.e., the people represented by a designated government offical or office holder).

4. What are the facts in this passage?

5. What does the word **adjourn** mean?

    A. to agree

    B. to a period of time

    C. to vote

    D. to end

6. After reading this passage you can conclude that

    A. Congress meets all year in Washington, D.C.

    B. Congress tries to pass all new bills in a regular session.

    C. Congress is not in session during the Christmas holiday season.

    D. Congress does not work except during regular sessions.

Read the passage and answer the questions.

The system of taxation in the United States is always being debated. Many Americans feel the tax system is not fair to all the citizens. Regressive taxes like the sales tax require everyone to pay the same amount of tax. People feel this type of tax is unfair, since people with higher incomes pay the same amount as people with lower incomes. Progressive taxes, like the personal income tax, appeal to these people. A progressive tax requires people with higher incomes to pay more than people with lower incomes.

7. What are the facts in this passage?

   _____

   _____

   _____

   _____

   _____

   _____

8. What do the terms **regressive tax** and **progressive tax** refer to?

   A. Taxes that fall and taxes that rise

   B. Taxes that are the same amount for everyone and taxes that vary depending on income

   C. Taxes that stay the same for all the citizens

   D. Taxes that are used to pay for the operations of the government

9. According to the passage, it can be concluded that

   A. people agree on taxation.

   B. people often disagree on taxation.

   C. the tax system in the United States is the best system in the world.

   D. the tax system in the United States is satisfactory to all U.S. citizens.

10. The process of a bill becoming a law involves the legislative and executive branches of government. The process is outlined in the chart below.

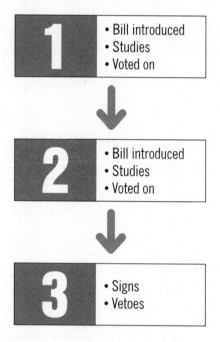

1
• Bill introduced
• Studies
• Voted on

2
• Bill introduced
• Studies
• Voted on

3
• Signs
• Vetoes

Using the numbers in the chart, indicate what role each of the following persons or entities takes in the legislative process.

President [ ]   House of Representatives [ ]   Senate [ ]

Social Studies Practice 1.1 Answers

1. Answers may vary. Facts include: In 1777, 13 states were required to ratify. The Founding Fathers decided that nine, a majority, was enough to qualify.

2. **B.**

Approve. Use context clues to determine what the word means. This passage is about the approval of changes by at least nine members.

3. **C.**

The Framers decided that a majority vote would enable them to make decisions quicker. This statement is the central idea of the passage. Option A may be true, but was not the reason the Founding Fathers wanted a majority vote. Option B is an opinion, and is not stated in the passage. Option D: the Articles of Confederation was a weak document for the needs of the nation, but, in United States history it was a very important document as it was the first governing document of the nation.

4.   Congress makes laws. Both senators and representatives are part of the process. There are at least two regular sessions, between or after which, Congress continues to work at home.

5.   **D.**

"Adjourn" means "to end." When the session ends (adjourns), each member of Congress returns to his or her home state.

6.   **B.**

Congress tries to prepare all new bills in a regular session.

Option A is incorrect since the passage states Congress members return to their home state to continue to work. There is no mention of Christmas; therefore, option C is not correct. The fact that Congress holds two regular sessions and all members return to their home states makes option D incorrect.

7.   Taxation is always being debated. Sales tax is a regressive tax. Income tax is a progressive tax.

8.   **B.**

Taxes that are the same amount for everyone and taxes that vary depending on income. This is the definition provided by the text. Options A and C are not given in this passage. Option D may be true, but is not in the passage. The answers must be supported by the information provided.

9.   **B.**

People often disagree on taxation. This statement is the central idea of the passage. Option A is clearly disputed in the passage. C is an opinion and cannot be supported by the text. Option D is not true and the opposite of the facts in the passage.

10. President: 3
    House: 2
    Senate: 1

Chapter 2

United States History

United States history makes up 20% of the GED® Social Studies test. These questions can cover time periods from exploration and settlement up to modern times. These questions often provide a document or excerpt of a document or passage, with or without a graphic image of some kind. The questions may ask you to draw conclusions based on the information provided, analyze events and ideas, or determine the purpose or the point of view being expressed.

Building Vocabulary Skills

Many people have difficulty comprehending words in social studies textbooks. Many times you encounter unknown terms, foreign words, names in relation to long-past events, abstract "isms," or words related to government, finance, and culture. As a reader, you need strategies to deal with vocabulary.

You probably have been told to "look it up" when you don't know a word. Using a dictionary is not the best strategy when it comes to taking the GED® test; after all, you won't have a dictionary at your side during the test. One reason you don't want to overly rely on the dictionary is that it provides a great deal more information than you need. You need to be able to know what the word means, or at least guess about it based on the context surrounding the term. Look for context clues. In other words, **context clues** (words before and after, how the unknown word is used in the sentence, what the passage is about) provide you hints to the meaning of the unknown word.

One strategy when an unknown word is encountered is to keep reading. A fluent reader keeps reading to determine if he or she can figure out the main idea without knowing the word. When you get to a word you don't know, don't get bogged down with it. Just keep reading. Often the text itself will tell you what the word means. For example, the word "arduous" could mean difficult (i.e., hard to accomplish), strenuous (i.e., indicating you are working really hard), tiring, and, by implication, perhaps unpleasant, challenging, daunting (i.e., frightening), and the like. Often the writer will explain the particular meaning he or she has in mind by following the use of the particular word with some further context. So, for example, instead of writing, "Sara was given an *arduous* task that she didn't want to do," the writer might say, "Sara was given an *arduous, or difficult,* task she didn't want to do." So, as you read, rather than stumble over the term "arduous," keep reading, and you will see that the writer means to say that an "arduous" task is one that is "difficult."

Another strategy is to separate words into meaningful parts. Knowing various parts like prefixes, suffixes, and root words can help you figure out the whole word's meaning. The following are a few common social studies word parts:

Prefix	Meaning
anthro-	man, mankind
chron-	time
circum-	around
counter-	against
contra-	against
fort-	strong
geo-	earth
terra-	earth
multi-	many
trans-	across
semi-	half

Suffix	Meaning
-arch	ruler
-crat	rules by
-ism	belief in, practice of
-ify	make

EXAMPLE

Use the word parts to help you determine the meaning of the following words.

1. *circumnavigate*

2. *fortify*

3. *multifaceted*

4. *activism*

5. *transcontinental*

ANSWERS

1. *Circum-* means *around*; *navigate* means *travel (a route); steer a course, determine a route*—hence: *travel around (a planned route)*.

   Example: Circumnavigate the globe.

2. *Fort* means *strong*; *-ify* means *make*—hence: *make strong*.

3. *Multi-* means *many*; *facet* comes from a French word that means *face* or *side* (like faces of a cut diamond, or sides of an issue or topic)—hence *many sided*.

4. *Act* means *to do something; ism* means *belief in* or *practice of*—hence *practice of a particular act,* or *belief in practicing a particular act,* or *belief in keeping active.*

5. *Trans* means *across; continent* means *one of the world's continuous expanses of land* (such as North America, or Asia)—hence *across a continent.*

It is a good idea to familiarize yourself with some terms common on the GED® Social Studies test. Here's a list to give you a working knowledge of the vocabulary you'll need to excel.

- Amend—to change or add

- Amendment—a change or addition (an addition or change to the U.S. Constitution)

- Annexation—forcible or lawful taking of property or territory

- Armistice—a temporary agreement to end hostilities (a battle timeout)

- Assimilate—to conform or adjust to the customs of other people

- Boycott—to withdraw from social or commercial relations with an entity (such as a store, company, or nation) as a means of punishment or protest (a refusal to buy or participate in trade)

- Dissenter—someone who disagrees with an opinion, policy, or law (often refers to disagreeing with government policy)

- Emancipation—freeing from restrictions (refers particularly to the freedom granted American slaves)

- Enfranchise—to give rights of citizenship to (especially with respect to the right to vote)

- Impeachment—to charge a public official formally with misconduct (usually involves removing someone from office)

- Inauguration—the beginning or introduction (e.g., presidential inauguration)

- Mercenary—a professional soldier hired to serve in a foreign army

- Naturalization—the process of foreign people becoming citizens of a country

- Ratify—to confirm by expressing consent (e.g., accepting an amendment, welcoming a state into the union, etc.)

- Suffrage—the right to vote

- Tenement—apartment, room, or small dwelling owned by someone other than the people living there

Landmark Documents

Important historical documents are often referred to as **landmark documents**. This means the writing had some significance in history and may have resulted in some major change or decision. Landmark documents include U.S. Supreme Court decisions. They could also be legal documents such as declarations, acts, or legislative actions. Landmark documents are important because they are the written proof of events throughout history.

Landmark documents will comprise a large portion of both government and history parts on the Social Studies test. While it is impossible to predict which documents will be included on your exam, it is helpful to understand the time period, historical, social, and political trends of the time. A helpful study aid would be a timeline of events. The timeline can help you remember the context in which the document was completed. Be sure and look for the date the document was written when you are completing your GED® test.

Here is an example of a timeline of some historical documents.[1]

DATE	EVENT
1215	Magna Carta
1620	Mayflower Compact
1776	Declaration of Independence
1777	Articles of Confederation

(continued)

[1] Source: U.S. Department of State, Office of the Historian.

DATE	EVENT
1789	U.S. Constitution
1791	Bill of Rights
1803	*Marbury v. Madison*
1819	*McCulloch v. Maryland*
1823	Monroe Doctrine
1857	*Dred Scott Decision*
1863	Emancipation Proclamation
1896	*Plessy v. Ferguson*
1917	Espionage Act
1919	*Schenck v. United States*
1948	Marshall Plan
1954	*Brown v. Board of Education*
1963	*Gideon v. Wainwright*; Dr. Martin Luther King Jr.'s *Letter from Birmingham Jail*; March on Washington for Jobs and Freedom (Civil Rights March on Washington)
1964	*Escobedo v. Illinois*
1966	*Miranda v. Arizona*
1971	*New York Times v. United States*
1991	Strategic Arms Reduction Treaty I

One important landmark document is the Declaration of Independence. This document literally represents the beginning of the United States government. To understand the American system of government, you need to understand the history and content of this document.

The American Revolutionary War began in 1775. The movement toward complete independence from Great Britain was growing. In 1776, the Continental Congress created a committee that included Thomas Jefferson, John Adams, and Benjamin Franklin. Think of the Congress as John Adams did: as a school for American leaders. The committee was to write a formal statement of the colonies' intentions. On July 4, Congress adopted the Declaration of Independence, written largely by Thomas Jefferson. This is why July 4 is celebrated as Independence Day.

Before the war, not many people wanted independence from Great Britain. But over the next few years Great Britain took actions, including taxing and restricting trade, that angered the colonists. Then, Thomas Paine wrote a pamphlet called "Common Sense" in which he urged people to make a stand for independence as it was a "natural right." Paine's razor-sharp, plainspoken prose rallied common people to the cause.

The Declaration listed grievances against the King, but the document is best known for this sentence:

> "*We hold these truths to be self-evident,* that all men are created equal, that they are endowed by their Creator with certain unalienable rights, that among these are life, liberty and the pursuit of happiness."

Another type of historical document could be something other than writing. Political cartoons are sometimes on the GED® test. Here is an example of two historical cartoons about the same topic.

Cartoon #1

Source: Puck Magazine, February 20, 1915

SUFFRAGETTES AT HOME.

He. "I SAY, THAT LADY OVER THERE LOOKS RATHER OUT OF IT."
She. "YES, YOU SEE, MOST OF US HERE HAVE BEEN IN PRISON TWO OR THREE TIMES, AND SHE, POOR DEAR, HAS ONLY BEEN BOUND OVER!"

Source: Punch Magazine, April 14, 1909.

These two political cartoons address women's suffrage. The two images are very different. Both are typical images of how women's suffrage was viewed in the late 1900s. You may be asked to analyze the point of view depicted in the images. Here's a list of questions that can help guide you in thinking about the message in each cartoon and how the two cartoons compare.

What people and objects are shown?

Cartoon No. 1.   A torch-bearing female called "Votes for Women" strides across the western states.

Cartoon No. 2.   Women of all shapes, sizes, and ages, a speaker's platform, some type of stage, pretty decorations, and a caption that reads, "The only way we can gain women's suffrage is by making our appeal through our charm, our grace, and our beauty."

What is happening in the image?

Cartoon No. 1.   The image symbolizes the awakening of America's women to the aspiration for suffrage. In 1915, when this cartoon appeared, women in the West had the right to vote, but not those in the East, which is why we see women there reaching out toward the torch bearer

Cartoon No. 2.   Women are gathered to hear other women speak about suffrage.

What did the creator of this source want people to think happened during the women's suffrage movement?

Cartoon No. 1.   The cartoonist has a distinct political bent. As it turns out, 1915 was the year New Yorkers cast ballots for the "Votes for Women" referendum, which went down to defeat in November 1915 but passed two years later, in 1917.

Cartoon No. 2.   Only women were for women's suffrage.

Based on the evidence in both cartoons and the knowledge that women did ultimately receive the right to vote, what was the point of view of each cartoon creator?

Cartoon No. 1.   The creator focused on the momentum on women's voting rights sparked in the West.

Cartoon No. 2.   The creator was in favor of women's suffrage and thought only women were supporting the movement.

Strategies to Understand Historical Documents

When you read a historical document there are some strategies you can practice to help you understand it better. Determine who wrote the document and when it was written. Sometimes this is given before the excerpt or after. Read the introduction. Knowing <u>who</u> the author was, <u>when</u> it was written, and <u>what</u> it is about can give you an idea of what you are looking for before you begin to read. Read the subtitles and notice how it is organized. Since these passages will be in a historical context, you might find unfamiliar words. In this case, try to use context to determine the meaning of the words.

Here is an example of a historical document. Before you start reading the text of the document, do the following:

- Determine the author.

- Identify the introduction.

- Determine when it was written.

- Identify the title and subtitles.

- Find any unfamiliar words. Consider the context of these words to determine the meaning.

The Pledge of Allegiance

The Pledge of Allegiance was written in August 1892 by the socialist minister Francis Bellamy (1855–1931). It was originally published in *The Youth's Companion* on September 8, 1892. Bellamy had hoped that the pledge would be used by citizens in any country.

In its original form it read:

> "I pledge allegiance to my Flag and the Republic for which it stands, one nation, indivisible, with liberty and justice for all."

In 1923, the words, "the Flag of the United States of America" were added. At this time it read:

> "I pledge allegiance to the Flag of the United States of America and to the Republic for which it stands, one nation, indivisible, with liberty and justice for all."

In 1954, in response to the Communist threat of the times, President Eisenhower encouraged Congress to add the words "under God," creating the 31-word pledge we say today. Bellamy's daughter objected to this alteration. Today it reads:

> "I pledge allegiance to the flag of the United States of America, and to the republic for which it stands, one nation under God, indivisible, with liberty and justice for all."

Section 4 of the Flag Code states:

> The Pledge of Allegiance to the Flag: "I pledge allegiance to the Flag of the United States of America, and to the Republic for which it stands, one Nation under God, indivisible, with liberty and justice for all", should be rendered by standing at attention facing the flag with the right hand over the heart. When not in uniform men should remove any non-religious headdress with their right hand and hold it at the left shoulder, the hand being over the heart. Persons in uniform should remain silent, face the flag, and render the military salute."

The original Bellamy salute, first described in 1892 by Francis Bellamy, who authored the original Pledge, began with a military salute, and after reciting the words "to the flag," the arm was extended toward the flag.

> At a signal from the Principal the pupils, in ordered ranks, hands to the side, face the Flag. Another signal is given; every pupil gives the flag the military salute — right hand lifted, palm downward, to a line with the forehead and close to it. Standing thus, all repeat together, slowly, "I pledge allegiance to my Flag and the Republic for which it stands; one Nation indivisible, with Liberty and Justice for all." At the words, "to my Flag," the right hand is extended gracefully, palm upward, toward the Flag, and remains in this gesture till the end of the affirmation; whereupon all hands immediately drop to the side.
>
> *The Youth's Companion,* 1892

Shortly thereafter, the pledge was begun with the right hand over the heart, and after reciting "to the Flag," the arm was extended toward the Flag, palm-down.

In World War II, the salute too much resembled the Nazi salute, so it was changed to keep the right hand over the heart throughout.[*2]

- **Author** — written by someone for the Independence Hall Association website, ushistory.org.

- **When** — Sometime after World War II (see last paragraph).

- **Introduction** — The Pledge of Allegiance was written in August 1892 by the socialist minister Francis Bellamy (1855–1931). It was originally published in *The Youth's Companion* on September 8, 1892. Bellamy had hoped that the pledge would be used by citizens in any country.

- **Title and Subtitles** — The Pledge of Allegiance; Section 4 of the Flag Code statutes.

- **Unknown words** might include "affirmation" or "Nazi."

The previous passage was somewhat difficult to read, but it was about a familiar topic. The familiarity makes it easier to put the information together.

When you are presented with any type of writing you should be able to evaluate the credibility of the author. An unknown author makes this more difficult. You can use these strategies to help you determine the writer's knowledge as well as the bias or point of view expressed. You won't be able to research the author's background or previous work during the test, so you will need to use the information provided for you and your own knowledge. First, examine the objectivity of the piece of writing. You can do this by skimming the document and looking for the answer to these types of questions.

Does the author state the goals for this article or passage?

Is he/she trying to inform, explain, or advocate?

Is this writing attempting to persuade you to do something or think in a certain direction?

Are both sides of the subject presented?

Does the writer acknowledge an opposing point of view?

Does the write cite sources used to uphold his point of view?

These questions are some that will help you to determine the point of view, the author's bias, and credibility on the subject.

---

[2] From "Historic Documents." ushistory.org, website of the Independence Hall Association. *http://www.ushistory.org/documents/pledge.htm.*

Graphic Organizers

As mentioned before, determining the point of view of the author is an important part of the exam. A good way to look at two opposing (or alternative) points of view is to divide a piece of paper into three columns. State the opposing points of view in the left and right columns. As you read, note in the left- and right-hand columns how the two viewpoints differ from one another. In the middle column list the ways the viewpoints are the same or are in agreement. Following is an example of what it might look like on your paper.

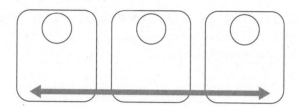

Another way to examine multiple points of view might be the Venn diagram. Following is an example of how to use a Venn diagram to sort out the different points of view. In this diagram, where the circles overlap one another list the ways the viewpoints agree, and in the remainder of the circle list the ways each respective viewpoint is different from the others.

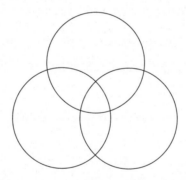

Making your own graphic is always a good way to sort through information. You could draw a diagram of steps in a process, or make a staircase or ladder diagram to list the steps in the correct order.

Cause and Effect

Another way to evaluate the author's viewpoint as you read a test problem is to analyze which events or circumstances the author considers to be the cause of other events or circumstances. That is: identify which events are the "cause" and which are the "effect." For example, look for cause and effect in the following prompt:

When the American colonists decided to become independent of Great Britain, they knew they needed a constitution. The first such document they developed was the Articles of Confederation. This document created a loose alliance of the states. However, the Articles of Confederation were not effective in creating a well-established country. For example, they did not provide for a president or leader, a court system, or a central government. The colonists feared strong central government. As a result, the Articles of Confederation left most of the powers to the states.

The weaknesses of the Articles of Confederation led to the writing of the United States Constitution. The Constitution allows the federal government and the states to exercise some separate, but also some nearly identical, powers.

The previous information could be used in supporting a cause-and-effect question. Here is an example of such a question:

During the Revolutionary War, the Americans borrowed millions of dollars from foreign governments and banks. This debt had to be paid. However, under the Articles of Confederation, the new government of the United States lacked the power to tax.

Which statement best describes why this situation occurred?

    A. The United States refused to pay its debt.

    B. The Articles of Confederation had no provisions for a central government.

    C. The people refused to pay taxes.

    D. There were no reasons to pay these taxes.

ANSWER: (B) The passage states the Articles of Confederation did not provide for a president or leader, a court system, or a central government.

Examining periods of history also can help you to focus on the attitudes and trends of the time. This can help you to understand the sequence of events or the events related to this time period. The cause-and-effect questions may ask you to connect one event to another.

EXAMPLE

Read the following excerpt; identify the cause and effects to answer the questions.

In 1852, Harriett Beecher Stowe wrote a novel entitled *Uncle Tom's Cabin*. This book described life as a slave. The book was very successful and was widely read by thousands of Americans.

This book helped to heighten the tension between antislavery and proslavery citizens. People who were proslavery claimed the book distorted how slaves were treated. People who were antislavery became more aware of the need to end slavery. Others who had not really formed an opinion about the issue of slavery began to question their own lack of a position on the issue. By the late 1850s, the issue of slavery in the United States became the center of the political and social debate across the country.

Identify the causes and effects from this excerpt.

ANSWER:

Cause: Thousands read *Uncle Tom's Cabin.*

Effects:

1. Helped heighten the tension between antislavery and proslavery people.

2. Increased awareness of the issue of slavery.

3. Brought the debate to the center of political and social arenas.

Remember, you can't always rely on time order. Instead you need to look for a connection between events.

EXAMPLE

Read the following excerpt to find the causes and effects.

Between 1880 and 1920, more than 24 million people immigrated to the United States. Many factors pushed them, including poverty, persecution, and wars in their homelands. Immigration resulted in large population increases in many cities. This large wave of newcomers also sparked protests by other Americans and led to laws limiting immigration.

1. What was the underlying event?

2. What were the causes of immigration?

3. What were the effects?

ANSWERS:

1. Immigration to the United States.

2. Poverty, persecution, and wars in the homelands of those immigrating to the United States.

3. Growth of cities, protests against newcomers, laws limiting immigration.

Another way to understand historical documents is to find how one is connected to another. A good example would be to compare and contrast the landmark U.S. Supreme Court cases *Plessy v. Ferguson* and *Brown v. Board of Education of Topeka*. Under Louisiana's two-year-old Separate Car Act, Homer Plessy was jailed in 1892 for sitting in the white section of an East Louisiana Railroad passenger train car. In the case, the Supreme Court established that separate facilities for blacks and whites were constitutional as long as they were equal. The "separate but equal" doctrine was quickly extended to cover many areas of public life, such as restaurants, theaters, restrooms, and public schools. But "separate but equal" was never the reality, as most facilities for blacks were not just unequal but notably inferior.

Decades later, in 1954, the *Brown* decision struck down "separate but equal." In the *Brown* case, eight-year-old Linda Brown traveled a long distance to attend school while whites were only a few blocks from their school. Her father testified that the only bus available to take his daughter on some days forced her to arrive up to 90 minutes before the school doors opened. When it reached the Supreme Court, *Brown* actually bundled several cases from different jurisdictions—all of them involving African American youngsters who had been denied admission to public schools based on laws decreeing segregation in public education. The plaintiffs argued that such segregation violated the Fourteenth Amendment's Equal Protection Clause.

A summary of the **periods of U.S. history** would be a good study aid for this type of question. Look at the timeline that follows.

U.S. History at-a-Glance

Colonial America (1492–1763)
Revolutionary Period (1764–1789)
The New Nation (1790–1828)
Western Expansion and Reform (1829–1860)
Civil War (1861–1865)
Reconstruction (1866–1877)
Gilded Age (1878–1889)
Progressive Era (1890–1920)
World War I and the Jazz Age (1914–1928)
Depression and World War II (1929–1945
Modern Era (1946–present)

One period in United States history that links one event to another is the time period of West-ward Movement. The California Gold Rush, the Homestead Act, and the conditions in the East (overcrowded cities, lack of employment, exhausted farm land) are a few reasons Americans wanted to move to the West. Many wanted to start new lives and own land. Thus, Manifest Destiny became a defining element of 19th-century America.

Manifest Destiny was an idea that America was destined by God and by history to expand its boundaries over a vast area, an area that included, but was not restricted to, the continent of North America. It was used as a creed as Americans settled the Midwest, West, and Southwest of the United States. It was later used as Americans exerted power and expansion in Central and South America.

Manifest Destiny the justification for the establishment of Texas and the war with Mexico. It was the creed as the Transcontinental Railroad was built. It was also used to justify the settlement of the land occupied by Native American Tribes. Adherence to this belief caused many conflicts between the American government and the native tribes.

During Andrew Jackson's administration, the Indian Removal Act was passed by Congress. Under this law the United States government moved the native tribes from their lands into reserva-tions. The "Trail of Tears" was the forced removal of the tribes, mostly the Cherokee, to reservations in Oklahoma onto what was known at the time as "The Great American Desert." Many Native Americans died during this forced march.

The Indian Removal Act of 1830 marked just the beginning of how the government dealt with Native Americans. The Indian Affairs Bureau made every attempt to eliminate the culture and traditions of the tribes including attempting to assimilate the children into the white culture. The tribes continued to resist even after World War II up to the time of the Cultural Revolution of the 1960s and '70s when the tribes organized the American Indian Movement.

Another example of how events and time periods are connected to one another is to look at the **Great Depression**. The Great Depression was a particularly difficult time in U.S. history. Most historians agree that the Great Depression had many causes, all of which followed either directly or indirectly from the aftermath of World War I. Below is a summary of those causes.[3]

1. **False sense of American prosperity.** The 1920s was a time when manufacturing created jobs, but 60% of people still were in poverty.

2. **European economic decline.** Most of Europe was still recovering from the devastation of World War I. America loaned Europe money, but Europe could not pay it back. In addition, foreign countries could not buy American goods.

3. **Speculation and bad investing.** In the postwar euphoria, people invested heavily in the stock market, causing stock prices to soar unreasonably.

---

[3] Source: *www.thegreatdepressioncauses.com.*

4. **Stock market crash.** After reaching astronomic heights, the Dow Jones Industrial Average plummeted nearly 13% on October 28, 1929. The next day, the market dropped nearly another 12%. By mid-November the Dow had lost roughly half its value.

5. **Bank failures.** With the loss of stock value, people panicked and began withdrawing their money from banks. By 1933, 44% of banks were closed.

6. **Lack of credit.** Banking problems made it impossible to borrow money in times of need.

7. **Consumers stopped buying.** Stung by the stock market plunge and the banking crisis, people either could not or would not spend oney.

8. **Unemployment spiked.** The unemployment rate climbed to 25%. People lost their jobs. No one was buying goods so industries stopped producing and laid off the workers.

9. **Dust Bowl.** A prolonged, devastating drought from 1930 to 1936 left the farms unable to produce crops. Farmers and their families had no jobs.

The new president's administration crafted a plan to provide rapid economic relief as well as bring about extensive reforms across all sectors of the economy.

New Deal

The **New Deal** was the most dramatic and important governent program in modern history. In fact, it changed the face of American government. The New Deal was President Franklin D. Roosevelt's program to relieve the distress of unemployment and poverty during the Great Depression.

Major Legislation of the New Deal

1933	Emergency Banking Act Economy Act Civilian Conservation Corps Agricultural Adjustment Act Tennessee Valley Authority National Industrial Recovery Act	Banking Act Federal Emergency Relief Act Home Owners' Refinancing Act Civil Works Administration Federal Securities Act
1934	National Housing Act Securities and Exchange Act	Home Owners' Loan Act
1935	Works Progress Administration National Youth Administration Social Security Administration National Labor Relations Act	Public Utilities Holding Company Act Resettlement Administration Rural Electrification Administration Revenue Act

(continued)

1936	Soil Conservation and Domestic Allotment
1937	Farm Security Administration National Housing Act
1938	Second Agricultural Adjustment Act
1939	Executive Reorganization Act

As you can see from this list, in just a few years President Roosevelt established many new government programs. Some of those programs are still a huge part of the government system. Other presidents have promoted similar social programs.

One other social program that was significant was the Great Society, the political slogan used by President Lyndon B. Johnson to describe an ambitious package of national reform. Johnson, who had served as vice president with President John F. Kennedy, assumed the presidency after Kennedy was assassinated. Kennedy had promised a "New Frontier" of domestic social and economic reform. Johnson's goal was to carry on Kennedy's programs, but also to add his own. Johnson pursued many reforms, including the "War on Poverty."

Here are some of Johnson's programs:

Medicaid and Medicare—health care for the poor and the elderly

Community Action Program—jobs for the poor providing valuable experience in administration and political work

Housing and Urban Development—housing at low costs

Immigration Act of 1965—maintained a strict limit on the number of newcomers to the country, but eliminated the "national origins" system of the 1920s

The "Great Society" was a costly attempt at ending poverty in the United States. The White House was successful in implementing sweeping legislation that included the Elementary and Secondary Education Act. Though Johnson's legislation did not end poverty, it did create many social reforms that still exist today.

The following could be a question related to the information about the Great Depression.

Fill in the missing links in this chain of events, using the list of causes presented on pages 589–590.

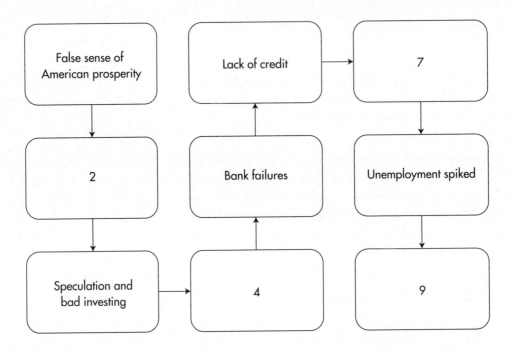

ANSWERS:

Event No. 2:   World War I left Europe devastated. America loaned money that was not paid back.

Event No. 4:   The stock market crash wiped out investments

Event No. 7:   Spooked by the stock market collapse and bank failures, consumers pulled their purse strings tight.

Event No. 9:   A devastating drought, known as the Dust Bowl and owing to overplanting, overswept the Great Plains.

The financial crisis that gripped the United States also descended upon Europe, where it caused political instability in many European nations. While the United States responded to the Great Depression with the New Deal, in Europe the response included the rise of fascism in Germany and Italy, and the threat of communism in other European countries, which propelled nations into conflict with one another. Looking for this cause-and-effect connection between one period of history and the next is a useful way to remember the sequence of such events.

By looking again at the preceding chart on successive periods of history, you can figure out that after the New Deal came World War II. One event leads to the next. Another way to connect periods of time in United States history is to understand the time before, during, and after wars.

Although wars are not a pleasant part of history, they do hold great significance and help put events in context.

One way to familiarize yourself with when and why wars occurred would be to examine major American wars in a timeline or chart. Examine the one below to get a sense of the order in which they occurred.

America's Wars

Time period*	Name of the war	Belligerents
1754–1763	French and Indian War	France, England, American colonists, Indian Tribes To establish borders in North America
1775–1783	American Revolution	Great Britain, Americans
1812	War of 1812	France, Great Britain, Americans, Indian Tribes
1846–1848	Mexican-American War	Mexico and United States
1861–1865	U.S. Civil War	United States (North vs. South)
1898	Spanish-American War	United States, Spain
1899–1902	Philippine-American War	United States, Filipino revolutionaries
1917–1918	World War I	Central powers vs. Allies
1941–1945	World War II	Axis powers vs. Allies
1950–1953	Korean War	U.S., Korea, China
1956–1975	Vietnam War	North and South Vietnam, U.S.
1990–1991	Persian Gulf War	Iraq, U.S., NATO allies
2003–2011	Iraq War	Iraq, U.S., Great Britain and other allies
2001–present	Afghanistan	War against terrorism led by U.S. against Taliban and Al-Qaeda (triggered by Sept. 11, 2001, terror attacks on the U.S.)

*Time period indicates period of American involvement.

Significance of Wars

To do well on the GED® Social Studies test, it will pay to sharpen your understanding of how causes and effects can become intertwined. Consider the American Revolution, for example, to see how cause-and-effect questions can have many facets. Far from being the result of any one thing, the Revolutionary War actually had a series of causes. Growing tensions between Great Britain and the American colonists stirred conflict. Tensions grew when Great Britain, heavily in debt after the French and Indian War, began taxing and restricting colonial trade. Over time, the colonists grew weary of these burdens and demanded their independence. This resulted in the writing of the

Declaration of Independence in which the colonists listed grievances against Great Britain. When the British sent troops to the colonies, the Revolutionary War began. The war itself was a step in the series of events that eventually led to the formation of an independent United States of America.

To understand the significance of major wars, we need to examine events before, during, and after the war. The events leading up to a conflict may be, and often are, considered the causes of the war while events afterwards are thought of as the results. For example, the War of 1812 was a major event in United States history that many people do not recognize or recall. During the Thomas Jefferson administration there was continuing tension in Europe. In 1803, that unease gave rise to the Napoleonic Wars between the British and French. Both sides took steps to prevent trade with the opposition. Meanwhile, the United States was experiencing conflicts with Native American tribes. Westward expansion was progressing at a rapid rate. This resulted in collisions with Native Americans who wanted to protect their homelands as well as their way of life and resisted white encroachment.

Soon the Native American conflicts became entwined with the European conflicts at sea. The trade problems led to the British and the French preventing the United States from trading with Europe. At the same time, the British had a policy of impressment, which meant they would search ships for deserting sailors, but often forced American sailors to serve on their ships. One incident, the Chesapeake-Leopard incident, during which the British impressed four American sailors, set off American rage toward the British. Meanwhile, the Indian problems continued as tribe leaders protested and resisted American advancement.

The Civil War (also known as the War Between the States) was extraordinarily significant in American history and can be best understood by taking into account events before, during, and after the war. One of the major causes of the war was the spread of slavery to new states and westward territories. This included areas of the Midwest, Texas, and the Oregon/California territories. At first, there was agreement that statehood would remain balanced. But as the number of states grew, tension and disagreement increased as well. It became a debate of sectionalism or nationalism. Sectionalism is the belief that states had the right to make their own decisions about slavery and other issues. The concept of "nullification," whereby states could nullify unwanted laws made by the federal government, soon grew to embrace the belief that those states could band together to become their own section of the nation and create their own laws and policies. This finally led to the divisions between the North and South and to the Civil War.

After the Civil War, there was a period and process known as "Reconstruction." This phase in United States history defined the conditions under which the states that had withdrawn from the Union could rejoin. It was also a time of rebuilding the Southern states after the devastation of the war. Changes in government policy and culture took place. In addition, during this period, the status of the African Americans who had been slaves was established.

The institution of slavery in the United States can also be viewed as a series of causes and effects. Slavery existed early in the American colonies. As the nation grew and became more industrialized, slavery grew with it. First, manufacturing of textiles became important in the North. As a result, cotton (which, with the invention of the cotton gin in 1793, saw explosive growth as a fiber of choice) became a major crop in the South. This caused an increase in the demand for slaves—because while the mechanization made possible by the cotton gin decreased the amount of labor required to remove the seeds from the plant, the slave labor needed to grow and the pick the cotton rose dramatically to keep pace with production.

Slavery was a central issue in the Civil War. Slavery also was the flash point in the heated debate over states' rights (that is, which powers rightly belonged to the states and which to the federal government). However, it's not that the South seceded over states' rights. As James Loewen, emeritus professor of sociology at the University of Vermont, has put it: "Confederate states did claim the right to secede, but no state claimed to be seceding for that right." It's important to consider what the Confederates themselves said about why they seceded. As Loewen recounted, when delegates gathered at South Carolina's secession convention on Dec. 24, 1860, they adopted a "Declaration of the Immediate Causes Which Induce and Justify the Secession of South Carolina from the Federal Union." The declaration noted "an increasing hostility on the part of the non-slaveholding States to the institution of slavery." In addition, the declaration cried foul over the Northern states' failure to "fulfill their constitutional obligations" by hindering the return of fugitive slaves to bondage.

Reconstruction Policies

President Andrew Johnson, who took office after President Lincoln's assassination, believed for the most part that the federal government should not tell states how to run their governments. Still, Johnson's reconstruction plan (known as Presidential Reconstruction (1865–67) stipulated that states would uphold the abolition of slavery, swear loyalty to the Union, and pay off war debts. Under his policy, all land that had been confiscated by the Union army was redistributed to the 4 million newly freed African American slaves by the Freedmen's Bureau (1865–72). In the South, the result was the "black codes," laws designed to restrict the activity of blacks and ensure their availability as a labor force.

Radical Reconstruction resulted when Republicans in Congress who believed Johnson hadn't gone far enough took hold of Reconstruction in the South. In 1867, following the ringing rejection of Johnson's approach in the 1866 congressional elections, the new policy divided the South into five military districts and outlined how governments based on universal (male) suffrage were to be organized. This created a more progressive society, resulting in schools, elections, and laws that were inclusive toward African Americans. In 1868 came the approval of the Fourteenth Amendment, granting citizenship and equal civil and legal rights to African Americans and slaves who had been emancipated after the Civil War.

As the process of reconstruction continued, some states in the South passed their own laws concerning the status of African Americans. It was then that the practice of segregation called "Jim Crow" began to take root.

Another way to connect periods of time in United States history is to understand the time before, during, and after wars. Although wars are not a pleasant part of history, these events inevitably hold a great deal of significance and help put surrounding events in context.

In modern history (1900–present), you will find that the time periods around war are more familiar and give a point of reference to questions or subjects you are exploring. The following are some brief descriptions of modern wars and other events that occurred around the same time span.

World War I and World War II

In many ways, the Russian Revolution of 1905 helped sow the seeds for the two world wars to come. Reeling from a humiliating defeat in the Russo-Japanese War, the Russian populace became increasingly uneasy with the government. Strikes and riots roiled the country.

In 1914, the now deeply divided factions within Russia saw World War I as an opportunity to make political gains. In fact, with the surge of patriotism the war prompted, the monarchy was briefly strengthened. But the ill-equipped Russian army suffered enormous losses in blood and treasure, with 2 million war casualties in 1915 alone.

By 1917, long-simmering social unrest had given way to open revolt, leading to the Revolution of 1917. With the average working woman spending 40 hours a week in bread lines to get her ration, bread riots, led by the women themselves, broke out. Czar Nicholas II called out the army to put down the protests, but the troops instead defected to join the revolt. Nicholas had lost the trust and respect of his people, the economy was in ruins, and his concessions to the opposition were too little, too late. His inept leadership ultimately left a dangerous power vacuum. The revolutionaries would accept nothing less than removal of the czar, and this they got when they deposed him in March. Then, the leftist revolutionaries led by Vladimir Lenin staged a takeover of the government. Lenin became a dictator. The government made peace with Germany, nationalized industry, and distributed land, eventually leading to the formation of the Union of Soviet Socialist Republics, or the USSR.

World War I (1914–1918) arose in Europe as the final clash between the old imperial powers of the German and Austro-Hungarian empires against the empires of Great Britain, France, and Russia. The United States wanted to stay out of it, but gradually the war tactics of Britain and Germany began to impact U.S. trade and freedom of the seas. So the United States entered the war as an ally of Great Britain, France, and Russia. In the United States, women fought for their independence and political rights. Therefore, the suffrage movement (women's voting rights) became strong. In addition, Russia was engaged in its communist revolution. At the end of the war, President Wilson created the League of Nations in an attempt to create international order and peace.

World War I created many problems worldwide. In Europe the economy suffered greatly from the war. Germany was in disarray with political and economic problems. Other countries also experienced political and economic turmoil as well as many changes in their leadership. When several governments fell to radical leaders, Europe became enveloped in another war. World War II (1939–1945) involved even more nations than the First World War.

The United States' role in World War II greatly influenced its results. At first, the United States planned to follow George Washington's warning to remain neutral in the conflicts in Europe. This "isolationism" had also been the strong theme of the Monroe Doctrine. As a result, Congress passed several laws called the Neutrality Acts. These laws allowed the United States to remain trade partners with all the participants involved in the war. These laws, however, became a problem when the United States government realized the war was escalating and it would be called upon to assist its allies. As the violence and invasions by Germany and the Axis Powers became more intense, Congress began to make changes to the Neutrality Acts. President Roosevelt pledged material aid to opponents of fascism, prime among them Great Britain. But U.S. law required that Great Britain pay cash for U.S. arms purchase. Roosevelt's solution to help the cash-strapped Brits was the Lend-Lease Act, which Congress passed in March 1941. Until it was ended in 1945 by the Truman administration, Lend-Lease gave the president the flexibility to aid any nation whose defense was deemed vital to U.S. interests by accepting repayment "in kind or property, or any other direct or indirect benefit which the president deems satisfactory."

The U.S., however, would not enter the war itself until the war came to its shores—with the Japanese surprise aerial attack on December 7, 1941, on the U.S. naval base at Pearl Harbor on the Pacific island of Oahu, Hawaii. At the War Department, the attack touched off fears that Japanese Americans were security risks. This led to a grim period in American history. Political leaders and the press fanned suspicions that Japanese immigrants could be spies, saboteurs, or enemy agents. In March 1942, the federal War Relocation Authority was established to "take all people of Japanese descent into custody, surround them with troops, prevent them from buying land, and return them to their former homes at the close of the war." After signing a loyalty oath, 17,600 Japanese Americans were allowed to enlist in the U.S. armed forces; many of their units earned commendations for bravery. Some German, Italian, and Aleut immigrants were also detained during the war. The war soon took a turn toward victory for the Allies.

After efforts to stop further Japanese attacks and advances, President Truman, who took office when FDR died, decided to use the atomic bomb on Japan. Bombs were dropped on two Japanese cities: Nagasaki and Hiroshima. A total of approximately 110,000 people were killed instantly by a weapon whose like the world had never seen. Soon after, the Japanese surrendered and the war ended. World War II resulted in far-reaching changes in world order.

In some ways, the causes and effects of war can be generalized. For example, war involves some tension or threat between two or more powers. Often these disputes are caused by economic problems, or the desire to gain territory. The effects or results of war are economic problems (war debts, inflation, unemployment, recession), shifts in borders, changes in types of government, immigration, and lingering suspicion and threats between rivals. One war, as in the case of World War I, can be seen to lead to another. World War I left European countries vulnerable and on edge with one another. The nations were torn apart and in economic crisis. This made it easier for strong, extreme leaders to gain influence and power, leading to the onset of World War II.

World War II greatly affected the entire world. Germany and its holdings as well as the city of Berlin were divided. The horrific extent of Adolf Hitler's policy of purification of the Aryan race became clear. Hitler and his party, the Nazis, had attempted to rid the country of non-Aryan peoples—particularly Jews—although those with disabilities, mental illness, the Roma Gypsies, Jehovah's Witnesses, gays, and many others were also targeted. In Germany and in territories captured by the Germans, these groups were gathered together and relocated, often to concentration camps. More than six million Jewish men, women, and children and millions of others were exterminated in gas chambers and other torturous ways. These systematic state-sponsored acts and policies were later known as the Holocaust. As the Allies moved through Europe, they freed captives from prison camps and concentration camps in what became known as the Liberation.

During World War II the United States had changed drastically. Many women and minorities had joined the workforce. The economy was strengthened by the war industries. But, when the war ended, the soldiers and sailors returned home to their jobs, families, and hometowns. Many soldiers had joined the war effort before completing their educations. Many were also disabled as a result of war injuries.

As a result, Congress passed the GI Bill (formally known as the Servicemen's Readjustment Act of 1944), which provided a comprehensive package of benefits for returning World War II veterans. Benefits included access to low-cost, low-interest loans for a home or business, coverage of college tuition, an avenue to a high school equivalency diploma (by passing a test called the GED®), vocational education, and one year of unemployment compensation. Historians and economists judge the GI Bill as a major political and economic success, as it created a pathway for great numbers of Americans to move into the middle class. The GI Bill was available after all wars after 1944. It was last updated in 2008.

As mentioned earlier, the war highlighted the gulf, dictated by law and policy, between minority Americans—as well as women of all races—and whites. For example, African Americans were barred from the Air Corps and the Marine Corps. In the Navy, they were segregated, allowed to enlist only in the all-black messmen's branch. But increasing numbers of blacks made it into the ranks of the U.S. military—many of them serving with valor. This, coupled with economic gains resulting from the opening of skilled, higher-paying jobs, fostered a deeper sense of their Americanism and self-confidence, presaging the civil rights movement. The war machine (that is, the defense industries) also thrust women into factories and shipyards, as epitomized by the iconic Norman Rockwell painting of "Rosie the Riveter."

Troops and civilians of minority or lower-class backgrounds who had served in Europe were treated with more respect and equality in other countries than they were in their homeland. Meanwhile, women showed they had what it took to compete in the workplace alongside their male counterparts. Though encouraged after the war to return to the domestic life of the household, some did not wish do so; this set the stage for demands for equality that would come in later years.

As the U.S. increased its leverage and influence worldwide, empires around the world saw their power wane. In South Asia where the British, Dutch, and French had long established great empires, revolutions evolved into independence for many countries. The Philippines, India, Indonesia, and Vietnam all experienced the struggles and victories of gaining independence. In the Middle East, Palestine became a new nation with the founding of Israel. North Africa, like Asia, had been part of the great empires, but the empires in this area collapsed. The power shift led to the creation of a large number of new nations. Decolonization forced Europe to reorganize and find a new status for its countries. Unfortunately, this process helped to bring about the Cold War.

The United States moved to a policy of containment to halt the spread of Communism. Part of this policy was to aid in the economic reconstruction of western Europe. Secretary of State George C. Marshall developed the Marshall Plan to carry out this goal, channeling $13 billion of American aid into Europe. The purpose was to rebuild European industrial production and boost the world economy. This lessened the strength of communism and created trade for the United States.

The policy known as the Truman Doctrine put the United States in a position to support free people resisting outside pressure from either armed or political threat. In other words, the Truman Doctrine was a pledge to contain the expansion of Communism. It became critical to the course of the Cold War.

In Germany after the war the U.S., Great Britain, and France agreed to merge their three zones of occupation into the West German Republic. In retaliation, the Soviets imposed a blockade around Berlin. The U.S. decided to airlifted badly needed supplies which included food and coal into the city. This was called the Berlin Airlift. It ended after almost a year, with the official division of Germany into two nations: the Federal Republic and the Democratic Republic. It also brought an agreement among twelve nations known as the North Atlantic Treaty Organization (NATO), which declared an attack on one was an attack on all. In response, the Soviet Union and seven of its European members signed a treaty establishing the Warsaw Pact. It was the counterpart of NATO for the Soviet bloc.

The Cold War

The Cold War (1947–1991) was not really a war, but rather an expression of the deep suspicion of the world's two superpowers: the United States and the Soviet Union. (The term itself was coined by George Orwell, the novelist famed for *Animal Farm* and *Nineteen Eighty-four*.) The two nations had very different political and economic agendas. The United States vowed to stop the spread of communism while the Soviet Union continued to move into small and poor countries. This caused both countries to develop weapons, including nuclear armaments, creating an arms race. The Cold War's superpower competition spawned several conflicts, including the Korean War (1950–1953), Cuban Missile Crisis (1962), and the Vietnam War (total period, 1955–1975; U.S. direct combat involvement, 1965–1973). It was also the reason for erecting the Berlin Wall (1961–1990), which was erected to split the nation of Germany into communist and noncommunist areas. In the latter years of the Cold War, both the United States and the Soviet Union felt the loss of support of their programs. In the 1970s and 1980s, the USSR experienced many problems with central planning as its economic system declined. Unemployment, low wages, and citizens' dissatisfaction with the government resulted. These problems called attention to the high costs of maintaining the military. At the same time, the USSR was embroiled in a conflict in Afghanistan that was costly and wore on for years. In addition, the USSR lost most of its top leaders to old age and sickness. New leadership made many changes and adopted new policies. Meanwhile, major revolutions and demand for independence erupted in several of the republics in the Soviet Union. With all these events, communism fell and the Soviet Union collapsed in 1991. The Berlin Wall itself came down in 1989 following the ouster of Germany's communist leadership.

Major Movements in United States History

The major movements in United States history also can help you to connect cause and effect. As with landmark documents or major events, the list of social movements or reform movements in American history can be connected in a cause-and-effect sequence. Below is a list and description of some of those movements.

The **Abolition Movement** was dedicated to ending slavery. The movement technically began among some of the earliest European settlers who came to America in the late 1600s. It became a formal movement in the early 1800s, and culminated in the freeing of slaves brought about by the Civil War (1861–1865). Famous abolitionists include Frederick Douglass, William Lloyd Garrison, and Sojourner Truth.

The **Progressive Era** (1890s–1920s) was a time of great reform movements. This was when Americans began to question many programs that were standard or the law in the United States, and ask for changes. Many movements originated in this period including the **Agrarian Movement** (farmers' movement), that eventually led to the rise of the People's Party, also known as the Populists, in 1892.

The **Temperance Movement** wanted to outlaw the manufacture and sale of alcoholic beverages in the United States. This movement was spearheaded by some famous women who also had a major role in the **Suffrage Movement** (the early women's movement to get the right to vote). The Temperance Movement was very successful, as it won ratification of an amendment to the United States Constitution. The Eighteenth Amendment made the manufacture and sale of liquor illegal. This created a strange period in history characterized by the appearance of speakeasies and bootlegging—full-fledged illegal economies unto themselves. Ultimately, in the teeth of the Great

Depression, federal prohibition was repealed (making it the only constitutional amendment to meet with that fate).

There were many more such events, but this short description gives an idea of how these movements could change the course of history.

The Civil Rights Movement

A critical period in United States history includes the events before, during, and after the end of World War II in 1945. Thousands of U.S. soldiers, sailors, Marines, and airmen returned from service and went back into the workforce; thus, many women and other minorities who had replaced them while they were away found themselves unemployed or underemployed. Also, the veterans had experienced European culture and ideas. In other countries, equality in employment, social settings, and services was commonplace. There was no separation of the races as was the norm in the United States. In addition, women, African Americans, Hispanics, Native Americans, and other minorities had served in the military alongside white men, performing the same tasks as their white counterparts. Some of these veterans had witnessed the horrors carried out by the Nazi regime. These factors combined to make returning minority-race American troops even more aware of the segregation, discrimination, and inequality they encountered at home. It was a violation of their guaranteed civil rights.

A series of events allowed the Civil Rights Movement to gather steam. The Supreme Court case *Brown v. Board of Education* was one of the most famous of these events. In this landmark case, Oliver Brown sued the Board of Education of Topeka, Kansas, when they would not allow his daughter to attend a "white-only" school. Brown took the case to the Supreme Court, which ruled in favor of Brown in 1954. This began the national movement toward integration of public schools.

Not long after the *Brown* decision, the NAACP set forth a plan to challenge segregation. In Montgomery, Alabama, **Rosa Parks** was the first to carry out this plan when she refused to give up her seat and move to the back of a public bus. When Mrs. Parks was arrested, the 381-day **Montgomery Bus Boycott** (December 1955–December 1956) began. This protest movement was spearheaded by the **Southern Christian Leadership Conference (SCLC)**, whose leader was the **Reverend Martin Luther King, Jr.** The bus boycott was the first of many protests.

In 1960 in Nashville, Tennessee, college students gathered to train in non-violent protests. These students planned a campaign to integrate lunch counters. Students in Greensboro, North Carolina, were the first to enter a lunch counter and stage a sit-in, refusing to leave when they were not served. This set off a series of similar protests around the nation. It also prompted the formation of an organization of college students who would lead the protest movements to end segregation, promote voter registration, and generally call attention to the violation of the civil rights of black people in the United States. This organization was called the **Student Nonviolent Coordinating Committee (SNCC)**.

The nonviolent training was modeled on the methods used by Mahatma Gandhi, who led the movement in India for independence from British rule. (India gained its independence in 1947. Ironically, Gandhi, the proponent of nonviolent political protest, was assassinated early the following year.) The protesters organized by SNCC (pronounced "Snick") refrained from any violent reaction when faced with violence. When the participants in the sit-ins were faced with violence, they continued to sit, refusing to respond in any other way. This type of protest proved to be very effective in many instances.

SNCC joined with the Congress of Racial Equality (CORE) to challenge segregation in interstate travel. Members of both organizations boarded Greyhound and Trailways buses in Detroit with the goal to travel all the way to New Orleans. The riders met violence once the buses entered the South. In Alabama, the buses were stopped by state police. Many people were arrested or forced off the buses. These **Freedom Rides** marked a new type of protest movement in the United States.

The next steps for the protesters were to challenge racially motivated restrictions on voting in the South. In order to get thousands of African Americans registered to vote, SNCC, CORE, and SCLC moved into the deep Southern states of Mississippi, Alabama, Georgia, and Louisiana. This part of the Movement was known as **Freedom Summer** (1964). Many college students and other young people joined the movement.

The news media brought the Civil Rights Movement into the homes of the entire nation. Television broadcast the events on the nightly news, and most newspapers published articles and photographs of the violence that was occurring on a daily basis. This media coverage also brought in famous people, bringing the Movement to the forefront of the nation's awareness.

As the movement continued, some participants felt it was proceeding too slowly and meekly. As a result, the Student Nonviolent Coordinating Committee took a new stance, and in 1996 became the **Black Power Movement.** This group of protesters and activists were *not* committed to non-violence but instead to militancy.

The Civil Rights Movement stands as the most significant protest movement in United States history. It was a mass movement that engaged young and old alike, and most importantly, it was the center of the country's attention. The movement used forms of nonviolent protest that effectively brought the problems of inequality and discrimination to everyone's attention and finally ended with legislative action to outlaw such conditions.

The Civil Rights Movement was the first of many Social movements in the modern era. It showed others that they, too, could protest conditions of inequality and injustice. The American Indian Movement, the Women's Movement, Gay Rights Movement, and the Environmentalist Movement were all spinoffs of the Civil Rights Movement, as were the antiwar demonstrations protesting the Vietnam War.

In 1964, the passage of the **Civil Rights Act** outlawed major forms of discrimination against racial, ethnic, national, and religious minorities, and racial segregation in schools, workplaces, and facilities that served the general public. The results also included the **Voting Rights Act,** which outlawed discriminatory voting practices.

The Civil Rights Movement also made its leaders famous: Dr. Martin Luther King, Jr., Rosa Parks, Medgar Evers, Jim Lawson, and John Lewis, to name just a few.

Between 1953 and 1969, the Warren Court, led by Supreme Court Chief Justice Earl Warren, made several landmark decisions. The Warren Court influenced public policy on many issues. Some of the most famous of the cases during his tenure include *Brown v. Board of Education*, the Civil Rights Act, the Voting Rights Act, and *Miranda v. Arizona.*

Following the massive September 11, 2001, terrorist attacks on the United States, the federal government enacted a series of sweeping new policies and laws—all in the name of taking extraordinary counterterrorism measures to protect Americans against future attacks. Chief among the bureaucratic changes was the establishment of the U.S. Department of Homeland Security, which consolidated more than 20 existing federal agencies. Not since 1947 had such extensive government restructuring occurred.

Homeland security now embraced the USA PATRIOT Act, which allowed for the centralization of surveillance data. The PATRIOT Act opened the door to extensive changes in telephonic and other electronic surveillance under the eye of the super-secret Foreign Intelligence Surveillance Court. This raised privacy concerns. Among the more visible aspects of the new measures were the National Terrorism Advisory System, which was created to alert the nation to terrorism threats, and stiffened security checkpoints at airports and other points of entry.

Identifying Sources

The GED® test relies heavily on **primary sources**. Primary sources are firsthand accounts, documents, artifacts, photographs, and other pieces of evidence created by an individual. Journals and diaries are very good primary sources. Letters and other correspondence between two or more people are good primary sources, as well.

Secondary sources are those created after the event took place. Secondary sources rely on and refer to primary sources as the evidence for the information. Biographies are secondary sources. A biography is an account of another person's life. The writers of biographies often use journals, diaries, and letters to support their writings.

Historic works of art also can be primary or secondary sources. Paintings, portraits, photographs, and other works of art can be useful tools for learning about history. Works of art can help us put a visual image in our minds of places, people, and events. Political cartoons or advertisements also can give us an image to connect to the events or time periods.

The GED® Social Studies test may include questions based on a primary source. Using the source, you will need to be able to determine what is being said and then use that information to make a claim based on evidence from the source. This skill can seem difficult when the source is a primary source such as a letter, speech, or diary. This example and the following guidelines can help you pull out the explicit language.

1812, February 3: Adams to Jefferson_____

Your Memoranda of the past, your Sense of the present and Prospect for the Future seem to be well founded, as far as I see. But the Latter i.e. the Prospect of the Future, will depend on the Union: and how is that Union to be preserved? *Concordiâ Res parve crescunt, Discordiâ Maximæ dilabuntur.* . . . .4 The Union is still to me an Object of as much Anxiety as ever Independence was. To this I have sacrificed my

Popularity in New England and yet what Treatment do I still receive from the Randolphs and Sheffeys of Virginia. By the Way are not these Eastern Shore Men? My Senectutal Loquacity has more than retaliated your "Senile Garrulity." . . . .

I walk every fair day, sometimes 3 or 4 miles. Ride now and then but very rarely more than ten or fifteen Miles. . . . I have the Start of you in Age by at least ten Years: but you are advanced to the Rank of a Great Grandfather before me.

(Library of Congress: The Papers of Thomas Jefferson, Prints & Photographs Division)

This letter, like all primary sources, does not speak for itself. It is difficult to read and understand. It has several foreign phrases and even contains Latin phrases. The reader has to interpret the letter for the information needed for a task. For example, if the question is for you to make an inference or to draw a conclusion or to make some claim, you would need to bring out the information for the specific task.

Although this is a difficult piece of writing to interpret, we can tackle it piece by piece by answering guiding questions.

Guiding Questions to Analyze a Primary Source

Question	Answer
Who wrote it?	President John Adams
What do you know about that person?	He was the second president of the United States (1797–1801) and its first vice president, under George Washington. His presidential successor was Thomas Jefferson (1801–1809). Jefferson also served as Adams's vice president—because he secured the second-highest number of electoral votes.
What are his or her biases?	Adams favored a stronger central government (while Jefferson favored states' rights and a more decentralized model).
Where, when, and why was it written?	The letter was written in 1812, long after the American Revolution had ended, and as the United States had begun to find its footing as an independent country, with its new government in full swing.
To what audience is it addressed?	Thomas Jefferson (now former president)
What kind of work is it? What is its purpose?	This letter is part of a larger exchange between Adams and his former friend and rival. You do not know this directly; however, consider the implication in a phrase such as "Your memoranda of the past . . . ," which invites the reader to consider the larger context of the letter. We certainly know the letter is in response to one that Jefferson had written to Adams. The discussion is about the country's future. The purpose of the letter may have been to persuade Jefferson to join Adams in some effort to change the politics (or political tone) of the time. Specifically, Adams does not speak well of the Virginians from the "Eastern Shore." This is evidence that Adams wants Jefferson to side with him instead of the Virginians in Jefferson's home state.
What do you know about the audience?	Jefferson felt Adams had trampled on Jefferson's executive prerogatives when Adams made appointments to the judiciary with just weeks to go in his term; these were the so-called midnight judges. In the wake of a divisive election, Adams snubbed Jefferson's inauguration in March 1801. So it's clear that the two had a falling-out, and Adams may now be working on patching up their friendship.
What are some of the key words and what do they mean?	• Adams expresses his "anxiety" over the nation's future. (He feels uneasy about the nation's prospects.) • He talks about the U.S. being "an immense structure," mention of which dovetails with his sense that the central government needs the powers to shoulder the nation's challenges. • In a touch of self-deprecating humor, Adams says, "My Senectutal Loquacity has more than retaliated your "Senile Garrulity." The joke lies in "loquacity" and "garrulity" being two ways to say the same thing: that both he and Jefferson are chatterboxes. Given the bitterness that had characterized their relationship, Adams's effort at lightening things up is important. • It's unlikely you'll know the meaning of the Latin phrase, "Concordiâ Res parve crescunt, Discordiâ Maximæ dilabuntur." It translates as "harmony makes small states great, while discord undermines the mightiest empires." If such a phrase were to appear on the GED® test, it would be translated for you.

(continued)

Question	Answer
What is the point of this document?	Adams is expressing concern over the preservation of the Union. He likens the societal storms he foresees tearing at the fabric of the nation to a violent storm (a "hideous tempest," as he puts it) he endured on a trans-Atlantic voyage to France in 1778.
What problem or issue does it address?	The issue addressed in this letter is nothing less than the preservation of the United States. We can infer that the country faced some dilemma that needed to be resolved. Adams may have been reaching out to Jefferson to help him defend the country in some way.
What is the historical context, and what problems, assumptions, arguments, ideas and values, if any, does it share with other sources from this period?	If you have studied a timeline of events in American history, you may recognize the year 1812 as being when the United States declared war on Great Britain, begetting the War of 1812 (which, contrary to its name, actually lasted 32 months—longer even than U.S. involvement in World War I).

First, we know this is a letter written by President John Adams in 1812 to President Thomas Jefferson. By 1812 the American Revolution had ended, the United States was an independent country, and the government was in full swing. The letter is in response to a letter that Jefferson had written to Adams. The discussion is about the future of the country. The purpose of the letter may have been to persuade Jefferson to join Adams—in their roles as elder statesmen—in some sort of effort to change the politics of the time. Adams does not speak well of the "eastern shore" Virginians. This is evidence that Adams wants Jefferson to distance himself from a certain group of politicos in Jefferson's home state.

The problem addressed in this letter is the preservation of the United States in the future. We can infer that the country faced some sort of challenge at the time. You may recognize the year 1812 as being when the United States declared war against Great Britain in the War of 1812. What the war's name obscures, however, is that the war actually lasted two years and eight months, not ending till January 1815.

Now, let's examine another primary source document; we'll then compare to another document by the same author to see how they link and what common claim can be extracted.

The Emancipation Proclamation

January 1, 1863

By the President of the United States of America:
A Proclamation.

(1) Whereas, on the twenty-second day of September, in the year of our Lord one thousand eight hundred and sixty-two, a proclamation was issued by the President of the United States, containing, among other things, the following, to wit:

(2) "That on the first day of January, in the year of our Lord one thousand eight hundred and sixty-three, all persons held as slaves within any State or designated part of a State, the people whereof shall then be in rebellion against the United States, shall be then, thenceforward, and forever free; and the Executive Government of the United States, including the military and naval authority thereof, will recognize and maintain the freedom of such persons, and will do no act or acts to repress such persons, or any of them, in any efforts they may make for their actual freedom.

(3) "That the Executive will, on the first day of January aforesaid, by proclamation, designate the States and parts of States, if any, in which the people thereof, respectively, shall then be in rebellion against the United States; and the fact that any State, or the people thereof, shall on that day be, in good faith, represented in the Congress of the United States by members chosen thereto at elections wherein a majority of the qualified voters of such State shall have participated, shall, in the absence of strong countervailing testimony, be deemed conclusive evidence that such State, and the people thereof, are not then in rebellion against the United States."

Second Inaugural Address, President Abraham Lincoln, delivered March 4, 1865

(1) At this second appearing to take the oath of the presidential office, there is less occasion for an extended address than there was at the first. Then a statement, somewhat in detail, of a course to be pursued, seemed fitting and proper. Now, at the expiration of four years, during which public declarations have been constantly called forth on every point and phase of the great contest which still absorbs the attention, and engrosses the energies of the nation, little that is new could be presented. The progress of our arms, upon which all else chiefly depends, is as well known to the public as to myself; and it is, I trust, reasonably satisfactory and encouraging to all. With high hope for the future, no prediction in regard to it is ventured.

(2) On the occasion corresponding to this four years ago, all thoughts were anxiously directed to an impending civil war. All dreaded it—all sought to avert it. While the inaugural address was

being delivered from this place, devoted altogether to *saving* the Union without war, insurgent agents were in the city seeking to *destroy* it without war—seeking to dissolve the Union, and divide effects, by negotiation. Both parties deprecated war; but one of them would *make* war rather than let the nation survive; and the other would *accept* war rather than let it perish. And the war came.

(3) One eighth of the whole population were colored slaves, not distributed generally over the Union, but localized in the Southern part of it. These slaves constituted a peculiar and powerful interest. All knew that this interest was, somehow, the cause of the war. To strengthen, perpetuate, and extend this interest was the object for which the insurgents would rend the Union, even by war; while the government claimed no right to do more than to restrict the territorial enlargement of it. Neither party expected for the war, the magnitude, or the duration, which it has already attained. Neither anticipated that the *cause* of the conflict might cease with, or even before, the conflict itself should cease. Each looked for an easier triumph, and a result less fundamental and astounding. Both read the same Bible, and pray to the same God; and each invokes His aid against the other. It may seem strange that any men should dare to ask a just God's assistance in wringing their bread from the sweat of other men's faces; but let us judge not that we be not judged. The prayers of both could not be answered; that of neither has been answered fully. The Almighty has his own purposes. "Woe unto the world because of offences! For it must needs be that offences come; but woe to that man by whom the offence cometh!" If we shall suppose that American Slavery is one of those offences which, in the providence of God, must needs come, but which, having continued through His appointed time, He now wills to remove, and that He gives to both North and South, this terrible war, as the woe due to those by whom the offence came, shall we discern therein any departure from those divine attributes which the believers in a Living God always ascribe to Him? Fondly do we hope—fervently do we pray—that this mighty scourge of war may speedily pass away. Yet, if God wills that it continue, until all the wealth piled by the bond-man's two hundred and fifty years of unrequited toil shall be sunk, and until every drop of blood drawn with the lash, shall be paid by another drawn with the sword, as was said three thousand years ago, so still it must be said "the judgments of the Lord, are true and righteous altogether."

(4) With malice toward none; with charity for all; with firmness in the right, as God gives us to see the right, let us strive on to finish the work we are in; to bind up the nation's wounds; to care for him who shall have borne the battle, and for his widow, and his orphan—to do all which may achieve and cherish a just and lasting peace, among ourselves, and with all nations.

(Abraham Lincoln: "Inaugural Address," March 4, 1865. Online by Gerhard Peters and John T. Woolley, The American Presidency Project. http://www.presidency.ucsb.edu)

In analyzing the preceding documents, the main questions to ask are *when* and *why*? The *who*, President Lincoln, is already established. Therefore, the reader must dive into the purpose and timeframe more carefully. Other relevant questions to consider are what events took place between the time the first one is written and the second speech and how the tone of the text has changed. This is key to answering the GED® test's source-based questions.

Timing, of course, can be crucial, and is often revealing. In the case of Lincoln's Emancipation Proclamation, January 1863 actually marked the second time the president had issued it. The so-called preliminary Emancipation Proclamation was issued in September 1862; it gave the Southern states a deadline of January 1, 1863, by which they were to cease their rebellion or have the Proclamation carried out. As you can see, that was the very date Lincoln delivered the Proclamation the second time.

The Proclamation served to profoundly reframe the Civil War. Before September 1862, the war's chief focus was to preserve the Union. But from that moment onward, achieving freedom for slaves became a major impetus. The Proclamation had far-reaching impact. In its wake, for instance, came the War Department of the United States' General Order No. 143: Creation of the U.S. Colored Troops. This paved the way for more than 200,000 African Americans to serve in the Union army and navy.

In the second document, Lincoln's Second Inaugural Address, delivered in March 1865, the president reflects on the enormous toll the war has taken on the country. The speech has strong religious overtones, describing "this terrible war" as God's punishment for the sin of slavery. Lincoln had begun this thread in the Emancipation Proclamation by declaring that all the people enslaved in the states in rebellion were free. In Lincoln's eyes, ending slavery had become nothing less than a moral imperative.

As you work your way through the Social Studies test, don't be put off by occasional big words you may see in a passage. Instead look for clues to what the words mean. When Lincoln talks about the roots of the war between the North and South, he says, "Both parties deprecated war; but one of them would *make* war rather than let the nation survive; and the other would *accept* war rather than let it perish. And the war came." Context clues provided in Lincoln's careful diction (choice of words) allow us to figure out the meaning of "deprecated" even if it's unfamiliar. The verb "deprecate" means "to seek to avert or avoid."

Facts and Opinions

When you are dealing with any passage, primary source, or secondary source, you need to separate fact and opinions. **Facts** are statements or events that can be proven based on some evidence. Facts are concrete and documented.

Here are three facts:

- Pearl Harbor was bombed on December 7, 1941.

- Richard Nixon resigned as president of the United States.

- July 4th is celebrated as Independence Day in the United States.

In contrast, an **opinion** is a belief, view, sentiment, or conception. An opinion is something that is subjective. Here are some opinions:

- Pearl Harbor was the worst day in U.S. history.

- Richard Nixon was not a bad president.

- Today was the best day ever.

At times, it may seem difficult to distinguish among facts and opinions. This is when it becomes necessary to understand how to detect **bias**. Opinion statements contain some type of judging word. For example, words like "good," "best," "worst," or adjectives that compare things or add feelings can be used as judging words.

EXAMPLE

Read the following passage; then read the numbered statements. Decide which statements are facts, which are opinions, and which are combined statements of both fact and opinion.

Frederick Douglass was born a slave. He escaped from slavery in 1838. After going to London, he returned to become an abolitionist leader and was the most important voice calling for an end to slavery. In 1847, he became the publisher of an abolitionist newspaper called *The North Star*. This newspaper was a very good source of information.

1. In 1838 Douglass escaped from slavery.

2. He became an abolitionist and the most important voice calling for an end to slavery.

3. He became the publisher of an abolitionist newspaper in 1847.

4. This newspaper was a very good source of information.

ANSWERS:

1. Fact

2. Fact and opinion

3. Fact

4. Opinion

Recognizing Bias

One of the skills you need when dealing with primary and secondary sources—whether they are written passages or images—is the ability to recognize **propaganda** or **bias** in the source. Propaganda uses persuasive writing or loaded language to draw the reader to the point of view it promotes. This type of writing plays on the reader's emotions. It is neither good nor bad writing, but a special kind of writing. It presents one point of view and works to win the reader to move to that point of view. Advertising uses persuasive writing and imagery to make the consumer want to buy the product or join a group. **Loaded language** uses words that spark an emotion in the reader.

There are some strategies that are helpful to determine if a document or image is biased. Ask yourself some questions. What is the purpose of this information? Does the author have a certain opinion? Is this one-sided? Does the style appeal more to emotions than to reason? After you have answered these questions in your mind, you can determine readily whether it is biased or not. Remember that works of art are just as likely to be biased or forms of propaganda as written materials. Artists are emotionally involved in their work. Therefore you must look at the works critically.

Loaded language also plays on the reader's emotions. It is the use of words or phrases that mean more than the simple definition of the words. For example, during the Revolutionary War period the colonists who favored independence often terrorized colonists who supported continued British rule ("British loyalists"). This meant that the colonists did things that made it uncomfortable for the loyalists to live in the American colonies. At that time, using terrorism against the British was considered heroic. Since the September 11, 2001, attacks by Al-Qaeda terrorists on U.S. soil, the words "terrorize," "terrorism," and "terrorists" have become highly charged for Americans. When a document or speech uses these words, the writer may be attempting to evoke fear or hate in the reader. This is the use of loaded language. Many words today have changed to negative or positive meanings over the years. "Liberal" and "conservative," or "far right" and "far left," are examples of simple words that have a great deal of meaning in advertising, political campaigns, speeches, or media documents in our current political climate.

Read the following three passages. The first is the background, next is Thomas Jefferson's letter, and the last is a letter from Abigail Adams.

Shays' Rebellion

During the 1780s, the United States faced hard times. Farmers in Massachusetts were especially hurt by a drop in crop prices, which left them without enough cash to pay debts. They asked the state legislature to let them pay with crops rather than money. When refused, farmers led by Daniel Shays rebelled. In January 1787, they tried to seize weapons from a government storehouse, but state troops stopped them. By February 1787 the rebellion had been crushed.

Letter from Thomas Jefferson to William Smith[4]

[C]an history produce an instance of rebellion so honorably conducted? . . . God forbid we should ever be 20 years without such a rebellion. . . . What country can preserve its liberties if their rulers are not warned from time to time that their people preserve the spirit of resistance? Let them take arms. . . . The tree of liberty must be refreshed from time to time with the blood of patriots and tyrants.

Letter from Abigail Adams to Thomas Jefferson[5]

Outlaws have persuaded a mob to follow their flag. They have complaints that exist only in their heads. . . . These rebels want to destroy the government all at once. But these people make up only a small part of the nation, when compared to the more sensible. They create much trouble and uneasiness.

The GED® test could ask you to click on emotionally charged or loaded words or phrases.

ANSWER: In the Jefferson letter, the loaded or charged words are "honorably," "preserve its liberties," "spirit of resistance," "patriots," and "tyrants." In Adams's letter, the words are "outlaws," "mob," "rebels," "trouble," and "uneasiness." These words are clues to the feelings of the writers of the letters about Shays' Rebellion.

The GED® test could also ask multiple-choice questions like this:

---

[4] Letter from Thomas Jefferson to William Smith, Library of Congress.
[5] Letter from Abigail Adams to Thomas Jefferson. From Ford, Paul I., ed. *The Annals of America*. Vol. 3. Chicago: Encyclopedia Britannica, 1968.

Which statement describes the two biases?

    A. Both Adams and Jefferson see the rebellion as a problem, but Jefferson is less bothered by it.

    B. Both Jefferson and Adams see the rebellion as a tragedy.

    C. Adams sees the revolt as a bad sign, but Jefferson sees it as a good sign.

    D. Jefferson sees the revolt as a bad sign, but Adams sees it as an encouraging sign.

ANSWER: (C) Adams thinks the rebellion is a threat, while Jefferson thinks it is part of a healthy democracy.

Point of View and Frame of Reference

To answer questions on the social studies test it is important to be able to understand frame of reference and point of view. **Point of view** is the perspective or opinion of the person writing the document. In order to understand the point of view, you need to know and understand the frame of reference. **Frame of reference** refers to the background of the person. Frame of reference includes factors that help to understand where this person is coming from.

These factors include:

- age

- gender

- personality

- family

- culture

- nationality

- social positions

- beliefs

- concerns

- experiences

All these factors play a part in shaping opinions and points of view.

To begin to understand point of view try taking the following steps. First, identify the topic or issue. Next, determine the person's opinion. Finally, consider the person's background and what shaped this opinion. These steps will lead to a conclusion on the person's point of view and frame of reference. This is particularly helpful in completing the extended-response questions.

Identifying the Historical Sequence

When you are asked to identify the historical sequence (the order in which things happen) of an event, there are several useful tools you can use. One is the timeline. As you read the passage or narrative, you could refer to the timeline of historical events. Knowing when significant events took place can help you put them in a historical context, and as a result help you understand the events more thoroughly. For example, knowing the Civil War took place from 1861 to 1865 could help you relate to other events that took place during this period. Using a diagram is another way to place narrative in the correct sequence or time order. For example, the narrative below discusses the events that led to the creation of the U.S. national park system. You should read the passage. Then note the series of events on your scrap paper in any way you best understand.

- Passage

- Timeline

- Steps

- Cluster

- Flowchart

Any of these methods can help you order the steps or events, as well as put them into historical perspective.

Here is an example of historical sequence:

The national park concept was generated by artist George Catlin, who, on a trip to the Dakotas in 1832, realized the impact westward expansion had on Indian civilizations, wildlife, and the wilderness. In part as a result of his efforts, in 1864 Congress donated Yosemite Valley to California for preservation as a state park. In 1872, Congress preserved Yellowstone "as a public park or pleasure ground for the benefit and enjoyment of the people." Yellowstone became the first national park. In the time period of the 1890s–1900s, Sequoia, Yosemite, Crater Lake, and Glacier became national parks. The Antiquities Act, passed in 1906, set aside Mesa Verde. Theodore Roosevelt used the Act to proclaim 18 national monuments before he left the presidency. This included the Grand Canyon. By 1916, the Department of the Interior was established and responsible for the development of 14 national parks and 21 national monuments.

Here is an example of how you might jot down chain-of-events based on the information presented on page 614:

1832	Catlin
1864	Congress donates Yosemite Valley
1872	Yellowstone
1890s–1900s	Several parks established
1906	Antiquities Act (Mesa Verde)
1916	Department of the Interior

For such questions on the GED® Social Studies test, be prepared to deal with a timeline or diagram that requires you to analyze the development of the U.S. National Park system.

Strategy for Analysis of Documents

The first step in completing an analysis is to read all the documents that are part of this task. Next, a good way to pull out the information is to "unpack" it one thing at a time. Follow a sequence of questions about the document. At first, it may seem slow and cumbersome, but like all such tasks, practice will make it easier and you will become more comfortable.

The basic "W" questions are a good starting point.

Who is in it or writing it?

What are the events?

What do the events have in common?

Where is it taking place?

When did it take place?

What were the reasons to write it?

What feelings do the ideas reflect?

When working with the task of analysis, the document may be broken down as steps in a process, by dates, by cause and effect, or the like.

PRACTICE!

Read the following passage and answer the questions that follow.

Background

The question of whether a U.S. territory that was about to become a new state should allow slavery was the focus of much debate and controversy in the United States during the 1850s. Several new states asked and qualified to enter the Union at this time. The geographical location of the state (north or south) had been the deciding factor in previous years, but as more people settled in the western part of the country, geographical location north and south became less of a determining factor.

Kansas-Nebraska Act

In 1854, Congress passed the Kansas-Nebraska Act, which allowed settlers in those areas to vote on the question of slavery. This created many conflicts over whether Kansas would enter the Union as a free state or a slave state. As a result, Kansas and Nebraska became areas of violence. These violent incidents caused Kansas to become known as "Bleeding Kansas." This issue became part of the struggle between the North and South and created more tension as the United States moved toward a civil war.

1. What was the event central to this passage?

2. What was the cause that led to this event?

3. What were the direct effects of these causes?

Read the following passage and answer the questions that follow.

On January 1, 1863, President Abraham Lincoln issued the Emancipation Proclamation. In this proclamation, President Lincoln announced that all slaves held in areas in rebellion against the United States were to be regarded as free. The North had the most to gain from the proclamation, as it encouraged Northerners who opposed slavery to support the war. It also deprived Southerners of manpower they needed to help carry on the war. It ensured that England would no longer help the South to be independent, because England had outlawed slavery and refused to support those who wanted to preserve it. Lastly, it encouraged free African Americans to join the United States army to fight against slavery.

4. Which of the following was an effect of the Emancipation Proclamation?

    A. The North's support of the war decreased.

    B. Southerners agreed to free their slaves.

    C. The war efforts in the South were weakened.

    D. England increased support for the South.

5. As stated in the paragraph, why did England eventually refuse to help the South during the Civil War?

    A. The English army was not strong enough.

    B. It was too far from England to be of interest to them.

    C. England did not support slavery.

    D. England was bitter about the American Revolution.

Read the following background summary and speech excerpt. Then answer the questions that follow.

Background on Theodore Roosevelt

As a young child, Theodore Roosevelt enjoyed learning. He was exposed to a routine of strenuous physical exercise and loved the outdoors. His political life was marked by efforts to involve the nation more in international affairs, protect the environment, and limit the power of large corporations. After visiting many of the nation's public lands, he pushed for laws to protect some 230 million acres. In 1908, he sponsored a meeting of governors on protecting natural resources.

Excerpt from a speech by Theodore Roosevelt

Preservation of the Forests, May 12, 1903, Leland Stanford Jr. University, Palo Alto, California

I appeal to you . . . to protect these mighty trees . . . for the sake of their beauty, but I also make the appeal just as strongly on economic grounds. . . . The interests of California in forests depends directly of course upon the handling of her wood and water supplies and the supply of material from the lumber woods, and the production of agricultural products on irrigated farms.

6. What were the factors in Roosevelt's background that led him to be a conservationist?

    A. He loved the outdoors.

    B. His political life was marked by efforts to involve the nation more in international affairs, protect the environment, and limit the power of large corporations.

    C. He pushed for laws to protect approximately 230 million acres.

    D. He had grown up in the city and had little experience with the outdoors.

7. Which of the following is the main topic of the speech?

    A. Conservation of the food supply

    B. Proper irrigation techniques in California

    C. Protection and use of California's forests

    D. Water conservation in California

8. What is the opinion Roosevelt states?

    A. California is being careful in its handling of forests.

    B. California should not allow further logging.

    C. California farms are not conserving water.

    D. Forests need to be protected for both their beauty and their economic uses.

9. What were some of Roosevelt's concerns for California's natural resources? (Use the techniques described above to develop an outline, citing specific evidence from the quoted passage and background.)

Social Studies Practice 2 Answers

1. Slavery and whether to allow slavery in new states.

2. Several new states asked to join the Union, which caused the hotly debated question to arise with greater frequency and intensity, leading to increased violence.

3. The Kansas-Nebraska Act and the conflicts in new territories. These conflicts led to "Bleeding Kansas."

4. **C.**

The war efforts in the South were weakened. Option A is untrue since the North greatly supported the war. Option B and D are also incorrect since England opposed slavery and the South did not want to free the slaves.

5. **C.**

England did not support slavery. England had abolished slavery in their country years before.

6. **A., B., C.**

A. He loved the outdoors.

B. His political life was marked by efforts to involve the nation more in international affairs, protect the environment, and limit the power of large corporations.

C. He pushed for laws to protect approximately 230 million acres.

7. **C.**

Conservation of the food supply, Option A, is too broad and not the central idea of Roosevelt's speech. Although irrigation is mentioned, he refers to the practices, so option B is not correct. Option D is part of the conservation plan, but is a supporting detail.

8. **D.**

Forests need to be protected for both their beauty and their economic uses. Roosevelt says he believes California should be more careful with handling the forests, logging practices, and agricultural practices. However, those are details that support his opinion in option D. Options A, B, and C are not the answer to this question.

9. Roosevelt's main concern was the conservation of the natural resources of California. He refers to the water and trees being handled properly, along with agricultural practices, which indicates a concern for the soil as well.

Economics

What is Economics?

Economics is the study of how people choose to use resources.

Resources include the time and talent people have available, the land, buildings, equipment, and other tools on hand, and the knowledge of how to combine them to create useful products and services.

Important choices involve how much time to devote to work, to school, and to leisure, how many dollars to spend and how many to save, how to combine resources to produce goods and services, and how to vote and shape the level of taxes and the role of government.

These decisions are made in different ways by each country. Most economists separate countries into two categories. Those that make these choices based on free enterprise and private ownership of property are called market economies, while those that use government planners to make these choices are called command economies.

Often, people appear to use available resources to improve their well-being. Well-being includes the satisfaction people gain from the products and services they choose to consume, from their time spent in leisure and with family and community as well as in jobs, and the security and services provided by effective government. Sometimes, however, people appear to use resources in ways that don't improve their well-being.

In short, economics includes the study of labor, land, and investments, of money, income, and production, and of taxes and government expenditures.[1]

The GED® test uses economic topics to make up 10% of the questions in the social studies section. The topics include types of markets, the effects of competition, credit and money management, supply and demand, as well as the global market.

Graphs, Charts, and Tables

This part of the GED® test uses many types of graphics to illustrate relevant topics or to provide information. Although graphics can be found throughout the exam, the economics section relies more on graphs, charts, tables, and diagrams than other sections. Graphics provide ways to organize data in visual and meaningful ways. Charts are visual displays of data usually arranged in columns and rows. In general, most charts are tables, although arranged in a special way. The best way to determine what data charts and graphs represent is to read the title. Pay attention to the order in which things are shown—particularly where numbers are involved. It may be least-to-greatest in one chart, but greatest-to-least in a graph, or the list could even be random. Be sure to read the entire chart or table before you begin.

Graphs are used to compare data. Line, bar, and pictorial graphs are built on a vertical and horizontal axis pattern. It is the same as columns and rows, but the information tells you about the comparisons. Each one should be labeled with important information to tell you what you are comparing.

Look at these bar graphs:

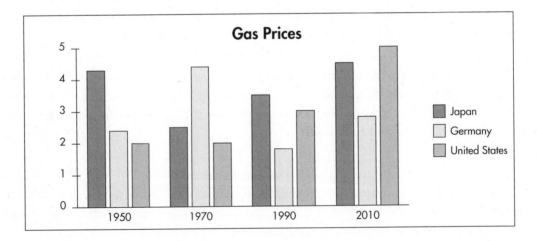

---

[1] American Economic Association.

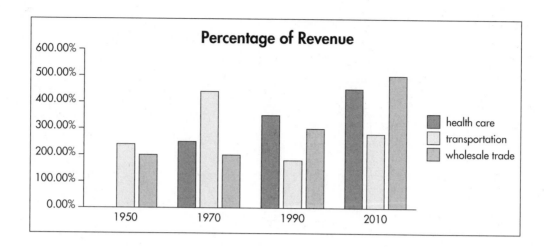

These are examples of bar graphs. It is important to read and understand the **key or legend.** This explains what the bars represent.

Line graphs are more complicated than bar graphs. Line graphs show trends or changes over time. To interpret line graphs, you need to be able to find specific points on the graph and identify the changes or differences. Another important but often misread aspect of line graphs is a point in the line where the change stops. *A flat line indicates that nothing happened or no change took place.*

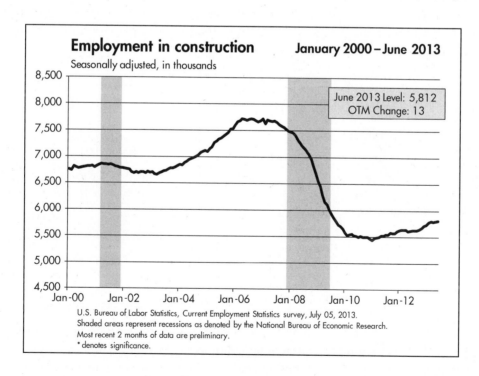

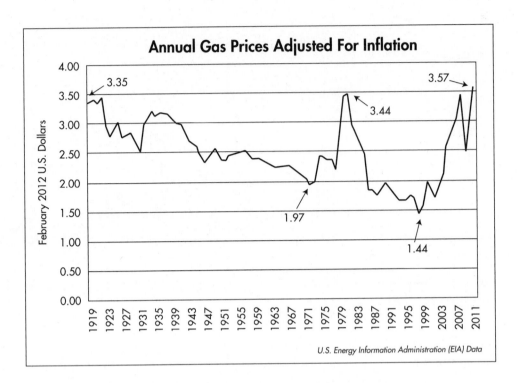

Circle graphs or pie charts represent part-to-whole data. Circle graphs show the size of data for comparisons. Often circle graphs will use percentages. To interpret correctly you need to know the whole number or amount. This is often given in the title or explanation of the graph. Remember the entire circle represents 100%.

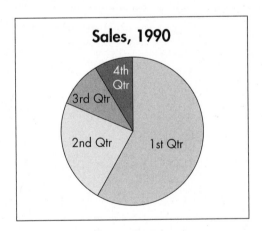

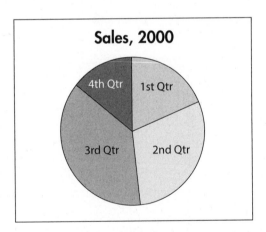

Another type of graph used to represent data in social studies is the **pictograph**. These graphs use some symbols or pictures to represent large numbers. As a result, it is very important to note the information in the key, 1 ☺ = 1,000,000 people. The idea is to estimate what numbers are depicted when the shape or symbol is not whole.

Population of states, 2012	
Tennessee	☺ ☺ ☺ ☺ ☺ ☺
New Jersey	☺ ☺ ☺ ☺ ☺ ☺ ☺ ☺ ☺
Montana	☺

1 ☺ = 1 million people

What is the population of New Jersey? It is about 9 million people.

Remember—the questions that ask you to make choices based on a graph must reflect the data. Your answer choice must be supported or given by the graph.

Other types of questions involving data will include calculations of mean, median, mode, and range of a dataset. This type of question could appear in any area of Social Studies. For example, in United States history you might see the ages of presidents when they were elected. In geography the questions might involve populations. It is common for such types of questions to concern economics or trends in markets.

This example can help you be prepared for these types of questions.

EXAMPLE

In 2008–2009 the United States housing market was at a peak. One analysis of the prices of homes in five cities found the following prices.

Location	Price of Home
Scranton, Pennsylvania	$84,000
Baton Rouge, Louisiana	$133,000
Columbia, South Carolina	$118,000
Springfield, Massachusetts	$180,000
Louisville, Kentucky	$105,950

1. What was the range of the prices of homes in these five cities?

The **range** of a dataset can be found by subtracting the lowest amount from the highest. 180,000 − 84,000 = $96,000.

2. What was the mean of the prices of homes in these five cities?

   The **mean** (average) is calculated by adding all the amounts and dividing by the number of prices. 84,000 + 133,000 + 118,000 + 180,000 + 105,950 = 620,950 divided by the number of prices or cities 5 = 124,190

3. What is the median price of homes in these five cities?

   The **median** is found by finding the middle prices. Arrange the numbers from least to greatest. 84,000, 105,950, 118,000, 133,000, 180,000. The middle number in this dataset is 118,000

   Mode is the number that occurs most often. This dataset has no mode since there is only one of each price.

These types of calculations are also used with data represented on graphs or tables.

Another type of question that is likely to be on the test is one which asks you to make a connection between correlation and causation. It could involve a graph like the one below:

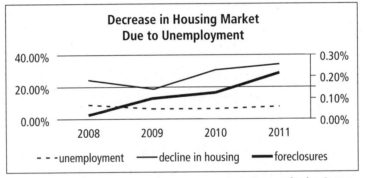

U.S. Bureau of Labor Statistics

The purpose of the graph is to show a correlation between the unemployment rates, decline in housing prices, and number of foreclosures. You may be asked to make a statement of the connection between the causes of the decline in home sales or the increase in foreclosures and the unemployment rate.

Types of Economic Systems

A nation's system of government often determines the type of economic system it uses. Here are a few examples:

Capitalism is an economic system based on private ownership of the resources of production. Investments are made by individuals rather than the government. The economic system in the United States is based on capitalism.

Socialism is a system in which goods and services are publicly and cooperatively owned and provide equal opportunity for all. Private ownership is permitted, although businesses and government together decide what goods are produced.

Communism is a system that does not permit private ownership. The government owns the property and distributes goods in accordance with the common good. The government decides what goods are produced and who should get them.

Some countries have **mixed economic systems**. For example, the United States operates by capitalism, but the government regulates some businesses. Government organizations like the Food and Drug Administration keep checks on the amount of products on the market and ensure the products' quality. Often, countries based on a market or capitalist model may offer different political liberties to citizens than those based on a command or communist model. Capitalist countries are inclined to reflect business interests and limit the role of government. Many communist systems have been closed one-party states which have been ruled as dictatorships.

The basic topics of economics are questions that help determine the type of economic system to use. What should be produced? What do members of society need and want? How should it be produced? Should each person make his or her own goods, or should businesses or the government be in charge of manufacturing goods for the entire service area? How should the products be distributed? Should the products be given to everyone equally or only to those who can afford to buy them? Societies develop economic systems to answer these fundamental economic questions.

Important factors in the production of goods and services are identified as **natural resources, capital**, and **labor**. Without these three components, the manufacturers and businesses could not produce their products. Below is a table that explains this more clearly.

Components	Definition	Examples
Natural resources	raw materials needed to make the product	trees ore to make steel
Capital	money to start the business, buy materials, hire workers equipment, machines, and factories	lumber to build houses steel to build cars machines used in making car parts
Labor	people who do the work	autoworkers construction workers carpenters

Free enterprise is another term for the capitalist economic system used in the United States. This system involves consumers and producers and how they buy and sell services and goods. Producers determine the kinds, amounts, and prices of services and goods, based on the choices of consumers and the opportunities in the market.

Car sales are a good example of the free enterprise system. Automobile manufacturers decide how many cars to make based on consumer demand or previous sales. If people bought more small cars over the last two years, manufacturers will produce more small cars this year. On the other hand, if the sale of large cars is down, then the production of large cars will be less.

Many other factors affect the market as well. Some outside factors change consumer activities. In the case of car sales, the price of gasoline plays a huge role in consumer demand. Free enterprise is a cycle with many factors. For example, if car sales are low and the manufacturers are not making many cars, then there is no need for workers. So, people who work in the automobile industry will lose their jobs, causing the unemployment rate to increase. The number of unemployed people creates a slump in consumer demand, since people have less money to spend and do not foresee having money in the future.

This analysis of car sales illustrates the free enterprise system. It also leads us to believe that the common questions about free enterprise would be cause-and-effect questions. Such questions are usually "why" questions. A strategy to answer cause-and-effect questions is to note (remember, make a list, etc.) causes and effects. The question is the effect. Why did car sales decrease in 2009? The answer would be because the price of gas increased that year (the cause). Why did unemployment increase among automobile industry workers? The answer is because car sales decreased.

The barter system has been used throughout history. It was the only system used in primitive societies. This system involved exchanging goods or services for other products. The barter system had both advantages and disadvantages. For example, there was no currency or money involved, so there was no banking system. On the other hand, bartering one good for another resulted in exchanges that may not have had the same value. It was based on need versus possession. Consequently, bartering allowed for more flexibility in the distribution of goods and services. However, there was the problem of a great need for a a particular product resulting in lowering of the exchange value of a more valuable good. For example, the treated hide of an animal ordinarily might have a high value, because of the difficulty in capturing and killing the animal, and preparing the hide. Ordinarily, that animal hide might be traded for ten baskets of grain, for example. However, if there was a period of drought and grain became scarce, the same animal hide might be exchanged for only five baskets of grain. The hide required the same effort to obtain, but its barter value in relation to grain was less.

Bartering was inefficient because it required a dual coincidence of wants: This meant that for a trade to take place, one person had to have what the second person wanted and the second person also needed to have what the first person wanted in return.

Another type of system to consider when looking at economic systems is monopoly versus competition. In a competitive market there are a large number of buyers and sellers. In a monopoly there is only one seller, but several buyers. The seller controls the price and can raise the price to an artificially high level. In addition, a competitive market creates or earns profit in the long term, while a monopoly has a higher profit and a smaller output of production.

Basic Economic Vocabulary

The economy is a topic of everyday conversations all over the world. An understanding of some terms used in those discussions can give you a better idea of how to answer questions about economics.

There are several important terms in economics that you should become familiar with in order to do well in this area.

One example is the cost of a college education. A student pays a great deal for tuition, housing, and books. These expenses are examples of accounting or monetary costs, but by no means provide a complete list of costs. The opportunities are often ignored in the estimation of the costs. For example, the wages that could be earned during the time spent attending class, the value of four years' job experience given up to go to school, the value of any activities missed in order to allocate time to study, and the value of items that could have been purchased with tuition money or the interest the money could have earned over four years.

Productivity measures how efficiently a given worker (or society) can produce a good or service. For example, Sally might be able perform four haircuts in an hour or mow a lawn in two hours. A producer has absolute advantage in making a good if she or he can make more of that good per unit of time than a neighbor. This also means producing each unit of output with fewer inputs than the other producer could. Put simply, the first producer is better at making that good. If Joe can do only two haircuts per hour, Sally has the absolute advantage in haircutting.

Comparative advantage means being able to make a unit of output with a lower opportunity cost than a neighbor. From the previous example, Sally sacrifices 8 haircuts every time she mows a lawn: That is her opportunity cost of mowing one lawn. If Joe can also mow one lawn per two hours (just the same as Sally, so neither has absolute advantage), then he has a comparative advantage in lawnmowing since he sacrifices only 4 haircuts per lawn he mows, a lower cost than Sally's.

One of the core principles of economics is specialization: the idea that people or societies should produce what they can make at a lower cost than their neighbors and trade for those things that neighbors can make at a lower cost. On an individual level, this means that Sally should be cutting hair and Joe should be mowing; internationally, this might mean that Chile should grow grapes and trade for corn from the United States.

Countries and individuals should focus on specializing based on the principle of comparative advantage and trade for the rest. This encourages us to be interdependent, relying on others for the things they can do at lower cost than we can. Looking around the world, those who enjoy the highest standards of living typically do not make all their own goods for themselves but rather rely heavily on this theory by specializing in what they can do at a lower cost than anyone else.

An **entrepreneur** is a person who takes an idea, product, or service and does whatever is necessary to introduce it to the marketplace where it can produce revenue. Although it is a risk-taking endeavor, it is also a way to become self-employed, fulfill goals, and create new markets for unknown or new products. Entrepreneurship is a common idea in the capitalist system. It may involve investors or investment of personal finances and credit, or both. Entrepreneurs are driven by the incentive of profit—they earn profits when the revenue they gain producing goods is greater than the costs they face buying resources to make those products.

One major component of economics goes back to individual choice. Consumers make choices based on their own needs and wants. It is always necessary to make choices because resources are scarce and competition is great. The real value of a product or service is how much you need it and what you have to give up to get it. Some of the components of individual choice involve how much you want or need it, how much is available, the amount of time it will take to get it, and the sacrifices you make to have what you want. So in the end all costs are opportunity costs when you consider the choices people make to purchase.

Recognizing these terms will be helpful when you face the passages, graphics, data, and questions about economics on the GED® test.

"Inflation," "deflation," "recession," and "depression" are words frequently heard in discussions of economics. Examining basic meanings of such words can give you a better idea of how to tackle the questions.

When too much money and credit are available, and not enough goods are available to satisfy demand, the dollar loses value. This causes the price of goods to increase. This creates **inflation**. On the other hand, when too little money and credit are available and more goods are available, prices for goods decrease. This is called **deflation**. During periods of deflation, factories and businesses have **layoffs**. Unless the situation is corrected, a **recession** will occur, because people who cannot find work do not have the means to purchase other people's products or services — even at deflated prices. An extended period of unemployment, high prices, and shortages of goods creates an economic **depression**.

A country's unemployment rate measures the percentage of workers in the labor force who do not have a job. The labor force is defined as the pool of workers who have a job or are actively seeking one. Thus, a worker needs to be looking for a job to be considered unemployed. In the United States, a healthy or typical rate of unemployment is about 5%--this is also referred to as the natural rate of unemployment. When about 5% of the labor force is unemployed there are about as many job vacancies as there are job seekers.

Oftentimes you will see a graph that helps to explain the factors in the previous paragraph. Here is an example:[2]

EXAMPLE

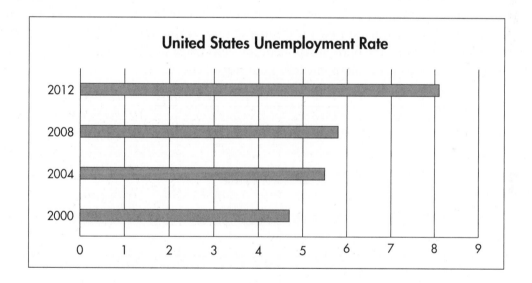

According to the graph, which of the following is an accurate statement?

    A. The unemployment rate was at its lowest in U.S. history in 2000.

    B. The unemployment rate experienced a large increase between 2008 and 2012.

    C. The job rate increased in 2008.

    D. In 2004, there was some job growth.

---

[2] U.S. Department of Labor.

ANSWER: (B) is the correct answer, since the graph shows the unemployment rate in 2008 was about 5.8%, but in 2012 it had increased to about 8.1%. The other choices are false or not supported by the information on the graph. (A) might be an attractive answer—but this graph is only for the years 2000 to 2012, not all of U.S. history.

Consumer economics is a type of economics you use in your daily life. Being able to apply economics to your daily life helps you become a better consumer. Consumer economics results in getting value for your money. For example, you have been considering purchasing a new pair of athletic shoes. The shoes you want are fashionable, but expensive. However, quality is another aspect of value. The shoes may fit better, function better, and last longer. As a result, the shoes are a better value for the price.

Consumer economics may involve skills like making comparisons or identifying cause-and-effect relationships. You also need to be able to analyze and evaluate information.

The U.S. Consumer Price Index (CPI) is the measure of change in prices of a group of goods or services that an average consumer would purchase. The rate of increase in the CPI from one year to the next is called the inflation rate. It is often quoted as the "rate of inflation." In the following chart, the numbers along the bottom represent the percentage rate by which prices increased during the period of the years listed along the left-hand side of the chart.

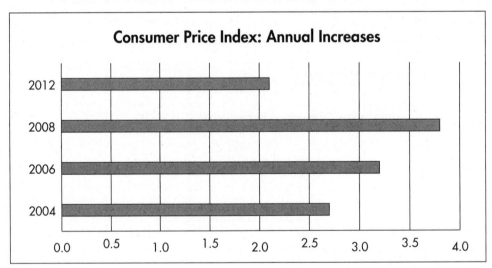

U.S. Bureau of Labor Statistics

Economic incentives involve a system that uses material or monetary means to motivate the production of products or types of production. Positive economic incentives reward the consumer for making choices or behaving in certain ways. Negative economic incentives punish consumers financially for making certain choices or behaving in certain ways.

Incentives usually involve money, but can include goods and services. Businesses and organizations use incentives in various ways. One example would be an offer of rebates when you purchase an item, or an offer of a lower insurance premium if you become involved in a wellness program. On the other hand, a punitive measure is also an incentive. An example of this type of incentive is the fine at the library for an overdue book or paying a higher premium if you continue to use tobacco products. Incentives also influence the behavior of business firms. Firms that are earning large profits (revenue taken in minus costs they face) are likely to produce more goods and grow in size. Firms that can't earn profits are likely to shrink, begin producing other goods, or may be forced to shut down operations. In this way, buyer demand for products is a signal to producers to use society's scarce resources in more efficient ways. This is a main reason why capitalist or market economies often use resources more efficiently than alternative systems.

Many incentives involve environmentally or socially conscious choices such as energy-saving doors and windows putting home heating at a lower price than when regular doors and windows are present. Tax breaks or deductions can also be economic incentives.

Microeconomics versus Macroeconomics

The study of how individual buyers and sellers interact and are affected by incentives is called Microeconomics. Households sell labor and other resources to business firms who use these resources to make finished goods and services to sell to households and other firms. These institutions work in a framework guided by government regulations and taxes.

Macroeconomics involves the study overall economic stability. Macroeconomists measure nationwide economic performance using Gross Domestic Product (GDP), inflation, and unemployment data, and form theories about when and how the major governmental institutions should act to help improve the health of the economy as a whole. These institutions are a country's central bank—in the U.S. this is the Federal Reserve System—and its fiscal policymakers—such as the President and Congress. The basic goal of all fiscal and monetary policy is to promote a high total output of goods and services (GDP) with close to full employment while keeping prices stable with a low inflation rate.

The United States Federal Reserve is responsible for setting the nation's monetary policy. It regulates the nation's supply of money and credit in order to keep the economy in balance. It does this by monitoring the *reserve ratio* and setting the *discount rate*. The reserve ratio is the amount of money banks are able to lend. During inflation this amount can be raised, which limits the amount the bank can loan. For example, the local bank has $100,000 in deposits. The reserve ratio is 10%. This means the bank must keep $10,000 on hand. However, if the Federal Reserve increases the reserve ratio to 20%, the bank must have a reserve of $20,000.

The discount rate is the rate of interest the federal government charges members and banks to borrow money. The banks make a profit by charging their customers a higher rate on loans than they pay in interest to other banks and the Federal Reserve to borrow money (the discount rate), or the interest they pay customers for their deposits in checking and savings accounts. For example, if a bank customer deposits $2,000 in a savings account that earns 2%, the bank will owe this person $2,040 at the end of the year. If another customer borrows $2,000 from the bank at a rate of 15% annual interest, this person owes the bank $2,300 at the end of the year. Comparing what the bank owes the first customer and what the bank is owed by the second customer, the bank earned $260 at the end of the year. It's clear, then, that banks want to lend money in order to make money.

The Federal Reserve controls the discount rate in order to set the supply of money available. The changes in the discount rate also affect the availability of credit. The availability of money and credit are influenced by the Federal Reserve. The government plays a role in the nation's economic conditions when it establishes **fiscal policy.** and can therefore encourage savings and investment. Business investment—the purchase of new capital equipment such as factories, machinery, and worker training—is a major driver of economic growth.

Fiscal policy is set through a process involving the elected branches of the government. First, the president creates a proposed annual budget. Then, Congress reviews the budget and decides what programs are needed and how they should be funded. Taxation is usually the source of funding. But another option could be the reallocation of funds by decreasing unneeded programs and government spending.

The decisions to raise or lower taxes or increase or decrease spending have a direct impact on a country's economic activity. Lower taxes and/or more government spending will increase economic activity, pushing up GDP and employment but also prices. A tax increase or a drop in government spending reduces GDP and employment and can reduce inflation. For example, the government might raise taxes during an inflationary time, or increase spending during a period of deflation.

A **budget surplus** results when the government spends less than it collects in taxes. The opposite situation results in a **budget deficit**. A balanced budget comes from taxes and spending being equal.

Taxes are an important way the government gains revenue to pay for the services and programs it provides. Tariffs are another source of income. Tariffs are the taxes charged on imports and exports. They are are often used for political reasons, and unpopular tariffs have caused political tensions and in some cases even revolutions. In spite of this, tariffs do generate money for the government.

Personal Finances and Banking

Most people depend on banks to control their personal finances. Employers provide paychecks through **direct deposit**. This means the company or business deposits the paycheck for its employees into their personal bank accounts electronically. The employee does not handle a paper paycheck. As a result, most people have a bank account. Understanding your bank account and the many features your bank offers is a huge part of managing personal finances.

There are two common types of bank accounts. The **checking account** is designed for daily transactions like paying bills, rent, utilities, or similar expenses. Checking accounts provide a list of your transactions and help you track your spending. However, it is very important to keep your balance updated so that you don't write a check or make a debit card payment for more money than you have in your account. The banks charge a hefty fee in these cases and this also may be a strike against you on your credit record. The credit record is used when lending agencies are deciding whether or not to loan you money.

Savings accounts are the other type of account available to consumers. The savings account is designed to help you prepare for emergencies and purchase high-priced items, such as a car or house. Also, savings accounts allow you to earn interest while your money is in the account. The savings account does have drawbacks. For example, there may be penalties for withdrawing your money, or fees if your balance drops below a certain point.

As people learn to manage their own personal finances they may find it necessary to borrow money for a short period of time. The most common types of credit are installment, revolving, and open credit. Installment credit is very often used for large purchase like buying a car. One option would be to apply for a short-term loan; this is installment credit. Revolving credit allows you to borrow a pre-established amount repeatedly as long as your credit is in good standing. Refinancing your home mortgage is a good example; however, a credit card is a more readily available and convenient way to obtain credit. Open credit requires that all money borrowed must be repaid in full every month. A business-expense credit card is one example, but another would be check-cashing service, which often charge large fees and huge penalties if you fail to repay or pay late.

Credit cards allow the consumer to buy goods and services quickly and easily, while paying the bill later, possibly in installment payments. The disadvantages to using credit cards often outweigh the benefits. The credit card companies charge large interest fees and service charges. In recent years credit card debt has become a great problem in the United States. This is particularly true for young people or those who suffer during economic downturns.

Credit card use seems like a quick fix for urgent problems. But smart consumers learn to read the fine print, compare rates and services, and choose carefully what types of bank accounts and credit cards that are right for their needs.

The terms of credit cards vary widely. Below is a list of features on three different credit cards being offered by the same company, Citibank. Examine the terms and decide which credit card would be best for each person's situation in the questions that follow.

	Annual percentage rate (APR) for purchases	Annual membership fee	Additional benefits	Credit rating
Citi Platinum Select Visa Signature® Card	15.2%	$95	30,000 American Airlines bonus miles after $1,000 in purchases within 3 months 1st checked bag is free Priority boarding and 25% off in flight services	Excellent credit rating required
Citi Simplicity® Card	0% APR on balance transfer and purchases for 18 months 12.9%–21.9% depending on credit status	$0	No late fees ever	All applicants considered; APR adjusted accordingly
Citi Diamond® Card	0% on balance transfers 11.9%–21.9%	$0	Excellent credit rating required	

1. Shaylah does not have a good credit rating. She does have a steady income with her new job. She would like a card to help her establish a better credit rating. Which card is best for her, and why? _____

2. Marion travels for her job. She spends a great deal on airline tickets. She has an excellent credit rating and income. Which card is best for her, and why? _____

3. Rebecca has excellent credit and pays her balance at the end of the month. Which card is best for her, and why? _____

ANSWERS: Shaylah should take the Simplicity card; a good credit rating is not required to get the card, and proper use of the card can improve her credit rating. Marion should take the Signature card; since she travels extensively, she can earn lots of bonus points on her credit card whenever she travels. Rebecca can handle the Diamond card; there is no membership fee, the interest rate on purchases is low, and in any event, she pays her balance in full each month, which means she would not incur interest on purchases anyway.

It is important to take notice that some of the information could be misleading if the customer does not read carefully. For example, 0% on transfer balances does not help any of these customers. That comes into play only if they want to transfer the balance of what they owe on another card to their new card. (Generally, the interest rate only remains at 0% for a limited period of time.)

Consumer credit laws are designed to protect households from unfair (or predatory) lending practices. These laws have changed over time and are necessary because lending institutions like banks and credit card companies have informational and other advantages over their potential customers.

The most important legal restriction on the practices of lenders and protection for credit consumers is the Consumer Credit Protection Act of 1969. This law and its amendments include the Truth in Lending Act, the Fair Credit Billing Act, the Fair Credit Reporting Act, the Equal Credit Opportunity Act, and the Credit Repair Organizations Act. Together these and other more recent laws protect customers who have had misleading or false offers from lenders, regulate what fees lenders can impose and how they can be charged, outlaw discrimination in lending, and ensure that unauthorized charges on credit cards are not owed by the cardholder. Some reform following the credit crisis of 2007-09 led to stronger mortgage lending regulations and requirements that credit card statements be more clear. It is important for credit customers to know about the protections they have under law, but also vital that they read and understand the terms of the loans they take out!

Most families have a personal budget. This is a plan for saving and spending their income or assets. Just like the government, individuals must consider how much they earn, what they need to spend, and where they want to spend their money.

Things a family must have, and for which there are regularly scheduled costs (like rent or mortgage, utilities, car payments, etc.), are called **fixed expenses**. Expenses that may vary from month to month, like food or medicine, are called **variable expenses**. The item a family wants to spend money on, but could live without, is called a **luxury expense**. A **fixed income** results where a person lives on a specific amount of money each month, like a social security payment or a monthly salary. A person on a fixed income must be careful to cover all fixed and variable expenses each month, and plan to spend for luxuries only if there is something left over at the end of the month to be saved from month to month until they can afford the luxury. A **flexible income** results when the amount of monthly income depends on, for example, how many hours the person works, or how many commissions they earn, or how well their investments are doing. A person on a flexible income may find it easier to incur expenses for luxuries, assuming they can be paid for just by working harder or longer the following month. But of course, it is not always certain that it will be possible to earn more next month, so persons on flexible income also have to be careful about budgeting for luxury expenses.

Average Budget for a Typical American Home

The chart below shows average spending by families in 2009–2011.[3] An average family unit in this chart consists of a wage earner who is 49.7 years old, with 2.5 persons living together.

	2009	2010	2011
Total income	$62,857	$62,481	$63,685
Food	$6,372	$6,129	$6,458
Housing	$16,895	$16,557	$16,803
Health Care	$3,126	$3,157	$3,313

What's missing? Answer each of the questions below.

1. The above chart is a snapshot of the average American budget. What factors should be considered to give a more accurate picture of these homes?

2. The income in 2011 is higher than in 2009, but so is the amount this family spent on food. What implications does this suggest?

   A. The family is consuming more food.

   B. As the family members grow older they eat more food.

   C. The cost of living (food) has increased as the income has increased.

   D. The father eats more expensive foods than before.

ANSWERS:

For question 1, you might have answered: transportation, utilities, education, personal care.

For question 2, the correct answer is (C). The cost of food has increased over the years.

[3] Source: U.S. Bureau of Labor Statistics.

Supply and Demand

When the same amount of a product is supplied as is demanded, a market is in equilibrium, and the price of the product is unlikely to change. If more is demanded than supplied, a shortage exists and the price is likely to rise. If more is supplied than is demanded, there is a surplus and price of the good will tend to fall.

The market forces of demand and supply (what famed economist Adam Smith referred to as the "invisible hand") help guide both buyers and sellers. Knowing prevailing prices can help producers and consumers make decisions about their willingness to sell or buy. As prices rise, buyers purchase less and firms produce more, rebalancing markets that had shortages before. If prices fall, buyers purchase more units while businesses supply less, eliminating surpluses. In this way, markets tend toward efficient use of resources most of the time.

Questions concerning supply and demand may have you look at cause and effect. Another typical question on this subject concerns prediction. For example, given a situation of high demand, you will be asked to predict what would occur with the demand.

EXAMPLE

Recently, the demand for organic food has risen steadily. Read this article and predict the result.[4]

The makers of the high-energy eat-and-run Clif Bar needed 85,000 lbs of almonds and the nuts had to be organic. But the nation's organic almond crop was spoken for. Shortages of apricots and blueberries, cashews and hazelnuts, brown rice syrup and oats had also occurred. America's appetite for organic food is so strong that supply just can't keep up with demand.

ANSWERS

What would you predict as possible outcomes of these facts? If you predicted the price of organic foods like nuts will increase, you would be correct. And if the price of ingredients goes up, it is quite likely that the price of Clif Bars also will increase. In addition, the demand for organic foods will drive farmers to produce more of these types of crops in the future.

You might be asked to make predictions about graphs or charts as well.

---

[4] "Appetite for Organic Food Proves Insatiable." Associated Press. 6 July 2006.

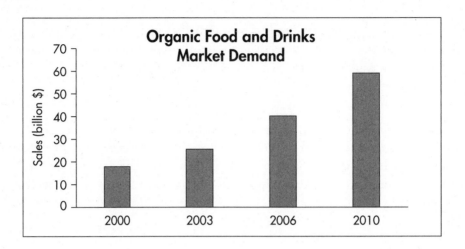

The figures on the left side of the chart represent billions of dollars. Let's say it is projected that by 2012, demand for organic food and drinks will rise by another 3.3% over 2010.

Based on the information in the graph, predict the market demand amount in 2014:

    A. $61 billion dollars.

    B. $75 billion dollars.

    C. $63 billion dollars.

    D. $100 billion dollars.

ANSWERS

You should have answered (C). In 2010, the graph shows that the amount was about $59 billion. An increase of 3.3% would raise it to $61 billion; then another 3.3% would raise it to around $63 billion. Answer (D) is too much and would not fit the pattern. The same is true for answer (B). Answer (A) is the amount for 2012. Your question has you predict beyond that to 2014.

When Markets Fail

Sometimes markets do not give us the results we want. This problem, called market failure, has many causes.

Sometimes there are so few sellers that the market becomes imbalanced, leading to underproduction and high prices; monopolies are extreme cases of this. Other times, either buyers or sellers have an information advantage over the other. Market failure also can be caused by external (or spillover) costs and benefits. If a product imposes costs to someone other than the seller, that part of the cost won't be factored into the price, and society will get too much of the product at too low a price—this is what happens when goods that result in industrial pollution are overproduced.

In order to fix market failures, governments may use incentives to adjust the output of a good toward the socially efficient level. Subsidies and taxes on specific goods are tools governments use to achieve this goal. At other times, governments regulate the industry's price or production quantity or can even take over the industry and run it publicly for free or a reduced price.

It is debatable whether government intervention and regulation help markets work better. Sometimes regulations and taxes prevent a sale even when a buyer values something more than a seller does. Most government programs and regulations cannot be perfectly enforced and implemented and many are quite costly to administer. Ideally, government action to disrupt markets should be done only if the benefits are greater than the costs.

Sadly, this isn't always the case. Economists and political scientists use the term "government failure" to describe times when government actions do not yield the socially efficient results. This can result from poor administration of laws and regulations, from politicians acting in their individual interests rather than for the general good, or because laws sometimes have unintended consequences that create greater harm than good.

Global Economy

Economic questions sometimes refer to the **global economy**. The global economic system increasingly is one of interdependence worldwide. International trade plays a huge role in the status of the global economy. Imports, exports, competition, and availability of raw materials affect trade all over the world. These factors can have both negative and positive effects. Below is some information explaining the basis of the global economy.

> The global economy is based on the economies of all of the world's countries. It cannot be separated from the geography and ecology of the Earth, and is not a monetary system.

> The widely accepted estimate of the global economy, and indeed the economy of any single country, is in terms of money. The main indicators for this assessment are the gross world product, industrial production figures of world trade, standards of living, and other economic and social indicators, which are expressed in terms of money, and as a percentage of base year.

Historical Events that Affect the Economy

Events in history have greatly driven the economy and changed how business was conducted. One important period was the Industrial Revolution—a time of great economic, technological, social, and cultural change. The decade of the 1830s is considered the first Industrial Revolution. Many new inventions were developed during this time. One was the automated loom which changed the textile industry. Another was the invention of the steam-powered engine, which changed transportation about 100 years before the invention of the internal combustion engine. The discovery of the process of changing iron into steel further revolutionized transportation and manufacturing. In the 1850s electric appliances and crude automobiles began to be developed. Many agree the automobile industry was an economic driver all around the world.

New inventions and technology was only a part of the changes the Industrial Revolution created. There were sweeping changes in how business was conducted. The development of the corporation was one of those changes. The corporation brought in investors. People who bought shares or stocks in a business the shared its profit or failure. The system of interchangeable parts made manufacturing cheaper and easier. In the late 1800s and early 1900s, the method called "Taylorism" which made workers able to move around where they were needed in the factory or business. The moving assembly line made it possible to produce goods (cars) rapidly and with ease. This made production cheaper and profits higher. In addition, wages increased for workers and the standard of living steadily increased as consumerism began to drive the markets.

Economic motives, such as the desire for more resources and more land, have often been reasons for expansion, whether to explore new lands, colonize territory, or wage war against neighboring countries. Wars and other conflicts between countries have in turn influenced economics in several ways. For centuries, war has involved invention of weapons and has been financed by government borrowing. These facts mean that wars often lead to useful technological innovations in production and have encouraged creative methods of lending and finance, helping economies to grow in the long run. On the other hand, wars involve ravaging land, destroying factories and productive tools, and killing potential consumers and workers. These factors leave countries with smaller resource bases and labor forces, which are not good for economic activity. The major world wars of the 20th century involved major restructuring of economies around weapons production and rationing of consumer goods and resulted in major changes in many countries' work forces—increasing the number of women in the labor pool of many Western countries.

Main Idea and Details to Support Conclusions

In the context of a global economy, questions on the GED® test could ask you to draw conclusions or make inferences. You can draw conclusions by reading the main idea. You can also find the details that support the conclusions. Both main idea and supporting details serve to help you make inferences. You figure out things that are not actually stated. By examining a car sales analogy, you can draw a conclusion that gas prices affect car sales or you could infer that higher gas prices result in lower car sales.

To find the main idea and details use these steps. First, identify the main idea. It is usually a central topic or can be stated in the text. Next, find the details that add information about the main idea. What stands out? What is the article or excerpt telling the reader? Now make a general statement about the information. This is your conclusion. Use the excerpt concerning global economy to practice your skills.

What is the general subject? _____

What are the details? _____

Make a general statement about the excerpt. _____

Predicting an Outcome

In **predicting an outcome** you try to guess what will happen next. However, in this case you can use the evidence in the readings or graphics to help you predict the outcome. In economics, you can examine the cause-and-effect relationship in one event to predict what would happen in a similar situation. For example, if the orange crops are destroyed in spring, what would be the outcome? Most likely, orange juice would be more expensive until the following year's crop produced more oranges.

In economics, as in science, when predicting an outcome it is important to consider only the change being asked about. If the question doesn't suggest a change in some factor, it is typically safe to assume that it remained the same. To stay on target, focus on the cause the question asks about!

PRACTICE!

Complete the sentences below.

1. Economics involves _____ .

2. Markets involve interactions between _____ .

Identify the types of graphs below and match each one with the most likely use of this type of graph. Use the drag-and-drop feature.

3.   A.

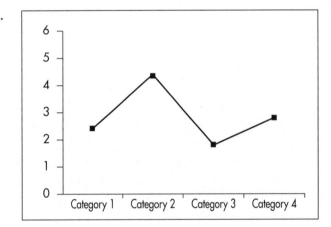

B.

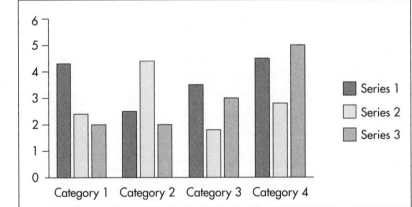

C.

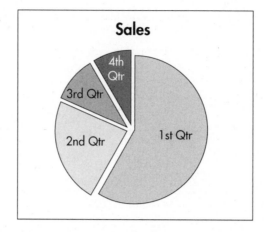

Sales

- 4th Qtr
- 3rd Qtr
- 2nd Qtr
- 1st Qtr

D.

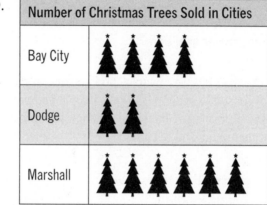

Number of Christmas Trees Sold in Cities	
Bay City	🎄🎄🎄🎄
Dodge	🎄🎄
Marshall	🎄🎄🎄🎄🎄🎄

🎄 Represents 100 trees.

For this paper-and-pencil setting, fill in the chart below with the letter of the correct type of graph.

	Line	Bar	Pie Chart	Pictograph
examine changes in data over time				
compare size/portions				
analysis data in large numbers				
compare several sets of data				

4. What are the factors of production or economic resources?

5. The government should 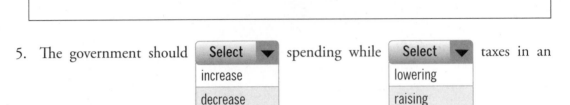 spending while taxes in an

Select ▼
increase
decrease

Select ▼
lowering
raising

economic recession.

6. When the government spends more than it collects in taxes, there is a budget

Select ▼
surplus.
deficit.

Read the following passage and answer question 7.

Technology has greatly changed the way people shop and spend money. Online shopping has changed many aspects of consumer economics. Many people find online shopping more convenient. As a result, stores and businesses have shifted advertising dollars to the Internet rather than newspapers, magazines, radio, and television.

7. Online shopping created several changes in American business practices. Which of the following is a result of online shopping?

    A. People buy more clothes.

    B. The amount of online stores have decreased.

    C. Stores have lowered their prices.

    D. Businesses have shifted advertising practices.

8. Which of the following is an example of the barter system?

    A. The bank loans $1,000 to John at a 5% interest rate.

    B. John exchanges his lumber with Mike, who wants to build a storage shed, for a truck Mike owns.

    C. John buys apples at $10 a bushel. Then, he sells the apples for $12 a bushel.

    D. Mary works at a factory for $10 an hour making chairs.

9. Write the economics-related definition for each of the following terms.

Inflation	
Deflation	
Recession	
Depression	

10. The year 2012 had several violent events that were reported in the news media. This resulted in a call for expanded gun control laws in the United States. What is the most likely reason the sale of firearms increased so dramatically since 2005?

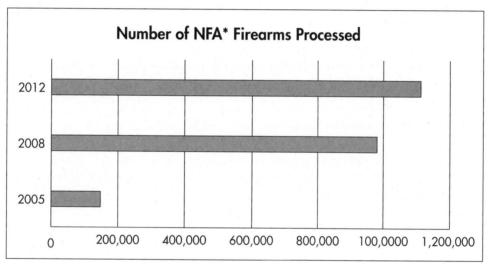

*National Firearms Act

A. More people want guns.

B. People fear that guns will not be available next year.

C. Guns are cheaper than before.

D. Guns are more popular than in 2005.

Social Studies Practice 3 Answers

1. resources and how people handle them.

2. consumers and producers.

3. A is a line graph — examine changes in data over time

    B bar graph — compare several sets of data

    C circle graph — compare size/portions

    D pictorial graph — analysis data in large numbers

4. **capital, raw materials, labor, and entrepreneurship**

5. **decrease — raising**

6. **deficit**

7. **D.**

    Businesses have shifted advertising practices. Options A, B, and C are incorrect and not supported by the passage.

8. **B.**

    John exchanges his lumber with Mike, who wants to build a storage shed, for a truck Mike owns. Option A is a bank loan with interest. Option C is buying and selling for profit. Option D is exchanging a service (work) for wages.

9. Inflation — a rise in prices and decline in purchasing power.

    Deflation — decrease in government, consumer, and investment spending results in increased unemployment.

    Recession — significant decline in economic activity spread across the economy.

    Depression — sustained downturn in economic activity.

10. **B.**

    People fear that guns will not be available next year. Option A is too broad a statement and not supported by the evidence. Option C is not supported by any of the information. Option D is the opposite of the information in the chart and graph.

Geography and the World

When you think of geography, you may picture in your mind maps and locations of places. You are correct, but don't be intimidated, as the geography part of the GED® test focuses more on global trends concerning climate, environmental issues, natural resources, and sustainability. Some other topics may include migration or movement of humans over time, and changes in population.

One great way to prepare for this part of the social studies exam is to become familiar with various types of maps. There are many. Therefore it is helpful to look at physical (land), political maps (names and locations of countries and states), but also very important are the climate and habitat maps (forests, deserts, etc.). Environmental and population maps also are important.

Knowing the climate of an area can help you conclude which crops would grow best in that area. Similarly, knowing the habitat features can help you reason what natural resources are found in an area, or how much precipitation that area receives. Remember that areas with sparse populations are likely to be farming areas or areas that are not convenient or comfortable places on which to live, while greater population density would suggest an area that has more urban development and industry. In addition, understanding weather and climate can help you reason why people move from one place to another.

The Five Themes of Geography

In general, there are five themes in geography. These five themes are identified as **location, place, human–environment interaction, movement, and region.** Since geography is the study of the Earth and how people use it, the five themes help to organize information in logical ways.

Understanding what the five themes mean can help you organize the information in a way you can remember it. First, *location* is where you can find a particular area or place. This is the idea most people have about geography. *Place* describes the physical features of a location. Things like landforms, climate, and bodies of water are examples of physical features. Natural resources are things from nature that people can use. Some examples are trees, oil, coal, and minerals like iron or gold. Physical features include man-made features—the things humans have created or put in the location. These are such things as buildings, roads, farms, schools, and stores.

Source: iStockphoto.com/thanarat27

Look at this picture of Benjakiti Park in Bangkok, Thailand. Now make a list of the things in the picture. Put the items in their category in the table below.

Physical	Natural	Human

This is one way to organize information to describe a location. When taking the GED® test you might not have time to notice everything, but if you practice this type of organizing data, you will find the specific details more quickly.

Human–Environment Interaction

Human–environment interaction is the main theme of geography. The interaction is why and how people live in a specific location, or why people move from one place to another. **Climate** is one major reason people stay or move. The climate and landform determine what you will eat or do in that place. For example, people who live in Florida live differently from people who live in Canada. The climate and landform of a location determine the kind of house in which people live, the crops grown there, even the type of automobiles people drive.

Movement is part of the human–environment aspect of geography. It simply means how and why people move from place to place. Movement includes transportation and communication. It also includes migration—the movement of groups of people from one region to another—as well as the emigration of individuals from one country to another. As it relates to geography, people may move from one place to another because of environmental reasons such as drought, flood, or earthquakes. (Distinguish this from movements of people brought about by developments in history, such as war; or in regional and global economy, such as financial recession in one area and prosperity in another; or in matters relating to government or society, such as persons fleeing political persecution or religious intolerance.) Sometimes, as in the case of the scattering of the Jews throughout the world after the Roman Empire destroyed their holy city of Jerusalem, a diaspora takes place. A diaspora is the scattering of any ethnic group.

Movement with a country is known as internal migration. People move in two major patterns: interregional and intraregional. Ineterregional migration is moving from one region in the country to another region, whereas intraregional migration is moving within a region, such as from a city to a suburb. As industrialization built up cities in the United States, more and more Americans migrated from farms to cities in a pattern of urban migration. A counterstream soon developed as people left crowded cities for suburbs.

The U.S. migration pattern has shifted its center of population consistently westward and in a southerly direction. During the Great Migration, which took place while the nation was fighting World War I, many southern African Americans moved north in search of industrial jobs not being filled by immigrants because of the war. By the 1970s, however, more African Americans were returning to the South than were moving north. This pattern is part of the trend by northerners, especially post-World War II baby boomers, moving south for better weather and increased job openings as U.S. factory jobs are lost. This aging of industrial-era factories in the U.S. has formed a Rustbelt in the Northeast and Midwest and a Sun Belt in the South.

Regions are areas that share one or more *features*. Regions are described in many ways. They could be based on location, climate, or landforms. These are just a few ways to describe regions. Culture is another. **Culture** is the traditions and practices of the people who live in the area. Culture includes language and customs. Examples of regions in the United States are areas like the Great Lakes region, which comprises states bordering the Great Lakes, or the Sun Belt, which comprises an area stretching from the South to the Southwest that is favored for its warm, sunny climate

When you are familiar with some common regions, you can understand what the information in the text or test question is based upon. It helps you to form an image in your mind about the information.

Examine these maps to learn about regions in the United States.

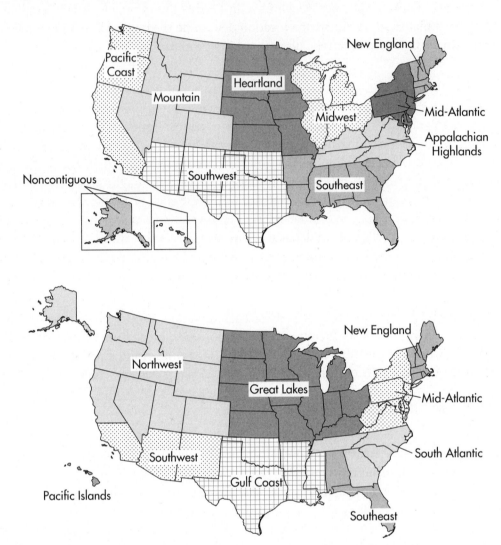

Regions of the world may be defined by climate, landforms, or language. Very often, location on the globe and direction (such as direction from Europe—more precisely, from the prime meridian, which is explained below—or from the Equator) are the deciding factors. For example, the Far East, Mideast, Eastern Europe, Central Europe, and Western Europe all are regions described by their directional location in relation to Europe. North America and South America are regions identified by their direction from the Equator. Europe, Asia, and Africa are regions identified by their location on the globe.

Types of Maps

There are many types of maps to consider when studying geography or any social studies subject. Here is a list of the many types of maps you might encounter and a brief description:

Physical maps—show locations of mountains, forests, deserts, and other land forms. Physical maps indicate the elevation of the land.

Political maps—tell the name of the countries, their capital cities, and borders.

Climate maps—provide information about the climate in an area or globally.

Economic maps—give an idea of the economic conditions in different locations.

Topographic maps—are often three-dimensional, designed to show the lay of (i.e., the contours of) the land, such as the depths of valleys, the heights of mountains, and the like.

Resource maps—show the resources of a region. This could be natural resources, economic resources, nonrenewable or renewable resources, population resources, and the like.

Road maps—show where the roads are and which ones to take to get from one location to another. Road maps have a great deal of information about the area, such as rest areas, state parks, national parks, even gas, food, and lodging.

Thematic maps—help to focus on a particular subject.

You can expect maps to be part of how you'll be tested on geography. However, you also need to be prepared for related graphs, charts, and tables. These types of questions may have you compare rainfall amounts of regions, or highest elevations on continents.

Globes are a special type of map. A globe is a model of Earth. Recognizing such things as the **Equator** (0° latitude, an imaginary line running east and west at the point exactly halfway between the North and South Poles), the **prime meridian** (0° longitude, an imaginary line running north and south around the globe and passing through Greenwich, England), and the **North** and **South Poles** (the points at the northern and southern "ends" of the globe that are on the Earth's axis—the imaginary line through the center of the globe around which the Earth rotates) will help you use globes more effectively. These lines, points, and other features on the globe help you to determine the location of hemispheres. **Hemisphere** means half a sphere, or in this case, half of the globe. The Eastern and Western Hemispheres are divided by the prime meridian; Northern and Southern Hemispheres are divided by the Equator. Below are examples of those definitions.

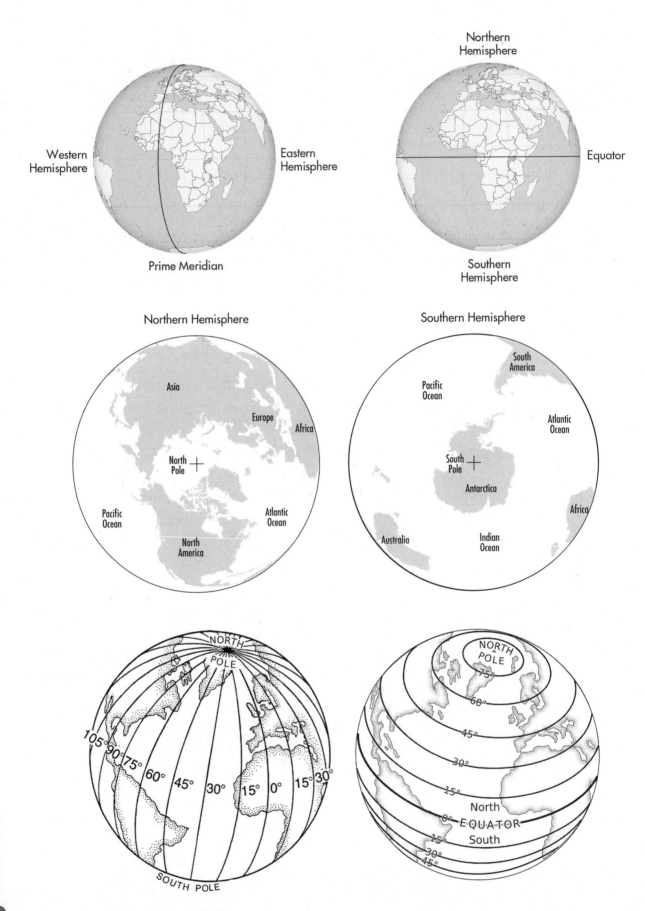

Western
Hemisphere

Eastern
Hemisphere

Prime Meridian

Northern
Hemisphere

Equator

Southern
Hemisphere

Northern Hemisphere

Asia

Europe

Africa

North
Pole

Pacific
Ocean

Atlantic
Ocean

North
America

Southern Hemisphere

South
America

Pacific
Ocean

Atlantic
Ocean

South
Pole

Antarctica

Africa

Australia

Indian
Ocean

NORTH
POLE

105° 90° 75° 60° 45° 30° 15° 0° 15° 30°

SOUTH POLE

NORTH
POLE

75°

60°

45°

30°

15°

North
0° EQUATOR
South

15°

30°

45°

The location of the Equator plays a great role in understanding climate. Since the location of the Equator is tropical, or very hot and humid, you can infer information about the climate in locations by knowing their distance from the Equator: the closer to the Equator a place is located, the more hot and humid its climate will most likely be. A question might have you order countries by their climate. If you know where the Equator is located, you can easily determine the order.

Understanding the difference between weather and climate will help you answer questions concerning several topics. **Weather** is the day-to-day conditions of the air—its temperature, humidity level, barometric pressure, cloud cover, and wind direction and speed. **Climate**, on the other hand, is the long-term patterns of weather of a place. Plainly said, weather is what you see when you look out the window. *Sunny, cloudy, rainy,* and *snowy* are some examples of weather terms. Climate can be described in terms like *tropical, subtropical, temperate,* or *arctic*.

Weather maps often show the temperatures and weather conditions for a short period of time. Here is an example:

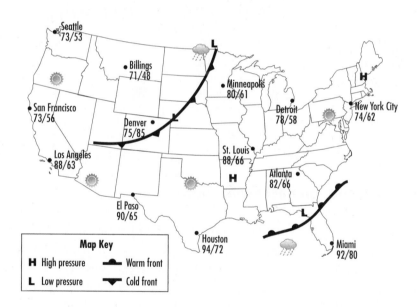

Climate is affected by many factors. Latitude (distance from the Equator) is a huge influence on climate, as mentioned previously. Another factor is the geographical features—the terrain—of a location, such as whether it is mountainous or flat, desert sands, rocky wastes, or fertile soil, coastland or interior. Terrain plays an important part in determining such things as the intensity of the sun's rays and the types of winds in the area. Warm moist air that blows over the ocean can be chilled as it passes over the mountain ranges. In this same way, the seas moderate the climate. The winds from the ocean bring rain. The wind passing over the warm Gulf Stream brings rain, while the currents of air over the Arctic ice bring blasts of cold air.

Climate maps tell more about the location and conditions based on long periods of time. The climate map below explains climate regions of North America.

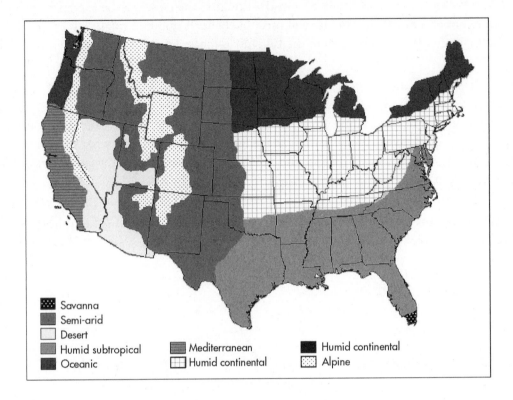

Legend:
- Savanna
- Semi-arid
- Desert
- Humid subtropical
- Oceanic
- Mediterranean
- Humid continental
- Humid continental
- Alpine

Geography's Influence on Past Civilizations

Geography impacted how past civilizations developed because it helped to determine how successful they became and how the geography (land, climate, weather, and water sources) benefited them or not. For instance, climate impacts what crops people grow, eat, and sell. Weather impacts where people want to live. Landforms play a role in activities necessary to function successfully in a particular location. In history, mountains provided protection from invasions of other people. Access to and location of waterways was very important. Rivers could provide food, water, and transportation.

An example is the region of the Mesopotamia. The word "Mesopotamia" comes from two Greek words meaning "the land between the rivers." This phrase refers specifically to the valleys of the Tigris and Euphrates Rivers, which is in modern-day Iraq. Another example is the land of Egypt, which was called "the gift of the Nile." During the fourth millennium B.C.E. (i.e., 4,000 years "before the common era," also referenced as "B.C.," for "before Christ"), the number of humans increased rapidly in Mesopotamia and Egypt. The map on the next page illustrates how Egypt was influenced by its location along the Nile River. It also shows the area of Mesopotamia and the location of the Fertile Crescent.

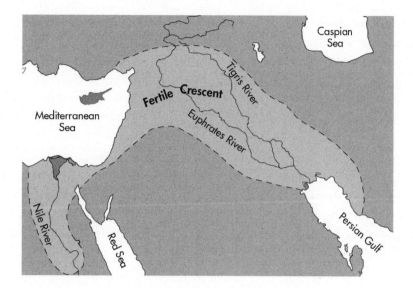

Several factors played important roles in the development of early complex societies. New ways of doing things created specialized labor, language, trade, metallurgy, and religion. These played a role in all societies that developed into classical civilization. The **classical civilizations** were vast and often widespread geographic regions, but several developed into nations.

"Nation" versus "State": What's the Difference?

The GED® Social Studies test requires that you be able to distinguish between nations and states. It's a distinction that can be confusing. Since you were a young child, you have probably thought of Spain, for example, as a country. Political geographers use a more precise term: "state." Even so, "state" and "country" can be used to mean the same thing. A state is a sovereign political unit with a permanent population, territorial boundaries recognized by other states, an effective government, and a working economy. Sovereignty is the internationally recognized control a state has over the people and territory within its boundaries. Germany, Russia, Japan, Indonesia, the United States, and Mexico are just some of the nearly 200 states (or countries). (The term "state" also serves to describe a division of a federal system, as is true of the United States' 50 states.)

The term "nation" refers to a group of people who share common bonds such as language, culture, religion, history, or ethnicity. The critical factor here is that these people identify as a cohesive group. The United States is often considered a nation because its people are unified around the idea of being American. But there are other cohesive groups whose ideas and principles can coexist within the nation that is the United States. For example, the United States formally recognizes 562 Indian nations within its borders. Some groups asserting nationhood have a state of their own, such as the Dutch, French, Egyptians, Hungarians, and Japanese; thus, their countries may be described as nation-states. Others want a state but do not have one, such as the Tibetans, the Palestinians, and the Chechens.

With nation building, exploration, and colonization comes the diffusion of culture. When peoples moved to other places they spread the culture from one place to another. This process served to change the society of their new area. In the same sense, the new peoples had to assimilate to the new culture. Often ethnic minority groups lost some of their cultural characteristics that made them different from the group in which they now live. All these factors are causes of changes people, even today, experience when they merge into another group or move to another area.

The questions on the test may ask you to look at the characteristics of a people and their geographic region and determine why they became a nation. You may need to infer that people isolated in one area learned the same language and formed bonds. Another aspect of this type of question involves thinking of the cultural similarities various peoples have and how they were being governed at the time. You can draw a conclusion or make inferences about how governments and their citizenries adopted a way of life.

How and why ancient civilizations became the classical civilizations and then nations is a process that may be covered on the test as well. It is important to recognize the cycle of sustainability to crisis to redevelopment. In early history, the use of fire and the hunt for certain foods made it possible for humans to go from a culture of constant movement to one of settlement. They learned to stay in one place where food could be gathered, and they could use fire to cook, heat, and use as a light source. The next phase was one of farming. People stayed in the place where they could grow food. Soon, though, the animals they hunted disappeared because of overhunting or because the land became depleted due to overfarming. This forced them to move to another place and form a new culture. During the Industrial Revolution, nations began to use fossil fuels, which placed a great demand on natural resources. This, of course, resulted in pollution and the depletion of the minerals, coal, and oil in the area. It caused these countries to become reliant on outside sources of fuel. This cycle continues even now as we face global warming, deforestation, and urban sprawl. The energy crisis and the environmental concerns have modern society searching for ways to become a sustainable society again.

In the same sense, technology also affected the development of society, civilizations, and nations. As more and more technology developed, so did the government and ideologies of different peoples. For example, the Iron Age brought technology that moved the ancient peoples to the next level of warfare, commerce, and transportation. This is also true of the Industrial Revolution when steam travel developed into the railroad industry. Manufacturing made it possible to become the electric, automated, automobile society we know today. The same is true as more and more advances develop. Now the computer has revolutionized communication across the globe, giving us modern interconnectedness so that we are able to conduct business in a global economy. Technology is one of the biggest drivers in the development of civilization and modern society.

Environmental Issues

Most environmental discussions or concerns have to do with the changes in the Earth's behavior. Climate and natural activities (earthquakes, volcanoes, storms, hurricanes, etc.) are some examples of those changes. In addition to natural causes, human activities have created many of the conditions for these types of events. **Deforestation** is one example. Much of the temperate zone in the Northern Hemisphere (the region between the tropics and the arctic circles, where temperatures are relatively moderate) once was covered in deciduous trees like ash, beech, elm, oak and maple. But **deciduous** trees are used for building things—homes and furniture. The trees also are used for fuel. In addition, trees are cut and sold to make way for more farmland so that profitable market crops can be grown. The result is that many of the forests that once covered the Northern Hemisphere have been cut down and are gone forever. This also can be seen in the increasing destruction of significant portions of the rainforest in South America, Central Africa, and Southeast Asia. Rainforest destruction resulted in extensive soil erosion, loss of habitat for animals, and loss of thousands of plant species. In addition, since the huge rainforest influences the weather and climate patterns, destroying rainforests in the Southern Hemisphere, or woodlands in the Northern Hemisphere, produces inevitable changes in the climate of those regions, and eventually disturbs climate patterns all around the globe.

Desertification—in which land that already is somewhat dry becomes increasingly arid and desert-like, with severe decline in soil moisture and vegetation—is the result of deforestation and the overuse of the land. It leaves the soil unusable and barren. Of course, pollution of air and water has created many environmental changes over the decades. Industrialization has created major problems that humankind is just beginning to regulate and to search for solutions. These changes, whether natural or manmade, are the issues that concern us and the Earth's future.

Let's look at some examples of how the GED® test might pose questions on these topics.

EXAMPLE

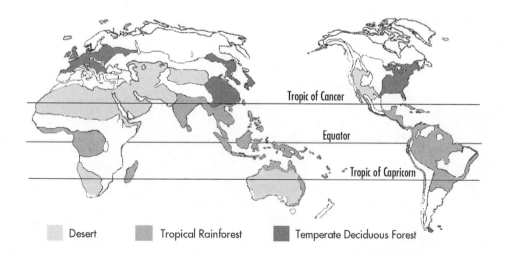

Put these in order of greatest to least risk of loss of natural habitat in the equatorial rainforests.

North Africa   Australia   Central Africa   Northern China

Be sure to examine the map legend. This tells you about the shades of gray on the map. The regions with greatest risk of loss of natural habitat in equatorial rainforests will be those identified as areas of tropical rainforest. Hence, greatest to least = Central Africa, Australia, Northern China, North Africa.

EXAMPLE

Consider the following maps of global population density (darker areas mean greater population density) and global comparison of income (based on gross domestic product) to population (the darkest regions are the wealthier regions in terms of gross domestic product):

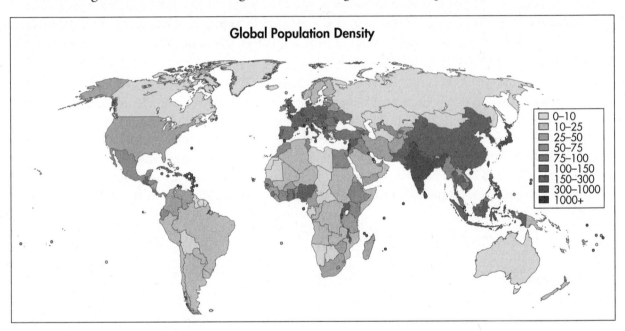

Global Population Density

0–10	
10–25	
25–50	
50–75	
75–100	
100–150	
150–300	
300–1000	
1000+	

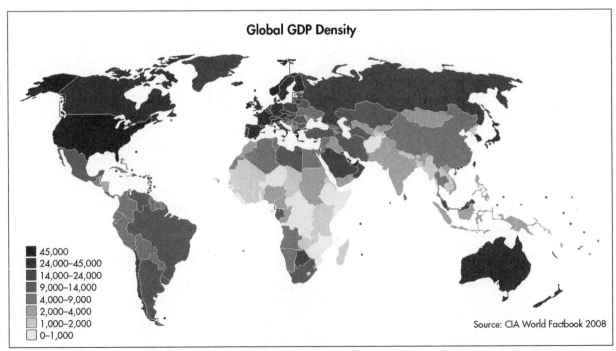

Global GDP Density

45,000	
24,000–45,000	
14,000–24,000	
9,000–14,000	
4,000–9,000	
2,000–4,000	
1,000–2,000	
0–1,000	

Source: CIA World Factbook 2008

According to these two maps, which areas are most likely to have more severe air and water pollution?

    A. China, United States, and Europe

    B. Brazil, Bolivia, and Uruguay

    C. Congo, Indonesia, and the South Pacific Islands

    D. Southern China, Canada, and the Arctic

It may seem as though you need to know about the location of the countries listed; however, you really don't. You do need to consider which of the countries are most industrialized and populated. Based on those two facts it is logical to choose (A). China, the United States, and countries of Europe are very industrialized, have dense populations, and hence are likely to create a great deal of water and air pollution.

Movement of people and changes in the territories of various nations are also important in the aspects of geography and the world. As to changes in the world map of countries, the two maps below show how Europe changed in terms of national borders from before World War I to after World War I.

Before World War I

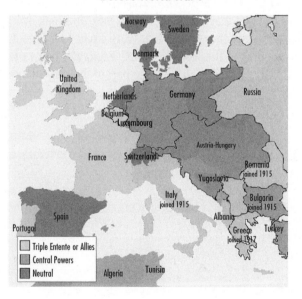

After World War I

Notice that one of the big differences in these two maps is the number of countries on the postwar map. This tells you that a large country, Austria-Hungary, was broken into several small countries. Germany also was reduced in size, and countries like Poland, Estonia, Latvia, and Lithuania were created out of what formerly was German territory. This map illustrates how drastically war often changes borders.

Shifts in population are important when thinking about geography. Weather and natural disasters are some reasons people move from one place to another, but human activity is also a factor. War, economic conditions, employment opportunities, and changes in governments are all reasons people move from one place to another. Below is a passage that provides information about one event in which people moved to another area for social and economic reasons.

> Between 1915 and 1970, more than 6 million African-Americans moved out of the South to cities across the Northeast, Midwest and West.
>
> This relocation— called the Great Migration— resulted in massive demographic shifts across the United States. Between 1910 and 1930, cities such as New York, Chicago, Detroit and Cleveland saw their African-American populations grow by about 40 percent, and the number of African-Americans employed in industrial jobs nearly doubled.
>
> "[The Great Migration] had such an effect on almost every aspect of our lives— from the music that we listen to, to the politics of our country, to the ways the cities even look and feel, even today," says Isabel Wilkerson. "The suburbanization and the ghettos that were created as a result of the limits of where [African-Americans] could live in the North [still exist today.] And ... the South was forced to change, in part because they were losing such a large part of their workforce through the Great Migration." [1]

According to this passage, several areas were changed because of the Great Migration. The South lost a large number of workers. The cities grew in population, which resulted in suburbanization and the creation of ghettos.

---

[1] *http://www.npr.org/templates/story/story.php?storyId=129827444.*

Immigration is the movement of people from one country to another. Immigration occurs for many reasons.

Below is a graph showing immigration facts.[2]

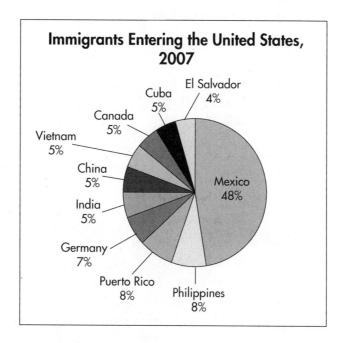

Migration and immigration are often the results of economic, political, and social changes. People leave the country they live in to find safety from violence or war in their homeland. When people leave their homes to escape violence, war, and persecution, they are called "refugees" because they want refuge from the problems in their place of origin.

---

[2] Source: *Migrationmap.net/USA/arrivals 2007.*

PRACTICE!

Use the map and passage to answer questions 1–3.

Climate Map of Africa

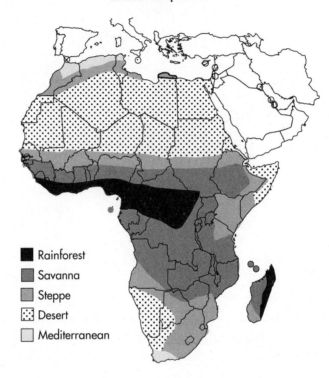

Rainforest
Savanna
Steppe
Desert
Mediterranean

The climate of Africa is governed by its position on the globe and can be broadly divided into five different climate types:

Rainforest—This region is characterized by very high temperatures and high rainfall throughout the year.

Savanna—This region has very high temperatures all year and rain during the summer season only.

Steppe—This region has high temperatures all year and only limited rainfall during the summer season.

Desert—High temperatures throughout the year, with very little rainfall.

Mediterranean—Warm-to-high temperatures, with rainfall in the autumn and winter months.[3]

_____

[3] Source: *naturalhistoryonthenet.com*.

1. According to the map, which of the following areas would most likely have the highest temperatures?

    A. Steppe

    B. Rainforest

    C. Mediterranean

    D. Desert

2. Which zone most likely attracts the lowest population density?

    A. Mediterranean

    B. Desert

    C. Savanna

    D. Steppe

3. How would you describe the most northern tip of Africa?

    A. Desert

    B. Steppe

    C. Mediterranean

    D. Rainforest

Read the following passage and answer the questions below.

One of the most important environmental issues is desertification. This is a type of soil erosion resulting from deforestation, overgrazing, and poor farming techniques. The soil is exposed to the wind and rain. In some regions, the once fertile land becomes barren desert. The Sabel region in Africa, which is south of the Sahara Desert, is one place where desertification is a major environmental problem.

4. In this passage, the word "barren" most likely means:

    A. Not able to sustain plant growth.

    B. Not identifiable.

    C. Not likely to grow.

    D. Lack of rain.

5. According to the information provided, desertification is the results of:

Select ▼
pollution
deforestation
soil erosion

6. The map below shows areas of flooding in Australia.

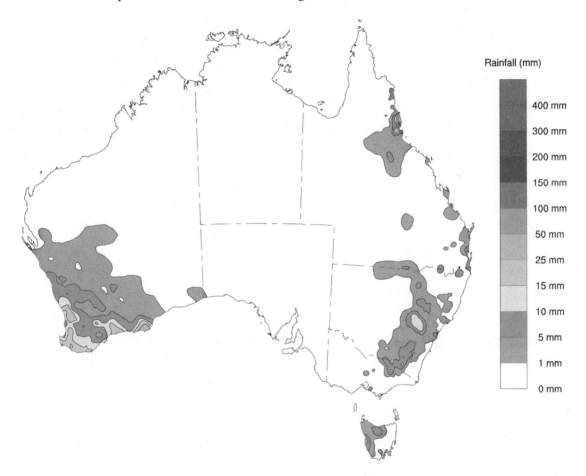

People who want to move to an area to avoid flood conditions most likely would choose which of the following?

A. The West Coast

B. The northern tip

C. The central part of the country

D. The East Coast

Lines of Latitude run east and west at equal distances from one another. Lines of Longitude run north and south, meeting at the poles.

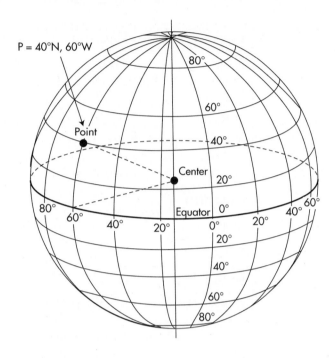

7. From the passage and the image, which of the following can be said about the point indicated?

    A. It is 60° longitude and 40° latitude.

    B. It is on the Equator.

    C. It is on the prime meridian.

    D. It is 40° latitude and 60° longitude.

8. What conclusion can be drawn by the information in the chart below?

Immigration to the United States—1840–1890

Country of origin	Population
Poland	5,000
Italy	15,000
Wales	15,000
Belgium	20,000
Scandinavia	30,000
Switzerland	30,000
Scotland	40,000
France	180,000
England	420,000
Ireland	2,900,000

Source: www.historyteacher.net

A. Poland did not have a large population in 1840.

B. Italian and Welsh immigrants followed one another.

C. Irish people accounted for the largest number of immigrants, 1840-1890.

D. Most immigrants were from countries at war with one another.

9. Which of the following conclusions can be drawn from the following map?

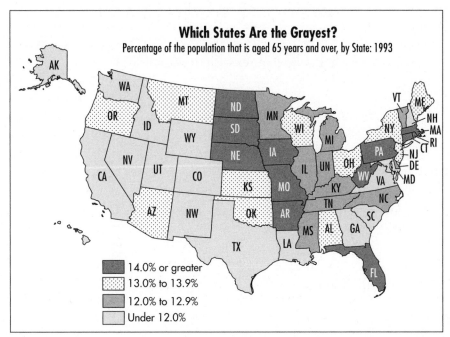

Which States Are the Grayest?
Percentage of the population that is aged 65 years and over, by State: 1993

14.0% or greater
13.0% to 13.9%
12.0% to 12.9%
Under 12.0%

Source: uscensus.gov

A. Elderly people move to warmer places.

B. The Western states have more to offer the elderly.

C. Northern states have more educated elderly people.

D. The Midwest has the largest percentage of elderly people.

10. Based on the information in the map, which of the following is most likely true for the state of Rhode Island?

A. This state needs more schools.

B. Rhode Island attracts a college-age population.

C. Rhode Island has a number of elder-care centers.

D. This state is warm and good for older people.

Social Studies Practice 4 Answers

1. **D.**

   Desert—very hot temperatures with dry conditions

2. **B.**

   Desert

3. **C.**

   Mediterranean

4. **A.**

   Not able to produce

5. deforestation

6. **C.**

   The central part of the country.

7. **D.**

   It is 40° latitude and 60° longitude. Option A is the opposite. The equator is the center of the latitude while the prime meridian is the center of the longitude.

8. **C.**

   Irish people accounted for the largest number of immigrants, 1840–1890.

9. **D.**

   The Midwest has the largest percentage of elderly people.

10. **C.**

    Rhode Island has a number of elder-care centers.

Practice Test Battery 1

- Reasoning Through Language Arts

- Mathematical Reasoning

- Science

- Social Studies

The GED® test, which is delivered on computer, has a built-in timer for each test section. Because it's computerized, the test uses an assortment of technology-enhanced questions. Such question types vary by test subject but may for instance require test-takers to highlight blocks of text, select answers from a list embedded within a text, classify and appropriately sequence information, or provide a numeric-entry response. REA's printed practice tests simulate the computerized GED® test as closely as possible.

PRACTICE TEST 1

REASONING THROUGH LANGUAGE ARTS
Section 1

40 questions
35 minutes

The Reasoning Through Language Arts test is 150 minutes, with a 10-minute break after Section 2 (the Extended Response portion of the test).

Practice Test 1: Reasoning Through Language Arts (RLA)

Read the following essay, "On Advertising for Marriage" by Charlotte Perkins Gilman. Then answer questions 1–8.

(1) Why not? Why not take every means in one's power to discover so important a person as one's husband or wife? What is the prejudice that exists against it?

(2) To say that such advertisements are used for improper purposes is saying nothing against using them properly. To say that "marriages are made in heaven;" that it is "tempting Providence" to speak of mysterious laws which bring people together, needs only for answer, Look at the majority of marriages now existing! If they are made in heaven let us try some earth-made ones. *The Alpha* and all common sense teaches that we should use reason and discrimination in a selection like this; and if one is desirous to marry and fails to find a fit mate in one's neighborhood or acquaintance, what reason is there that he or she should not look farther?

(3) They have no surety that fate will bring them the desired one without effort on their part, for behold! Many of their friends are unmarried and many more mismarried. What certainty have they of a better lot?

(4) I do believe that if we obeyed all the laws of our life as the birds do, we should find mates as they do; but we do not.

(5) One reasonable argument may be adduced against me, namely, that people brought together from different parts of the county would be dissimilar in their tastes and habits, and so suffer when united; also that *one* must be separated from home and friends.

(6) To the latter I reply that in the case of true marriage it would be a small evil, that under ordinary circumstances the separation need not be complete, and that it frequently happens under the present method.

(7) To the former, that people whose local tastes and habits were stronger than their individualities, who shared the feelings of the neighborhood to such an extent that change would be painful, would not be likely to miss mating, for they would be satisfied with local character.

(8) Conversely, those who found no mate in the home influence and were so constituted as to demand something different would find full compensation in what they gained for all they lost.

(9) It may be said that if the match proved unhappy they would bitterly regret having meddled with fate, and wish they had waited patiently; but in like cases those who meet by chance, or are thrown together in the natural course of events, as bitterly curse fortune, or their own folly, and wish the same.

(10) Errors of judgment need be no more frequent than now, and even in case of mistaking, surely it is better to look back on an earnest attempt to choose wisely than the usual much-extolled drifting.

(11) Surely *The Alpha* teaches that marriage should result not from the will and judgment led by passion, but the opposite. If a man sees a fair woman before he knows her; feels the charm of her presence before he begins to understand her character; if first aroused to the necessity of judging by his strong inclination; surely he stands less chance of a cool and safe decision than one who begins knowingly, learns a character from earnest letters, loves the mind before he does the body. And that first love would improve and be more to him yearly, growing ever richer, stronger, and more lovely with advancing age.

(12) The other does not. I see in writing still another consideration.

(13) It would if it became a general custom, teach both sexes to cultivate the mind and the power of expression in writing more than the beauty of the body and its sexual attraction.

(14) Also when marriage was seen to depend more upon real value and worth coolly inquired into than upon feminine charms and snares and masculine force and persistence, that would be a huge power enlisted on the side of good. Young women would take more interest in the affairs of the world if they knew the chance of a happy marriage might depend on such knowledge; that they might be written to by such a man as they would love and honor, and expected to sympathize with his ideas, appreciate his work, understand and help him; and man might condescend to think a women's nature worth studying a little if their hopes rested also in genuine sympathy and appreciation.

(15) (Not her sexual nature! Heaven defend us! They have studied that long and well, but the *rest* of her, the "ninety-nine parts human!")

(16) Will someone explain what harm would result from Advertising for Marriage?

1. What is the purpose of this passage?

    A. To condemn arranged marriages due to the lack of buy-in from the couple.

    B. To inform the reader about the benefits of advertising for marriage.

    C. To convince the reader that advertising for marriage would result in happier unions.

    D. To dissuade the audience from advertising for marriage based on the negative effects doing so would have on the institution.

2. Indicate which claims are supported by reasons and evidence in the text. Place the letters of your selections in the boxes.

Claims Supported by the Text

A. To say that "marriages are made in heaven;" that it is "tempting Providence" to speak of mysterious laws which bring people together, needs only for answer, Look at the majority of marriages now existing!

B. *The Alpha* and all common sense teaches that we should use reason and discrimination in a selection like this; and if one is desirous to marry and fails to find a fit mate in one's neighborhood or acquaintance, what reason is there that he or she should not look farther?

C. What certainty have they of a better lot?

D. Conversely, those who found no mate in the home influence and were so constituted as to demand something different would find full compensation in what they gained for all they lost.

E. If a man sees a fair woman before he knows her; feels the charm of her presence before he begins to understand her character; if first aroused to the necessity of judging by his strong inclination; surely he stands less chance of a cool and safe decision than one who begins knowingly, learns a character from earnest letters, loves the mind before he does the body.

F. And that first love would improve and be more to him yearly, growing ever richer, stronger, and more lovely with advancing age. The other does not.

G. Not her sexual nature! Heaven defend us! They have studied that long and well, but the *rest* of her, the "ninety-nine parts human!"

3. What can you infer about marriage at the time of this essay?

    A. People were forced into marriage based on socio-economic status.

    B. One in three marriages ended or was unhappy.

    C. Women who advertised for marriage had loose moral standards.

    D. Advertising for marriage was considered socially unacceptable.

4. Which sentence best employs an appeal to emotion?

    A. It may be said that if the match proved unhappy they would bitterly regret having meddled with fate, and wish they had waited patiently; but in like cases those who meet by chance, or are thrown together in the natural course of events, as bitterly curse fortune, or their own folly, and wish the same.

    B. Errors of judgment need be no more frequent than now, and even in case of mistaking, surely it is better to look back on an earnest attempt to choose wisely than the usual much-extolled drifting.

    C. It would if it became a general custom, teach both sexes to cultivate the mind and the power of expression in writing more than the beauty of the body and its sexual attraction.

    D. Surely *The Alpha* teaches that marriage should result not from the will and judgment led by passion, but the opposite.

5. Which best gives an example of the author anticipating the claim of the opposition and negating it?

    A. Why not take every means in one's power to discover so important a person as one's husband or wife? What is the prejudice that exists against it?

    B. One reasonable argument may be adduced against me, namely, that people brought together from different parts of the county would be dissimilar in their tastes and habits, and so suffer when united . . . To the former, that people whose local tastes and habits were stronger than their individualities, who shared the feelings of the neighborhood to such an extent that change would be painful, would not be likely to miss mating, for they would be satisfied with local character.

    C. Also when marriage was seen to depend more upon real value and worth coolly inquired into than upon feminine charms and snares and masculine force and persistence, that would be a huge power enlisted on the side of good.

    D. Young women would take more interest in the affairs of the world if they knew the chance of a happy marriage might depend on such knowledge; that they might be written to by such a man as they would love and honor, and expected to sympathize with his ideas, appreciate his work, understand and help him; and man might condescend to think a women's nature worth studying a little if their hopes rested also in genuine sympathy and appreciation.

6. What technique does Gilman most employ to construct her argument?

    A. Appeal to tradition

    B. Authoritative warrant

    C. Citation of commonly held beliefs

    D. Appeal to logic

7. What type of relationship is drawn in the sentence that follows?

    Also when marriage was seen to depend more upon real value and worth coolly inquired into than upon feminine charms and snares and masculine force and persistence, that would be a huge power enlisted on the side of good. (from paragraph 14)

    A. A parallel relationship between love and money

    B. A contrasting relationship between monetary value and actual attraction

    C. A dependent relationship between men and women

    D. A parallel relationship between the past and the present

8. Which statement would most imply that the author may be a feminist?

    A. "*The Alpha* and all common sense teaches that we should use reason and discrimination in a selection like this; and if one is desirous to marry and fails to find a fit mate in one's neighborhood or acquaintance, what reason is there that he or she should not look farther?"

    B. "Conversely, those who found no mate in the home influence and were so constituted as to demand something different would find full compensation in what they gained for all they lost."

    C. "If a man sees a fair woman before he knows her; feels the charm of her presence before he begins to understand her character; if first aroused to the necessity of judging by his strong inclination; surely he stands less chance of a cool and safe decision than one who begins knowingly, learns a character from earnest letters, loves the mind before he does the body."

    D. "Young women would take more interest in the affairs of the world if they knew the chance of a happy marriage might depend on such knowledge; that they might be written to by such a man as they would love and honor, and expected to sympathize with his ideas, appreciate his work, understand and help him . . ."

Use the excerpt from the essay "On Being Idle" by Jerome K. Jerome and the chart regarding unemployment to answer questions 9–14.

(1) It is impossible to enjoy idling thoroughly unless one has plenty of work to do. There is no fun in doing nothing when you have nothing to do. Wasting time is merely an occupation then, and a most exhausting one. Idleness, like kisses, to be sweet must be stolen.

(2) Many years ago, when I was a young man, I was taken very ill—I never could see myself that much was the matter with me, except that I had a beastly cold. But I suppose it was something very serious, for the doctor said that I ought to have come to him a month before, and that if it (whatever it was) had gone on for another week he would not have answered for the consequences. It is an extraordinary thing, but I never knew a doctor called into any case yet but what it transpired that another day's delay would have rendered cure hopeless. Our medical guide, philosopher, and friend is like the hero in a melodrama—he always comes upon the scene just, and only just, in the nick of time. It is Providence, that is what it is.

(3) Well, as I was saying, I was very ill and was ordered to Buxton for a month, with strict injunctions to do nothing whatever all the while that I was there. "Rest is what you require," said the doctor, "perfect rest."

(4) It seemed a delightful prospect. "This man evidently understands my complaint," said I, and I pictured to myself a glorious time—a four weeks' *dolce far niente* with a dash of illness in it. Not too much illness, but just illness enough—just sufficient to give it the flavor of suffering and make it poetical. I should get up late, sip chocolate, and have my breakfast in slippers and a dressing-gown. I should lie out in the garden in a hammock and read sentimental novels with a melancholy ending, until the books should fall from my listless hand, and I should recline there, dreamily gazing into the deep blue of the firmament, watching the fleecy clouds floating like white-sailed ships across its depths, and listening to the joyous song of the birds and the low rustling of the trees. Or, on becoming too weak to go out of doors, I should sit propped up with pillows at the open window of the ground-floor front, and look wasted and interesting, so that all the pretty girls would sigh as they passed by.

(5) And twice a day I should go down in a Bath chair to the Colonnade to drink the waters. Oh, those waters! I knew nothing about them then, and was rather taken with the idea. "Drinking the waters" sounded fashionable and Queen Anne-fied, and I thought I should like them. But, ugh! after the first three or four mornings! Sam Weller's description of them as "having a taste of warm flat-irons" conveys only a faint idea of their hideous nauseousness. If anything could make a sick man get well quickly, it would be the knowledge that he must drink a glassful of them every day until he was recovered. I drank them neat for six consecutive days, and they nearly killed me; but after then I adopted the plan of taking a stiff glass of brandy-and-water immediately on the top of them, and found much relief thereby. I have been informed since, by

various eminent medical gentlemen, that the alcohol must have entirely counteracted the effects of the chalybeate properties contained in the water. I am glad I was lucky enough to hit upon the right thing.

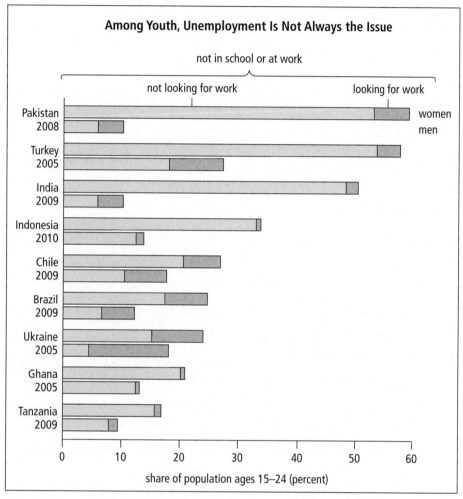

Source: World Development Report 2013, The World Bank

9. What information can you infer that is common to these two pieces?

    A. More men are unemployed than women.

    B. Youth will not support the country due to their increasing idleness.

    C. Youth may choose to be idle.

    D. The reason youth are idle is because they are lazy.

10. Indicate each word that describes the narrator's attitude in his essay and thus belongs in the blank ovals in the narrator traits web.

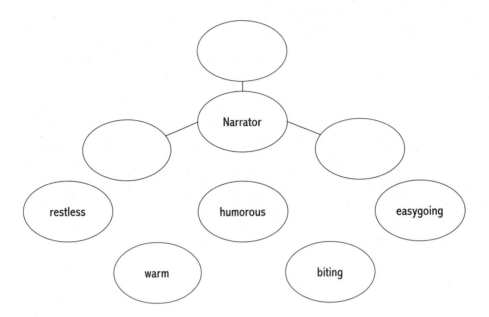

11. What motivating message might one find in both texts for an audience of young, unemployed youth?

    A. There is little competition amongst young people, so one can easily distinguish oneself from his peers if he applies himself.

    B. There are many jobs available if young people would only attempt to motivate themselves.

    C. Because young women are far less likely to look for jobs than men, it is likely possible to find more work in feminized professions such as teaching.

    D. Being idle will not keep you from finding a job if you are charming.

12. How does the chart differ from the essay in terms of purpose?

    A. The chart serves to scare the population into motivation, whereas the essay celebrates being idle.

    B. The essay instructs one on the methods of being idle and reflects on the joys of it, while the chart simply reports on the idleness of the youth as it relates to unemployment.

    C. The essay is simply a reflection on being unemployed, while the chart serves to uncover a mystery about the unemployed youth.

    D. The chart seeks to improve the status of our youth, whereas the essay encourages more idleness.

13. What do these texts say about the nature and future of the workforce?

    A. The future of the workforce is doomed because the youth will grow up to be incompetent and lazy adults.

    B. The workforce will keep production exactly as it is.

    C. The youth will have to grow out of their idleness before they can become competent members of the workforce.

    D. The youth will ultimately ruin the workforce with their idleness.

14. What is the contrast between these two pieces?

    A. There is no contrast; both pieces convey the same tone and information.

    B. There is no evidence of the author's country of origin, and so the chart may have no bearing on his experience whatsoever.

    C. The essay is cautionary, while the chart is rational and detached.

    D. The essay celebrates idleness, but the title of the chart indicates judgment towards the unemployed, idle youth.

Read the following excerpt from Charles Dickens' *A Christmas Carol*. Then answer question 15–21.

(1) When Scrooge awoke, it was so dark, that looking out of bed, he could scarcely distinguish the transparent window from the opaque walls of his chamber. He was endeavouring to pierce the darkness with his ferret eyes, when the chimes of a neighbouring church struck the four quarters. So he listened for the hour.

(2) To his great astonishment the heavy bell went on from six to seven, and from seven to eight, and regularly up to twelve; then stopped. Twelve. It was past two when he went to bed. The clock was wrong. An icicle must have got into the works. Twelve.

(3) He touched the spring of his repeater, to correct this most preposterous clock. Its rapid little pulse beat twelve: and stopped.

(4) 'Why, it isn't possible,' said Scrooge, 'that I can have slept through a whole day and far into another night. It isn't possible that anything has happened to the sun, and this is twelve at noon.'

(5) The idea being an alarming one, he scrambled out of bed, and groped his way to the window. He was obliged to rub the frost off with the sleeve of his dressing-gown before he could see anything; and could see very little then. All he could make out was, that it was still very foggy and extremely cold, and that there was no noise of people running to and fro, and making a

great stir, as there unquestionably would have been if night had beaten off bright day, and taken possession of the world. This was a great relief, because "Three days after sight of this First of Exchange pay to Mr. Ebenezer Scrooge on his order," and so forth, would have become a mere United States security if there were no days to count by.

(6) Scrooge went to bed again, and thought, and thought, and thought it over and over, and could make nothing of it. The more he thought, the more perplexed he was; and, the more he endeavoured not to think, the more he thought.

(7) Marley's Ghost bothered him exceedingly. Every time he resolved within himself, after mature inquiry that it was all a dream, his mind flew back again, like a strong spring released, to its first position, and presented the same problem to be worked all through, "Was it a dream or not?"

(8) Scrooge lay in this state until the chime had gone three-quarters more, when he remembered, on a sudden, that the Ghost had warned him of a visitation when the bell tolled one. He resolved to lie awake until the hour was passed; and, considering that he could no more go to sleep than go to heaven, this was, perhaps, the wisest resolution in his power.

(9) The quarter was so long, that he was more than once convinced he must have sunk into a doze unconsciously, and missed the clock. At length it broke upon his listening ear.

(10) "Ding, dong!"

(11) "A quarter past," said Scrooge, counting.

(12) "Ding, dong!"

(13) "Half past," said Scrooge.

(14) "Ding, dong!"

(15) "A quarter to it," said Scrooge. "Ding, dong!"

(16) "The hour itself," said Scrooge triumphantly, "and nothing else!"

(17) He spoke before the hour bell sounded, which it now did with a deep, dull, hollow, melancholy ONE. Light flashed up in the room upon the instant, and the curtains of his bed were drawn.

(18) The curtains of his bed were drawn aside, I tell you, by a hand. Not the curtains at his feet, nor the curtains at his back, but those to which his face was addressed. The curtains of his bed were drawn aside; and Scrooge, starting up into a half-recumbent attitude, found himself face to face

with the unearthly visitor who drew them: as close to it as I am now to you, and I am standing in the spirit at your elbow.

(19) It was a strange figure—like a child: yet not so like a child as like an old man, viewed through some supernatural medium, which gave him the appearance of having receded from the view, and being diminished to a child's proportions. Its hair, which hung about its neck and down its back, was white as if with age; and yet the face had not a wrinkle in it, and the tenderest bloom was on the skin. The arms were very long and muscular; the hands the same, as if its hold were of uncommon strength. Its legs and feet, most delicately formed, were, like those upper members, bare. It wore a tunic of the purest white, and round its waist was bound a lustrous belt, the sheen of which was beautiful. It held a branch of fresh green holly in its hand; and, in singular contradiction of that wintry emblem, had its dress trimmed with summer flowers. But the strangest thing about it was, that from the crown of its head there sprung a bright clear jet of light, by which all this was visible; and which was doubtless the occasion of its using, in its duller moments, a great extinguisher for a cap, which it now held under its arm.

15. Place the events into the proper sequence by selecting the correct lettered choice for each box in the order of events.

    A.   Scrooge tries to rationalize his confusion with time.

    B.   Scrooge's room lights up.

    C.   Scrooge is met by a ghost.

    D.   Scrooge awakens to incorrect chiming of the clock.

    E.   Scrooge realizes the ghost has light coming from its head.

    F.   Scrooge remembers a ghost is supposed to visit him at one o'clock.

Order of Events

↓
↓
↓
↓
↓

16. Which is an example of fallacious reasoning?

    A. The quarter was so long, that he was more than once convinced he must have sunk into a doze unconsciously, and missed the clock.

    B. The curtains of his bed were drawn aside, I tell you, by a hand.

    C. "The hour itself," said Scrooge triumphantly, "and nothing else!"

    D. But the strangest thing about it was, that from the crown of its head there sprung a bright clear jet of light, by which all this was visible; and which was doubtless the occasion of its using, in its duller moments, a great extinguisher for a cap, which it now held under its arm.

17. What can you infer about Scrooge's character?

    A. Scrooge is an incredibly imaginative and creative person.

    B. Scrooge is a fearful person who reacts to any small stimulus.

    C. Scrooge is an angry person who approaches change and fear with violence.

    D. Scrooge tends to dwell in all things rational; he does not give into imagination easily.

18. What is the central theme in this particular passage?

    A. Ghosts are terrifying.

    B. Fear can drive people mad.

    C. Not everything is as it seems.

    D. One should always sleep with the doors locked.

19. Which example best reflects the paradoxical experience Scrooge is having?

    A. "It was past two when he went to bed. The clock was wrong. An icicle must have got into the works. Twelve."

    B. "Every time he resolved within himself, after mature inquiry that it was all a dream, his mind flew back again, like a strong spring released, to its first position, and presented the same problem to be worked all through, 'Was it a dream or not?'"

    C. "He spoke before the hour bell sounded, which it now did with a deep, dull, hollow, melancholy ONE. Light flashed up in the room upon the instant, and the curtains of his bed were drawn."

    D. "It held a branch of fresh green holly in its hand; and, in singular contradiction of that wintry emblem, had its dress trimmed with summer flowers."

20. What effect does the following sentence from paragraph 18 have on the reader?

> The curtains of his bed were drawn aside; and Scrooge, starting up into a half-recumbent attitude, found himself face to face with the unearthly visitor who drew them: as close to it as I am now to you, and I am standing in the spirit at your elbow.

    A. It makes the reader fully empathize with Scrooge in this instance because it seems as if Charles Dickens is like the ghost that Scrooge is facing.

    B. It creates an eerie sensation by shifting out of omniscient point of view into first-person perspective, bringing the reader into the text and heightening the drama.

    C. It serves to describe the ghost in full detail and make the reader have a clearer picture of the person drawing back Scrooge's curtains.

    D. It makes the reader question the authenticity of the narrator because breaking the fourth wall in this instance violates his credibility.

21. What can you infer about the relationship between Scrooge and Marley in this passage?

    A. Scrooge has always been petrified of Marley.

    B. Marley is incredibly angry at Scrooge and wants to exact revenge by scaring him.

    C. There is some degree of companionship between Scrooge and Marley.

    D. Scrooge considers Marley's ghost a figment of his imagination, showing that Scrooge has no regard for Marley whatsoever.

Read the following excerpt from the essay, "On Washerwomen" by Leigh Hunt. Then answer questions 22–27.

(1) Writers, we think, might oftener indulge themselves in direct picture-making, that is to say, in detached sketches of men and things, which should be to *manners*, what those of Theophrastus are to *character*.

(2) Painters do not always think it necessary to paint epics, or to fill a room with a series of pictures on one subject. They deal sometimes in single figures and groups; and often exhibit a profounder feeling in these little concentrations of their art, than in subjects of a more numerous description. Their *gusto*, perhaps, is less likely to be lost, on that very account. They are no longer Sultans in a seraglio, but lovers with a favourite mistress, retired and absorbed. A Madonna of Correggio's, the Bath of Michael Angelo, the Standard of Leonardo da Vinci, Titian's Mistress, and other single subjects or groups of the great masters, are acknowledged to be among their greatest performances, some of them their greatest of all.

(3) It is the same with music. Overtures, which are supposed to make allusion to the whole progress of the story they precede, are not always the best productions of the master; still less are choruses, and quintetts, and other pieces involving a multiplicity of actors. The overture to Mozart's *Magic Flute (Zauberflöte)* is worthy of the title of the piece; it is truly enchanting; but what are so intense, in their way, as the duet of the two lovers, *Ah Perdona,*—or the laughing trio in *Cosi Fan Tutte,*—or that passionate serenade in Don Giovanni, *Deh vieni alla finestra*, which breathes the very soul of refined sensuality! The gallant is before you, with his mandolin and his cap and feather, taking place of the nightingale for that amorous hour; and you feel that the sounds must inevitably draw his mistress to the window. Their intenseness even renders them pathetic; and his heart seems in earnest, because his senses are.

(4) We do not mean to say, that, in proportion as the work is large and the subject numerous, the merit may not be the greater if all is good. Raphael's Sacrament is a greater work than his Adam and Eve; but his Transfiguration would still have been the finest picture in the world, had the second group in the foreground been away; nay, the latter is supposed, and, we think, with justice, to injure its effect. We only say that there are times when the numerousness may scatter the individual gusto;—that the greatest possible feeling may be proved without it;—and, above all, returning to our more immediate subject, that writers, like painters, may sometimes have leisure for excellent detached pieces, when they want it for larger productions. Here, then, is an opportunity for them. Let them, in their intervals of history, or, if they want time for it, give us portraits of humanity. People lament that Sappho did not write more: but, at any rate, her two odes are worth twenty epics like Tryphiodorus.

(5) But, in portraits of this kind, writing will also have a great advantage; and may avoid what seems to be an inevitable stumbling-block in paintings of a similar description. Between the matter-of-fact works of the Dutch artists, and the subtle compositions of Hogarth, there seems to be a medium reserved only for the pen. The writer only can tell you all he means,—can let you into his whole mind and intention. The moral insinuations of the painter are, on the one hand, apt to be lost for want of distinctness; or tempted, on the other, by their visible nature, to put on too gross a shape. If he leaves his meanings to be imagined, he may unfortunately speak to unimaginative spectators, and generally does; if he wishes to explain himself so as not to be mistaken, he will paint a set of comments upon his own incidents and characters, rather than let them tell for themselves. Hogarth himself, for instance, who never does anything without a sentiment or a moral, is too apt to perk them both in your face, and to be over-redundant in his combinations. His persons, in many instances, seem too much taken away from their proper indifference to effect, and to be made too much of conscious agents and joint contributors. He "o'er-informs his tenements." His very goods and chattels are didactic. He makes a capital remark of a cow's horn, and brings up a piece of cannon in aid of a satire on vanity. It is the writer only who, without hurting the most delicate propriety of the representation, can leave no doubt of all his intentions,—who can insinuate his object, in two or three words, to the dullest conception; and, in conversing with the most foreign minds, take away all the awkwardness of interpretation. What painting gains in universality to the eye, it loses by an infinite proportion in power of suggestion to the understanding.

22. What is the central argument in this passage?

    A. Writing is the best art form known to man.

    B. Painting has certain advantages over both writing and music.

    C. Many authors find stimulation from other art forms.

    D. Quality is more important than quantity.

23. What can you infer about the author's position on writing's advantage over painting?

    A. Although both are provocative, writing has an advantage in allowing the audience to fill in the gaps of interpretation; whereas a painting must provide it for us.

    B. Writing has an advantage in that it can be entirely exact; painting always leaves room for interpretation.

    C. The author prefers writing over painting because she is a writer, and to celebrate painting instead would be a conflict of interest.

    D. The author believes that painting can elicit a more emotional response than writing can because of its lack of words.

24. Which sentence best supports the inference about the author's thoughts about writing versus painting?

    A. "Writers, we think, might oftener indulge themselves in direct picture-making, that is to say, in detached sketches of men and things, which should be to *manners*, what those of Theophrastus are to *character*."

    B. "But, in portraits of this kind, writing will also have a great advantage; and may avoid what seems to be an inevitable stumbling-block in paintings of a similar description."

    C. "We do not mean to say, that, in proportion as the work is large and the subject numerous, the merit may not be the greater if all is good."

    D. "What painting gains in universality to the eye, it loses by an infinite proportion in power of suggestion to the understanding."

25. Which word best describes the author's tone towards art?

    A. turgid

    B. accusatory

    C. critical

    D. fervent

26. What effect would removing paragraph 3 have on the work?

    A. The scope of the discussion on art would be more limited.

    B. The argument would be tipped in favor of painting as the superior art form for communicating emotions.

    C. The author would seem ignorant of the finer subtleties of writing without the comparison to music.

    D. There would be no change.

27. Which definition best matches the use of the word **lament** in the last sentence of paragraph 4?

    A. to cheer

    B. to mourn

    C. to wonder

    D. to regret

Consider the following essays: Michel de Montaigne's "Of the Education of Children" and "The Tyranny of Facts" by Elisabeth Morris. Then answer questions 28–34.

Of the Education of Children

(1) Madam, science is a very great ornament, and a thing of marvellous use, especially in persons raised to that degree of fortune in which you are. And, in truth, in persons of mean and low condition, it cannot perform its true and genuine office, being naturally more prompt to assist in the conduct of war, in the government of peoples, in negotiating the leagues and friendships of princes and foreign nations, than in forming a syllogism in logic, in pleading a process in law, or in prescribing a dose of pills in physic. Wherefore, madam, believing you will not omit this so necessary feature in the education of your children, who yourself have tasted its sweetness, and are of a learned extraction (for we yet have the writings of the ancient Counts of Foix, from whom my lord, your husband, and yourself, are both of you descended, and Monsieur de Candale, your uncle, every day obliges the world with others, which will extend the knowledge of this quality in your family for so many succeeding ages), I will, upon this occasion, presume to acquaint your ladyship with one particular fancy of my own, contrary to the common method, which is all I am able to contribute to your service in this affair.

(2) The charge of the tutor you shall provide for your son, upon the choice of whom depends the whole success of his education, has several other great and considerable parts and duties required in so important a trust, besides that of which I am about to speak: these, however, I shall not mention, as being unable to add anything of moment to the common rules: and in this, wherein I take upon me to advise, he may follow it so far only as it shall appear advisable.

(3) For a, boy of quality then, who pretends to letters not upon the account of profit (for so mean an object is unworthy of the grace and favour of the Muses, and moreover, in it a man directs his service to and depends upon others), nor so much for outward ornament, as for his own proper and peculiar use, and to furnish and enrich himself within, having rather a desire to come out an accomplished cavalier than a mere scholar or learned man; for such a one, I say, I would, also, have his friends solicitous to find him out a tutor, who has rather a well-made than a well-filled head;—["'Tete bien faite,' an expression created by Montaigne, and which has remained a part of our language."—Servan.]— seeking, indeed, both the one and the other, but rather of the two to prefer manners and judgment to mere learning, and that this man should exercise his charge after a new method.

(4) 'Tis the custom of pedagogues to be eternally thundering in their pupil's ears, as they were pouring into a funnel, whilst the business of the pupil is only to repeat what the others have said: now I would have a tutor to correct this error, and, that at the very first, he should according to the capacity he has to deal with, put it to the test, permitting his pupil himself to taste things, and of himself to discern and choose them, sometimes opening the way to him, and sometimes leaving him to open it for himself; that is, I would not have him alone to invent and speak, but that he should also hear his pupil speak in turn. Socrates, and since him Arcesilaus, made first their scholars speak, and then they spoke to them—[Diogenes Laertius, iv. 36.]

(5) Obest plerumque iis, qui discere volunt,
auctoritas eorum, qui docent.

(6) ["The authority of those who teach, is very often an impediment to those who desire to learn."—Cicero, De Natura Deor., i. 5.]

(7) It is good to make him, like a young horse, trot before him, that he may judge of his going, and how much he is to abate of his own speed, to accommodate himself to the vigour and capacity of the other. For want of which due proportion we spoil all; which also to know how to adjust, and to keep within an exact and due measure, is one of the hardest things I know, and 'tis the effect of a high and well-tempered soul, to know how to condescend to such puerile motions and to govern and direct them. I walk firmer and more secure uphill than down.

The Tyranny of Facts

(1) Of late, I notice, the same thing that happened in my house has happened in my head. There was a time when I loved to collect information. Facts—all facts—were precious to me, and I loved to feel them making piles and stacks and rows in my brain. Everything was welcome, from the names of the stars to the prepositions that governed the Latin ablative, from the dynasties of Egypt to the geography lists of "state products"—"corn, wheat, and potatoes," "rice, sugar, cotton, and tobacco." While this mania was upon me, dictionaries allured me, cyclopaedias held me spellbound. I was even able to read with interest the annals of the "Swiss Family Robinson,"

a book which presents more facts per page than any other volume in that great and unclassified mob called "fiction" . . .

(2) . . .But following my feeling of amazement there usually comes one of relief—how glad I am that I don't know all that now! I still love "Nature," but when I have found the lovely flower in the meadow or the deep wood, I do not hasten to pick it and bring it home and analyze it and press it. I am content to lie down beside it a while and enjoy its companionship, its beauty, its fragrance, whatever it has of charm and comeliness, and then I leave it and pass on. When I hear a sweet bird-note, I pause and listen as it comes again and yet again. But I do not pursue the bird with an opera-glass to count its feathers and estimate its dimensions, and then hurry home to my "bird books" to "look it up" and make a marginal note of the date. When I see butterflies fluttering about the lilacs and the syringas and the phlox, I stand quiet and watch them—those huge pale yellow ones banded with black that love to hang about lavender flowers—do they know what a lovely chord of color they strike? those dark ones with blues and greens splashed on their wing-edges, those rich rusty-red ones, with pure silver flashes on their under sides, those little jagged-winged beauties with all the colors of an Oriental rug—old reds, old blues, old yellows—all mottled together. Ah, they are all delightful, and as I watch this favorite and that, holding my breath lest I scare him into flight, I find myself smiling to think, I knew his name once!

(3) But most of my friends still know their names. They have opera-glasses and note books, and a prodigious amount of information. They keep tally of the number of birds they see in a day or on a walk or on a drive, of the number of new birds or flowers they recognize in a season. They call me up by telephone to tell me that the beautiful creature we had seen in a certain tree was, after all, not the *Apteryx Americanus*, but the *Apteryx Warrensis*, a much rarer variety of the same species, with longer tail feathers and two more white feathers in the wing than his commonplace cousin.

(4) Amid such whirlpools of information I feel that I am unable to hold my own, and so I try to drift out, but now and again I am drawn in, and I find myself growing stupid as I bend over my friends' bird books. I give myself headaches looking at their butterfly cabinets—real butterflies on the phlox and the lilacs never seem to give me headaches.

28. What is the central disagreement between these two pieces of writing?

    A. People need to be educated, or they will not have the proper tools for experiencing the world.

    B. Education by way of fact-gathering is the quintessential method of experiencing the world knowledgeably.

    C. Without education, people will not have the upper hand against their peers.

    D. Boys learn differently than girls.

29. How is the word **whirlpools** used in this sentence from paragraph 4 in "The Tyranny of Facts"?

> Amid such whirlpools of information I feel that I am unable to hold my own, and so I try to drift out, but now and again I am drawn in, and I find myself growing stupid as I bend over my friends' bird books.

A. literally

B. metaphorically

C. churlishly

D. petulantly

30. What is one argument upon which the two authors may agree?

A. Facts are essential to understanding the world around us.

B. Being able to produce facts will improve one's standing in the world.

C. Having facts about what one experiences will improve one's enjoyment of that experience.

D. One's method of obtaining knowledge can have a great effect on a person's life.

31. Which statement best upholds the claim that experience is preferred to facts?

A. "Facts—all facts—were precious to me, and I loved to feel them making piles and stacks and rows in my brain."

B. "I still love "Nature," but when I have found the lovely flower in the meadow or the deep wood, I do not hasten to pick it and bring it home and analyze it and press it."

C. "They have opera-glasses and note books, and a prodigious amount of information."

D. "I give myself headaches looking at their butterfly cabinets—real butterflies on the phlox and the lilacs never seem to give me headaches."

32. What rhetorical strategy does Morris use most?

A. appeal to emotion

B. appeal to tradition

C. appeal to logic

D. appeal to authority

33. What rhetorical strategy is most employed by Montaigne?

    A. appeal to emotion

    B. appeal to tradition

    C. appeal to logic

    D. appeal to authority

34. Which statement shows the author considering the opposition's point of view?

    A. "Madam, science is a very great ornament, and a thing of marvellous use, especially in persons raised to that degree of fortune in which you are."

    B. "Wherefore, madam, believing you will not omit this so necessary feature in the education of your children, who yourself have tasted its sweetness, and are of a learned extraction (for we yet have the writings of the ancient Counts of Foix, from whom my lord, your husband, and yourself, are both of you descended, and Monsieur de Candale, your uncle, every day obliges the world with others, which will extend the knowledge of this quality in your family for so many succeeding ages), I will, upon this occasion, presume to acquaint your ladyship with one particular fancy of my own, contrary to the common method, which is all I am able to contribute to your service in this affair."

    C. "For a, boy of quality then, who pretends to letters not upon the account of profit (for so mean an object is unworthy of the grace and favour of the Muses, and moreover, in it a man directs his service to and depends upon others), nor so much for outward ornament, as for his own proper and peculiar use, and to furnish and enrich himself within, having rather a desire to come out an accomplished cavalier than a mere scholar or learned man; for such a one, I say, I would, also, have his friends solicitous to find him out a tutor, who has rather a well-made than a well-filled head . . ."

    D. "It is good to make him, like a young horse, trot before him, that he may judge of his going, and how much he is to abate of his own speed, to accommodate himself to the vigour and capacity of the other."

Read the following essay entitled "Fashionable Advice for a Career Wardrobe on a Budget." Then answer questions 35–40.

(1) In the workforce, as the job market becomes more competitive, appearances can either make or break you. Yet, many Americans don't have the money to keep up with their bills, much less update their wardrobe with fashion-forward staples. But looking professional doesn't have to require a bank loan. It just takes a little clothing-care know-how.

(2) According to a recent national survey sponsored by Woolite, 70 percent of American women surveyed admitted to throwing away clothing at least once a year due to misinformed laundry decisions that resulted in pilling, fading, stretching or bleeding of clothes. In fact, nearly $2 billion worth of clothing was ruined last year due to laundry-related mistakes.

(3) Stacy London, co-host of TLC's fashion show, "What Not to Wear," offers these tips for the working fashionista looking to maintain her look on a budget:

(4) • First and foremost, take care of the clothes you have. Avoid ruining the clothes you already own by following each garment's cleaning instructions. Using a non-harsh detergent, like Woolite, on all of your favorite fashions can help to protect your style investments and extend an outfit's life.

(5) • Shop your closet. A-line skirts and simple cardigans never go out of style, so if you already own a few, stop pushing them to the back of the closet. Combine that A-line skirt with a colorful blouse and a curve-complementing blazer, and you'll be more than ready for your next presentation.

(6) • Invest in versatile pieces. When you do shop for professional clothing, look for pieces that can be worn in and out of the office. The blazer is an easy flattering transition piece that can be translated from day to night. Find a "little black dress" in three-season fabrics to get the most wear all year round.

(7) Having recently partnered with Woolite to create the "Find the Look, Keep the Look" program, London is dedicated to educating clothes-minded individuals on looking their best every day. Ten boutique owners from across the country have also joined this partnership to offer their insight on regional style trends. Together, they created the "Look Book," a compilation of basic wardrobe must-haves. The entire book is available online for free at *www.findthelookkeepthelook.com.*

35. What is the main purpose of this article?

   A. To make people aware of the way fashion portrays them in the workforce.

   B. To help professionals make money-saving decisions about clothing, its maintenance, and its appeal.

   C. To sell Woolite products.

   D. To invoke the help of experts to instruct an unknowing audience on the correct steps to look good in the workplace.

36. What is the intended effect of citing Woolite and Stacy London?

    A. The author is promoting Woolite and "What Not to Wear."

    B. The author cites commonly held beliefs.

    C. The author makes references to beloved items the audience knows and trusts.

    D. The author invokes authority to give credence to the arguments.

37. What conclusions can be drawn about the intended audience of this article?

    A. They are young men who have no awareness of what to wear to be professional.

    B. They are fashionable, but not wealthy enough to make decisions that reflect this.

    C. They are affected by tight economic times, and likely are women who need fashion guidance.

    D. They wear non-flattering clothing most of the time.

38. What can you infer is the definition of the word, **fashionista**?

    A. A person who is lost in the subtleties of fashion.

    B. A person who is diametrically opposed to fashion.

    C. A person who is a practical expert on fashion.

    D. A person who is a student of fashion.

39. What is the main method the author employs in conveying information in this text?

    A. listing

    B. argument

    C. embellishment

    D. anecdote

40. What is the underlying assumption in this article?

    A. If you can't afford to look like a professional, you should look for another job that better fits your budget.

    B. If you are not dressed appropriately, you will not make the proper impression in the workforce.

    C. If you do not use Woolite on your clothing, you will ruin it too quickly.

    D. If you cannot afford professional clothing, it does not matter what type of detergent you use.

REASONING THROUGH LANGUAGE ARTS
Section 2

One Extended Response Essay
45 minutes (followed by a 10-minute break)

Practice Test 1: Reasoning Through Language Arts (RLA)

Section 2 (Extended Response)

> **Analyze the thoughts and arguments presented in the essay excerpt in Passage #1 and in the article in Passage #2.**
>
> In your response, develop an argument in which you explain how one position on the aging process is better supported than the other. Incorporate relevant and specific evidence from both sources to support your argument on how young people can transition both themselves and their seniors into old age.
>
> Remember, the better-argued position is not necessarily the position with which you agree. You must complete this task in 45 minutes. Your response should contain 4 to 7 paragraphs of 3 to 7 sentences each, or about 300 to 500 words.
>
> If possible, type your response on a computer. Be sure to time yourself.

Reflections on Aging Stimulus Passage #1

Excerpt from "An Essay on an Old Subject" by Alexander Smith

One does not like to be an old fogie, and still less perhaps does one like to own to being one. You may remember when you were the youngest person in every company into which you entered; and how it pleased you to think how precociously clever you were, and how opulent in Time. You were introduced to the great Mr. Blank,—at least twenty years older than yourself,—and could not help thinking how much greater you would be than Mr. Blank by the time you reached his age. But pleasant as it is to be the youngest member of every company, that pleasure does not last forever. As years pass on you do not quite develop into the genius you expected; and the new generation makes its appearance and pushes you from your stool. You make the disagreeable discovery that there is a younger man of promise in the world than even you; then the one younger man becomes a dozen younger men; then younger men come flowing in like waves, and before you know where you are, by this impertinent younger generation—fellows who were barely breeched when you won your first fame—you are shouldered into Old Fogiedom, and your staid ways are laughed at, perhaps, by the irreverent scoundrels into the bargain. There is nothing more wonderful in youth than this wealth in Time. It is only a Rothschild who can indulge in the amusement of tossing a sovereign to a beggar. It is only a young man who can dream and build castles in the air. . . .

My experience is of use only to myself. I cannot bequeath it to my son as I can my cash. Every human being must start untrammelled and work out the problem for himself. . . . The blooming apple must grate in the young man's teeth before he owns that it is dust and ashes. Young people will take nothing on hearsay.

If a new generation were starting with the wisdom of its elders, what would be the consequence? Would there be any love-making twenty years after? Would there be any fine extravagance? Would there be any lending of money? Would there be any noble friendship such as that of Damon and Pythias, or of David and Jonathan, or even of our own Beaumont and Fletcher, who had purse, wardrobe, and genius in common? It is extremely doubtful. . . .

(Source: Smith, Alexander. "An essay on an old subject." 1866. Quotidiana. Ed. Patrick Madden. 19 Oct. 2007.)

Reflections on Aging Stimulus Passage #2

How to Help Seniors Age Independently

Ask most seniors if they want to age independently in their own homes, and they likely will say yes. Surveys show 95 percent of people over the age of 75 desire to age in place, and about a quarter of seniors live alone.

These numbers are just the beginning. Baby Boomers are now turning 65 at a rate of about 8,000 a day, according to AARP. But what if you're the adult child of one of those independent-minded seniors? What if, like Alison Jacobson, whose SafetyMom.com blog has a loyal following, you find yourself frequently worrying about your parents' well-being?

"While aging-in place is the goal for most seniors, how do you, as the adult child, ensure they're safe?" she asks.

Here are some tips for dealing with the situation:

- Preventing falls. Falls are a leading cause of injury and death for seniors. Like the worry Jacobson describes, a new survey by market researchers Toluna found that a far greater number of caregivers were concerned about seniors being injured than seniors themselves were (76.1 percent vs. 33 percent). One simple first step is to remove all scatter rugs and make sure electric cords don't extend into high-traffic areas.

- Upgrading lights. While seniors sometimes may be reluctant to admit it, vision diminishes with age. So, brighten lights in kitchen work areas to reduce the risk of burns and cuts.

- Tech fix. The latest technology is the answer to substantial research highlighting the importance of staying connected for both seniors and caregivers. Harvard University researchers found that the odds of mental decline doubled for seniors with no social ties, for example, while Toluna's survey looked at the emotional toll on those trying to help loved ones age in place.

"For caregivers, ease of communication with the seniors they love relieves stress, reduced guilt and builds rich relationships," says expert on successful aging Adriane Berg.

Enter the new CareLine home safety telephone system from VTech. The product includes three individual pieces designed for optimal usability, even for those with vision, hearing and dexterity issues. The pieces are the corded base phone with photo displays for frequent contacts, a cordless handset and a very handy pendant that can also be snapped onto a belt and easily kept with the user. The pendant can make and receive calls, access voicemail, and receive automatic reminders about medications and appointments.

If you don't have a computer handy, use this box to write your response.

PRACTICE TEST 1 (cont'd)

REASONING THROUGH LANGUAGE ARTS
Section 3

50 questions
60 minutes

Read the following excerpt of a student's paper on the dangerous effects of drug use. Then answer questions 1–7.

(1) It's a common experience these days to see a man on the street overcome with his lot in life. How did he get this way? He used drugs. This individual, who was probably unloved by his parents and unsupported by his teachers, is not ultimately to blame. We must, instead, look to the harmful effects of drugs on the human body. First and foremost, drugs cause addiction. Secondly, drugs can affect the brain and other fine motor functions. Finally, drugs can inhibit a persons ability to make correct choices.

(2) There is a popular television show called "breaking bad." In this show, a drug addict named Jesse is addicted not only to crystal meth, but also to the lifestyle that goes along with selling drugs. After all, why get a real job when you can make "fat stacks" by taking the easy way out and selling drugs? He doesn't need to go to school. He doesn't have to get up early to go to work; he doesn't even have to be responsible for himself. This guy. Simply gets too do what he wants when he wants. Furthermore, the use of drugs has him addicted, which causes him to continue to covet them. He will do anything to get a hit when he needs it, even though this causes much stress between him and Walt, the other major character. Walt's normal life is constantly made worse by drugs.

(3) Whose to say that drugs aren't a viable way to relieve stress? The American Medical Association, that's who. According to a recent study done by the AMA, prolonged drug use of even "minor" drugs such as tobacco and alcohol can cause irrevocable brain damage. The AMA cites problems such as: vomiting, memory loss, to have paranoia, and aggression as common side-effects of repeated drug use.

(4) Finally, as we see over and over again in "Breaking Bad," drug use causes people to make poor decisions. Jesses decisions constantly come back to haunt him. These evil substances are the reason so many people are homeless on the streets. If these people would make the right choices and stay in school and not do drugs they would probably be a lot happier and they would be able to make better decisions in the long run. Drugs kill people and make a cycle of misery that would be easy to avoid if people just never started on them in the first place.

(5) Don't experiment with drugs. You're going to end up homeless and miserable. Not to mention it's against the law. Is jail a place you want to go to?

1. What word should replace the word **whose** in the following sentence from paragraph 3?

    Whose to say that drugs aren't a viable way to relieve stress.

    A. Who's
    B. Who
    C. Whom
    D. No change.

2. Correct the capitalization errors in the following sentence from paragraph 2.

    There is a popular television show called 'breaking bad.'

    A. Breaking
    B. Breaking Bad
    C. Bad
    D. No change.

3. Edit the following sentence to show proper grammatical structure.

    The AMA cites problems such as: vomiting, memory loss, to have paranoia, and aggression as common side-effects of repeated drug use.

4. Correct the following sentence from paragraph 4.

    If these people would make the right choices and stay in school and not do drugs they would probably be a lot happier and they would be able to make better decisions in the long run.

    A. "If these people would make the right choices and stay in school and not do drugs, they would probably be a lot happier, and they would be able to make better decisions in the long run."

    B. "If these people would make the right choices and stay in school and not do drugs they would probably be a lot happier; they would be able to make better decisions in the long run."

    C. "If these people would make the right choices, stay in school, and not do drugs, they would probably be a lot happier because they would be able to make better decisions in the long run."

    D. No change.

5. Correct the punctuation in the following two sentences from paragraph 2.

    This guy. Simply gets to do what he wants when he wants.

6. What word needs to be adjusted to ensure proper possession in the following sentence?

    Finally, drugs can inhibit a persons ability to make correct choices.

    A. drug's

    B. person's

    C. persons'

    D. No change.

7. How can the following sentence from paragraph 5, be rewritten to avoid the dangling preposition?

    Is jail a place you want to go to?

    A. Is jail a place you want?

    B. Is jail where you want to go to?

    C. Is jail a place you want to go?

    D. No change.

Read the following letter from a citizen to an elected official. Then answer questions 8–15.

(1) Dear Representative Smith,

(2) My wife has suggested I write to you because she's tired of hearing me complain about how many potholes there is in our streets. I live in Waterville (near where you grew up). You must of driven over here recently, right? Then you know it is bad.

(3) I have worked for 19 years as a mechanic. So I know what it does to cars. You think people like to get their cars worked on? Well, I like it (ha, ha), but you know what I mean. Most people would rather spend a hundred bucks on date night than on a new tie rod. Not to mention having the car in the shop for a day (or two). I try hard to keep my house looking nice.

(4) Would you believe there are nine potholes just on Main Street? Well, believe it. Me and my wife took a drive last Sunday to get an accurate count for you. We counted a total of 27.

(5) Even though I'm just a mechanic, I complained to city hall, but it didn't do any good. They say that they know their is a problem they can't put it on this year's budget because there is not enough money.

(6) Between you and I, let us admit there is money in government. What happens to all my tax money isn't it to fix some holes in the road? My whole point is that I would like you to see what you can do about this problem.

(7) My neighbors would appreciate it too. Joe is afraid to buy a new car because it might get damaged. That ain't good for new-car sales.

(8) I had a sign for you in the last election in my yard. I voted for you. So, please, if you can help out, it will be appreciated.

(9) Sincerely,

Matthew Ford

8. Correct the subject-verb agreement in the following sentence from paragraph 2.

My wife has suggested I write to you because she's tired of hearing me complain about how many potholes there is in our streets.

A. My wife has suggested I write to you because she's tired of hearing me complain about how many potholes there are in our streets.

B. My wife has suggested I write to you because she's tired of hearing me complain that there is so many potholes in our streets.

C. I am writing to you to complain about how many potholes there is in our streets.

D. No change.

9. Correct the verb usage error in the sentence from paragraph 2.

You must of driven over here recently, right?

A. You must drive over here.

B. You must've driven over here recently, right?

C. You must of driven here, right?

D. No change.

10. Correct the use of the objective pronoun **me** in the following sentence from paragraph 4.

Me and my wife took a drive last Sunday to get an accurate count for you.

A. Myself and my wife took a drive last Sunday to get an accurate count for you.

B. My wife and me took a drive last Sunday to get an accurate count for you.

C. My wife and I took a drive last Sunday to get an accurate count for you.

D. No change.

11. Rewrite the following paragraph to improve it as a whole, but specifically to eliminate the following errors: overly informal (casual) language; a sentence fragment; the ambiguous (unclear) pronoun "it" in the second sentence; and the sentence that is not consistent with the main idea of the paragraph.

I have worked for 19 years as a mechanic. So I know what it does to cars. You think people like to get their cars worked on? Well, I like it (ha, ha), but you know what I mean. Most people would rather spend a hundred bucks on date night than on a new tie rod. Not to mention having the car in the shop for a day (or two). I try hard to keep my house looking nice.

_____

_____

_____

_____

_____

_____

12. Correct the misuse of the subjective pronoun **I** in the following sentence from paragraph 6.

Between you and I, let us admit there is money in government.

A. Between you and me, let us admit there is money in government.

B. Between you and myself, let us admit there is money in government.

C. Between I and you, let us admit there is money in government.

D. No change.

13. How can the run-on be corrected in the following sentence?

What happens to all my tax money isn't it to fix some holes in the road?

    A.   What happens to all my tax money, isn't it to fix some holes in the road?

    B.   What happens to all my tax money. Isn't it to fix some holes in the road?

    C.   What happens to all my tax money? Isn't it to fix some holes in the road?

    D.   No change.

14. The following sentences contain nonstandard language usage. Select the best choice to address the problem.

Joe is afraid to buy a new car because it might get damaged. That ain't good for new-car sales.

    A.   Joe is afraid to buy a new car because it might get damaged. That isn't good for new-car sales.

    B.   Joe is afraid to buy a new car because it might get damaged, which ain't good for new-car sales.

    C.   Joe is afraid to buy a new car because it might damage sales.

    D.   No change.

15. The location of the prepositional phrase **in my yard** in the following sentence creates confusion. How should the sentence be revised to make it more clear?

I had a sign for you in the last election in my yard.

    A.   I put a sign for you in the last election in my yard.

    B.   I had a sign in my yard for you in the last election.

    C.   In the last election, I put a campaign sign for you in my yard.

    D.   No change

Read the following advertisement to answer questions 16–23:

Teachers Make the World Go Round

(1) So you're thinking about becoming a teacher? That's great! Join the exciting and demanding world of education and find yourself on the path to having one of the most respectable careers ever.

(2) Teachers are not just professional babysitters; they are the people that shape the future of our world. Can you remember your favorite teacher? What about a really terrible teacher? We all can. That's why it's necessary to fill the profession with really talented individuals like yourself to ensure that all will be right with the world in the future.

(3) Join our career switchers' movement. If you're reading this advertisement, it's probably because you are unsatisfied with your current job. Who can blame you? You're probably sitting at a cubicle all day or making coffee for someone who is not nearly as talented and qualified as you, just giving your job up to someone you know is not the best. Did you go to school to be a literature major? Can't find a job that satisfies? Try teaching! There is no other profession where you can talk about books all day long.

(4) Our program will prepare you for all the difficulties you might encounter while teaching. If you have teacher friends, then you probably already know about all the demands that teaching puts on you. Our program will prepare you for this by helping you understand the alphabet soup that comes along with education. IEP? SOL? We'll teach you all of that but not only that we'll help you become masters of classroom management and pedagogical theory.

(5) The world needs good teachers, and you are the right person to do it! Did you know that the average teacher's salary has increased by approximately $1,500 a year in the last twenty years? People say teachers don't make much money, and although that may be true, our program will also help you get involved in the perfect teachers' unions to help you find all the resources you need to fight for your rights in the profession. People may say that teaching is the most under-valued job on the market these days. It is up to talented individuals like yourself to change this mindset! Get in there, be professional, teach kids, be exciting, and to help adjust the world's mindset one classroom at a time.

(6) Our program will train you to be the most competitive new teacher on the market. Because job shortages are prevalent in these tough economic times, so join our programs and you will find yourself leaps and bounds ahead of the game as we teach you how to present yourself with your best foot forward. Don't believe it? Perhaps the testimony from our graduates will help you! John Gordon and Michael Birchoff both graduated from here, and now they're teaching in the same school. He said he was sure he'd never been happier, and if he hadn't taken the program, he would probably still be making coffee instead of living his dream as a science teacher.

(7) Remember: teachers make the world go round. Get on the bandwagon today! It doesn't matter where you're at; it only matters where you're going.

16. Correct the reflexive pronoun in the following sentence from paragraph 2.

That's why it's necessary to fill the profession with really talented individuals like yourself to ensure that all will be right with the world in the future.

A. myself

B. him

C. you

D. No change.

17. Rewrite this sentence from paragraph 3 to eliminate awkward construction.

You're probably sitting at a cubicle all day or making coffee for someone who is not nearly as talented and qualified as you, just giving your job up to someone you know is not the best.

_____

_____

_____

_____

_____

_____

18. Edit this sentence from paragraph 5 to ensure proper possession.

People say teachers don't make much money, and although that may be true, our program will also help you get involved in the perfect teachers' unions to help you find all the resources you need to fight for your rights in the profession.

A. teacher's; teachers

B. teachers'; teachers'

C. teachers; teacher's

D. No change.

19. Which of the following revises the following sentence from paragraph 5 to ensure proper coordination?

Get in there, be professional, teach kids, be exciting, and to help adjust the world's mindset one classroom at a time.

A. "Get in there, be professional, teach kids, be exciting, and help adjust the world's mindset one classroom at a time."

B. "Get in there, be professional, be exciting, teach kids, and to help adjust the world's mindset one classroom at a time."

C. "Get in there, be professional, teach kids, be exciting, and to help to adjust the world's mindset one classroom at a time."

D. No change.

20. Correct the punctuation in the following sentence from paragraph 4.

We'll teach you all of that but not only that we'll help you become masters of classroom management and pedagogical theory.

21. How might the following sentence from paragraph 6 be rewritten to show clear pronoun use?

> He said he was sure he'd never been happier, and if he hadn't taken the program, he would probably still be making coffee instead of living his dream as a science teacher.

A. He said he was sure he'd never been happier, and if John hadn't taken the program, he would probably still be making coffee instead of living his dream as a science teacher.

B. John said he was sure he'd never been happier, and if he hadn't taken the program, Michael would probably still be making coffee instead of living his dream as a science teacher.

C. Michael said he was sure he'd never been happier, and if he hadn't taken the program, he would probably still be making coffee instead of living his dream as a science teacher.

D. No change.

22. How should this sentence from paragraph 6 be rewritten to show more logical construction?

> Because job shortages are prevalent in these tough economic times, so join our programs and you will find yourself leaps and bounds ahead of the game as we teach you how to present yourself with your best foot forward.

A. "Job shortages are prevalent in these tough economic times, so join our programs and you will find yourself leaps and bounds ahead of the game as we teach you how to present yourself with your best food forward."

B. "Because job shortages are prevalent in these tough economic times, join our programs and you will find yourself leaps and bounds ahead of the game as we teach you how to present yourself with your best foot forward."

C. "Because job shortages are prevalent in these tough economic times, so join our programs and you will find yourself leaps and bounds ahead of the game."

D. No change.

23. How can this sentence from paragraph 7 be rewritten to avoid the dangling preposition?

> It doesn't matter where you're at; it only matters where you're going.

A. It only matters where you are going.

B. It doesn't matter where you are; it only matters where you're going.

C. It doesn't matter where you're at. It only matters where you are going.

D. No change.

Read this excerpt from a student's paper on Arundhati Roy's *The God of Small Things*. Then answer questions 24–31.

(1) Often, authors take it upon themselves to expose injustice in the world. Writers fancy themselves the moral guardians of culture, or the peaceful weapon which might enact some form of change in a corrupt society. Therefore, because writers take this burden upon their work, they must communicate their messages in the most effective means possible. This usually includes a balance of the most shocking and yet simultaneously believable means of suffering imaginable, that way the truth behind corruption is exposed in a memorable and passionate way. The reason authors will not simply allow children to be children is because they need to use a child's innocence to exploit the wrongs adults commit.

(2) As a society, we are immune to the terrors we inflict upon each other, validating our choices with logic and reason, but we find ourselves ready to gather with pitch forks and torches when we encounter those that would do harm to our children. Children are our last great enterprise, our future. Indian author Arundhati Roy strips children of their childhoods in order to expose larger problems in society, thus calling an audience to act upon injustice or reflect upon their own choices. In Roy's *The God of Small Things*, the social commentary involves the Indian caste system and feudal state of political unrest. Roy explores the effect these adult choices have on the children who must experience them as well, but have no control in the unfolding. Therefore, by exposing the readers to the children's experiences, Roy makes more poignant commentary that forces her audience into a hard swallowing of the wrongs in society.

(3) In *The God Of Small Things*, Estha and Rahel, the "two egg twins," suffer more by the age of ten than most adults have suffered in a lifetime. The tragedy Arundhati Roy crafts in the story is necessary to fuel the plot surely but at times it seems excessive. Is it not enough for Estha and Rahel to find there dead cousin in the water and to bear the guilt of her accidental death? Is it not enough for them to see the man they love like a father beaten so badly that the wounds ultimately claim his life? Is it not enough for them to be separated from each other, but to also lose their mother? Is it not enough for Estha to be molested by the Orangedrink Lemondrink man and for Rahel to be told she is loved "a little less"? The misery never seems to let up. These children suffer more than their fair share, and Roy seems relentless in punishing them with not only the events themselves, but also with her haunting, repetitive phrases that constantly serve as reminders of the horrific events of their past.

(4) Roy mimics childlike speech and thought patterns throughout the novel, choosing to obsess over small symbols like Rahel's Love in Toyko and Estha's "Elvis the Pelvis Puff." She spells out words in childish ways, even backwards, and writes American songs phonetically. She does this to create a child's frame of reference within the reader. We ought to feel it along with them. Within this frame she tortures Estha and Rahel, and then allows them occasional third person limited narration, so the reader, too, experiences the damaging and obsessive thoughts the children have to endure throughout the text. Although the children age to a "viable, die-able age" of 31 in the

work, even their adult choices smack of the ghosts of childhood. They sleep together to ease the grief of childhood wounds left untreated. Neither are able to sustain healthy adult relationships, and Estha becomes mute because he suffered so extensively as a child. Roy cannot let Estha and Rahel be children because she needs them to suffer. She needs them to suffer so the reader will walk away with this message: if we do not protect our children, they grow up to be THIS. This. If we do not change, we are responsible for this.

(5) Roy's commentary lies within the idea that "that *personal* despair could never be desperate enough. That something happened when personal turmoil dropped by at the wayside shrine of the vast, violent, circling, driving, ridiculous, insane, unfeasible, public toil of a nation." The commentary in *The God of Small Things* is not a critique of Ammu's parenting, but of India's state of existence. It is not entirely the fault of any of the abusers that the children suffered as they did. The fault lies within the state of the country when a woman cannot love the man she loves because they are of a different caste. It is the fault of the country that a man exacts his revenge for his lot in life on the rich children whose lives should be worry-free. It is the fault of the country that the police are able to manipulate the truth and kill a man whose only crime was love. The children are tortured not because of karmic or situational reasons, but for political judgment. Estha and Rahel are the victims in Arundhati Roy's outcry against political and economic inequalities because Roy knows a tale of one child's suffering due to these inequities is far more influential and heart-wrenching than nuclear war among adults."

24. Identify the word that should replace the word **there** in this sentence from paragraph 3 to avoid confusion.

> Is it not enough for Estha and Rahel to find there dead cousin in the water and to bear the guilt of her accidental death?

   A. his

   B. they're

   C. their

   D. No change.

25. How could the one-word sentence, "This" (from the last line of paragraph 4), be rewritten to avoid the fragmentation?

   A. They do this.

   B. This childish act.

   C. This effect on the children.

   D. No change.

26. What can be done to eliminate the informal usage in the following sentence from paragraph 4?

We ought to feel them.

A. Roy wants us to feel them.

B. Roy wants the audience to experience the world along with them.

C. Roy creates an experience where the audience can feel the characters.

D. No change.

27. How can the following sentence from paragraph 5 be corrected?

Estha and Rahel are the victims in Arundhati Roy's outcry against political and economic inequalities because Roy knows a tale of one child's suffering due to these inequities is far more influential and heart-wrenching than nuclear war among adults."

A. Estha and Rahel are the victims in Arundhati Roy's outcry against political and economic inequalities because Roy knows a tale of one child's suffering due to these inequities are far more influential and heart-wrenching than nuclear war among adults

B. Estha and Rahel is the victims in Arundhati Roy's outcry against political and economic inequalities because Roy knows a tale of one child's suffering due to these inequities are far more influential and heart-wrenching than nuclear war among adults

C. Estha and Rahel are the victims in Arundhati Roy's outcry against political and economic inequalities because Roy knows a tale of one child's suffering due to these inequities will far more influential and heart-wrenching than nuclear war among adults

D. No change.

28. Correct the punctuation in the following sentence from paragraph 3.

The tragedy Arundhati Roy crafts in the story is necessary to fuel the plot surely but at times it seems excessive.

29. Which word needs to be corrected for capitalization in the following sentence from paragraph 3?

In *The God Of Small Things*, Estha and Rahel, the "two egg twins," suffer more by the age of ten than most adults have suffered in a lifetime.

A. of

B. Twins

C. god

D. No change.

30. Correct the following sentence from paragraph 4 to show proper subject-verb agreement.

Neither are able to sustain healthy adult relationships, and Estha becomes mute because he suffered so extensively as a child.

A. "Neither are able to sustain healthy adult relationships, and Estha becomes mute because he suffered so extensively when he was a child."

B. "Neither is able to sustain healthy adult relationships, and Estha becomes mute because he suffered so extensively as a child."

C. "Neither are able to sustain healthy adult relationships, and Estha become mute because he suffered so extensively as a child."

D. No change.

31. Rewrite the following sentence from paragraph 1 to avoid awkward construction.

Therefore, because writers take this burden upon their work, they must communicate their messages in the most effective means possible.

_____

_____

_____

_____

_____

Read the following speech from the president of a high school's environmental club to her classmates. Then answer questions 32–37.

(1) Students of Jefferson High School, I stand before you today to talk about the biggest problem plaguing our humanity: Plastic Bottles. Yes, plastic bottles. Have you seen our hallways? They are overrun with plastic bottles piling out of our trashcans. I've even seen plastic bottles in the stalls in the girls' bathroom. They are on our steps, left in the windowsills, under desks, absolutely choking the cafeteria's floor, and if you ask any given freshman, I bet he will tell you he's got at least four empty Gatorade bottles at the bottom of his locker. What are we going to do about this terrible plight?

(2) First, let me tell you why plastic bottles are terrible. The biggest problem with plastic bottles in this school is that they aren't even ending up in the recycling bins! The environmental club holds 48 bake sales last year to purchase one blue recycling bin per classroom. At the end of every single school day, I walk around with Gloria to empty them. Do you know what I end up doing? Picking plastic bottles out of the regular trash can! YES! I have to role up my sleeves and sort through banana peels, pencil shavings and empty deodorant aerosol cans to pick out YOUR plastic bottles. We have an apathy problem, people. Are you too good to take the four extra seconds it requires to determine whether or not the waste receptacle into which you are depositing your plastic bottle is for trash or recyclable goods? Let me answer that for you. No. You are not.

(3) Thirdly, let's talk about your over-dependence on bottled WATER. Bottled water. Really, people, really? Why do you need to buy a water bottle? We have 16 water fountains in this school and on most occasions there is more than one in each hallway. WHY on earth do you need to buy a bottle of water? Oh—I know why—just to annoy me so you can throw your water bottle into the trash instead of the recycling bin, right? Come on, people! Tap water is subjected to far more tests for purity than bottled water. I could take water out of my toilet and put it in an Evian bottle, and would you even know the difference? What do you think is stopping big companies from doing the exact same thing? Your tap water is infinitely safer than bottled water, and if you just brought a water bottle to school, you could cut down significantly on waste production every year. Sure, they're recyclable, but do you know how much energy is wasted recycling something that you don't even need in the first place? More than you can imagine.

(4) The world's leader in recycling, in Japan, people are subjected to hundreds of dollars' worth of fines for not recycling properly. I think we should adopt their hard-nosed approach to the subject. To that end, I have approached our instructional leadership team with a plan, and it's a plan that has been approved by our principal. From now on, every time you throw away a plastic bottle into the trash can instead of the recycling bin, you will be given a detention. Fifteen minutes for the first offense, thirty for the second, and it just keeps going up from there until you reach two hours. Is that what you want? No? Then recycle!

32. What word should replace the word **role** in the following sentence from paragraph 2?

I have to role up my sleeves and sort through banana peels, pencil shavings, and empty deoderant aerosol cans to pick out YOUR plastic bottles.

A. pull

B. roil

C. roll

D. No change.

33. How can the following sentence from paragraph 1 be rewritten to avoid awkward construction?

They are on our steps, left in the windowsills, under desks, absolutely choking the cafeteria's floor, and if you ask any given freshman, I bet he will tell you he's got at least four empty Gatorade bottles at the bottom of his locker.

A. They are on our steps, left in the windowsills, under desks, absolutely choking the cafeteria's floor; and if you ask any given freshman, I bet he will tell you he's got at least four empty Gatorade bottles at the bottom of his locker.

B. They are on our steps, left in the windowsills, under desks, and absolutely choking the cafeteria's floor. If you ask any given freshman, I bet he will tell you he's got at least four empty Gatorade bottles at the bottom of his locker.

C. They are on our steps, left in the windowsills, under desks, absolutely choking the cafeteria's floor. If you ask any given freshman, I bet he will tell you he's got at least four empty Gatorade bottles at the bottom of his locker.

D. No change.

34. How can the subject-verb agreement be corrected in the following sentence from paragraph 2?

The environmental club holds 48 bake sales last year to purchase one blue recycling bin per classroom.

A. Replace the word "holds" with "held."

B. Replace the word "holds" with "hold."

C. Replace the phrase "to purchase" with "purchased."

D. No change.

35. How can the following sentence from paragraph 4 be written to avoid illogical construction?

> The world's leader in recycling, in Japan, people are subjected to hundreds of dollars' worth of fines for not recycling properly.

    A. The world's leader in recycling, Japan, people are subjected to hundreds of dollars' worth of fines for not recycling properly.

    B. In Japan, the world's leader in recycling, people are subjected to hundreds of dollars' worth of fines for not recycling properly.

    C. Japan, the world's leader in recycling, people are subjected to hundreds of dollars' worth of fines for not recycling properly.

    D. No change.

36. Punctuate this sentence from paragraph 3 correctly.

> We have 16 water fountains in this school and on most occasions there is more than one in each hallway.

37. Correct the transitional word in this sentence: "Thirdly, let's talk about your over-dependence on bottled WATER."

    A. Replace "Thirdly" with "However"

    B. Replace "Thirdly" with "Therefore"

    C. Replace "Thirdly with "Next"

    D. No change.

Read the following letter of recommendation. Then answer questions 38–44.

(1) Institute Members:

(2) I am writing to recommend Amber Jordan for admission into your program. I am the english department chair, and have worked with Amber for seven years. She is the director of the highly successful Writing Center, and she is also one of the most competent teachers I have ever known. Amber has taught a variety of levels and subjects in English, and she is successful in leading all of them. Currently Amber teaches ninth grade honors English and Advanced Composition, but she was also a corner-stone teacher of International Baccalaureate English HL for years. She demonstrates a fluid ability to plan and show flexibility in her schedule. Amber has a strong rapport with her students and colleagues and shows particular strength in working with freshmen, which I consider an incredibly laudable talent indeed. Amber's commitment to professionalism is second to none. She ensures that she is up to the minute with all the latest and greatest trends in the teaching of writing.

(3) Amber is actively involved in the community. She has coached lacrosse for years, and she is at work until untold hours making sure all her lesson plans are as effective as possible. Because of her responsibility advising the Writing Center, Amber has had the opportunity to work collaboratively with nearly every person in our school, and her has forged meaningful and lasting relationships with the administrators, students, and faculty beyond her own department. Amber has managed to foster a school-wide culture of writing across the curriculum. She is fiercely committed to her visions to the point of self-sacrifice. Amber gives up her lunch time every day except Friday so she can work with her Writing Center Tutors at all available lunches. The notoriety of the Writing Center is national at this point. Amber began the program from nothing, and it now serves as a model for the entirety of the county. She helped write the County's Program of Study for Advanced Composition. The Writing Center has been mentioned on NPR, and it is currently being featured on the National Writing Project's radio.

(4) Amber demands excellence. She demands it of herself, her students and her colleagues. I am a senior teacher, and for years have benefited from the rigor Amber has fostered in our department. The students coming from Amber's classes are prepared, quick, reflective and informed. They approach literature with a keen eye for detail and a vast arsenal of strategies, thoughtful and reflective, for literary criticism. She manages to engender a love for reading and learning in all her students, not just the ones destined to become English majors. Amber prepares every single student to the best of his ability because she differentiates her instruction beautifully. The rigor she has implemented in the English 9 team is unparalleled. Her focus on excellence is data driven, and her mastery of technology put her on the cutting edge of reaching students. She meets students on their turf and demands they excel. She is an inspiration to all who work with her.

(5) Amber has an admirable and indomitable thirst for expanding her world views. She is an avid traveler, and journeys at every given opportunity. She will often bring students along for educational trips over the summer whenever she is able. My impression of Amber's ambition regarding her personal interests is parallel to my impression of her as a teacher: she demands excellence. My assessment of Amber is she does nothing half-way, and while she is careful to be well-rounded, she is discerning in the endeavors which take up her time, because she is the embodiment of integrity. I truly believe Amber will reject additional hobbies or opportunities if she knows she does not have the time or resources to make them as meaningful as she possibly can. Amber seems to me self-actualized and a true Renaissance woman. I imagine Amber is good at nearly everything she attempts.

(6) I unabashedly recommend Amber for your program. She is bright, vocal, competent and capable. Her work ethic is unparalleled, and her contributions to meaningful discussion are absolutely delightful.

(7) Sincerely,

Katarina Dvorzhinskaya

38. How can this sentence from paragraph 4 be rewritten to show correct possession?

The students coming from Amber's classes are prepared, quick, reflective and informed.

A. The students coming from Ambers classes are prepared, quick, reflective and informed.

B. The students coming from Ambers' classes are prepared, quick, reflective and informed.

C. The students coming from Amber's classes' are prepared, quick, reflective and informed.

D. No change.

39. Correct the pronoun agreement in this sentence from paragraph 3.

Because of her responsibility advising the Writing Center, Amber has had the opportunity to work collaboratively with nearly every person in our school, and her has forged meaningful and lasting relationships with the administrators, students, and faculty beyond her own department.

A. Because of she responsibility advising the Writing Center, Amber has had the opportunity to work collaboratively with nearly every person in our school, and her has forged meaningful and lasting relationships with the administrators, students, and faculty beyond her own department.

B. Because of her responsibility advising the Writing Center, Amber has had the opportunity to work collaboratively with nearly every person in our school, and she has forged meaningful and lasting relationships with the administrators, students, and faculty beyond her own department.

C. Because of her responsibility advising the Writing Center, Amber has had the opportunity to work collaboratively with nearly every person in our school, and they has forged meaningful and lasting relationships with the administrators, students, and faculty beyond her own department.

D. No change.

40. Correct the subject-verb agreement in this sentence from paragraph 4.

> Her focus on excellence is data driven, and her mastery of technology put her on the cutting edge of reaching students.

A. Her focuses on excellence is data driven, and her mastery of technology put her on the cutting edge of reaching students.

B. Her focus on excellence are data driven, and her mastery of technology put her on the cutting edge of reaching students.

C. Her focus on excellence is data driven, and her mastery of technology puts her on the cutting edge of reaching students."

D. No change.

41. How can the following sentence from paragraph 4 be rewritten to correct the misplaced modifier?

> They approach literature with a keen eye for detail and a vast arsenal of strategies, thoughtful and reflective, for literary criticism.

A. They approach literature, thoughtful and reflective, with a keen eye for detail and a vast arsenal of strategies, for literary criticism.

B. They approach literature with a keen eye for detail, thoughtful and reflective, and a vast arsenal of strategies for literary criticism.

C. They approach literature with a keen eye for detail and a vast arsenal of thoughtful and reflective strategies for literary criticism.

D. No change.

42. Correct the following run-on sentence from paragraph 5.

> My assessment of Amber is she does nothing half-way, and while she is careful to be well-rounded, she is discerning in the endeavors that take up her time, because she is the embodiment of integrity.

_____

_____

_____

_____

_____

43. Correct the capitalization in this sentence from paragraph 1.

I am the english department chair, and have worked with Amber for seven years.

A. English Department Chair

B. English department chair

C. English Department chair

D. Correct as is.

44. Correct the punctuation in this sentence from paragraph 2.

Amber has a strong rapport with her students and colleagues and shows particular strength in working with freshmen which I consider an incredibly laudable talent indeed.

Read the following public health announcement about dieting. Then answer questions 45–49.

Don't Just Sit There

(1) It's the same old story. You're overweight and you are unhappy with your appearance. Well instead of sitting there feeling sorry for yourself why don't you get up and take a walk around your neighborhood! Companies keep trying to come out with new and improved diets and pills, but guess what? None of them work like the tried and true method of eating healthy foods and maintaining an active lifestyle.

(2) We are inundated with advertisements about the newest, "guaranteed" diet for weight loss. Atkins, South Beach, and Weight Watchers. We've seen supplements like Guarana and Ephedra crowd the shelves of dieting supplements in health food stores, only to find out that they are dangerous to our health. We've been told to eat nothing but cantaloupe and fish. Cut out carbs, no exercise necessary.

(3) Let's break it down in the same way that it's been broken down for centuries: eat fruits and vegetables. Get some exercise. Don't eat tons of sugar, but don't deny yourself too often either (that just causes more cravings). If you need to have that cookie, fine, eat the cookie, but then go for a bike ride. It's simple: you have to burn more calories a day than you eat. There is no magic solution that will negate this fact. It might not be what you want to hear, but our real problem in this country is not that we are obese, it's that we are uneducated and lazy. Why will you spend days torturing yourself on an unsatisfing diet you can't possibly sticks to instead of going for a jog for 30 minutes?

(4) We need to change our mindset. Are you within two miles of your work? Walk or bike there. It won't kill you, I promise, and you can spend the time listening to audiobooks or just enjoying

nature. Dieting is a lame fad that needs to go away. The only answer is to eat in moderation and exercise. Look at the French. Their diet is loaded with fats, but are the French fat people? No. Why? They walk everywhere. They buy fresh foods every day, and they DO NOT eat at McDonald's. You are probably like the rest of us and obsessed with convenience so you can work harder. Spare yourself the stress and frustration and make a meal with fresh foods instead of those Extra Value meals. You start making smart choices and exercising, and I promise you will see your weight adjust to a normal healthy ratio.

45. How can this sentence from paragraph 2 be rewritten to avoid the fragment?

    Atkins, South Beach, and Weight Watchers.

    A. We have patiently endured Atkins, South Beach, and Weight Watchers.
    B. Atkins, South Beach, and Weight Watchers, three trying diets.
    C. Atkins. South Beach. Weight Watchers.
    D. No change.

46. Correct the non-standard language in this sentence.

    Dieting is a lame fad that needs to go away.

    A. Dieting is a lame fad that needs to die out.
    B. Dieting is old school.
    C. Dieting is a passing trend whose time has come and gone.
    D. No change.

47. Correct the subject-verb agreement in this sentence from paragraph 3.

    Why will you spend days torturing yourself on an unsatisfying diet you can't possibly sticks to instead of going for a jog for 30 minutes?

    A. Why will you spend days torturing yourself on an unsatisfying diet you can't possibly stick to instead of going for a jog for 30 minutes?
    B. Why will you spend days torturing yourselves on an unsatisfying diet you can't possibly sticks to instead of going for a jog for 30 minutes?
    C. Why will you spend days torturing yourself on an unsatisfying diet you can't possibly sticks to instead of go for a jog for 30 minutes?
    D. No change.

48. How can this sentence from paragraph 2 be rewritten to show logical clarity?

We've seen supplements like Guarana and Ephedra crowd the shelves of dieting supplements in health food stores, only to find out that they are dangerous to our health.

A. We've seen supplements like Guarana and Ephedra crowd the shelves of dieting supplements, only to find out that they are dangerous to our health.

B. We've seen supplements like Guarana and Ephedra crowd the shelves of dieting supplements in health food stores, only to find out that these drugs are dangerous to our health."

C. We've seen supplements like Guarana and Ephedra in health food stores, only to find out that they are dangerous to our health.

D. No change.

49. Correct the punctuation in this sentence from paragraph 1.

Well instead of sitting there feeling sorry for yourself why don't you get up and take a walk around your neighborhood!

50. The passage that follows is incomplete. For each "Select…" option, choose the response that correctly completes the paragraph or sentence.

The Beauty of Speleotherms

Dripstone features are called speleotherms, and they can take several beautiful forms. When these structures are highlighted by lanterns or electric lights, they transform the cave into a natural wonderland. The most familiar dripstone features are stalactites and stalagmites. Stalactites hang from the ceiling and are formed as drops of water slowly trickle through cracks in the cave roof.

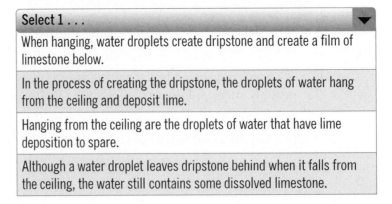

Select 1 . . .

When hanging, water droplets create dripstone and create a film of limestone below.

In the process of creating the dripstone, the droplets of water hang from the ceiling and deposit lime.

Hanging from the ceiling are the droplets of water that have lime deposition to spare.

Although a water droplet leaves dripstone behind when it falls from the ceiling, the water still contains some dissolved limestone.

As a result, the lime deposition from above creates stalagmites, which in all their glorious formations grow upward from the floor of the cave. An impressive column forms when a stalactite and stalagmite grow until they join. A curtain or drapery begins to form an inclined ceiling when the drops of water trickle along a slope.

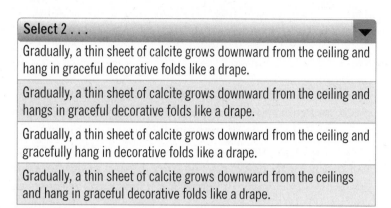

Select 2 ... ▼
Gradually, a thin sheet of calcite grows downward from the ceiling and hang in graceful decorative folds like a drape.
Gradually, a thin sheet of calcite grows downward from the ceiling and hangs in graceful decorative folds like a drape.
Gradually, a thin sheet of calcite grows downward from the ceiling and gracefully hang in decorative folds like a drape.
Gradually, a thin sheet of calcite grows downward from the ceilings and hang in graceful decorative folds like a drape.

These impressive and beautiful features appear in caves in almost every state, making for easy access for tourists looking for a thrill. In addition, the size and depth of many caves in the United States

Select 3 ... ▼
also impress even the most experienced tourist accustomed to many very unique sights.
impress even the most experienced tourist accustomed to many unique sights.
also impress very experienced tourists accustomed to very unique sights.
impressed the most experienced tourist also accustomed to very unique sights.

Seven caves have more than 15 passage miles, the longest being the Flint-Mammoth Cave system in Kentucky with more than 169 miles. The deepest cave in the United States is Neff Canyon in Utah. Although many people seem to think that the deepest cave is Carlsbad Caverns, located in New Mexico. However, Carlsbad Caverns boasts the largest room, the Bog Room, which covers 14 acres. These are sights not to be missed by those who appreciate the handiwork of Mother Nature.

Answers: Reasoning Through Language Arts—Practice Test 1

Section 1

1. **C.**

   It is important to acknowledge the word "convince." The entire essay is a persuasive piece, and goes about its rhetoric in a variety of ways, mostly through rhetorical questions and negation of opposition through logical construction. Choice (A) is incorrect because it only deals with a small section of the piece and misses the main idea. Choice (B) is incorrect because although it may be true, it is not as developed of an answer as choice (C), and misses the key element of persuasion. Choice (B) dismisses the text as simply informational. Choice (D) is incorrect because it is based on a misreading of the text.

2. **(A., B., E.)**

   (A) is supported by the evidence of "marriages now existing"—an appeal to common knowledge; choice (B) is an authoritative claim, supported by the evidence, citing *The Alpha;* choice (E) is supported by logical reasoning, the if-then cause-and-effect thought process. Choice (C) is simply a question with no context. Choices (D) and (F) are based on supposition and conjecture rather than evidence or logical construction. Choice (G) is a parenthetical qualifier and exclamation.

3. **D.**

   Choice (D) is correct—you can infer this based on the strong persuasive appeal employed by the author to support advertising for marriage as an acceptable practice. Choices (A), (B), and (C) are incorrect because there is nothing in the text to support these claims, nor is there anything indicated in the text from which you could draw such inferences.

4. **A.**

   The correct answer is choice (A). The emotionally charged language ("unhappy," "bitterly," and "regret") helps to create an investment for the reader. Additionally, the use of a personal example helps the reader to imagine herself in the situation Gilman describes. Choice (B) is an appeal to logic, considering its call to judgment. Choice (C) is an appeal to tradition, an ethical appeal, as is choice (D), which is an appeal to ethical construction through its citation of an authority.

5. **B.**

In this instance, Gilman acknowledges the argument against her—people from different backgrounds would have different interests and an unhappy marriage—and negates it by saying that those people who preferred to remain with what they know would not venture out to find partners anyway. Choices (A), (C), and (D) do not present counterarguments.

6. **D.**

Although Gilman does appeal to emotion, which includes choices (A) and (C), she most often uses these appeals in tandem with her logical negation of them. It is important to remember that Gilman is trying to change the minds of people whose minds are only made up this way due to tradition (A) and normalcy (C). Gilman does use authoritative warrants (B), especially when she cites *The Alpha*, but this, too, is an appeal to logic.

7. **B.**

This sentence pits against each other the past view of marriage as a business arrangement and the potential nouveau view of marriage as a result of flirtation and interest. It is true that there is a relationship implied here between love and money, but it is contrasting, not parallel (A). There is no warrant that links a relationship between men and women in this instance—though both are mentioned as one part of one relationship (C). Finally, though there is a relationship drawn between the past and the present (D), the relationship is not parallel, it is contrasting.

8. **D.**

Although this entire essay should help cement the idea that Gilman was an early feminist, choice (D) is the answer which most strongly portrays it because she discusses a woman's sensibility and intelligence and views her as an independent half of a couple, rather than property to be bargained for. Choice (A) is incorrect because it is merely an appeal to common sense and choice (B) is simply a modifying statement. Choice (C) is the next best answer because it discusses a couple's right to have physical interaction before marriage, but this is dealing more with the man's perspective on that case than with the woman's.

9. **C.**

The idea that youth may choose to be idle is supported by the essay when the gentleman describes his desire to "do nothing," and by the chart, which proves that most youth are not currently looking for employment. Choice (A) is incorrect because it is not supported by either piece; choice (B) is an inference that is a reasonable assumption, but not supported by the text, and choice (D) is refuted by the first line of the essay excerpt, which says: "It is impossible to enjoy idling thoroughly unless one has plenty of work to do."

10. **humorous, easygoing, warm**

The author's attitude is humorous, easygoing, and warm. Neither "biting" nor "restless" fit. The former would require Jerome's humor to be scathing and satirical, which it is not. And rather than showing signs of restlessness, the author is actually a model of patience—intent on enjoying lazing about to the hilt.

11. **A.**

In both the narrative essay and the chart, we are given the information that the youth population, in general, is idle. To this end, it is a simple inference to realize that with effort put forth, a young individual can easily set himself apart from his peers. Choice (B) might seem a logical choice, but it takes for granted that there are jobs available for unemployed youth, and this is not stated explicitly in either text. Choice (C), too, is another jump in logic that is only remotely discussed in the chart, not in the essay. Choice (D) is entirely unsubstantiated in either text.

12. **B.**

The speaker actually tells the audience how to be idle for pure enjoyment and then tells us of the instances in which he was most successful at the endeavor. The chart shows the ratio of unemployed youth who are seeking employment versus those who are not. There is nothing about the chart that could be viewed as scaring youth into motivation (A). Choice (C) is the next best answer because it is mostly correct, but choice (B) is better because it goes into more precise depth. Choice (D) is incorrect because there is information in the chart that bears on improving the status of youth.

13. **C.**

Choice (C) is the only response that does not make assumptions about the intentions of the pieces. For choices (A) and (D) to be correct, one or both of the pieces would have to indicate that there is no cure for idleness, or that there is a fear inherent in the writing that would indicate some sort of disaster is looming in the workforce. Choice (B) makes no comparison at all, so it is an incomplete conclusion.

14. **D.**

The title of the chart, "Among youth, unemployment is not always the issue," indicates that there is a further issue, and when the information is analyzed, it is easy to see that the additional "issue" is the fact that youth are not even seeking employment. Meanwhile, the essay says right off the bat that doing nothing is enjoyable. From this information you can rule out choices (A) and (C) immediately. Choice (B) may in fact be a correct statement, but it has nothing to do with the conflicting nature of the two pieces.

15.

Order of Events

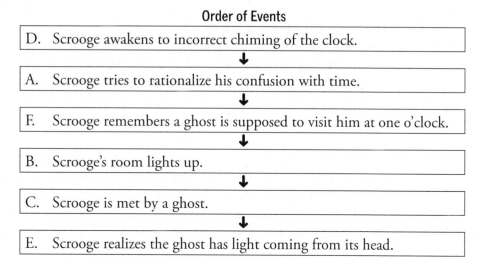

D.	Scrooge awakens to incorrect chiming of the clock.
A.	Scrooge tries to rationalize his confusion with time.
F.	Scrooge remembers a ghost is supposed to visit him at one o'clock.
B.	Scrooge's room lights up.
C.	Scrooge is met by a ghost.
E.	Scrooge realizes the ghost has light coming from its head.

16. **A.**

This should be a relatively easy answer to find, as choice (A) is the only response that includes any reasoning at all. However, you can tell that it is fallacious because Scrooge is trying to convince himself of something that is clearly not true. Although choice (B) has a bit of hyperbole, it is not a fallacy. Choice (C) is the next best answer, but it does not demonstrate reasoning, only the conclusion. Finally, choice (D) is simply a description.

17. **D.**

You can tell that Scrooge does not believe in the imaginative very much because he attempts to rationalize all aspects of the supernatural as things are happening to him. This negates choice (A). You might infer that Scrooge is a very fearful person (B) because he cannot go back to sleep, but when you consider the circumstances (a ghost visiting him), it is quite a stretch to apply to his character all the time. There is no evidence in the text to conclude that Scrooge is angry or violent (C).

18. **C.**

This is a common theme in literature, and it is highlighted in this instance by Scrooge's confusion over the time. It may be true that ghosts are terrifying (A), but this is more of an observation than a message. Choice (B) might seem an appealing option, but this is not entirely substantiated by the text—Scrooge does not necessarily demonstrate madness to any discernible degree in this excerpt. Finally, though choice (D) might be good advice, it is not a theme that applies in this scenario—especially when the ghost is coming in through the window!

19. **D.**

The ghost himself represents a paradox by the very nature of his dress. Choice (A) might seem appealing because it shows the absurdity of the event itself and its confusing nature, but it is not *by itself* contradictory, and is simply Scrooge trying to reassure himself that there is a logical explanation. Choice (B) is simply an observation made to heighten the senses of the reader in the passage. Choice (C) is simply a narrative progression of the plot.

20. **B.**

The author echoes Scrooge's experience for the reader by directly addressing the reader in this sentence, something that does not happen elsewhere in this passage. This same idea is crafted in choice (A), but it is not as developed. Also, the words "fully empathize" are a bit of a stretch when considering the situation Scrooge is in compared to the one the reader is in. Choice (C) is incorrect because very little detail is given about the ghost in this instance; that detail comes later. Choice (D) is an unsubstantiated claim that is suppositional and personal at best.

21. **C.**

You really only have two sentences that give any detail about Scrooge and Marley's relationship: "Marley's Ghost bothered him exceedingly," and, "Scrooge lay in this state until the chime had gone three-quarters more, when he remembered, on a sudden, that the Ghost had warned him of a visitation when the bell tolled one." You must infer from the words "bothered" and "warned" that there is some type of familiarity between them. Scrooge is not "petrified" by seeing Marley's ghost (A), and the ghost did provide Scrooge with some type of roadmap for the events of the evening. Therefore, you must infer that there is some degree of friendship between the two. There is no evidence that Marley is "angry" at Scrooge (B). Additionally, although Scrooge does try to convince himself that Marley's ghost is a figment of his imagination, there is no conclusive warrant to show that this means Scrooge disregards him (D); indeed it is quite the opposite since Scrooge stays awake worrying about what Marley said to him.

22. **D.**

The author says on several occasions that less is more, and the assertion can be backed up by the claim about Sappho's two poems having greater weight than a wealth of inferior works. The author points out the advantages of all aspects of art, including music, writing and painting, so you can rule out choices (A) and (B). While choice (C) may be a correct statement, it is not directly supported by the text.

23. **A.**

The assertion in choice (A) is made by the author when she says, "What painting gains in universality to the eye, it loses by an infinite proportion in power of suggestion to the understanding." Choice (B) is incorrect because it is a direct contradiction to this statement. Neither choice (C) nor choice (D) offers any textual evidence to back up this claim.

24. **D.**

The reasoning for choice (D) is suggested in the answers to question No. 23; this is simply the follow-up question, which forces you to identify the sentence for yourself. Choice (A) is simply the beginning of the argument, but does not shed light on the inference about the difference between painting and writing. Choice (B) is an attractive answer because it mentions that writing has an advantage, but it has no clear delineation for what that advantage is. Choice (C) is simply a clarifying statement that makes a concession about the argument itself.

25. **C.**

The author is very critical about all aspects of art—in writing, painting, and music. She is not pompous (A), as she makes several humbling statements and concessions in her argument. Nor is she accusatory (B), because there is no victim in her argument. Though she is passionate (D), this is not the *best* choice because the author carefully lays out the argument and is more logical than inflammatory.

26. **A.**

Without the analysis of the tendencies in music, the author would not seem ignorant (C), but simply more limited in her analysis of art, as she would be leaving out a widely known and loved method of expression. There is no basis to choose choice (B), because the paragraph has nothing to do with painting, though emotions are mentioned. Choice (D) may seem an attractive answer because the paragraph is not about painting or writing, the two main subjects, but taking it out would indeed change it in some manner—namely by limiting the scope of discussion (A).

27. **D.**

Choice (D) is correct. Though choices (B) and (D) are not only close but in fact both actual dictionary definitions of "lament," "to mourn" (B) is too intense for the sentence, which expresses a wish that Sappho, a talented poet, would have written more during her lifetime. This makes "to regret" (D) the best answer. "To cheer" (A) is a near-antonym (opposite) to the correct answer, while choice (C)—"to wonder"—misses the mark because it means "to be in a state of astonishment" or "to feel surprise, curiosity, or doubt." The sadness of Sappho not producing more poetry is measured against the value of what she did produce.

28. B.

The core difference between these two pieces of writing is the approach to education. Montaigne advocates learning by way of facts, and Morris advocates that facts may not be as important as experience. Both authors agree that education is important (A). While choice (C) is an argument both authors discuss, it is not the central disagreement between the pieces. Finally, though choice (D) might be an observation one could make by reading the pieces, neither author uses this as an argument for the essays.

29. B.

"Whirlpools" is used metaphorically in the phrase "whirlpools of information." Morris does this to further her narrative about trying to absorb a dizzying array of information. "Literally" (A) is the opposite of "metaphorically"—a physical swirling rather than the vortex spinning in her mind. Choices (C) and (D) are near-homonyms of each other that indicate an attitude (lacking civility in the case of "churlishly") and (peevishness in the case of "petulantly") of which there is no evidence in the text.

30. D.

Both authors discuss the impact education has had on their lives. Because Morris argues that she prefers enjoying her experiences rather than analyzing them, you can rule out choice (A). Similarly, choice (B) is unsubstantiated by Morris's claim that although she gets frustrated by her peers' fact-gathering, she prefers her own method of education. Finally, Morris also negates choice (C) by discussing her pleasure of experiencing her outings without the "tyranny of facts."

31. D.

This is the only instance in which the author makes a direct distinction between facts ("butterfly cabinets") and experience ("real butterflies"). In this way, she proves that experience is preferred because it does not "give [her] headaches." Choice (A) negates the argument entirely, and though choice (B) does mention her preference for experience, it does not mention that this entails a preference for fact-gathering itself. Choice (C) is simply a notation of the difference between the speaker and her friends.

32. A.

Morris discusses her own personal experience, which gives her argument an emotional appeal. She does not discuss "tradition" (B); and although she does employ logical construction (C), she does not use traditional rhetorical strategies for logic, such as cause and effect. Morris cites no authority in her argument, so choice (D) is out.

33. **C.**

Montaigne employs many logical constructions in his argument, specifically his citation of great thinkers (e.g., Socrates) and the analysis of their ideas. He also employs cause
and effect and other logical construction to advance his argument about the importance of
education. Although he does cite emotion (A) by imploring the boy's mother to consider her
son's well-being, this is not part of the crux of his argument. Similarly, he discusses tradition
(B) only in the sense that challenges the value of the teacher lecturing without encouraging
dialogue. Finally, as mentioned, he does cite authority (D), but he does build a logical case,
not as the essay's central ethical appeal.

34. **B.**

In this instance, Montaigne considers the view of the "madam," taking into account
that she will not "omit" education for her children even as he looks to build upon the educational foundation she has put in place for her child. Although choice (A) may seem an
appealing answer, ultimately he is simply addressing the woman, not acknowledging her
difference of opinion. Choices (C) and (D) are both extensions of Montaigne's own argument, and cite no additional or oppositional claims.

35. **B.**

This article focuses on two things: budget and investment in appealing, classic clothing.
Choice (A) is mentioned in the text as part of a motivating factor for the larger argument.
Although the article may come across as a plug for Woolite (C), this is not its main purpose.
Finally, choice (D) is partially correct, but it ignores the financial aspect of this, which is a
critical focus of the text as indicated by the title ("Fashionable Advice for a Career Wardrobe
on a Budget").

36. **D.**

By citing research done by Woolite and Stacy London, a well-known expert, the author
brings weight to her own argument. Although there is a certain degree of promotionalism
(A), this is a byproduct of a credible argument stitched together with genuinely helpful,
reliable advice. There is no commonly held belief inherent in citing an authority (B), and
though the author does make reference to beloved items (C), this response is not relevant
to why the author cites the Woolite and London research.

37. **C.**

It can be inferred by the word "budget" in the title, that money is an issue in the writing
of this article, and because the author references skirts, blouses and "little black dresses," it's
likely that the intended audience is women. This rules out choice (A). We don't know from
the text that the audience is fashionable (B), especially given that the advice is directed at more

basic ideas than fashion. There is also no support in the text to deduce that the audience usually wears non-flattering clothing (D).

38. **C.**

You can infer that because the author is providing steps to build a career wardrobe, a fashionista, in this instance, is a person who is well-versed in fashion. This would rule out a person who does not understand fashion (A) and a person who does not like fashion (B). Choice (D) might be an attractive option, but because the text says it's offering "tips for the working fashionista," you can infer that such a person is not merely a student of fashion.

39. **A.**

Nearly half of the article is a list of steps to help someone become a "fashionista." This piece, in general, is not an argument, but rather an informative text (B). There is very little embellishment (C) employed in this piece, as most ideas are simply stated rather than elaborated upon. Similarly, the author usess no anecdotal stories (D) to help convey the information.

40. **B.**

The article assumes that every person in the business world is concerned with making the right impression, and that without the right clothes, a person's professional reputation might be affected. Choice (A) is completely unsupported by the text, and though choice (C) might seem logical, it is not even implied in the text. Finally, choice (D) is not substantiated by any of the information presented in the article.

Section 2: Extended Response

Outline for response:

In order to write an accurate response to this prompt, you need to focus on the thesis stem given to you in the wording of the prompt: **how the youth can transition both themselves and their seniors into old age.** This should be the focus of your entire response; don't stray from whatever argument you construct.

Before you begin, it is important to pause to analyze both pieces of information presented to you. In this instance you have a first-person narrator discussing what it is like to grow old, and an article that discusses the consequences of aging on the family. Notice that the narrator in the piece has a stubborn approach to aging, and the article encourages discussion. This is a source of conflict between the two works, and thus your thesis would do well to address this.

A good thesis may be something along the lines of this:

> The youth can transition both themselves and their seniors into old age by first having difficult, candid discussions amongst themselves about the aging process, and then creating a plan for the next steps.

This is an easy-to-discuss argument, and it is relevant to both pieces.

As you structure your response, keep your thesis in mind. Because this thesis is an easy roadmap to follow, you know that your first order of business is to talk about the kind of conversations that youth can have with seniors. As you do this, you should make reference to both the essay and the article about the advice given therein. Some relevant quotes you should probably include are, from the essay:

- "If a new generation were starting with the wisdom of its elders, what would be the consequence?"

- "One does not like to be an old fogie, and still less perhaps does one like to own to being one."

- "For the plant Experience to be of any worth a man must grow it for himself."

It would be a good idea to couch your response in the knowledge that the senior is likely to begin a discussion about the aging process with quotes such as these in protest to the plan.

Then, you can counter with the evidence from the article, using quotations such as:

- "'For caregivers, ease of communication with the seniors they love relieves stress, reduced guilt and builds rich relationships,' says expert on successful aging Adriane Berg."

- "Ask most seniors if they want to age independently in their own homes, and they likely will say yes."

These quotes will help you construct the argument that, with persistent, difficult questions, a plan can be laid for even the most hesitant of seniors to discuss the issue without making them feel like a burden.

After you have structured this part of your essay, you can transition into the next, which deals with coming up with a plan. Here you can use a quotation from the essay such as:

- "My experience is of use only to myself. I cannot bequeath it to my son as I can my cash."

This quotation will help to structure the argument that every aging person knows a plan is necessary for the next steps, even if they are hesitant. The essay seems to offer up its own solution to the problem: The aging narrator knows that he has experience to offer to his family regarding his own fate. In this way you can argue that the evidence from the article (dealing with falls, the technology fix, etc.) are all excellent ways to help create a viable option for the aging process which will ensure the senior's *dignity*. Including this piece of information offers a way to tie together the narrative and the advice in the article.

Finally, you will end your essay with a conclusion that succinctly restates your thesis. A good rule is to end with something new for the audience to think about. One such example would be, "Perhaps if this conversation were part of an ongoing lifelong discussion, it would not be as difficult to discuss when it actually becomes a pressing issue."

Section 3

1. **A.**

   "Whose" is a homonym for the word "who's," which is a contraction made up of, "who" and "is." This sentence should read, "Who is to say. . . ."Choice (B) is incorrect because it removes the verb, which would create a sentence fragment. Choice (C) has the same problem.

2. **B.**

   "Breaking Bad" is a title, so, as a general rule, you should capitalize the first, last, and any important words—except articles, coordinating conjunctions, and short prepositions. This means choices (A) and (C) are both incomplete.

3.

   The correction should read:

   > The AMA cites problems such as vomiting, memory loss, paranoia, and aggression as common side-effects of repeated drug use.

   This is a question of correct parallel structure. "To have paranoia" does not fit in with the correct structure of the list; otherwise it would read, "to vomit, to lose memory, to have aggression," and so on. In addition, the colon after "such as" should be deleted because phrases like "for example," "including," and "such as" already indicate that a list will follow.

4. **C.**

This sentence has many errors, but the most evident is that it is a run-on. To correct it, the coordination should be adjusted into a list, and the dependent clause should be subordinated by the word "because." Choice (A) is incorrect because it is still a run-on sentence. Choice (B) is incorrect because, although it does fix the main run-on, it does not adjust for the punctuation needed in the first independent clause.

5.

The correct answer is,

> This guy simply gets to do what he wants, when he wants.

These two fragments need to be connected into a full sentence. Additionally, it requires a comma between the words "wants" and the word "when."

6. **B.**

The word "person" is a singular subject, which requires a possessive to indicate his ability. In this sentence, "drugs" (A) are not showing ownership, and the word "person" is not plural. Though choice (C) does offer a possessive, it is not correct in number.

7. **C.**

In this sentence, the preposition "to" is dangling. It needs another word to create its syntactical relationship. However, it can be eliminated, and the sentence still makes logical sense. The easiest way to fix the problem in this instance is just to remove the preposition. Choice (A) obscures the meaning behind the sentence, and choice (B) still leaves the preposition dangling.

8. **A.**

"Potholes" is plural, so you must use the plural verb "are" to create agreement. Choice (B) is incorrect because simply changing the order of the wording does not fix the error. Choice (C) is a simpler, more direct sentence, but the subject–verb agreement error remains.

9. **B.**

The correct usage is the contraction "must've," never "must of" (or "could of," "should of," "would of"). "Must" is a modal verb, which expresses necessity or possibility. Choice (A) changes the meaning, telling the representative he must drive to the town; this is not what the writer intends. In choice (C), simply removing the adverb "recently" does not fix the usage error, and it removes a time reference that might aid meaning, as the potholes may have become only worse over time.

10. **C.**

"Me" is an objective pronoun and can never serve as the subject of a sentence. Replacing "me" with "myself" (A) creates another problem: As a reflexive or emphatic pronoun, "myself" can also never be used as a subject of a sentence. Changing the position to the second spot in a compound subject does not fix the problem. You are still asking "me" to be a subject, which it cannot be. Choice (C) is the correct choice, as "I" is a subjective pronoun.

11. Suggested revision:

> I have worked for 19 years as a mechanic, so I know what potholes can do to cars. You think people like to get their cars worked on? Car damage is good for my business, but you know what I mean. Most people would rather spend a hundred dollars on date night than on a new tie rod, not to mention how inconvenient it is to have the car in the shop for a day (or two).

12. **A.**

Choice (A) corrects the error. Merely changing the order (C) does not remove the error. The subjective pronoun "I" is used incorrectly. "Myself" (B) is a reflexive or emphatic pronoun and can never be used as a subject or an object.

13. **C.**

Choice (A) is incorrect. Two sentences can never be connected with a comma. Choice (B) adds a period, which is the correct way to punctuate a declarative sentence, which this is not. Choice (C) is the correct answer because the first sentence is an interrogative sentence and needs a question mark at the end, not a period.

14. **A.**

Choice (A) corrects the nonstandard usage ("ain't"). Choice (B) perpetuates the usage error. Choice (C) makes it appear as if Joe's fear of buying a new car stems from a belief that a purchase will harm, not help, car sales.

15. **C.**

Placement of modifying phrases matters. In the wrong place, the meaning becomes unclear. The original sentence makes it sound like the election was held in Mr. Ford's yard. In choice (A), changing "had" to "put" does nothing to fix the problem. Choice (B) is an improvement since it is clear that it is the sign that is in the yard, not the election. Choice (C) is best because Mr. Ford's point about supporting the candidate in the election by placing a sign in his yard is what he wishes to convey.

16. **C.**

The reflexive pronoun "yourself" should only be used when the pronoun "you" has already been used in the sentence. For example, "You saw yourself in this position." To that end, you can rule out the reflexive pronoun "myself" (A) as well. Choice (B) may be grammatically correct, but it alters the meaning of the sentence and negates the advertisement.

17.

Answers will vary, but a correct response may read,

> You're probably sitting in a cubicle all day or making coffee for someone who is not nearly as talented and qualified as you. Meanwhile, you're giving your job up to someone you know is not the best.

The awkwardness in this sentence results from its length and structure. The sentence should be broken into two sentences, and the "just giving up your job . . ." sentiment should be qualified with some type of modifier, such as "meanwhile."

18. **D.**

This sentence is already grammatically correct in terms of the possession. The first "teachers" is not possessive, so it does not need an apostrophe, which means you can rule out (A) and (B) immediately. The second "teachers'" is possessive, but it refers to the plural possessive, "teachers'," which is already correctly indicated by the sentence. Choice (C) indicates a singular possessive, which is incorrect.

19. **A.**

This response has a problem in the coordination of the list—the phrase "to help" leaves the standard command in the rest of the sentence—be, do, teach, etc. "To help" creates passive voice, and is incorrect. Choice (A) is correct because it transitions the last verb into the active voice. Choice (B) might be interesting, but all it does is coordinate the "be" verbs together. This does not solve the problem of the "to help" issue. Choice (C) is incorrect because it, too, ignores the "to help" problem. Had it removed the "to" and just written "help to adjust," this could have been a correct response.

20.

The correct answer is,

> We'll teach you all of that, but not only that, we'll help you become masters of classroom management and pedagogical theory.

This sentence requires a comma before the coordinating conjunction "but" and it requires another one before the next dependent clause.

21. B.

Because the previous sentence mentions both John and Michael, you know that you must include them both in this sentence; otherwise, it would have mentioned only one of them. Therefore, the pronoun use becomes incredibly unclear. Choice (B) is the only option that provides a solution for both individuals, and makes a clear, coherent sentence. Choice (A) indicates only John is the subject, as choice (C) indicates only Michael is the subject.

22. A.

This sentence removes the subordinate word "Because," which is unnecessary in this sentence. Choice (B) seems like a legitimate choice, but the problem with it is the subordinate word because indicates that the rest of the sentence will solve the job shortage problem, which it does not. Choice (C) only removes half of the sentence, but does not solve the problem of agreement.

23. B.

In this sentence, the dangling preposition is the word "at." Prepositions such as "at," "on," and "in" are used to link a noun, pronoun, or noun phrase to another part of the sentence. In this instance, however, the preposition fails to link to anything else, so it is "dangling." Choice (B) fixes this problem by simply removing the preposition, which in this case, has no function. Choice (A) is incorrect because, although it does fix the problem of the dangling preposition, it also changes the intention of the sentence. Choice (C) is incorrect because the preposition is now dangling at the end of a sentence, rather than in the middle of it.

24. C.

The antecedent to the pronoun in this case is "Estha and Rahel," which is plural, and thus requires the pronoun "their." The way the sentence is written, the word "their" is replaced with its homonym, "there." Choice (B) presents its other homonym, "they're," which is a contraction of "they" and "are." Choice (A) is incorrect because the pronoun must be plural, and "his" is singular.

25. A.

This is the only option that creates a complete sentence with a subject and a verb. Here, "they" is the subject, and "do" is the verb. Choices (B) and (C) both offer incomplete thoughts or dependent clauses.

26. B.

The colloquialism in this sentence is the use of the verb "feel." This is an informal term, and it should be avoided unless the word is contextualized—after all, we are not "feeling" the children—they are intangible beings, and do we really want to touch them, anyway? The word "feel" could be used if the sentence read, "Roy intends for the audience to feel the children's emotions along with them." No sentence provided, however, avoids this error, so the best option is response (B). Choices (A) and (C) both keep the informal use of the word "feel," so you can rule both out.

27. D.

The sentence is correct as it stands. The skill tested in the alternative choices is subject-verb agreement in more complicated situations. This sentence has two subjects—Estha and Rahel as the first, and one child's suffering as the second. "Estha and Rahel" is plural, and receives the plural verb "are," and "one child's suffering" is singular, so it receives a singular verb, "is." Choice (A) is incorrect because it confuses the number of the second subject as plural, which it is not. Similarly, choice (B) makes the first subject singular, which it is not. Finally, choice (C) does not complete the verb "will be," but even if it did, it would change the sentence's tense to future, which is not correct.

28.

The correct answer is,

> The tragedy Arundhati Roy crafts in the story is necessary to fuel the plot, surely, but at times it seems excessive.

This sentence requires commas around its interjection, "surely."

29. A.

In titles, prepositions are not capitalized. Choice (A) corrects this error. There is no reason to capitalize "twins" (B) because it is not a proper noun. However, "God" should be capitalized because it is both a proper noun and a noun in the title of the book.

30. B.

The word "neither" requires a singular verb, which in this case is the word "is." Choice (B) is the only option that corrects this error. Choice (A) makes a change ("when he was a child") that is unnecessary and does not fix the error, as does choice (C). Choice (C), however, complicates the problem by further creating subject-verb disagreement between "Estha" and the verb "become," which is a plural verb with a singular subject.

31.

Answers will vary, but one correct answer is,

> Because writers take this burden upon their work, they must communicate their messages in the most effective means possible.

The awkward construction in this case is the inclusion of the transitional word "therefore." In this instance, it is unnecessary and sets up a definitive, conclusive statement for which there is no logical predicate.

32. **C.**

The words "role" and "roll" are often confused. "Role" is a part played by an actor or by any person in a specific situation, and "roll" means to move in a circular fashion. Clearly, in this instance the student intended to write "roll" but was confused by two words that sound the same. "Pull" (A) may be an acceptable substitute, but when possible, it is always best to leave the author's intentions intact. Choice (B) is a word that makes no sense in the context of the sentence, as it means "churning."

33. **B.**

The problem with this sentence is that it is both long and awkward. This can be solved in choice (B) by adding a comma before "and absolutely . . ." to complete the coordination correctly, and by starting a new sentence at "If you ask . . .." Choice (A) does not solve either of these problems. Though a semicolon is a fine idea for combining this sentence with two shorter ones, it should replace the word "and" as well.

34. **A.**

Because this sentence is referencing the past—last year—you know the sentence needs to be constructed in past tense. The word "holds" is present tense, and is incorrect. Choice (A) fixes this problem. Choice (B) confuses tense and number agreement; the club is singular and "hold" is a plural verb. Choice (C) completely ignores the problem in the sentence and focuses instead on an irrelevant and non-problematic construction.

35. **B.**

The problem with this sentence is the misplaced modifier in the phrase, "The world's leader in recycling." Choice (B) rearranges this so that it is correctly modifying Japan. Choice (A) is not correct because it leaves the sentence a fragment, as it has no proper subject and verb. Similarly, choice (C) fixes the modified clause, but removes a needed verb.

36.

> The correct answer is,
>
> We have 16 water fountains in this school, and on most occasions there is more than one in each hallway."

This sentence simply needs a comma before the coordinating conjunction, "and," which joins the two independent clauses.

37. **C.**

"Thirdly" is an illogical construction because the student has only said "First." "Third" is an illogical leap, and leaves out the second point the student might have made. Choice (A) is incorrect because there is no reason to assume the previous statement was conflicting with this new information. Choice (B) is incorrect because this is not a conclusion that can be drawn from synthesizing previous problems.

38. **D.**

This sentence is written correctly, with "Amber's" showing correct possessive construction—since the classes belong to Amber. Choice (A) is incorrect because it removes the possession altogether. Choice (B) is incorrect because it indicates that there is more than one Amber, which is not true. Choice (C) is incorrect because it gives possession to the word "classes," which is not necessary in this instance.

39. **B.**

In this instance, the antecedent is "Amber," and the pronoun is "she." This text places the incorrect antecedent "her" in, but this is the wrong case. Choice (A) makes the same mistake at the beginning of the sentence, as does choice (C), which replaces "she" with the incorrect plural case, "they."

40. **C.**

The subject-verb agreement error in this sentence is the subject, "mastery," and the verb, "put." "Mastery" is a singular noun, and "put" is a plural verb case, so it must be adjusted to the correct case, so it's "Mastery *puts* . . ." Choice (A) is incorrect because it changes "focus" to a plural noun, so it's unnecessary and incorrect. Choice (B) indicates that the letter writer has more than one focus, but leaves that verb singular. Both choices (A) and (B) ignore the subject-verb agreement error later in the sentence.

41. **C.**

This sentence places the modifier where it belongs—in front of the "strategies" it modifies. Although it could be said that "thoughtful and reflective" might modify "literature" (A), or "detail" (B), in each of these other choices, the modification is unclear and awkward. So it is best to place the modification directly preceding its intended subject.

42.

The run-on may be corrected by creating two sentences:

> Because she is the embodiment of integrity, my assessment of Amber is she does nothing half-way. While she is careful to be well-rounded, she is discerning in the endeavors that take up her time."

This sentence may also be corrected by using a semicolon:

> Because she is the embodiment of integrity, my assessment of Amber is she does nothing half-way; while she is careful to be well-rounded, she is discerning in the endeavors that take up her time.

The run-on occurs when a comma links the two independent clauses. To be correct, they either each need to be independent sentences or linked with a semicolon.

43. **B.**

The sentence should appear as follows:

> I am the English department chair, and have worked with Amber for seven years.

44.

The correct answer is,

> Amber has a strong rapport with her students and colleagues, and shows particular strength in working with freshmen (which I consider an incredibly laudable talent, indeed).

The compound sentence requires a comma before the conjunction, and the parenthetical notation requires the parentheses to differentiate the thought from the rest of the sentence. In addition, a comma should set off the modifying word "indeed."

45. **A.**

The only option that creates a full sentence, including a subject and a verb, is choice (A). The subject is "We" and the verb is "endured." Choice (B) has a subject, but no verb, and choice (C) just creates three new fragments.

46. **C.**

The non-standard use is found in the phrase "lame fad," and "needs to go away" is not that properly formal, either. The GED® follows the fules and norms of standard written English. The correct answer is choice (C) because it takes a colloquial sentence and turns it into a respectable idea. Choice (A) leaves in the slang terminology, and choice (B) replaces it with another colloquial phrase, "old school."

47. **A.**

The subject-verb agreement in this case is problematic with the subject "you" and the verb "sticks." Choice (A) corrects this with "you . . . stick." The problem with choice (B) is that it leaves the subject verb agreement error and creates an unnecessary reflexive pronoun. Similarly, choice (C) changes the tense and case agreement by substituting "going for" with "go."

48. **B.**

The word "they" in this sentence is an ambiguous pronoun. Are the drugs or health food stores dangerous to our health? Choices (A) and (C) are both structurally acceptable, but they both also alter the intention of the sentence. Choice (B) is the only option that keeps the integrity of the sentence intact.

49.

The correct answer is

Well, instead of sitting there feeling sorry for yourself, why don't you get up and take a walk around your neighborhood?

The sentence requires a comma after the interjectory comment, and the correct punctuation for a question requires a question mark.

50.

Select 1 correct answer is Choice (D): Although a water droplet leaves dripstone behind when it falls from the ceiling, the water still contains some dissolved limestone.

This choice avoids the redundancy in choices (A), (B), and (C) that results from describing the water droplets *hanging from the ceiling*—the stalactites are described similarly—while maintaining the logic established earlier and bridging effectively to discussion of how the stalagmites on the cave floor are formed.

Select 2 correct answer is Choice (B): Gradually, a thin sheet of calcite grows downward from the ceiling and hangs in graceful decorative folds like a drape.

This response is correct because both verbs must agree with the singular noun "sheet." Response option (A) brings the noun in accordance with "grow" and "hang" by changing it to the plural "sheets," but it leaves the singular article "a" instead of removing it. Option (C) uses "gracefully" as an adverb correctly, but does not correct the verb agreement problem. Though option (D) may initially appear correct ("hang" would be correct if it modified the plural "ceilings") it modifies "sheet" and thus must be used in its singular form.

Select 3 correct answer is Choice (B): impress even the most experienced tourist accustomed to many unique sights.

Choice (B) is the best option because it avoids the use of the intensifier "very," as seen in options (A), (C), and (D), as well as the repetitive "also" (made so by following the transition "In addition") in options (A) and (C). We want to avoid using "very" to modify "unique" because in the passage's context, "unique" means "one of a kind." Used this way, a thing is either unique or it is not. ("Unique" in a sense not used in this passage can also mean "peculiar," in which case the modifying qualifier "very" would be fitting.)

PRACTICE TEST 1

Mathematical Reasoning

(Part 1: Non-Calculator)

5 questions
10 minutes*

You may not use a calculator on this section.

---

*Test-takers are advised to pace themselves by spending no more than 10 to 12 minutes on the non-calculator portion of the Mathematical Reasoning test so they can move on to the calculator-active portion.

Mathematics Formula Sheet

Area

parallelogram: $A = bh$

trapezoid: $\dfrac{1}{2}h(b_1 + b_2)$

Surface Area and Volume

rectangular/right prism: $SA = ph + 2B$ $\qquad V = Bh$

cylinder: $SA = 2\pi rh + 2\pi r^2$ $\qquad V = \pi r^2 h$

pyramid: $SA = \dfrac{1}{2}ps + B$ $\qquad V = \dfrac{1}{3}Bh$

cone: $SA = \pi rs + \pi r^2$ $\qquad V = \dfrac{1}{3}\pi r^2 h$

sphere: $SA = 4\pi r^2$ $\qquad V = \dfrac{4}{3}\pi r^3$

(p = perimeter of base B; $\pi \approx 3.14$)

Algebra

slope of a line: $m = \dfrac{y_2 - y_1}{x_2 - x_1}$

slope-intercept form of the equation of a line: $y = mx + b$

point-slope form of the equation of a line: $y - y_1 = m(x - x_1)$

standard form of a quadratic equation: $y = ax^2 + bx + c$

quadratic formula: $y = \dfrac{-b \pm \sqrt{b^2 - 4ac}}{2a}$

Pythagorean Theorem: $a^2 + b^2 = c^2$

simple interest: $I = prt$

(I = interest, p = principal, r = rate, t = time)

Practice Test 1: Mathematical Reasoning (Part 1)

1. A rope, 8 feet 6 inches long, is divided into six equal lengths. If there is no waste, what is the measure of each length?

    A. 11 inches

    B. 1 foot 2 inches

    C. 1 foot 5 inches

    D. 1 foot 8 inches

2. A number divided by 6 is two less than the number. What is the number?

    A. 2.4

    B. 2.6

    C. 4

    D. 4.2

3. A pair of running shoes sells for $80.00. After one week, the vendor reduced the cost of the shoes by 20%. After two weeks, he raised the current price by 20%. What is the cost of the running shoes after two weeks?

    A. $88.48

    B. $80.00

    C. $78.00

    D. $76.80

Questions 4 and 5 refer to the graph below.

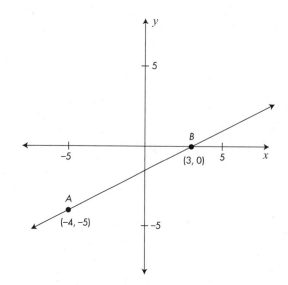

4. What is the slope of $\overleftrightarrow{AB}$?

    A. $-\dfrac{5}{7}$

    B. $\dfrac{7}{5}$

    C. $\dfrac{5}{7}$

    D. $-\dfrac{7}{5}$

5. Which of the following points lies on $\overleftrightarrow{AB}$?

    A. $\dfrac{11}{7}, \dfrac{2}{7}$

    B. $3, \dfrac{2}{7}$

    C. $7, \dfrac{20}{7}$

    D. $(-6, 6)$

PRACTICE TEST 1 (cont'd)

Mathematical Reasoning

(Part 2: Calculator)

41 questions
105 minutes*

You may use a calculator on this section.

---

*Timing is based on the total available time of 115 minutes for the Mathematical Reasoning test. Test-takers are advised to spend no more than 10 to 12 minutes on the non-calculator portion so they can invest more time on the more complex questions that show up in the calculator-active section that follows.

6. A rectangle has a width measuring 3 inches and an area that measures 85.5 in². What is the perimeter of the rectangle? Place your answer in the box below.

```
[                              ]
```

7. An expression is shown.

$$\sqrt{18} \cdot \sqrt{10}$$

Simplify the expression completely. Leave your answer in radical form.

   A. $5\sqrt{6}$

   B. $6\sqrt{5}$

   C. $18\sqrt{10}$

   D. $10\sqrt{18}$

8. The sum of three consecutive odd integers is 111. What is the second of the three consecutive odd integers? Place your answer in the box below.

```
[                              ]
```

9.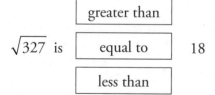

$\sqrt{327}$ is [greater than / equal to / less than] 18

10. A parallelogram has vertices located at A (3, 2), B (–3, 2) and C (1, –1). Highlight the point on the coordinate grid below at the location of the fourth vertex, D.

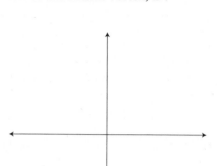

Questions 11 and 12 refer to the pie chart below.

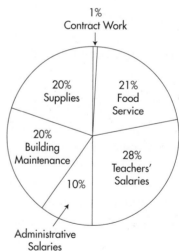

1%
Contract Work

20%
Supplies

21%
Food Service

20%
Building Maintenance

28%
Teachers' Salaries

10%

Administrative Salaries

11. The chart refers to the monthly $400,000 cost to run a local high school. What is the monthly expenditure for food service?

   A. $86,000

   B. $84,000

   C. $80,000

   D. $68,000

12. What is the measure of the central angle formed by the slice showing building maintenance in the chart? Place your answer in the box below (ignore the degree symbol).

13. A square photograph, 9 inches on a side, is surrounded by a square frame. If the frame's width is 3 inches, what is its area?

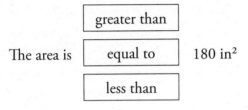

The area is [greater than / equal to / less than] 180 in²

14. What is the value of the following expression?

$$2^3 - 3(4 - 6)^3 - |-12|$$

Place a check mark next to the correct answer.

___ −20   ___ −16   ___ 12   ___ 20

15. Jamie is considering two different car rental agencies for a one-day rental. One service offers $30 per day and $0.25 per mile. The other service offers $40 per day and $0.20 per mile. At what number of miles is the cost for the two services equal?

A. 400

B. 200

C. 80

D. 20

16. A ladder leaning against a wall reaches a point 12 feet above the ground. If the bottom of the ladder is 5 feet from the wall, how long is the ladder?

A. 13 feet

B. 14 feet

C. 15 feet

D. 16 feet

17. Which of the following graphs represents the following compound inequality?

$$-2 < 2x + 4 \le 10$$

A. ━●━━━━━┼━━━━●━
　　　−3　　0　　3

B. ━━○━━━━┼━━━━○━
　　−2　　　0　　　　5

C. ━━○━━━━┼━━━●━
　　−3　　　0　　　3

D. ━━●━━━━┼━━━●━
　　−3　　　0　　　3

18. The mean of four numbers is 18. If a fifth number is added to the set, the mean increases to 22. What is the fifth number?

The fifth number is [less than / equal to / greater than] 38

19.

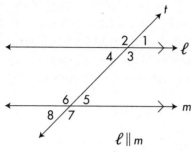

$\ell \parallel m$

$m\angle 4 = (3x - 40)°$

$m\angle 8 = (x + 30)°$

$m\angle 6 = ?$

Place your answer in the box below.

20. A sock drawer contains 3 pairs of white socks, 6 pairs of black socks, and 1 pair of blue socks. If two pairs are removed from the drawer without replacing them, what is the probability that both pairs of socks are black?

A. $\dfrac{1}{4}$

B. $\dfrac{3}{10}$

C. $\dfrac{1}{3}$

D. $\dfrac{11}{90}$

21. A truck in a movie measures 16 feet across a screen that is 36 feet long. What is the measure of the same truck, *in inches,* on a television screen that is 2 feet wide?

A. $\dfrac{8}{9}$

B. $\dfrac{9}{8}$

C. $10\dfrac{2}{3}$

D. $11\dfrac{5}{6}$

22. A trapezoid has height of 8 feet and one base that measures 16 feet. If the area of the trapezoid is 168 ft², what is the length of the other base? Place your answer in the box below.

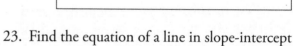

23. Find the equation of a line in slope-intercept form that is perpendicular to $y = -\dfrac{2}{3}x + \dfrac{15}{2}$ and passes through $(6, -4)$. Place your answer in the boxes below from the choices offered.

$-\dfrac{2}{3}$ $[x]$ $[-13]$

$\dfrac{3}{2}$ $[y]$ $[5]$

$y = \boxed{}\boxed{} + \boxed{}$

24. Simplify the following expression.

$$\frac{(-2x^3y^2)^3(3xy)^2}{-6xy^4}$$

   A. $x^{10}y^4$

   B. x^9y^2

   C. $12x^9y^2$

   D. $12x^{10}y^4$

25. What is the positive solution to the equation $x^2 + 2x - 6 = 0$?

   A. 3

   B. $-1 + \sqrt{7}$

   C. 2

   D. $2 + \sqrt{3}$

26. A light-year, the distance light travels in one year, is about 6×10^{12} miles (6 trillion miles). If the distance to the Andromeda Galaxy is 2,200,000 light-years, what is its distance expressed in miles? (Express your answer in scientific notation.)

   A. 13.2×10^{18}

   B. 1.32×10^{19}

   C. 0.132×10^{20}

   D. 8.2×10^{19}

27. Bamboo can grow up to 1.5 feet per day. A bamboo plant was 1.8 feet tall on day 2 and 5.1 feet on day 5. If the plant grows at the same rate, what will its height be on day 10? Place your answer in the box below.

   [   ]

28. A container of oatmeal is in the shape of a cylinder. If its diameter is 6 inches and its height is 10 inches, find its surface area after the top has been removed. Use $\pi = 3.14$ and round your answer to the nearest tenth.

   A. 602.9 inches^2

   B. 489.8 inches^2

   C. 244.9 inches^2

   D. 216.7 inches^2

29. The probability of rain for the next three days is given in the table.

	Sunday	Monday	Tuesday
Probability of rain	45%	80%	30%

Based on the data in the table, what percent is the probability that it will rain on Sunday and Monday but not Tuesday? Place your answer in the box below and ignore the percent sign.

   [   ]

30. The graph below shows the downloads of a popular song over a six-week period. What was the number of downloads during the fifth week?

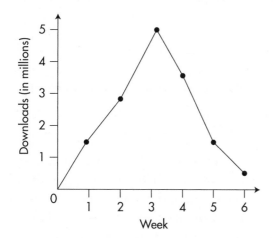

A. 4,500,000

B. 2,000,000

C. 1,500,000

D. 1,000,000

31. The volume of a cube is 5,359.375 cm³. What is the area of one of its faces? Place a check mark next to the correct answer.

___1,786.47 cm²   ___480.62 cm²
___306.25 cm²   ___17.5 cm²

32. Juan needs to replace one row of square tiles in his kitchen. If the tiles are 8 inches wide and the kitchen floor is 24 feet wide, how many tiles will he need? Place your answer in the box below.

33. Two six-sided dice are thrown. What is the probability that the first die will land on a prime number and the second will land on a number greater than 4?

A. $\dfrac{5}{6}$

B. $\dfrac{1}{2}$

C. $\dfrac{1}{3}$

D. $\dfrac{1}{6}$

Questions 34 and 35 refer to the graph below.

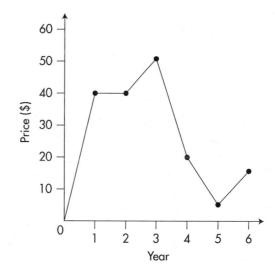

34. What was the largest percent drop in stock price from one year to another?

Percent drop is
less than
equal to	15
greater than

35. What was the greatest decrease in stock price in the graph? Place your answer in the box below.

[ ]

Questions 36 and 37 refer to the information below.

A business measures its profit by using the following profit function:

$$P(x) = 11,000x - 6750$$

"x" is the number of units the company sells in a three-month period.

36. If the company sold 1,740 units in a three-month period, what was its profit?

    A. $19,140,000

    B. $19,133,250

    C. $18,242,360

    D. $1,913,325

37. If the company's profit over a three-month period was $9,321,250, how many units did it sell?

    A. 848

    B. 849

    C. 851

    D. 904

38. What is the area of the right triangle below?

Place your answer in the box below.

[ ]

39. A bicycle tire with a 28-inch diameter makes 6 revolutions. How many inches did the tire travel. Round your answer to the nearest tenth of an inch. ($\pi = 3.14$.) Place a check mark next to the correct answer.

    ___432.6   ___   527.5
    ___3,692.6   ___14,770.6

40. Which of the following points lies on the parabola $y = -1.5x^2 + 6.5x - 9$?

    A. $(-5, -79)$

    B. $(2, 2)$

    C. $(4, 7)$

    D. $(-7, -102)$

41. The following chart represents the scores of students on a French quiz.

		X	X	
		X	X	
X		X	X	
X	X	X	X	X
20%	40%	60%	80%	100%

Place an "X" in the column for the quiz grade that another student must earn to make the mean score for the class equal to 60%.

42. In $\triangle ABC$, $\overline{AC} = 9$, $\overline{AB} = 6$, and $\overline{BC} = 4$. From greatest to least, what is the correct order of the measures of the angles?

    A. $\angle B > \angle A > \angle C$

    B. $\angle C > \angle A > \angle B$

    C. $\angle A > \angle B > \angle C$

    D. $\angle B > \angle C > \angle A$

43. If $2^{4x} = 64$, then what is the value of x?

    A. 1

    B. 1.5

    C. 2.5

    D. 6

44. What is the quotient of $x^2 - 5x + 6$ and $x^2 - 9$?

    A. $x + 3$

    B. $x - 3$

    C. $x - 2$

    D. $\dfrac{x - 2}{x + 3}$

45. The following price sheet indicates the cost of purchasing bottled water.

Quantity	Price
24-pack	$9.95
12-pack	$5.95
Individual Bottle	$1.15

What is the lowest price available for 39 bottles of water?

The cost is   [less than]   [equal to]   [greater than] $19.35

46. The chart below represents the hourly pay rates of X-ray technicians at a certain hospital.

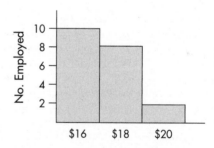

Pay Rate per Hour

What is the median hourly pay of the X-ray technicians?

    A. $16

    B. $17

    C. $18.50

    D. $19.25

1. **C.**

   Convert 8 feet 6 inches into inches and divide by 6.

   $$(8 \times 12) + 6 = 102 \text{ inches}$$

   $$102 \div 6 = 17 \text{ inches}$$

   $$17 \text{ inches} = 1 \text{ foot } 5 \text{ inches}$$

2. **A.**

   Let x = the number

   $$\frac{x}{6} + 2 = x$$

   $$(6) \, \frac{x}{6} + 2 = x \, (6)$$

   $$12 + x = 6x$$

   $$12 = 5x$$

   $$2.4 = x$$

3. **D.**

   Find the cost of the shoes after one week:

   $$\$80.00 - (.20)(\$80.00) = \$64.00$$

   Add 20% to $64.00 to find the cost after two weeks.

   $$\$64.00 + (.20)(\$64.00) = \$76.80$$

4. **C.**

   Use the slope formula, $m = \dfrac{y_2 - y_1}{x_2 - x_1}$, to calculate the slope.

   $$\frac{0 - (-5)}{3 - (-4)} = \frac{5}{7}$$

5. **C.**

   Find the equation of $\overleftrightarrow{AB}$ in slope-intercept form.

   1) Find the slope.

   $$m = \frac{y_2 - y_1}{x_2 - x_1} = \frac{0 - (-5)}{3 - (-4)} = \frac{5}{7}$$

   2) Substitute the coordinates of one of the points for x and y. (3,0)

   $$0 = \frac{5}{7}(3) + b$$

   $$0 = \frac{15}{7} + b$$

   $$-\frac{15}{7} = b$$

   The equation for $\overleftrightarrow{AB}$ is $y = \dfrac{5}{7}x - \dfrac{15}{7}$.

   Substitute $7, \dfrac{20}{7}$ for x and y.

   $$-\frac{20}{7} = \frac{5}{7}(7) - \frac{15}{7}$$

   $$\frac{20}{7} = \frac{20}{7} \checkmark$$

6. **63**

   The perimeter of the rectangle is found by using the formula $P = 2l + 2w$ where l and w are the length and width, respectively. Find the length by placing 3 and 85.5 in the formula for the area of a rectangle.

   $$A = l \times w$$

   $$85.5 = (l)(3)$$

   $$28.5 = l$$

   $$P = 2(28.5) + 2(3) = 63$$

7. **B.**

Multiply the two radicals.

$$\sqrt{18} \cdot \sqrt{10} = \sqrt{180}$$

Find the prime factorization of 180.

$$\sqrt{180} = \sqrt{2 \times 2 \times 3 \times 3 \times 5}$$

$$= \sqrt{2^2 \times 3^2 \times 5}$$

Extract the perfect squares from under the radical.

$$\sqrt{2^2}\sqrt{3^2}\sqrt{5} = (2)(3)\sqrt{5} = 6\sqrt{5}$$

8. **37**

Let x = the smallest odd integer

$x + 2$ = second odd integer

$x + 4$ = third odd integer

$x + x + 2 + x + 4 = 111$

$3x + 6 = 111$

$3x = 105$

$x = 35$

The middle integer is $x + 2$.

$35 + 2 = 37$

Although the numbers were consecutive odd integers, we add 2 to each to get to the next one. For example, the next odd integer after 9 is $9 + 2 = 11$.

9. $\sqrt{327}$ is greater than 18. Since $\sqrt{324} = 18$, then $\sqrt{327}$ is greater than 18.

10. The fourth vertex is located at (–5, –1).

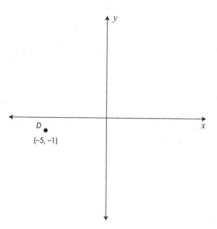

The opposite sides of a parallelogram are parallel and equal in measure. Measure the length of side *AB*; its length is 6 units. Thus the length of *CD* must also be 6 units. Count 6 units to the left of (1, –1) to arrive at (–5, 1).

11. **B.**

Find 21% of $400,000 by multiplying $400,000 by 0.21.

$$\$400,000 \times 0.21 = \$84,000$$

12. **72**

A circle measures 360°. Given that building and maintenance costs represent 20% of all costs, find 20% of 360.

$$360 \times 0.20 = 72$$

13. The area is less than 180 in²

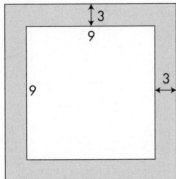

Find the area of the larger square and subtract the area of the smaller square.

$$15 \times 15 = 225$$

$$9 \times 9 = 81$$

$$225 - 81 = 144 \text{ in}^2$$

14. ___ −20   ___ −16   ___ 12   _✓_ 20

Use the order of operations to simplify the expression.

Parentheses:

$$2^3 - 3(4 - 6)^3 - |{-12}| = 2^3 - 3(-2)^3 - |{-12}|$$

Exponents:

$$2^3 - 3(-2)^3 - |{-12}| = 8 - 3(-8) - |{-12}|$$

Multiplication/Division:

$$8 - 3(-8) - |{-12}| = 8 - (-24) - |{-12}|$$

Addition/Subtraction:

$$8 - (-24) - |{-12}| = 8 + 24 - 12 = 20$$

15. **B.**

Let x = the number of miles for the two rental costs to be equal.

$$40 + 0.20x = 30 + 0.25x$$

$$40 + 0.20x - 0.20x = 30 + 0.25x - 0.20x$$

$$40 = 30 + 0.05x$$

$$10 = 0.05x$$

$$200 = x$$

16. **A.**

The ladder, the wall, and the ground form a right triangle.

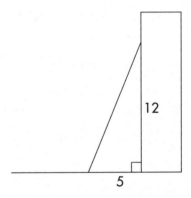

Use the Pythagorean Theorem to find the length of the ladder.

$$5^2 + 12^2 = c^2$$

$$25 + 144 = c^2$$

$$169 = c^2$$

$$\sqrt{169} = \sqrt{c^2}$$

$$13 = c$$

The length of the ladder is 13 feet. 5-12-13 is an example of a Pythagorean triple.

17. C.

Solve the compound inequality as two separate inequalities.

$$-2 < 2x + 4 \le 10$$

$$-2 < 2x + 4 \quad \text{and} \quad 2x + 4 \le 10$$

$$-6 < 2x \quad \text{and} \quad 2x \le 6$$

$$-3 < x \quad \text{and} \quad x \le 3$$

$$-3 < x \le 3$$

Choose a number, such as 0, to test the inequality.

$$-3 < 0 \le 3? \text{ yes}$$

Thus, the graph will be the area of the line between −3 and 3. Remember, −3 is not part of the graph, so we put an open circle at −3. 3 *is* part of the graph, so we darken the circle at 3.

18. The fifth number is equal to 38.

If four numbers have an average of 18, their sum is 72 because 4 × 18 = 72. If five numbers have an average of 22, their sum must be 110 because 5 × 22 = 110. Subtract 72 from 110 to find the fifth number.

$$110 - 72 = 38$$

19. 115

The measures of ∠4 and ∠8 are congruent because corresponding angles are equal when lines are parallel. Set their values equal and solve for *x*.

$$3x - 40 = x + 30$$

$$2x - 40 = 30$$

$$2x = 70$$

$$x = 35$$

$$m\angle 8 = 35 + 30 = 65°$$

∠6 and ∠8 are supplementary angles. Subtract 65 from 180 to find the measure of ∠6.

$$180 - 65 = 115$$

20. C.

Of the 10 pairs of sock in the drawer, 6 are black. Thus, the probability of removing a black pair of socks on the first draw is $\frac{6}{10}$. With one pair of black socks removed, 5 of the remaining 9 pairs of socks are black $\frac{5}{9}$. In order for two events to occur in succession, multiply the probability of each event.

$$\frac{6}{10} \times \frac{5}{9} = \frac{30}{90} = \frac{1}{3}$$

21. C.

Use the proportion $\dfrac{\text{truck length}}{\text{screen length}} = \dfrac{\text{truck length}}{\text{screen length}}$ to find the length of the truck on the television screen.

$$\frac{16}{36} = \frac{x}{2}$$

$$36x = 32$$

$$x = \frac{8}{9}$$

The truck will measure $\frac{8}{9}$ of a foot on the television screen. Since the question requires the answer to be expressed in inches, convert $\frac{8}{9}$ foot into inches.

$$\frac{8}{9} \times 12 = 10\frac{2}{3}$$

22. **26 feet**

The area of a trapezoid is found by using the formula

$$A = \frac{1}{2}(h)(b_1 + b_2)$$

Input the known data to calculate the length of the unknown base.

$$168 = \frac{1}{2}(8)(16 + b_2)$$

$$168 = 4(16 + b_2)$$

$$168 = 64 + 4b_2$$

$$26 = b_2$$

23. $y = \frac{3}{2}[x] + [-13]$

The slopes of perpendicular lines are the opposite reciprocals of one another. The slope in the equation $y = -\frac{2}{3}x + \frac{15}{2}$ is $-\frac{2}{3}$, so the slope of a line that is perpendicular is $\frac{3}{2}$. Substitute 6 and -4 for x and y, respectively, to find the y-intercept.

$$y = \frac{3}{2}x + b$$

$$-4 = \frac{3}{2}(6) + b$$

$$-4 = 9 + b$$

$$-13 = b$$

$$y = \frac{3}{2}x + -13$$

24. **D.**

When raising one exponent to another, multiply the exponents. Remember, the coefficients are also raised to the exponent outside the parentheses.

$$\frac{(-2x^3 y^2)^3 (3xy)^2}{-6xy^4} = \frac{(-8x^9 y6)(9x^2 y^2)}{-6xy^4}$$

When multiplying like terms, add the exponents.

$$\frac{(-8x^9 y6)(9x^2 y^2)}{-6xy^4} = \frac{-72x^{11} y^8}{-6xy^4}$$

When dividing like terms, subtract the exponents.

$$\frac{-72x^{11} y^8}{-6xy^4} = 12x^{10} y^4$$

25. **B.**

There are no factors of -6 with sum of 2, so this equation cannot be factored. Use the quadratic formula to calculate the positive solution to $x^2 + 2x - 6 = 0$.

$$x = \frac{-b \pm \sqrt{b^2 - 4ac}}{2a}$$

$$a = 1, b = 2, c = -6$$

$$\frac{-2 \pm \sqrt{(2)^2 - 4(1)(-6)}}{2(1)} =$$

$$\frac{-2 \pm \sqrt{28}}{2} = \frac{-2 \pm 2\sqrt{7}}{2} =$$

$$-1 + \sqrt{7}; \ -1 - \sqrt{7}$$

$$x = -1 + \sqrt{7} \approx 1.65$$

$$x = -1 - \sqrt{7} \approx -3.65$$

$x = -1 + \sqrt{7}$ is the positive root of $x^2 + 2x - 6 = 0$

26. B.

Convert the light-years to the Andromeda Galaxy into scientific notation.

$$2{,}200{,}000 = 2.2 \times 10^6$$

Next, multiply the number of miles in a light-year by 2.2×10^6 to find the number of miles to the Andromeda Galaxy.

$$2.2 \times 10^6 \times 6 \times 10^{12} =$$
$$13.2 \times 10^{12+6} =$$
$$13.2 \times 10^{18}$$

An answer expressed in scientific notation is the product of a number greater than or equal to 1 and less than 10 ($1 \le x < 10$) and 10 to some exponent. Change 13.2×10^{18} into scientific notation by moving the decimal point one place to the left and adding an additional power of 10.

$$13.2 \times 10^{18} = 1.32 \times 10^{19}$$

27. 10.6

This problem requires solving by using a linear equation. Solve the problem by using the slope formula:

$$m = \frac{y_2 - y_1}{x_2 - x_1}$$

(Day, Height): (2, 1.8) (5, 5.1)

$$\frac{5.1 - 1.8}{5 - 2} = 1.1$$

The slope of the line is 1.1. Input 1.1 for m in the formula $y = mx + b$ and substitute either data point for x and y.

$$y = 1.1x + b$$
$$1.8 = 1.1(2) + b$$
$$-0.4 = b$$
$$y = 1.1x - 0.4$$

Substitute 10 for x to find the plant's height on day 10.

$$y = 1.1(10) - 0.4 = 10.6$$

The plant will measure 10.6 feet on day 10.

28. D.

The formula for the surface area of a cylinder is $SA = 2\pi rh + 2\pi r^2$ with r representing the radius of the cylinder and h representing its height. Since the top, which is a circle, is removed, the formula becomes $SA = 2\pi rh + \pi r^2$. Input the known values for radius and height. Remember to divide the diameter, 6, by 2 to find the radius.

$$SA = 2(3.14)(3)(10) + (3.14)(3)^2$$
$$= 216.7 \text{ inches}^2.$$

Selection C fails to subtract the area of the top from the entire surface area of the cylinder. Selections A and B use the diameter, rather than the radius, in the calculation.

29. 25.2

Solving this problem requires knowledge of compound probability. Begin by converting each percentage into a decimal. Since we want to know the probability of no rain on Tuesday, subtract 30% from 100%.

$$100\% - 30\% = 70\%$$

Next, convert each percentage into a decimal:

$$45\% = 0.45$$
$$80\% = 0.80$$
$$70\% = 0.70$$

To find the probability of rain on Sunday and Monday but not Tuesday, multiply the three probabilities together.

$$(0.45)(0.80)(0.70) = 0.252$$

Finally, convert the decimal into a percent.

$$0.252 = 25.2\%$$

30. **C.**

The *x*-axis in the graph represents time measured in weeks while the *y*-axis represents the number of downloads measured in millions. At week 5, the sales volume is midway between 1,000,000 and 2,000,000. Thus, the number of downloads during the fifth week was 1,500,000.

31. ___ 1,786.47 cm²   ___ 480.62 cm²
    ✓ 306.25 cm²   ___ 17.5 cm²

The formula for the volume of a cube is *volume = edge³* ($V = e^3$). Find the length of an edge by finding the cube root of 5,359.375.

$$\sqrt[3]{5{,}359.375} = 17.5$$

Find the area of a square face by using the formula area = side² in which a side is 17.5.

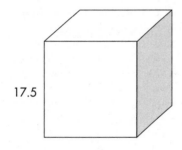

17.5

Area = 17.5² = 306.25

32. **36**

Convert the width of the kitchen into inches.

$$24 \times 12 = 288$$

Divide 288 by 8 to find the number of tiles Juan needs.

$$288 \div 8 = 36$$

33. **D.**

Find the probability of each event and then multiply the two probabilities.

$$\frac{\text{prime numbers}}{\text{all numbers}} = \frac{2, 3, 5}{1, 2, 3, 4, 5, 6} = \frac{1}{2}$$

Remember, 1 is not a prime number.

$$\frac{\text{numbers} > 4}{\text{all numbers}} = \frac{5, 6}{1, 2, 3, 4, 5, 6} = \frac{1}{3}$$

$$\frac{1}{2} \times \frac{1}{3} = \frac{1}{6}$$

34. The greatest percent drop is greater than 15. The greatest drop, as a percentage, occurred between years 4 and 5.

Year 4: $20

Year 5: $5

Use the formula $\dfrac{\text{decrease}}{\text{original}} = \dfrac{n}{100}$ to find the percent decrease.

$$\frac{15}{20} = \frac{n}{100}$$

$$20n = 1{,}500$$

$$n = 75\%$$

35. **$30**

In year 3, the stock price was $50. In year 4, the stock price decreased to $20.

$$50 - 20 = 30$$

36. **B.**

Replace *x* with 1,740, the number of units sold in a three-month period.

$$P(1{,}740) = 11{,}000(1{,}740) - 6{,}750$$
$$= \$19{,}133{,}250$$

37. A.

Replace $P(x)$ with $9,321,250$, the company's profit.

$$9,321,250 = 11,000x - 6,750$$
$$9,328,000 = 11,000x$$
$$848 = x$$

38. 720 units²

Use the Pythagorean Theorem to calculate the length of the base.

$$a^2 + b^2 = c^2$$
$$18^2 + b^2 = 82^2$$
$$324 + b^2 = 6,724$$
$$b^2 = 6,400$$
$$b = 80$$

Use the formula for the area of a triangle to calculate the area.

$$A = \frac{1}{2}(\text{base})(\text{height})$$

$$A = \frac{1}{2}(80)(18) = 720 \text{ units}$$

39. ___432.6   ✓527.5
___3,692.6   ___14,770.6

The revolution of a tire is the same as its circumference. Find the circumference of the tire and multiply that number by 6.

Circumference = $\pi \times$ diameter

$$6 \times 3.14 \times 28 = 527.5$$

40. A.

Any point that lies on the parabola must satisfy its equation. Substitute -5 for x and -79 for y and verify that it satisfies the equation.

$$-79 = -1.5(-5)^2 + 6.5(-5) - 9$$
$$-79 = -1.5(25) - 32.5 - 9$$
$$-79 = -79 \quad ✓$$

41. 40%

		X	X	
		X	X	
X	**X**	X	X	
X	X	X	X	X
20%	40%	60%	80%	100%

An "x" has been placed at 40%.

Add the scores of all twelve of the students.

$$(2 \times 20) + (1 \times 40) + (4 \times 60) +$$
$$(4 \times 80) + (1 \times 100) = 740$$

In order for 13 students to average 60%, the class must amass 780 points because $13 \times 60 = 780$.

Since the first 12 students accumulated 740 points, then the thirteenth student must score a 40% on his/her test because $780 - 740 = 40$.

42. D.

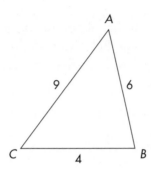

The largest angle in a triangle is opposite the longest side. Similarly, the middle and smallest angles are opposite the middle and smallest sides. In $\triangle ABC$, $AC > AB > BC$; therefore $\angle B > \angle C > \angle A$.

43. B.

$64 = 2^6$, so $2^{4x} = 2^6$. With the bases being equal we get:

$$4x = 6$$

$$x = 1.5$$

44. D.

Factor $x^2 - 5x + 6$ and $x^2 - 9$ and cancel any equal quantities in the numerator and the denominator.

$$\frac{x^2 - 5x + 6}{x^2 - 9} = \frac{(x-2)\,\cancel{(x-3)}}{(x+3)\,\cancel{(x-3)}} = \frac{x-2}{x+3}$$

45. Equal to $19.35

Calculate the cost per bottle of a 24-pack and a 12-pack.

$$\$9.95 \div 24 \approx \$.41 \text{ per bottle}$$

$$\$5.95 \div 12 \approx \$.50 \text{ per bottle}$$

Minimize the cost by purchasing one 24-pack, one 12-pack and three individual bottles.

$$\$9.95 + \$5.95 + (3 \times \$1.15) = \$19.35$$

46. B.

Array the data from least to greatest.

16 16 16 16 16 16 16 16 16 16 18 18 18 18 18 18 18 18 18 20 20

The median is the value in the middle. In this chart, 16 and 18 are located in the middle so find their mean.

$$\frac{16 + 18}{2} = \frac{34}{2} = 17$$

PRACTICE TEST 1

SCIENCE

50 questions
90 minutes

1. The process that releases energy for use by the cell is known as

   A. photosynthesis.

   B. aerobic metabolism.

   C. anaerobic metabolism.

   D. cellular respiration.

2. In hamsters, the gene for short hair (H) is dominant to the gene for long hair (h). Which is the most likely genotype of the parents if 4 of their 8 offspring have long hair?

   A. $Hh \times hh$

   B. $Hh \times Hh$

   C. $HH \times hh$

   D. $hh \times hh$

3. The change of state from liquid to solid or solid to liquid involves a phase where the temperature remains constant. This phase is known as the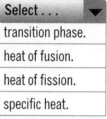

4. Which of the following is NOT a step in the carbon cycle?

   A. Carbon is taken in by plants and used to form carbohydrates through photosynthesis.

   B. Carbon is dissolved out of the air into ocean water, combined with calcium to form calcium carbonate, used by mollusks to form their shells.

   C. Carbon is taken in by animal respiration and used to form carbohydrates.

   D. Detritus feeders return carbon to elemental form.

5. In the following unbalanced reaction, once the reaction is balanced, how many moles of hydrogen ions are needed to react with each mole of aluminum hydroxide?

$$Al(OH)_3 + H^+ \rightarrow Al^{3+} + H_2O$$

    A. 1

    B. 2

    C. 3

    D. 4

6. Which of the following is a limiting factor that is density-independent?

    A. an outbreak of disease

    B. a forest fire caused by lightning

    C. immigration of new predators

    D. competition for scarce resources

7. If the Earth completely shades the Moon as seen by an earthbound observer, there is a

    A. total solar eclipse.

    B. total lunar eclipse.

    C. partial lunar eclipse.

    D. partial solar eclipse.

8. A certain enzyme oxidizes ethanol. If a genetic defect prevents the enzyme from being produced, which outcome do you predict would occur?

    A. Ethanol would undergo reduction, which is the opposite process of oxidation.

    B. The oxidation of ethanol would proceed only in certain locations in the cell.

    C. The cell would employ a different enzyme to oxidize ethanol.

    D. The oxidation of ethanol in the cell would happen very slowly or not at all.

Questions 9–12 consist of four lettered terms followed by a list of numbered phrases. For each numbered phrase, select the one term that is most closely related to it. Each term may be used once, more than once, or not at all. Write your letter choice for each at the end of the corresponding description.

    (A) Secretory Vesicle

    (B) Smooth Endoplasmic Reticulum

    (C) Microvilli

    (D) Nucleolus

9. extensions that provide extra surface area for absorption

10. contain digestive enzymes

11. packets that carry substances (hormones, fats, etc.) synthesized within the cell

12. network of membranes that deliver lipids and proteins throughout the cytoplasm

13. Which of the following is a key difference between mitosis and meiosis?

    A. Mitosis allows for genetic variation, while meiosis results in generations of organisms with stable characteristics.

    B. Mitosis produces offspring more slowly, while meiosis has the advantage of producing offspring more quickly and easily.

    C. Mitosis produces cells that are almost identical genetically, while meiosis produces cells that differ genetically from each parent or from each other.

    D. Mitosis has two cell divisions, while meiosis has only one.

14. Which of the following BEST describes osmosis?

    A. the movement of water molecules out of a cell, resulting in cell shrinkage

    B. the movement of small, uncharged molecules across the lipid bilayer to a state of equilibrium

    C. the movement of charged molecules and larger molecules into and out of the cell

    D. the movement of water molecules across the selectively permeable plasma membrane

15. GAPDH is an enzyme that serves as a catalyst for the sixth step in glycolysis, which is a vital part of cellular respiration. The chart below shows the percentage of similarity between the GAPDH gene in humans and some other species.

Species	Percentage Similarity to Humans for the GAPDH Gene
Chimpanzee	99.6%
Dog	91.3%
Fruit Fly	72.4%
Roundworm	68.2%

Which of the following conclusions might be drawn from this chart?

A. Humans evolved directly from the chimpanzee.

B. The fruit fly and roundworm are not genetically related to humans.

C. Of the species shown, the roundworm has the closest evolutionary relationship to humans.

D. Of the species shown, the chimpanzee has the closest evolutionary relationship to humans.

Use the following terms to answer questions 16–19. Write the letter next to the corresponding line of text.

A. Water Cycle

B. Carbon Cycle

C. Phosphorous Cycle

D. Nitrogen Cycle

16. Interaction with lightning provides energy for a component in this cycle to become available.

17. Pathways in this cycle include living cells, the atmosphere, oceans, rocks, and fossil fuels.

18. The main pathways include condensation, evaporation, transpiration, and precipitation.

19. This cycle includes only solid and dissolved forms, no gases.

20. In their early stage of life, insects such as mosquitoes and flies exist as aquatic larvae. Huge numbers of mosquitoes and flies swarm in the Arctic tundra during the summer. Which of the following BEST explains this?

    A. Pools of water from melting permafrost in the summer make excellent breeding grounds for the insects.

    B. Adult mosquitoes and flies lay thousands of eggs beneath the ice of frozen lakes.

    C. Intense cold eliminates all predatory organisms even in the Arctic summer.

    D. Frequent rain in the Arctic summer replenishes ponds and lakes that went dry during the fall and winter.

Read the following passage and use it to answer questions 21–22.

Builders of a new housing community were asked to do an ecological study of the land features before laying out the housing plans to ensure that local wildlife would be able to continue to thrive in the nearby ponds and waterways. A simplified version of the major species found in one of the ponds is shown in the food web below.

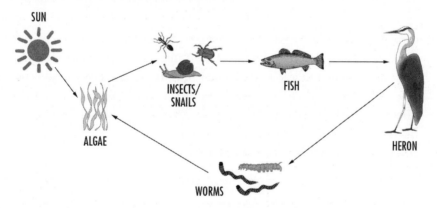

The pond ecosystem was deemed to be healthy as it was, so the building plan included the following features:

1. Leave space between the houses and the pond and to build a running trail around the pond at a distance that would not disturb the nests of birds or other wildlife.

2. No boating or swimming would be allowed in the pond.

3. Install a dock where community members could fish.

21. Place the following terms in the pyramid diagram to show the members of the food web as they would be designated in a food pyramid.

Food Pyramid

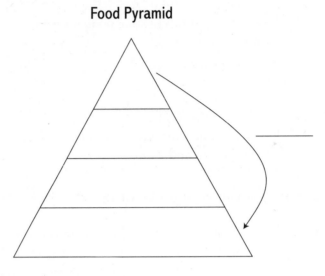

ALGAE   FISH   HERON   INSECTS/SNAILS   WORMS

22. One year after the pond recreation area became active, runners and picnickers in the area began complaining of an increased number of mosquitoes and insects in the area. They also noticed that the herons that once frequented the pond ecosystem had stopped coming around. There was even less of the green algae covering the pond than there once was. Considering the three policies of the planning board, which one was most likely to have influenced a change in this ecosystem, and how? Explain how the change could have impacted the food pyramid as a whole.

_____

_____

_____

_____

_____

_____

_____

_____

23. Look at the illustration below.

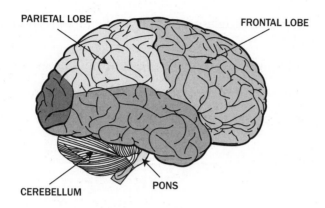

The part of the brain where reasoning, planning, speech, movement, emotions, and problem solving occurs is the

    A. parietal lobe.

    B. frontal lobe.

    C. cerebellum.

    D. pons.

24. What type of wave is a sound wave?

    A. compression

    B. transverse

    C. inverse

    D. converse

25. A small non-protein molecule such as iron that works with enzymes to promote catalysis is known as

    A. a protein.

    B. an inorganic cofactor.

    C. a coenzyme.

    D. a hormone.

26. The BEST way for a geologist to determine when an igneous rock formed (i.e., its age) is by

    A. comparing the amounts of decayed and undecayed radioactive isotopes in the rock.

    B. examining its relative placement in an outcropping of rocks.

    C. examining the environment where the rock is found.

    D. comparing the sizes of crystals found in the upper and lower portions of the rock.

27. Look at the diagram of an animal cell.

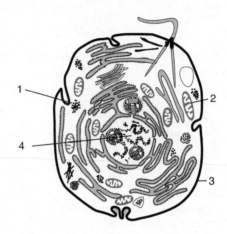

    In which part of the cell does aerobic respiration take place?

    A. 1

    B. 2

    C. 3

    D. 4

28. Which of the following is TRUE concerning Einstein's theory of relativity?

    A. As energy increases, the speed of light increases and mass is constant.

    B. As energy increases, mass increases and the speed of light is constant.

    C. As energy increases, the speed of light decreases and mass is constant.

    D. As energy increases, mass decreases and the speed of light is constant.

29. Crossing over is a process that occurs during meiosis. Which of the following BEST describes why this results in increased genetic diversity?

    A. During prophase I, homologous chromosomes pair up and exchange DNA segments, causing different combinations of alleles.

    B. During prophase I, there is independent assortment of homologous chromosomes, creating a variety of genetic outcomes.

    C. During prophase II, each pair of chromatids lines up in the middle of the cell, allowing for the exchange of DNA before the chromatids split and move to either side of the cell.

    D. During prophase II, fragments of DNA spontaneously separate from certain chromosomes and attach themselves to the end of other chromosomes, producing new genetic sequences.

30. A marathoner's leg muscles often feel heavy and prone to cramping after 20 or more miles. Which of the following is the BEST explanation for this?

    A. A marathoner's muscle cells cannot store glucose for use as energy.

    B. A marathoner's muscle cells contract when glucose reacts with oxygen.

    C. A marathoner's circulatory system cannot take in sufficient oxygen, and the muscle cells must switch to anaerobic respiration for energy.

    D. A marathoner's circulatory system takes in too much oxygen during a race, which causes muscle cramping.

Questions 31–35. In the year 2030, scientists on Earth send out a probe (Gnome Probe) on a trip to visit two planets in a distant solar system. It arrives back on Earth in the year 2067 carrying valuable data. Use the information in the illustration below and the data given in the questions to answer questions 31–35.

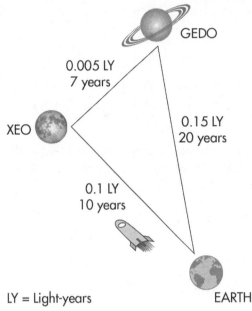

GEDO

0.005 LY
7 years

XEO

0.15 LY
20 years

0.1 LY
10 years

LY = Light-years

EARTH

For question 31, write the correct answer in the box.

31. The speed of the Gnome Probe for the trip from Earth to XEO to GEDO and back to Earth is [   ].

32. Which of the following is TRUE regarding the portion of the trip from GEDO to Earth?

    A. The probe decelerated for this portion compared to the average velocity of the trip from Earth to GEDO.

    B. The probe traveled at the same rate for this portion of the trip compared to the average velocity of the trip from Earth to GEDO.

    C. The probe accelerated for this portion of the trip compared to the average velocity of the trip from Earth to GEDO.

    D. The probe accelerated for a portion of the trip so the average was the same as the average velocity of the trip from XEO to GEDO.

33. One data table from the Gnome Probe showed the following for the trip:

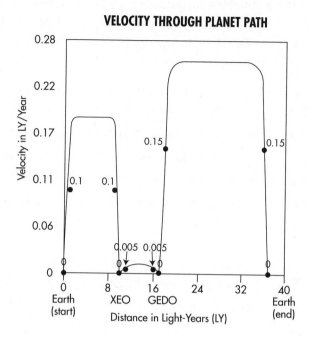

VELOCITY THROUGH PLANET PATH

Which of the following is NOT a correct analysis of the data on this graph?

A. As the Gnome Probe left the gravitational field of each planet, it accelerated quickly to near the sustained flight velocity for the majority of the trip between planets.

B. The average velocity for each segment is represented by the nearly straight bar at the top of the curves.

C. There was an anomaly between XEO and GEDO that kept the Gnome Probe from reaching its normal flight velocity (possibly a high gravity field from asteroids, etc.).

D. Time in years is not directly shown on this graph, but is figured into the velocity, which represents distance/time.

34. The Gnome Probe collected a video in flight of two asteroids colliding. According to the video, and the accompanying data, Asteroid Alpha, with a mass of 750 kg and traveling at a velocity of 20 km/sec, struck Asteroid Omega head on. Asteroid Omega had a mass of 500 kg and was traveling at 25 km/sec. Which of the following would NOT be true about the collision?

    A. Both asteroids had momentum coming into the crash, which results in energy that would be transferred to the other asteroid on impact.

    B. The asteroids had no inertia as they crashed since the impact occurred in space.

    C. Since energy cannot be created or destroyed, the energy at impact from inertia and momentum would cause an explosion of shattering pieces of asteroid.

    D. As the impact occurred, the smaller pieces of asteroid were propelled into their own asteroid orbits.

35. The Gnome Probe was built for speed and durability and has a mass of 4500 kg. The mass of XEO is 1.5 times the mass of Earth, while the mass of GEDO is 0.9 times the mass of Earth. What was the mass of the Gnome Probe when it landed on GEDO?

    A. 4050 kg

    B. 6750 kg

    C. Approaching 0 kg

    D. 4500 kg

36. **Scurvy** is a disease caused by a lack of Vitamin C, which leaves the body unable to build enough collagen (a major component of connective tissue). The most plausible explanation for this malfunction is that vitamin C | Select . . . ▼ |

Select . . .
A. is an amino acid component of collagen.
B. is a coenzyme required in the synthesis of collagen.
C. destroys collagen.
D. is produced by collagen.

37. Which of the following BEST explains why carbohydrates are excellent molecules for storing energy?

   A. Carbohydrates consist of three elements—carbon, hydrogen, and oxygen.

   B. Carbohydrates consist of long chains of monomers.

   C. Carbohydrates contain many carbon-hydrogen bonds.

   D. Sugars tend to function as the building blocks for larger molecules.

38. Which of the following will NOT inhibit enzymatic reactions?

   A. temperature

   B. pH level

   C. particular chemical agents

   D. lack of substrate

39. Ocean currents are influenced by all of the following EXCEPT

   A. plankton concentration.

   B. temperature gradients.

   C. salinity.

   D. depth.

40. Scientists have found that a mutation that disrupts a single protein they call Sonic Hedge Hog (SHH) is responsible for extra digits in organisms. This mutation has been found in Ernest Hemingway's famous six-toed cats, in certain kinds of mice, and in humans with extra fingers or toes. What does this indicate about evolutionary relationships?

   A. Organisms with mutations all have similar gene patterns.

   B. Genetic patterns in humans, cats, and mice are very similar, showing that they are all closely related organisms.

   C. The mutation in the Sonic Hedge Hog gene shows that natural selection does not work for humans, cats, and mice.

   D. Over time, all humans, cats, and mice will develop extra digits due to stabilizing selection.

41. Which of the following statements about enzymes is NOT true?

   A. High temperatures destroy most enzymes.

   B. Enzymes only function within living things.

   C. An enzyme is unaffected by the reactions it catalyzes, so it can be used over and over again.

   D. Enzymes are usually very specific to certain reactions.

42. When a person hyperventilates, he or she is often given a paper bag to breathe into for relief. Which of the following explains the purpose for this?

   A. to increase the acidity of the person's blood

   B. to limit the amount of oxygen in the person's lungs

   C. to decrease the level of carbon dioxide in the person's blood

   D. to increase the level of carbon dioxide in the person's blood

43. What is the energy-generating mechanism of the stars, including the Sun?

   A. fission

   B. fusion

   C. spontaneous generation

   D. combustion

44. Which of the following uses energy to move substances across the plasma membrane and against their concentration gradient from areas of low concentration to areas of high concentration?

   A. osmosis

   B. facilitated diffusion

   C. exocytosis

   D. the sodium-potassium pump

45. The portion of the electromagnetic spectrum (EMS) that transmits thermal energy (heat) and has longer wavelengths than visible light is

    A. ultraviolet rays (UV).

    B. radio waves.

    C. white light.

    D. infrared waves (IR).

Use the following equations to answer questions 46–49. For questions 46–47, write the letter of your answer choice in the box.

(A) $12H_2O + 12NADP + 18ADP \rightarrow 6O2 + 12NADPH + 18ATP$

(B) $6CO_2 + 12NADPH + 18ATP \rightarrow C_6H_{12}O_6 + 12NADP + 18ADP + 6H_2O$

(C) $6CO_2 + 12H_2O \overset{light}{\rightarrow} C_6H_{12}O_6 + 6H_2O + 6O_2$

(D) $C_6H_{12}O_6 + 6O_2 \rightarrow 6CO_2 + H_2O + energy$

46. Which of the reactions is NOT balanced properly?

    [   ]

47. Which reaction represents cellular respiration?

    [   ]

48. Reaction equation (C) describes the overall process of photosynthesis. Which type of chemical reaction is this?

    A. replacement

    B. combination

    C. exothermic

    D. decomposition

49. What is the function of ATP (Adenosine Triphosphate), which is formed in reaction (A)?

_____

_____

_____

_____

_____

_____

50. The following graph shows the change in CO_2 levels between 1960 and 1990.

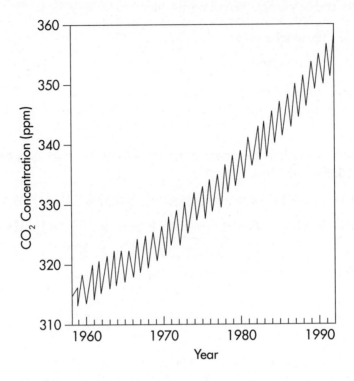

What is a plausible prediction for the cause of the increase in CO_2 concentration for this time period?

    A.   decreased UV light

    B.   increased fossil fuel usage

    C.   decreased greenhouse gas production

    D.   increased planting of replacement forests

Answers: Science Practice Test 1

1. **D.**

   Respiration is the process that releases energy for use by the cell. There are several steps involved in cellular respiration; some require oxygen (aerobic) and some do not (anaerobic). Photosynthesis is the process of harnessing the Sun's energy and storing it as energy in chemical bonds for later use as energy. Metabolism is the use of energy for cellular functions in order to sustain life.

2. **A.**

   If 4 of the 8 hamster offspring have long hair, then 4 have short hair, and the ratio of long hair to short hair is 1:1. A 1:1 ratio means that the parents are *H/h* and *h/h*. Since half of the offspring have short hair, each of the parents must contribute a recessive (*h*) allele. And one of the parents must have two recessive (*h*) alleles. The cross looks like this:

	h	*h*
H	*Hh*	*Hh*
h	*hh*	*hh*

3. **B.**

   Heat of fusion is correct. Although there is a transition from one state of matter to another, there is no term "transition phase" to describe this process. The term "fission" is used in nuclear physics to describe the breaking apart of nuclear particles. It is not used to describe changes in the state of matter. "Specific heat" is the amount of energy in calories required to raise one gram of a substance by 1°C.

4. **C.**

   Animal respiration releases carbon dioxide back into the atmosphere in large quantities; it does not take in carbon dioxide for use. Most of the carbon within organisms is derived from the production of carbohydrates in plants through photosynthesis. Carbon is also dissolved directly into the oceans, where it is combined with calcium to form calcium carbonate—used by mollusks to form their shells. Detritus feeders include worms, mites, insects, and crustaceans that feed on dead organic matter, returning the carbon to the cycle through chemical breakdown and respiration. Organic matter that is left to decay may, under conditions of heat and pressure, be transformed into coal, oil, or natural gas—the fossil fuels. When fossil fuels are burned for energy, the combustion process releases carbon dioxide back into the atmosphere, where it is available to plants for photosynthesis.

5. **C.**

3, since the balanced reaction is as follows:

$$Al(OH)_3 + 3H^+ \rightarrow Al^{3+} + 3H_2O$$

6. **B.**

Limiting factors are density-independent when they occur without regard to population size and have effects that are not worsened as population increases. Natural disasters such as fires, floods, and tornadoes are density-independent factors. The other answer choices are all density-dependent.

7. **B.**

The eclipse must be a lunar eclipse because the Earth is between the Moon and the Sun. The lunar eclipse is total because the Earth's disk shades (or eclipses) the Moon completely.

8. **D.**

An enzyme accelerates the rate of a biochemical reaction by lowering its required activation energy. Should the enzyme not be produced due to genetic mutation, the biochemical reaction (in this case, the oxidation of ethanol) either would proceed at a much slower rate or not occur at all.

9. **C.**

Microvilli are filaments that extend from the cell membrane, particularly in cells that are involved in absorption (such as in the intestine). These filaments increase the surface area of the cell membrane, increasing the area available to absorb nutrients.

10. **C.**

Microvilli also contain enzymes that are involved in digesting certain types of nutrients.

11. **A.**

Secretory vesicles are packets of material packaged by either the Golgi apparatus or the endoplasmic reticulum. The secretory vesicle carries the substance produced within the cell to the cell membrane. The vesicle membrane fuses with the cell membrane, allowing the substance to escape the cell.

12. B.

The smooth endoplasmic reticulum is a network of continuous membranous channels that connect the cell membrane with the nuclear membrane and is responsible for the delivery of lipids and proteins to certain areas within the cytoplasm. The smooth endoplasmic reticulum lacks attached ribosomes.

13. C.

Mitosis decreases genetic diversity because the cells produced by this process are almost identical genetically. This is a key difference from meiosis, which allows for genetic change and improvement through the mixing of parental genetic material. This key difference is mistakenly reversed in choice (A). Choices (B) and (D) also mistakenly reverse mitosis and meiosis in describing their rates of producing offspring and the number of cell divisions in each process.

14. D.

The movement of water molecules across the plasma membrane from a hypotonic (low-salt) solution to a hypertonic (high-salt) solution is called osmosis. Vesicular transport moves large molecules and food particles across the plasma membrane using vesicles or other organs. Active transport is the movement of molecules against a concentration gradient. Facilitated diffusion is the movement of charged molecules, such as potassium ions, and larger molecules, such as glucose, across the cell membrane.

15. D.

The chart shows that the percentage similarity for the GAPDH gene is closest between humans and the chimpanzee. This supports the proposition that humans have a much closer evolutionary relationship to chimpanzees than to the other species shown. The chart does not indicate that humans evolved from chimpanzees.

16. D.

Interaction with lightning provides energy for a nitrogen to combine with water to form ammonia in the Nitrogen Cycle.

17. B.

Pathways in the Carbon Cycle include living cells, the atmosphere, oceans, rocks, and fossil fuels.

18. **A.**

The main pathways of the Water Cycle include condensation, evaporation, transpiration, and precipitation.

19. **C.**

The Phosphorous Cycle includes only solid and dissolved forms, no gases.

20. **A.**

The aquatic larvae breed easily in the pools of melting water during the Arctic summer. This is an example of an abiotic factor improving the conditions necessary for a population to grow.

21.

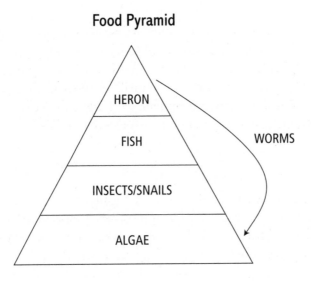

22.

(*4 pts. possible*) The policy most likely to have influenced this change was the fishing policy. (1 pt.) An overfishing event in the pond could cause a change in the overall balance of the energy pyramid in several ways. By having fewer fish, the number of insects would increase since the fish are not eating them. This would be why the residents are noticing more mosquitoes and other insects. (+1 pt.) It would also indicate why fewer algae are seen because there are more insects consuming more algae. (+1 pt.) In addition, with fewer fish in the pond, the herons have less food and have gone to find other places to nest. (+1 pt.) [*The rubric for this is 1 pt. for the first sentence; for each additional idea one point is added, for a total possible 4 pts.*]

23. B.

The part of the brain where reasoning, planning, speech, movement, emotions, and problem solving occur is the Frontal Lobe. The Parietal Lobe is associated with movement, orientation, recognition, and perception of stimuli. The Cerebellum is the location of regulation and coordination of movement, posture, and balance for the body. The Pons is the part of the brainstem involved in motor control and sensory analysis.

24. A.

A sound wave is a compression or longitudinal wave, which means that it compresses and rarefies as it moves through a medium. Transverse waves oscillate up and down as they move through a medium.

25. B.

Inorganic cofactors are small non-protein molecules that promote proper enzyme catalysis. These molecules may bind to the active site to the substrate itself. The most common inorganic cofactors are metallic atoms such as iron, copper, and zinc.

26. A.

Comparing the amounts of decayed and undecayed radioactive isotopes in the rock is the best way to determine the age of the igneous rock. This procedure is called **radiometric** dating, a technique used to date materials based on a comparison between the observed abundance of a naturally occurring radioactive isotope and its decay products, using the known decay rates of the isotopes. The most common techniques are radiocarbon dating, potassium-argon dating, and uranium-lead dating.

27. B.

Cellular respiration is carried out in the mitochondria. Label 2 (B) is a single mitochondrium. An active cell may contain more than 2,000 mitochondria. Aerobic cellular respiration is how the cell obtains energy (as ATP) from carbohydrates. Label 1 (A) is ribosomes. Label 3 (C) is the plasma membrane. Label 4 (D) is the nucleolus.

28. B.

Einstein's energy equation, $E = mc^2$, is based on the premise that the speed of light for all observers is constant, and that energy is directly proportional to mass. As energy increases, so does its mass. The speed of light is considered constant; the mass and energy values must increase or decrease directly and proportionately.

29. **A.**

It is the exchange of DNA between homologous chromosomes during prophase I that results in the mixing of maternal and paternal DNA and greater genetic diversity. Independent assortment occurs during metaphase I and anaphase I, so answer (B) is incorrect. Answers (C) and (D) incorrectly describe how genetic information is exchanged during meiosis.

30. **C.**

A person's body cannot store oxygen as it can glucose, and a marathoner cannot take in sufficient oxygen to keep up with energy needs for a long race. Thus, the marathoner's muscle cells must switch to anaerobic respiration for energy. Instead of reacting with oxygen, the glucose in the muscles forms lactic acid for energy. This lactic acid builds up in the muscles, leading to feelings of heaviness and cramping.

31. **0.0069 LY/year**

The speed of the Gnome Probe for the entire trip is 0.0069 LY/year. First, add all the distances: $0.1 + 0.150 + 0.100 = 0.255$ LY. Then, add the time: 10 years + 7 years + 20 years = 37 years. Speed = distance/time. S= $\dfrac{0.255 \text{ LY}}{37 \text{ years}}$ = 0.0069 LY/year.

32. **C.**

The Gnome Probe went faster for this portion of the trip as evidenced by the following calculations. The average velocity from Earth to GEDO was $\dfrac{(0.005 \text{ LY} + 0.1 \text{ LY})}{17 \text{ years}}$ = 0.0062 LY/year whereas the average velocity from GEDO to Earth was $\dfrac{0.15 \text{ LY}}{20 \text{ years}}$ = 0.0075 LY/year. Also, the trip from XEO to GEDO was much slower at $\dfrac{0.005 \text{ LY}}{7 \text{ years}}$ = 0.00071 LY/year.

33. **B.**

The only statement that is NOT a true analysis of the data is, "The average velocity for each segment is represented by the nearly straight bar at the top of the curves." The average velocity for each segment is represented by the labeled points (0.1, 0.005, 0.15).

34. B.

The only statement that is NOT true is, "The asteroids had no inertia as they crashed since the impact occurred in space." Objects in space have inertia and momentum the same as anywhere else in the universe.

35. D.

4500 kg is correct since mass does not change dependent on change in gravity. If we were considering weight, 4050 kg would be the weight of the probe on GEDO since the gravity there would be 0.9% of the gravity on earth since the mass is 0.9 % of Earth's mass. The weight on XEO would be 6750 kg, and while traveling in space it would approach 0 kg (weightlessness).

36. B.

Vitamins are organic cofactors or coenzymes that are required by some enzymatic reactions. In this case, it is the coenzyme required for the process of synthesizing collagen.

37. C.

Carbohydrates have numerous carbon-hydrogen bonds, which release energy upon interaction with oxygen molecules. This makes carbohydrates an excellent means of storing energy that the body can access quickly.

38. B.

Environmental conditions such as heat or acidity inhibit enzymatic reactions by changing the shape of the active site and rendering the enzyme ineffective. Certain chemicals inhibit enzymatic reactions by changing the shape of the enzyme's active site. If there is a lack of substrate, the enzyme will have no substance to affect. Thus, all of these factors may inhibit enzymatic reactions.

39. A.

Ocean currents are not known to be influenced by plankton concentration. However, temperature gradients, salinity, and depth all contribute to the currents that move ocean water.

40. B.

The fact that the mutation that disrupts the SHH gene results in extra digits in humans, cats, and mice shows that these species are all closely related on the evolutionary scale. In fact, mice are often used to test the effects of new medicines because their biochemical makeup is so similar to that of humans'.

41. B.

The only statement that is NOT true is, "Enzymes only function within living things." In fact, enzymes are useful for many functions in the nonliving world as well, including as cleaning agents.

42. D.

When a person breathes too fast, as in hyperventilation, he or she loses carbon dioxide from the blood too quickly. This makes the blood too alkaline (reduced acidity) and causes the person to feel faint and dizzy. Breathing into a paper bag forces the person to inhale some of the carbon dioxide that is exhaled into the bag, thus increasing levels of carbon dioxide in the blood and relieving the symptoms.

43. B.

Astrophysicists speculate that just 1/100 of a second after the Big Bang, the entire universe was filled with elementary particles (i.e., electrons, protons, positrons, neutrinos, photons, etc.). At 1 second, the temperature was 10^{10} K, which was still too hot for neutrons and protons to stay together in the nuclei by the strong nuclear force. After about 3 minutes, it had cooled to about 10^9 K. Electrons and positrons were annihilated, generating photons neutrinos, anti-neutrinos, and a small number of neutrons and protons. The universe was now as hot and dense as the core of a star undergoing nuclear fusion. However, it wasn't until 300,000 years later that the nuclei could hold on to the electrons, clearing the vast fog. The process then continued to cool, coalesce, and expand through **fusion**, forming stars and galaxies in the visible universe. Fission does not occur until much later in stellar evolution. Spontaneous generation, disproven by Pasteur, has nothing to do with the evolution of stars. Combustion is common in various exothermic processes in a general way. Stellar explosions indicative of the latter stages of stellar evolution generally occur toward the end of a star's life, not at the origination.

44. D.

The sodium-potassium pump (also called the cell membrane pump) uses energy to move sodium ions and potassium ions across the cell membrane and against the concentration gradient. It is also important in maintaining a difference in charge across the plasma membrane.

45. D.

The portion of the electromagnetic spectrum (EMS) that transmits thermal energy (heat) and has longer wavelengths than visible light is infrared waves (IR).

46. D.

The correct balanced equation should be: $C_6H_{12}O_6 + 6O_2 \rightarrow 6CO_2 + 6H_2O +$ energy.

47. D.

Choices (A) and (B) are the light and dark reactions, which are two portions of the overall photosynthesis reaction (C).

48. B.

Photosynthesis is a combination reaction, combining water and carbon dioxide to form energy-storing bonds in the presence of light. This is an endothermic reaction (not exothermic).

49.

ATP is one molecule that stores energy for use by cells in its chemical bonds. $\boxed{\text{1 pt.}}$

Photosynthesis produces carbohydrates such as glucose ($C_6H_{12}O_6$). However, at the cellular level, glucose must be broken down into smaller packets in order to be usable in cell activities. $\boxed{\text{+1 pt.}}$

ATP (and ADP) are smaller molecules that store energy in their efficient high energy covalent bonds. $\boxed{\text{+1 pt.}}$ The rubric for this test item is 1 point for the first sentence; if either of the second or third ideas is there, another point is added; if both, 2 points added, for a total possible 3 points.

50. B.

Increased fossil fuels could increase the CO_2 levels since burning fossil fuels for energy releases CO_2 into the atmosphere. UV light is blocked by the atmosphere but it does not impact CO_2 levels. CO_2 is a greenhouse gas. Trees use CO_2 and produce O_2.

PRACTICE TEST 1

SOCIAL STUDIES

49 questions
70 minutes

Practice Test 1: Social Studies

Questions 1–2 refer to the following table.

Region	Colonies	Date founded or claimed by England	Reason for founding
New England	Plymouth	1620	Religious freedom, farming, trade
	Massachusetts Bay	1630	Puritan commonwealth, farming, trade
	Connecticut	1635	Religious freedom, farming, trade
	Rhode Island	1636	Religious freedom, farming, trade
	New Hampshire	1638	Farming, trade
Middle Colonies	New York	1664 (Dutch 1624)	Farming, trade
	New Jersey	1664 (Dutch 1629)	Farming, trade
	Pennsylvania	1681	Farming, trade
	Delaware	1701 (Dutch 1638)	Farming, trade
Southern Colonies	Virginia	1607	Search for gold, farming
	Maryland	1634	Religious freedom, farming, trade
	Carolina	1670 (divided into North and South Carolina in 1729)	Trade, farming
	Georgia	1733	Refuge for poor, farming, buffer from Spanish Florida

1. By examining the reasons the British American colonies were founded, the most accurate conclusion is which of the following?

    A. Religious freedom was the primary reason the English settled in America.

    B. When Georgia was founded, the colonies feared an attack from Spain.

    C. People who settled in the Middle Colonies were searching for gold.

    D. Most colonists were poor.

2. According to the table, [   ] and [   ] were the most common reasons people settled in America.

An idea that America was destined by God and by history to expand its boundaries over a vast area, an area that included, but was not restricted to the continent of North America. It was used as a creed as Americans settled the Midwest, West, and Southwest of the United States. It was later the excuse when Americans exerted power and expansion in Central and South America.

Manifest Destiny was used to justify Americans settling in Texas and the war with Mexico. It was the creed as the Transcontinental Railroad was built and the settlement in the land occupied by Native American Tribes. This resulted in many conflicts between the American government and the tribes.

3. According to the passage, the results of Manifest Destiny resulted in all of the following EXCEPT

       A.   the Mexican War.

       B.   the annexation of Texas.

       C.   the Civil War.

       D.   the Indian Wars.

Questions 4 and 5 refer to the following graph.

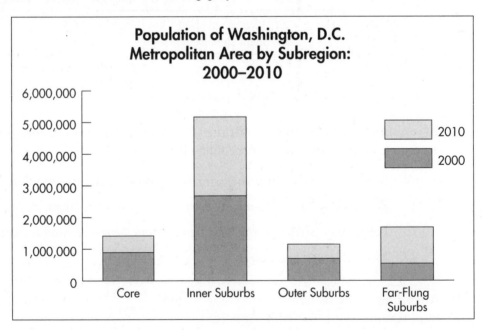

4. Which subregion of Washington, D.C., had the greatest rate of change in population from 2000–2010? [   ].

5. What trend does the population increase in the suburban regions indicate?

    A. More people live outside the core of the city due to the abundance of residential housing.

    B. More people live in the inner suburbs.

    C. Housing is less expensive in the core.

    D. Housing is more expensive in the inner suburbs.

Questions 6–8 are based on the following information.

How Nations Face the World

	Policy	Definition
I.	Nationalism	The policy of asserting the interests of one's own nation, viewed as separate from the interests of other nations or the common interests of all nations.
II.	Imperialism	The policy of extending the rule or authority of an empire or nation over foreign countries, or of acquiring and holding colonies and dependencies.
III.	Militarism	The policy of maintaining a large military establishment; the tendency to regard militarism as the supreme law of the state and to subordinate all other interests to those of the military.
IV.	Isolationism	The policy of isolating one's country from the affairs of other nations by declining to enter into alliances, foreign economic commitments, or international agreements.

6. During World War II, Germany attempted to conquer and rule much of Europe. According to the table, this is an example of:

    A. I.

    B. II.

    C. III.

    D. IV.

7. Germany built many airplanes, bombs, tanks, and ships to use in its attempt to conquer and rule other European nations. According to the table, this is an example of:

    A. I.

    B. II.

    C. III.

    D. IV.

8. Prior to the outbreak of World War II, at the time Germany was building up its military and threatening to attack its neighbors, the United States wanted to stay out of the affairs of the European nations and avoid conflict. This is an example of:

    A. I.

    B. II.

    C. III.

    D. IV.

Question 9 is based on the following information.

From the study of history, it is obvious that groups of people or countries have colonized and settled other areas. The list below describes some of the factors that motivate colonization and settlement.

Motivating Factors for Colonization

Political—to make the country stronger by gaining more territory and for the prestige that becoming an empire brings.

Economic—to gain resources and trade in order to to increase the wealth of the nation.

Religious—to avoid persecution from others for religious beliefs, to pursue the freedom to participate in a self-chosen religion, and to spread religious ideas to others.

Social—to leave problems in one society and create a new society.

9. Spain financed many expeditions to explore the New World. The voyages to South America brought both soldiers and priests. Which motivating factors caused Spain to send both soldiers and priests?

    A. Political and economic

    B. Political and religious

    C. Political and social

    D. Social and religious

10. During World War II, the countries that were trying to conquer and rule others formed an alliance called the Axis. The countries that the Axis was trying to conquer formed their own alliance called the Allies. Some countries remained neutral during the war. Below is a map showing which countries belonged to each alliance during the period of 1937–1942. Using the map as a reference, place each country in its appropriate category.

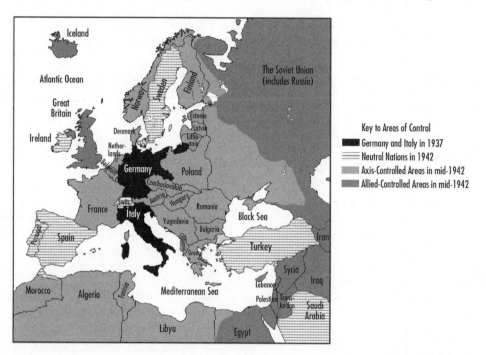

Axis	Allies	Neutral

Spain

France

Poland

Soviet Union

Libya

Turkey

Great Britain

Questions 11–13 are based on the following information.

The Founding Fathers of the United States were influenced by several sources. Some of these sources included John Locke's natural rights philosophy and the ancient Roman ideas of republicanism. This chart provides a comparison and contrast of the two concepts.

Understanding the Differences between Natural Rights Philosophy and Classical Republicanism

Natural Rights Philosophy	Classical Republicanism
1. The individual has the right to life, liberty, and property.	1. Promote the common good above the right of the individual.
2. Society is a collection of individual behaviors and is motivated by self-interest.	2. Individuals should be motivated by **civic virtue**.
3. Society is a collection of individuals, each sharing the same right to pursue his or her own welfare.	3. Individual rights are limited to privacy, belief, expression, and opportunities to read, think, and earn money. If people had unlimited freedom to pursue such interests and activities, they might stop being reliable and fully dedicated to the common good.
4. People's opportunities should not be limited by the situation or group into which they are born.	4. Discourage diversity of beliefs, wealth, and ways of life. Stress small communities where people know and care for each other. Discourage citizens from traveling, earning money, and reading and thinking about things that had nothing to do with their governments.
5. The main purpose of government should be to protect natural rights. The state existed to serve the interests of the individual.	5. Avoid the formation of factions or interest groups that might endanger the common good. Citizens should participate fully in the government to promote the common good.
6. To preserve natural rights, governments guarantee specific rights, such as civil rights (freedom of conscience and privacy) and political rights (vote, run for office).	6. The importance of political rights such as voting, expressing ideas and opinions about government, and serving in public office.

We the People: The Citizen and the Constitution, Center for Civic Education, 1995

11. Which of the following do both the natural rights philosophy and the classical republicanism philosophy support?

    A. Voting, expressing ideas, and serving in public office

    B. The belief that everyone must be very much alike

    C. Economic inequality is destructive to the common good.

    D. One established set of religion and moral standards creates stability and is good for a nation.

12. In this chart, the term **civic virtue** most likely means

    A. a good understanding of government.

    B. working to better oneself.

    C. promoting the common good of the community.

    D. fair treatment by government officials.

13. The United States has a system of government that represents people of different cultural backgrounds, economic conditions, and religious beliefs. Identify the statement of the natural rights philosophy that best supports this idea.

    A. Statement 1

    B. Statement 6

    C. Statement 2

    D. Statement 5

Read the following definition and then answer question 14.

Opportunity cost is defined as the value of a forgone activity or alternative when another item or activity is chosen. Opportunity cost comes into play in any decision that involves a tradeoff between two or more options.

14. Using this definition, all of the following involve a tradeoff EXCEPT:

    A. An attorney has the chance to represent a client who is wealthy in a very large lawsuit in which both council and client are sure to profit.

    B. A college student attends classes, even though he could be working at a job with good wages. However, he chooses to continue his education because it will provide a long-term payoff.

    C. A worker at a factory decides to take a higher paying job even though he will have less time to play golf, which is his favorite pastime.

    D. A doctor chooses to leave a good practice to join a lower-paying position in a practice in a small town.

15. Popular sovereignty is the basic idea of democracy. Popular sovereignty means that the people are the ultimate source of the authority of their government. In which type of government is popular sovereignty found?

    A. monarchy

    B. democracy

    C. theocracy

    D. dictatorship

16. According to the definition of *popular sovereignty*, which of the following best describes the ultimate political authority?

    A. senators

    B. president

    C. U.S. Supreme Court justice

    D. citizens

17. Under the definition of *popular sovereignty*, in a democracy political authority comes from the people, not from the state. How is this idea practiced in a political system?

    A. by participating in political campaigns

    B. by voting in elections

    C. by debating political issues

    D. by court trial

18. It is an abuse of power for a democratic government to claim more powers than the people have delegated to it. Government may not assign itself powers.

In the statement above, the term **abuse of powers** most likely means which of the following?

    A. misuse of power

    B. police brutality

    C. use of the military

    D. too much power

Questions 19 and 20 are based on the following information.

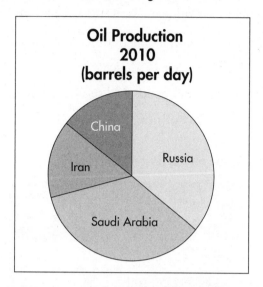

Country	Barrels per Day
Russia	10,270,000
Saudi Arabia	10,520,000
Iran	4,252,000
China	4,073,000

U.S. Energy Information Administration

Gross domestic product (GDP) is the total market value of all the goods and services produced within the borders of a nation during a specified period.

Country	2010 GDP (Gross Domestic Product) (In millions of U.S. dollars)
Russia	1,525,353
Saudi Arabia	526,811
Iran	419,118
China	5,930,393

19. According to the graph, [Select 1 . . . ▼] produced the most oil in 2010.

    A. China
    B. Russia
    C. Saudi Arabia
    D. Iran

20. According to the definition and the table, Russia has a lower GDP than China. One of the statements below provides an accurate explanation. Which statement is true?

    A. China's oil is more valuable than Russia's oil.

    B. China produces other products.

    C. Russia exports fewer goods and services than China.

    D. China is larger than Russia in size.

Questions 21 and 22 are based on the poster below.

U.S. National Archives and Records Administration

21. The poster most likely was used to

    A. show that women were stronger than men.

    B. illustrate the strength of the American housewife.

    C. recruit women to work in factories during World War II.

    D. provide information on the abilities of women.

22. The poster is an example of

    A. propaganda.

    B. advertising.

    C. faulty language.

    D. loaded language.

23. The Fifteenth Amendment of the United States Constitution gave citizens the right to vote regardless of race, color, or former status of servitude. Later methods of trying to get around the Fifteenth Amendment and continue to deprive Negroes of the chance to vote included:

    A. poll taxes and literacy tests.

    B. requiring landownership.

    C. requiring church membership.

    D. requiring selective service status.

Question 24 is based on the following passage and table.

The Civil War in the United States was the result of many underlying factors. It was a time of great change. People had different ideas about how that change would affect the nation. The chart below identifies some of the inventions of the time preceding the war and how the inventions changed America. Those changes had an influence on bringing about the Civil War and on how the war was fought.

Inventions That Had a Major Impact on the Civil War

Invention	Date	Contributions to the war
Power loom	1780	Made the manufacturing of textiles easier and quicker. Increased the demand for cotton, bringing wealth to the South that helped finance the war against the Union.
Cotton gin	1793	Made the cleaning of cotton easier; increased the demand for cotton; helped fuel the economy in the South.
Interchangeable parts	1801	Made it easier to manufacture goods—guns, sewing machines, etc.
Telegraph	1837	Made communication easier and spread news quicker.
Steamboat	1793	Made the transportation of goods easier across long distances.
Railroad	1830	Made transportation of people and goods easier, less expensive, and faster.

24. According to the passage and the chart, the Civil War had a number of causes. Which of the following is likely to be one of the factors that led to the outbreak of the war?

    A. the competition in trade

    B. the desire to go places fast

    C. the need for more clothes

    D. the demand for more guns

Read the following definition and then answer question 25.

The Rule of Law requires that everyone, including those in government positions, exercise authority under the law and that every citizen is subject to the law.

25. After reading the definition of the Rule of Law, one can infer that

    A. the president is the only person above the law.

    B. members of Congress are the only people above the law.

    C. state government officials are above the law.

    D. no person is above the law.

Questions 26 refers to the following table.

The World's Most Populous Urban Areas

1900	1950	2012
New York 4,242,000	New York 12,463,000	Shanghai, China 13,831,900
Paris 3,330,000	London 8,860,000	Mumbai, India 13,991,000
Berlin 2,707,000	Tokyo 7,000,000	Karachi, Pakistan 12,991,000
Chicago 1,717,000	Paris 5,900,000	Delhi, India 12,565,900
Vienna 1,698,000	Shanghai, China 5,406,000	Istanbul, Turkey 12,517,000
Tokyo 1,497,000	Moscow 5,100,000	Sao Paulo 11,244,360
St. Petersburg, Russia 1,439,000	Buenos Aires, Argentina 5,000,000	Moscow 10,563,038
Manchester, England 1,435,000	Chicago 4,906,000	Seoul, South Korea 10,464,051
Philadelphia 1,000,000	Ruhr, Germany 4,900,000	Beijing, China 10,123,000

26. Which statement best describes the changes in urban growth from 1900 to 2012?

    A. Urban growth has shifted from North America to Asia.

    B. Urban growth has occurred in areas of North and South America, but not in Eastern Europe.

    C. Urban growth has shifted over the last century to the Middle Eastern and Asian countries.

    D. Urban growth has changed the most in countries with new cities.

Refer to the following passage for question 27.

An Excerpt from "The Man with the Muck Rake," a speech delivered by President Theodore Roosevelt

(1) In "Pilgrim's Progress" the Man with the Muck Rake is set forth as the example of him whose vision is fixed on carnal instead of spiritual things. Yet he also typifies the man who in this life consistently refuses to see aught that is lofty, and fixes his eyes with solemn intentness only on that which is vile and debasing.

(2) Now, it is very necessary that we should not flinch from seeing what is vile and debasing. There is filth on the floor, and it must be scraped up with the muck rake; and there are times and places where this service is the most needed of all the services that can be performed. But the man who never does anything else, who never thinks or speaks or writes, save of his feats with the muck rake, speedily becomes, not a help but one of the most potent forces for evil.

(3) There are in the body politic, economic and social, many and grave evils, and there is urgent necessity for the sternest war upon them. There should be relentless exposure of and attack upon every evil man, whether politician or business man, every evil practice, whether in politics, business, or social life. I hail as a benefactor every writer or speaker, every man who, on the platform or in a book, magazine, or newspaper, with merciless severity makes such attack, provided always that he in his turn remembers that the attack is of use only if it is absolutely truthful.

(4) The liar is no whit better than the thief, and if his mendacity takes the form of slander he may be worse than most thieves. It puts a premium upon knavery untruthfully to attack an honest man, or even with hysterical exaggeration to assail a bad man with untruth.

(5) An epidemic of indiscriminate assault upon character does no good, but very great harm. The soul of every scoundrel is gladdened whenever an honest man is assailed, or even when a scoundrel is untruthfully assailed.

U.S. President Theodore "Teddy" Roosevelt. "The Man with the Muck Rake." Delivered 14 April 1906.
Text courtesy of the Program in Presidential Rhetoric, Texas A&M University.

27. Journalism that exposes corruption in business or government is known as muckraking. But when President Theodore Roosevelt coined the term in the 1906 speech excerpted above, he saw not just the valuable role the press could play in highlighting political and business abuses, but also was concerned that muckraking could go too far, leading to irresponsible and sensational attacks. Place the letter of the appropriate sentence from the excerpt of "The Man with the Muck Rake" in the correct column to indicate whether it is an aspect of muckraking that Roosevelt criticizes or supports.

President Theodore Roosevelt's Split Views on Muckraking

Criticism	Support

(A) "There is filth on the floor, and it must be scraped up with the muck rake; and there are times and places where this service is the most needed of all the services that can be performed." (paragraph 2)

(B) "But the man who never does anything else, who never thinks or speaks or writes, save of his feats with the muck rake, speedily becomes not a help but one of the most potent forces of evil." (paragraph 2)

(C) "There are in the body politic, economic and social, many and grave evils, and there is urgent necessity for the sternest war upon them." (paragraph 3)

(D) "The liar is no whit better than the thief, and if his mendacity takes the form of slander he may be worse than most thieves." (paragraph 4)

Read the following excerpt from the First Amendment to the U.S. Constitution to answer question 28.

Congress shall make no law respecting an establishment of religion, or prohibiting the free exercise thereof; or abridging the freedom of speech, or of the press.

28. This excerpt reflects which of the following concepts?

    A. individual rights

    B. executive powers

    C. popular sovereignty

    D. checks and balances

29. The United States has several methods to carry out its foreign policy. The chart below shows some of these methods and their purpose. Examine the information in the chart. Then match each of the following statements from the lettered list below to the box in the table that corresponds with the appropriate method of foreign policy.

Methods Used to Carry Out Foreign Policy

Method	Purpose	Example
1. Treaties	Defense treaties allow the United States to use military force to defend other nations, protect interests abroad, and promote peace.	
2. Alliances	Agreements between the United States and other nations to help each other for economic and military reasons.	
3. Military Force	Use of troops to fight in any part of the world.	
4. Peace Corps	Work with people in poorer countries around the world to improve health care, agriculture, and education.	
5. Negotiations	Used to settle problems and disputes with other nations and to decide the extent of foreign aid the U.S. gives to other nations.	
6. The United Nations	The U.S. is a member of the United Nations, which works to maintain peace throughout the world.	

A. In 1990, President George H. W. Bush sent American military forces to Saudi Arabia to join with other nations in the fight against Iraq.

B. NATO is an agreement between the U.S., Canada, and fourteen other nations to defend one another.

C. In 1979 President Carter helped Israel and Egypt agree to end their long conflicts.

D. In 2012, medical specialists worked as maternal attendants in Malawi, Africa.

E. In 1987, the U.S. and the Soviet Union signed the I.N.F. Treaty, which required both nations to destroy large numbers of nuclear weapons.

F. In 2012, peacekeeping forces provided by various nations were present in the Democratic Republic of the Congo.

Question 30 refers to the map below.

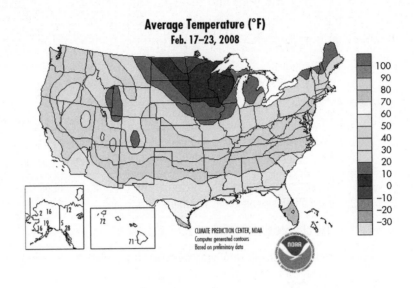

30. According to the map, the coldest area in the 48 contiguous states is:

    A.   the center border with Canada.

    B.   the light gray area in the center of the country.

    C.   the area along the West Coast.

    D.   the lower half of the country.

31. As used in the previous question, the word **contiguous** most likely means which of the following?

    A.   lower

    B.   middle

    C.   center

    D.   connected

Refer to the following passage to answer questions 32 and 33.

The Fifth Amendment protects people who are accused of crimes in three ways. First, people cannot be forced to speak against (*incriminate*) themselves in court proceedings. The government must have evidence and prove that the accused person is guilty of the crime charged. Next, the Fifth Amendment provides for due process, or fair treatment of the accused person, including a guarantee that established court procedures will be followed in determining whether the person is guilty, and that the person will have the opportunity to confront his or her accusers. The third protection is to prevent double jeopardy. A person who has been declared not guilty by a jury cannot be tried for the same crime again.

32. According to the information in the passage, which of the following is NOT provided for by the Fifth Amendment?

    A. fair treatment

    B. being tried for the same crime after being declared not guilty

    C. the right to an attorney

    D. being forced to speak against oneself

33. According to the passage, **due process** most likely means

    A. speaking against oneself.

    B. being tried for the same crime two or more times.

    C. fair treatment.

    D. petitioning the government.

Use the information in the following table to answer questions 34–36.

Department	Major Agencies	Responsibility
Agriculture	Food Safety and Inspection Food and Nutrition Service Commodity Credit Corporation	Inspect dairy, meat, and poultry Oversee school lunches and food stamps program Provide farmer assistance
Commerce	International Trade Administration Census Bureau Patent and Trademark Office National Weather Service	Promote international trade Conduct census Issue patents Protect economic growth
Defense	Joint Chiefs of Staff Departments of Armed Forces	Advise the President on security and military affairs Maintain armed forces Build military bases

(continued)

Department	Major Agencies	Responsibility
Education	Elementary and Secondary Education Educational Research and Improvement	Study problems in education Advise the president about education programs
Energy	Conservation and Renewable Energy Nuclear Energy	Find sources of energy Protect the energy supply Control the use of nuclear energy
Health and Human Services	Social Security Administration Food and Drug Administration Public Health Services	Manage Social Security and Medicare Programs Approve new medicines Manage health and welfare programs
Housing and Urban Development	Housing Public Housing and Indian Housing	Assist state and local governments with urban problems Provide housing for low-income people
Homeland Security	Federal Emergency Management Transportation Security Administration U.S. Immigration and Customs Enforcement U.S. Coast Guard Customs and Border Protection Secret Service	Enhance domestic security Enforce laws concerning terrorism, immigration, travel Enforce border control, customs, trade, and immigration Protect U.S. borders along the sea coast, polices maritime trade, and saves those in peril on the sea Protect against entry into the country by illegal immigrants, illegal drugs, terrorists, and terrorist weapons Safeguard the nation's financial infrastructure and payment systems, and protects national leaders, visiting heads of state, and government-designated sites
Justice	Alcohol, Tobacco, Firearms, and Explosives. Drug Enforcement Administration FBI U.S. Parole Commission U.S. Marshals Service INTERPOL Washington	Enforce drug, immigrations, and customs laws Protect against import, manufacture, and sale of illegal drugs Protect against terrorist and foreign intelligence threats, and uphold Federal criminal laws Supervise paroled criminal offenders Protect federal courts and judges, transport prison inmates, carry out arrests and other police functions for courts Facilitate law enforcement cooperation with police agencies of other nations
Labor	OSHA (Occupational Safety and Health Administration) VETS Bureau of Labor Statistics	Enforce labor laws and safety laws Aids military veterans to find employment Provide data on employment, wages, inflation, productivity, and many other topics.

(continued)

Department	Major Agencies	Responsibility
State	Arms Control Global Affairs Public Diplomacy US mission to the United Nations	Development and implement foreign policy
Interior	Indian Affairs Land Management Fish and Wildlife Geological Parks Mining	Protect and provide access to national, natural, and cultural heritage
Treasury	Engraving and Printing IRS US Mint	Maintain and monitor financial well-being
Transportation	Federal Aviation Administration (FAA) National Transportation Safety Board	Development and safety of transportation
Veterans Affairs	Veterans Benefits Administration (VBA) Veterans Health Administration (VHA) National Cemetery Association (NCA)	The department's mission is to serve U.S. veterans and their families comprehensively—as their principal advocate in ensuring that they receive medical care, benefits, and social support; and to promote the health, welfare, and dignity of all veterans in recognition of their service to the nation.

Source: USA.gov

34. According to the table, the Department of the Interior is in charge of which of the following?

    A. determining where and when people may enter the country

    B. determining where and when people may hunt deer

    C. determining where and when people may travel to other countries

    D. determining where and when people may build a factory

35. The information in the table could best help you do which of the following?

    A. locate the agency that regulates hospitals

    B. locate the agency that regulates manufacturing

    C. locate the agency that oversees the Peace Corps

    D. locate the agency that will help in a legal case

36. Which department would most likely be in charge of granting permission to a company that wants to mine for zinc?

    A. Department of State

    B. Department of Labor

    C. Department of Transportation

    D. Department of the Interior

Question 37 refers to the following information.

> The theory of natural rights held that rights come from God and cannot be taken away without consent.

The following statement is from *The Federalist Papers* penned by some of the Founding Fathers of the United States.

> "The majority has no legislative power to vote away or otherwise abridge the natural rights of political, ethnic, religious, and other minorities."

37. According to these statements, which groups have equal and natural rights?

    A. women who are citizens

    B. all minority groups

    C. African Americans

    D. all immigrants to the United States

Questions 38–41 are based on the following excerpt.

The French and Indian War ended in 1763. This war created a huge debt for England. In an effort to raise revenue, the British Parliament and King George III passed the Stamp Act of 1765. This Act required the British colonies in America to pay a fee for all official documents. The fee was not extravagant, but it foretold the methods England would use in dealing with the colonies in the future.

In response to the Stamp Act and similar laws, the American colonists began to rebel. The instigators called on others to join in a revolution. The colonists began to harass loyalists, boycott British goods, and speak against British rule. In time, the Revolutionary War broke out and ended with independence for the colonies.

38. According to the passage, the colonists reacted to the Stamp Act of 1765 in all the following ways EXCEPT

    A. boycotting British goods.

    B. harassing loyalists.

    C. shooting at British troops.

    D. speaking out against British rule.

39. From the information in the passage, it can be inferred that the word **boycott** most likely means

    A. using young boys to fight.

    B. refusing to buy British goods.

    C. making British goods themselves.

    D. refusing to buy the required tax stamp.

40. The Stamp Act of 1765 was a(n) [＿＿＿＿＿＿＿] of the French and Indian War and a [＿＿＿＿＿＿＿] of the American Revolution.

41. What was the purpose of the Stamp Act?

    A. to punish the colonists

    B. to counteract hostilities toward the British

    C. to raise money to pay war debts

    D. to gain control of taxes in the colonies

Questions 42 and 43 are based on the following pie chart.

Top 5 Occupations for Employed Women in the U.S., 2010

Nursing, psychiatric, and home health aides 15%

Secretaries and administrative assistants 25%

Cashiers 19%

Registered nurses 22%

Elementary and middle school teachers 19%

U.S. Department of Labor, Bureau of Labor Statistics, Annual Averages 2010.

42. According to the pie chart, nearly half of U.S. working women in 2010 were employed as _____ and _____.

43. Which of the following is a fact you can find in this chart?

    A. Women like to be with children.

    B. Women's role as caregivers is growing.

    C. More than one-fifth of the women in the workforce are registered nurses.

    D. Women make better workers than men.

Questions 44–47 refer to the following background information and letter.

The modern American civil rights movement is best known for the nonviolent protests that took place in the 1950s and '60s. The movement involved many areas of the South and several organizations. From these organizations and events came some of the most famous American leaders to date. People were arrested, imprisoned, beaten, and even killed as a result of their actions to end segregation in the United States, but particularly in the "Jim Crow" South.

This is a letter Dr. Martin Luther King, Jr., wrote while in jail in Birmingham, Alabama, in 1963.

You may well ask: "Why direct action? Why sit-ins, marches, etc.? Isn't negotiation a better path?" You are exactly right in your call for negotiation. Indeed, this is the purpose of direct action. Nonviolent direct action seeks to create such a crisis and establish such creative tension that a community that has constantly refused to negotiate is forced to confront the issue. It seeks so to dramatize the issue that it can no longer be ignored. I just referred to the creation of tension as a part of the work of the nonviolent resister. This may sound rather shocking. But I must confess that I am not afraid of the word tension. I have earnestly worked and preached against violent tension, but there is a type of constructive nonviolent tension that is necessary for growth. Just as Socrates felt that it was necessary to create a tension in the mind so that individuals could rise from the bondage of myths and half-truths to the unfettered realm of creative analysis and objective appraisal, we must see the need of having nonviolent gadflies to create the kind of tension in society that will help men to rise from the dark depths of prejudice and racism to the majestic heights of understanding and brotherhood. So the purpose of the direct action is to create a situation so crisis-packed that it will inevitably open the door to negotiation. We, therefore, concur with you in your call for negotiation. Too long has our beloved Southland been bogged down in the tragic attempt to live in monologue rather than dialogue.

Dr. Martin Luther King, Jr. "Letter from a Birmingham Jail." 16 April 1963.

44. According to the letter, the methods used in protests included

    A. engaging in long fasts.

    B. engaging in riots.

    C. engaging in sit-ins.

    D. engaging in long speeches in Congress.

45. Dr. King refers to which Greek philosopher when he writes the following? "Just as _____ felt that it was necessary to create tension in the mind so that individuals could rise from bondage. . . ."

46. It can be implied from the background paragraph and the letter that the Civil Rights movement took place mainly in the

    A. North.

    B. West.

    C. East.

    D. South.

47. In the 1950s and '60s, the term **Jim Crow** meant

    A. a man's name.

    B. to eat your words.

    C. a bird used as a symbol.

    D. a system of segregation in the American South.

Read the following passage and answer questions 48–49.

On June 23, 1948, all road, rail, and canal links from West Berlin through East Germany (which was under Communist control) were closed, cutting off West Berlin from West Germany, both of which were under the control of the United States, Britain, and France. The aim was to force the Western Powers to withdraw from the city by reducing it to a point of starvation. General Clay, the American Commander in Berlin, predicted, "[W]hen Berlin falls, western Germany will be next. If we withdraw . . . , Communism will run rampant."

The Western Powers decided to fly supplies into the city. Over the next ten months, two million tons of supplies were airlifted to the blockaded city. This is known as the Marshall Plan, as it was developed by Secretary of State George Marshall. After this blockade finally ended, the Cold War began.

The Cold War continued for decades, as is evident in President Kennedy's words:

All free men, wherever they may live, are citizens of Berlin, and, therefore, as a free man, I take pride in the words "*Ich bin ein Berliner* [I am a Berliner]."

President John F. Kennedy, "Speech from the Rathaus Schöneberg, Berlin, Germany." 26 June 1963.

48. The policy of containment was developed by President Harry Truman, who led the United States from 1945 to 1953. To which of the following did the policy of containment refer?

    A. stopping the spread of Communism all over the world

    B. stopping the spread of China's forces in Asia

    C. stopping the spread of terrorism in the Middle East

    D. stopping the spread of racism throughout the world

49. Based on the passage, the word **blockade** most likely means

    A. a war measure that isolates some area of importance to the enemy.

    B. to make some goods or services accessible.

    C. to begin a war with violent measures.

    D. a way to stop people from immigrating to another country.

Answers: Social Studies Practice Test 1

1. **B.**

   The chart states that a reason for founding Georgia was to serve as a buffer from Spanish Florida. It can be inferred from this information that the colonists feared an attack from Spain. Choice A might seem likely, but farming and trade are listed more times than religion. The other choices are not supported by the chart.

2. **Farming and trade**

   The chart lists this reason more often than the others; therefore, it is the best answer.

3. **C.**

   This is the only choice that was not a result of Manifest Destiny. Be sure to pay attention to the word "except" in the question. All the other options are mentioned in the passage.

4. **Far-flung suburbs**

   Far-flung suburbs had the largest rate of change, more than doubling their population. Though the Inner Suburbs had the largest number of new residents, the rate of growth was not as great.

5. **B.**

   Choice (B) is the only statement among the choices that can be proven by the chart. The other reasons cannot be supported by this chart. Choices (A), (C), and (D) are generalizations not based on facts from the chart.

6. **B.**

   Imperialism is the policy of extending rule or authority over an empire.

7. **C.**

   This is an example of militarism—building up and using military force.

8. **D.**

   Isolationism—the policy of isolating one's country from the affairs of other nations by declining to enter into alliances, foreign economic commitments, or international agreements.

9. **B.**

Political and religious factors are represented by soldiers and priests.

10.

Axis	Allies	Neutral
Poland France Libya	Great Britain Russia	Spain Turkey

11. **A.**

Both documents support all these components.

12. **C.**

Promoting the common good of the community. Choice (A) is not stated by either. Choice (B) is a trait of republicanism, not natural rights philosophy, and choice (D) is not correct because republicanism may promote it, but natural rights philosophy does not.

13. **C.**

Statement 2 supports this conclusion in saying that society is a collection of individual behaviors motivated by self-interest.

14. **B.**

The college student provides an example of opportunity cost as he takes the risk of losing money while attending school. The other options are not consistent with the definition.

15. **B.**

"Democracy" means "rule by the people."

16. **D.**

The citizens are "the people."

17. **B.**

Voting.

18. **A.**

Misuse of power.

19. **C.**

Saudi Arabia. Although Russia and Saudi Arabia appear to have similar oil production per day on the graph, Russia does not have the largest numbers in the table.

20. **C.**

China has more diverse trade than Russia. Answer choice (A) is just an opinion without supporting evidence. Although answer choice (D) may be possible, there is no information in the graph or chart to prove this. Answer choice (B) is a true statement, but does not explain why China would have a greater GDP than Russia, since Russia also produces other products besides oil.

21. **C.**

During World War II, women worked in factories producing war materiel, since so many working-age men were serving in the military. The poster was part of an effort by Westinghouse Electric to promote the war effort. Created by artist J. Howard Miller, it was neither intended to be, nor known at the time as, "Rosie the Riveter"—though over time that was the name that stuck. The original "Rosie" appeared on the magazine cover of the Saturday Evening Post on May 29, 1943. Its illustrator: Norman Rockwell. The other answer choices are opinions unsupported by the image.

22. **A.**

Propaganda. It uses an image to persuade people to do something that will further the cause of, in this case, winning the war.

23. **A.**

After the Fifteenth Amendment passed, states in the South made it difficult for blacks to vote by charging a fee or requiring a reading test.

24. **A.**

Competition in trade is the only logical answer among the choices.

25. **D.**

The rule of law states that every citizen is subject to the law.

26. **C.**

In 2012, China, India, and Pakistan have the largest population.

27. **The chart shows the correct answers.**

President Theodore Roosevelt's Split Views on Muckraking

Criticism	Support
Sentence (B). "But the man who never does anything else, who never thinks or speaks or writes, save of his feats with the muck rake, speedily becomes not a help but one of the most potent forces of evil."	**Sentence (A).** "There is filth on the floor, and it must be scraped up with the muck rake; and there are times and places where this service is the most needed of all the services that can be performed."
Sentence (D). "The liar is no whit better than the thief, and if his mendacity takes the form of slander he may be worse than most thieves."	**Sentence (C).** "There are in the body politic, economic and social, many and grave evils, and there is urgent necessity for the sternest war upon them."

Roosevelt makes it clear in the very first sentence of the excerpt that he is concerned about American journalists who, like the Man with the Muck Rake (a manure rake) in Bunyan's "Pilgrim's Progress," a spiritual allegory, cast their gaze only downward—in the muck. On the one hand, he says, muckrakers can be the source of excessive "raking" (B) and reckless attacks (D) – often called "yellow journalism"—that risk being worse than the problems being written about. But then in sentence (A), he welcomes responsible critiques, and in sentence (C) points to the necessity of rooting out abuses in politics, business, and society-at-large. As you reflect on "The Man with the Muck Rake" speech, consider the historical context: Roosevelt's pivotal role, following the speech, in enactment of the Pure Food and Drug Act (1906), the Meat Inspection Act (1906), and other reforms, coming on the heels of Upton Sinclair's *exposé* on the meat-packing industry, *The Jungle*, which was published a few months before the president's speech. Roosevelt invited Sinclair to the White House to get his advice on how to make meat inspections safer.

28. **A.**

Individual rights to freedom of religion, speech, and the press.

29. The correct matchups are as follows:

   1. E

   2. B

   3. A

   4. D

   5. C

   6. F

30. **A.**

   The darkest area gets as cold as 0° and below.

31. **D.**

   In question No. 30, the term *contiguous states* does not include Hawaii and Alaska, because their borders are not connected with the borders of any of the other states.

32. **C.**

   This choice—the right to an attorney—is not mentioned in the excerpt, but the others are.

33. **C.**

   Fair treatment is stated as a context clue.

34. **B.**

   Fish and Wildlife. Answers (A) and (C) are responsibilities of the Department of Homeland Security, and (D) is the Department of Labor's domain.

35. **C.**

   Answer (C) is listed in the chart. The other choices are not in the chart and thus irrelevant.

36. **D.**

   The Department of the Interior is in charge of mining. This is stated in the chart.

37. B.

The passage states that the majority cannot abridge or overrule the rights of any group. All minorities would qualify for equality.

38. C.

There is no mention of shooting troops. The other choices are stated in the passage.

39. B.

This choice best fits the description in the passage and the use of the word in context.

40. Effect (or result) and cause.

These responses can be inferred from the information and the sequence of events in the passage.

41. C.

The passage states that the reason for the Stamp Act was to raise money to pay Britain's debts from the French and Indian War. The other choices are not stated in the passage.

42. Secretaries/administrative assistants and registered nurses.

These two occupations are the top 2 categories, representing 47% of the total number of women employed in the top 5 occupations. Forty-seven percent is just under half.

43. C.

Only choice (C) is a fact found in the chart; none of the other choices have any basis in the chart.

44. C.

Sit-ins are stated. The other choices are not stated in the passage. Choice (A) is a non-violent action taken by some protesters, but not during the Civil Rights Movement in the United States. Choice (B) is violent action. Choice (D) is not correct; although Dr. King is famous for making speeches, this passage is not a speech.

45. Socrates

Socrates is a detail in the passage.

46. D.

Southland is mentioned, and the letter is written from a jail in Birmingham, Alabama, a Southern state.

47. D.

The information is not stated, but is a common reference in writings, speeches, or documents relating to segregation in the United States.

48. A.

Since the passages are focused on Communism in Germany, as well as the Kennedy quote, you should draw the conclusion that the containment policy was put in place to stop the spread of Communism. The other choices are not mentioned in this passage, nor would the time period would not be appropriate for these subjects.

49. A.

Based on the information in the passage, the United States took supplies to Berlin. This information allows the reader to infer that a blockade isolates an area from supplies of food or weapons. The other answer choices are not mentioned in the passage.

Practice Test Battery 2

- Reasoning Through Language Arts

- Mathematical Reasoning

- Science

- Social Studies

The GED® test, which is delivered on computer, has a built-in timer for each test section. Because it's computerized, the test uses an assortment of technology-enhanced questions. Such question types vary by test subject but may for instance require test-takers to highlight blocks of text, select answers from a list embedded within a text, classify and appropriately sequence information, or provide a numeric-entry response. REA's printed practice tests simulate the computerized GED® test as closely as possible.

PRACTICE TEST 2

REASONING THROUGH LANGUAGE ARTS
Section 1

40 questions
35 minutes

The Reasoning Through Language Arts test is 150 minutes, with a 10-minute break after Section 2 (the Extended Response portion of the test).

Practice Test 2: Reasoning Through Language Arts (RLA)

Section 1

Read the following excerpt from Thomas de Quincey's essay "The Vision of Sudden Death." Then answer questions 1–7.

What is to be thought of sudden death? It is remarkable that, in different conditions of society it has been variously regarded as the consummation of an earthly career most fervently to be desired, and, on the other hand, as that consummation which is most of all to be deprecated. Caesar the Dictator, at his last dinner party, (cœna,) and the very evening before his assassination, being questioned as to the mode of death which, in his opinion, might seem the most eligible, replied — "That which should be most sudden." On the other hand, the divine Litany of our English Church, when breathing forth supplications, as if in some representative character for the whole human race prostrate before God, places such a death in the very van of horrors. "From lightning and tempest; from plague, pestilence, and famine; from battle and murder, and from sudden death, — Good Lord, deliver us." Sudden death is here made to crown the climax in a grand ascent of calamities; it is the last of curses; and yet, by the noblest of Romans, it was treated as the first of blessings. (In that difference, most readers will see little more than the difference between Christianity and Paganism. But there I hesitate. The Christian church may be right in its estimate of sudden death; and it is a natural feeling, though after all it may also be an infirm one, to wish for a quiet dismissal from life — as that which seems most reconcilable with meditation, with penitential retrospects, and with the humilities of farewell prayer. There does not, however, occur to me any direct scriptural warrant for this earnest petition of the English Litany. It seems rather a petition indulged to human infirmity, than exacted from human piety. And, however that may be, two remarks suggest themselves as prudent restraints upon a doctrine, which else may wander, and has wandered, into an uncharitable superstition. The first is this: that many people are likely to exaggerate the horror of a sudden death, (I mean the objective horror to him who contemplates such a death, not the subjective horror to him who suffers it,) from the false disposition to lay a stress upon words or acts, simply because by an accident they have become words or acts. If a man dies, for instance, by some sudden death when he happens to be intoxicated, such a death is falsely regarded with peculiar horror; as though the intoxication were suddenly exalted into a blasphemy. But that is unphilosophic. The man was, or he was not, habitually a drunkard. If not, if his intoxication were a solitary accident, there can be no reason at all for allowing special emphasis to this act, simply because through misfortune it became his final act. Nor, on the other hand, if it were no accident, but one of his habitual transgressions, will it be the more habitual or the more a transgression, because some sudden calamity, surprising him, has caused this habitual transgression to be also a final one? Could the man have had any reason even dimly to foresee his own sudden death, there would have been a new feature in his act of intemperance — a feature of presumption and irreverence, as in one that by possibility felt himself drawing near to the presence of God. But this is no part of the case supposed. And the only new element in the man's act is not any element of extra immorality, but simply of extra misfortune.

1. What is the main idea in this text?

    A. Death, by any method, is horrible.

    B. Slow death is preferable to sudden death.

    C. The positive or negative qualities of sudden death are debatable.

    D. Sudden death is preferable to slow death.

2. What can you infer about the relationships presented in this text?

    A. Religion and philosophy agree that sudden death is to be preferred over other methods.

    B. There are conflicting viewpoints about sudden death between philosophy and religion.

    C. Alcohol and sudden death are matters that seem to go hand in hand.

    D. A pious life determines whether a person will die suddenly or slowly.

3. What is the meaning of the word **prostrate** as it is used in the following sentence from the text?

> On the other hand, the divine Litany of our English Church, when breathing forth supplications, as if in some representative character for the whole human race prostrate before God, places such a death in the very van of horrors.

    A. vertically positioned

    B. up in arms against

    C. angrily opposing

    D. at the mercy of

4. What role does the follwing sentence play in the development of the purpose of this text?

> What is to be thought of sudden death?

    A. It forces the reader to question this for themselves.

    B. It lays the premise for the rest of the paragraph's development of the scope of this idea.

    C. It lays out the author's direction of his opinion that sudden death is preferable.

    D. It implores a more knowledgeable person to answer the question.

5. Which claim is NOT supported by reason?

    A. "Sudden death is here made to crown the climax in a grand ascent of calamities; it is the last of curses; and yet, by the noblest of Romans, it was treated as the first of blessings."

    B. "There does not, however, occur to me any direct scriptural warrant for this earnest petition of the English Litany."

    C. "The first is this: that many people are likely to exaggerate the horror of a sudden death, (I mean the objective horror to him who contemplates such a death, not the subjective horror to him who suffers it,) from the false disposition to lay a stress upon words or acts, simply because by an accident they have become words or acts."

    D. "If a man dies, for instance, by some sudden death when he happens to be intoxicated, such a death is falsely regarded with peculiar horror; as though the intoxication were suddenly exalted into a blasphemy."

6. Which sentence best supports the main idea of this passage?

    A. "It is remarkable that, in different conditions of society it has been variously regarded as the consummation of an earthly career most fervently to be desired, and, on the other hand, as that consummation which is most of all to be deprecated."

    B. ". . . being questioned as to the mode of death which, in his opinion, might seem the most eligible, replied—"That which should be most sudden."

    C. "From lightning and tempest; from plague, pestilence, and famine; from battle and murder, and from sudden death,—Good Lord, deliver us."

    D. "And the only new element in the man's act is not any element of extra immorality, but simply of extra misfortune."

7. How would the tone of the sentence differ if the word **infirmity** were to be replaced with the word **suffering**?

It seems rather a petition indulged to human infirmity, than exacted from human piety.

    A. By replacing "infirmity" with the weaker word "suffering," the tone would seem more in favor of the English Litany's position.

    B. By replacing "infirmity" with the stronger word "suffering," the tone would seem more in favor of the English Litany's position.

    C. By replacing "infirmity" with the stronger word "suffering," the tone would seem more condemnation for the English Litany's position.

    D. There would be no change in tone.

Consider the following two articles, "As Food Imports Rise, So Do Safety Concerns" and "Two Concerns Addressed with One Stone" to answer questions 8–15.

As Food Imports Rise, So Do Safety Concerns

(1) From New Zealand lamb to Mexican papaya and Colombian coffee, your local grocery store provides a truly international experience. And while plantains, eddoes and avocados expand culinary horizons, importing these foods raises legitimate safety concerns.

(2) Americans rely heavily on imported food—the U.S. now imports nearly 85 percent of its fish consumption, and fruit and vegetable imports have doubled since 1998. Even products made in the United States may contain foreign products, such as Chinese wheat gluten or Mexican green onions. And while many countries enforce safety standards equal to those used in the U.S., newly industrialized or industrializing nations may not have the resources or infrastructure to meet safety and quality benchmarks.

(3) Unfortunately, the U.S. Food and Drug Administration (FDA) cannot pick up the slack. The FDA reports that, due to its own lack of resources, 99 percent of the imports that enter the U.S. are not inspected.

(4) Experts agree that prevention, not inspection, will best ensure food safety. One life sciences company, Global Food Technologies, Inc., has developed an organic processing method that ensures that foods do not become contaminated during processing or packaging. By destroying the microbes in the food without harmful chemicals, the company achieves higher safety standards than the minimum required by law. The processing method, designated by the iPura brand name, is currently being used to produce seafood in several overseas nations. Any product bearing the iPura label is guaranteed to be a result of its comprehensive Source-to-Retail food safety program.

(5) The Centers for Disease Control and Prevention (CDC) reports that 325,000 Americans are hospitalized and 5,000 die annually from foodborne illnesses. A food company that does not adhere to food safety practices will eventually be driven out of business, a fact that tends to encourage good practices and results in a relatively safe food supply. Yet reports of new outbreaks continually surface, indicating that more work must be done to safeguard the food supply.

Two Concerns Addressed with One Stone

(1) A global recession has a wearied public in its grip as consumers tighten their belts. Policymakers are engaging in a fierce battle for short-term and long-term solutions while ordinary Americans go about their daily lives with hopes that the situation won't get any worse.

(2) Nearly one trillion dollars has been injected into the faltering system, but immediate success has yet to materialize. Fears about the sagging pocketbook are coupled with feelings of insecurity about the safety and quality of products being imported from overseas, especially the food being imported into the U.S. at an unprecedented rate. Americans currently import over 80 percent of seafood meals consumed, while statistics indicate that seafood is the leading cause of foodborne illnesses. With the FDA able to inspect less than one percent of the shipments into U.S. ports, consumers have expressed deep concern about the safety of their families.

(3) A California-based life sciences company, Global Food Technologies (GFT), is primed to take advantage of the current economic situation by offering its first product into the market, iPura. The first of its kind, iPura is a food-safety company with a unique approach combining techno-logical hardware and methods with trained technicians to ensure that the very highest standards have been implemented in the delivery of seafood imported from overseas.

(4) Including an organic "clean step" that reduces disease-causing pathogens, iPura escorts the product from foreign-based factories to the U.S.-held fork with a seal of authenticity that includes temperature monitoring, traceability, and full transparency for the consumer.

(5) "iPura instills confidence in foreign-sourced seafood by giving consumers the peace of mind they deserve," says GFT President Keith Meeks.

(6) With the wild volatility of most sectors on Wall Street, household goods and staples have not fallen as much as the others, reflective of the trend for consumers to take care of essentials before discretionary purchases such as electronic goods and new automobiles. As food safety has become a major concern for food company executives, with 84 percent in a recent survey stating that food safety is their main priority, iPura offers investors a chance to profit in a time of uncertainty and economic downturn by meeting market demand.

8. What thematic idea do these two articles share?

    A. Foods imported from other countries can be dangerous to Americans' health.

    B. The economic crisis has caused Americans to import more foods.

    C. Imported foods make up the vast majority of our diet.

    D. Americans cannot produce their own foods fast enough to make enough produce to feed themselves without relying on imports.

9. According to the first text, the Food and Drug Administration inspects what percentage of food imports entering the United States?

    A. 85 percent

    B. 1 percent

    C. 15 percent

    D. 99 percent

10. What is one point about which the authors would disagree?

    A. Imports are responsible for our failing economy.

    B. Imports have a role in many of our health problems.

    C. The biggest factor dealing with imported foods is the economy.

    D. America should do more to increase its own food production.

11. How does the impact of these two texts differ?

    A. The first article encourages readers to buy organic foods, while the second article urges readers to consider more healthfully treated foods.

    B. The first article broadens the scope of imports to many kinds of foods, whereas the second article simply deals with seafood.

    C. The first article urges Americans to be more health conscious, while the second encourages us to be more fiscally conservative.

    D. The first article informs readers of the potential impacts of imported food on our health, and the second encourages readers to seek other solutions.

12. How is the idea of iPura differently emphasized in these two articles?

    A. The first article uses it as a scare tactic, while the second article examines the role it can play in ensuring American safety.

    B. The first article discusses iPura as a business model, while the second discusses its beneficial qualities as a scientific endeavor.

    C. The first article mentions it as a new method to ensure safety, and the second article furthers this idea by highlighting it as a vehicle for helping America's failing economy.

    D. The first article examines it as a business model, and the second article uses it to emphasize the dangers of imported foods.

13. What is the purpose of the first article?

    A. to warn Americans about the potential hazardous impacts of imported foods

    B. to discuss the beneficial qualities of the company iPura

    C. to encourage Americans to grow their own food

    D. to criticize the FDA for not inspecting our imports

14. What is the purpose of the second article?

    A. to applaud iPura for its revolutionary business model

    B. to comment on the impacts a failing economy can have on America's consumer habits

    C. to inform Americans about alternatives to imported foods

    D. to warn Americans about the harmful effects of imported foods

15. What is something these two authors would agree about?

    A. A struggling economy creates innovative companies.

    B. Reliance on imported foods should be diminished.

    C. Consumer safety should be the No. 1 priority when dealing with imported foods.

    D. Failing health creates innovative companies.

Read the following article, "What Every Woman Should Know About Long-Term Care," to answer questions 16–21.

(1) With women generally outliving men, planning for long-term care becomes more urgent for them in their pre-retirement years. After all, while longevity definitely has its upside—including more time to enjoy travel and family—there's no denying its biggest potential downside: the increased risk of health problems that can make caring for oneself difficult.

(2) Today, seven in 10 nursing home residents are women.

(3) They also represent a whopping 76 percent of assisted living residents, according to the latest statistics, and two-thirds of all home-care recipients.

(4) And that care isn't necessarily what many would consider "affordable"—unless you're perhaps lucky enough to have the opportunity to enroll in the likes of the Federal Long-Term Care Insurance Program (FLTCIP).

(5) "Like other forms of health care, long-term care is expensive, and costs continually increase," says Paul Forte, CEO of Long Term Care Partners, which administers the FLTCIP. The program is specifically designed to help current and retired federal employees safeguard their retirement income and savings while maintaining their independence and avoiding reliance on their children.

How Will You Pay for Care?

(6) The most recent John Hancock Cost of Care Study puts the national average cost of a licensed home health aide at $20 per hour, with private and semiprivate nursing home rooms going for $235 and $207, respectively, a day.

(7) Those costs aren't generally covered by health plans such as Medicare, the Defense Department's TRICARE, TRICARE for Life, or even the regular Federal Employees Health Benefits Program. And as for Medicaid, as Forte notes, "it covers long-term care only for those with very low income and assets, so the responsibility for paying may fall on you."

(8) Now suppose you're a woman who is eligible for the FLTCIP, but you haven't yet applied. Ask yourself these four questions:

(9) • Considering your health and family history, might you live a long life with health conditions that could hinder caring for yourself?

(10) • Do you live alone?

(11) • If you don't live alone, how might tending to you disrupt the professional and personal lives of others, and do you wish to be dependent on them?

(12) • If you do live alone, will you have the resources not just to pay for care, but to also maintain a comfortable lifestyle?

The Advantages of the Federal Long-Term Care Insurance Program

(13) Established by an act of Congress in 2000 and overseen by the U.S. Office of Personnel Management, the program is tailored exclusively to meet the budgetary and lifestyle needs of what's referred to as "the federal family." And as so often is the case with the federal workforce, the cost to enrollees is surprisingly affordable.

How affordable?

(14) Well, there's a choice of four prepackaged plans that combine the most popular program features, with customizable plans also available.

(15) So, say you're a 45-year-old woman who chooses the FLTCIP's most popular prepackaged plan (Plan B, with the 4 percent inflation rider). You'd pay a biweekly premium of $33.90—less than $68 per month, or slightly more than $2 a day—for protection that can save you thousands of dollars in future care costs.

(16) The program's consumer-friendly website lets you calculate the premium rate for your age and choice of plans, and view current and past informational webinars. Personal consultants can also walk you through the entire process, including plan design and applications.

(17) Again, not everyone is eligible for FLTCIP, and certain medical conditions, or combinations of conditions, will prevent some from being approved for coverage. Premiums are set with the expectation that they'll suffice, but aren't guaranteed. While the group policy is in effect, the Office of Personnel Management must approve an increase in premium.

16. What is the underlying premise of this article?

   A. Men should take better care of themselves so they can live as long as their female partners.

   B. The assumption that women outlive men.

   C. Without proper planning for the future, people can suffer serious consequences.

   D. People should find ways to care for themselves rather than moving into assisted living facilities.

17. Which sentence proves the author has taken other, potentially conflicting factors into consideration before making this argument?

   A. "After all, while longevity definitely has its upside—including more time to enjoy travel and family—there's no denying its biggest potential downside: the increased risk of health problems that can make caring 'for oneself difficult.'"

   B. "Today, seven in 10 nursing home residents are women."

   C. "Established by an act of Congress in 2000 and overseen by the U.S. Office of Personnel Management, the program is tailored exclusively to meet the budgetary and lifestyle needs of what's referred to as 'the federal family.'"

   D. "Again, not everyone is eligible for FLTCIP, and certain medical conditions, or combinations of conditions, will prevent some from being approved for coverage."

18. Identify the text's stated advantages of the Federal Long-Term Care Insurance Program by placing the choice letter (A, B, C, etc.) to go in each of the three blank boxes.

Advantages of Federal Long-Term Care Insurance Program

A. Helps protect retirement assets
B. Provides coverage not available through Medicaid
C. Avoids reliance on private insurers
D. Customizable plans available
E. Locked-in premiums

19. What is the inherent cause-and-effect argument presented in this article?

    A. If you do not raise your children properly, they will not take care of you when you are old.

    B. Longevity will impact choices you will have to make.

    C. The cost of living will not rise in the future.

    D. Living longer will not impact the future.

20. How can this information be applied to readers in different situations?

    A. Readers can be encouraged to make smart decisions (such as saving money) for their future.

    B. Readers can take more time to spend with their children to ensure a healthier relationship.

    C. Readers can ensure they take the right steps to care for themselves in the future.

    D. Readers can visit the websites provided to receive the care mentioned in this article.

21. Place all the supporting details for the main idea in the four blank boxes. Use the letters to make your selections.

Supporting Details

A.	With women generally outliving men, planning for long-term care becomes more urgent for them in their pre-retirement years.
B.	They also represent a whopping 76 percent of assisted living residents, according to the latest statistics, and two-thirds of all home-care recipients.
C.	The program is specifically designed to help current and retired federal employees safeguard their retirement income and savings while maintaining their independence and avoiding reliance on their children.
D.	The most recent John Hancock Cost of Care Study puts the national average cost of a licensed home health aide at $20 per hour, with private and semiprivate nursing home rooms going for $235 and $207, respectively, a day.
E.	And as for Medicaid, as Forte notes, "it covers long-term care only for those with very low income and assets, so the responsibility for paying may fall on you."
F.	How affordable?
G.	Personal consultants can also walk you through the entire process, including plan design and applications.

Consider the following two pieces of information: the article, "Crowdfunding Brings Relief to Student Debt Burden," and the graph, "Crowdfunded Projects on Kickstarter, 2012" to answer questions 22–28.

Crowdfunding Brings Relief to Student Debt Burden

(1) Whether you're a supportive parent, an eager high school grad, or an adult looking to return to school, the reality of higher education is gloomy. Tuition keeps climbing, the job market isn't

improving fast enough, and the mountain of student loan debt passed the $1 trillion mile marker and kept on trucking with enthusiasm.

(2) Successful entrepreneur and owner of NBA team the Dallas Mavericks, Mark Cuban blogged a great question, "We freak out about the trillions of dollars in debt our country faces. What about the trillion dollar plus debt college kids are facing?"

(3) Student debt is a growing problem for more than 37 million Americans. People are falling behind on student loans at a worse level than before. Now, long-term delinquency rates for student loans are higher than delinquency rates for car loans, mortgages, and home equity loans.

(4) These dismal statistics aren't surprising, considering a recent labor analysis by the Associated Press indicating that over half the adults below 25 with a bachelor's degree are under-employed or can't find a job at all.

(5) "Although the situation is growing worse, the federal government hasn't been able to find a real solution to the student loan crisis," says Amy Mintz, founder of *Student Body of America Association* (SBAA). SBAA is a nonprofit organization that offers information, support, and viable solutions to the student debt crisis and escalating costs of higher education through several programs including movie production and disbursement of funds for U.S. students.

(6) SBAA is the fiscal sponsor of CrowdFundEDU—a new and potentially integral piece in the student debt puzzle. CrowdFundEDU is a social fundraising platform with tangible results and real-world applications.

(7) "CrowdFundEDU is basically Kickstarter for education," explains Mintz. "People hold an online fundraiser for any education-related goal. That includes tuition, student loans, seminars, equipment, study-abroad programs, activities, you name it."

(8) Much like Kickstarter, CrowdFundEDU relies on social networks to stir interest and urge supporters to donate to a good cause. People can make direct contributions to fundraisers or a general donation to SBAA, which is tax-deductible and allocated to student and school fundraisers. As with other online fundraisers, seeing strangers and acquaintances alike rally to help someone is inspiring. Get a glimpse of the CrowdFundEDU mentality at *www.projectpayitforward.org*, SBAA's documentary film currently in pre-production.

(9) CrowdFundEDU can be used for all levels of education, including grades K–12 up to a Ph.D. plus trade school degrees and certifications. But, given the heightened interest in the skyrocketing costs of education, the platform sparked special interest in its potential to alleviate the student debt problem. To learn more about the unsustainable student loan system mired in higher education, visit *www.thefallenamericandream.com*.

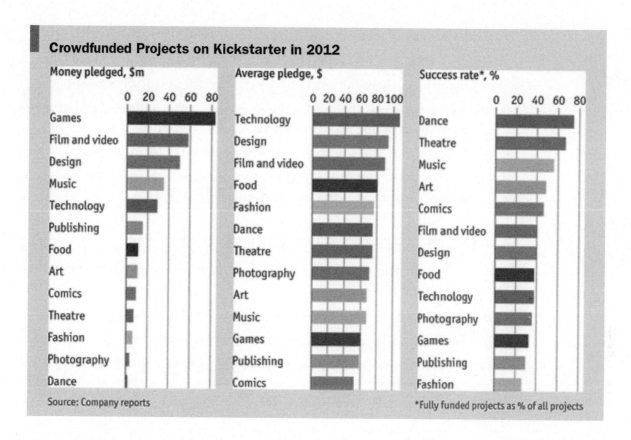

Crowdfunded Projects on Kickstarter in 2012

Money pledged, $m

Games, Film and video, Design, Music, Technology, Publishing, Food, Art, Comics, Theatre, Fashion, Photography, Dance

Average pledge, $

Technology, Design, Film and video, Food, Fashion, Dance, Theatre, Photography, Art, Music, Games, Publishing, Comics

Success rate*, %

Dance, Theatre, Music, Art, Comics, Film and video, Design, Food, Technology, Photography, Games, Publishing, Fashion

Source: Company reports

*Fully funded projects as % of all projects

22. How does the information in the chart clarify the information presented in the article?

   A. The chart negates all information presented in the article because it does not show specific scholarship awards through crowdfunding.

   B. The chart indicates that only fine arts majors, such as photography, music, and dance, will have any success with Kickstarter.

   C. Certain Kickstarter projects have made nearly $80 million dollars, which gives proof there is a substantial amount of money to be made through this avenue.

   D. The chart indicates that technology projects receive the highest pledge value, but games have the most interest.

23. What is the common theme between the two pieces of information?

   A. Crowdfunding can help fund major projects.

   B. Crowdfunding is an unfair and unethical manner to raise money.

   C. Kickstarter is only successful with independent projects that will yield returns.

   D. Patrons do not want to support the arts.

24. How will the graph potentially affect the intended audience of the article?

    A. Students will be incredibly pleased with the graph because it will give them many ideas about the types of projects they can potentially crowdsource.

    B. Students will be angered by the graph because it indicates that traditional methods of paying for school are no longer available to them.

    C. Students with full scholarships will not be affected by the graph.

    D. Students may be disappointed by the information presented by the graph, as it does not show the data regarding educational projects.

25. What conclusions can be drawn from the information presented?

    A. A person will likely come up against many obstacles when attempting to crowdfund his education.

    B. Education is becoming more and more costly as times progress.

    C. Without a college degree, a person cannot be successful in life.

    D. A person must have the proper tools and motivation to make money off of crowdfunding.

26. How can the overall impact of this information be applied to different situations?

    A. People looking to crowdfund might find the best opportunities for projects other than education given the information presented in the chart.

    B. People will find that education is no longer a necessary commodity and will enter the workforce.

    C. People will learn how to use the internet as a tool to build businesses.

    D. People will become more interested in attending or supporting projects backed by crowdfunding websites such as Kickstarter.

27. How does the data in the chart support the author's claims?

    A. The chart indicates that crowdfunding can be lucrative.

    B. The chart indicates that many crowdfunded projects fail.

    C. The chart indicates that education is directly affected by Kickstarter.

    D. The chart indicates that crowdfunding is a time-consuming effort.

28. What conclusions can be drawn from the article and the chart?

    A. Kickstarter projects ultimately make people happy.

    B. Funding through crowdfunding is the solution to tough economic times.

    C. Crowdfunding will pave the way for more independent film projects.

    D. Crowdfunding is a legitimate option for funding one's education.

Read the following excerpt from Ralph Waldo Emerson's essay "Illusions." Then answer questions 29–34.

(1) I own, I did not like the cave so well for eking out its sublimities with this theatrical trick. But I have had many experiences like it, before and since; and we must be content to be pleased without too curiously analyzing the occasions. Our conversation with Nature is not just what it seems. The cloud-rack, the sunrise and sunset glories, rainbows, and northern lights are not quite so spheral as our childhood thought them; and the part our organization plays in them is too large. The senses interfere everywhere, and mix their own structure with all they report of. Once, we fancied the earth a plane, and stationary. In admiring the sunset, we do not yet deduct the rounding, coordinating, pictorial powers of the eye.

(2) The same interference from our organization creates the most of our pleasure and pain. Our first mistake is the belief that the circumstance gives the joy which we give to the circumstance. Life is an ecstasy. Life is sweet as nitrous oxide; and the fisherman dripping all day over a cold pond, the switchman at the railway intersection, the farmer in the field, the negro in the rice-swamp, the fop in the street, the hunter in the woods, the barrister with the jury, the belle at the ball, all ascribe a certain pleasure to their employment, which they themselves give it. Health and appetite impart the sweetness to sugar, bread, and meat. We fancy that our civilization has got on far, but we still come back to our primers.

(3) We live by our imaginations, by our admirations, by our sentiments. The child walks amid heaps of illusions, which he does not like to have disturbed. The boy, how sweet to him is his fancy! how dear the story of barons and battles! What a hero he is, whilst he feeds on his heroes! What a debt is his to imaginative books! He has no better friend or influence, than Scott, Shakespeare, Plutarch, and Homer. The man lives to other objects, but who dare affirm that they are more real? Even the prose of the streets is full of refractions. In the life of the dreariest alderman, fancy enters into all details, and colors them with rosy hue. He imitates the air and actions of people whom he admires, and is raised in his own eyes. He pays a debt quicker to a rich man than to a poor man. He wishes the bow and compliment of some leader in the state, or in society; weighs what he says; perhaps he never comes nearer to him for that, but dies at last better contented for this amusement of his eyes and his fancy.

29. What is the theme of this passage?

   A. At some point in our lives, we all must grow up and abandon the illusions of our youth.

   B. Imagination is detrimental to achievement.

   C. People's imaginations and attitude are what shape our experience of events.

   D. Illusions color our perceptions of reality.

30. What is the meaning of the word **fop** as it is used in the fifth line of paragraph 2?

   A. goat

   B. fancy gentleman

   C. angry

   D. rubbish

31. What is the author's attitude toward illusions?

   A. Illusions are sentimental aspirations, which, while necessary, should be kept separate from our professional lives.

   B. Illusions are what help us become better people.

   C. Illusions are only to be embraced because to deny them would be a distraction that keeps us from being productive.

   D. Illusions are a necessary and integral part of our lives, and grow with us from childhood into adulthood.

32. How does the structure of the following sentence affect its message?

   Life is sweet as nitrous oxide; and the fisherman dripping all day over a cold pond, the switchman at the railway intersection, the farmer in the field, the negro in the rice-swamp, the fop in the street, the hunter in the woods, the barrister with the jury, the belle at the ball, all ascribe a certain pleasure to their employment, which they themselves give it.

   A. The use of figurative language helps to draw the reader into believing that life is very sweet.

   B. The use of dependent clauses as part of a run-on sentence helps to sway the reader into the melodious nature of imagination.

   C. The listing employed helps to portray a universal aspect of the idea that all walks of life require imagination and joy.

   D. The semicolon joins the two sentences together, making them a coherent argument.

33. What is the main rhetorical approach employed by Emerson in this passage?

    A. Emotional appeal

    B. Appeal to tradition

    C. Logical persuasion

    D. Ethical appeal

34. What is the author's implicit purpose in this text?

    A. To encourage readers to reflect on what makes them so lucky in life.

    B. To encourage readers to embrace imagination and live life joyously.

    C. To encourage readers to be nicer to each other.

    D. To encourage readers to live every day as if it was their last.

Read the following passage from *Jane Eyre* by Charlotte Brontë. Then answer questions 35–40.

(1) It is in vain to say human beings ought to be satisfied with tranquility: they must have action; and they will make it if they cannot find it. Millions are condemned to a stiller doom than mine, and millions are in silent revolt against their lot. Nobody knows how many rebellions besides political rebellions ferment in the masses of life which people earth. Women are supposed to be very calm generally: but women feel just as men feel; they need exercise for their faculties, and a field for their efforts, as much as their brothers do; they suffer from too rigid a restraint, too absolute a stagnation, precisely as men would suffer; and it is narrow-minded in their more privileged fellow-creatures to say that they ought to confine themselves to making puddings and knitting stockings, to playing on the piano and embroidering bags. It is thoughtless to condemn them, or laugh at them, if they seek to do more or learn more than custom has pronounced necessary for their sex.

(2) When thus alone, I not unfrequently heard Grace Poole's laugh: the same peal, the same low, slow ha! ha! which, when first heard, had thrilled me: I heard, too, her eccentric murmurs; stranger than her laugh. There were days when she was quite silent; but there were others when I could not account for the sounds she made. Sometimes I saw her: she would come out of her room with a basin, or a plate, or a tray in her hand, go down to the kitchen and shortly return, generally (oh, romantic reader, forgive me for telling the plain truth!) bearing a pot of porter. Her appearance always acted as a damper to the curiosity raised by her oral oddities: hard-featured and staid, she had no point to which interest could attach. I made some attempts to draw her into conversation, but she seemed a person of few words: a monosyllabic reply usually cut short every effort of that sort.

(3) The other members of the household, viz., John and his wife, Leah the housemaid, and Sophie the French nurse, were decent people; but in no respect remarkable; with Sophie I used to talk French, and sometimes I asked her questions about her native country; but she was not of a descriptive or narrative turn, and generally gave such vapid and confused answers as were calculated rather to check than encourage inquiry.

(4) October, November, December passed away. One afternoon in January, Mrs. Fairfax had begged a holiday for Adele, because she had a cold; and, as Adele seconded the request with an ardour that reminded me how precious occasional holidays had been to me in my own childhood, I accorded it, deeming that I did well in showing pliability on the point. It was a fine, calm day, though very cold; I was tired of sitting still in the library through a whole long morning: Mrs. Fairfax had just written a letter which was waiting to be posted, so I put on my bonnet and cloak and volunteered to carry it to Hay; the distance, two miles, would be a pleasant winter afternoon walk. Having seen Adele comfortably seated in her little chair by Mrs. Fairfax's parlour fireside, and given her her best wax doll (which I usually kept enveloped in silver paper in a drawer) to play with, and a story-book for change of amusement; and having replied to her "Revenez bientot, ma bonne amie, ma chere Mdlle. Jeannette," with a kiss I set out.

35. Indicate the order of events in this passage by placing the correct letter in each box.

    A.   Jane discusses the need for women to have an occupation.

    B.   Jane invites Adele for a holiday.

    C.   Jane sees Grace Poole steal beer from the kitchen.

    D.   Jane speaks with Sophie, the French nurse.

    E.   Jane hears the strange laugh of Grace Poole.

    F.   Jane goes for a walk.

Order of Events

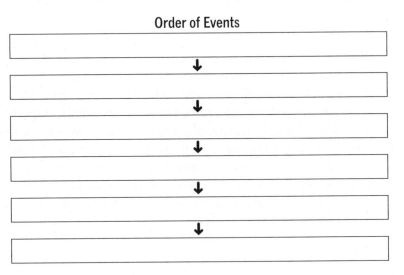

36. Which sentence best indicates that Brontë may be a feminist?

    A.   Women are supposed to be very calm generally: but women feel just as men feel; they need exercise for their faculties, and a field for their efforts, as much as their brothers do; they suffer from too rigid a restraint, too absolute a stagnation, precisely as men would suffer; and it is narrow-minded in their more privileged fellow-creatures to say that they ought to confine themselves to making puddings and knitting stockings, to playing on the piano and embroidering bags.

    B.   There were days when she was quite silent; but there were others when I could not account for the sounds she made.

    C.   The other members of the household, viz., John and his wife, Leah the housemaid, and Sophie the French nurse, were decent people; but in no respect remarkable; with Sophie I used to talk French, and sometimes I asked her questions about her native country; but she was not of a descriptive or narrative turn, and generally gave such vapid and confused answers as were calculated rather to check than encourage inquiry.

    D.   One afternoon in January, Mrs. Fairfax had begged a holiday for Adele, because she had a cold; and, as Adele seconded the request with an ardour that reminded me how precious occasional holidays had been to me in my own childhood, I accorded it, deeming that I did well in showing pliability on the point.

37. How does Jane feel toward Grace Poole?

    A. interested

    B. caring

    C. judgmental

    D. anxious

38. What is the effect of the figurative language used in the following sentence?

> Nobody knows how many rebellions besides political rebellions ferment in the masses of life which people earth.

A. Repeating the word "rebellions" helps to cement the author's feeling that mutiny is a way of life.

B. Using the word "ferment" to describe internal struggles indicates a rising boil of passion within a person, inflaming the audience's senses.

C. The phrase, "masses of life which people earth" is particularly effective in indicating the sheer number of people who live on earth.

D. No figurative language is used in this sentence.

39. What is the effect of paragraph 1 on the rest of the selection?

A. It sets the stage for the events to unfold.

B. It describes the characters in the rest of the piece.

C. It sets the tone for the entire novel.

D. It indicates Jane's fierce independence.

40. What can you conclude about Jane's character?

A. Jane is weak.

B. Jane is more interested in the affairs of others than she is in her own.

C. Jane is curious and strong-willed.

D. Jane is cruel-hearted.

REASONING THROUGH LANGUAGE ARTS
Section 2

One Extended-Response Essay
45 minutes (followed by a 10-minute break)

Practice Test 2: Reasoning Through Language Arts (RLA)

Section 2 (Extended Response)

> **Analyze the thoughts and arguments presented in the book excerpt in Passage #1 and in the excerpt of the speech in Passage #2.**
>
> **In your response, develop an argument in which you explain how one way of invention is better supported than the other. Incorporate relevant and specific evidence from both sources to support your argument.**
>
> **Remember, the better-argued position is not necessarily the position with which you agree. You ust complete this task in 45 minutes. Your response should contain 4 to 7 paragraphs of 3 to 7 sentences each, or about 300 to 500 words.**
>
> **If possible, type your response on a computer. Be sure to time yourself.**

Innovation and Invention Stimulus Passage #1

Excerpt from *Nature's Teachings* by John George Wood

It is tolerably evident that the first raft was nothing more than a tree-trunk. Finding that the single trunk was apt to turn over with the weight of the occupant, the next move was evidently to lash two trunks side by side.

Next would come the great advance of putting the trunks at some distance apart, and connecting them with cross-bars. This plan would obviate even the chance of the upsetting of the raft, and it still survives in that curious mixture of the raft and canoe, the outrigger boat of the Polynesians, which no gale of wind can upset. It may be torn to pieces by the storm, but nothing can capsize it as long as it holds together.

Laying a number of smaller logs or branches upon the bars which connect the larger logs is an evident mode of forming a continuous platform, and thus the raft is completed. It would not be long before the superior buoyancy of a hollow over a solid log would be discovered, and so, when the savage could not find a log ready hollowed to his hand, he would hollow one for himself, mostly using fire in lieu of tools. The progress from a hollowed log, or "dug-out," as it is popularly called, to the bark canoe, and then the built boat, naturally followed, the boats increasing in size until they were developed into ships.

Now, let us ask ourselves whether, in creation, there are any natural boats which existed before man came upon the earth, and from which he might have taken the idea if he had been able to reason on the subject. The Paper Nautilus is, of course, the first example that comes before the mind; but although, as we have seen, the delicate shell of the nautilus is not used as a boat, and its sailing and rowing powers are alike fabulous, there is, as is the case with most fables, a substratum of truth, and there are aquatic mollusks which form themselves into boats, although they do not propel themselves with sails or oars.

(Source: Wood, J.G., 1907. Nature's Teachings: Human Invention Anticipated by Nature. *London: The Gresham Press, Unwin Brothers, Ltd.)*

Innovation and Invention Stimulus Passage #2

Excerpt of Inaugural Address of President John F. Kennedy
Washington, D.C.

The world is very different now. For man holds in his mortal hands the power to abolish all forms of human poverty and all forms of human life. And yet the same revolutionary beliefs for which our forebears fought are still at issue around the globe—the belief that the rights of man come not from the generosity of the state but from the hand of God.

We dare not forget today that we are the heirs of that first revolution. Let the word go forth from this time and place, to friend and foe alike, that the torch has been passed to a new generation of Americans—born in this century, tempered by war, disciplined by a hard and bitter peace, proud of our ancient heritage—and unwilling to witness or permit the slow undoing of those human rights to which this nation has always been committed, and to which we are committed today at home and around the world.

Let every nation know, whether it wishes us well or ill, that we shall pay any price, bear any burden, meet any hardship, support any friend, oppose any foe, in order to assure the survival and the success of liberty.

This much we pledge—and more.

To those old allies whose cultural and spiritual origins we share, we pledge the loyalty of faithful friends. United there is little we cannot do in a host of cooperative ventures. Divided there is little we can do—for we dare not meet a powerful challenge at odds and split asunder.

To those new states whom we welcome to the ranks of the free, we pledge our word that one form of colonial control shall not have passed away merely to be replaced by a far more iron tyranny. We shall not always expect to find them supporting our view. But we shall always hope to find them strongly supporting their own freedom—and to remember that, in the past, those who foolishly sought power by riding the back of the tiger ended up inside.

(Source: John F. Kennedy Presidential Library and Museum)

If you don't have a computer handy, use this box to write your response.

PRACTICE TEST 2 (cont'd)

REASONING THROUGH LANGUAGE ARTS
Section 3

50 questions
60 minutes

Practice Test 2: Reasoning Through Language Arts (RLA)

Section 3

Read the following blog entry and answer questions 1–9.

Battle of the Sexes

(1) Today a man actually said, out loud, to me, "Only a woman would be so selfish." He was talking about my very legal, very public right to park my Vespa—unobtrusively at that—at a bicycle rack on a sidewalk. I suppose it is up for debate whether it is selfish of me to: drive a scooter, take an insignificant and unclaimed slice of the sidewalk, protect my expensive belonging by securing it to an immoveable object designed for such a purpose, live and breathe at all . . . but whether or not my actions caused this guy some inconvenience or strife for which I should have been aware of my need to apologize to him is actually irrelevant. What really startled me, of course, was his blatant sexism.

(2) This man did not appear to be uneducated, in fact, he was really quite dapper, and albeit rotund (so he must be making decent enough money). He wasn't notably older than me and didn't have a southern drawl—though DC is still south of the Mason-Dixon line, no matter which way you slice it—so there was no reason to believe he had grown up around such ardently expressed, vocal prejudice. (I only refer to the south as a seed of such sexism because I remember my science teacher in Fayetteville in the 7th grade telling me in front of the class that my effort to get an A was a waste of time, women belonged in the kitchen.) This was just an average, middle class white guy.

(3) I channeled Esther Greenwood. I have never met a woman-hater before.

(4) So I started thinking, what makes men hate women? Generally, I think it is women who tend to be the ones big on the slandering of the opposite sex. Stereotypically, gals have all the right ammunition to fire against men: rape, oppression, promiscuity, abandonment, blah blah blah . . . But what does our sex, in general, do to paint ourselves as fundamentally selfish to the menfolk?

(5) I did see a special on social networking sites about women searching for men to be her "Sugar Daddies," but it seems to me that this is often a consensual, upfront arrangement, like prostitution (which I'm neither championing nor denouncing, just noting it as a contractual agreement), in which money and goods are exchanged for services. Sure, these "Sugar Babies" may have some pretty questionable motives, but is it necessarily selfish? It seems to me both parties are receiving benefits. I think women, yes, can be good with manipulation, particularly that of the emotional variety, but that makes us coercive, not selfish. I guess in the past women have typically been the ones to survive off their husband's much fatter paychecks, but still, they cook, clean, mother children, entertain at least five full-time-stay-at-home-OTHER jobs at that, AND work on a budget of what is allowed them. I don't really see that as selfish, but I guess some men might.

(6) I wonder if this particular man's wife left him and took the car and the house in the 'burbs, and that's why he was at union station in the first place—to take the metro to his measly intern-esque, low-paying job, only to kiss the profit goodbye to pay her alimony and child support while she's off with Mr. Older and Much Richer. That would score him some right to be bitter chips, I guess. But to be bitter to ALL women? Me? I never dated him, never would, actually, and had never given him any reason to judge and exploit my character flaws. Let alone those of my whole sex.

(7) Effectively quieting the notion that he may have been speaking to someone else, what further eludes me about this situation is why he would articulate this thought while looking me dead in the eyes. Wouldn't it have been more productive, if I was indeed BEING selfish, to say something like, Hey. You know, that's kind of rude, what you're doing there. I don't have a bike with me, but if I did, I might like to park it there, instead of at the other, far less accessible to YOU, but not anyone with a bicycle space. Why don't you move somewhere else? Or, Hey. You're in the way of my invisible entourage. Move it.

(8) I probably would have taken ACTION in his best interest if he had approached me with a more logical and concerted effort. Nope. Instead all I get is snarky bitterness because I'm a woman. Of course, I have to fight the urge to retort with an equally debasing, dehumanizing sexist remark, because I realize: it's not because he's a man that he made that remark. It's because he's _____. I've inserted several colorful invectives in that sentence to pass the time in commute between work and home.

(9) Maybe insult was added to injury because I towered over him. Strong, tall women. Man, we rock. We scare men into making derogatory comments at us just because they're intimidated.

1.   How can this sentence be rewritten to avoid the error?

I wonder if this particular man's wife left him and took the car and the house in the 'burbs, and that's why he was at union station in the first place—to take the metro to his measly intern-esque, low-paying job, only to kiss the profit goodbye to pay her alimony and child support while she's off with Mr. Older and Much Richer.

A.   "I wonder if this particular man's wife left him and took the car and the house in the 'burbs, and that's why he was at Union Station in the first place—to take the metro to his measly intern-esque, low-paying job, only to kiss the profit goodbye to pay her alimony and child support while she's off with Mr. Older and Much Richer.

B.   "I wonder if this particular man's wife left him and took the car and the house in the 'burbs, and that's why he was at union station in the first place—to take the metro to his measly intern-esque, low-paying job, only to kiss the profit goodbye to pay her alimony and child support while she's off with Mr. older and much richer.

C. "I wonder if this particular man's wife left him and took the car and the house in the 'burbs, and that's why he was at union station in the first place—to take the metro to his measly intern-esque, low-paying job, only too kiss the profit goodbye to pay her alimony and child support while she's off with Mr. Older and Much Richer.

D. No change.

2. Rewrite this segment from paragraph 6 to avoid the fragmentation.

I never dated him, never would, actually, and had never given him any reason to judge and exploit my character flaws. Let alone those of my whole sex.

_____

_____

_____

_____

_____

_____

3. How can the following sentence from paragraph 5 be rewritten to avoid the pronoun confusion?

I did see a special on social networking sites about women searching for men to be her "Sugar Daddies," but it seems to me that this is often a consensual, upfront arrangement, like prostitution (which I'm neither championing nor denouncing, just noting it as a contractual agreement), in which money and goods are exchanged for services.

A. I did see a special on social networking sites about women searching for men to be her "Sugar Daddies," but it seems to me that this is often a consensual, upfront arrangement, like prostitution (which I'm neither championing nor denouncing, just noting it as a contractual agreement), when money and goods are exchanged for services.

B. I did see a special on Social Networking sites about women searching for men to be her "Sugar Daddies," but it seems to me that this is often a consensual, upfront arrangement, like prostitution (which I'm neither championing nor denouncing, just noting it as a contractual agreement), in which money and goods are exchanged for services.

C. I did see a special on social networking sites about women searching for men to be their "Sugar Daddies," but it seems to me that this is often a consensual, upfront arrangement, like prostitution (which I'm neither championing nor denouncing, just noting it as a contractual agreement), in which money and goods are exchanged for services.

D. No change.

4. How should the following sentence from paragraph 8 be rewritten to avoid the subject-verb agreement error?

> Of course, I have to fight the urge to retort with an equally debasing, dehumanizing sexist remark, because I realize: it's not because he's a man that he made that remark.

   A. "Of course, I have to fight the urge to retort with an equally debasing, dehumanizing sexist remark, because I realized: it's not because he's a man that he made that remark."

   B. "Of course, I have to fight the urge to retort with an equally debasing, dehumanizing sexist remark, because I realize it's not because he's a man that he made that remark."

   C. "Of course, I had to fight the urge to retort with an equally debasing, dehumanizing sexist remark, because I realize: it's not because he's a man that he made that remark."

   D. No change.

5. Correctly punctuate the following excerpt from the text:

> Wouldn't it have been more productive, if I was indeed BEING selfish, to say something like, Hey. You know, that's kind of rude, what you're doing there. I don't have a bike with me, but if I did, I might like to park it there, instead of at the other, far less accessible to YOU, but not anyone with a bicycle spaces. Why don't you move somewhere else? Or, Hey. You're in the way of my invisible entourage. Move it.

6. How can the following sentence be rewritten to avoid the informal register—that is, to not come off as casual?

> I wonder if this particular man's wife left him and took the car and the house in the 'burbs, and that's why he was at union station in the first place—to take the metro to his measly intern-esque, low-paying job, only to kiss the profit goodbye to pay her alimony and child support while she's off with Mr. Older and Much Richer.

   A. I wonder if this particular man's wife left him and took the car and the house in the suburbs, and that's why he was at Union Station in the first place—to take the metro to his measly intern-style, low-paying job, only to kiss the profit goodbye to pay her alimony and child support while she's off with Mr. Older and Much Richer.

   B. I wonder if this particular man's wife left him and took the car and the house in the 'burbs, and that's why he was at Union Station in the first place—to take the metro to his measly intern-esque, low-paying job, only to kiss the profit goodbye to pay her alimony and child support while she's off with someone else.

   C. I wonder if this particular man's wife left him and took the car and the house in the suburbs, and that's why he was at union station in the first place—to take the metro to his measly intern-esque, low-paying job, only to kiss the profit goodbye to pay her alimony and child support while she's off with Mr. Older and Much Richer.

  D. No change.

7. Which word should replace the word **their** in the following sentence?

    I guess in the past women have typically been the ones to survive off their husband's much fatter paychecks, but still, they cook, clean, mother children, entertain at least five full-time stay-at-home OTHER jobs at that, AND work on a budget of what is allowed them.

  A. they're

  B. there

  C. her

  D. No change.

8. How should this sentence be rewritten to ensure proper coordination?

    I suppose it is up for debate whether it is selfish of me to: drive a scooter, take an insignificant and unclaimed slice of the sidewalk, protect my expensive belonging by securing it to an immoveable object designed for such a purpose, live and breathe at all . . . but whether or not my actions caused this guy some inconvenience or strife for which I should have been aware of my need to apologize to him is actually irrelevant.

  A. I suppose it is up for debate whether it is selfish of me to drive a scooter, take an insignificant and unclaimed slice of the sidewalk, protect my expensive belonging by securing it to an immoveable object designed for such a purpose, live and breathe at all . . . but whether or not my actions caused this guy some inconvenience or strife for which I should have been aware of my need to apologize to him is actually irrelevant.

  B. I suppose it is up for debate whether it is selfish of me to drive a scooter, take an insignificant and unclaimed slice of the sidewalk, protect my expensive belonging by securing it to an immoveable object designed for such a purpose, or live and breathe at all . . . but whether or not my actions caused this guy some inconvenience or strife for which I should have been aware of my need to apologize to him is actually irrelevant.

  C. I suppose it is up for debate whether it is selfish of me to: drive a scooter; take an insignificant and unclaimed slice of the sidewalk; protect my expensive belonging by securing it to an immoveable object designed for such a purpose; live and breathe at all . . . but whether or not my actions caused this guy some inconvenience or strife for which I should have been aware of my need to apologize to him is actually irrelevant.

  D. No change.

9. How should this sentence be rewritten to fix the awkward construction?

> Effectively quieting the notion that he may have been speaking to someone else, what further eludes me about this situation is why he would articulate this thought while looking me dead in the eyes.

 A. Effective to quiet the notion that he may have been speaking to someone else, what further eludes me about this situation is why he would articulate this thought while looking me dead in the eyes.

 B. Effectively quieting the notion that he may have been speaking to someone else, what further eludes me about this situation is why he would have possibly articulated this thought while looking me dead in the eyes.

 C. What further eludes me about this situation is why he would articulate this thought while looking me dead in the eyes, effectively quieting the notion that he may have been speaking to someone else.

 D. No change.

Read the following business memo. Then answer questions 10–18.

Success Prep: Helping Struggling Students

(1) Yesterday Melanie Harris and I visited Carver High School to investigate their LEARN model. They have been working on intervention strategies for 10 years, and are perhaps the most progressive school in the county in terms of being a truly established PLC. It is imperative we change our model to follow theirs.

(2) We met with students, teachers, administrators, student services and testing coordinators, and came back with more information than I can share in a succinct email. To put it simply, Carver's successful plan boils down to three pieces:

(3) 1) They use their **Success Prep** classes to directly intervene with students who are struggling. These kids, as it was beautifully put, are the ones they hope become AVID kids. The rules for scheduling students are: no IEPs. 1.5-2.5 GPA, no behavioral problems, no big weakness. SP is a course that organizes binders, checks homework, assigns LEARN, teaches study strategies, etc. They choose their teachers carefully. There are 3 sections arranged by grade level (9, 10 and 11). They are an English teacher, a math teacher and a science teacher, and they are the "jack of all trades" in the departments. They teach IB courses, but CHOOSE to also work with these kids to establish a rapport with them, encourage them and help them succeed. These teacher's were paid for 8 hours to meet in the summer to plan the year, they all have the same planning block and they have every resource necessary in their classrooms. (10th grade SP has every 10th grade textbook, etc.). SP meets the same block so the teachers can send kids to the math expert if that is where the student is struggling. The classes started very small (around 7) so students could be added through the year as they were identified. At March they have about 15–20.

(4)   2) **LEARN** has two levels of teacher support, advisor and mentor. LEARN has 3 levels of Standing: Good, Monitored, and Supervised. Good students have all Cs or above Monitored have 1 D or F and Supervised have multiple Ds and Fs. Carver has PDAs for students to check in, but they do not assign LEARN unless a student is in Supervised Standing. They keep records about where everyone goes, though, and once a quarter, the LEARN advisor disseminates a LEARN report along with the interim. This report is created by the Testing Coordinator. The LEARN report shows the child where they have gone, and this is a useful tool for the teacher at parent conferences. Carver has LEARN 4 times a week (not Wednesday, the day the school begins late for teacher collaboration). The students said they hate Wednesdays because they NEEDS LEARN, and that the 36 minutes is not nearly enough time.

(5)   3) Carver staffs an IA who runs **ISS**, but this is an ACADEMIC intervention for the most part, with only occasional behavioral referrals. When kids are not attending assigned LEARN, or when they are chronically at the "Supervised" level, teachers can send their students to ISS teachers know they are monitored there. The IA is gifted in math, and he establishes a good rapport with the students and forces them to do work. This runs all day.

(6) A few things the crew at Carver communicated very strongly:

(7)   1) One time a week is not nearly enough to make this model work in any kind of productive fashion.

(8)   2) Student choice is very important, and you have to trust the kids to do the right thing so the atmosphere does not become negative. Someone said this profound statement, "Why make a rule that only applies to 10% of the kids that 100% of the people have to follow?" There was some disagreement about whether or not the cafeteria should be open to students as a place to hang out, but at first the general sentiment was that it was a good strategy for a reward. Of course, there is a gate keeper, and students not in Good Standing CANNOT enter. This is easy to determine by the PDAs.

(9)   3) All the work for success is done on the front end.

(10)   4) ILT uses their time to talk about the 10% of kids who keep failing. However, they've begun the new LEARN model, they have decreased their failure rate to 8%. They have the highest IB scores in the county, and the largest number of students sitting for exams because their culture is such: give the kids the resources they need to take really hard classes and they will do it.

(11) Finally, we learned that Carver is a really excellent school for teachers, parents, administrators and students to be at.

10. Fix the apostrophe in the following sentence from paragraph 3.

These teacher's were paid for 8 hours to meet in the summer to plan the year, they all have the same planning block and they have every resource necessary in their classrooms.

    A. These teachers' were paid for 8 hours to meet in the summer to plan the year, they all have the same planning block and they have every resource necessary in their classrooms.

    B. These teacher's were paid for 8 hours to meet in the summer to plan the year, they'll have the same planning block and they have every resource necessary in their classrooms.

    C. These teachers were paid for 8 hours to meet in the summer to plan the year, they all have the same planning block and they have every resource necessary in their classrooms.

    D. No change.

11. How should this sentence from paragraph 8 be rewritten to give it more clarity?

There was some disagreement about whether or not the cafeteria should be open to students as a place to hang out, but at first the general sentiment was that it was a good strategy for a reward.

    A. At first there was some disagreement about whether or not the cafeteria should be open to students as a place to hang out, but the general sentiment was that it was a good strategy for a reward.

    B. There was some disagreement about whether or not the cafeteria should be open to students as a place to hang out, but the general sentiment was that it was a good strategy for a reward at first.

    C. There was some disagreement about whether or not the cafeteria should at first be open to students as a place to hang out, but the general sentiment was that it was a good strategy for a reward.

    D. No change.

12. How should this sentence be rewritten to avoid the run-on?

When kids are not attending assigned LEARN, or when they are chronically at the "Supervised" level, teachers can send their students to ISS teachers know they are monitored there.

A. When kids are not attending assigned LEARN or when they are chronically at the "Supervised" level teachers can send their students to ISS teachers know they are monitored there.

B. When kids are not attending assigned LEARN, or when they are chronically at the "Supervised" level, teachers can send their students to ISS; teachers know they are monitored there.

C. When kids are not attending assigned LEARN, or when they are chronically at the "Supervised" level, teachers can send their students to ISS teachers. Know they are monitored there.

D. No change.

13. Correct the punctuation in this sentence from paragraph 4.

Good students have all Cs or above Monitored have 1 D or F and Supervised have multiple Ds and Fs.

_____

_____

14. How should this sentence be properly worded?

Finally, we learned that Carver is a really excellent school for teachers, parents, administrators and students to be at.

A. Finally, Carver is a really excellent school for teachers, parents, administrators and students to be.

B. Finally, we learned that Carver is a really excellent school for teachers, parents, administrators and students.

C. Finally, we learned that Carver is a really excellent school.

D. No change.

15. Which word should replace the word **to** in the sentence?

One time a week is not nearly enough to make this model work in any kind of productive fashion.

A. too

B. two

C. that

D. No change.

16. Fix the subject-verb agreement in this sentence:

The students said they hate Wednesdays because they needs LEARN, and that the 36 minutes is not nearly enough time.

A. The students said them hate Wednesdays because they needs LEARN, and that the 36 minutes is not nearly enough time.

B. The students said they hate Wednesdays because they need LEARN, and that the 36 minutes is not nearly enough time.

C. The students said they hate Wednesday's because they needs LEARN, and that the 36 minutes is not nearly enough time.

D. No change.

17. What change needs to be made to fix the transitional word in the following sentence?

However, they've begun the new LEARN model, they have decreased their failure rate to 8%.

A. Change "However," to "Since."

B. Change "However," to "Therefore" and remove the comma.

C. Change "However," to "Since" and remove the comma.

D. No change.

18. Rewrite this sentence to eliminate wordiness:

It is imperative that we must change our model to follow theirs.

_____

_____

_____

_____

_____

_____

_____

Read the following pre-service teacher's essay. Then answer questions 19–26.

How I Knew I Wanted to be an Engligh Teacher

(1) I knew that I wanted to be an English teacher NOT in my English class. I was actually in speech, practicing an oratory about imaginary friends to the sand hills of North Carolina just beyond the second story window of my high school. I was very seriously discussing the negative impacts

of growing up too quickly when a marvelous event unfolded. The AP Physics teacher ran out of space for a very complicated equation on his chalkboard. It was the first clear and mildly warm day (in February), and they decided to bring his class outside to finish the problem on a seemingly endless chalkboard: the sidewalk. The commencement of the public chalking intrigued me. I stood in awe as I watched the fifteen student's mark up the sidewalk for the better part of an hour with what looked to me like hieroglyphics.

(2)   I hate physics. I am no good at math and equations. But this man made me want to drop my other interests, meander outside and take part in finding the solution. In science. I remember thinking to myself—Wow. If that man can make physics—a curriculum in which I have absolutely zero interest—look appealing to me, imagine what I could do with English.

(3)   Being that I wanted to become a high school English teacher, I've never forgotten this day. When I was a junior in high school, a purpose for my life began to develop as I watched this teacher change the lives of his students, my peers, heck, even me—the irrelevant spy and innocent bystander, mauled by physics. My purpose was stemmed in an emerging belief, a belief that everyone deserves the opportunity to make meaningful connections to frustrating tasks, and sometimes we require the service of a talented guide to help us make those connections. I am lucky enough to be on the path to becoming one such a guide.

(4)   In my experience as a Student teacher, I have learned that in my job, content is secondary. I believe that high school English classes are not about Literature with a capital L. Reading and writing are merely byproducts of the work we do with kids. In a classroom where we compete with texting, homecoming, budding adulthood, celebrities, fashion and bullying, we have to find ways to use their interests, their problems, and their lives to relates to the program of studies we are required to teach. Teaching high school English is about opening students' minds to possibility. I believe English classes are about preparing students for life outside of high school, and if we're lucky enough, to create one or two English majors along the way. If we're really lucky, we'll engender a lifelong love of learning and reading. Our real job is singular: to help them develop their ability to think. Our means are simply works of Literature.

19. Which of the edits eliminates the fragment in this example?

> But this man made me want to drop my other interests, meander outside and take part in finding the solution. In science.

   A. "This man made me want to drop my other interests, meander outside and take part in finding the solution. In science."

   B. "But this man made me want to drop my other interests, meander outside and take part in finding the solution, in science."

   C. "But this man made me want to drop my other interests, and meander outside and take part in finding the solution. In science"

   D. No change.

20. How should the following sentence be edited to correct the pronoun agreement?

It was the first clear and mildly warm day (in February), and they decided to bring his class outside to finish the problem on a seemingly endless chalkboard: the sidewalk.

A. Replace "they" with "he."

B. Replace "they" with "him."

C. Replace "his" with "their."

D. No change.

21. Edit the illogical word order in this sentence:

But this man made me want to drop my other interests, meander outside and take part in finding the solution.

A. Replace "meander" with "wander."

B. Replace "other" with "current."

C. Replace "But" with "However."

D. No change.

22. Correct the capitalization in this sentence:

In my experience as a Student teacher, I have learned that in my job, content is secondary.

A. "In my experience as a Student Teacher, I have learned that in my job, Content is secondary."

B. "In my experience as a student Teacher, I have learned that in my job, content is secondary."

C. "In my experience as a student teacher, I have learned that in my job, content is secondary."

D. No change.

23. Correct the awkward wording in this sentence:

Being that I wanted to become a high school English teacher, I've never forgotten this day.

A. "Because I wanted to become a high school English teacher, I've never forgotten this day."

B. "I've never forgotten this day, being that I wanted to become a high school English teacher."

C. "I wanted to become a high school English teacher, I've never forgotten this day."

D. No change.

24. Correct the subject-verb agreement with the interceding phrase in this sentence from paragraph 4:

> In a classroom where we compete with texting, homecoming, budding adulthood, celebrities, fashion and bullying, we have to find ways to use their interests, their problems, and their lives to relates to the program of studies we are required to teach.

A. In a classroom where we compete with texting, homecoming, budding adulthood, celebrities, fashion and bullying, we have to find ways to use their interests, their problems, and their lives to relates to the program of study we are required to teach

B. In a classroom where we compete with texting, homecoming, budding adulthood, celebrities, fashion and bullying, we have to find ways to use their interests, their problems, and their lives to relate to the program of studies we are required to teach

C. In a classroom where we compete, we have to find ways to use their interests, their problems, and their lives to relates to the program of studies we are required to teach

D. No change.

25. Which word should replace the word **knew** in the following sentence?

> I knew that I wanted to be an English teacher NOT in my English class.

A. new

B. know

C. think

D. No change.

26. How should the informal use be corrected in the following sentence?

> When I was a junior in high school, a purpose for my life began to develop as I watched this teacher change the lives of his students, my peers, heck, even me—the irrelevant spy and innocent bystander, mauled by physics.

A. Remove the word "heck" and the comma following it.

B. Replace the word "mauled" with "intrigued."

C. Remove the phrase "When I was a junior in high school."

D. No change.

Read the following information to answer questions 27–34.

Your First Time as a Forensics Judge?

(1) Since everyone must start somewhere—here are a few tips . . .

(2) • Bring a reliable stopwatch, pen and/or pencils. Arrive at the high school where the tournament is being held ON TIME!! Late judges result in fines for the school, and late starts equal long days!

(3) • When you arrive, check in with the coaches (usually in the judges' lounge or near the TAB ROOM). Find out where and when the Judges' Meeting will be held & GO!

(4) • Your coach will give you a judge code. This code is used to identify your judging assignments—no switching judge codes! (It results in BIG problems!)

(5) • Claim a comfortable spot in the judge's lounge. So wear comfortable clothing, it can be a long day; bring reading material and food. Some schools feed you like royalty, but others aren't quite so generous.

(6) • After the judges' meeting, the meet organizer will "post" the Round I listings. If your code is posted go to the Tab Room, or ballot table to pick up your ballots and the list of students in your room. Go to the room where you've been assigned. Tip: go to the restroom on route if in doubt, because it can be a long round. Judging is already difficult to do and much harder when you are uncomfortable.

(7) • Review the criteria and ballots—if in doubt, ask another adult before you go to the room, competent. Event rules change from league to league. After you have judged a few times this will become second nature.

(8) • Fill out the information on the top parts of each ballot. To save time and prevent hand cramps, some judges ask students to fill it out (that is okay to do).

(9) • Start once all students have arrived. Although it is not necessary, most judges have students sign in on the board with their speaker code, title and author of selection. Some may have signed in on the board with an asterisk (*) or "D.E." next to their speaker code. This means they are double entered and will return after going to their other event (or, they may ask to speak first and leave to go to their other event.)

(10) A good forensics judge is four main things:

(11) 1. S/he is familiar with the rules.

(12) 2. S/he is willing to be flexible in accepting the student's interpretation of a piece of literature.

(13)   3. S/he is capable of communicating nonverbally during a performance. This is the only form of immediate feedback a student will receive! It is okay to laugh, cry and make eye contact, etc. if you feel that it is appropriate.

(14)   4. S/he is well-read and familiar with various forms of literature and current events.

(15)   Focus on the selection choice, how it was prepared and delivered, and how the author's expression of meaning and feeling was communicated. Justify and support your decisions! Remember it is constructive criticism, and the students are LEARNING! Find a balance between praise and criticism. To receive a rank and score from a judge without any comments to justify or support the decision, nothing is more frustrating! Be consistent!

(16)   • Have students perform in the order they are listed. Double entered students are the exception. She should perform first and be permitted to leave OR they can perform when they return. Do NOT give oral critiques.

(17)   • Keep accurate time and give hand signals. This is essential for Impromptu and Extemp. Most events have a 30 second grace period.

(18)   • Once all students have performed, they may be dismissed. Finalize your comments and rankings (first through sixth). Make sure your rankings on the individual ballots matches the master ballot. Check it again.

(19)   • Assign a numeric score (1–100). Scores should NOT go below an 85 (unless it was terrible). No two performers can have the same score or rank.

27. Correct the subordination in this sentence:

So wear comfortable clothing, it can be a long day; bring reading material and food.

A. So where comfortable clothing, it can be a long day; bring reading material and food.

B. It can be a long day, so wear comfortable clothing; bring reading material and food.

C. So wear comfortable clothing, it can be a long day.

D. No change.

28. Correct the punctuation in this sentence:

If your code is posted go to the Tab Room, or ballot table to pick up your ballots and the list of students in your room.

_____

_____

_____

_____

29. Show correct possession in this sentence:

Claim a comfortable spot in the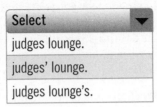

30. Correct the pronoun agreement in this sentence:

She should perform first and be permitted to leave OR they can perform when they return.

A. Replace "She" with "They."

B. Replace "they" with "she."

C. Replace "they" with "them."

D. No change.

31. Correct the misplaced modifier in this sentence:

Review the criteria and ballots—if in doubt, ask another adult before you go to the room, competent.

A. "Review the competent criteria and ballots—if in doubt, ask another adult before you go to the room."

B. "Review the criteria and ballots—if in competent doubt, ask another adult before you go to the room, competent."

C. "Review the criteria and ballots—if in doubt, ask another competent adult before you go to the room."

D. No change.

32. Rewrite this sentence to ensure logical clarity:

To receive a rank and score from a judge without any comments to justify or support the decision, nothing is more frustrating!

_____

_____

_____

_____

_____

_____

33. Which word should replace the word **matches** in the following sentence to demonstrate proper subject-verb agreement?

Make sure your rankings on the individual ballots matches the master ballot.

A. matched

B. match

C. matching

D. No change.

34. Which word should be capitalized in the following sentence?

Although it is not necessary, most judges have students sign in on the board with their speaker code, title and author of selection.

A. judges

B. title

C. author

D. No change.

Read the following letter of recommendation. Then answer questions 35–42.

Letter of Recommendation for Jennifer Fountain

(1) To Whom It May Concern:

(2) I am writing to recommend Jennifer Fountain for your program. I have known Jennifer since August of this year, when she came to school a week before it began to find out if she was eligible to take IB English.

(3) Jennifer was particularly memorable to me not only because of her initiative, but because of her story. She had been homeschooled until this year, and still managed to take and excel in AP courses. She was curious to find out if she could also add the additional burden of IB to her senior year in high school. When I explained all the catching up she would have to do, she did not flinch. She simply responded ecstatically You mean I can still do the IB work I don't have to be enrolled in regular English 12? I will do anything you ask me to do!

(4) To hear that from a parent is one thing, but to hear it from a student is something else entirely. Its novel. I haltingly gave her a book to read for the summer reading assignment, which was due less than a week from the day I was giving it to her. She did not blink. Instead, she read the entire novel over the weekend, and submitted her work first thing with the other students. The behavior impressed me, as did the quality of her work. Indeed, it is rare that I write a recommendation for a student in the first quarter of my class for a November deadline if I have not taught her before. Jennifer has done nothing but impress me as good natured, hard-working, thoughtful and diligent.

(5) Jennifer takes every opportunity to improve her already excellent work. I allow for re-writes in my class, and Jennifer re-writes everything. This knowledge of the writing process and willingness to improve shows a philosophy it takes most students four years of college to master: writing is re-writing. Jennifer demonstrates an ideology that is the embodiment of the striving for perfection; though I doubt she would be so cliché as to word it like that. When it is true, though, it is true. She never takes offense, either, when I criticize her work. She is earnest in her desire to improve, and seeks me out for counsel often. Jennifer is brilliant, she tries her best.

(6) Jennifer's accomplishments are not simply limited to the classroom, therefore. I coach volleyball and was surprised to see her leading the way on our track team at after-school practices. Though I barely know her, it takes a lot of courage to submerge into public school in the way Jennifer has, I am incredibly proud and in awe of her drive. She is very friendly, and her interests expand beyond school and its sports. She also has experience with the responsibility of caring for horses, teaching lessons and organizing events on a larger scale with her church youth group.

(7) It is without a moment's hesitation that I recommend Jennifer Fountain. I finds her competent, capable, enjoyable and exceptionally intrinsically motivated, which I believe is likely from the years of home schooling. Jennifer is a wonderful student, and I am certain she will make a wonderful addition to your University. Please do not hesitate to contact me if you have any questions about Jennifer.

35. Eliminate the wordiness in this sentence:

I haltingly gave her a book to read for the summer reading assignment, which was due less than a week from the day I was giving it to her.

A. "I gave her a book to read for the summer reading assignment, which was due less than a week from the day I was giving it to her."

B. "I haltingly gave her a book for the summer reading assignment, which was due less than a week from the day I was giving it to her."

C. "I haltingly gave her a book, which was due less than a week from the day I was giving it to her."

D. No change.

36. Select the correct answer.

Jennifer's accomplishments are not simply limited to the classroom,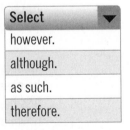

37. Correct this run-on sentence:

Jennifer is brilliant, she tries her best.

A. Jennifer is brilliant, and she tries her best.

B. Jennifer is brilliant she tries her best.

C. Jennifer is brilliant, tries her best.

D. No change.

38. How should the following sentence be properly punctuated?

She simply responded ecstatically You mean I can still do the IB work I don't have to be enrolled in regular English 12? I will do anything you ask me to do!

_____

_____

_____

_____

39. What should replace the word **its** in the following sentence?

Its novel.

A. A

B. It is

C. Its'

D. No change.

40. How can this sentence be reworded to avoid the dangling modifier?

Though I barely know her, it takes a lot of courage to submerge into public school in the way Jennifer has, I am incredibly proud and in awe of her drive.

A. I barely know her, it takes a lot of courage to submerge into public school in the way Jennifer has, I am incredibly proud and in awe of her drive.

B. I am incredibly proud and in awe of her drive, though I barely know her, it takes a lot of courage to submerge into public school in the way Jennifer has.

C. It takes a lot of courage to submerge into public school in the way Jennifer has, and though I barely know her, I am incredibly proud and in awe of her drive.

D. No change.

41. What word should be replaced to avoid informal usage in the following sentence?

Jennifer demonstrates an ideology that is the embodiment of the striving for perfection; though I doubt she would be so cliché as to word it like that.

    A. cliché

    B. ideology

    C. embodiment

    D. No change.

42. Correct the subject-verb agreement in the following sentence.

I finds her competent, capable, enjoyable and exceptionally intrinsically motivated, which I believe is likely from the years of home schooling.

    A. I find her competent, capable, enjoyable and exceptionally intrinsically motivated, which I believe is likely from the years of homeschooling.

    B. I found her competent, capable, enjoyable and exceptionally intrinsically motivated, which I believe is likely from the years of homeschooling.

    C. I finding her competent, capable, enjoyable and exceptionally intrinsically motivated, which I believe is likely from the years of homeschooling.

    D. No change.

Read the following report about a blind cook who turned into a Master Chef. Then answer questions 43–49.

(1) If you watched season three of Fox TV's reality cooking show *MasterChef* you remember the big smile that lit up Christine Hà's face every time she impressed the judges with her bold flavors and especially when her threecourse meal of Vietnamese comfort food won Hà the "MasterChef" title.

(2) What viewers casually may not have realized right away is that the amateur cook from Houston, Texas, is blind. In 2003, Hà was diagnosed with neuromyelitis optica (NMO), a rare neurological condition that deteriorates the optic nerves and spinal cord. By 2007, Hà had lost most of her vision. But she had regained her love of reading, through help from the National Library Service for the Blind and Physically Handicapped (NLS).

(3) "[NLS] reignited my love for literature. It was what kept me sane when I went through my first bouts of NMO," says Hà, who also authors the blog *theblindcook.com*. "When I went through some of my worst health issues in 2003—complete paralysis from my neck down due to spinal inflammation, and complete blindness—all I could do was lie in bed and listen to NLS audiobooks."

(4) NLS, part of the Library of Congress, oversees a free reading program for U.S. residents and citizens living abroad who are blind, have low vision, or cannot holds a book because of a physical disability. NLS patrons may choose from tens of thousands of books and dozens of magazines in audio and braille—including dozens of cookbooks, such as "O, the Oprah Magazine Cookbook" and titles by Julia Child, James Beard, and other famous foodies. NLS also loans the portable playback equipment needed to read its audiobooks. Computer-savvy patrons' may access books online through the NLS Braille and Audio Reading Download (BARD) service.

(5) Hà, who is pursuing a master of fine arts degree at the University of Houston, always has a book checked out from NLS. Recently she was reading Gail Caldwell's "Let's take the long way home" in braille. And she currently is working on her "MasterChef" cookbook, which is set for a spring 2013 release.

(6) Disabilities do not need to stand in the way of our dreams; this is something that has been proven throughout the ages. If you have a problem, you can always find a way to get over it, get through it, or around it.

43. Correct the subject-verb agreement in this sentence from paragraph 4:

NLS, part of the Library of Congress, oversees a free reading program for U.S. residents and citizens living abroad who are blind, have low vision, or cannot holds a book because of a physical disability.

A. "NLS, part of the Library of Congress, oversees a free reading program for U.S. residents and citizen living abroad who are blind, have low vision, or cannot holds a book because of a physical disability."

B. "NLS, part of the Library of Congress, oversee a free reading program for U.S. residents and citizens living abroad who are blind, have low vision, or cannot holds a book because of a physical disability."

C. "NLS, part of the Library of Congress, oversees a free reading program for U.S. residents and citizens living abroad who are blind, have low vision, or cannot hold a book because of a physical disability."

D. No change.

44. Which word should replace **through** in the following sentence?

But she had regained her love of reading, through help from the National Library Service for the Blind and Physically Handicapped (NLS).

A. thorough

B. threw

C. thru

D. No change.

45. How should the parallelism be properly written in the following sentence?

If you have a problem, you can always find a way to get over it, get through it, or around it.

    A. "If you have a problem, you can always find a way to get over it, get through it, or get around it."

    B. "If you have a problem, you can always find a way to get over it, through it, or get around it."

    C. "If you have a problem, you can always find a way to get over it."

    D. No change.

46. Correct the capitalization in this sentence:

Recently she was reading Gail Caldwell's "Let's take the long way home" in Braille.

    A. "Let's Take the long Way Home"

    B. "let's take the long way home"

    C. "Let's Take the Long Way Home"

    D. No change.

47. Correct the possession in the following sentence:

Computer-savvy patrons' may access books online through the NLS Braille and Audio Reading Download (BARD) service.

    A. patron's

    B. savvy's

    C. patrons

    D. No change.

48. Insert the proper punctuation marks into this sentence:

If you watched season three of Fox TV's reality cooking show *MasterChef* you remember the big smile that lit up Christine Hà's face every time she impressed the judges with her bold flavors and especially when her threecourse meal of Vietnamese comfort food won Hà the "MasterChef" title.

49. Eliminate the wordiness in the following sentence.

Hà, who is pursuing a master of fine arts degree at the University of Houston, always has a book checked out from NLS.

A. Hà, who is pursuing a master of fine arts degree at the University of Houston, has a book checked out from NLS.

B. Hà, pursuing a master of fine arts degree at the University of Houston, always has a book checked out from NLS.

C. Hà, who is pursuing a master at the University of Houston, always has a book checked out from NLS.

D. No change.

50. The passage that follows is incomplete. For each "Select . . ." option, choose the response that correctly completes the sentence.

How Stock-Car Racing Became Popular

Stock-car racing is a major spectator sport in this country,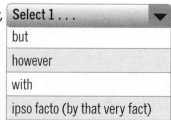

an estimated 30 percent of Americans claiming to be fans of this more than half-century-old sport. However, racing has not always been so popular. As a matter of fact, it had a rather shaky start, with a negative reputation and problems with the law. During the 1920s, with Prohibition came moonshining; and with moonshining came

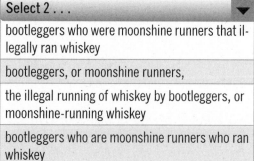 from the illegal stills to the markets. These

drivers ran races with the law; the losers were subject to jail time and steep fines. Soon racing among the bootleggers became a weekend sport; they used their "whiskey run" cars to prove who was the fastest. And of course folks from the area came out to watch.

These races became popular. They continued even after the end of Prohibition. In 1938 Bill France organized the first Daytona Beach race. Winners received such prizes as rum, cigars, and motor oil. After a hiatus during World War II, in the late 1940s France held a meeting of promoters. This three-day meeting [Select 3 ▼] the establishment of the rules,

Select 3 ▼
reinstated
emphasized
nevertheless led to
resulted in

specifications, and official name of the organization—the National Association of Stock Car Auto Racing, or NASCAR.

Answers: Reasoning Through Language Arts—Practice Test 2

Section 1

1. **C.**

   This article considers both the positive and negative aspects of sudden death, and discusses the differing opinions about it. The text does not give a specific opinion about death itself being good or bad (A), and although the author may seem to imply that sudden death is the better option (D), he makes no definitive statement regarding this. The author only states that religion seems to prefer a slow death (B).

2. **B.**

   The author discusses the conflicting stance between religion and Roman philosophy as to whether sudden death is or is not preferable. Because this conflict is true, you can rule out choice (A). Although the author does discuss intoxication, he points out that the mere coincidence of "some sudden death when [one] happens to be intoxicated" could be "falsely regarded with peculiar horror"—implying "extra immorality" when in actuality "extra misfortune" may be at work. (C). Finally, while the author does discuss a person's excessive drinking habits in terms of intoxication (D), he makes no claim that the regularity of such habits will determine a person's fate.

3. **D.**

   You can infer the meaning of "prostrate" from the sentence in which it appears: "On the other hand, the divine Litany of our English Church, when breathing forth supplications, as if in some representative character for the whole human race **prostrate** before God, places such a death in the very van of horrors." This is because the sentence means the Church thinks it has the corner on human servitude (supplication) to God. In this light, "vertically positioned" (A), "up in arms against" (B), and "angrily opposing" (C) simply do not make sense.

4. **B.**

   By beginning with this question, the author indicates he will answer, or at least flesh out, the implications of this idea. You should already know that he presents conflicting information in this paragraph, so you can rule out choice (C). Although it may have the effect of forcing the readers to ask themselves this question, this does not warrant the development or assertion of a main idea itself (A). Because the author endeavors himself to answer this question, you can tell that he is not asking someone else to answer it for him, as choice (D) indicates.

5. B.

This answer is a reason, not a claim. It is indicating that the scripture does not provide evidence for the claim, thus it is the reasoning and evidence itself. Choice (A) is a claim that is supported by the sentence immediately preceding it. Choice (C) is a claim with its reasoning coupled in the same sentence. Choice (D) is a claim the author spends the rest of the paragraph reasoning out.

6. A.

This sentence is, in fact, the main idea, which is that different parts of society view sudden death as either desirable or despicable. Choice (B) is a bit of reasoning that supports one conflicting side of the argument, as is choice (C). Neither of these is explicitly the main idea, though both are connected to it. Choice (D) is simply a conclusive statement that, when placed in the context of the whole passage, helps to support the main idea—that the method of death is up for debate—but on its own is simply reasoning regarding the drunkard's method of death.

7. C.

"Infirmity" indicates illness or weakness, which is not directly qualified by "suffering," though it can be inferred. "Suffering" is a harsher word that takes human emotion into consideration. To that end, if the author had used "suffering" instead of "illness," he would indicate more directly that the Church is cruel for allowing the misery to continue. Therefore, you can rule out both choices (A) and (B), which indicate the author would be in favor of the Church's position—which should have been clear simply from the sentence itself. There is definitely a change in tone, so you can rule out choice (D).

8. A.

Both articles address this issue. Although choice (B) is somewhat handled by the second article, it is not a thematic idea presented in the first. Similarly, choice (C) is discussed in the first article, but it is not a large enough focus of the second to be considered a theme. Finally, while choice (D) might be something you can infer from the information presented in both articles, it is not a theme for either.

9. B.

The correct is choice (B), 1 percent. Notice that the question asks you what percentage *is* inspected, which is the flip side of how the statistic is presented in the text: the 99% of food imports *not* inspected. When you're asked a question like this, be careful not to latch on to the wrong data.

10. **C.**

It seems the first article is more concerned with the safety aspect of imports, while the second article deals more with the economic hardships regarding importation. Though the second article does mention food safety concerns, it is far more concerned with the United States' failing economy. Choice (A) is incorrect because it is likely that both authors would agree that this idea is false. The authors would probably agree to (rather than dispute) both choices (B) and (D).

11. **D.**

Though the purpose of both articles is to inform, the second article offers positive, hopeful motivation that the first does not. Choice (A) is incorrect because it misses the point of both articles entirely. While choice (B) may be a correct observation of the two articles, it does not discuss the impact these articles intend to create. Finally, choice (C) is halfway correct, but it misinterprets the aim of the second article—which deals with fiscal impacts, but does nothing to encourage readers to be more thrifty.

12. **C.**

Both articles mention iPura, but the first one simply uses it as part of a hopeful discussion of a means to help decrease food safety issues. The second article realizes the potential for American business to become successful by recognizing the problem of food import safety. Both articles consider iPura to be positive, so you can rule out (A), which describes it as a "scare tactic." (B) has the emphasis jumbled between the two articles, as does (D).

13. **A.**

The article is designed to educate Americans about the health problems imported foods can cause. Though iPura is mentioned as a benefit (B), showcasing it is not the intended purpose of the article; rather it is used as a side comment. Though this article may encourage readers to grow their own food (C), this would be a side benefit, as the text gives no specific direction to do so. Finally, the FDA is actually pardoned within the article by "experts" for its lack of inspection, so you can rule out choice (D).

14. **B.**

The article seeks to educate its readers on a successful business model, which seems to solve two problems at once—hence the title. The article does applaud iPura (A), but this is an example to strengthen the commentary, not part of the overall purpose. The article does not deal with alternatives to imported foods (C), which would center on guidance on how to buy American produce. Although choice (D) is mentioned in the article, this is the main purpose of the first article, and is only used by the second as a mitigating factor.

15. **B.**

Both articles deal with the problems created by imported foods, but one couches this in terms of economic hardship and the other highlights health problems. This indicates that the underlying problem is reliance on imported foods. Although both articles deal with an innovative company, iPura, the two authors would likely disagree on the reasons this company came into existence, so you can rule out choices (A) and (D). Although both authors agree that public health is a factor with imported foods (C), the articles indicate a disagreement about the priority of food safety, as one discusses food safety in tandem with money.

16. **C.**

A *premise* is the major argument or impact of an article, and in this one the author encourages readers to make their own plan for the future so as not to suffer the consequences. Although choice (A) might be an inference a reader could make, it is certainly not the focus of the article. Choice (B) is a correct observation, but it does not directly answer the question. Finally, choice (D) might be a potential point a reader might take away from the article, but it certainly is not the point the author attempts to convey.

17. **A.**

This sentence assumes there is an argument made that "it is better to live longer." The author, in this instance, considers this and its positive outcomes before moving on to discuss the true purpose of the article: planning for the downside of what happens when you outlive your spouse. Choice (B) is a piece of information that supports the main argument, but does not indicate conflict. Similarly, choices (C) and (D) are simply additional pieces of information that support the main ideas presented in the piece. Neither (C) nor (D) indicates a conflicting point of view.

18. **A., B., and D.**

This item asks you to select three details mentioned in the article. The correct answers are (A), (B), and (D):

Helps protect retirement assets
Provides coverage not available through Medicaid
Customizable plans available

In terms of the remaining two response options, (C) and (E), note that the article is silent on avoiding "reliance on private insurers" and says the U.S. Office of Personnel Management must approve premium increases, not that premiums will not rise.

19. **B.**

At its basal level, the article assumes the cause-and-effect relationship that living longer causes you to face up to decisions to make about how you want to plan for your future. The article makes no argument about how to raise children (A); indeed, it encourages readers to take the burden off their children. The argument about the cost of living is actually negated in the article (C), and choice (D) runs opposite the premise of the entire article.

20. **A.**

Because the question asks for different situations, you can immediately rule out choices (C) and (D) because those responses deal with the argument presented within this article. The problem with choice (B) is that although children and relationships are mentioned, there are no steps provided—such as "employ better communication skills" to help apply to building a relationship. So, choice (A) is the best answer because it employs the same skills mentioned in this article to a similar scenerio that happens to deal with different subject matter.

21. **The correct answer is: B, C, D, and E.**

Choice (A) is the main idea of the text, so you can tell immediately that it is not a supporting detail. Choice (F) simply asks a question, so you should immediately rule it out. Finally, choice (G) is a comment in the nature of advice, not a detail that supports the main idea. Choices (B), (C), (D), and (E) all support the main idea that women are outliving men and need to consider planning for long-term care.

22. **C.**

Because the question asks about clarification, you must draw the parallel relationship between the two pieces of information. Choice (C) is the only response option that presents an accurate distinction. Although choice (A) may seem like a legitimate response, this would be an answer to a question that asks how the chart disagrees with the article rather than how it clarifies it. Although choice (B) may be a correct observation—that the fine arts projects seem to have the greatest success—these are independent projects, not crowdfunded options for education. Finally, choice (D) is another correct observation, but it does not consider the article, so no relevant comparison or clarification is offered.

23. **A.**

The reader can infer from the article and graph that there is a distinctive parallel between crowdfunding and success rates for financial gain. Because the article is suggesting the use of crowdfunding websites, you can rule out choice (B). Similarly, the article indicates that there has been some success with crowdfunded projects such as Kickstarter in regards to helping fund education, so choice (C) is also ruled out. Clearly, the graph indicates that the arts are supported by crowdfunding (D).

24. D.

Although choice (C) may be a true statement, you can assume that the intended audience for the article is students looking to fund their education, so you can rule it out as a reaction. Choice (D) is correct because it is a logical assumption to make that the students, not seeing education listed in the graph, might consider it an endeavor not worth their effort. Finally, the graph does not indicate in any way that traditional methods of financing school are obsolete, so you can rule out choice (B) as well.

25. D.

A person must have vision and drive, but both the article and the graph support the idea that there is money to be made in the internet world of crowdfunding. Although choice (A) may be true, this information is clearly negated in the chart as it indicates most projects come close to the $1 million mark. Although choices (B) and (C) are both easily inferred from the article, they are not supported by the graph.

26. A.

Once readers consider the evidence in the chart, it is a fair, logical conclusion to draw that they may be swayed to attempt other Kickstarter projects such as gaming or photography endeavors. Choice (B) is incorrect because it does not reference the graph, and makes a claim not supported by the article. Choice (C) may be an attractive answer, but the Kickstarter information is applicable to projects, and does not give instructions about how to build a business. Finally, choice (D) may be an outcome of the two pieces of information, but it is not an *application* of the information, so it does not answer the question.

27. A.

The chart supports the author's claim that Kickstarter or other crowdfunding websites can be successful in garnering financial backing. Even if choice (B) might be true in the success ratio column of the graph, this does not support the author's claim and should be ignored. Choice (C) is incorrect because the chart does not directly address education as a potential project on Kickstarter. Finally, the chart makes no mention of the time involved in running a Kickstarter project (D).

28. D.

Because the chart shows the success of projects on Kickstarter, it is logical to conclude that it is a viable option for funding one's education. There is no basis to decide that Kickstarter makes people happy (A) or that it will be the necessary conclusive item that makes more independent film projects (C). Although choice (B) might seem correct, ultimately crowdfunding is presented as an *option*, not the ultimate or sole solution to trying economic times.

29. C.

Throughout the passage, the author argues that illusion, imagination, and attitude are the elements that make life enjoyable. The author discusses how even adults employ illusion in their jobs, so you can rule out choices (A) and (B). Although choice (D) is the next best response, it is only mentioned in a tertiary, and positive way. The tone of choice (D) is negative, so you should rule it out as well.

30. B.

Technically "fop" is a "dandy," but from context clues and the subject of the sentence—people's occupations—you should at least be able to determine it is some kind of human. This information rules out choices (A), (C), and (D).

31. D.

Although choice (B) may seem like a viable option, the author would likely argue that illusions are a part of us that we cannot separate ourselves from, they do not necessarily make us better people, they are simply a part of who we are. Choice (D) is correct because it embodies this idea. Because of this, you can rule out choices (A) and (C), which both negate the idea that illusions are integral parts of our personae.

32. C.

The author's sincere effort to include a variety of jobs through a seemingly endless list helps to indicate that no one is immune to imagination and attitude. Choice (A) might seem a viable option, but it deals with figurative language—diction—rather than the syntax—sentence structure—which is what the question asks about. Choice (B) is interesting, but ultimately it is an incorrect assessment—the sentence is not a run-on, so you can rule it out. Choice (D) is a correct observation, but it does not address the second part of the question, which deals with how this structure helps convey the message.

33. A.

Emerson plays on people's emotions as he connects adults to their youth, as well as appealing to our sense of belonging as he describes our own jobs and relates to us. He makes no reference to tradition (B), and though the piece is logically constructed (C) in an easy-to-follow manner, there is very little analysis of cause and effect or use of statistics to argue his point. The piece uses very little ethical appeal (D), such as the citation of authority or research to prove the author's integrity.

34. **B.**

The author's main goal here is to personally connect with the audience and encourage them to enjoy life and approach it with a positive attitude. The piece does not deal with fate or luck (A), and though choice (C) might seem like a logical answer, it would be more of a side-glance than a direct outcome of this text. Similarly, choice (D) is an acceptable answer, but it is not as precise in the analysis of the author's intent as choice (B).

35.

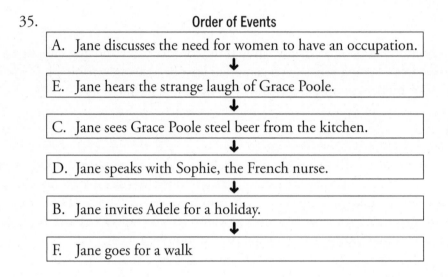

36. **A.**

In this line, Brontë indicates that women have equally as passionate feelings about work and occupations as men do, which was a relatively unorthodox view at the time of Brontë's writing. Nonetheless, the explicit mentions of equality between the sexes in this sentence should answer this question, provided you know the definition of feminist: someone who believes women should be treated equally to men. To that end, choice (B) is incorrect because it does not deal with equality among men and women; choice (C), too, is incorrect not least because it describes Sophie as vapid, which is an insult. Choice (D) is incorrect as well, though it may be alluring because it shows Jane has a modicum of power in decision making, but it is not as precise in answering the question as choice (A).

37. **C.**

Jane is judgmental of Grace Poole, as is evidenced by her parenthetical note regarding Grace's alcohol use. "Interested" (A) may vie for your attention, but it's not the best answer because Jane's initial attempts at showing interest by striking up a conversation with Grace are met with "few words," which is discouraging. Instead of "caring" (B), Jane actually adopts a superior attitude toward Grace. Finally, choice (D) should be eliminated because Jane exhibits no signs of anxiety in the course of assessing Grace's "oddities" and flaws.

38. B.

This is an exaggerated description of internal conflict, and using fermentation to describe it indicates a sour feeling and building pressure within. Choice (A) might seem a viable answer, but it is incorrect because repetition is not figurative language. Choice (C), too, is incorrect because it does not talk about the effect itself, but merely indicates that the phrase is a good choice of description. Finally, choice (D) is incorrect because ferment is both a metaphor and hyperbole.

39. D.

You can tell from Jane's diatribe regarding female occupation that Jane is not the type of person to sit idly by. This is substantiated in the final paragraph when she endeavors a two-mile walk to post a letter, and in the descriptions of her attempts to engage Sophie in conversation. Choice (A) is incorrect; the events in this section do not definitively relate back to this particular paragraph. Choice (B) is incorrect because no character other than Jane herself is described (D). Finally, you cannot choose option (C) because even if it is correct, you have no basis for comparison unless you have read the entire novel, and this question assumes you have not.

40. C.

Jane is interested in many things, as illustrated in this passage, and she discusses her beliefs at length. Choice (A) is incorrect because Jane actually demonstrates a great deal of strength in this passage. Although Jane is interested in other characters (B), as is evidenced by her discussion of them, there is no reason to determine she cares more about them than she does herself, especially given the information presented in the first paragraph. Finally, there is no reason to determine Jane is cruel (D). Even if she calls Sophie vapid, she invites Adele to visit and suffers Grace Poole, who she considers slightly morally reprehensible.

Extended Response—Section 2

Let's consider how you would approach building a solid essay on the topic at hand.

Start by brainstorming. For this prompt, two passages have been presented that showcase the physical invention of the boat and the mental and emotional invention of ideas and innovation. While it seems as if both texts are arguing very different ideas, both are still speaking of invention.

First, consider how each passage frames new knowledge (invention). Then, noticed how each passage delivers that information to you as the reader.

When selecting which passage is stronger than the other, it may help to select which argument *you naturally believe in*. From there, pull which parts of the passage make the argument so strong.

Remember: There is no right answer here, so you may find it to be more comfortable to discuss in your writing how that passage is better or stronger because you naturally believe this to be true. Although this may be your personal opinion, however, it is important that you avoid using the personal pronoun of "I," as your argument must remain objective in looking at the two passages. Nothing in your argument can be self-evident — there has to be a reason behind everything you say. The better you clarify what that reason is, the better and more persuasive your argument will be.

Below is a four-paragraph structure to help you craft your extended-response essay. This four-paragraph structure happens to be on the short end of GED Testing Service's recommended four- to seven-paragraph length. Having the confidence to collect your thoughts and make your case in four compelling paragraphs will tend to lift your entire response.

In fact, aiming for four paragraphs will help you to focus and organize your attention on the most important pieces of the task itself, especially since you are being timed.

The opening statement will allow you to present your position — that one passage delivers a better argument than the other. The next two paragraphs (the body paragraphs) are where you should (a) present supporting evidence as to how one passage is more effective than the other, and (b) provide information as to how, *specifically*, the other passage's position is weaker. When you cite information from the passages, be sure to select key words, phrases, and examples of tone that support your claims that one passage is ultimately more successful than the other.

This leaves the closing statement, which not only allows you to add emphasis as you work to drive your points home, but also to summarize the overall strengths of the passage you favor (for example, in tone and word choices). Let's boil it down in an outline:

How to Organize Your Extended-Response Essay at the Paragraph Level

Paragraph 1: Opening Statement

- Discuss how Passage #1 delivers its information.

- Discuss how Passage #2 delivers its information.

- Select which passage delivers its position on invention better. Put this in the last sentence of the paragraph. This is your thesis statement.

After you read through this primer, be your own best critic. You may spot weaknesses in your essay. It's not test day yet, so you still have time to can take another shot. Be sure to have someone you trust read your work. Then listen carefully to their criticisms. Let's look at a bad introduction versus a good one to give you a feel for how you should have approached this prompt.

> **Bad opening statement…**
>
> Passage #1 focuses on the past while Passage #2 focuses on the future. After all, how much can one accomplish by building a boat?
>
> (short, dismissive, simplistic—lacking explanation)
>
> **Good opening statement…**
>
> Passage #1 uses workmanlike language—literal, concrete descriptions of the history of boat-making. It plods along, describing what it takes to build a boat—and asks us to consider how the invention of the boat may have come about. Passage #2, on the other hand, uses soaring language and the power of metaphor to appeal to our highest sense of ourselves and what we, as human beings, can accomplish when we collaborate. Thus, the stronger position of the two is found in President Kennedy's inaugural address, which paints a picture of the American ideal that is the beacon for freedom for people everywhere.
>
> (thoughtful and analytical—and properly lengthy)

Paragraph 2: Laying Out the Evidence & Defending Your Position

- This paragraph and the next are where the heart of your analysis will be.

- Discuss first key strength/argument of the better passage in the first sentence of this paragraph.

- Support your point by citing information from that passage that shows how that first key strength is conveyed.

- Contrast the weaker passage's approach with your favored passage's first key strength.

Paragraph 3: Laying Out the Evidence & Defending Your Position

- This paragraph continues the analysis begun in Paragraph 2.

- Discuss the second key strength/argument of the better passage in the first sentence of this paragraph.

- Support your point by citing information from that passage that shows how that second key strength is conveyed.

- Contrast the weaker passage's approach with your favored passage's second key strength.

Paragraph 4: Concluding Statement

- Emphasize how one passage makes its argument in a better way than the other.

- Address how tone may be more impactful in that overall passage versus the other (which then contributes to the passage's argument).

- Address how key words or phrases may be more impactful in that overall passage versus the other (which then shows how the passage's argument is stitched together as a whole).

Section 3

1. **A.**

   Union Station is a proper noun and needs to be capitalized. Choice (B) is incorrect because "Mr. Older and Much Richer," too, is a proper noun and is correctly capitalized in the sentence. Choice (C) is also incorrect because it fails to capitalize the proper noun, and replaces the correctly written word "to" with its incorrect homonym "too."

2. The correct answer is:

   I never dated him, never would, actually, and had never given him any reason to judge and exploit my character flaws, let alone those of my whole sex."

   (This is a long, complex sentence but "let alone those of my whole sex" is a dependent clause that requires combination with the independent clause preceding it.)

3. **C.**

   The word "their" refers to the women who are searching for men. The word "women" is plural, so the pronoun that goes along with it must be plural as well. "Her" is singular. Choice (A) changes the wording to something potentially correct, but ignores the pronoun agreement error. Choice (B) makes a capitalization error and ignores the pronoun error.

4. **C.**

   This is a tricky question. The present tense of the word "realize" would indicate that the speaker should speak in the present tense for the entire sentence. Alternatively, the sentence should all be written in past tense. This sentence continues in the past, reflective tense of the rest of the passage ("had") and then switches to the present tense to make an observation about the speaker herself at ALL times—including the present time of writing. This means changing "realize" to "realized" (A) is incorrect because the problem of tenses is switched. Choice (B) simply removes the colon, a stylistic choice that by itself could be correct, but ignores the tense problem.

5.   This should read:

> Wouldn't it have been more productive, if I was indeed BEING selfish, to say something like, "Hey. You know, that's kind of rude, what you're doing there. I don't have a bike with me, but if I did, I might like to park it there, instead of at the other, far less accessible to YOU, (but not anyone with a bicycle) spaces. Why don't you move somewhere else?" Or, "Hey. You're in the way of my invisible entourage. Move it."

There should be quotation marks around the dialogue, and because the first sentence is very long, it required some parentheses around the parenthetical side comment. Additionally, due to length, the fragment has been left in for style in the second sentence.

6.   **A.**

To avoid the informal usage, the sentence must eliminate the colloquial version of the word "suburbs" ("'burbs") correct the capitalization error and fix the made-up word "internesque." Choice (B) is incorrect because it deals only with the capitalization error and adjusts a proper noun, which, while perhaps sarcastic, is not necessarily informal. Similarly, choice (C) only fixes half of the problem with informal register.

7.   **D.**

The pronoun agreement is correct, as "women" is plural and requires a plural pronoun. Choice (A) is an incorrect homonym meaning "they are," which does not make sense in context, as is "there" (B), the homonym meaning "that place." "Her" (C) would be correct if the sentence was written for just one woman, as in "I guess in the past the woman has typically been the one to survive off her husband's much fatter paycheck, but still, a woman cooks, cleans, mothers children, entertains at least five full-time stay-at-home OTHER jobs at that, AND works on a budget of what is allowed to her."

8.   **B.**

To ensure proper coordination, the sentence requires the conjunction "or" to make the first half of it an independent clause. Choice (A) removes the colon, which is necessary for such a massive list. Choice (C) is the second best answer as it shows another plausible way to separate a list, but does not fix the error in coordination.

9. **C.**

The first half of this sentence is a dependent clause, which, while technically acceptable, confuses the intention of the sentence by placing this clause first. This is corrected by reversing the clause order. Choice (A) is incorrect because it does not fix the awkward sentence; indeed it, like choice (B), makes the sentence even *more* awkward.

10. **C.**

"Teachers" is not a possessive noun, so it does not require an apostrophe. Choice (A) changes it to plural possessive case, but again, "teachers" is only plural in this sentence, not possessive. Choice (B) ignores the error and changes a different word, "they'll," which is a contraction for "they will," which is contrary to "they all" in the sentence.

11. **A.**

"At first" is a conditional modifier, so it is important to place it in a section of the sentence that makes the most sense. You must consider the context of the sentence. Choice (B) indicates that allowing students to hang out in the Cafeteria became a bad strategy, and nothing indicates that in the following sentence. Similarly, choice (C) indicates that the Cafeteria's status would change, but this, too, is unsubstantiated. Written as is, the sentence indicates that the sentiment has changed, which does not make sense since there was "some disagreement."

12. **B.**

The run-on happens between the two independent clauses, the second of which reads, "teachers know they are monitored there." There are two ways to fix this sentence: The first is choice (B). The other is to split this into two complete sentences: "When kids are not attending LEARN, or when they are chronically Supervised, teachers can send their students to ISS. Teachers know they are monitored there." Choice (C) attempts this, but puts the period and capitalization in the wrong place. Choice (A) compounds the run-on by removing the commas.

13. The correct answer is:

> Good students have all Cs or above, Monitored have 1 D or F, and Supervised have multiple Ds and Fs.

(Only lowercased letters require an apostrophe when they are used as plurals; there need to be commas between the items in the list: Good students, Monitored students, and Supervised students.)

14. **B.**

The problem with the sentence written as it is, is the dangling preposition at the end. Although this is corrected in choice (A), by removing the phrase "we learned," the meaning of the sentence is thereby changed, and that is not what the question asks you to do. Choice (B) fixes it without leaving the awkward infinitive at the end—and fixes the incorrect assumption that the parents will be "at" school. Choice (C) completely alters the meaning of the sentence.

15. **D.**

This sentence is correctly written, and replacing the word "to" with either of its homonyms, "too" (A) or "two" (B), the sentence meaning shifts respectively to: "not nearly enough also make this model work . . ." and "not nearly enough 2 make this model work . . ." (C) is incorrect because replacing the word "to" with "that" simply makes the sentence incoherent.

16. **B.**

"Students" is a plural noun, and therefore needs the verb constructed to plurality, which in this case is "need." Students need. (A) is incorrect because it does not fix the error and replaces "they" with "them"—an incorrect pronoun for the case. (C) is incorrect because it ignores the error and creates another one by making a possessive noun out of a plural one.

17. **C.**

The first clause is a dependent, conditional clause that requires a conditional word, like "Since." The transitional word "However" indicates that there would be some contrary information presented from the previous sentence, which in this case is not correct. (A) is incorrect because it would leave in the comma, which does not make grammatical sense. Changing "However" to "Therefore" (B) would indicate that the sentence will provide some sort of conclusive argument, which the sentence does not.

18. The correct answer is:

We must change our model to follow theirs.

In this instance, "It is imperative" is redundant and unnecessary to the meaning of the sentence, which is simply a declarative statement: "We must change our model to follow theirs."

19. **B.**

The fragment in this instance is the phrase "In science" because it does not contain a subject and a verb. Although choice (A) corrects the conjunction at the beginning of the sentence, it does not address the fragment, which is what you're asked to do. Choice (C) is also incorrect because it creates a run-on sentence and does not correct the fragment.

20. **A.**

In this instance, the pronoun is referring to the subject in a previous sentence, "the AP Physics teacher." This is one person, so the pronoun selected must be singular—in this instance, "he." Choice (B) is incorrect because "him decided" is an incorrect pronoun-verb agreement. Finally, although choice (C) does create pronoun agreement between "they" and "their," it fails to achieve agreement with the antecedent, "AP Physics teacher."

21. **C.**

A formal correct sentence never begins with a conjunction. Therefore, it must be replaced with a different transitional word. "However" works in this instance because it is hinged upon the idea presented in the previous sentiments—that the speaker does not like science or math. Choices (A) and (B) deal only with diction, failing to correct the problem with transition.

22. **C.**

"Student Teacher" is not a proper noun and should not be capitalized. Choice (A) is incorrect because "content" is not a proper noun. Choice (B) is close to correct, but it assumes "teacher" is a proper noun, which it is not.

23. **A.**

The problem with this sentence is that it begins with a dependent clause in a conditional sense. Choice (A) corrects this by replacing the phrase "being that" with "Because," which corrects the subordination. Choice (B) might sound correct, but it does not fix the error in subordination. Choice (C) would be correct if the comma were changed to a semicolon. Otherwise, it is a run-on sentence.

24. **B.**

The subject of the sentence is "we," and though the infinitive verb "to relate" comes well after the interceding phrase, it still must agree with the subject. We "relate," not "relates." Choice (A) is incorrect because it ignores this problem and changes an arbitrary word, "stud." Choice (C) is incorrect because it, too, ignores the problem even though it removes the intercession.

25. D.

"Knew" is the correct past tense of "know," and it is the correct word in this sentence. Replacing it with the homonym "new" (A) changes the meaning of the sentence, and makes no logical sense. Using the present tense "know" (B) would disrupt the past tense used in the rest of the essay. Replacing it with the word "think" (C) creates the same problem.

26. A.

The word "heck" is a slang term used for effect in this instance, but it is not standard, formal English. Choices (B) and (C) are simply stylistic, failing to not remove the colloquialism, "heck."

27. B.

The dependent clause "so wear comfortable clothing" must hinge logically behind its independent clause because of the word "so." It makes logical sense to switch the order of the sentence rather than rewrite the entire thing, which may change the meaning of it. Choice (A) simply changes a homonym, but does not fix the subordination problem. Choice (C) would be correct if the comma was replaced with a semicolon and the word "so" were removed.

28. The correct answer is:

> If your code is posted, go to the Tab Room or ballot table to pick up your ballots and the list of students in your room.

This sentence requires a comma between the dependent clause "if your code is posted" and the rest of the independent, declarative sentence. The additional comma between "Room" and "or" is not necessary because it is not a conjunction.

29. judges' lounge

You can tell from the sentence—"Claim a spot"—that there is more than one judge enjoying the lounge; otherwise, there would be no need to claim anything because the reader of the sentence would be the only judge. Plural possessives require an apostrophe after the "s." Therefore, "judges lounge" is incorrect because it does not show possession. "Judges lounge's" is incorrect because it incorrectly assigns the possession to the lounge. "Judge's lounge" is incorrect because it is singular possessive.

30. A.

The pronoun "she" is actually referring to the "students" in the previous sentence. Because the antecedent is plural, so, too, must the pronoun be. In this instance, "she" should be replaced with "they." Replacing the "they"s with "she"s (B) will only continue to confuse the pronoun and the subject-verb agreement, "she can perform when she return" would require "return" to be adjusted to "returns." Choice (C) does not correct the number agreement and chooses the incorrect pronoun.

31. **C.**

"Competent" means capable, and so you should know that it is modifying the word "adult" (C). The sentence does not make sense if you modify the "criteria" (A) or "doubt" (B) with "capable."

32. **The correct answer is:**

> Nothing is more frustrating than to receive a rank and score from a judge without any comments to justify or support the decision!

The original sentence creates a dependent clause where none should exist. Rewriting it in this way creates one full, declarative sentence.

33. **B.**

"Rankings" is plural and requires a plural verb form of the word "match" — "rankings match." You can tell that you do not need to go change the verb tense to past (A) because "Make sure" is a present tense command. It would make sense to change the word "matches" to "matching" (C) if the word "are" were to be placed before it; however, this would be passive voice.

34. **D.**

This sentence contains no proper nouns, and there is no reason to consider "judges" (A), "title" (B), or "author" (C) proper.

35. **B.**

This sentence becomes wordy with the repetition of the word "read" and its other form, "reading." This can be eliminated by removing "to read." The meaning of the sentence remains intact. Choice (A) simply removes the word "haltingly," which does not affect the wordiness of the sentence. Choice (C) is illogical since it would indicate the book itself was due less than a week later, which changes the meaning of the sentence.

36. **however**

The sentence as it appears in the given text includes a transitional word, "therefore," which does not make sense in context. This sentence does not provide a conclusive, definitive statement; rather, it is contrary or enlightening the transition from the information presented earlier, so the transitional cue should be "however." In context, "although" makes no sense, and "as such" is not only awkwardly placed but also misused, because its definition is "in the capacity previously spelled out" or "in itself." "As such" could work here only if, for example, the discussion of "classroom" were extended metaphorically. Instead, the text shifts to the athletic field.

37. **A.**

Though it is short, this is a run-on sentence because it fuses two short, independent clauses together. Fixing this requires use a conjunction (A). Removing the comma does not correct the problem (B), nor does removing the word "she" (C).

38. The correct answer is:

> She simply responded ecstatically, "You mean I can still do the IB work? I don't have to be enrolled in regular English 12? I will do anything you ask me to do!"

When punctuating dialogue, there must be a comma before the quotation marks, and because the line the child delivers is interrogative, her first sentence should end with a question mark.

39. **B.**

The two-word sentence "It is" (B) is correct because it has just what it needs to function as a sentence: a subject and a verb. Only a simple spelling error keeps choice (C), the contracted form of "it is" or "it has," from being correct; "Its'" (with the apostrophe after the "s" instead of before it). If the contraction misrendered in choice (C) were to show the apostrophe in the correct position ("It's"), this option would be an acceptable answer. Choice (A) would create a sentence fragment, and choice (D) is incorrect because "its" is the possessive form of the word "it." Learning the distinction between "its" and "it's" (covered elsewhere in this test guide) will save you lots of headaches—including on the job and other situations where it's vital to communicate clearly.

40. **C.**

The problem with the modifier in this sentence is that it is modifying the "courage" clause rather than the "pride" clause. This is only true in (C). Choice (A) simply removes the word "Though," which does not fix the modification problem. Choice (B) is actually a run-on sentence, which replaces one error with another.

41. **D.**

None of the answer choices—"cliché" (A), "ideology" (B), or "embodiment" (C) represents informal usage; in fact, each word is particularly formal.

42. **A.**

The subject, "I," is singular and requires a singular form of the verb "find." This is found in choice (A). Choice (B) may seem like a correct response, but it is incorrect because it shifts tense in the sentence—"I believe," rather than "I believed." It is generally best to maintain the same tense. Choice (C) is incorrect because it would require "I am finding" in order to be grammatically sound, and this is wordy and in passive voice.

43. **C.**

This is a complex sentence with multiple subjects. The first is NLS, which is singular; the second is "residents and citizens" which is plural. The second subject is not part of an independent clause, so the word "holds" is the problem in this sentence because it is not a verb belonging to the second subject. Choice (C) is the only response which handles this. Choice (A) merely changes the word "citizens" to its singular form, which creates more problems with agreement in the sentence. Choice (B), too, creates a problem with agreement—"NLS oversee" does not work because subject and verb do not agree.

44. **D.**

The sentence as written employs the correct word "through" to indicate a means to an end. Replacing it with either of its homonyms: "threw" (B) does changes the meaning to indicate throwing, and "thru" (C) though technically acceptable creates a different problem: informality. "Thorough" (A) is an entirely different word; including it would alter the meaning of the sentence, nor is it grammatically sound.

45. **A.**

The problem with the parallelism in this sentence is the removal of the final repetitive construction, "get _____." To achieve correct parallel structure, all aspects of the list should be structured in the same manner. Choice (A) fixes this problem, but choice (B) simply moves the incorrect parallel to a different part of the list. Choice (C) removes the parallel structure entirely.

46. **C.**

The first word in book titles must always be capitalized, so you can immediately rule out choice (B). In addition, all proper nouns, verbs, adjectives, adverbs, and subordinating conjunctions should also be capitalized, which would include the adjective "Long" (A). The article "the" does not need to be capitalized in a title, so the correct choice is option (C).

47. **C.**

In this instance, there is no need for the word "patrons"—nor for "savvy" to be possessive—choices (A) and (B), respectively. Choice (D) is also incorrect because in its current state, the possessive is for a plural, which is still unnecessary.

48. The correct answer is:

> If you watched season three of Fox TV's reality cooking show, "_MasterChef_," you remember the big smile that lit up Christine Ha's face every time she impressed the judges with her bold flavors, and especially when her three-course meal of Vietnamese comfort food won Ha the "MasterChef" title.

When introducing a modifier, in this case, "MasterChef," it must be set off by commas. Additionally, the title should be underlined. A comma must be inserted to create a correct compound sentence before the "and," and "three-course" must be hyphenated.

49. **B.**

Although this sentence is technically acceptable as it stands, the wordiness comes into play with the unnecessary phrase "who is." This should be eliminated. This is dissimilar to choice (A), which indicates it is unusual for Ha to have a book checked out by eliminating the word "always." Similarly, removing "fine arts degree" (C) takes away some of the important information presented.

50.

Select 1 correct answer is Choice (C): with

Here, "with" is used as a function word to indicate a means, cause, agent, or instrumentality. In this case, the popularity of NASCAR racing is established by the fact that nearly one-third of the Americans describe themselves as fans. "But" (A) and "however" (C) do not fit because they signal a contrast rather than a reinforcing phrase. Choice (D) could fit the intended meaning, but only if the sentence were flipped around to read something like this, "An estimated 30 percent of Americans claim to be fans of stock-car racing, making it ipso facto a major spectator sport."

Select 2 correct answer is Choice (B): bootleggers, or moonshine runners,

Choice (B) is the best answer because it advances the narrative logically while avoiding wordiness. It correctly uses a comma to set apart the appositive "or moonshine runners," which is used to explain the noun, "bootleggers." Choice (A) creates the redundancy of "illegally" and "illegal" in the same sentence. It also contains the unneeded words "who were also called . . . because." Choice (C) is ungrammatical and contains the tangled illogical phrase "moonshine-running whiskey." Choice (D) shifts from past tense to present tense, while the repetition of the word "who" is awkward though grammatically correct.

Select 3 correct answer is Choice (D): resulted in

Choice (D) is the correct answer. The context tells you that the promoters came together to advance the prospects of stock-car racing. "Reinstated" (A) would have to involve restoring some kind of status, which is illogical because NASCAR's founding stemmed from the meeting. "Emphasized" (B) is off the mark because nothing is being emphasized over anything else; there's just a simple list of achievements. "Nevertheless led to" would make it seem as if the meeting's agenda had been challenged in some way; however, the passage offers no such evidence. Rather, the passage indicates that the promoters knew what they wanted to do, and they went and did it.

Mathematical Reasoning

(Part 1: Non-Calculator)

5 questions
10 minutes*

You may not use a calculator on this section.

---

*Test-takers are advised to pace themselves by spending no more than 10 to 12 minutes on the non-calculator portion of the Mathematical Reasoning test so they can move on to the calculator-active portion.

Mathematics Formula Sheet

Area

parallelogram: $A = bh$

trapezoid: $\dfrac{1}{2}h(b_1 + b_2)$

Surface Area and Volume

rectangular/right prism: $SA = ph + 2B$ $V = Bh$

cylinder: $SA = 2\pi rh + 2\pi r^2$ $V = \pi r^2 h$

pyramid: $SA = \dfrac{1}{2}ps + B$ $V = \dfrac{1}{3}Bh$

cone: $SA = \pi rs + \pi r^2$ $V = \dfrac{1}{3}\neq r^2 h$

sphere: $SA = 4\pi r^2$ $V = \dfrac{4}{3}\neq r^3$

(p = perimeter of base B; $\pi \approx 3.14$)

Algebra

slope of a line: $m = \dfrac{y_2 - y_1}{x_2 - x_1}$

slope-intercept form of the equation of a line: $y = mx + b$

point-slope form of the equation of a line: $y - y_1 = m(x - x_1)$

standard form of a quadratic equation: $y = ax^2 + bx + c$

quadratic formula: $y = \dfrac{-b \pm \sqrt{b^2 - 4ac}}{2a}$

Pythagorean Theorem: $a^2 + b^2 = c^2$

simple interest: $I = prt$

(I = interest, p = principal, r = rate, t = time)

1. Convert 12 yards 3 feet and 8 inches into inches.

    A. 288

    B. 324

    C. 468

    D. 476

2. Twice a positive integer squared less 3 is 95. What is the integer?

    A. 5

    B. 7

    C. 11

    D. 13

3. Place the point (8, –6) on the coordinate plane below.

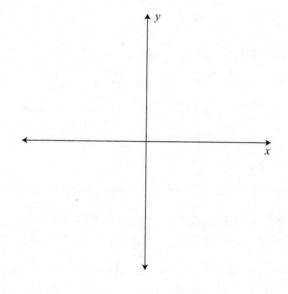

A.

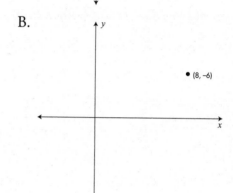

B.

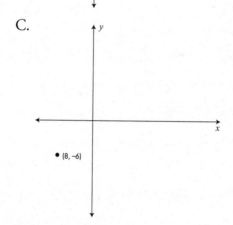

C.

D.

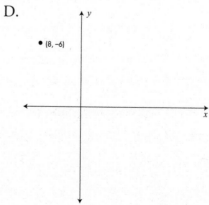

4. A jacket costing $120 is discounted 20%. After a week, the jacket is discounted another 20% and is sold. What expression below can be used to calculate the cost for which the jacket was sold?

    A. (120)(0.40)

    B. 120 – 120(0.40)

    C. 120 – (120)(.20) – [120 – (0.20)(120)](0.20)

    D. 120 – (120)(0.40) – [120 – (120)(0.40)]

5. Which of the following points lies on the line $y - 2 = 3(x - 4)$?

    A. (4, –2)

    B. (4, 2)

    C. (–4, –2)

    D. (6, –2)

PRACTICE TEST 2 (cont'd)

Mathematical Reasoning

(Part 2: Calculator)

46 questions
105 minutes*

You may use a calculator on this section.

---

*Timing is based on the total available time of 115 minutes for the Mathematical Reasoning test. Test-takers are advised to spend no more than 10 to 12 minutes on the non-calculator portion so they can invest more time on the more complex questions that show up in the calculator-active section that follows.

6. What is the diameter of a circle that has area equal to 484π? Place your answer in the box below

[   ]

7. Simplify the following expression.

$$\sqrt{12} + 3\sqrt{27} + \sqrt{3}$$

A. 108

B. $3\sqrt{42}$

C. $12\sqrt{3}$

D. $3\sqrt{3} + 3\sqrt{27}$

8. Select the correct answer.

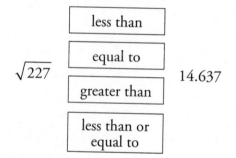

A. less than

B. equal to

C. greater than

D. less than or equal to

9.

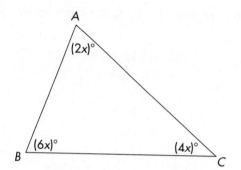

$\triangle ABC$ is what type of triangle?

A. Obtuse

B. Equiangular

C. Isosceles

D. Right

10. A 1.5 gallon jug needs to be filled with water. If the jug is filled one pint at a time, how many pints are needed to fill the jug? Place your answer in the box below

[   ]

11. Simplify the following expression.

$$5 - 2(3 - 5)^3 + 2^2 - (-11)$$

A. 20

B. 26

C. 30

D. 36

Questions 12 and 13 refer to the chart below.

Wilson High School 2012
Total Students = 1,200

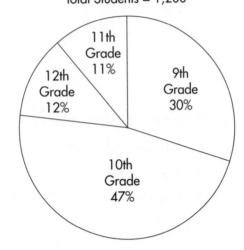

12. The number of 9th graders attending the high school in 2014 is expected to be 20% greater than the 2012 total. How many 9th graders are expected to be at the high school in 2014?

    A. 422

    B. 432

    C. 660

    D. 900

13. What is the measure of the central angle created by the sum of the 9th and 11th graders?

    A. 147.6°

    B. 151.2°

    C. 163.7°

    D. 180°

14. Which of the following graphs represents the following inequalities?

$$y < \frac{2}{3}x - 4$$

$$y \geq -3x + 3$$

A.

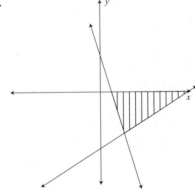

B.

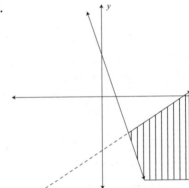

C.

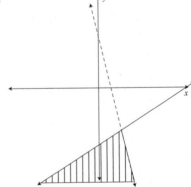

D.

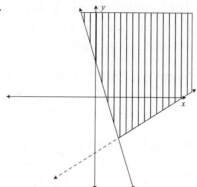

15. A rectangular television screen is sold by the length of its diagonal. If the diagonal is 45 inches and the height of the screen is 27 inches, what is the area of the screen?

    A. 972 in²

    B. 1,008 in²

    C. 1,215 in²

    D. 1,620 in²

16. Which of the following graphs represents the compound inequality $-8 \leq 2x - 8 < 8$?

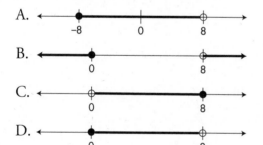

17. A board game uses a six-sided die and a spinner with the colors red, yellow and blue. What is the probability of throwing a 4 or 6 and spinning red or blue?

    A. $\dfrac{2}{3}$

    B. $\dfrac{1}{3}$

    C. $\dfrac{2}{9}$

    D. $\dfrac{1}{9}$

18. If $x^2 + 6x = 40$, what are the values of $x - 6$?

    A. 16, –2

    B. –16, –2

    C. 10, –4

    D. –20, 2

19. What is the slope of a line that is perpendicular to the line $2x - 7y = -37$?

    A. $\dfrac{2}{7}$

    B. $\dfrac{-2}{7}$

    C. $\dfrac{7}{2}$

    D. $\dfrac{-7}{2}$

20.

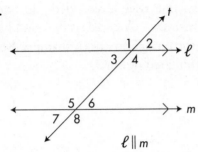

$\ell \parallel m$

If the measure of $\angle 5 = (3x)°$ and the measure of $\angle 2 = (2x)°$, what is the measure of $\angle 8$?

A. 98°

B. 102°

C. 108°

D. 110°

21. Elena has an exercise routine in which she runs uphill, rests and bikes downhill (not in any set order).

The graph below shows her routine on a given day.

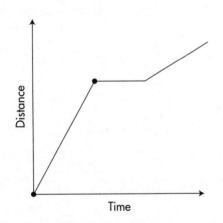

What is the order in which Elena rested, biked, and ran?

A. ran, biked, rested

B. biked, rested, ran

C. rested, biked, ran

D. ran, rested, biked

22. The supplement of an angle is four times the measure of its complement. What is the measure of the angle?

Select the correct answer below.

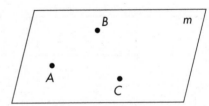

the angle's measure is [less than / equal to / greater than] 60°

23. The following points lie on a certain line.

x	y
−2	−11
1	−5
4	1
6	5

What is the equation of the line?

A. $y = -4x + 2$

B. $y = -3x + 3$

C. $y = 2x - 3$

D. $y = 2x - 7$

24.

In the figure above, points A, B, and C are

A. Collinear and coplanar

B. Collinear only

C. Non-collinear and coplanar

D. Adjacent and supplementary

25. What is the product of $(-2x^2y^3)^3(3xy^2)^2$?

    A. $-6x^8y^{13}$

    B. $-72x^7y^{10}$

    C. $72x^7y^{10}$

    D. $-72x^8y^{13}$

26. James placed $7,500 in a certificate of deposit (CD) at his local bank. The interest the CD generated was $731.25. If the interest rate was 6.5%, for how many months was the money deposited?

    A. 1.5

    B. 2.5

    C. 12

    D. 18

27. A rectangle has a diagonal that is 5 inches long and a height of 1.4 inches. What is the perimeter of the rectangle? Place your answer in the box below.

    A. 8.3

    B. 10.6

    C. 12.4

    D. 14.8

28. What is the solution to the equation

$$x^2 + 4x - 14 = 0?$$

Round your answer to the nearest tenth.

    A. 2.3

    B. −6.3

    C. 2.3, −6.3

    D. 4.4, −4.1

29. Lori needs an 85% average in her math class to move on to the next class. On her first three exams, she earned scores of 81%, 78%, and 97%. What must Lori score on her fourth and final test to earn an 85% grade for the class?

    A. 84%

    B. 86%

    C. 92%

    D. 96%

30. What is the perimeter of a square that has an area of 1,459.24 square meters?

    A. 164.4 meters

    B. 152.8 meters

    C. 144 meters

    D. 139.8 meters

Questions 31 and 32 refer to the chart below.

Carbon-14 has a half-life of 5,700 years. The graph below shows the decay of a 10 kilogram sample over several thousand years.

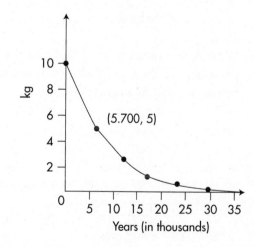

31. What is the best estimate of the weight of the carbon-14 sample after 19,000 years?

    A. 1.4 kg

    B. 0.9 kg

    C. 0.2 kg

    D. 0.08 kg

32. Approximately how many years have passed when the carbon-14 sample decays to 4.1 kg?

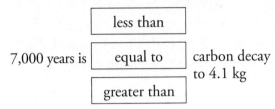

7,000 years is | less than / equal to / greater than | carbon decay to 4.1 kg

33. The scale on a state map of Connecticut indicates that 1 inch = 6.5 miles. If the distance between Bristol and New Haven is 31 miles, what is the distance on the map? (Round your answer to the nearest tenth of an inch.)

    A. 3.9 inches

    B. 4.2 inches

    C. 4.7 inches

    D. 4.8 inches

34. What is the measure of $\angle BOC$ in the diagram below? Place your answer in the boxes below (ignore the degrees symbol).

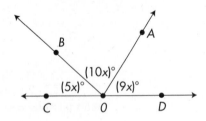

    A. 35.7°

    B. 37.5°

    C. 73.5°

    D. 33.2°

35. What is the slant height of a cone with a surface area that measures 435.675 in² and a radius that measures 7.5 inches? ($\pi = 3.14$).

    A. 10.6

    B. 11

    C. 11.2

    D. 12.4

36. The width of a wavelength in the visible light region of the electromagnetic spectrum is 4.6×10^{-6} meters. Another wavelength in the microwave portion of the electromagnetic spectrum has a width of 3.22×10^{-2}. How many wavelengths of the visible light, if laid side to side, would fit within one length of the microwave wavelength? Express your answer in scientific notation.

    A. 7×10^4

    B. 7.2×10^3

    C. 7×10^3

    D. 6.85×10^{-3}

37. A vendor of ornamental rope charges $0.15 per inch or $1.55 per foot. What is the savings on an order of 7 yards of chain if it is purchased on a per foot-basis rather than a per inch basis?

    A. $5.25

    B. $3.75

    C. $3.65

    D. $2.45

38. A local fishing pier recorded the following catches (in pounds) for a six-day period.

Day	Weight
1	108
2	112
3	104
4	109
5	118
6	112

What is the difference between the median and the mean of these weights?

A. 10

B. 8

C. 5

D. 0

39. Find the missing y-coordinate if $(7, y)$ and $(4, -3)$ lie on a line that has slope $-\dfrac{2}{5}$.

A. 4.8

B. −2.6

C. −4.2

D. −7.8

40. Katie can spend up to $100 on some inexpensive skirts. If each skirt costs $8, which of the following expressions reflects the conditions of Katie's purchase?

A. $s + 8 = 100$

B. $s + 8 < 100$

C. $8s < 100$

D. $8s \leq 100$

41. Simplify the following expression:

$$\frac{x^3 + 6x^2 - 16x}{x^2 - 2x}$$

A. $\dfrac{x + 8}{x - 2}$

B. $\dfrac{x(x - 8)}{x + 2}$

C. $x + 8$

D. $x - 2$

42. $\sqrt{2x + 2} - 3 = 15$

Find the value of x and place your answer in the box below.

Place your answer in the box below.

43. If $19.50 represents a 22% discount off the price of a tennis racquet, what were the *cents* of the racquet's original price? (Round your answer to the nearest cent.)

    A. 63

    B. 64

    C. 71

    D. 96

44. A cruise line ship left Port A and traveled 90 miles due west and then 400 miles due north.

At this point, the ship docked at Port B. What is the shortest distance between Port A and Port B?

Place your answer in the box below.

+------------------------------------+
| |
+------------------------------------+

45. Select the graph that represents the following inequalities:

$$-8x + 2 > -12 \text{ or } 4x - 6 \geq 16$$

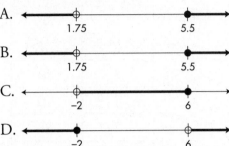

46. A rope measures 30 yards in length. How many circles of radius 5 feet can be created from this length of rope. Drag your answer to the boxes below.

Hundreds [0] [1]

Tens [0] [1] [3] [4]

Ones [1] [2] [3] [5]

Hundreds ☐ Tens ☐ Ones ☐

1. **D.**

   Convert 12 yards into inches.

   1 yard = 36 inches (3 feet)

   $12 \times 36 = 432$

   Convert 3 feet into inches.

   $3 \times 12 = 36$

   Add 432, 36 and 8 to find the inches in 12 yards 3 feet and 8 inches.

   $432 + 36 + 8 = 476$

2. **B.**

   Let x = the number

   $2x^2 - 3 = 95$

   $2x^2 = 98$

   $x^2 = 49$

   $x = 7$

   Although -7 is also a solution to the equation, the answer to the question is 7, the positive integer that satisfies the equation.

3. **A.**

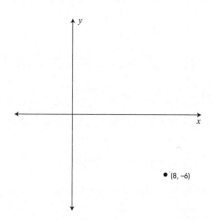

4. **C.**

   After the first 20% discount we get:

   $120 - (0.20)(120) = 96$

   After the second 20% discount we get:

   original – first discount – second discount

   $120 - (120)(.20) - [120] - (0.20)(120)]$
   $(0.20) = \$76.80$

5. **B.**

   Substitute $(4, 2)$ into the line $y - 2 = 3(x - 4)$.

   $2 - 2 = 3(4 - 4)$

   $0 = 3(0)$

   $0 = 0$ ✓

   $y - 2 = 3(x - 4)$ is the equation of a line expressed in point-slope form.

6. **44**

   Find the radius of the circle by setting 484π equal to the area formula.

   $A = \pi r^2$

   $484\pi = \pi r^2$

   $r^2 = 484$

   $r = 22$

   Find the diameter by multiplying the radius by 2.

   $2 \times 22 = 44$

7. C.

Simplify each radical and add like terms.

$$\sqrt{12} = \sqrt{4} \times \sqrt{3} = 2\sqrt{3}$$

$$3\sqrt{27} = 3 \times \sqrt{9} \times \sqrt{3}$$

$$= 3 \times 3 \times \sqrt{3} = 9\sqrt{3}$$

$$\sqrt{3} = 1\sqrt{3}$$

All of the radicals are like terms.

$$\sqrt{12} + 3\sqrt{27} + \sqrt{3} =$$

$$2\sqrt{3} + 9\sqrt{3} + 1\sqrt{3} = 12\sqrt{3}$$

8. C.

$\sqrt{227}$ is greater than 14.637. Since $\sqrt{225} =$ 15, then $\sqrt{227}$ must be greater than 14.637.

9. D.

The sum of the measures of the angles in a triangle is 180°. Solve for x by using the equation

$$2x + 4x + 6x = 180.$$

$$2x + 4x + 6x = 180$$

$$12x = 180$$

$$x = 15$$

Since $x = 15$ we can conclude:

$$6x = 90$$

$$4x = 60$$

$$2x = 30$$

$\triangle ABC$ has one angle that measures 90°, a right angle, so it is a right triangle.

10. 12

Find the number of quarts in 1.5 gallons.

Since 4 quarts equal one gallon, then 1.5 gallons equal 6 quarts because $1.5 \times 4 = 6$. Each quart equals 2 pints, so 6 quarts equals 12 pints.

11. D.

Use the order of operations to simplify the expression.

Parentheses:	$5 - 2(3 - 5)^3 + 2^2 - (-11) =$ $5 - 2 (-2)^3 + 2^2 - (-11)$
Exponents:	$5 - 2(-2)^3 + 2^2 - (-11) =$ $5 - 2(-8) + 4 - (-11)$
Multiply/Divide:	$5 - 2(-8) + 4 - (-11) =$ $5 + 16 + 4 - (-11)$
Add/Subtract:	$5 + 16 + 4 - (-11) =$ $25 + 11 = 36$

12. B.

Find the current enrollment of 9th graders by calculating 30% of 1,200.

$$(0.30)(1,200) = 360$$

Find 20% of 360 and add that number to 360.

$$360 + (0.20)(360) = 360 + 72 = 432$$

13. A.

The percent of the students attending 9th and 11th grade is 41% because $30 + 11 = 41$. Calculate the measure of the central angle formed in the chart by the 9th and 11th graders by finding 41% of 360°.

$$(360)(0.41) = 147.6°$$

14. **B.**

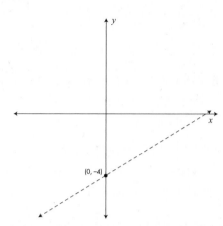

Graph $y \geq -3x + 3$. Remember to draw a solid line because of the "$\geq$" symbol.

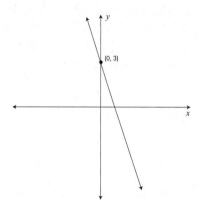

Find the shaded area by testing $(0,0)$ in the inequality.

$$0 < \frac{2}{3}(0) - 4$$

$$0 < -4$$

0 is not less than -4 so shade below the line.

Find the shaded area by testing $(0,0)$ in the inequality.

$$0 \geq -3(0) + 3$$

$$0 \geq 3$$

0 is not greater than or equal to 3, so shade to the right of the line. The correct graph is the intersection of the shaded areas.

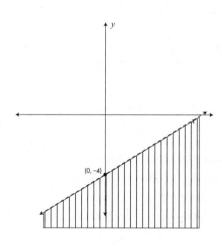

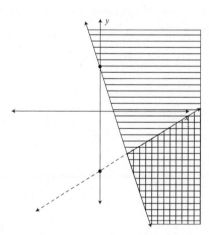

15. A.

The diagonal of a rectangle creates two right triangles. The diagonal of the television is the hypotenuse while the height of the screen is one of the legs. Use the Pythagorean theorem to calculate the measure of the screen's base.

$$27^2 + b^2 = 45^2$$

$$729 + b^2 = 2025$$

$$b^2 = 1{,}296$$

$$b = 36$$

Note that the lengths 27-36-45 are multiples of a 3-4-5 Pythagorean triple because $9 \times 3 = 27$, $9 \times 4 = 36$ and $9 \times 5 = 45$.

Find the area of the rectangular screen by using the formula for the area of a rectangle.

$$\text{Area} = \text{base} \times \text{height}$$

$$\text{Area} = 27 \times 36 = 972 \text{ in}^2$$

16. D.

Solve the compound inequality by writing it as two separate inequalities.

$$-8 \le 2x - 8 \qquad \text{and} \qquad 2x - 8 < 8$$

$$0 \le 2x \qquad\qquad\qquad 2x < 16$$

$$0 \le x \qquad\qquad\qquad\quad x < 8$$

$$0 \le x < 8$$

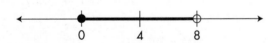

Remember, the dot at 0 is filled because 0 is a part of the graph. The dot at 8 is open because 8 is *not* part of the graph. Double-check your work by testing a point on the number line. We will try 4.

$$-8 \le 2(4) - 6 < 8$$

$$-8 < 2 < 8$$

Testing 4 satisfied the inequality confirming the line is shaded between 0 and 8.

17. C.

Find the probability of each event by using the formula $\dfrac{\text{desired outcomes}}{\text{all outcomes}}$.

Probability of throwing a 4 or 6:

$$\frac{4, 6}{1, 2, 3, 4, 5, 6} = \frac{2}{6} = \frac{1}{3}$$

Probability of spinning red or blue:

$$\frac{\text{red, blue}}{\text{red, blue, yellow}} = \frac{2}{3}$$

Find the probability of both events occurring by finding the product of the two probabilities.

$$\frac{1}{3} \times \frac{2}{3} = \frac{2}{9}$$

18. B.

Subtract 40 from both sides of $x^2 + 6x = 40$ and factor.

$$x^2 + 6x = 40$$

$$x^2 + 6x - 40 = 0$$

The factors that add to 6 and have a product of -40 are 10 and -4 because $10 + -4 = 6$ and $10 \times -4 = -40$

$$(x + 10)(x - 4) = 0$$

$$x + 10 = 0 \quad \text{or} \quad x - 4 = 0$$

$$x = -10 \text{ or } x = 4$$

Substitute both values in the expression $x - 6$.

$$-10 - 6 = -16$$

$$4 - 6 = -2$$

19. D.

The slopes of perpendicular lines are the opposite reciprocals of one another. Find the slope of $2x - 7y = -37$ by transforming the equation into slope-intercept form.

$$2x - 7y = -37$$

$$-7y = -2x - 37$$

$$\frac{-7}{-7}y = \frac{-2}{-7}x - \frac{37}{7}$$

$$y = \frac{2}{7}x + \frac{37}{7}$$

The slope of the line is $\frac{2}{7}$; therefore, the slope of a line perpendicular to $2x - 7y = -37$ is $-\frac{7}{2}$.

20. C.

$\angle 5$ and $\angle 2$ are supplementary angles so set their sum equal to $180°$.

$$3x + 2x = 180$$

$$5x = 180$$

$$x = 36$$

The measure of $\angle 5 = 108°$ because $3 \times 36 = 108$. The measure of $\angle 2 = 72°$ because $2 \times 36 = 72$.

$\angle 5$ and $\angle 8$ are vertical angles and thus are equal in measure. Therefore, the measure of $\angle 8$ equals $108°$.

21. B.

The first section of the graph shows a relatively large distance covered in a relatively small amount of time. Presumably, her bike route covered a great distance in a short time, so biking was the first part of the exercise routine.

The second section of the graph shows time increasing without any distance being covered. Therefore, resting was the next aspect of her routine.

The final section of the graph shows both distance and time being increased. Compared to the first section, more time is being spent per unit of distance covered. Therefore, running uphill was the final part of Elena's exercise routine.

22. equal to

60 is equal to the measurement of the angle.

Let $x =$ the angle's measure

$180 - x =$ the angle's supplement

$90 - x =$ the angle's complement

$$180 - x = 4(90 - x)$$

$$180 - x = 360 - 4x$$

$$3x = 180$$

$$x = 60$$

Check your solution. If x is $60°$, then the supplement is $180 - 60 = 120$ and the complement is $90 - 60 = 30$.

$$120 = 4 \times 30$$

$$120 = 120 \quad \checkmark$$

23. D.

Since all the points lie on the line, we could take any two points and find the slope and y-intercept. However, a quicker way to solve this problem is to substitute the coordinates for x and y. The correct answer will satisfy all four of the points in the table.

$$y = 2x - 7$$

Substitute $(-2, -11)$

$$-11 = 2(-2) - 7$$
$$-11 = -11 \quad \checkmark$$

Substitute $(1, -5)$

$$-5 = 2(1) - 7$$
$$-5 = -5 \quad \checkmark$$

Substitute $(4, 1)$

$$1 = 2(4) - 7$$
$$1 = 1 \quad \checkmark$$

Substitute $(6, 5)$

$$5 = 2(6) - 7$$
$$5 = 5 \quad \checkmark$$

24. C.

Points that are not on the same line are called non-collinear points. Three non-collinear points determine a plane so they are also coplanar.

25. D.

Simplify each parentheses separately.

$$(-2x^2y^3)^3 = -8x^6y^9$$
$$(3xy^2)^2 = 9x^2y^4$$

Next, multiply the two simplified quantities.

$$(-8x^6y^9)(9x^2y^4) = -72x^8y^{13}$$

26. D.

Use the formula Interest = Principal $\times$ Rate $\times$ Time (where time is usually expressed in years) and input the known information.

Let t = the time in years of the certificate of deposit

$$731.25 = 7{,}500 \times 0.065 \times t$$
$$731.25 = 487.5t$$
$$1.5 = t$$

Convert 1.5 years to months by multiplying it by 12.

$$1.5 \times 12 = 18$$

27. C.

The diagonal of a rectangle creates two right triangles. Use the Pythagorean theorem to calculate the base of the rectangle.

$$a^2 + b^2 = c^2$$
$$1.4^2 + b^2 = 5^2$$
$$1.96 + b^2 = 25$$
$$b^2 = 23.04$$
$$b = 4.8$$

The perimeter of a rectangle is found by using the formula $P = 2l + 2w$.

$$P = (2)(4.8) + (2)(1.4) = 12.4$$

28. C.

Since there are no numbers with product -14 and sum 4, use the quadratic formula to solve this equation.

$$x^2 + 4x - 14 = 0$$

$$x = \frac{-b \pm \sqrt{b^2 - 4ac}}{2a}$$

$$a = 1, b = 4, c = -14$$

$$\frac{-4 \pm \sqrt{4^2 - 4(1)(-14)}}{2(1)} =$$

$$\frac{-4 \pm \sqrt{16 - (-56)}}{2} =$$

$$\frac{-4 \pm \sqrt{72}}{2} =$$

$$\frac{-4 \pm 8.5}{2} =$$

$$x = 2.25 \quad x = -6.25$$

Rounded to the nearest tenth, the solution set is $x = 2.3$ and $x = -6.3$

29. A.

The average of Lori's test scores is calculated by finding the sum of the four scores and then dividing by four.

Let x = Lori's fourth test score

$$\frac{81 + 78 + 97 + x}{4} = 85$$

$$\frac{256 + x}{4} = 85$$

$$(4)\ \frac{256 + x}{4} = 85\ = (85)(4)$$

$$256 + x = 340$$

$$x = 84$$

30. B.

The area of a square is found by using the formula $A = s^2$, where s is the length of one side. Input 1,459.24 for the area to find the length of one side.

$$1,459.22 = s^2$$

$$\sqrt{1,459.22} = \sqrt{s^2}$$

$$38.2 = s$$

The perimeter of a square is found by using the formula $P = 4s$. Input 38.2 for s and calculate.

$$P = 4 \times 38.2 = 152.8$$

31. B.

The graph shows that after decaying for 19,000 years, approximately 0.9 kg of the 10 kg sample remains.

32. greater than

The graph shows that the 10 kg sample has decayed to 4.1 kg after approximately 6,000 years have passed.

33. D.

Use the proportion $\dfrac{\text{inches}}{\text{miles}} = \dfrac{\text{inches}}{\text{miles}}$ to find the inches on the map between Bristol and New Haven.

$$\frac{1}{6.5} = \frac{n}{31}$$

Cross-multiply and solve for n.

$$1 \times 31 = 6.5 \times n$$

$$31 = 6.5n$$

$$4.76 = n$$

Rounded to the nearest tenth of an inch, the distance between Bristol and New Haven is 4.8 inches on the map.

34. B.

The three angles create a straight line so their sum is 180°. Add the three angles and solve for x.

$$5x + 10x + 9x = 180$$

$$24x = 180$$

$$x = 7.5$$

Replace x with 7.5 for $\angle BOC$.

$$5x = 5(7.5) = 37.5$$

35. B.

The surface area of a cone is found by using the formula $SA = \pi r^2 + \pi r l$ where r represents the measure of the radius and l represents the measure of the slant height. Input the known data and solve for the slant height.

$$SA = \pi r^2 + \pi r l$$

$$435.675 = (3.14)(7.5^2) + (3.14)(7.5)(l)$$

$$435.675 = 176.625 + 23.55l$$

$$259.05 = 23.55l$$

$$11 = l$$

36. C.

Divide the longer microwave wavelength by the smaller visible light wavelength.

$$\frac{3.22 \times 10^{-2}}{4.6 \times 10^{-6}}$$

Divide 3.22 by 4.6 and then divide 10^{-2} by 10^{-6}. Remember, when dividing numbers with the same base, subtract the exponents.

$$3.22 \div 4.6 = 0.7$$

$$10^{-2} \div 10^{-6} = 10^{-2-(-6)} = 10^4$$

Thus far we have 0.7×10^4. A number expressed in scientific notation is the product of a number greater than or equal to 1 and less than 10 multiplied by 10 to some power. To change 0.7×10^4 into scientific notation, move the decimal point one place to the right and decrease the power of ten by 1.

$$0.7 \times 10^4 = 7 \times 10^3$$

37. A.

Find the number of feet and inches in 7 yards.

1 yard = 36 inches

7 yards = 252 inches

1 yard = 3 feet

7 yards = 21 feet

Find the cost of 252 inches.

$$(252)(\$0.15) = \$37.80$$

Find the cost of 21 feet.

$$(21)(\$1.55) = \$32.55$$

$$\$37.80 - \$32.55 = \$5.25$$

38. D.

The median of a set of numbers is the value in the middle when the numbers are arranged in order. The mean of a set of numbers is the sum of the numbers divided by the number of values.

Find the median by arranging the weight in order.

$$104 \quad 108 \quad 109 \quad 112 \quad 112 \quad 118$$

There are two numbers in the middle, 109 and 112. Find their mean to get the median.

$$(109 + 112) \div 2 = 110.5$$

Find the mean:

$$(104 + 108 + 109 + 112 + 112 + 118) \div 6 = 110.5$$

Subtract the mean from the median.

$$110.5 - 110.5 = 0$$

39. C.

Find the value of y by using the slope formula and inputting the known data.

$$m = \frac{y_2 - y_1}{x_2 - x_1}$$

$$x_1 = 7$$
$$y_1 = y$$
$$x_2 = 4$$
$$y_2 = -3$$

$$\frac{-3 - y_1}{4 - 7} = -\frac{2}{5}$$

$$\frac{-3 - y_1}{-3} = -\frac{2}{5}$$

Cross-multiply and solve for y_1.

$$-3(-2) = 5(-3 - y_1)$$
$$6 = -15 - 5y_1$$
$$21 = -5y_1$$
$$-4.2 = y_1$$

40. D.

The variable s represents the number of skirts Katie can purchase. Since each skirt costs \$8, $8s$ represents the cost of Katie's purchase. The phrase "up to \$100" means the cost can equal \$100 or be some dollar value less. Thus, the inequality $8s \leq 100$ reflects the maximum number of skirts Katie can buy with \$100.

41. C.

Factor the numerator and denominator completely

$$\frac{x^3 + 6x^2 - 16x}{x^2 - 2x} =$$

$$\frac{x(x^2 + 6x - 16)}{x(x - 2)} =$$

$$\frac{x(x + 8)(x - 2)}{x(x - 2)} =$$

$$\frac{\cancel{x}(x + 8)\cancel{(x - 2)}}{\cancel{x}\cancel{(x - 2)}} =$$

$$x + 8$$

42. 161

Begin by isolating the variable.

$$\sqrt{2x + 2} - 3 = 15$$

$$\sqrt{2x + 2} = 18$$

Eliminate the radical by squaring both sides.

$$(\sqrt{2x + 2})^2 = 18^2$$

$$2x + 2 = 324$$

Solve the equation as you normally would.

$$2x + 2 = 324$$
$$2x = 322$$
$$x = 161$$

43. B.

Use the formula $\dfrac{\text{part}}{\text{whole}} = \dfrac{n}{100}$ to calculate the original price of the racquet.

$$\frac{19.50}{x} = \frac{22}{100}$$

Cross-multiply and solve for x.

$(19.50)(100) = 22x$

$1,950 = 22x$

$\$88.636 = x$

Rounded to the nearest cent, the racquet's original price was $88.64. Thus, the cents portion of the price was 64.

44. 410

The path of the ship creates the legs of a right triangle.

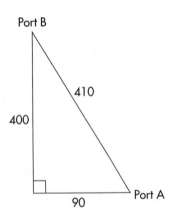

The shortest distance between Port A and Port B is the hypotenuse of the right triangle. Use the Pythagorean theorem to calculate the distance.

$90^2 + 400^2 = c^2$

$8,100 + 160,000 = c^2$

$168,100 = c^2$

$410 = c$

45. A.

Solve each inequality separately.

$-8x + 2 > -12$

$-8x > -14$

$x < 1.75$

Remember to reverse the direction of the inequality when you divide by -8.

$4x - 6 \geq 16$

$4x \geq 22$

$x \geq 5.5$

Test each inequality with a sample value.

$-8x + 2 > -12$ Use 0 to test the inequality

$-8(0) + 2 > -12$

$2 > -12$ ✓

Shade to the left where 0 is located. Remember, the circle is open because 1.75 is not part of the graph.

$4x - 6 \geq 16$ Use 6 to test the inequality

$4(6) - 6 \geq 16$

$24 - 6 \geq 16$

$18 \geq 16$ ✓

Shade to the right of 5.5, where 6 is located. The circle at 5.5 is filled because 5.5 is part of the graph.

46. Hundreds $\boxed{0}$ **Tens** $\boxed{0}$ **Ones** $\boxed{2}$

Find the circumference of a circle that has a radius of 5 feet. Use the formula Circumference =2πr.

$C = (2)(3.14)(5) = 31.4$ feet.

Convert 30 yards into feet and divide that value by 31.4.

1 yard = 3 feet

$30 \times 3 = 90$ feet

$90 \div 31.4 \approx 2.87$

There is enough rope to make 2 full circles.

PRACTICE TEST 2

SCIENCE

50 questions
90 minutes

Practice Test 2: Science

1. All of the following may inhibit enzymatic reactions EXCEPT:

   A. temperature

   B. pH level

   C. excess of substrate

   D. lack of substrate

2. All of the following are steps of photosynthesis EXCEPT:

   A. Chlorophyll is absorbed through plant roots.

   B. During photolysis a photon of light is absorbed by the chlorophyll pigment, which then is in an excited (higher energy) state.

   C. Water is separated into hydrogen and oxygen atoms.

   D. An ADP molecule is phosphorylated to ATP.

3. Which has the least mass?

   A. proton

   B. neutron

   C. electron

   D. hydrogen atom

4. Most animals have internal or external skeletons for structure and support. Which of the following parts provide a similar function in plant cells?

   A. cytoplasm

   B. chloroplasts

   C. cell membranes

   D. cell walls

Match the following terms to their definitions to answer questions 5–8.

   A. Gravity

   B. Force

   C. Inertia

   D. Momentum

5. Mass times acceleration

6. Acts at a distance and attracts bodies of matter toward each other

7. Mass times velocity

8. A particle at rest will stay at rest and a particle in motion will stay in motion until acted upon by an outside force.

Use the text and diagram to answer questions 9–10.

The crust is the outermost layer of what we think of as "the Earth." It includes the mountains, valleys, continents, continental shelves, ocean basins, etc. The crust is rich in oxygen, silicon, and aluminum, with lesser amounts of other elements like iron, nickel, etc. It has low density (2.5 to 3.5 gm/cm³), that floats on the denser mantle. Several separate tectonic plates float beneath it on the surface of the mantle. The tectonic plates touch but magma can leak between the plates, at times causing volcanoes or the formation of underwater ocean ridges of new rock.

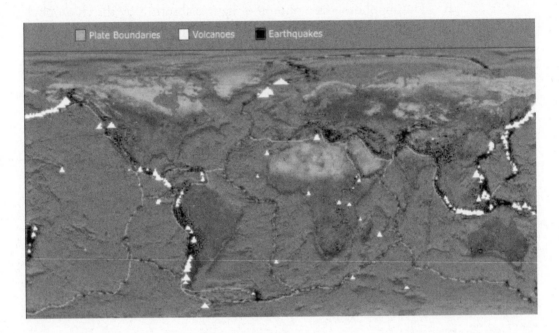

9. There is a line of volcanic activity that shows up in white on this map. It stretches through the Aleutian Islands of Alaska, around the Eastern shore of Asia, Japan, and the Pacific Islands, to the Western shore of South America and Central and North America. This area has been nicknamed the "Ring of Fire" due to its highly volatile volcanic activity. Explain using evidence from the map and text why this area would be subject to high volcanic disruption.

_____

_____

_____

_____

_____

10. Many of Earth's major landforms are features that occurred due to _____ hitting each other.

      A. continental shelves

      B. continents

      C. tectonic plates

      D. faults

11. Pathogens in the form of airborne droplets are most likely to cause which of the following illnesses?

      A. throat infection

      B. stomach virus

      C. AIDS

      D. malaria

12. In glycolysis, a molecule of glucose is broken down into all of the following EXCEPT

      A. pyruvic acid

      B. ATP

      C. CO_2

      D. H^+

13. When astronomers observe the redshift of light from a faraway star, this means that the star is

      A. moving away from us.

      B. moving toward us.

      C. ready to explode.

      D. a dwarf star.

14. Rabbits are not native to Australia, having been brought there from England by sailors in the 18th century. Yet rabbits have thrived and have, in fact, overpopulated Australia. In addition, rabbits and certain native Australian wallabies, although not closely related, resemble each other as to body structure and habits. Which idea about evolution is supported by these facts?

    A. Mass extinctions of species and the emergence of new species can be studied by examining the fossil record.

    B. Different species originally developed because of changes in some shared ancestral genetic code.

    C. Many species have body parts that look similar because they evolved from the same ancestral mammal.

    D. Species evolve in similar ways when they react to similar surroundings.

Use the following list to answer questions 15–17.

    A. Radiation

    B. Convection

    C. Irradiation

    D. Conduction

15. An athlete with a sore shoulder places a warm compress on it to transfer energy to soothe the muscle.

16. On a cold February morning, a blower system in a car warms up after several minutes and blows air through vents in the floor, dashboard, and under the windshield. Eventually, the driver is able to unbutton his coat and stay warm even though the outside temperature is still 23°F.

17. Getting ready for a fall cruise inspires a young lady to spend a couple of weeks going to a local spa and reclining under a tanning lamp. However, such practices might result in dangerous overexposure to ultraviolet rays that can lead to cancer or premature aging of the skin.

Use the following passage and graph, as instructed, to answer questions 18–20.

Fish health in ponds depends on dissolved oxygen mostly produced through the process of photosynthesis by phytoplankton (microscopic plants).

$$6CO_2 \quad + \quad 6H_2O \xrightarrow[\text{nutrients}]{\text{sunlight}} C_6H_{12}O_6 \quad + \quad 6O_2$$

Carbon dioxide   Water   Carbohydrate   Oxygen

The equation above illustrates the process of photosynthesis. Photosynthesis occurs during the day producing oxygen. At night the process of respiration occurs in the phytoplankton, represented by the equation below. It uses dissolved oxygen and produces carbon dioxide.

$$6O_2 \quad + \quad C_6H_{12}O_6 \xrightarrow[\text{nutrients}]{\text{sunlight}} 6CO_2 \quad + \quad 6H_2O \quad + \quad \text{Energy}$$

Oxygen   Carbohydrate   Carbon dioxide   Water

Changes in pond's dissolved oxygen saturation level over a 24-hour period

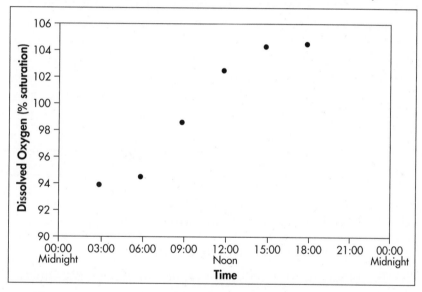

18. The graph above shows the pattern of dissolved oxygen in a pond over a 24-hour period due to the photosynthetic and respiration processes. Think about how you would complete the last two points on the graph for the hours of 21:00 and 00:00 (midnight) on day 2. The last two points on the graph would

    A. go a lot higher.

    B. drop quite a bit.

    C. go up a little.

    D. drop a bit.

19. The respiration reaction shown below and that occurs at night is a  reaction.

Select . . . ▼
decomposition
combination
replacement
double replacement

$$6O_2 \quad + \quad C_6H_{12}O_6 \quad \longrightarrow \quad 6CO_2 \quad + \quad 6H_2O \quad + \quad Energy$$

Oxygen Carbohydrate Carbondioxide Water

20. Considering the information provided in the text and the graph, explain what effect shortening days of sunlight in winter would have on the pond ecosystem.

_____

_____

_____

_____

_____

_____

_____

_____

21. Energy flows through the food chain from

   A. producers to consumers to decomposers.

   B. producers to secondary consumers to primary consumers.

   C. decomposers to consumers to producers.

   D. secondary consumers to producers.

Normal skin color in mice is dominant to albino. In the following questions, N stands for normal skin color and n for albino.

22. Three offspring of two normal-skinned parents have normal skin, but one is albino. Which of the following must be true?

    A. One parent must have the NN genotype.

    B. Both parents must have the NN genotype.

    C. One parent must have the nn genotype.

    D. Both parents must have the Nn genotype.

23. The albino offspring from the F_1 generation described above produces one albino offspring and one normal offspring in the F_2 generation. What must be the genotype of the albino's mate?

    A. either Nn or NN

    B. either Nn or nn

    C. Nn

    D. nn

24. What percentage of the offspring of two albino parents would most likely be normal?

    A. 100%

    B. 50%

    C. 10%

    D. 0%

25. What are the chances that two normal parents each carrying recessive genes for albinism could have a heterozygous normal offspring?

    A. 1 out of 2

    B. 3 out of 4

    C. 2 out of 3

    D. 0 out of 4

26. Which of the following chemical equations is NOT properly balanced?

    A. $FeCl_3 - 3NaOH \rightarrow Fe(OH)_3 - 3NaCl$

    B. $CH_4 + O_2 \rightarrow CO_2 + 2H_2O$

    C. $C_3H_3 + 5O_2 \rightarrow 3CO_2 + 4H_2O$

    D. $2NaCL + F_2 \rightarrow 2NAF + CL_2$

27. The 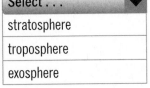 is the densest atmospheric layer, accounting for most

Select... ▼
stratosphere
troposphere
exosphere

of the mass of the atmosphere. It contains 99% of the water vapor found in the atmosphere.

Use the following information to answer questions 28–29.

The formation of holes in the Earth's ozone layer due to chemicals used by humans allows more ultraviolet (UV) light to reach the oceans. Increased UV light can kill phytoplankton, marine algae, and other microorganisms.

28. Which statement BEST describes how a large decrease in phytoplankton and marine algae would affect the ocean food web?

    A. The effect would not be drastic since the organisms are so small.

    B. The number of marine animals would decrease due to the decrease in producers.

    C. The number of consumers in the food web would increase as the producers decrease.

    D. The number of decomposers would increase as the phytoplankton and marine algae die.

29. Which of the following explains the MOST LIKELY effect of increased UV light on alpine and polar lakes that are very clear?

    A. The increase in solar UV radiation would increase the rate of mutation in microorganisms such as phytoplankton and algae, so that they would no longer be a healthy food source for marine animals.

    B. The UV light would raise the temperature of the alpine and polar lakes, which would help the microorganisms repair themselves.

    C. The UV light would stimulate photosynthesis, resulting in a more stable ecosystem.

    D. The UV light would penetrate to a greater depth in lakes that have clear water, potentially doing greater damage to the ecosystem.

30. Why does a food chain generally have no more than five trophic levels?

    A. There is a loss of energy at each trophic level.

    B. There is no way to determine the upper trophic levels.

    C. Many organisms have multiple food sources.

    D. The loss of biodiversity has limited the variety of organisms.

31. Which of the following statements is correct in comparing and contrasting prokaryotes and eukaryotes?

    A. Eukaryotes are much larger than prokaryotes, but otherwise they share the same structure.

    B. Cytoplasm is found in both prokaryotes and eukaryotes but in a slightly different form in each.

    C. Both prokaryotes and eukaryotes are mainly multicellular.

    D. Prokaryotes and eukaryotes both have distinct organelles, although prokaryotes have fewer of them.

32. Which of the following is NOT included in the body's first line of defense against disease-causing agents?

    A. stomach acid

    B. mucous membranes

    C. phagocytes

    D. cilia

33. A ball rolling at a velocity of 12 m/sec hits a wall after 36 seconds. What is the acceleration of the ball?

    A. −23.334 m/sec

    B. 23.334 m/sec

    C. 0.334 m/sec^2

    D. −0.334 m/sec^2

34. A food pyramid is shown below.

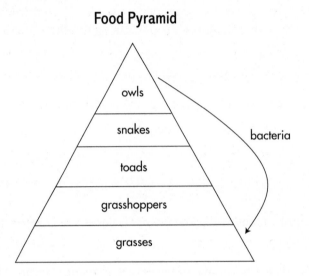

Food Pyramid

In this food pyramid, toads are which of the following?

    A. primary consumers

    B. secondary consumers

    C. producers

    D. tertiary consumers

35. Look at the population graph below.

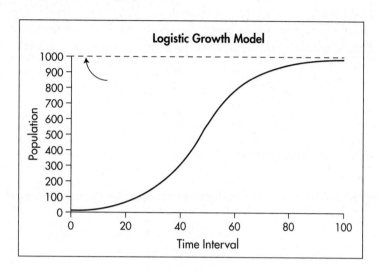

Which of the following population factors does the dotted line represent?

A. lack of competitors

B. carrying capacity

C. migration

D. frequency of reproduction

36. The Florida panther once roamed widely in the southeastern United States. The number of Florida panthers was drastically reduced due to loss of habitat, hunting, and even collisions with automobiles. By the 1970s, the estimated number of Florida panthers had shrunk to only six. Which of the following describes the most likely next stage in this situation?

A. genetic defects in the population due to inbreeding

B. genetic diversity due to interbreeding with other free-roaming puma species

C. improvement of the Florida panther's gene pool due to inbreeding

D. development of two new breeds of Florida panther

37. Cyclooxygenase-2 (COX-2) is an enzyme vital to the production of the prostaglandins, but also contributes to the inflammation of joints in medical conditions such as arthritis. New medications that block the production of prostaglandins by COX-2 enzymes and thereby relieve the symptoms of arthritis are a type of which of the following?

    A. hormone

    B. chemical inhibitor

    C. ion

    D. prosthetic group

Use the diagram below of the human female reproductive system to answer question 38.

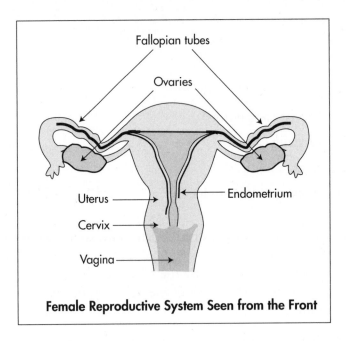

Female Reproductive System Seen from the Front

38. In human sexual reproduction, the fertilized ovum attaches to which of the following?

    A. fallopian tube

    B. uterus

    C. endometrium

    D. vagina

39. A person who contracts chicken pox as an adult lacks which of the following?

    A. memory cells

    B. memory cells for a specific pathogen

    C. plasma cells

    D. B lymphocyte cells

40. The water molecule has many special properties. Which of the following occurs because of water's cohesive behavior?

    A. Water is able to cool down and heat up slowly.

    B. Water is able to float in solid form.

    C. Water is able to dissolve many substances.

    D. Water is able to move from the roots to the leaves of plants.

41. Which of the following is NOT one of the ways in which the carbon cycle uses carbon to build organic compounds?

    A. plant and animal respiration

    B. transpiration

    C. photosynthesis

    D. combustion

Use the following terms to answer questions 42–43.

    A. Cellular respiration

    B. Fermentation

    C. Krebs Cycle

    D. Photosynthesis

42. Anaerobic process producing two ATP molecules per glucose molecule.

43. Breaks down pyruvic acid molecules into CO_2 molecules, H^+ (protons), and 2 ATP molecules.

A student wants to know how temperature affects the rate of the catalyzed reaction for the stomach enzyme pepsin. She sets up an experiment in the lab using reaction chambers set at varying temperatures.

44. Identify the independent variable and dependent variable for this experiment and place the correct component into the boxes:

Independent	Dependent

Variables

Pepsin
Rate of reaction
Temperature (°C)
Catalyzation reaction

45. In which step of the nitrogen cycle do bacteria and fungi break excess nitrates back into their elements and release elemental nitrogen back into the atmosphere?

    A. ammonification

    B. denitrification

    C. nitrogen fixing

    D. decomposition

46. Which graph shows the MOST LIKELY result of this experiment?

A.

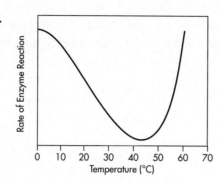

B.

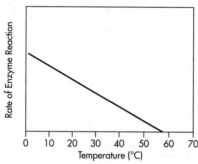

C.

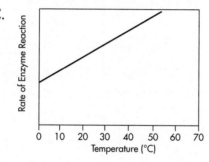

D.

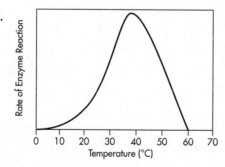

47. The gravity from the Moon pulls the ocean, causing it to bulge and rise on one side while it lowers on the other as the Earth rotates and the Moon orbits, forming tides. The Sun has some gravitational effect on tides, but not as much as the Moon. Tides rise and fall daily with the rotation of the Earth. Especially high (spring) tides occur during which of the following positions of the Sun/Earth/Moon?

A.

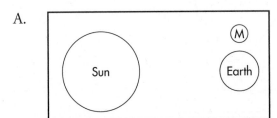

B.

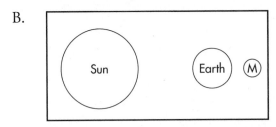

C.

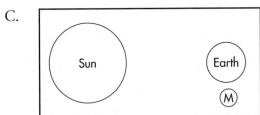

D.

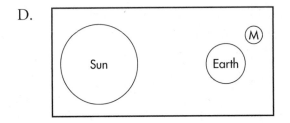

Use the information in the following table to answer questions 48–50.

Properties of Substances				
Substance	Reaction with Water	Phase at Room Temperature	Reaction to Flame	Density
Hydrogen (gas)	none	gas	explosive	0.00009 g/ml
Sodium	bubbling	solid	explosive	0.97 g/ml
Mercury	none	liquid	none	13.6 g/ml

48. Which substance would be considered most highly reactive?

    A. hydrogen

    B. sodium

    C. mercury

    D. argon

49. It was concluded from these tests that the phase of a substance determines how reactive it would be. Is this a reasonable conclusion from the data included in the table?

    A. It is a reasonable conclusion since both gases do not react with water

    B. It is a reasonable conclusion since the solid is the most reactive

    C. It is a reasonable conclusion since not all substances can be reactive

    D. It is a poor conclusion since the two gases have very different reactions

50. Which of the tests noted in the table measured physical properties?

    A. density, reaction to flame

    B. reaction to flame and water

    C. density, phase

    D. phase, reaction to water

Answers: Science Practice Test 2

1. **C.**

   Environmental conditions such as heat or acidity inhibit enzymatic reactions by changing the shape of the active site and rendering the enzyme ineffective. Certain chemicals inhibit enzymatic reactions by changing the shape of the enzyme's active site. If there is a lack of substrate, the enzyme will have no substance to affect. Thus, all of these factors may inhibit enzymatic reactions except an excess of substrate, which would not inhibit those reactions.

2. **A.**

   Chlorophyll is not absorbed through plant roots; it is synthesized within plant cells. Photolysis, in which a photon of light is absorbed by the chlorophyll pigment, which then is in an excited (higher energy) state, is the first step in the photosynthetic process. The light reaction is a decomposition reaction that separates water molecules into hydrogen and oxygen atoms utilizing the energy from the excited chlorophyll pigment. Oxygen that is not needed by the cell combines to form O_2 (gas) and is released into the environment. The free hydrogen is grabbed and held by a particular molecule (called the hydrogen acceptor) until it is needed.

3. **C.**

   An electron has nearly no discernible mass. A proton has a mass of 1 atomic mass unit (AMU) as does a neutron. According to the Periodic Table of Elements, an atom of hydrogen has a mass on average of 1AMU (1.007) since the most common isotope of hydrogen has no neutrons and is a single proton.

4. **D.**

   Rigid cell walls made of cellulose serve the same function of structure and support in plant cells as skeletons do in animals.

5. **B.**

   Force equals mass times acceleration.

6. **A.**

   Gravity is defined as the force that acts at a distance and attracts bodies of matter toward each other.

7. **D.**

Momentum is equal to mass times velocity.

8. **C.**

Inertia is the property of matter that allows a particle at rest to stay at rest and a particle in motion to stay in motion until acted upon by an outside force.

9.

[3 pts. possible]

> The ring of fire is located at the edge of large tectonic plates. (1pt.) Not only is this area at the edge of tectonic plates but it also is where continental plates meet and one slides under the other, making it easy for magma to leak. (1pt.) These features, as shown on the map, make these areas more prone to volcanic activity than the center of a plate would be. (1pt.)

10. **C.**

Many of Earth's major landforms are features that occurred due to tectonic plates rubbing against each other. Such action causes the folding of rock into mountains or the slipping of one plate under another to form a continental shelf. Careful study of the tectonic plates and the land formations between them reveals how the formations came to be.

11. **A.**

A respiratory illness such as a throat infection is the most likely sickness to be caused by pathogens in airborne droplets spread by sneezing or coughing. A virus might be caught by surface contact; AIDS is a bloodborne disease and must be passed by direct blood contact; and malaria is spread by parasites such as the mosquito.

12. **C.**

CO_2 is not a product of glycolysis. Each molecule of glucose is broken down into two molecules of pyruvic acid (pyruvate), two ATP molecules, and two hydrogen atoms (attached to NADH, nicotinamide adenine dinucleotide).

13. **A.**

A redshift in the electromagnetic spectrum of the light from a faraway star means that the star is moving away from the observer. In the 1920s, Edwin Hubble (1889–1953) observed that galaxies around the Milky Way were moving away from us because of this redshift, and those farther away are moving away from us even more rapidly; it is not moving toward us.

14. **D.**

Though rabbits and wallabies are not closely related and their geographic origins are distant, their similarities and the rabbit's ability to survive in similar habitat supports the idea that widely divergent species can evolve in similar ways when reacting to similar biogeographical environments.

15. **D.**

Conduction is the transfer of molecules by collisions, passing heat through one material into another.

16. **B.**

Convection is caused by the flow of heated liquid or gas through a volumetric medium.

17. **A.**

Radiation is waves traveling through space to transfer heat away from the energy source.

18. **B.**

On the actual GED® test, you would mark two **hot spots**. Answers in the range of the box are acceptable. It is important to understand from the text that the oxygen levels will drop significantly. It is also important to know how to graph this appropriately.

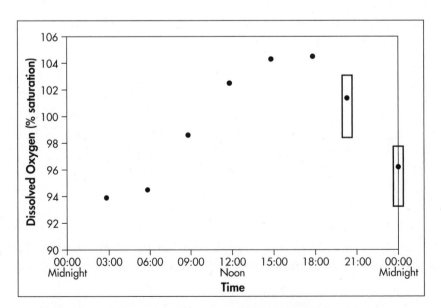

Changes in pond's dissolved oxygen saturation level over 24-hour period.

19. decomposition

The respiration reaction discussed in the text is an exothermic reaction, releasing energy for the cell's use. It is also a decomposition reaction rather than a combination or replacement reaction.

20.

[3 pts. possible]

> As the amount of daylight per day decreases in autumn and winter there is less photosynthesis and more respiration. (1 pt.) The oxygen levels in the pond will decrease and the pond will not be able to support as many fish. (1 pt.) The population of fish will drop off until the sunlight begins to increase again. (1 pt.)

21. A.

Energy flows through the entire ecosystem in one direction, from producers to consumers and on to decomposers through the food chain.

22. D.

As shown in the following Punnett square, the only way offspring could be albino is if each parent has at least one recessive gene for albinism. Since both have a normal phenotype, both must have the Nn genotype. Each parent must also have one recessive allele for albinism in order to produce one nn child.

	N	n
N	NN	Nn
n	Nn	nn

23. C.

The albino parent from the F_1 cross must have the nn genotype. As shown in the following Punnett square, if the mate was albino (nn) all the offspring would be albino, and if the mate was homozygous (NN), then all the offspring would be normal. In order to produce both phenotypes, the second parent must be heterozygous (Nn).

	n	n
N	Nn	Nn
N	nn	nn

24. D.

All offspring of two albino parents (each must have the genotype nn) will be albino, so the answer is 0%.

25. A.

Referring to the Punnett square in answer 22, it is clear that the Nn × Nn cross would yield 1 out of 4 albino (homozygous), 1 out of 4 homozygous normal (NN), and 2 out of 4 heterozygous normal (Nn) children.

26. B.

The correct balanced equation is:

$$CH_4 + 2O_2 \rightarrow CO_2 + 2H_2O$$

27. troposphere

The troposphere is the densest atmospheric layer. Accounting for most of the mass of the atmosphere, it contains 99% of the water vapor found in the atmosphere.

28. B.

The numbers of marine animals that are primary consumers in the ocean food web would decrease because of the decrease in phytoplankton and marine algae that these animals depend on. The small size of the organisms does not affect their importance to the ecosystem (A). The number of consumers would decrease, not increase, with the loss of microorganisms. Decomposers would also decrease due to the overall effect on the ocean food web.

29. D.

The most likely effect is that clear waters in alpine (mountain) and polar lakes would allow UV radiation to penetrate to a greater depth, which would increase the potential damage to the organisms in the lakes and thus to the entire ecosystem. By affecting rates of photosynthesis and reproduction, this abiotic factor would probably decrease biodiversity and limit the carrying capacity of each lake.

30. A.

A food chain is usually limited to no more than five trophic levels because of a nearly 90% loss of energy at each trophic level. Loss of energy is caused by such factors as heat loss from chemical reactions, energy lost as waste, and the fact that not all lower-level organisms are consumed by organisms at the next-highest level.

31. B.

Both prokaryotic cells and eukaryotic cells have cytoplasm. However, the cytoplasm in the prokaryote is granular and viscous, and the nuclear material floats freely without a nuclear membrane. Eukaryotes are indeed much larger than prokaryotes, but the latter has a much more primitive structure. Prokaryotes are unicellular and do not have distinct organelles.

32. C.

Phagocytes are special cells that ingest invasive microbes as part of the body's nonspecific immune response in the second line of defense against disease. The other answer choices are all part of the first line of defense.

33. D.

Acceleration is determined with the following equation:

$$\text{average acceleration} = \frac{\text{change in velocity}}{\text{time}}$$

$$a = \frac{v_2 - v_1}{t} = \frac{0 - 12 \text{ m/sec}}{36 \text{ sec}} = -0.334 \text{ m/sec}^2$$

34. B.

In this food pyramid, toads are secondary consumers that feed on the herbivore grasshoppers, which are primary consumers.

35. B.

The dotted line in the graph represents the point at which the habitat's carrying capacity is reached and population growth therefore levels out. Factors such as lack of competitors and frequency of reproduction would affect the carrying capacity of a habitat but are not specifically represented by the dotted line. Limiting factors (disease, predators, toxic environment, natural disasters, etc.) are those that prevent a population from growing to its biotic potential.

36. A.

The Florida panther, with its drastically reduced numbers, was subject to the bottleneck effect. Population bottlenecks take place when a population's size is decreased for at least one generation. A reduced population must survive by inbreeding and is thus much more vulnerable to the effects of certain alleles than usual. This frequently results in genetic defects in the population. This is, in fact, what happened to the Florida panther. While it has avoided extinction, its population now has certain genetic defects including a hole in the heart.

37. B.

Substances that compete to attach to an enzyme's active site are called inhibitors. If they attach to the enzyme first, the cellular reaction (in this case the synthesis of prostaglandins) will not take place. A hormone is a specific chemical messenger used throughout the endocrine system. The COX-2 inhibitor is a molecule, not an ion. Prosthetic groups and cofactors are substances that work with enzymes to enhance certain reactions, whereas an inhibitor will limit the reaction.

38. C.

The fertilized ovum attaches to the endometrium, which is the inside wall of the uterus.

39. B.

Memory cells are a kind of T cell that is created when an antigen such as the chicken pox virus appears. Unlike plasma cells, which fight an antigen for about two weeks, memory cells remain in a person's system for a very long time, ready to reactivate immediately should the same antigen reappear. Memory cells are always specific to a pathogen, so an adult person who has never had a certain virus will not have memory cells in his or her system to attack that antigen. That person may, however, have memory cells keyed to another antigen.

40. D.

The cohesive properties of water are due to the hydrogen bonding between water molecules. This aids in capillary action, in which water moves upward in the narrow fibers of a plant or tree from the roots to the leaves. The ability of water to cool down and heat up slowly (A) is due to its high heat capacity, not its strong cohesion. Water floats as a solid (B) because it expands upon freezing. It is a universal solvent (C) because it is a highly polar molecule.

41. B.

Transpiration is part of the water cycle, and is the process by which plants release water vapor into the air.

42. **B.**

Fermentation is an anaerobic process producing two ATP molecules per glucose molecule.

43. **C.**

The Krebs Cycle breaks down pyruvic acid molecules into CO_2 molecules, H^+ (protons), and 2 ATP molecules and liberates two electrons as the second step of cellular respiration.

44. **The correct answers are as follows:**

Independent Variable

Temperature (°C)

Dependent Variable

Rate of Reaction

45. **B.**

Various species of bacteria and fungi break excess nitrates back down into elements, a process that releases elemental nitrogen back into the air. This process is called denitrification. Ammonification and decomposition are both processes that break substances down but do not release nitrogen into the air. Nitrogen fixing makes nitrogen available to plant roots.

46. **D.**

As temperature increases, the reaction rate of an enzyme also increases. However, above an optimal temperature, the reaction rate decreases rapidly. This is because the enzyme molecules become altered as their hydrogen bonds begin to break. The enzyme then becomes "denatured," or incapable of fitting with its substrate and catalyzing the reaction. Choice (D) shows this situation, with the graph line peaking at 37° then falling off.

47. **B.**

Choice (B) shows the Sun/Earth/Moon alignment of the full moon. During a full moon, as during a new moon, the spring tide is in effect since the gravitational pull of the sun and moon work together in a 180° force to pull the tides into the highest tides of any time.

48. **B.**

Sodium would be considered most highly reactive.

49. **D.**

Based on the data n the chart, it is a poor conclusion because the two gases have very different reactions.

50. **C.**

Density and phase measured physical properties in the table.

PRACTICE TEST 2

SOCIAL STUDIES

49 questions
70 minutes

Practice Test 2: Social Studies

Use the following chart to answer questions 1–3.

Amendments to the U.S. Constitution

1	Guarantees freedom of religion, speech, assembly, and press, and the right to petition the government
2	Protects the rights of states to maintain a militia and of citizens to bear arms
3	Restricts the quartering of troops in private homes
4	Protects against unreasonable searches and seizures
5	Assures the right not to be deprived of life, liberty, and property without due process of law
6	Guarantees the right to a speedy and public trial by an impartial jury
7	Assures the right to a jury trial in cases involving the common law, the law established by previous court decisions
8	Protects against excessive bail or cruel and unusual punishment
9	Provides that people's right are not restricted to those specified in the first eight amendments
10	Restates the Constitution's principle of federalism by providing that powers not granted to the national government nor prohibited to the states are reserved to the states and to the people

1. The chart above lists the first 10 amendments to the United States Constitution. The First Amendment includes

     A. the Rights of the Accused.

     B. the Five Freedoms.

     C. the Preamble.

     D. the Bill of Rights.

2. Amendments four to eight are referred to as

     A. the Rights of the Accused.

     B. the Five Freedoms.

     C. the Preamble.

     D. the Bill of Rights.

3. In the Third Amendment, the word **quartering** means which of the following?

    A. cutting

    B. blocking

    C. housing

    D. measuring

Use the following chart to answer question 4.

The graph below shows the year 2013 purchasing power of having $50 in previous years.

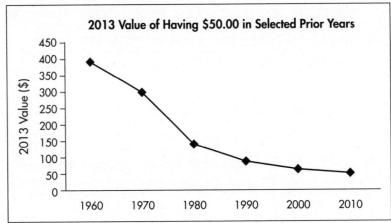

Source: Federal Bureau of Labor Statistics

4. According to the graph above, which decade experienced the fastest rate of inflation?

    A. 1960s

    B. 1970s

    C. 1980s

    D. 1990s

Use the graph below to answer questions 5 and 6.

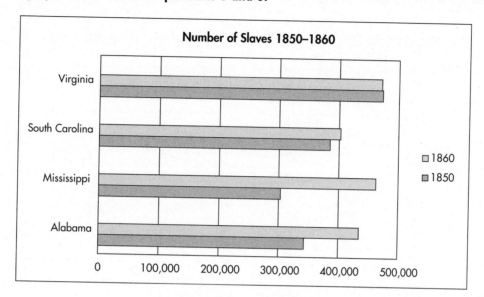

5. According to this graph, [Select ▼] had almost as many slaves in 1850

Select
Virginia
South Carolina
Mississippi
Alabama

as it did in 1860?

6. According to the graph, [Select ▼] had the greatest increase in the num-

Select
Virginia
South Carolina
Mississippi
Alabama

ber of slaves in 1860?

Use the following graph to answer question 7.

7. Which of the following statements is supported by the graph?

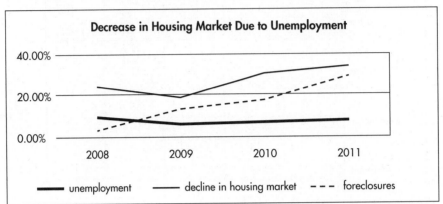

U.S. Bureau of Labor and Statistics

A. The unemployment rate increased from 2008 to 2011, causing the number of foreclosures to increase.

B. The unemployment rate remained steady from 2009 to 2011; however, the decrease in the housing market increased.

C. The unemployment rate, decline in housing market, and number of foreclosures are unrelated.

D. Foreclosures increased steadily throughout the period between 2008 and 2011 with little or no correlation to the unemployment rate.

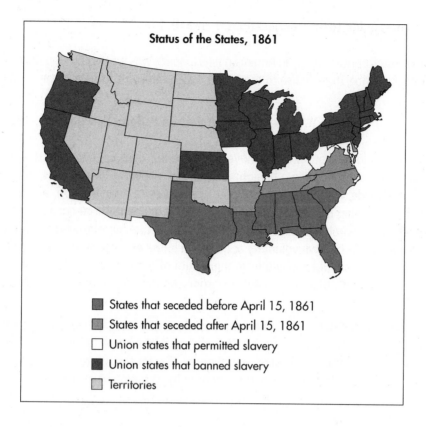

Status of the States, 1861

- States that seceded before April 15, 1861
- States that seceded after April 15, 1861
- Union states that permitted slavery
- Union states that banned slavery
- Territories

8. According to the above map, April 15, 1861 was significant. What conclusion can be made about this date?

    A. The United States had a new president.

    B. The line drawn by the Missouri Compromise in 1850 did not apply to California.

    C. The territories did not have slavery.

    D. The Southern states had seceded from the Union.

Use this information to answer questions 9 and 10.

This letter, printed widely in American newspapers, was written by George W. Harkins, chief of the Choctaw tribe, in response to the brutal Indian removals to new homes in the West.

George W. Harkins to the American People, February 25, 1832

Yet it is said that our present movements are our own voluntary acts — such is not the case. We found ourselves like a benighted stranger, following false guides, until he was surrounded on every side, with fire and water. The fire was certain destruction, and a feeble hope was left him of escaping by water. A distant view of the opposite shore encourages the hope; to remain would be inevitable annihilation. Who would hesitate, or who would say that his plunging into the water was his own voluntary act? Painful in the extreme is the mandate of our expulsion. We regret that it should proceed from the mouth of our professed friend, for whom our blood was co-mingled with that of his bravest warriors, on the field of danger and death.

I ask you in the name of justice, for repose for myself and for my injured people. Let us alone — we will not harm you, we want rest. We hope, in the name of justice, that another outrage may never be committed against us, and that we may for the future be cared for as children, and not driven about as beasts, which are benefited by a change of pasture.

Courtesy of the Center on Congress at Indiana University

9. In his letter, George W. Harkins is referring to which of the following?

   A. Indian Removal Act

   B. Civil Rights Movement

   C. American Indian Movement

   D. People's Protest at the University of California at Berkeley

10. Which conclusion can you draw from the information in the Harkins letter?

   A. The Choctaw tribe was leaving their lands voluntarily.

   B. The Choctaw tribe was being forced to leave their lands.

   C. The Choctaw tribe had no land.

   D. The Choctaw tribe wanted to move to another place.

Use the following map to answer question 11

11. Based on the map, which of the following is the most likely conclusion one could draw?

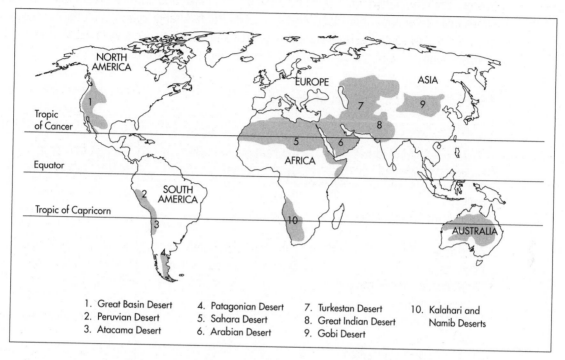

1. Great Basin Desert
2. Peruvian Desert
3. Atacama Desert
4. Patagonian Desert
5. Sahara Desert
6. Arabian Desert
7. Turkestan Desert
8. Great Indian Desert
9. Gobi Desert
10. Kalahari and Namib Deserts

A. Most desertification occurs near the equator.

B. A large area of desert can be found in Northern Africa.

C. There is a large desert area in South America.

D. There is no desert in Australia.

Use the following information to answer questions 12 and 13.

The Constitution allows the federal government and the states to exercise some nearly identical powers. Both the federal and state governments can make and enforce similar laws. For example, states make laws regulating state elections, while the federal government controls congressional and presidential elections. Both state legislatures and Congress can levy taxes, charter banks, and borrow money. Powers that exist at both levels are called concurrent powers.

The Federal System: Division of Powers

Powers Delegated to the Federal Government	Powers Shared by the Federal and State Governments	Powers Reserved to the States
Declare war Regulate interstate and foreign trade Coin money Establish post offices Set standards for weights and measurements Admit new states Establish foreign policy Establish laws for citizenship Regulate patents and copyrights Pass laws necessary for carrying out its powers	Enforce laws Borrow money Levy taxes Establish charter banks Provide for general welfare	Establish local governments Regulate commerce within a state Provide for public safety Create corporation laws Establish schools Make marriage laws Assume all the powers not granted to the federal government or prohibited by the Constitution

12. Which of the following are shared powers of the Federal and State governments?

    A. Make it possible for an immigrant to become a citizen of the United States

    B. Provide the legal basis and charter for a new bank in the state of Wyoming

    C. Establish a new school system in Shelby County, Tennessee

    D. Admit Puerto Rico as a new state

13. In the introduction to this chart the word **concurrent** most likely means which of the following?

    A. Next to one another

    B. Shared by both federal and state

    C. Occurring in two geographic places at the same time

    D. Near but not next to one another

Use the following table to answer question 14.

Trends in Urban Populations—Current and Projected

1975		2000		2025	
1. Tokyo, Japan	26.6	1. Tokyo, Japan	34.5	1. Tokyo, Japan	36.4
2. New York- Newark, USA	15.9	2. Mexico City, Mexico	18	2. Bombay, India	26.4
3. Mexico City, Mexico	10.7	3. New York-Newark, USA	17.9	3. Delhi, India	22.5
4. Osaka-Kobe, Japan	9.8	4. São Paulo, Brazil	17.1	4. Dhaka, Bangladesh	22
5. São Paulo, Brazil	9.6	5. Bombay, India	16.1	5. São Paulo, Brazil	21.4
6. Los Angeles-Long Beach-Santa Ana, USA	8.9	6. Shanghai, China	13.2	6. Mexico City, Mexico	21
7. Buenos Aires, Argentina	8.8	7. Calcutta, India	13.1	7. New York-Newark, USA	20.6
8. Paris, France	8.6	8. Delhi, India	12.4	8. Calcutta, India	20.6
9. Calcutta, India	7.9	9. Buenos Aires, Argentina	11.9	9. Shanghai, China	19.4
10. Moscow, Russian Federation	7.6	10. Los Angeles-Long Beach-Santa Ana, USA	11.8	10. Karachi, Pakistan	19.1

Source: United Nations, World Urbanization Prospects, The 2007 Revision.

14. Based on the information in the chart above, 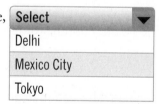 will be the most

populous city in the world in 2025.

Use the following pie chart to answer questions 15 and 16.

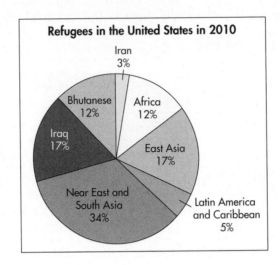

15. According to the graph, what conclusion can be made about refugees in the United States in 2010?

    A. More than half the refugees in the United States were from Asia.

    B. Latin America and the Caribbean were a great source of refugees in 2010.

    C. Refugees come to the United States from Europe.

    D. Iran and Iraq had a large number of refugees.

16. The smallest number of refugees in the United States came from [ ] and [ ].

Use the following information to answer questions 17–19.

Text 1: The Aftermath of the Alien and Sedition Acts

In 1798, Congress passed the Alien and Sedition Acts. The acts came in response to fears of going to war with France. The Alien Act gave the president the right to imprison or expel aliens (non-citizens) deemed "dangerous to the peace and safety of the United States." The Sedition Act was adopted to restrict speech critical of the government. Some people believed these acts violated the Constitution. In fact, Thomas Jefferson and James Madison wrote resolutions that argued that the federal government lacked authority to exercise power not specifically given to it by the Constitution. Kentucky and Virginia passed these resolutions. The Kentucky Resolution, penned by Jefferson, went further than Madison's Virginia Resolution, declaring that states had the right to nullify such an act of Congress.

This debate made its way into the presidential election of 1800. Jefferson and Aaron Burr ran against John Adams and Charles Pinckney. The election resulted in a tie, so the House of Representatives had to decide the winner. Ultimately, Jefferson was declared the winner. But because the election created so many problems, the 12th Amendment was added to the U.S. Constitution.

Text 2: Amendment XII

Passed by Congress December 9, 1803. Ratified June 15, 1804.

. . . The person having the greatest number of votes for President, shall be the President, if such number be a majority of the whole number of Electors appointed; and if no person have such majority, then from the persons having the highest numbers not exceeding three on the list of those voted for as President, the House of Representatives shall choose immediately, by ballot, the President. But in choosing the President, the votes shall be taken by states, the representation from each state having one vote; a quorum for this purpose shall consist of a member or members from two-thirds of the states, and a majority of all the states shall be necessary to a choice. . . .

Source: National Archives and Records Administration

17. Place the four events into the flow chart to show the order in which they occur in Text 1.

Event Flow Chart: What Happened After the Alien and Sedition Acts Became Law

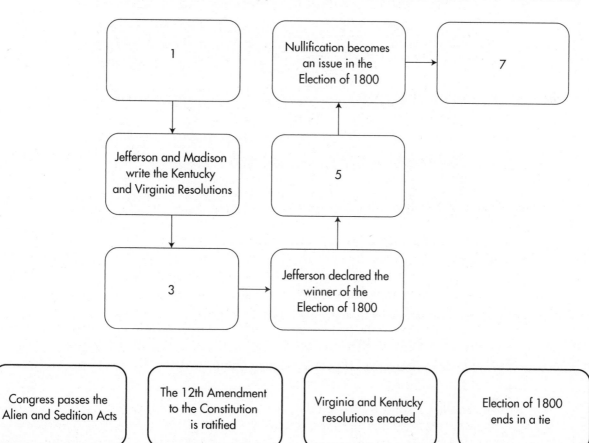

18. In the text, the word **nullify** most likely means which of the following?

    A. to bring about

    B. to strike down

    C. to add to the Constitution

    D. to become higher in rank

19. The 12th Amendment was one important result of the election of 1800. According to the excerpt, what was the purpose of passing this amendment?

    A. To make Thomas Jefferson the president of the United States

    B. To provide a way to decide who is president in the event of an equal number of votes

    C. To help the House of Representatives make Thomas Jefferson the president

    D. To give the electoral college more power

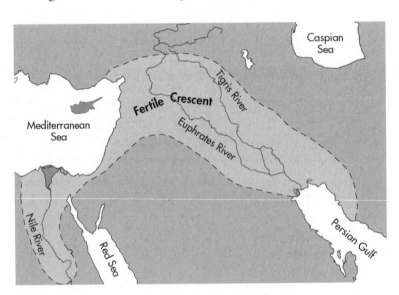

20. The area on the map above is known as the Fertile Crescent. What is the reason for this name?

    A. It is a place of large population

    B. It is an area where people travel a great deal

    C. It is between two rivers which makes the land very productive

    D. It is a place where people migrate often

21. The Fertile Crescent is between the [＿＿＿＿＿＿] and the [＿＿＿＿＿＿] rivers.

Read the passage below and then answer questions 22 and 23.

John Adams was about to leave the office of President when he made several last minute appointments including judges and court officials. President Jefferson ordered his Secretary of State, James Madison, not to deliver the appointment papers. William Marbury was one of those appointments. He went to the Supreme Court in a case against Madison. Chief Justice John Marshall ruled that Marbury had no right to appeal. This was the first time the Supreme Court ruled a law unconstitutional.

The very essence of civil liberty certainly consists in the right of every individual to claim the protection of the laws, whenever he receives an injury. One of the first duties of government is to afford that protection. [The] government of the United States has been emphatically termed a government of laws, and not of men. It will certainly cease to deserve this high appellation, if the laws furnish no remedy for the violation of a vested legal right. . . .

By the constitution of the United States, the President is invested with certain important political powers, in the exercise of which he is to use his own discretion, and is accountable only to his country in his political character, and to his own conscience. To aid him in the performance of these duties, he is authorized to appoint certain officers, who act by his authority and in conformity with his orders.

In such cases, their acts are his acts; and whatever opinion may be entertained of the manner in which executive discretion may be used, still there exists, and can exist, no power to control that discretion. The subjects are political. They respect the nation, not individual rights, and being entrusted to the executive, the decision of the executive is conclusive. . . .

National Archives and Records Administration

22. *Marbury v. Madison* is one of the most important Supreme Court rulings in United States history. Since the decision, many cases have gone before the Courts. Based on this information and the information in the previous paragraphs, why was this ruling so significant?

    A. Denied Adams's right to make midnight appointments

    B. Upheld Adams's right to make midnight appointments

    C. Confirmed Congress's power to expand judicial authority

    D. Affirmed the power of the court to declare a law unconstitutional

23. The process established in the case of *Marbury v. Madison* is called judicial review. It extends the power of the [Select ▼] branch of U.S. government.

    executive

    legislative

    judicial

24. What organization was often the target of mass demonstrations, a few of them violent, against globalization?

    A. WTO–World Trade Organization

    B. CBC–Canadian Broadcasting Corporation

    C. NATO– North Atlantic Treaty Organization

    D. NASA–National Aeronautics and Space Administration

Use this chart to answer questions 25.

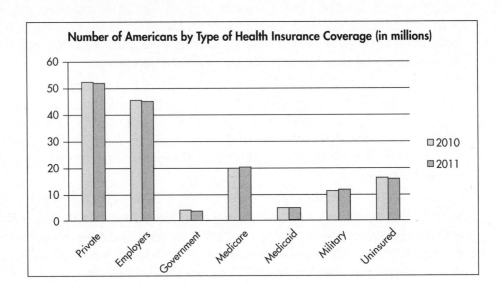

25. Based on the information in this chart, what are the implications concerning health insurance?

    A. More people were insured in 2011 than in 2010.

    B. The number of uninsured have increased.

    C. The number of insured overall have increased.

    D. More people are insured by Medicare and Medicaid.

Use the following statement to answer question 26.

According to the Kaiser Family Foundation, the Great Recession (2007-2009) triggered a big increase in the number of Americans without health insurance from 2008 to 2010 "as a high jobless rate led millions to lose their employer-sponsored coverage." Meanwhile, the new federal Affordable Care Act (ACA), with a key goal of reducing the number of uninsured, was signed into law by President Obama in 2010.

26. Based on the above statement, what would be a reasonable prediction for 2011 about the rate of uninsured in relation to the total American population?

    A. Uninsured rates would be expected to rise as the economy improved and early provisions expanding coverage under the ACA went into effect.

    B. There would be no uninsured Americans left because, under the ACA, all Americans are mandated to carry health insurance.

    C. Newly insured Americans would place a strain on the Medicaid system.

    D. Uninsured rates would be expected to drop as the economy improved and early provisions expanding coverage under the ACA went into effect.

Read the passage below. Then answer questions 27 and 28.

The Fair Credit Reporting Act (FCRA) requires each of the nationwide credit reporting companies — Equifax, Experian, and TransUnion — to provide you with a free copy of your credit report, at your request, once every 12 months. The FCRA promotes the accuracy and privacy of information in the files of the nation's credit reporting companies. The Federal Trade Commission (FTC), the nation's consumer protection agency, enforces the FCRA with respect to credit reporting companies.

A credit report includes information on where you live, how you pay your bills, and whether you've been sued or have filed for bankruptcy. Nationwide credit reporting companies sell the information in your report to creditors, insurers, employers, and other businesses that use it to evaluate your applications for credit, insurance, employment, or renting a home.

Your credit report has information that affects whether you can get a loan — and how much you will have to pay to borrow money. You want a copy of your credit report to:

- make sure the information is accurate, complete, and up-to-date before you apply for a loan for a major purchase like a house or car, buy insurance, or apply for a job.

- help guard against identity theft. That's when someone uses your personal information — like your name, your Social Security number, or your credit card number — to commit fraud. Identity thieves may use your information to open a new credit card account in your name. Then, when they don't pay the bills, the delinquent account is reported on your credit report. Inaccurate information like that could affect your ability to get credit, insurance, or even a job

27. According to the excerpt, what information is found in your credit report?

    A. your education level, income amount, and debt amounts

    B. your payment and credit history

    C. your parents' or other family members' credit history

    D. your bank account numbers

Read the following passage and answer questions 28–31.

Amendment VI

In all criminal prosecutions, the accused shall enjoy the right to a speedy and public trial, by an impartial jury of the State and district wherein the crime shall have been committed, which district shall have been previously ascertained by law, and to be informed of the nature and cause of the accusation; to be confronted with the witnesses against him; to have compulsory process for obtaining witnesses in his favor, and to have the Assistance of Counsel for his defence.

Source: National Archives and Records Administration

28. Which of the following is NOT provided for in the Sixth Amendment?

    A. A mistrial

    B. An innocent person convicted of crimes he did not commit

    C. A lengthy trial

    D. The services of an attorney

29. As it is used in the above text, what does the word *impartial* mean?

    A. half

    B. fair

    C. long

    D. large

30. Some trials do not take place in the "district wherein the crime shall have been committed" when the attorney of the accused asks for a "change of venue." What does the term "change of venue" mean?

    A. more people to select as jurors

    B. a different location for the trial since it may be difficult to find an impartial jury in the area the crime was committed

    C. a larger location in the event of a large attendance

    D. a different attorney since the accused cannot pay

Use the following map of the exploration route of Hernando de Soto to answer question 31.

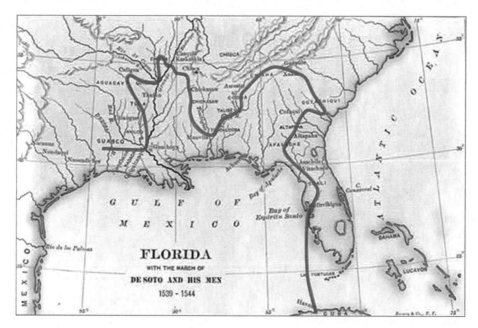

Source: Library of Congress

31. Based on the map, Hernando de Soto explored the [Select ▼] regions of

| northeast |
| northwest |
| southeast |
| southwest |

the United States.

Use the chart below to answer questions 32–34.

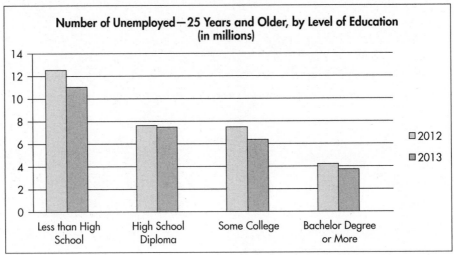

Source: *Bureau of Labor Statistics, April 2013*

32. Based on the information in the chart 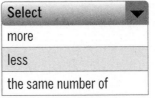 people with high school

Select
more
less
the same number of

    diplomas are unemployed than those with a bachelor's degree.

33. Based on the information in the chart, the best prediction about the unemployment rate for people over 25 years old is that it 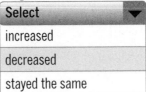 in 2013 when

Select
increased
decreased
stayed the same

    compared to 2012.

34. Which of the following conclusions about the connection between education level and unemployment rate is best supported by the data in the chart?

    A. Education will not make a difference in the unemployment rate for people in the future.

    B. Education plays a significant role in finding and keeping a job now and in the future.

    C. People who have less than a high school diploma can get good paying jobs.

    D. People with a high school diploma do not need to further their education in order to find and keep jobs.

Read the passage and answer question 35.

President Reagan's 1986 State of the Union Message to Congress was originally scheduled for the day of the Challenger explosion, January 28, 1986, but was postponed by a week in response to the accident. Reagan begins his message by paying tribute to "the brave seven" Challenger crew members and later reiterates the nation's commitment to the space program. This is a select page from the official copy Reagan handed to the President of the Senate before the address. The text differs slightly from the final speech made by the President.

RG 46, Records of the U.S. Senate

Feb 4, 1986
P P T
PM-106
Table
PT

TO THE CONGRESS OF THE UNITED STATES:

Thank you for allowing me to delay my address until this evening. We paused together to mourn and honor the valor of our seven Challenger heroes. And I hope we are now ready to do what they would want us to do -- go forward America, reach for the stars. We will never forget those brave seven, but we shall go forward.

I have come to review with you the progress of our Nation, to speak of unfinished work, and to set our sights on the future. I am pleased to report the state of our Union is stronger than a year ago, and growing stronger each day. Tonight, we look out on a Rising America -- firm of heart, united in spirit, powerful in pride and patriotism -- America is on the move!

But, it wasn't long ago that we looked out on a different land -- locked factory gates and long gasoline lines, intolerable prices and interest rates turning the greatest country on Earth into a land of broken dreams. Government growing beyond our consent had become a lumbering giant, slamming shut the gates of opportunity, threatening to crush the very roots of our freedom.

(continued)

(continued)

What brought America back? The American people brought us
back -- with quiet courage and common sense; with undying faith
that in this Nation under God the future will be ours, for the
future belongs to the free.

Tonight the American people deserve our thanks -- for
37 straight months of economic growth; for sunrise firms and
modernized industries creating 9 million new jobs in 3 years;
interest rates cut in half and inflation falling from over
12 percent in 1980 to under 4 today; and a mighty river of good
works, a record $74 billion in voluntary giving last year alone.

Despite the pressures of our modern world, family and
community remain the moral core of our society, guardians of our
values and hopes for the future. Family and community are the
costars of this great American comeback. They are why we say
tonight: Private values must be at the heart of public policies.

35. This document refers to the *Challenger* explosion several times. Based on the information in the text, which of the following describes the *Challenger*?

    A. an airplane crash

    B. a war mission in Cuba

    C. a space shuttle

    D. a missile launched, but failed to fire

Use the following information to answer question 36.

The United States' involvement in war has been costly throughout history. However, it becomes increasingly more expensive as the technology is improved. The American Revolution, which lasted eight years, cost $101 million. The War of 1812, lasting only 3 years, cost $90 million. The Civil War, which waged for only four years, was intense and widespread, costing an estimated $5 billion. Once warfare spread to other countries and grew in technological capabilities, it became much more expensive. World War I cost $20 billion in the four years of American involvement. However, World War II, which lasted six years, cost $296 billion.

36. Which of the following graphics supports the information in the paragraph?

A.

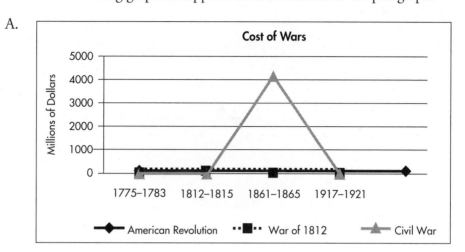

B.

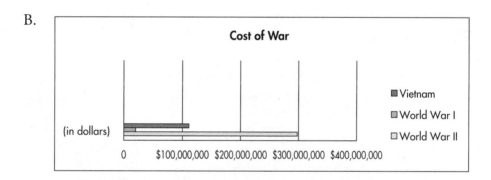

C.

War	Duration	Cost
American Revolution	8 years	$101,000,000
War of 1812	3 years	$90,000,000
Civil War	4 years	$5,000,000,000
WWI	4 years	$20,000,000,000
WWII	6 years	$296,000,000,000

D.

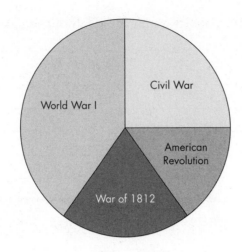

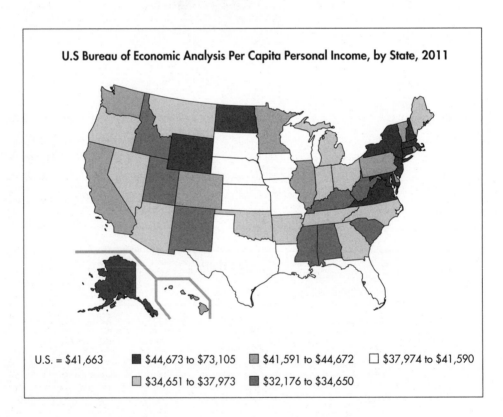

U.S Bureau of Economic Analysis Per Capita Personal Income, by State, 2011

U.S. = $41,663   ■ $44,673 to $73,105   ■ $41,591 to $44,672   □ $37,974 to $41,590

■ $34,651 to $37,973   ■ $32,176 to $34,650

37. Based on the map above, the states with the lowest per capita person income in 2011 were found in which of the following locations?

A. north and west

B. northeast

C. no specific area, but all parts of the nation

D. around large cities

Read the following passages to answer questions 38 and 39.

After the terrorist attacks on U.S. soil on September 11, 2001, the United States government saw a need for more security. As a result, the Department of Homeland Security was created. This federal department was first charged with the duties of preventing terrorism. However, the role of Homeland Security expanded, creating a vast organization with far-reaching duties. Below is a summary of the agency's work.

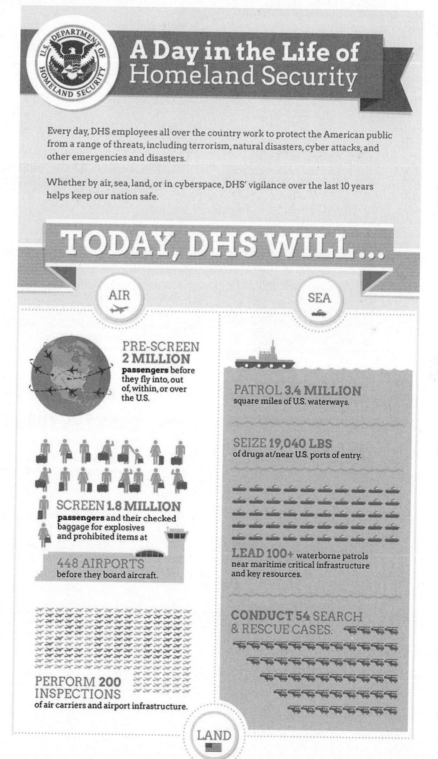

LAND

TRAIN **350 MEMBERS** of law enforcement, faith-based, academic, and private sector communities to respond to active shooter scenarios.

SCREEN 100% of cargo and vehicles entering the U.S. from Canada and Mexico.

NATURALIZE **3,200 NEW** U.S. CITIZENS.

PROCESS **ONE MILLION** travelers entering the U.S. by air, sea, and land.

SEIZE **$500,000** in counterfeit U.S. currency before it is introduced into circulation.

CANADA

MEXICO

VERIFY THE IDENTITIES OF **109,000+** APPLICANTS for visas or border-crossing cards.

TRAIN

5,880+ federal, state, local, tribal, and territorial emergency management and response personnel.

2,100+ officers and agents from **90+** federal agencies, as well as **125+** state, local, rural, tribal, territorial, and international officers and agents.

94 stakeholders from critical infrastructure sectors to identify, mitigate, and respond to cyber attacks.

PROVIDE **$3.7+ MILLION** in federal disaster grants to individuals and households, following presidentially-declared disaster declarations.

 ENGAGE THE **PUBLIC** every day through "If You See Something, Say Something™."

PROVIDE SECRET SERVICE protection for an average of **30** U.S. government officials and their families.

CYBER

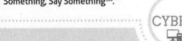

PREVENT **$6.8 MILLION** in potential losses through cyber crime investigations.

RESPOND TO **70** CYBERSECURITY incidents per month while issuing warnings for each.

ISSUE **20+** ACTIONABLE cyber alerts for public and private sector to protect their systems.

Note: Data is approximate and represents daily averages based on annual Department-wide statistics. "If You See Something, Say Something™" used with permission by the New York Metropolitan Transportation Authority (MTA).

In addition to the tasks listed on the excerpt of the DHS website, this department is also in charge of immigration and citizenship services and immigration enforcement.

38. Based on the information, which of the following would be an area Homeland Security would investigate?

    A. searching for drug smugglers in Mexico

    B. going to Iran to find terrorist groups

    C. providing assistance after an earthquake in California

    D. investigating a shooting in Peru

39. As used in the excerpt, the word **vigilance** most likely can be defined by which of the following?

    A. a religious ritual

    B. an alert watchfulness

    C. a long ceremony

    D. an attack on the country

Use the following chart and graph to answer questions 40 and 41.

The Transatlantic Slave Trade, 1451–1870					
Number of Slaves Transported (in thousands)					
	1451–1600	1601–1700	1701–1810	1811–1870	Totals
British North America	—	—	348.0	51.0	399.0
Spanish America (Including the Sp. Caribbean)	75.0	292.5	578.6	606.0	1552.1
Caribbean Islands (Dutch, British, and French)	—	483.5	3,233.7	96.0	3,813.2
Portuguese Brazil	50.0	550.0	1,891.4	1,145.4	3,636.8
Europe, Africa, and Asia	149.9	25.1	—	—	175.0
Totals	274.9	1,235.1	6,051.7	1,898.4	9,576.1

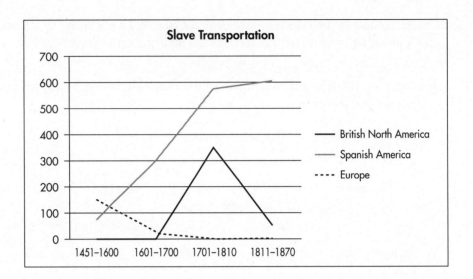

Slave Transportation

40. According to the chart and graph, the transportation of slaves increased sharply in which of the following areas?

   A.   Europe

   B.   the United States

   C.   Spanish America

   D.   British North America

41. The slave trade drastically decreased in British North America. Which of the following is the best explanation for this drop in numbers in 1811–1870?

   A.   There were no more Africans to become slaves.

   B.   There were no crops or work for which slave labor was needed.

   C.   Great Britain abolished slavery in all of its colonies.

   D.   Spanish America had more resources to purchase and transport slaves.

Use the following passage and map to answer questions 42 and 43.

Louisiana Purchase Treaty, 1803

"Let the Land rejoice, for you have bought Louisiana for a Song."

Gen. Horatio Gates to President Thomas Jefferson, July 18, 1803

Robert Livingston and James Monroe closed on the sweetest real estate deal of the millennium when they signed the Louisiana Purchase Treaty in Paris on April 30, 1803. They were authorized to pay France up to $10 million for the port of New Orleans and the Floridas. When offered the entire territory of Louisiana—an area larger than Great Britain, France, Germany, Italy, Spain and Portugal combined—the American negotiators swiftly agreed to a price of $15 million.

Although President Thomas Jefferson was a strict interpreter of the Constitution who wondered if the U.S. Government was authorized to acquire new territory, he was also a visionary who dreamed of an "empire for liberty" that would stretch across the entire continent. As Napoleon threatened to take back the offer, Jefferson squelched whatever doubts he had, submitted the treaty to Congress, and prepared to occupy a land of unimaginable riches.

The Louisiana Purchase added 828,000 square miles of land west of the Mississippi River to the United States. For roughly 4 cents an acre, the United States had purchased a territory whose natural resources amounted to a richness beyond anyone's wildest calculations.

Source: National Archives and Records Administration

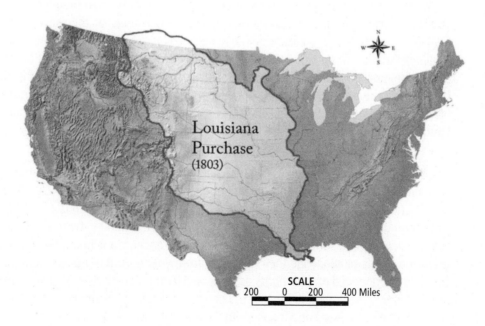

42. President Jefferson was reluctant to agree to the purchase of the Louisiana Territory because

    A. He was unsure the Constitution allowed him to make the agreement.

    B. He was afraid the Indians would be upset.

    C. He thought New Orleans would become a large trade center and difficult to control since it was so far from Washington, D.C.

    D. Spain had claimed the area as theirs, so Jefferson feared it might cause a war with Spain.

43. Jefferson was a Democratic-Republican. When the Federalists learned about the Louisiana Purchase, they were upset. Which of the following can be inferred about the reason the Federalists were upset?

    A. The Federalists thought the British were involved in the deal.

    B. The Federalists feared more slave states would enter the Union.

    C. The Federalists were concerned that more states would become Republican.

    D. The Federalists understood that the Constitution did not authorize the purchase.

Read the following passage and then answer questions 44–46.

The woman suffrage movement was first seriously proposed in the United States at Seneca Falls, NY, July 19, 1848, in a general declaration of the rights of women prepared by Elizabeth Cady Stanton, Lucretia Mott, and several others. The early leaders of the movement in the United States—Susan B. Anthony, Elizabeth Cady Stanton, Lucretia Mott, Lucy Stone, Abby Kelley Foster, Angelina Grimké, Sarah Grimké, and others—were usually also advocates of temperance and of the abolition of slavery. When, however, after the close of the Civil War, the 15 Amendment (1870) gave the franchise to newly emancipated African American men, but not to the women who had helped win it for them, the suffragists for the most part confined their efforts to the struggle for the vote.

The National Woman Suffrage Association, led by Susan B. Anthony and Elizabeth Cady Stanton, was formed in 1869 to agitate for an amendment to the U.S. Constitution. Another organization, the American Woman Suffrage Association, led by Lucy Stone, was organized the same year to work through the state legislatures. In the 1870s, disheartened by the response to the proposed Federal amendment, suffragists also tried other approaches to winning the vote. These included using the courts to challenge their exclusion from voting on the grounds that, as citizens, they could not be deprived of their rights as protected by the Constitution. In 1872, Susan B. Anthony attempted to vote, hoping to be arrested and to have the opportunity to test this strategy in the courts. She was arrested and indicted for "knowingly, wrongfully and unlawfully vot[ing] for a representative to the Congress of the United States." Found guilty and fined, she insisted she would never pay a dollar of it. Virginia Minor, a suffrage leader in St. Louis, succeeded in getting the issue before the United States Supreme Court, but in 1875 the Court ruled unanimously that citizenship did not automatically confer the right to vote and that the issue of female enfranchisement should be decided within the states.

These differing approaches—i.e., whether to seek a Federal amendment or to work for state amendments—kept the woman suffrage movement divided until 1890, when the two societies were united as the National American Woman Suffrage Association. Later leaders included Anna Howard Shaw and Carrie Chapman Catt. Several of the states and territories (with Wyoming first, in 1869) granted suffrage to the women within their borders. By 1913, 12 states and territories had granted voting rights to women, so the National Woman's party, under the leadership of Alice Paul, Lucy Burns, and others, resolved to use the voting power of the enfranchised women to force a suffrage resolution through Congress and secure ratification from the state legislatures. In 1920 the 19th Amendment to the Constitution granted nationwide suffrage to women.

The 19th amendment guarantees all American women the right to vote. Achieving this milestone required a lengthy and difficult struggle; victory took decades of agitation and protest. Beginning in the mid-19th century, several generations of woman suffrage supporters lectured, wrote, marched, lobbied, and practiced civil disobedience to achieve what many Americans considered a radical change of the Constitution. Few early supporters lived to see final victory in 1920.

Source: National Archives and Records Administration

44. According to the excerpt, Suffragettes were involved in several other movements as well. Which of the following includes the other causes these women championed?

    A. war protests

    B. environmental protests

    C. temperance and abolition of slavery

    D. world peace

45. According to the excerpt, the women suffragists used several methods to gain attention for their cause including:

(place a check beside the correct answers)

    ____ formed organizations   ____ held meetings

    ____ went to the courts   ____ participated in parades

46. Which suffragist made a daring attempt to challenge the denial of women's vote by attempting to vote anyway? She was arrested, convicted, and fined.

    A. Elizabeth Cady Stanton

    B. Lucy Stone

    C. Virginia Minor

    D. Susan B. Anthony

Read the following passage and then answer question 47.

In 1972, Richard Nixon assumed the United State Presidential office as a popular incumbent. However, his tenure in the office was a turbulent time for the nation. In June 1972, police arrested five men who had broken into the Democratic National Convention headquarters in the Watergate office building in Washington DC. The media discovered those arrested were members of the committee to reelect the President. One worked at the White House. As a result, people began to question whether the President was aware of this plot. Then, during the investigation, the White House staff engaged in steps to hide evidence pointing to the President. By 1974 the evidence had mounted against the President who resigned from the office of United States President.

47. After reading the passage, arrange the following information in the order of the events which lead to the resignation of President Richard Nixon.

    A. Steps to cover up the president's knowledge of the Watergate crime

    B. The Supreme Court Case of *United States v. Richard Nixon*

    C. Discovery that White House staff members were involved

    D. Break-in at the Democratic National Convention headquarters

"It is common sense to take a method and try it. If it fails, admit it frankly and try another. But above all, try something."

— *Franklin D. Roosevelt*

48. Which of the following is President Roosevelt referring to in the above quote?

    A. his plan for the future

    B. his disability

    C. his New Deal

    D. his job as President

49. Which of the following is used to release a person from improper imprisonment?

    A. a writ of mandamus

    B. a writ of habeas corpus

    C. the Supreme Court's decision in *Roe v. Wade*

    D. *ex post facto* laws

Answers: Social Studies Practice Test 2

1. **B.**

   The Five Freedoms. Option A is part of the Bill of Rights. The entire chart presents the first 10 amendments, known as the Bill of Rights (D). Option (C) is the beginning of the Constitution.

2. **A.**

   The Rights of the Accused. The four amendments contain information concerning being arrested, searched, and trials.

3. **C.**

   Housing. As used in the context of the sentence housing soldiers in private homes. The other three options do not match the meaning of the word.

4. **C.**

   Calculate the mean by adding the numbers and dividing.

5. **Virginia**

   Since the graph shows the bars are almost equal in size.

6. **Mississippi**

   The 1860 line for Mississippi is longer than the other choices.

7. **D.**

   The decrease in housing may not be due to unemployment. The graph is inconclusive and shows there is no correlation of the two.

8. **D.**

   The Southern states had seceded from the Union. Options (A) and (B) are not found on this map. Option (C) is not true since the laws had not been determined for the territory.

9. **A.**

Indian Removal Act. Option (C) might be a possible answer except the AIM was a protest movement in the 1960s. Option (B) and (D) do not relate to the document.

10. **B.**

The Choctaw tribe was being forced to leave their lands. In Harkins' letter he states that his people are said to go voluntarily, but that is false. Option (A) is the opposite of the correct answer. Options (C) and (D) are not stated in the letter.

11. **B.**

An area of desert can be found in Northern Africa. In fact, the subtropical Sahara is the largest hot desert in the world—but this is not knowable fro the map.

12. **B.**

Provide the legal basis and charter for a new bank in the state of Wyoming. Option (A) and (D) are powers of the federal government. Option (C) is a power of the state.

13. **B.**

Shared by both federal and state. The last sentence of the passage clearly states the definition of *concurrent*.

14. **Tokyo.**

You should pay attention to the chart's information and structure.

15. **A.**

The Near East and South Asia combined with East Asia is 51%.

16. **Iran, Latin America, and the Caribbean.**

17. • Box #1 = Congress passes the Alien and Sedition Acts
   • Box #3 = Virginia and Kentucky resolutions enacted
   • Box #5 = Election of 1800 ends in a tie
   • Box #7 = The 12th Amendment to the Constitution is ratified

Here is what your filled-in flow chart should look like:

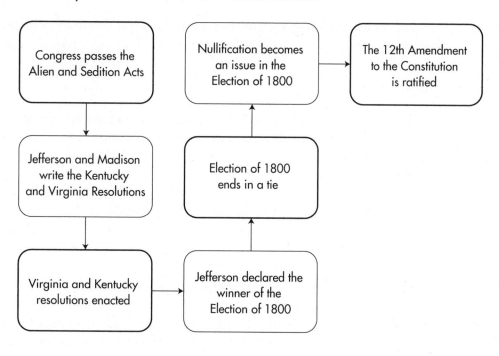

18. **B.**

In the text, the word *nullify* means "to strike down."

19. **B.**

To provide a way to decide who is president in the event of an equal number of votes. Options (A) and (C) are incorrect since the amendment was not added for the purpose of winning elections. Option (D) is the opposite since the amendment was made to clarify the role of the electoral college.

20. **C.**

It is between two rivers which makes the land very productive. Options (A), (B), and (D) are not supported by the map.

21. **Tigris and Euphrates**

These are the only rivers on the map.

22. **D.**

Marbury v. Madison affirmed the power of the Court to declare a law unconstitutional.

23. Judicial

Judicial review allows the court to review a case to determine whether a law is unconstitutional.

24. A.

WTO—World Trade Organization. None of the others is a global organization; therefore, they cannot reasonably be connected to globalization.

25. D.

More people are insured by Medicare and Medicaid.

26. D.

Once recovery was under way, employers would be expected to start rehiring and thus more Americans would be expected to have access to employer-sponsored health insurance plans. In addition, with the Affordable Care Act having been launched explicitly to reduce the number of uninsured in the United States, it is entirely reasonable to assume that the number of uninsured would begin to drop as a result. Choice (A) is the opposite of what would reasonably be expected to happen. Choice (B) should be ruled out because, even if though a mandate may exist, your response must draw upon the information in the statement alone. Choice (C) again goes beyond what you're given; thus, it must not be the correct answer.

27. B.

Your payment and credit history. Although debt amounts may be included, income and education level would not. This rules out option (A). No information for parents or family is needed, and no bank account numbers would be included.

28. C.

A lengthy trial. This amendment guarantees a speedy and public trial.

29. B.

in this passage *impartial* means "fair."

30. B.

A different location for the trial since it may be difficult to find an impartial jury in the area the crime was committed.

31. **Southeast**

The line which represents De Soto's route is entirely located in the Southeast.

32. **More**

The chart shows "high school diploma" to have the greatest number of unemployed. You should remember to read the titles of charts to determine what information is being measured.

33. **Decreased**

According to the bar graph, the unemployment rate for people over 25 decreased. However, this may be explained by the fact that fewer people reported the status for this report. The graph must support the data even if it seems illogical.

34. **B.**

Education plays a significant role in finding and keeping a job now and in the future. The other options are not supported by the information

35. **C.**

A space shuttle

36. **C.**

B is incorrect since the passage does not mention Vietnam.

37. **C.**

No specific area, but all parts of the nation. Option (D) is incorrect since no cities are shown. The other options are not supported by the map.

38. **C.**

Providing assistance after an earthquake in California. Homeland security does not investigate in other countries.

39. **B.**

An alert watchfulness

40. **C.**

Spanish America has the greatest increase on the chart and in the numbers.

41. **C.**

Great Britain abolished slavery in all of its colonies.

42. **A.**

He was unsure the Constitution allowed him to make the agreement.

43. **C.**

The Federalists were concerned that more states would become Republican.

44. **C.**

Temperance and abolition of slavery. The other options are not supported by the passage.

45. The suffragists **formed organizations**, **held meetings**, and **went to the courts**.

46. **D.**

Susan B. Anthony attempted to vote.

47. **D, A, C, B.**

Break-in at the Democratic National Committee's headquarters

Steps to cover up the president's knowledge of the Watergate crime

Discovery that White House staff members were involved

The Supreme Court case of *United States v. Richard M. Nixon*

48. **C.**

His New Deal is the only option possible. The other options are not supported by the quote in any logical way.

49.

The primary function of a writ of habeas corpus is to effect the release of someone who has been imprisoned without due process of law.

Appendix

Rubric for GED® RLA Test Extended Response

RLA ER Rubric — Trait 1

Score	Description
Trait 1: Creation of Arguments and Use of Evidence **A**	
2	• generates text-based argument(s) and establishes a purpose that is connected to the prompt **B** • cites relevant and specific evidence from source text(s) to support argument (may include few irrelevant pieces of evidence or unsupported claims) **C** • analyzes the issue and/or evaluates the validity of the argumentation within the source texts (e.g., distinguishes between supported and unsupported claims, makes reasonable inferences about underlying premises or assumptions, identifies fallacious reasoning, evaluates the credibility of sources, etc.) **D**
1	• generates an argument and demonstrates some connection to the prompt • cites some evidence from source text(s) to support argument (may include a mix of relevant and irrelevant citations or a mix of textual and non-textual references) • partially analyzes the issue and/or evaluates the validity of the argumentation within the source texts; may be simplistic, limited, or inaccurate
0	• may attempt to create an argument OR lacks purpose or connection to the prompt OR does neither • cites minimal or no evidence from source text(s) (sections of text may be copied from source) • minimally analyzes the issue and/or evaluates the validity of the argumentation within the source texts; may completely lack analysis or demonstrate minimal or no understanding of the given argument(s)

Non-scorable Responses (Score of 0/Condition Codes)

• Response exclusively contains text copied from source text(s) or prompt

• Response shows no evidence that test-taker has read the prompt or is off-topic

• Response is incomprehensible

• Response is not in English

• Response has not been attempted (blank)

Note: The annotations to the rubric, A through D, appear on the next page.

A

- Trait 1: Responses are scored according to the criteria outlined in all three bullets.

- Each bullet represents a distinct **dimension** or **quality of writing** that involves the creation of arguments and use of evidence. Each score point describes the same dimensions, but at varying levels of mastery.

- Responses may exhibit qualities indicative of more than one score point. For instance, a response may contain a logical text-based argument and sufficient support (a 4-point response), but the integration of claims might be simplistic (a 2-point response).

- When a response shows mixed evidence of proficiency levels, it will receive a score that reflects a balanced consideration of each quality, with no one dimension weighted more than the others.

B

- The first dimension relates to making claims or assertions.

- At higher score points, arguments will be focused on close reading and analysis of the source texts. As responses ascend the scale in this dimension, they will become more focused on making arguments.

C

- The second dimension focuses on a test-taker's ability to use information from the source texts to support their claims or assertions.

- As responses ascend the scale in this dimension, they will use evidence that is progressively more tied to the text.

- At lower score points, the test-taker may rely more heavily on evidence drawn from personal experience with the topic rather than from text-based evidence.

- While responses that argue the test-taker's own opinion on the issue are acceptable, test-takers who focus more specifically on the task outlined in the prompt, which asks them to analyze source texts to determine which position is better supported, will be more likely to score highly on this dimension.

- More specifically, responses that establish criteria for the evaluation of the source texts and then apply these criteria to specific text-based evidence are most likely to score highest in this dimension.

D

- The third dimension focuses on a test-taker's ability to critically evaluate the rhetorical strategies and argumentation demonstrated by the authors of the source texts.

- While responses that argue the test-taker's own opinion on the issue are acceptable, test-takers who focus more specifically on the task outlined in the prompt, which asks them to analyze source texts to determine which position is better supported, will be more likely to score highly on this dimension.

RLA ER Rubric — Trait 2

Score	Description
Trait 2: Development of Ideas and Organizational Structure **E**	
2	• contains ideas that are well developed and generally logical; most ideas are elaborated upon **F** • contains a sensible progression of ideas with clear connections between details and main points **G** • establishes an organizational structure that conveys the message and purpose of the response; applies transitional devices appropriately **H** • establishes and maintains a formal style and appropriate tone that demonstrate awareness of the audience and purpose of the task **J** • chooses specific words to express ideas clearly **K**
1	• contains ideas that are inconsistently developed and/or may reflect simplistic or vague reasoning; some ideas are elaborated upon • demonstrates some evidence of a progression of ideas, but details may be disjointed or lacking connection to main ideas • establishes an organization structure that may inconsistently group ideas or is partially effective at conveying the message of the task; uses transitional devices inconsistently • may inconsistently maintain a formal style and appropriate tone to demonstrate an awareness of the audience and purpose of the task • may occasionally misuse words and/or choose words that express ideas in vague terms
0	• contains ideas that are insufficiently or illogically developed, with minimal or no elaboration on main ideas • contains an unclear or no progression of ideas; details may be absent or irrelevant to the main ideas • establishes an ineffective or no discernable organizational structure; does not apply transitional devices, or does so inappropriately • uses an informal style and/or inappropriate tone that demonstrates limited or no awareness of audience and purpose • may frequently misuse words, overuse slang or express ideas in a vague or repetitious manner

Non-scorable Responses (Score of 0/Condition Codes)

• Response exclusively contains text copied from source text(s) or prompt

• Response shows no evidence that test-taker has read the prompt or is off-topic

• Response is incomprehensible

• Response is not in English

• Response has not been attempted (blank)

Note: The annotations to the rubric, E through K (with no letter I [EYE] being used), appear on the next page.

E

- The five bullets, or dimensions, in Trait 2 must be considered together to determine the score of any individual response.

- No one dimension is weighted more than any other.

- Each score point describes the same dimensions, but at varying levels of mastery.

F

- The first dimension relates to the depth and breadth of explanation exhibited in the response. While support for ideas should come from the source texts (like in Trait 1), fully developed ideas are often extended with additional evidence that builds upon central assertions.

- High-scoring papers will tend to contain multiple ideas that are fully elaborated upon and help articulate a central thesis.

- Responses that develop ideas insufficiently, unevenly, or illogically fall into the lower score ranges with regard to this dimension.

G

- The second dimension focuses on how effectively the response builds from one idea to the next as well as the degree in which details and central ideas are linked.

- High-scoring responses will maintain coherence and a sense of progression that help convey the writer's central thesis.

- Responses at lower score points demonstrate an increasingly disjointed or unclear progression of ideas. Details are increasingly unrelated to central ideas, or even absent.

H

- The third dimension relates to how well the response is organized. Though paragraphs may lend structure to many responses, it is possible for a well-organized, logical, nonparagraphed response to receive a high score.

- However, responses that contain circular, list-like, or scattered organizational structure, as well as those that do not fully integrate effective transitions between ideas, are often indicative of lower score points.

J

- The fourth dimension is associated with how well the response demonstrates an understanding of audience and purpose.

- Responses that score highly in this dimension will establish and maintain a formal style and objective tone while attending to the norms and conventions of argumentative writing.

K

- The fifth dimension focuses on word choice. Effective word choice does not necessarily suggest that test-takers must employ a great deal of advanced vocabulary.

- Advanced vocabulary used correctly is often associated with a higher score on Trait 2, but responses that reflect a precision in word choice are just as likely to score well in this dimension.

- At lower score points, imprecise, vague and/or misused words are more prevalent.

RLA ER Rubric — Trait 3

Score	Description
	Trait 3: Clarity and Command of Standard English Conventions 🄻

2	• demonstrates largely correct sentence structure and a general fluency that enhances clarity with specific regard to the following skills: 🄼
	  1) varied sentence structure within a paragraph or paragraphs
	  2) correct subordination, coordination and parallelism
	  3) avoidance of wordiness and awkward sentence structures
	  4) usage of transitional words, conjunctive adverbs and other words that support logic and clarity
	  5) avoidance of run-on sentences, fused sentences, or sentence fragments
	• demonstrates competent application of conventions with specific regard to the following skills: 🄽
	  1) frequently confused words and homonyms, including contractions
	  2) subject-verb agreement
	  3) pronoun usage, including pronoun antecedent agreement, unclear pronoun references, and pronoun case
	  4) placement of modifiers and correct word order
	  5) capitalization (e.g., proper nouns, titles, and beginnings of sentences)
	  6) use of apostrophes with possessive nouns
	  7) use of punctuation (e.g., commas in a series or in appositives and other non- essential elements, end marks, and appropriate punctuation for clause separation)
	• may contain some errors in mechanics and conventions, but they do not interfere with comprehension; overall, standard usage is at a level appropriate for on-demand draft writing. 🄿

1	• demonstrates inconsistent sentence structure; may contain some repetitive, choppy, rambling, or awkward sentences that may detract from clarity; demonstrates inconsistent control over skills 1–5 as listed in the first bullet under Trait 3, Score Point 2 above • demonstrates inconsistent control of basic conventions with specific regard to skills 1–7 as listed in the second bullet under Trait 3, Score Point 2 above • may contain frequent errors in mechanics and conventions that occasionally interfere with comprehension; standard usage is at a minimally acceptable level of appropriateness for on-demand draft writing.
0	• demonstrates consistently flawed sentence structure such that meaning may be obscured; demonstrates minimal control over skills 1-5 as listed in the first bullet under Trait 3, Score Point 2 above • demonstrates minimal control of basic conventions with specific regard to skills 1–7 as listed in the second bullet under Trait 3, Score Point 2 above • contains severe and frequent errors in mechanics and conventions that interfere with comprehension; overall, standard usage is at an unacceptable level for on-demand draft writing. OR • response is insufficient to demonstrate level of mastery over conventions and usage

Non-scorable Responses (Score of 0/Condition Codes)

- Response exclusively contains text copied from source text(s) or prompt

- Response shows no evidence that test-taker has read the prompt or is off-topic

- Response is incomprehensible

- Response is not in English

- Response has not been attempted (blank)

Note: The annotations to the rubric, L through P, appear below. (Note that the annotations do not use the letter O to avoid confusion with the number 0.)

L

- As in the previous two traits, each of the three dimensions of Trait 3 must be weighed together to determine the score.

- Each score point describes the same dimensions, but at varying levels of mastery.

M

- This dimension relates to sentence structure and variety. Scoring will focus only on these skills essential to the development of sentence structure.

- High-scoring responses mix simple and compound sentences and purposefully incorporate a variety of clauses to enhance overall fluidity.

- Repetitive, choppy, rambling, and/or awkward sentence constructions are indicative of responses at the lower score points.

N

- The second dimension focuses on how well the response maintains specific conventions of standard English. Responses will be scored on the basis of a test-taker's demonstrated mastery over the particular language skills listed in this dimension. Though there are many other conventions that come into play in a test-taker's writing, these essential skills are the ones on which they will be scored.

- Further, the longer the response, the greater tolerance for errors. For example, 10 errors in a 10-line response will likely receive a lower score than a response that contains 20 errors but is 60 lines long.

P

- The third dimension pertains to overall fluency with conventions and mechanics.

- In order to receive a score higher than 1, test-takers must sustain their writing long enough to demonstrate their level of proficiency with all the skills listed in the two previous dimensions.

- Then, writing samples are evaluated for level of grammatical and syntactical fluency appropriate for on-demand, draft writing.

Index

Index

NOTES

NOTES

NOTES

NOTES

NOTES

NOTES

NOTES

NOTES

NOTES

NOTES

Also Available from REA...

NEW 2nd Edition

GED® Math Test Tutor

CONTENT ALIGNED · GED TESTING SERVICE®

Sandra Rush, M.A.

$$c^2 = a^2 + b^2$$

$$30\% = .30 = \frac{3}{10}$$

All the Tools You Need to Succeed

- Diagnostic pretest pinpoints strengths and weaknesses
- Focused coverage for the GED® Mathematical Reasoning test
- Hundreds of hints, shortcuts, and exercises reinforce key points
- 2 Full-Length GED® Math practice exams

GED® is a registered trademark of the American Council on Education (ACE) and may not be used or reproduced without express written permission. The GED® and GED Testing Service® brands are administered by GED Testing Service LLC under license from ACE. ACE and GED Testing Service LLC have not approved, authorized, endorsed, been involved in the development of, or licensed the substantive content of this material.

Research & Education Association
For more information, visit us at: www.rea.com